LIST OF
ILLUSTRATIONS

GENERAL EDITORS'
PREFACE

The Arden Shakespeare is now nearly one hundred years old. The earliest volume in the first series, Edward Dowden's edition of *Hamlet*, was published in 1899. Since then the Arden Shakespeare has become internationally recognized and respected. It is now widely acknowledged as the pre-eminent Shakespeare series, valued by scholars, students, actors, and 'the great variety of readers' alike for its readable and reliable texts, its full annotation and its richly informative introductions.

We have aimed in the third Arden series to maintain the quality and general character of its predecessors, preserving the commitment to presenting the play as it has been shaped in history. While each individual edition will necessarily have its own emphasis in the light of the unique possibilities and problems posed by the play, the series as a whole, like the earlier Ardens, insists upon the highest standards of scholarship and upon attractive and accessible presentation.

Newly edited from the original quarto and folio editions, the texts are presented in fully modernized form, with a textual apparatus that records all substantial divergences from those early printings. The notes and introductions focus on the conditions and possibilities of meaning that editors, critics and performers (on stage and screen) have discovered in the play. While building upon the rich history of scholarly and theatrical activity that has long shaped our understanding of the texts of Shakespeare's plays, this third series of the Arden Shakespeare is made necessary and possible by a new generation's encounter with Shakespeare, engaging with the plays and their complex relation to the culture in which they were – and continue to be – produced.

THE TEXT

On each page of the play itself, readers will find a passage of text followed by commentary and, finally, textual notes. Act and scene divisions (seldom present in the early editions and often the product of eighteenth-century or later scholarship) have been retained for ease of reference, but have been given less prominence than in the previous series. Editorial indications of scene have been removed to the textual notes or commentary.

In the text itself, unfamiliar typographic conventions have been avoided in order to minimize obstacles to the reader. Elided forms in the early texts are spelt out in full in verse lines wherever they indicate a usual late twentieth-century pronunciation that requires no special indication and wherever they occur in prose (except when they indicate non-standard pronunciation). In verse speeches, marks of elision are retained where they are necessary guides to the scansion and pronunciation of the line. Final -ed in past tense and participial forms of verbs is always printed as -ed, without accent, never as -'d, but wherever the required pronunciation diverges from modern usage a note in the commentary draws attention to the fact. Where the final -ed should be given syllabic value contrary to modern usage, e.g.

Doth Silvia know that I am banished?
(*TGV* 3.1.221)

the note will take the form

221 **banished** banishèd

Conventional lineation of divided verse lines shared by two or more speakers has been reconsidered and sometimes rearranged. Except for the familiar *Exit* and *Exeunt*, Latin forms in stage directions and speech prefixes have been translated into English and the original Latin forms recorded in the textual notes.

COMMENTARY AND TEXTUAL NOTES

Notes in the commentary, for which a major source will be the *Oxford English Dictionary*, offer glossarial and other explication of verbal difficulties; they may also include discussion of points of theatrical interpretation and, in relevant cases, substantial extracts from Shakespeare's source material. Editors will not usually offer glossarial notes for words adequately defined in the latest edition of *The Concise Oxford Dictionary* or *Merriam - Webster's Collegiate Dictionary,* but in cases of doubt they will include notes. Attention, however, will be drawn to places where more than one likely interpretation can be proposed and to significant verbal and syntactic complexity. Notes preceded by * involve readings altered from the early edition(s) on which the text is based.

Headnotes to acts or scenes discuss, where appropriate, questions of scene location, Shakespeare's handling of his source materials, and major difficulties of staging. The list of roles (so headed to emphasize the play's status as a text for performance) is also considered in commentary notes. These may include comment on plausible patterns of casting with the resources of an Elizabethan or Jacobean acting company and also on any variation in the description of roles in their speech prefixes in the early editions.

The textual notes are designed to let readers know when the edited text diverges from the early edition(s) on which it is based. Wherever this happens the note will record the rejected reading of the early edition(s), in original spelling, and the source of the reading adopted in this edition. Other forms from the early edition(s) recorded in these notes will include some spellings of particular interest or significance and original forms of translated stage directions. Where two early editions are involved, for instance with *Othello*, the notes will also record all important differences between them. The textual notes take a form that has been in use since the nineteenth century. This comprises, first: line reference, reading adopted in the text and closing square bracket; then: abbreviated reference, in italic, to the earliest edition to adopt the accepted reading, italic semi-colon and noteworthy alternative reading(s), each with abbreviated italic reference to its source.

Conventions used in these textual notes include the following. The solidus / is used, in notes quoting verse or discussing verse lining, to indicate line endings. Distinctive spellings of the basic text (Q or F) follow the square bracket without indication of source and are enclosed in italic brackets. Names enclosed in brackets indicate originators of conjectural emendations when these did not originate in an edition of the text, or when this edition records a conjecture not accepted into its text. Stage directions (SDs) are referred to by the number of the line within or immediately after which they are placed. Line numbers with a decimal point relate to SDs more than one line long, with the number after the point indicating the line within the SD: e.g. 78.4 refers to the fourth line of the SD following line 78. Lines of SDs at the start of a scene are numbered 0.1, 0.2, etc. Where only a line number precedes the square bracket, e.g. 128], the note relates to the whole line; where SD is added to the number, it relates to the whole of a SD within or immediately following the line. Speech prefixes (SPs) follow similar conventions, 203 SP], referring to the speaker's name for line 203. Where a SP reference takes the form e.g. 38+ SP, it relates to all subsequent speeches assigned to that speaker in the scene in question.

Where, as with *King Henry V*, one of the early editions is a so-called 'bad quarto' (that is, a text either heavily adapted, or reconstructed from memory, or both), the divergences from the present edition are too great to be recorded in full in the notes. In these cases the editions will include a reduced photographic facsimile of the 'bad quarto' in an appendix.

INTRODUCTION

Both the introduction and the commentary are designed to present the plays as texts for performance, and make appropriate reference to stage, film and television versions, as well as introducing the reader to the range of critical approaches to the play. They discuss the history of the reception of the texts within the theatre and scholarship and beyond, investigating the interdependency of the literary text and the surrounding 'cultural text' both at the time of the original production of Shakespeare's works and during their long and rich afterlife.

The Editor

T. W. Craik is Emeritus Professor of English in the University of Durham. He is the author of *The Tudor Interlude* and *The Comic Tales of Chaucer*, and has edited plays by Marlowe and Massinger for the New Mermaids, a selection of Elizabethan tragedies for Everyman's Library, Beaumont and Fletcher's *Maid's Tragedy* for The Revels Plays, and *The Merry Wives of Windsor* for The Oxford Shakespeare. He was joint editor of *Twelfth Night* in the second series of The Arden Shakespeare.

PREFACE

My acquaintance with *Henry V* goes back to September 1939. I was twelve years old, in the fourth form of the Boteler Grammar School, Warrington, and this was the first of Shakespeare's plays that I had studied in class. The master, Mr W. N. Havard, a young graduate of Durham University, got us to read the play aloud, distributing the parts among us, and I can still remember how the class responded to particular phrases: 'Tennis-balls, my liege'; 'Will you shog off? I would have you *solus*'; 'Read them, and know I know your worthiness'; 'and all was as cold as any stone'; 'Scorn and defiance; slight regard, contempt' (as it was punctuated in the edition we used); 'And down goes all before them'; 'The game's afoot'; 'To the mines? Tell you the Duke it is not so good to come to the mines'. The list would be a long one, not forgetting the King's 'How now, what's the matter?', which, following hard upon Warwick's 'How now, how now, what's the matter?', proved a real show-stopper.

I do not know whether the outbreak of the Second World War had anything to do with the choice of *Henry V* as our Shakespeare play for study, though I fancy not. I am sure that nothing was said in class about the matter. At the present time, when one school of criticism is much concerned to show how often Shakespeare has been 'appropriated' for undesirable ends, it is worth putting on record that Mr Havard did not preach patriotism to us. He encouraged us to enjoy *Henry V* as a play, and by getting us to perform it, though not in action, he made sure that we did enjoy it. That still seems to me the most important thing to do with a play, to enjoy it in performance, whether in a reading-aloud, or on a stage, or in the theatre of the mind. Accordingly, in the major section of the following Introduction, 'The play', I try to convey a sense of how *Henry V* works, as a stage play, by following its development from scene to scene and sometimes from speech to speech. To some readers – but, I hope, not to many – this method will appear an elementary one, little better than telling the story, especially as I have done my best to avoid bringing the play's progress to a standstill by extensive comments of my own. Elementary or not, it seems worth adopting, as there is no shortage of criticism that analyses the play by different methods.

In the twentieth century the cinema and television have presented *Henry V* to a larger audience than any stage production can reach, and most readers will have seen one or more of the versions directed in 1944 by Laurence Olivier, in 1979 by David Giles for the BBC, and in 1989 by Kenneth Branagh. It is interesting to compare them, and any stage versions that one may have seen, with each other, and with their Shakespearean original – noticing, for instance, that though they all make cuts they do not always cut the same passages.

By 'their Shakespearean original' I mean the script of the play, and by that I mean the text printed in the collection of Shakespeare's comedies, histories and tragedies published in 1623 (the First Folio). A text had appeared in 1600, soon after the play's first performance in 1599. This text (the First Quarto) is an inaccurately reconstructed version of the one that was being performed in the playhouse. Since it is a much shortened version (less than half the length of the Folio text), and since in the Agincourt scenes it substitutes Bourbon for the Dauphin, the possibility has to be considered that it may reflect cuts and other changes made to the script before the play began to be shown to audiences. This is why the Introduction, after briefly discussing the play's date and sources, cannot proceed to the play itself without first giving reasons for regarding the Folio text not only as the version written by Shakespeare but also as the version performed in the playhouse.

The section on 'The play', as I have said, is an account of *Henry V* as it appears to me, and I have therefore mentioned alternative interpretations only in passing, reserving further mention of them to the two following sections, 'Critical opinions of the play and its hero' and '*Henry V* in performance'. The final section of the Introduction contains a more detailed discussion of the earliest printed texts of the play than was proper in assessing the reliability of the Quarto and the Folio, and concludes by explaining the editorial procedure of the present edition.

In the commentary notes I have tried always to bear in mind the needs of actors and directors, and have examined afresh the stage action that the lines imply, avoiding as far as possible the overloading of the text with editorial stage directions. Since the lines were written to be spoken, not silently read, I have indicated in the commentary all the words which for metrical or other reasons are to be given a different pronunciation from that which they have in modern prose. As to the meaning of the words, I have done my best to explain everything that might now be obscure or misleading, while recognizing with Samuel Johnson that 'it is impossible for an expositor not to write too little for some, and too much for others'. Much ambiguity and word-play has been sought (and therefore found) in Shakespeare's language; where I think it exists I have noted it, but I have not thought it necessary to record all such instances as I reject. As to the genuineness of the words as they have come down to us, the Folio provides a generally reliable text of *Henry V*, but it naturally contains some errors, and every editor has to engage in debate about whether this or that passage is corrupt. I have sometimes defended the Folio reading, sometimes accepted a Quarto reading or another editor's emendation, and sometimes proposed an emendation of my own; on a few occasions I have emended passages hitherto unrecognized as corrupt – always remembering Johnson's advice about 'keeping the middle way between presumption and timidity'.

The Quarto and Folio texts contain so many differences, of lineation and sentence structure as well as of vocabulary, that it can be misleading to compare a word from one with a word from the other in attempting to establish which of them gives the correct reading. The Quarto text is therefore included, in reduced photographic facsimile, as an appendix to this edition, so that readers can see the whole evidence for themselves. The Folio, because of its large format, cannot be so reproduced, but I have given at the foot of each page of text every substantive departure from its readings, as well as recording some of its most interesting spellings.

Like Shakespeare's other plays from history, whether English or Roman, *Henry V* is heavily indebted to its chief historical source, often following it in close verbal detail. To allow readers to see this readily, I have placed quotations from Holinshed's *Chronicles* in the commentary notes, beneath the passages in the text to which they relate, instead of relegating them to an appendix. This arrangement necessarily puts Holinshed's passages in Shakespeare's order instead of allowing them to form their own continuous narrative, and so for the convenience of readers I have stated in parentheses how these passages connect with each other. I have also supplied a genealogical table and maps to make clearer the allusions to persons and places.

I am grateful to Professor Richard Proudfoot and Professor David Scott Kastan for their care in overseeing this volume as General Editors, to my colleagues David Crane and David Fuller for reading and commenting on parts of the Introduction, to Dr Z. P. Zaddy for answering my queries about sixteenth-century French usage, and to Dr Janette Dillon and Professor Graham Holderness for letting me see unpublished work of theirs. What I owe to previous editors and commentators on the play will be obvious from my frequent references to them. I am also grateful to the University of Durham for a term of study leave granted to me while working on the edition, and to the owners of copyright in the illustrations for permission to reproduce them. I dedicate the volume to the memory of three editors of Shakespeare, Harold Brooks, George Hibbard and Arthur Humphreys, all of whom I am proud to have had among my friends and whose example I have tried to follow.

T. W. Craik
Durham

I have taken advantage of reprinting to introduce some corrections in the editorial material. The text of the play remains as in the first impression. I am also glad to have the opportunity of thanking my copy-editor Linden Stafford for her many helpful suggestions when the volume was first being prepared for the press.

1997   *T. W. C.*

INTRODUCTION

DATE

A passage in *Henry V* provides an almost undisputed indication
of the date of the play. Describing the King's triumphant
return to England and entry into London after his victory at
Agincourt, the Chorus says:

> But now behold,
> In the quick forge and working-house of thought,
> How London doth pour out her citizens.
> The Mayor and all his brethren in best sort,
> Like to the senators of th'antique Rome
> With the plebeians swarming at their heels,
> Go forth and fetch their conquering Caesar in;
> As, by a lower but as loving likelihood,
> Were now the General of our gracious Empress,
> As in good time he may, from Ireland coming,
> Bringing rebellion broached on his sword,
> How many would the peaceful city quit
> To welcome him! Much more, and much more cause,
> Did they this Harry.
>
> (5.0.22–35)

Nearly everyone agrees that in these lines 'the General' is
Robert Devereux, Earl of Essex, a popular figure because of
his successful assault on Cadiz in 1596 when he was still under
thirty years old. On 25 March 1599 he was appointed lieutenant
and governor-general of Ireland, and two days later he left

1

London, cheered and blessed by the people. The rebellion that he was expected to slay (as Saint George slew the dragon) and bring back spitted on his sword was led by Hugh O'Neill, second Earl of Tyrone, who had destroyed an English force in August 1598 and overrun Munster in October. Essex landed at Dublin from Beaumaris on 15 April 1599, and after an inconclusive campaign returned to Dublin in July with a weary, sick and depleted army. Later that month he received peremptory orders from Elizabeth I to attack Tyrone's forces, and duly left Dublin on 28 August, but apart from minor skirmishes could not engage with the Irish. Tyrone, who was a skilful manipulator of political situations, called for a parley, Essex agreed, and their meetings on 6 and 7 September concluded in a truce. Elizabeth wrote to Essex angrily dissociating herself from this action of his, whereupon he appointed a deputy to command his army and returned to London, where he arrived with some half-dozen attendants on 28 September, and had an immediate interview with the Queen. Though she received him kindly, he presently found himself placed under house arrest for leaving his command, and on 6 June 1600 he was tried by a special court and sentenced to the loss of all offices of state. He did not regain his liberty till 26 August. In the following January he plotted to seize Whitehall palace and require, or compel, the Queen to dismiss her counsellors. The plot was discovered, and the discovery precipitated a premature rising by Essex and his followers on 8 February. The Londoners, though they had been sympathetic towards him in his fall from power, did not rally to his support; he surrendered, was convicted of compassing the Queen's death, and was beheaded on 25 February.

It has sometimes been suggested that the allusion is not to Essex but to his friend and fellow soldier against the Spaniards, Charles Blount, Lord Mountjoy, who was asked to succeed him in his Irish post in October 1599 and in November agreed to do so. He left for Ireland in February 1600, and on 24

December 1601 gained a decisive victory over Tyrone's army and their 4,000 Spanish allies at Kinsale. By December 1602 he had forced Tyrone to sue to the Queen for pardon (which was granted by her successor James I in April 1603), and he continued to control Ireland till his recall to England on 26 May 1603.

A complimentary allusion to Blount would hardly have been effective before his victory at Kinsale, and he could never be said to have rivalled Essex as a popular hero. Moreover, Gower's allusion to 'a beard of the General's cut', although it can be understood as applying to any general of any English army, points clearly to Essex's characteristic 'Cadiz beard' and must have been meant to raise a topical smile (see 3.6.76n.). This allusion to the General's beard is found as early as 1600, in the first published version of *Henry V*, the Quarto of that year. The allusion to the General's hoped-for return is not in the Quarto, which lacks all the Chorus's speeches, but it is in the Folio edition of Shakespeare's plays, in which they were first collected in 1623.

If the allusions are to Essex they imply that *Henry V* was acted between March 1599, once it was generally known that Essex was going to Ireland, and September of that year. The play might, of course, have been written well before that time, and the choruses, or these lines in this particular one, added later. However, the passage does not look like an addition,[1] the choruses look like an integral part of the design, and there are other reasons for thinking 1599 a probable date for the play's composition.

The Prologue dwells on the impossibility of presenting so great an object as Agincourt on 'this unworthy scaffold', in 'this cockpit' and 'within this wooden O'. It was in 1599 that the Lord Chamberlain's Men occupied their new playhouse,

---

1 The completion of l. 35, 'Now in London place him', is necessary to prevent an abrupt transition from l. 28 ('Go forth and fetch their conquering Caesar in') to ll. 36-7 ('As yet the lamentation of the French / Invites the King of England's stay at home').

3

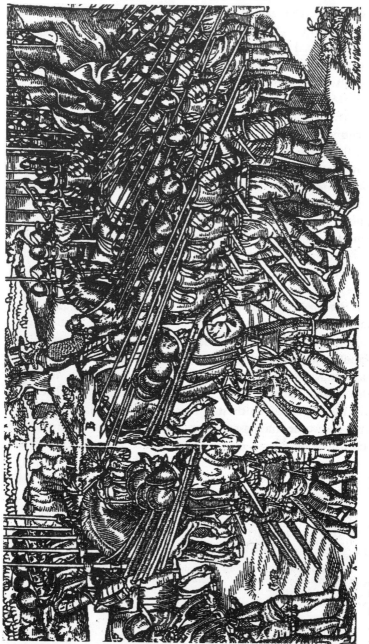

1 An English army on the march in Ireland. John Derricke, *The Image of Ireland* (London, 1586)

the Globe, built on the Bankside in Southwark with the materials of their old one, the Theatre, which they had ferried over the Thames after dismantling it on 28 December 1598 in consequence of a dispute with their ground landlord. How soon it was ready for use is not known; *Henry V* may have had its first performance at the Curtain playhouse, which like the late Theatre was over twenty years old. But when Shakespeare was composing the Prologue he must have been expecting the play to remain in the repertoire for some time, in which case the derogatory remarks about the playhouse – granted that they would apply to any playhouse as regards staging the unstageable – would have a humorous point when applied to a scaffold that the Lord Chamberlain's Men did not think in the least unworthy.

Henry V would have been written if the Earl of Essex had never gone to Ireland and if the Lord Chamberlain's Men had never gone to the Globe. It was the promised culmination of Shakespeare's second sequence of plays on subjects from English history, beginning with *Richard II*. Whether or not he had projected the four-play series from the first, and whether or not he originally meant to divide *Henry IV* into the two plays of which it consists, at the end of *2 Henry IV* he knew what he would next be writing. In the final dialogue Prince John and the Lord Chief Justice observe that the newly crowned King has called· his parliament and is thinking of invading France. In the Epilogue more specific promises are made:

> If you be not too much cloyed with fat meat, our humble author will continue the story with Sir John in it, and make you merry with fair Katherine of France; where, for anything I know, Falstaff shall die of a sweat – unless already 'a be killed with your hard opinions.

In the Epilogue to *Henry V* Shakespeare reverts to this wording ('Our bending author hath pursued the story'), and in the final scene the opening phrase of the wooing, 'Fair Katherine, and most fair', echoes 'fair Katherine of France'. Perhaps he was already composing the courtship dialogue, in his mind if not on paper. His comparing of Henry V's triumphal entry to Caesar's may likewise suggest that when drawing towards the end of *Henry V* he was planning his next play, *Julius Caesar*, which a Swiss visitor to England, Thomas Platter, saw performed at the Globe on 21 September 1599 – just a week before Essex's return.

SOURCES

For *Julius Caesar* and his later tragedies on subjects from ancient history Shakespeare turned towards Plutarch and away from Raphael Holinshed, whose *Chronicles of England, Scotland and Ireland* (1577), in the edition of 1587 revised and enlarged after its author's death, had been his chief source for his second quartet of English history plays. He had also used Edward Hall's *The Union of the Two Noble and Illustre Families of Lancaster and York* (1548; revised and enlarged, 1550).

Hall's history, as its title suggests, is shaped by the happy conclusion to which it is always, however indirectly, tending. It celebrates the reigns of the first two Tudor kings, Henry VII (the Richmond of *Richard III*), who by his marriage to Edward IV's daughter had united the families, and his son Henry VIII, with whose reign it concludes. Holinshed's history is more neutral in tone, lacking Hall's colourful chapter headings, 'The unquiet time of King Henry the Fourth', 'The victorious acts of King Henry the Fifth', and so on. As a narrator Holinshed condenses what Hall amplifies, but he often follows Hall's phrasing closely. Where their phrasing diverges, Shakespeare is closer to Holinshed in this play than to Hall. A number of details from Holinshed, such as the wish of 'one of the host' for more soldiers from England (4.3.16–18) and the conversion of a trumpet's banner into an improvised standard by one of the French lords (4.2.59–61), are not in Hall. Occasionally the opposite is the case, as when the Scots' habit of invading England whenever the English army goes overseas is mentioned (1.2.146–54). Some of the echoes of Hall, particularly Canterbury's reference to 'the last king's reign' as a 'scambling and unquiet time' (1.1.4), would have come readily to Shakespeare's memory without book; but in setting down the details of the parliamentary bill to confiscate church property (1.1.1–19) or those of Canterbury's refutation of the Salic law (1.2.33–95) he was evidently transcribing from Holinshed's prose and versifying it as he went along.[1]

Holinshed's chronicle underlies the whole historical action of *Henry V*, though the play is far from being a transcript of the chronicle. Shakespeare selects and reshapes his historical material with his usual dramatic skill. He also works in a few details from other historical sources. For example, the two chantries that the King has built (4.1.298–9) come from Robert Fabyan's chronicle (1516), but they have been transformed from a monastery and a nunnery, and the weekly memorial services for Richard were not held there but at Westminster. The 'gun-stones' into which the Dauphin's tennis-balls have been turned (1.2.283) may come from a chronicle printed by William Caxton in 1482; the fact that Shakespeare nowhere else uses the word makes this borrowing probable.

The other major source for *Henry V* (and also for *1 Henry IV* and *2 Henry IV*) is an anonymous play entered in the Stationers' Register on 14 May 1594 and printed by Thomas Creede in 1598 with the title *The Famous Victories of Henry the fifth: Containing the Honourable Battell of Agin-court*. This title, which recalls Hall's chapter heading, is applicable only to the play's second half, its first half dealing with the hero's wild doings in London as Prince of Wales, his conversion at his

---

1 A substantial series of extracts from Holinshed is in Bullough, 4.376–408. For full references to works cited in the Introduction, textual notes and commentary notes, see Abbreviations and references, pp. 406–15.

father's deathbed and his dismissal of his former companions. Thereafter there is a dialogue, corresponding to 1.2, in which Canterbury outlines the King's claim to France, he and Oxford respectively propose invading Scotland and invading France first, and a French ambassador is admitted (here the Archbishop of Bourges) who offers from the French King 50,000 crowns a year and the Princess Katherine's hand in marriage; the King replies, in a speech typical of the play's style,

> Why then belike your Lord and maister,
> Thinks to puffe me vp [*read* putte me of] with
>   fifty thousand crowns a yere,
> No tell thy Lord and maister,
> That all the crownes in *France* shall not serue me,
> Except the Crowne and kingdome it selfe:
> And perchance hereafter I will haue his daughter.[1]

The Dauphin's tennis-balls are then presented, the Ambassador expressing diffidence about declaring the message and being reassured by the King, as in 1.2.238–46 (not in Holinshed). This time the King's response (not in Holinshed) is

> My lord prince *Dolphin* is very pleansant [*read* pleasant]
>   with me:

which Shakespeare has taken over almost unaltered (1.2.260). Instead of a businesslike closing speech, however, *The Famous Victories* ends the scene with the King reconciling himself with the Lord Chief Justice (as in *2 Henry IV*, 5.2) and putting him in charge of the kingdom during the French campaign. There follows a comic scene (x) in which a captain recruits John Cobler, Dericke the carrier and a thief (all of whom have appeared in earlier scenes) for the wars; John and his aggressive wife 'part louingly' with 'kissing and crying'. After this episode the action shifts to France, as in Shakespeare's 2.4, where the

---

1 *Famous Victories* [scene ix], ll. 821–6. Bullough (4.299–343) reprints the text and adds scene numbers and continuous line numbers.

opening exchange of opinions about King Henry corresponds to the dialogue here (see 2.4.0n.); the rest of the scene (xi) develops differently, and ends with the decision to fight the English and with the French King's refusal of the Dauphin's request to take part, as in Shakespeare's 3.5 and in Holinshed (see 3.5.64–6n.). Enough has been said to indicate the degree of resemblance, and the degree of difference, between *Henry V* and *The Famous Victories*, but two more scenes of the latter should be mentioned, a farcical encounter between Dericke and a French soldier in which each conquers the other in turn and neither is hurt (xvii), and a courtship dialogue between King Henry and the Princess Katherine (xviii) in which he says

> tell me in plaine termes,
> Canst thou loue the King of England?

and she replies

> How should I loue him, that hath dealt so hardly
> With my father.

These scenes may have influenced Shakespeare's 4.4 and 5.2.

There may have been other plays about Henry V as well as *The Famous Victories*. Thomas Nashe, defending plays against cullions and club-fisted usurers in *Pierce Pennilesse* (1592), writes:

> All Artes to them are vanitie: and, if you tell them what a glorious thing it is to haue *Henrie* the fifth represented on the Stage, leading the French King prisoner, and forcing both him and the Dolphin to sweare fealty, I, but (will they say) what do we get by it?
>
> (Nashe, 1.213)

He seems here to be referring to an actual play rather than an imaginary one (he has just praised the representation of Talbot's death, clearly referring to *1 Henry VI*), but what he describes does not occur in *The Famous Victories*, though Burgundy and the Dauphin do both swear fealty and kiss King Henry's sword at the end of that play. Philip Henslowe, the owner of the Rose playhouse, mentions in his diary a play of 'harey the v' performed there by the Admiral's Men on 28 November 1595; he calls it 'ne' (i.e. new) and lists a dozen more performances up to 15 July 1596. Whether this can have been *The Famous Victories*, in either its printed form or some other, seems impossible to decide.[1] In any case, what Shakespeare may have owed to lost plays, or to lost versions of extant ones, can never be known.

On the available evidence, Holinshed and *The Famous Victories* between them provided all the material from which he created the dramatic action of *Henry V*. Suggestions that English translations of Tacitus' *Annals* and Homer's *Iliad*, both published in 1598, contributed events to the first scene of Act 4 (the King's encouragement of his colleagues; his nocturnal walk about the camp; his meditation and prayer) are not persuasive.[2] All these elements of the scene Shakespeare could have created for himself, given the King's circumstances and character. As for the incognito encounters with Pistol and the three soldiers, they spring from a dramatic tradition current in the 1590s (and still available to Shakespeare for *Measure for Measure*) in which a ruler in disguise mingles with his subjects.[3] *Henry V* greatly benefits from this infusion of 'comical history', and although it would be wrong to ignore the more serious aspect of the latter encounter it would be equally wrong to

---

1   Foakes and Rickert, in Henslowe, 33, 34, 36, 37, 48 and (on Henslowe's use of 'ne') xxx. The title-page of *Famous Victories* includes 'As it was plaide by the Queenes Maiesties Players', and a jest-book anecdote (printed in Bullough, 4.289–90) connects their leading comedian Richard Tarlton, who died in 1588, with the play, or at any rate with one in which the Prince of Wales struck the Lord Chief Justice.
2   Bullough, 4.361–3 (Grenewey's Tacitus) and Oxf[1], 52–5 (Chapman's Homer).
3   Barton discusses Shakespeare's use of this tradition.

underestimate the comic element in its dramatic irony.[1] Another dramatic tradition, that of the military play from *Tamburlaine* onwards, contributed to *Henry V*, particularly in the scene before the walls of Harfleur (compare the scene before the walls of Angiers in *King John*) and in the English victory against overwhelming odds and vainglorious opponents (compare the Prince of Wales's victory at Crécy in *Edward III*, a play in which Shakespeare may have had a hand). However, the influence of these traditions does not yield anything as concrete as a source, in the sense that Holinshed and *The Famous Victories* are sources.

HENRY V: THE QUARTO AND FOLIO TEXTS

By the middle of August 1600 anyone wishing to read Shakespeare's play could buy, for sixpence, an unbound quarto copy. The title-page announced the play as 'THE / CRONICLE / History of Henry the fift, / With his battell fought at *Agin Court* in / *France*. Togither with *Auntient / Pistoll*.' To make its identity even clearer there followed the sentence '*As it hath bene sundry times playd by the Right honorable / the Lord Chamberlaine his seruants*.' Beneath the printer's personal device, which had appeared on many books, among them *The Famous Victories*, were the words 'LONDON / Printed by *Thomas Creede*, for Tho. Milling- / ton, and Iohn Busby. And are to be / sold at his house in Carter Lane, next / the Powle head. 1600.'

---

1   *Sir John Oldcastle* (Munday, Drayton, Wilson and Hathaway), first performed 16 October 1599 (Henslowe, 125, 126), contains two consecutive scenes (3.4, 4.1) which suggest how contemporaries regarded the episode of Williams and the glove. The disguised Henry V is robbed by the highwayman-priest Sir John of Wrotham, whom he tells he is 'one of [the King's] chamber'; later he wins all his money back from him at dice, they draw swords on each other, and Sir John is nonplussed when a third party identifies the King, who orders Sir John to be hanged but presently relents. A coin which Sir John breaks in two at their first encounter serves as a recognition token at their second, and the dialogue of both scenes is full of humorous irony. Text in Brooke.

Let us suppose that one of Millington's and Busby's customers was a young man of twenty, perhaps a student at one of the Inns of Court. (We shall need to suppose him again, still in London and still buying books, when he is forty-three.) What might he make of the play as this text presented it to him?

On the first page, after a repeat of the full title (as on the first page of *The Famous Victories* and of other plays), he would find the stage direction '*Enter King* Henry, Exeter, 2. *Bishops*, Clarence, *and other Attendants*.' Clearly the scene is laid in the English court, for Exeter begins the play by asking, 'Shall I call in Thambassadors my Liege?' The King replies:

> Not yet my Cousin, till we be resolude
> Of some serious matters touching vs and *France*.

One of the two Bishops who has entered with the rest now rather surprisingly exclaims:

> God and his Angels guard your sacred throne,
> And make you long become it.

The King, evidently not surprised, thanks him and bids him

> proceed
> Why the Lawe *Salicke* which they haue in *France*,
> Or should or should not, stop vs in our clayme:

The Bishop argues the case, exhorting him to go to war, and after a general discussion of policy the King announces his decision:

> Call in the messenger sent fro[m] the Dolphin,
> And by your ayde, the noble sinewes of our land,
> *France* being ours, weele bring it to our awe,
> Or breake it all in peeces:
> Eyther our Chronicles shal with full mouth speak
> Freely of our acts,
> Or else like toonglesse mutes
> Not worshipt with a paper Epitaph.

The Dauphin's messengers present the tennis-balls, the King makes a spirited reply, and the scene ends with his couplet:

Therefore let euery man now taske his thought,
That this faire action may on foote be brought.

The stage being cleared, '*Enter* Nim *and* Bardolfe.' Bardolph asks, 'What is antient *Pistoll* and thee friends yet?', and, gathering from Nym's reply that they are not, observes obliquely:

Yfaith mistresse quickly did thee great wrong,
For thou weart troth plight to her.

Presently the stage direction '*Enter* Pistoll *and Hostes Quickly, his wife*' confirms his meaning; Nym and Pistol quarrel, and Bardolph reconciles them while the Hostess goes to tend the Boy's sick master, whom our reader, if familiar with *2 Henry IV*, would know to be Falstaff, though nothing is said that identifies him until the Hostess returns and names him as Sir John. The men go with her to comfort him. Exeter now reappears, with Gloucester (a new character), who says, 'Before God my Lord, his Grace is too bold to trust these traytors.' ('What traitors?' our reader might ask, unless he knew the answer from Holinshed.) Gloucester is particularly indignant that the King's own bedfellow should betray him 'for a forraine purse', and Exeter comments, 'O the Lord of *Massham*.' Now '*Enter the King and three Lords*', whom the King addresses as

My Lord of *Cambridge*, and my Lord of *Massham*,
And you my gentle Knight,

this third traitor being at last named – and named in full – when the King is giving them their commissions: 'And sir *Thomas Gray* knight of *Northumberland*, this same is yours.' They are presently denounced and sent to execution; the King foretells success in France now that God has 'cut off this dangerous treason lurking in our way'; and the play returns to

Pistol and his companions, who take leave of the Hostess after hearing her account of Sir John's death, Nym saying:

> Shall we shog off?
> The king wil be gone from *Southampton*.

– Southampton evidently having been the location of the previous scene, in which the King's opening line was 'Now sirs the windes faire, and we wil aboord.' Once they are off stage, '*Enter King of* France, Bourbon, Dolphin, and others.' The French King's first speech shows the present state of affairs:

> Now you Lords of *Orleance*,
> Of *Bourbon*, and of *Berry*,
> You see the King of England is not slack,
> For he is footed on this land alreadie.

Presently Exeter arrives as an ambassador, demanding the crown for King Henry and threatening 'Bloody co[n]straint' if it is withheld. He conveys his king's defiance to the Dauphin and makes a crushing answer to the Dauphin's defiant reply. The French King briefly concludes the scene:

> Well for vs, you shall returne our answere backe
> To our brother England.

Then '*Enter* Nim, Bardolfe, Pistoll, Boy', evidently in the field, for Nym's opening line is 'Before God here is hote seruice.' Presently '*Enter* Flewellen *and beates them in*'; the Boy has a short speech about his wish to leave them, and there follow the consecutive stage directions '*Exit* Nim, Bardolfe, Pistoll, *and the Boy*' and '*Enter* Gower.' Gower summons Fluellen 'To the Mines, to the Duke of *Gloster*', and Fluellen criticizes the mines, pointing out that they may be blown up by French countermines. Then '*Enter the King and his Lords alarum*.' The King demands 'How yet resolues the Gouernour of the Towne?' which he presently names as 'the halfe atchieued Harflew'.

14

'*Enter Gouernour*', and makes a seven-line reply to the King's twelve-line speech, ending:

> Enter our gates, dispose of vs and ours,
> For we no longer are defensiue now.

There is no exit marked for anyone here (nor was there one for Gower and Fluellen at the end of their short dialogue), and a new scene begins with '*Enter* Katherine, Allice.' At the end of the lesson in English vocabulary ('*Exit omnes.*'), '*Enter King of* France *Lord Constable, the Dolphin and* Burbon.' The French King states that King Henry 'is past the Riuer Some'; he ends the scene by ordering that Montjoy shall be sent to him 'To know what willing raunsome he will giue', and that the Dauphin shall stay in Rouen. In the next scene Gower meets Fluellen (whose entrance is not marked) and hears from him of the bridge's capture and of Pistol's valour. Pistol enters, quarrels with Fluellen about repriuing Bardolph, and goes, Gower warning Fluellen in a long speech about being taken in by such counterfeits. The King enters with 'Clarence, Gloster *and others*', hears from Fluellen of Bardolph's execution, and replies to Montjoy's message. The battle is now imminent:

> *Glos.* My Liege, I hope they will not come vpon vs now.
> *King.* We are in Gods hand brother, not in theirs:
> To night we will encampe beyond the bridge,
> And on to morrow bid them march away.

No exit is marked, but '*Enter* Burbon, Constable, Orleance, Gebon' shows that we are now in the French camp. Bourbon boasts about his horse and his valour, and is impatient for morning. The Constable is told that 'the English lye within a hundred / Paces of your Tent' and ends the scene with the couplet:

> Come, come away:
> The Sun is hie, and we weare out the day.

'*Exit omnes.*' Then '*Enter the King disguised, to him* Pistoll.' Their dialogue begins immediately, without any preliminary soliloquy by the King to tell why, or how, he is disguised. When Pistol goes, Fluellen and Gower enter, and the King overhears their conversation. When they go, '*Enter three Souldiers*', whom the disguised King accosts; he explains to them that 'Euery mans seruice is the kings: / But euery mans soule is his owne', and presently is drawn into a quarrel and an exchange of gloves with one of them. '*Exit the souldiers*', and '*Enter the King, Gloster, Epingam and Attendants*' – a stage direction that will astonish our reader, as the King is not only still on stage but proceeds to pray that God will strengthen his soldiers' courage and will not remember his father's usurpation and the death of Richard II. At the end of his prayer, '*Enter Gloster*':

> *Glost.* My Lord, the Army stayes vpon your presence.
> *King.* Stay *Gloster* stay, and I will go with thee,
> The day my friends, and all things stayes for me.

By now our reader will probably have concluded that the astonishing stage direction has somehow got misplaced and must belong to some later scene; but his difficulties regarding Gloucester are not over, for now '*Enter* Clarence, Gloster, Exeter and Salisburie' – and Warwick too, for he has the first and third speeches, and (immediately after the stage direction '*Enter King*') expresses a wish for ten thousand more men from England, thus prompting the King's Saint Crispin's day speech. Montjoy comes again, and a proposal of ransom is again rejected. York asks, and is granted, the leading of the vaward, and the King commits the outcome of the battle to God. Thereafter it is nearly all plain sailing for our reader. Four points alone may have puzzled him. First, after a scene showing the French lords in defeat, and another showing a French soldier yielding to Pistol and following him off stage, Pistol is immediately back again in the stage direction '*Enter the King and his Nobles*, Pistoll.' There seems to be nothing for Pistol to do in this scene, which chiefly consists of Exeter's moving account of how York and Suffolk died; but then, at its end, as the King is replying,

> *Alarum soundes.*
> What new alarum is this?
> Bid euery souldier kill his prisoner.
> *Pist.* Couple gorge.   *Exit omnes.*

Secondly, when the King has given Fluellen the soldier's glove and sent him to find Gower he gives the order 'Follow *Flewellen* closely at the heeles' to some person or persons whom he also tells to 'Go see there be no harme betweene them'; but no one has an exit, and when Fluellen meets the soldier no one arrives before the King himself ('*Enter the King, VVarwicke, Clarence, and Exeter*'). Thirdly, Fluellen and Gower enter for the leek-eating scene immediately after the end of the previous one, where Fluellen has spoken the penultimate speech. The fourth puzzling matter is the inclusion of '*the Duke of* Burbon' in the stage direction at the beginning of the final scene, when he was last heard of in the list of prisoners; but within half a dozen lines it becomes clear that this should be not 'Burbon' but 'Burgondie'.

We have been assuming all this while that our reader has not yet seen the play on the stage (rather an improbable assumption if he is an Inns of Court student, but let that pass), and we must now assume (more improbably still) that he is not tempted by the Quarto to do so. We meet him again in 1623 reading '*The Life of Henry the Fift*' in the Folio ('MR. WILLIAM / SHAKESPEARES / COMEDIES, / HIS-TORIES, & / TRAGEDIES. / Published according to the True Originall Copies. / *LONDON* / Printed by Isaac Iaggard, and Ed. Blount. 1623'). He may have noticed that a second quarto appeared in 1602, and another, curiously dated 1608, in 1619, but a quick glance would have shown him that these were substantially reprintings of the text that he had already read.

In the Folio he will read a large double-column page and a half before he reaches the point where the Quarto began. There is a prologue, followed by a long scene of dialogue between Canterbury and Ely. When the court scene does begin, it becomes clear that Canterbury says 'God and his angels guard your sacred throne, / And make you long become it' because he has just made his entrance. Many other problematical points are cleared up in this way, but there is no need to enumerate them now, because the Folio text is the basis of the present edition, as it has been of all editions unto this day, howbeit most editors have incorporated some verbal emendations from the Quarto and a few of them have incorporated larger elements from it. The major differences are as follows. The Folio text, besides its prologue, has four chorus speeches and an epilogue, while the Quarto has none of these. Its opening scene is not in the Quarto; nor is the scene (3.1) consisting of a single long speech in which the King encourages his soldiers, beginning 'Once more unto the breach, dear friends, once more'; nor is the second of two scenes (3.7, 4.2) between the French lords before the battle, though the final couplet of the latter scene is found at the end of the scene that is included in the Quarto. Two consecutive scenes in the Quarto, the scene of the French lords in defeat and the scene between Pistol and his French prisoner, are placed in reverse order in the Folio (4.4, 4.5). In the Quarto the French lord who boasts about his horse is Bourbon; in the Folio he is the Dauphin, who also appears in the second scene before the battle (the one absent from the Quarto) and in the scene of their defeat, a scene in which Bourbon is on stage too. Jamy and Macmorris, who enter in the Folio when Gower and Fluellen are speaking of the mines (3.2), do not appear in the Quarto. Finally, the Folio text is just over twice as long as the Quarto one (3,381 lines to 1,622 lines).

Before we take leave of our supposed reader, we may imagine him turning again to the Folio's subtitle, 'Published according to the True Originall Copies', and then to its preface '*To the great Variety of Readers. /* From the most able, to him that can but spell.' In this preface, signed by John Heminges and Henry Condell, fellow shareholders with Shakespeare in the company of actors to which they all belonged, the readers are told that

> where (before) you were abus'd with diuerse stolne, and surreptitious copies, maimed, and deformed by the frauds and stealthes of iniurious impostors, that expos'd them: euen those, are now offer'd to your view cur'd, and perfect of their limbes; and all the rest, absolute in their numbers, as he conceiued the[m].

Strong words, these; and it would be strange if our particular reader did not apply them to the version of *Henry V* that he first read in 1600, considering how much it differed from the one that he had just been reading.

'BAD QUARTOS', 'FOUL PAPERS' AND 'PERFORMANCE-BASED TEXTS'

Heminges and Condell and their readers had had recent cause to be wary of maimed and deformed texts of Shakespeare's plays. The Third Quarto of *Henry V*, which had appeared in 1619 with the false date 1608 on its title-page, was one of ten plays (eight by Shakespeare and two falsely attributed to him) reprinted from earlier quartos by William Jaggard for the publisher Thomas Pavier. Pavier had intended to issue them as a collection in one volume, but on 3 May 1619 a letter from the Lord Chamberlain to the Stationers' Company caused them to prevent any further publication of plays belonging to the King's Men (as the Lord Chamberlain's Men had become on James I's accession) without their consent, and Pavier had to change his plan. Five of his quartos had already been printed, with the correct date 1619, but he put false dates, and in some cases false publishers' names, on the other five to make them seem to date from before the prohibition order.

Not all of Pavier's reprinted texts were maimed and deformed (the 1600 quarto of *The Merchant of Venice* was good enough to serve as printers' copy for the Folio); Heminges and Condell's preface was aimed at him only in so far as he had put bad texts back into circulation. Their complaint was against the bad texts themselves, the 'bad quartos' as they began to be called early in the present century.[1]

The text of a play (by Shakespeare or any other dramatist of his time) published in a 'good quarto' is one that has been printed from manuscript copy supplied by the author or, if an actors' company owned the play, by the company. This would be less probably the promptbook (which, if the play was still in the repertoire, would still be in use in the playhouse and might be considered too valuable to trust outside it) than the author's manuscript from which the promptbook had been prepared. Such a manuscript was known as the author's papers: Heminges and Condell tell their readers that Shakespeare wrote with such fluency 'that wee haue scarse receiued from him a blot [i.e. a deletion] in his papers'. A rough draft was called 'foul papers', and, if it contained so much alteration as to make it hard to read, the author might need to make a fair copy for the use of whoever was to prepare the promptbook.

The text of a 'bad quarto', on the contrary, derives not from manuscript copy of this sort but from manuscript copy

---

1 The term was coined by A. W. Pollard in 1909: see G. Blakemore Evans, 229, who provides an introduction to the textual study of Shakespeare (ibid., 222–38). A recent account of the 'memorial reconstruction' of texts is given in *Textual Companion*, 23–8. Though aspects of the hypothesis have been criticized (Urkowitz; Werstine; Holderness & Loughrey), in general terms it continues to give the best available explanation of the nature of such texts: the view that they represent Shakespeare's early versions of the plays in question, still occasionally put forward, is disproved by their characteristic features (see p. 21 below). The term 'bad quarto' is used in this edition in a descriptive sense rather than in an opprobrious one.

compiled by some process involving memorization of the text as performed in the playhouse. Its invariable characteristics are abbreviation, paraphrase and the misplacing of lines or phrases at earlier or later points than those where they properly belong. It may also contain phrases recollected from other plays and phrases interpolated by the actors in performance. The use of shorthand would not produce all these characteristics, so memorization must have been the method, which is why 'bad quartos' are also known as 'reported texts'. Who reported them, someone in the audience or someone on the stage, is debatable, though sometimes an unusually accurate piece of text points to the actor who spoke it. In the Quarto of *Henry V* the speech that Gower makes to Fluellen about counterfeit soldiers (3.6.66–80) must be of this kind, particularly as prose is harder to remember accurately than verse.[1]

Some of the passages already quoted from the Quarto illustrate the characteristics just mentioned. In the King's speech before receiving the Dauphin's messengers (1.2.222–34) one passage is omitted (from 'Or there we'll sit' to 'no remembrance over them'). This omission can – though it need not – be regarded as a theatrical cut; but cutting cannot account for the change from

> Now are we well resolu'd, and by Gods helpe
> And yours, the noble sinewes of our power,
>
> > (Folio)

to

> And by your ayde, the noble sinewes of our land,
> > (Quarto)

where not only is the versification destroyed but so is the

---

1 That the actor playing Gower helped in the compiling of Q was first suggested by Price. See also Irace, cited at p. 106 below.

continuity of thought after 'Call in the messenger sent fro[m] the Dolphin'. Even worse is the change from

> or else our graue
> Like Turkish mute, shall haue a tonguelesse mouth,
> Not worshipt with a waxen Epitaph.
>
> (Folio)

to

> Or else like toonglesse mutes
> Not worshipt with a paper Epitaph:
>
> (Quarto)

which is so incoherent as not even to be a paraphrase. (The badness cannot be attributed to any compositorial error such as the omission of a line – 'Our grave shall have a Turkish mouth', perhaps.) Examples of misplaced passages occur in the Quarto's version of 2.4. In the opening speech the French King says:

> You see the King of England is not slack,
> For he is footed on this land alreadie.
>
> (Quarto)

The first of these lines anticipates 'You see this chase is hotly followed, friends', which later occurs in its right place, 2.4.68, with 'Lords' substituted for 'friends', and the second belongs in Exeter's speech near the end of the scene demanding a speedy answer (2.4.141–3). At the end of the scene the Quarto reads:

> *King.* Well for vs, you shall returne our answere backe
> To our brother England.

This corresponds to the Folio's 2.4.113–15, in which the French King replies to the part of Exeter's message addressed to him, the Dauphin then echoing his expression with

> For the Dolphin,
> I stand here for him: what to him from England?

22

In the Quarto this immediate echoing is lost when the French King is not allowed to answer Exeter until the Dauphin has had his say. The real end of the scene, the exchange between Exeter and the French King (2.4.140–6), has completely vanished from the Quarto's text because of these misplacements of dialogue, which must cast some doubt on the widely held opinion that the actor playing Exeter was one of the reporters of the text. If the scene had ended with a rhymed couplet the reporter would have been less likely to have got it wrong. But even a rhymed couplet can become detached from its right scene. It has been mentioned already that the Quarto has only the earlier of the two scenes in the French camp before the battle (3.7 and 4.2), and the concluding couplet of that scene in the Quarto has been quoted:

> Come, come away:
> The Sun is hie, and we weare out the day.

This belongs at the end of the later of the two scenes, the one absent from the Quarto, when battle is just about to be joined. The earlier scene ends in the Folio with the couplet:

> It is now two a Clock: but let me see, by ten
> Wee shall haue each a hundred English men.

– very properly, as it is still the middle of the night. The Dauphin, some time before, has announced: ' 'Tis Mid-night, Ile goe arme my selfe.' In the following chorus (4.0.16) it is stated that the clocks are striking three. It could be argued, by someone trying to make a case for the Quarto, that because it omits this chorus (as it omits all the others) and because its version of the Dauphin's speech is 'Well ile go arme my selfe, hay', what we have here is a deliberate compression of time; but this argument would ignore the long night scene (four pages of the Quarto) in the English camp that immediately follows, and the obvious explanation is that the reporter found the wrong couplet easier to remember than the right one.

More will need to be said about the Quarto presently, but it is now time to turn briefly to the Folio's text of the play. There is general agreement that it was printed from Shakespeare's 'foul papers', though there is room for disagreement about some of the details with which this opinion has been supported. Stage directions calling for flourishes, tuckets, sennets, cannon-effects and alarums were perfectly within Shakespeare's experience and he did not need to leave them to be added at the promptbook stage. Some of the entry directions, such as '*Enter the King and all his Traine before the Gates*' (3.3.0.1) and '*Drum and Colours. Enter the King and his poore Souldiers*' (3.6.86.1–2), look as though they were also set down by him as he was writing the lines, and the speech prefixes for Fluellen in 3.2.68–139, who becomes '*Welch*' just before Macmorris and Jamy enter and bring with them their Irish and Scottish characteristics, seem to reflect his purpose in this dialogue: Gower, a bystander without peculiarities of speech, does not become '*English*', but Jamy is '*Scot*' and Macmorris '*Irish*'. The name '*Beaumont*' in the entry direction for the second French lords' scene (4.2.0.1) is presumably there because Shakespeare contemplated bringing in a new character so called. The only sign of interference with his papers is the division of the play into acts. As the drama of Shakespeare's time was drama of continuous action he would have been unlikely to introduce act divisions, but the Folio's conventions of layout required them. They were added carelessly: Act 2 should begin with the chorus that follows the first two scenes, but this chorus was overlooked and '*Actus Secundus*' was placed before the next one, so that the next act division was similarly misnumbered and a false act division ('*Actus Quartus*') had to be created at the beginning of 4.7.

The Folio text makes the play one of the longest in the volume (only five others are longer), and as the Quarto text is particularly short the question of theatrical cutting naturally arises. The Quarto may reconstruct a shortened version of the play intended for taking on tour when the company was not playing in London. Another possibility is that it reconstructs the play as adapted from Shakespeare's long script for the company's London performances. A third possibility is that the cuts originated with the Quarto itself. These possibilities need not be mutually exclusive, for the Quarto text may contain cuts of more than one kind.

The no longer topical reference to Essex's future victorious return from Ireland (5.0.22–35) would have to be cut by September 1599, but that is no reason why the whole chorus and all the other choruses should go. They are the play's most distinctive feature, and to omit them would seem an act of folly. That the London performances did not omit them is shown by the Quarto's inclusion of the verse line 'Sir Thomas Grey, knight, of Northumberland' (2.0.25) in its version of 2.2.66–8 and by its incorrect immediate re-entry for Fluellen at the beginning of 5.1. Admittedly the choruses require an experienced actor, who will therefore not be able to take any of the major roles which adjoin his exits and entrances (Canterbury, the King, Exeter, the Constable, Fluellen), but there are plenty of other roles, notably Montjoy, that he can double. Only if the Quarto text is regarded as reconstructing a performance by a very small number of actors can its omission of the choruses be ascribed to casting difficulties.

Casting difficulties, even with a drastically reduced number of actors, cannot explain the omission of the first scene, Canterbury's dialogue with Ely, an omission which may be due to various causes: a desire to suppress the clergy's self-interested motive, a desire to begin the play with a big scene instead of leading up to one, a desire simply to shorten the acting time, or (from a reporter's point of view) a desire to save the trouble of remembering a scene of more length than importance. The same causes, or any combination of them, may account for the omission of four consecutive encouraging speeches by Ely, Exeter, Westmorland and Canterbury in the second scene

(1.2.115–35). The next substantial cut occurs when the King is enlarging on Scroop's unnatural betrayal of him (2.2.105–42). As the physical action here stands still, and as the King has already made his point, it is possible that Shakespeare, if he needed to shorten a long play, may have agreed to the cut or made it himself. But he can hardly have agreed to the total omission of the first scene before Harfleur (3.1), an omission which makes the campaign start with Pistol and his companions instead of with the King. If the omission is due to the exigencies of casting the play for a very small touring group, one wonders why they thought the play worth performing at all. It is hard to see any other reason for this cut – if it is indeed a cut, and not an omission caused by the loss of a sheet of Quarto copy – because the speech is so memorable that anyone who had seen the play more than once, let alone acted in it, could make a shot at reproducing it.

The Quarto also lacks all the dialogue of the four captains (3.2.65–142), Fluellen's criticism of the mines being immediately followed by the King's ultimatum to Harfleur, the second line of which is 'This is the latest parley weele admit'. The sounding of a parley and Gower's reference to it are in the missing passage, so if this is a theatrical cut it is an unskilful one. The King's ultimatum speech is itself heavily cut (3.3.11–43 omitted), perhaps to save acting time or a reporter's trouble, perhaps to remove its terrible details; and his final speech disappears, for no apparent reason, since it is short, allows him to reply to the Governor, expressly states his merciful intentions towards Harfleur's inhabitants, and points towards the next phase of the action, the march towards Calais.

The scenes in the French court and the French camp are shorter in the Quarto than in the Folio. More than thirty consecutive lines (3.5.27–60) are omitted from the first; they can be spared, but their omission does not improve the scene. In the second scene the boasting about the horse, and the consequent verbal fencing, are shortened, apparently through memorial failure (3.7.45–59 is reduced to five lines, and the sequence of the argument is muddled); then, after the Messenger's entrance, the end of the scene is treated as though it were the end of 4.2 after Grandpré's, and 4.2 itself is omitted. This is inept, and the omission of 4.2 causes trouble later when two scenes in the English camp involving the immediate re-entry of one of the characters have to occur consecutively (4.1 and 4.3).

The first of these English camp scenes lacks its opening dialogue, including the King's borrowing of Erpingham's cloak and his stated wish to be private awhile (4.1.1–34), which are necessary to make sense of what follows, in which there are omissions (as is to be expected in reported prose) but no evident cuts. After the dialogue with the soldiers the soliloquy beginning 'Upon the King!' (4.1.227–81), which follows naturally from it, is omitted in favour of the prayer beginning 'O God of battles', which does not. This is not a rational cut, and the stage direction that precedes the prayer is nonsense. The second English camp scene has omissions that seem due merely to lapses of memory (4.3.20–9, 81–8). So do the omissions in Pistol's scene with the French Soldier (see the commentary at 4.4.7), apart from the total omission of the Boy's closing soliloquy, another irrational cut whereby the link between his death and the attack on the tents is destroyed. In the King's speech about the French losses there is a gap (4.8.83–91), but the awkward repetition in 'that in the field lyes slaine. / Of Nobles bearing banners in the field' proclaims the reason to be not a cut but memorial failure. When Fluellen has cudgelled Pistol, Gower loses his moralizing speech and his exit (5.1.69–80) – surprisingly, in view of his well-reported speech at 3.6.66–80; possibly some of the printer's copy has been lost. The long final scene is marked by large omissions: Burgundy's eloquent and emotional appeal for peace is reduced from forty-four lines to four, the wooing dialogue is a faint echo of the original, and the lighthearted dialogue between Burgundy and

King Henry is completely removed, with some following speeches (5.2.278–323). These omissions look less like theatrical cuts than a relaxation of memorial effort as the play's end comes in sight.

It is clear that the Quarto is not an accurate record of a systematically cut version of the play, and therefore that it can give no firm grounds for deciding what cuts, if any, were made for the London performances. Its text could not be acted without some correction of its errors of stagecraft, particularly the immediate re-entry of the same characters to begin a new scene. If it were a reconstruction of a shortened version recently taken on tour these errors of stagecraft would surely not exist, and in any case there seems to have been no occasion for a tour between the summer of 1599 and the summer of 1600 – since there was no plague epidemic or other special circumstance to close the playhouses – unless the actors happened to travel during Lent.[1] Probably it was compiled simply to provide a reading text of the play.

With all its faults, however, the Quarto cannot be disregarded, for it is based on the recollection of the play as it was performed in 1599–1600, and it may therefore embody, in however imperfect a form, changes made between composition and performance. Much attention has lately been paid to this aspect of dramatic texts. For instance, the editors of the Oxford Shakespeare write, of *Hamlet*, 'We believe that the 1604 quarto represents the play as Shakespeare first wrote it, before it was performed, and that the Folio represents a theatrical text of the play after he had revised it' (Oxf, xxxvi); they accordingly base their edited text on the Folio, printing as an appendix the passages that occur only in the 1604 quarto. When two good texts of the same play exist, they argue, conflation of them

---

1 'Probably during 1588–91, and certainly during 1595–1602 and 1610–16, plague was so far absent as to be practically negligible' (Chambers, 1.329). Between 28 July and 10 October 1597 there had been an inhibition of playing, in the interests of public order (ibid., 1.298–9), but no such inhibition occurred in 1599–1600. Performances were traditionally inhibited during Lent (ibid., 1.315–16).

may result in 'a version that never existed in Shakespeare's time'.

As far as *Henry V* is concerned there is no question of conflating two good texts. The Folio text is so evidently the better that it must be the basis of a modern edition. But one major difference between it and the Quarto does require an editorial decision, the latter's substitution of Bourbon for the Dauphin in 3.7.

The Folio names Bourbon only twice in stage directions, in 4.5 (when he enters with the other defeated French lords, including the Dauphin) and 4.7 (when he enters, mute, among King Henry's prisoners). These two scenes constitute his role in the Folio, and he dominates the first of them with his vivid picture of the degradation that awaits anyone 'that will not follow Bourbon now' and with his final line, 'Let life be short, else shame will be too long.' It is true that in 3.5 he is among those exhorted by the French King to 'hie to the field', but the list is nineteen names long and is far from requiring his presence among the '*others*' called for in the opening stage direction. The Quarto brings him on stage as early as 2.4 (and includes his name in the French King's opening address to his nobles), reintroduces him in 3.5 (and assigns to him the speech which the Folio assigns to Britain), substitutes him for the Dauphin in 3.7, and gives him the same part in 4.5 that he takes in the Folio. The prisoners among whom he appears in the Folio's 4.7 are not included in the Quarto's corresponding stage direction, and, as already stated, the Quarto omits 4.2.

The Dauphin disappears from the Quarto after 3.5, which ends in both texts with his father's insistence on his remaining in Rouen while the other lords go to fight the English. In keeping him away from Agincourt the Quarto is consistent with Holinshed and also with *The Famous Victories*, in which King Henry ironically expresses his regret that he and the Dauphin cannot play a tennis match with cannon-balls. Holinshed reports that after Agincourt the Dauphin died, either of grief or of some physical illness, whereas in *The Famous Victories* he is present in the final scene and has to swear allegiance to King Henry. The Folio's version of his role, in which he is present at Agincourt but thereafter melts into thin air, thus differs from all the other versions, historical or theatrical.

That deliberate alteration of the Folio's handling of the Dauphin and Bourbon has occurred in the Quarto is beyond debate. What is debatable is the significance of the alteration and its consequences for a modern editor. On the one hand it can be argued that the Quarto records changes made after Shakespeare's manuscript was delivered to the actors, that these changes mark a final resolution on a matter over which Shakespeare had been hesitating, that they were incorporated into performances, and therefore that in this respect the Quarto gives the authentic theatrical version of the play, which should be adopted by an editor. On the other hand it can be argued that the Folio preserves Shakespeare's conception of the Dauphin's and Bourbon's roles in the play, that he did not mind the inconsistency between the Dauphin's being forbidden to go to Agincourt and his later presence there, that the Quarto's changes may not have had his approval (if made for the stage) or even his knowledge (if made by whoever compiled the Quarto), and therefore that the Folio's version should be adopted by an editor. Of recent editions the Oxford Shakespeare and the New Cambridge Shakespeare adopt the Quarto's version, while the present one adopts the Folio's for the following reasons.[1] When Shakespeare was completing the manuscript of the play he did not go back to 3.5 and remove

---

1 Oxf[1] (and Oxf), Cam[2]. The fact that both the Dauphin and Bourbon appear in the Folio version of 4.5 requires further decisions by editors who follow the Quarto in removing the Dauphin from the Agincourt scenes. Cam[2], which retains all the Folio's lines in 4.5, gives Bourbon the Dauphin's speeches as well as his own. Oxf[1], which combines lines from the Folio with lines from the Quarto, creates a third text of the scene, giving the Folio and Quarto versions in an appendix. It is probable that both Oxf[1]'s and Cam[2]'s conflations are versions that never existed in Shakespeare's time.

the French King's veto, nor did he insert any explanation of the Dauphin's apparent defiance of it, either of which he could easily have done if inconsistency troubled him or if he felt it might trouble his audience. He may never have contemplated following *The Famous Victories* in making the Dauphin swear allegiance, or in introducing him into the final scene to be deprived of his inheritance: that final scene is one of rec- onciliation after conflict, and the Dauphin of the play (still less his rebellious successor the Dauphin of *1 Henry VI*) could never have been assimilated into it; 'out of sight, out of mind' is a common enough principle in Shakespeare's dramatic art. (It is also just possible that he had followed Holinshed and killed the Dauphin off in the two lost half-lines of the Act 5 chorus.) It seems unlikely that he could be bullied into altering his play by some friend with a stronger regard for historical truth (Jonson, perhaps), or by his fellow sharers in the Lord Chamberlain's Men (imagine Burbage as Bottom: 'There are things in this history of Henry the Fifth that will never please'). And even if he had been persuaded to make the changes, would he have made them in such a perfunctory fashion, with barely more than the stroke of a pen?

> *Gebon.* The Duke of *Burbon* longs for morning.

> *Or.* Well the Duke of *Burbon*, is simply,
> The most actiue Gentleman of *France*.

(Not even 'my lord of Bourbon', as idiomatic usage between equals would surely require.) Would he have countenanced the inconsistency of character (no principle of his dramatic art) created by fusing the man who prates about his horse like an ass with the man who indignantly rallies his comrades for a final assault? And who is this Gebon who replaces Rambures in the Quarto's versions of 3.7 and 4.5? It is sometimes suggested that Gebon stands for the name of some actor, a most unlikely suggestion in view of the Quarto's probable origin as a memorially reconstructed text.[1] More probably his name is meant to be a French one (there is a Frenchman called Gobin de Graie in *Edward III*, printed in 1596), and he comes out of the same stable as '*Gerard* and *Verton*', who are the Quarto's substitutes for Beaumont and Marle in the list of French dead which the Folio transcribes from Holinshed in 4.8. In short, he comes out of the head of whoever compiled the Quarto, on whose initiative it is possible that the substitution of Bourbon for the Dauphin was made.

THE PLAY

In a memorable phrase in his *Defence of Poesy* Sir Philip Sidney describes the historian as 'captived to the truth of a foolish world'. Sidney is here undertaking to show that poetry teaches better moral lessons than history because the poet is at liberty to reward virtue and punish vice in his fictions whereas the historian must record what actually happened to virtuous and vicious persons; but his contrast can be applied in a more general sense to the poet's greater freedom, and the contrast is specially interesting when the poet is not simply imagining events but reshaping historical ones. Even in Sidney's particular sense it can be applied to dramatic fictions based on the life of Henry V: both *The Famous Victories* and Shakespeare's play (in the Folio version) show pride going before a fall in the case of the Dauphin.

Though Shakespeare read history attentively he was not fettered by it.

> O, that it could be proved
> That some night-tripping fairy had exchanged
> In cradle clothes our children where they lay,
> And called mine Percy, his Plantagenet!
> Then would I have his Harry, and he mine.

---

1 Texts in which actors' names occur are usually thought to derive either from authorial manuscript copy or from promptbook copy (*TxC*, 12, 169, 176, 274, 371).

Henry IV's wistful reflection (*1 Henry IV*, 1.1.85–9) makes Hotspur, who was born in 1364, contemporary with Prince Henry, who was born in 1387. This liberty taken with the facts is essential to Shakespeare's dramatic design. In his interview with the Prince (3.3.93–6) the King returns to the contrast between the two young men:

> For all the world
> As thou art to this hour was Richard then,
> When I from France set foot at Ravenspurgh,
> And even as I was then is Percy now.[1]

The Prince, in reply, vows that 'in the closing of some glorious day' he will 'redeem all this on Percy's head':

> for the time will come
> That I shall make this northern youth exchange
> His glorious deeds for my indignities.

His prophecy is fulfilled at the end of the play when he kills Hotspur at Shrewsbury.

What served Shakespeare's purpose for Shrewsbury would not have served his purpose for Agincourt. Though Holinshed reports that 'the king that daie shewed himselfe a valiant knight' and describes his hand-to-hand fight with the Duke of Alençon, the only use that Shakespeare makes of that combat is to supply the King with an invented reason why Fluellen should wear in his cap the glove that was actually the soldier Williams's pledge given to the disguised King in their nocturnal argument. The King could have no personal antagonist corresponding to Hotspur: the Dauphin, sender of the tennis-balls, to whom he returns through Exeter's mouth 'Scorn and defiance, slight regard, contempt', and who has never shown his valour except in beating his unresisting lackey, is out of the question. (In the Olivier film of the play, riding a white

---

1 As a matter of fact, Richard II and Henry IV *were* born in the same year, 1367 – three years after Hotspur.

horse, the King concludes the battle by striking down the Constable riding a black one.) The battle of Agincourt is so presented as to justify the King's comment on the disproportionate lists of French and English dead: 'O God, thine arm was here.' And with God fighting for the English it was not necessary or desirable to show the English fighting lustily for themselves; though the Chorus apologizes in advance for a battle represented by 'four or five most vile and ragged foils / Right ill-disposed in brawl ridiculous', the audience in fact sees no such thing. Not a word is said, either, about the sharpened stakes that the King caused to be pitched before his men to defend them against the French cavalry, though Holinshed describes this 'politike inuention' (his marginal note) in detail, and *The Famous Victories* dwells upon it ('But *Robin*, didst thou see what a pollicie / The King had, to see how the French men were kild / With the stakes of the trees'). If the King has fought bravely, he has done so as the leader of a 'band of brothers' facing fearful odds. He returns home to a hero's welcome, of course, but he refuses to let 'His bruised helmet and his bended sword' be borne before him,

> Giving full trophy, signal and ostent
> Quite from himself to God.

There is no mention in *1 Henry IV* of God's part in the victory at Shrewsbury, but it will be remembered that in *2 Henry IV* 'God, and not we, hath safely fought today' is Prince John's comment on his bloodless capture of the Yorkshire rebels.

Whatever the audience is expected to make of Prince John's conviction that God's arm was present in his own stratagem, it is not encouraged to be sceptical about Agincourt. *Henry V* is a celebratory play, commemorating a famous victory. The refrain of Southey's poem on the battle of Blenheim will come to mind, no doubt; the old countryman tells his grandchildren,

> 'They say it was a shocking sight
> After the field was won;

34

> For many thousand bodies here
>   Lay rotting in the sun;
> But things like that, you know, must be
> After a famous victory.'

Shakespeare was no less conscious than Southey of the cost of war, as he showed in speeches by Williams, Montjoy, Burgundy and King Henry himself, but the politically inspired irony of Southey's poem (first published in *The Morning Post* of 9 August 1798) is foreign to *Henry V*.

Agincourt was the predetermined climax of the play. Its position in the dramatic action was predetermined too. *The Famous Victories* had followed the victory with the peace and the betrothal, and the Epilogue to *2 Henry IV*, mentioning Katherine, shows that Shakespeare meant his play to do the same. The action of *1 Henry IV* had been completed with the victory at Shrewsbury, but the action of *Henry V* would have been incomplete without the final re-establishment of harmony – final, that is, as far as the play is concerned. To have prolonged it to the King's death, from camp fever, while fighting renewed wars in France, would have made the play a quite different one, and can hardly have crossed Shakespeare's mind. ('And shall I die, and this unconquered?', the poignant burden of the dying Tamburlaine, would here have been out of place.) Shakespeare's Epilogue, sometimes regarded as derogating from Henry V's achievements, actually sets the seal on them.

With the end of the play predetermined, Shakespeare then had to dispose the chief historical events that led up to Agincourt. They must have virtually disposed themselves. The taking of Harfleur, the one conspicuous military success of the campaign, had to occupy the middle of the play, leaving the tennis-balls incident and the discovery of the conspiracy for the first two acts. Whether or not Shakespeare had the term 'act' in mind, his introduction of the Chorus created a five-act structure more obviously in this play than in any other. The

Chorus, the play's most distinctive feature, turns *Henry V* into a 'history' – 'Admit me Chorus to this history' – in the sense of an epic poem in scenes.

There remained the question of how the comic element was to be managed. A comic element there had to be, after the two *Henry IV* plays, in which Falstaff had been so popular with audiences. Falstaff had been promised, as had Katherine, in the Epilogue to *2 Henry IV*, but after his rejection by the newly crowned Prince Henry his occupation was gone. A reformed Falstaff, if that were thinkable, would be worse than no Falstaff; an unreformed Falstaff could not be allowed near Harfleur or Agincourt; and, with the action transferred from England to France, Falstaff could not have independent adventures at home. Pistol would have to be moved up into his place. He could be to Harfleur and Agincourt as Falstaff was to Shrewsbury and Gaultree Forest; he could even capture a readily yielding prisoner, as Falstaff captured Coleville. Nym (created for *The Merry Wives of Windsor*) and Bardolph would provide supporting humour. Mistress Quickly, who had been prominent in all three of the Falstaff plays (her transformation from a hostess to a housekeeper in *The Merry Wives* testifies to her popularity), may have seemed difficult to place in *Henry V* until Shakespeare thought of Falstaff's dying on the eve of the French campaign. Had he already thought of this when he made the Epilogue of *2 Henry IV* humorously foretell that Falstaff would 'die of a sweat', or was that just a joke at the time but one that continued to echo in his mind? Whenever he thought of it, once he had done so everything fell into place. Falstaff was indeed 'in' the new play, after a fashion, and the Epilogue's promise kept. Mistress Quickly, describing his death, had an important role, even though it was limited to the first half of the play. By marrying her to Pistol, Shakespeare contrived a leave-taking to match Falstaff's farewell to Doll Tearsheet in *2 Henry IV*. By making Nym her jilted suitor he contrived a lively quarrel in which

Bardolph had something to do as peacemaker, and even Doll Tearsheet could be mentioned. The Boy, Falstaff's page in *2 Henry IV* and *The Merry Wives*, could go with the men to France.

What were they to do when they got there? Pistol's capture of the French Soldier was a fairly obvious development (*The Famous Victories* had included something of the sort), with the Boy's role of interpreter and commentator as a thoroughly Shakespearean bonus, but what else could they do, and who could share their scenes in a play where the low comedy would have to be kept well clear of the King's heroics? Shakespeare's answer was to create Fluellen, a Welsh captain who is both comic and respectable. (The Welsh parson Sir Hugh Evans, who has much in common with him, must have been a success in *The Merry Wives*.) Did Shakespeare think first of the leek-eating incident and work backwards from it? It could have been an episode complete in itself, with Pistol mocking at the leek and Fluellen cudgelling him, but that would never have satisfied Shakespeare. To prepare for it at a long distance by making Pistol and Fluellen quarrel over Bardolph's reprieve, and at the same time to identify Bardolph as the soldier in Holinshed who was hanged for robbing a church, was a master-stroke, and another was to make Pistol announce his threat to knock Fluellen's leek about his pate to the disguised King on the eve of Agincourt. Thus Pistol and the King do meet, though the nature of the play might have seemed to make their meeting impossible.

By this time, with Fluellen in the play and with the King disguised, comedy was opening up in all directions. Fluellen can meet Macmorris and Jamy, can give Gower advice on the eve of Agincourt, can moralize to Pistol upon Fortune's mutability and to Gower upon King Henry's resemblance to Alexander the Great, can speak to the King as one Welshman to another, and in terms of action can be ignorantly involved in the King's practical joke with the soldier's glove. The

2 'The last scene in the life of Sir John Falstaff'. *The Life of Sir John Falstaff*. Illustrated by George Cruikshank. With a biography of the knight from authentic sources by R. B. Brough (London, 1858)

disguised King's exchange of gloves with the soldier, and the quarrel that provokes it, arise from an encounter rich in serio-comic dramatic irony. No doubt it was for the sake of that encounter that Shakespeare made the King borrow Erpingham's cloak; and once the King was wearing the cloak his encounter with Pistol was a happily invented development.

The danger of the next day's battle hangs over the common soldiers and the King alike, and during their dialogue it is never forgotten, even though the exchange of gloves -- not to mention the audience's knowledge that the English will win the battle -- is a guarantee that comedy will reassert itself. Williams survives for a second encounter with the King (in his own person this time), and it can fairly be hoped that Bates and Court are not among the five and twenty commoners who lose their lives. But Bardolph and Nym lose theirs, for stealing, and so does the Boy when the luggage of the camp is plundered by French stragglers -- another of Shakespeare's brilliant applications of Holinshed's facts to the characters in his own play. Falstaff has died already, and in his final speech Pistol reveals that Mistress Quickly is dead too. In the *Henry IV* plays no comic characters die: Falstaff is never more alive than when he is shamming death at Shrewsbury. In *Henry V* Pistol is the sole survivor. It is hard not to see this difference as Shakespeare's announcement that he had come to the end of this particular road.

In the meantime he was shaping the present play. Did he modify the design as he went along? Is the dialogue between the four captains, in which Fluellen's speech prefixes become '*Welch.*', an amplified substitute for a shorter dialogue between him and Gower? Is the final couplet of the chorus before Act 2 a postscript made necessary by the splitting of one Eastcheap scene, originally intended to follow the scene of the conspirators at Southampton, into two? These are questions which seem incapable of resolution. Shakespeare must have recognized that Falstaff's death could not be crushed into the end of the quarrel scene and be immediately followed by the departure for Southampton and France, but did he try to write such a scene before the recognition dawned? The two scenes that we have, separated by the Southampton scene, are very different in character. The first is lively, given an unexpected development when the Boy enters with the news of Falstaff's sickness; the second is elegiac, allowing the audience to digest the fact that they will see Falstaff no more. Yet the final couplet of the Act 2 chorus does look like an afterthought, after the jocular couplet (to all appearances a final one) that precedes it. And yet, again, that final couplet may not be an afterthought but the dramatic representation of one, with the Chorus turning back to the audience, in the act of making his exit, to give them a piece of confidential information.

Towards the end of the second Eastcheap scene Nym says, 'Shall we shog? The King will be gone from Southampton.' Since the Southampton scene had ended with the King's order to set sail for France, nothing is more certain; but nothing is more certain than that Nym and the rest will not be left behind. Shakespeare's willingness to sacrifice consistency to dramatic effect is well known, and *Henry V* affords many examples of it; one of the most notable is the scene where Fluellen cudgels Pistol into eating the leek just after Saint David's day (1 March) and Pistol resolves to pretend that he got his broken pate 'in the Gallia wars' when he returns to England – all this occurring just after the Chorus has recounted the King's return to England (with his army) and has asked the audience to excuse the long lapse of time between Agincourt (Saint Crispin's day, 25 October) and the King's return to France. Obviously there is no fitting this scene into the time-scheme of the play, and just as obviously no one who sees the play staged in the fluent Elizabethan manner will care. What matters is the effect that it will make in performance – and no small part of that effect is the pleasurable surprise of seeing Pistol and Fluellen again when it seemed that Shakespeare had done with them. He might be saying to the audience, 'You have forgot the leek I told you of.'

Performance needs to be constantly borne in mind by anyone who reads a play or writes about one, assuming that the play was written to be performed. In *Henry V*, thanks to the interventions of the Chorus, it is easier than usual to imagine oneself sitting or standing in the playhouse, sharing the expectations of the original audience (as far as twentieth-century spectators can share those of sixteenth-century ones), and responding to the sequence of dramatic impressions which the performance offers.

The stage action begins with what may come as a surprise. After the exalted tone of the Prologue, picturing the 'two mighty monarchies' that confront each other across the English Channel and inviting the spectators to deck with their thoughts the actors' kings, the first two persons to appear are two bishops, their minds occupied with a parliamentary bill to confiscate the temporal lands of the clergy. We almost seem to be at the wrong play – until, with the line 'The King is full of grace and fair regard', they begin to contemplate Prince Henry's reformation when he succeeded to the throne, and Canterbury dwells on his astonishing grasp of all that a king should understand, and even of theology into the bargain. Those spectators who had seen the *Henry IV* plays would know about his reformation (and his deeper character), but those who had not would need to be told about it if his response to the Dauphin's taunting message in the next scene was to make its proper effect. When the bishops revert to the bill and the support that they hope to obtain from the King, we are told of the royal claim to France and the arrival of the French ambassador, and are led towards the second scene. The bishops' self-interested motive, which cannot be ignored, has often been a stumbling-block, but in view of its function in getting the action started it is doubtful whether it should be allowed to colour Canterbury's part in the next scene, not to mention the whole Agincourt campaign. Canterbury himself, with his shrewd humour (''Twould drink the cup and all'; 'Which I could with a ready guess declare / Before the Frenchman speak a word of it'), is not presented unattractively.

This opening scene, which in the days of editorial scene locations used to be situated in an antechamber, is followed by what might have been expected in its place as an opening scene, the King in courtly splendour. The contrast heightens this second scene's effect. Here again there is a surprise, when the ambassador's admittance is postponed by the King so that he can hear Canterbury's exposition of the royal claim's validity. In the opening scene Canterbury's private exposition was said to have been broken off by the ambassador's request for audience. The discrepancy will not trouble many spectators,[1] and the dramatic point is made that the King controls events and is not controlled by them, while Canterbury's exposition now becomes public and prompts a general display of enthusiasm for pursuing the royal claim by force of arms. It hardly needs saying that his speech about the Salic law is to be taken as seriously by a theatre audience as it is by the stage one, and that the King's subsequent line, 'May I with right and conscience make this claim?', is not expressing bewilderment or suspicion but reinforcing the 'conjuration' that he laid upon Canterbury to unfold the case 'justly and religiously'. It is dramatically important that in this scene where everyone is urging him to emulate his valiant ancestors the King should seem not passive but active, and not hot-headed but level-headed; thus it is he who raises the topic of defence against Scottish invaders, and when that matter has been settled he orders 'the messengers sent from the Dauphin' to be admitted. From this point onwards Shakespeare gives the actor of the King more rein, with the powerful lines beginning 'Now are

1 Shakespeare covers it by conspicuously naming the time of the audience as four o'clock – not explaining why Canterbury could not finish his talk with the King once the audience had been promised.

we well resolved'. A touch of displeasure at the fact that the Dauphin, not the French King, has sent the ambassadors is appropriate, and gives additional cause for the ambassador's apprehension about how his message may be received.[1] While it is being delivered, every eye, on stage and in the theatre, will be on the King; at its end, when the tennis-balls are displayed, his reply is the climax of the scene. He is sure to rise to his feet, on which he will remain till the general exit.[2]

The Chorus voices the universal enthusiasm for the war, his hyperboles enlivened with wit ('They sell the pasture now to buy the horse'). The tone then changes, as the traitors are named, to one of apprehension:

> And by their hands this grace of kings must die,
> If hell and treason hold their promises,
> Ere he take ship for France, and in Southampton.

Here is a forecast of excitement to come, with which the speech almost ends. But not quite. The afterthought couplet, postponing Southampton, allows Eastcheap to erupt into the play. Bardolph and Nym, Pistol and the Hostess, are welcome arrivals: comedy has been delayed in this play compared with the two *Henry IV* ones, and all the physical swaggering, the drawing and sheathing of swords, is welcome too. Then, with the Boy's message about Falstaff's sickness, the mood changes: 'The King has killed his heart.' More swaggering follows, but the Hostess's return reasserts the sombre tone, and the exit line, 'Let us condole the knight, for, lambkins, we will live', confirms that Falstaff is dying.

Now we reach Southampton and the conspiracy. In a different kind of play it might have been given dramatic development over several scenes, but here it is already discovered and all

---

1   Shakespeare does not mention the French King's occasional lapses into insanity, during which the Dauphin acted as regent, but makes it appear that the Dauphin has behaved presumptuously.
2   His throne, which has been twice mentioned by Canterbury, will have been brought on at the beginning of the scene and will be removed at its end.

that remains is exposure and denunciation. The exposure, making use of the pardoned drunkard and of the royal commissions, is inventive (on Shakespeare's part, not on the King's), and the denunciation is eloquent, with the utmost emphasis laid on the ingratitude of a close friend (always a strong theme of Shakespeare's). The traitors' contrition – even that of Cambridge, who hints at his dynastic ambitions – makes even them retrospectively patriotic, justifying the King's confidence that now, thanks to God's disclosure of the conspiracy, 'every rub is smoothed on our way'.

The ringing tone of his final couplet throws into relief the despondent prose as Pistol and his fellows leave the tavern after Falstaff's death. Yet even in despondency they have vitality, and the Hostess's warm-hearted account of his last moments even has humour (unconscious, of course): 'Now I, to comfort him, bid him 'a should not think of God; I hoped there was no need to trouble himself with any such thoughts yet.'[1] Finally swagger reappears: 'To suck, to suck, the very blood to suck!'

'Thus comes the English with full power upon us.' The French King's opening line may have a whiff of incongruity considering who were the last English to leave the stage, but his speech about fortifying France casts our minds back to King Henry's 'No king of England, if not king of France'. The Dauphin's belittlement of the English threat is rebutted by the Constable, whom he airily contradicts, and by the French King, who fears a renewal of Crécy. Exeter, arriving as ambassador, virtually personifies his fear, especially when he foretells the slaughter of those 'for whom this hungry war / Opens his vasty jaws' if the royal pedigree that he presents is not enough to ensure the yielding up of the crown. The Dauphin, still impervious to rebuke, is threatened for his sending of the

---

1 This has the true Shakespearean stamp, like Sir Andrew's challenge: 'Fare thee well, and God have mercy upon one of our souls. He may have mercy upon mine, but my hope is better, and so look to thyself' (*TN* 3.4.163–5).

tennis-balls. Exeter dominates the stage from his arrival to the end of the scene; the last few speeches are a further demonstration of his authority, though the French King maintains his dignity.

The war is now ready to begin, as the Chorus, after an imagination-feeding picture of the ships sailing to Harfleur, announces: 'Work, work your thoughts, and therein see a siege.' Even while he is still speaking the cannon are heard, and it is against a background of 'Alarums' and soldiers carrying scaling-ladders that King Henry makes his rallying speech: 'Once more unto the breach, dear friends, once more.' Harfleur is proving a hard nut to crack, and any spectator who expects the scaling-ladders to be placed against the tiring-house and the siege to be over now that the King is on stage will be disappointed. Satisfaction of a different kind is provided by 'On, on, on, on, on, to the breach, to the breach!' from Bardolph. But this first appearance of the Eastcheap soldiers in France is very short – shorter than the Boy's soliloquy after their exit[1] – and the comedy that follows is from Fluellen and the other captains as they discuss military matters, the mines being appropriate to the protracted siege. Their argument is neatly brought to an end when 'The town sounds a parley', which, in the next scene, brings the King before the walls of Harfleur. What the assaults on the breach and the digging of the mines have failed to do is finally accomplished by the dreadful threats of his speech, coupled with the Dauphin's failure to raise the siege. It can be argued that if the defenders, who have called for the parley, were going to surrender anyway there is no need for the speech, but to stage the surrender without it would have been an anticlimax. As it is, Shakespeare has it all ways: the King is prepared to be ruthless if the war needs ruthlessness, but he views the consequences as a horror which he will gladly

---

1 His soliloquy was undoubtedly added by Shakespeare during composition, after he had decided that Bardolph and Nym would be hanged for their thefts (so this first appearance in France is also their last) and that the Boy would be killed.

avoid if Harfleur, by yielding, will let him, and when Harfleur does yield he bids Exeter 'Use mercy to them all'. Then comes his announcement,

> For us, dear uncle,
> The winter coming on and sickness growing
> Upon our soldiers, we will retire to Calais.

– not at this moment, obviously, for they must enter Harfleur with the flourish of victory.

The end of the siege calls for a change of mood. If one considers how unsuitable a reversion to Pistol and the rest would be, one appreciates all the more the first appearance of Katherine. The marriage negotiations lately referred to by the Chorus, though premature and abortive, will have made it clear who she is, and this scene foreshadows her betrothal to King Henry in the final one. The light humour of her language lesson bridges the passage of time between the departure from Harfleur and the next reported stage of the English march:

> 'Tis certain he hath passed the river Somme.

The whole theme of this scene in the French court is that King Henry must be intercepted before he reaches Calais; he must be defeated or compelled to yield to ransom. That established, we are ready to return to him, but before he enters we have Shakespeare's master-stroke, already mentioned, of Pistol's encounter with Fluellen, so that he enters to hear not only the news of Exeter's capture of the bridge but also the news of Bardolph's execution – so naturally introduced when, apart from him, 'the Duke hath lost never a man'. The audience's recollection that in his younger days King Henry had been familiar with Bardolph gives piquancy to Fluellen's casual phrase 'one Bardolph, if your majesty know the man'. Of course Fluellen has no notion that he does know him; he merely thinks that because of Bardolph's fiery and pimply face, which he describes, the King might have noticed even a common soldier who looked like that. And, equally of course, the King gives no verbal sign of recognition or feeling: 'We would have all such offenders so cut off.'[1] With that, Montjoy's arrival with the French demand for surrender changes the mood, and the King's reply, expressing a determination to fight if forced to do so even though his men are sick and hungry, leads to yet another sounding of what has become the keynote of his being: 'We are in God's hand, brother, not in theirs.'

Shakespeare hurries events forward now. No sooner have King Henry and his forces left the stage, to cross the bridge, camp beyond the river and continue their march next day, than it is the eve of Agincourt and we are in the French camp: 'Tut, I have the best armour of the world. Would it were day!' The Dauphin gives another display of his self-importance, and the mutual hostility between him and the Constable, suggested in the first French court scene, comes out more clearly. This scene allows the Chorus to plunge straight into a description of the two camps without any narrative preliminaries. Into this tableau comes the figure of the King, 'Walking from watch to watch, from tent to tent', radiating warmth and confidence, 'Thawing cold fear' in his soldiers. 'And so our scene must to the battle fly' – the apologetic lines bringing our minds back from that transcendent vision to theatrical realities, and thereby to the next scene, in which an alternative or supplementary version of the King's walk among the tents is to be given – Shakespeare having it both ways, as he so often does.

What the opening of this scene and the transcendent vision have in common is comradeship and cheerfulness in the face of danger. The King's serious enough reflection on the moral usefulness of the enemy's presence has its humorous touches, and Sir Thomas Erpingham's 'Now lie I like a king' is witty.

---

1   What sign do his adverse critics want him to give? An aside, perhaps ('Bardolph, art thou gone?')? Shakespeare leaves us to guess what he feels. As to reprieving Bardolph, there can be no question of that, and in any case he seems to be past reprieving by this time.

The tone is being set for what will follow after the King has borrowed Erpingham's cloak. No reason is given for borrowing it, unless one is implied in 'I and my bosom must debate awhile', and some have suggested that Shakespeare originally meant to proceed straight to the prayer beginning 'O God of battles'. If this is so (and Erpingham's reappearance just before the prayer can be regarded as an awkward join), one can only marvel at the abundance of his invention. But one can marvel at that even if he had planned the scene in advance. Observe how naturally Pistol's grandiose tribute to the King arises from the exchange of greetings between strangers, and is immediately followed by 'What is thy name?' (which, with the reply, highlights the dramatic irony), and how naturally the dialogue turns Pistol's thoughts to Fluellen. Having given the fico to Fluellen earlier, it is inevitable that he should now give it to Fluellen's kinsman, an unwitting abuse of the King's royal person that outdoes Williams's later derision of the stranger's 'foolish saying'. The brief and characteristic appearance of Fluellen himself, passively witnessed by the King, gives a breathing-space between the King's incognito dialogues with Pistol and with the three soldiers, Bates, Court and Williams.[1]

Who could have foreseen this second dialogue? So far, everything that has happened since the King assumed Erpingham's cloak has been humorous and theatrical (and none the worse for that). Now comes a different sort of naturalness from the one that has been noticed in the dialogue with Pistol: 'We see yonder the beginning of the day, but I think we shall never see the end of it.' Apart from Nym's recognition at Harfleur that 'the knocks are too hot' (itself humorous and theatrical) there has been nothing to show the common soldiers' natural fear of death, a fear now heightened by the fearful odds in the

---

1 Only the first-mentioned of these is ever named in the dialogue: 'Brother John Bates, is not that the morning which breaks yonder?' Probably it was this opening line, indicating that they are not literally brothers, that led Shakespeare to give them all full names. Williams needs a surname for the stage directions and speech prefixes of the later scenes in which he appears without the other two.

enemy's favour. This is the cold fear that, according to the Chorus, the King's sun-like eye thawed as he cheered his troops, and it would be possible to imagine the King now unmuffling to inspire them with confidence. That was not Shakespeare's way. He maintains the King's incognito and with it the dramatic irony: 'I think the King is but a man, as I am'; 'I think he would not wish himself anywhere but where he is'; 'Methinks I could not die anywhere so contented as in the King's company'. Moreover, he allows him to be drawn into an argument, not about the justice of his cause but about any king's responsibility for the souls of such soldiers of his as die in a battle on his behalf.[1] His long speech, which begins as a refutation ('by your rule'), ends as an informal sermon on readiness for death. It convinces the soldiers. The quarrel that leads to his exchange of gloves with Williams has a quite different origin, when the conversation reverts to whether the King will be ransomed if defeated. The King's remarks resume the dramatic irony that has been suspended during his long speech, but this is necessarily lost on Williams, who seizes scornfully on 'I will never trust his word after'. By now the present situation is visibly setting up a future ironic one ('Well, I will do it, though I take thee in the King's company'), and the audience is bound to ask whether Williams will then actually strike the King, and, if not, how that will be avoided. The soldiers' exit, with Bates's reproof to 'you English fools' and the King's genially quibbling reply, is well managed, but it does not lead the audience to expect the anguished soliloquy beginning 'Upon the King!' This soliloquy presently moves from the particular to the general: 'subject to the breath / Of every fool whose sense no more can feel / But his own

---

1   It is Williams who shifts the discussion to this point with 'I am afeard there are few die well that die in a battle, for how can they charitably dispose of anything when blood is their argument?' Probably it was in Shakespeare's interest to make him do so, not least because we do not want a recapitulation of the royal claim to the French throne. What is important to recognize is that the King is not disingenuously shifting the discussion, as some of his detractors say.

wringing' can hardly refer to Williams's serious reflections in the face of imminent death, and recalls rather the railing drunkard of the Southampton scene. In fact it turns into a set piece on the theme of Henry IV's soliloquy ending 'Uneasy lies the head that wears a crown', and it is not clear why Shakespeare protracts it in this way, unless to make sure that when Erpingham arrives he does find the King in meditation. The prayer that follows Erpingham's exit is another matter. It too has a double theme, the fortifying of his soldiers' hearts and the pardoning of his father's fault; this second theme brings out an impassioned tone. This scene has shown both the King's serious confidence and, latterly, his serious misgivings. It quells any suspicion that he is presuming on the divine aid that he so often invokes. Its end, with Gloucester's interruption of the prayer (an interruption foreshadowed by Erpingham's statement that the King's nobles are seeking him), is finely judged, as can be seen if one imagines the prayer ending with a couplet and the King springing off stage.

A short return to the French camp exhibits the Dauphin again and paints a further picture of the wretched English host, but its chief dramatic effect is suspense – an army poised for the command 'To the field!', which is finally given. Suspense is also a large element in the scene in the English camp that follows, beginning with the nobles' talk of the enemy's strength and with Salisbury's exit to take up his place in the battle-line. But the suspense is intermittent. There is room for the King's characteristic response to the overheard wish for more men from England, which leads into his Saint Crispin's day speech, a speech which is nicely balanced between the acknowledgement of danger and the hope of victory. For the audience, knowing the outcome, it is a prophecy of legendary glory to come:

> And Crispin Crispian shall ne'er go by
> From this day to the ending of the world

> But we in it shall be remembered,
> We few, we happy few, we band of brothers.

At its end, suspense returns with Salisbury's announcement that the French are ready to charge. But immediately the shock of battle is averted by Montjoy's arrival. This second invitation to surrender and pay ransom is from Holinshed (who had not mentioned ransom on the occasion of Montjoy's earlier visit), and nothing in the previous scene has prepared for it – nor, indeed, allowed it. Shakespeare, as so often, is playing fast and loose. In postponing the fighting it is an anticlimax, but in putting the King under further strain it is intensely dramatic: 'Good God, why should they mock poor fellows thus?' He is equal to the occasion, and his rejoinder, like the Crispin speech, is a gift to the actor – with its grand and macabre image of even the English dead wreaking destruction on their enemies, and with its ironical reference to the 'slovenry' of him and his army – and it calls for a warm response from the soldiers, the stage audience: 'But by the mass, our hearts are in the trim'. Now, at last, battle can be joined, and the 'excursions' which the Folio's stage direction here specifies will not look like a 'brawl ridiculous' to the theatre audience after such preparation. But before this stage action has time to grow stale Pistol is on view again, receiving the surrender of the French soldier. The comic virtue of this scene is in the dialogue, and it is easy to spoil it by overloading it with action, specially as the Boy's concluding soliloquy must not look like a dispensable append-age. It is to be the last we see of him, and his last confidential remark about the undefended luggage needs to be delivered to the audience as engagingly as the actor can do it. The next scene, with the French lords in defeat, is the last we are to see of the Dauphin, whose actor had better make the point clear by taking the door opposite to Bourbon's for his exit. (In the Olivier film he is seen to turn his horse for flight.) Now King Henry reappears, with prisoners, and hears from Exeter a moving account of York's and Suffolk's deaths – another of Shakespeare's additions, and presumably included in order to vary the pace and the mood of the battle scenes, as well as to acknowledge York and Suffolk more memorably than by simply including them in a list of dead so short that it risks making light of the loss of twenty-nine lives. To bring the scene to an end, the sound of a French rally prompts the order to kill the prisoners, the impression of cause and effect making it clear that this order is dictated by military necessity. At the beginning of the next scene, however, Gower represents it as justifiable revenge for the slaughter of the boys. The probable explanation is that Shakespeare needed to mention the boys' deaths, saw the opportunity of doing so in a characteristic dialogue between Fluellen and Gower (a lull in the battle is to be assumed), and did not foresee the critical attention that the discrepancy would later receive. There may be a moment of surprise in the theatre over it, but that is all. When the King enters, with the words 'I was not angry since I came to France / Until this instant', he will probably – and probably rightly – be understood to be referring to the slaughter of the boys, and his threat to cut more prisoners' throats (in a passage significantly altered from Holinshed) will be taken as a further demonstration of his anger. Montjoy's third arrival averts any such action, but without anticlimax, because now he has come on different business from formerly, to concede defeat: 'The day is yours.' The King's single-line reply, 'Praised be God, and not our strength, for it!', says all that needs to be said, and when he has named the battle Fluellen can take over, eagerly talking of past victories and Welsh valour, while with the entry of Williams the whole business of the exchanged gloves comes back into the foreground. Fluellen is kept prominent in all this ('What think you, Captain Fluellen, is it fit this soldier keep his oath?'), so that the audience has a dawning glimmer of what is going to happen, for the sake of which every spectator should willingly turn a blind eye to Fluellen's failure to connect the two glove stories. The next scene shows the sequel, letting the King play out the comedy with a straight face until the very last minute, when all ends in harmony between him, Williams and Fluellen. The English herald, almost as though he has had to wait for his cue, can now enter, bringing the details of losses on both sides, and the act ends with the King's renewal of thanks to God (varied, and enriched, by the interpolation of a couple of short prose speeches for Fluellen), and with a rounding-off of this long phase of the action:

> Let there be sung *Non nobis* and *Te Deum*,
> The dead with charity enclosed in clay,
> And then to Calais, and to England then,
> Where ne'er from France arrived more happy men.

The Chorus chronicles his loyal and enthusiastic welcome at Dover and into London.

The other business of the Chorus is to pass over the events of the five years between Agincourt and the peace treaty. Nothing is said of King Henry's second campaign in France: Agincourt, the decisive victory, is here the end of the war, and 'Harry's back return again to France' is a peaceful one, taking place after a decent interval to allow the French to mourn their dead.

This last section of the play needs to contain something more than the peace treaty and the betrothal if it is not to look like short measure, and what better than Fluellen's settling of the score with Pistol? 'If I find a hole in his coat, I will tell him my mind', he had said to Gower after the quarrel over Bardolph, and now, sporting his leek and armed with his cudgel after being provoked by Pistol the day before, he says 'I will tell him a little piece of my desires.' This understatement, and the unfailing politeness with which he invites Pistol to eat the leek while heaping abuse on him, give the scene its zest. Pistol, cudgelled by Fluellen and preached to by Gower, is still, and rightly, allowed the last word, in his soliloquy – another of Shakespeare's gifts to the actor.

The ceremonious opening of the final scene is all the more grand for its contrast with what has just taken place. Burgundy's long speech, traditionally delivered from stage centre to the English and French ranged on either side, is wholly Shakespeare's invention. Besides embodying the earnest hope of peace, so welcome at the end of this play largely devoted to war, it counterpoises the long wooing dialogue which is to be the main action of the scene. That dialogue begins in verse, the medium of the whole scene so far:

> Fair Katherine, and most fair,
> Will you vouchsafe to teach a soldier terms
> Such as will enter at a lady's ear
> And plead his love-suit to her gentle heart?

Katherine's reply puts an immediate stop to this: 'Your majesty shall mock at me; I cannot speak your England.' King Henry takes up her statement in well-turned prose, with a reply that sums up the courtship to follow: 'O fair Katherine, if you will love me soundly with your French heart I will be glad to hear you confess it brokenly with your English tongue.' Here the full value of the English lesson in Act 3 becomes evident. At the time it seemed like an interlude brought in to change the mood and to give a brief sight of a character who would be needed later. Now Katherine's imperfect English requires the King to take the major part in a dialogue where they cannot meet on equal terms. He is both victor and suitor, and she is his 'capital demand' in the articles of peace, so that their betrothal is a virtual certainty, whatever her wishes. All the more reason why he should try to make his wishes hers, and hence the length and liveliness of his courtship speeches. He has to work at his wooing (one recalls Gratiano's 'For wooing here until I sweat again, / And swearing till my very roof was dry / With oaths of love'), but the work comes easily to him, and she is more than half won from the first: '*O bon Dieu, les langues des hommes sont pleines de tromperies!*' and 'Your majesty

54

'ave *fausse* French enough to deceive de most *sage demoiselle* dat is *en France*' can hardly be spoken other than playfully. Physical attraction there must be, on both sides, and the more Henry protests (too much?) his want of good looks the more he is affirming his strength of body and of character, just as his alleged want of eloquence (to which his actual, though unconventional, eloquence gives the lie) is an affirmation of his sincerity. For patriotic reasons the audience will not want him to be too humble a suitor, but (also for patriotic reasons) he must not woo like a tyrant. Observe how deftly Shakespeare turns one particularly dangerous corner, just after Henry has made his second, more elaborate, proposal of marriage:

> KATHERINE   Is it possible dat I sould love de enemy
> of France?
> KING   No, it is not possible you should love the
> enemy of France, Kate: but in loving me you should
> love the friend of France; for I love France so well
> that I will not part with a village of it; I will have
> it all mine: and Kate, when France is mine, and I
> am yours, then yours is France, and you are mine.

Henry's repartee will delight an audience that was half afraid of seeing him on the defensive, but the next moment he is offering Katherine mutual exchange and possession. (He then has to translate, which further lightens their dialogue.) Towards the end of the courtship he reverts to this theme, without any direct mention, this time, of his own acquisition of France:

> take me by the hand, and say 'Harry of England, I am
> thine': which word thou shalt no sooner bless mine
> ear withal but I will tell thee aloud 'England is thine,
> Ireland is thine, France is thine, and Henry Plantagenet
> is thine...'

The generous tone of this can be questioned only by a mean-spirited spectator (or reader).

The bargain is sealed with a kiss, itself born of comedy when Henry exploits Katherine's self-disparaging reluctance to let him kiss her hand, and followed with 'Here comes your father' – which always, no doubt as Shakespeare intended, gets a laugh in the theatre. Burgundy's dialogue with Henry keeps the tone light, though what he calls 'the frankness of my mirth', with its Mercutio-like sexual innuendo, is usually shortened or omitted altogether on the modern stage, and cannot have been particularly easy to handle even on Shakespeare's: this 'mean dialogue for princes' (as Johnson called it) hardly suits so public a scene as this one has now become, and probably the best way to perform it, then as now, is to bring the two young men downstage, Henry turning to the stage audience and raising his voice at 'and you may some of you thank love for my blindness', which lets the French King into the conversation, while at his mention of 'one fair French maid that stands in my way' he can indicate Katherine, who has remained upstage. One last hitch in the peace negotiations, King Henry's title in official correspondence, is soon shaken out, and another kiss, this time taken with due formality, leads into the prayer for every sort of harmony:

> God, the best maker of all marriages,
> Combine your hearts in one, your realms in one!

The prayer, at least as regards England and France, was not granted, and Shakespeare had not the option of pretending that it was. As the Chorus says in the Epilogue, he has 'pursued the story' only 'thus far'. The loss of France, and the wars of York and Lancaster, are duly mentioned, with regret, but the final emphasis is not on the disappointing historical facts but on the plays which have so acceptably staged them. *Henry V* is now to join the repertoire at the Globe.

That repertoire was well known to regular spectators, and of course to Shakespeare himself who had created much of it. The question therefore arises how far *Henry V* depends on prior knowledge of the history plays that had led up to it, and whether such knowledge modifies the play. Two aspects are particularly relevant, Prince Henry's reformation and his father's usurpation of the crown.

The usurpation is referred to only once in *Henry V*, but is given strong emphasis by being the main theme of the King's prayer before Agincourt. 'The fault / My father made in compassing the crown' puts the matter unequivocally, and the efforts that the King has made to expiate Richard II's murder, a crime for which the usurper was indirectly responsible, also bear witness to his sense of inherited guilt. It is possible to conclude from this soliloquy that the King has no true claim to the crown of England, let alone to that of France; a comparison has sometimes been drawn with King Claudius's effort to repent his brother's murder in *Hamlet*, when his conscience has been caught by the play-acting ('May one be pardoned and retain th'offence?'), and the suggestion made that King Henry ought to resign his crown if he is sincere.[1] However, nothing that he says questions his right to the crown, and in *2 Henry IV*, during the interview between the Prince and his dying father, the right has been insisted on: the father admits his devious path to the crown and the unhappiness its possession has brought him, but is confident that it will descend to his son 'with better quiet', a view that the son accepts and amplifies:

> My gracious liege,
> You won it, wore it, kept it, gave it me;
> Then plain and right must my succession be.
> (*2 Henry IV*, 4.3.349–51 [5.220–2])

This confidence can, admittedly, be regarded sceptically, and in the long term the scepticism may be legitimate in view of

---

1 But to whom? Edmund Mortimer, Earl of March, who had in 1398 succeeded his father both as earl and as proclaimed heir of Richard II, is never mentioned in *Henry V* (on the connection between his claim and Cambridge's conspiracy see 2.2.155–7n.); in *1 Henry IV*, where he is confused with his uncle Sir Edmund Mortimer, he is discredited by his willingness to partition the realm between himself, Hotspur and Glendower.

what is to happen (and in Shakespeare's first series of histories has already happened) to Henry VI: 'I know not what to say – my title's weak' (*3 Henry VI*, 1.1.135). Probably a distinction should be made between the immediate context and the long-term view. In the same scene the father advises the son, for the avoidance of trouble at home, to 'busy giddy minds / With foreign quarrels'; but in *Henry V* there is not the slightest invitation to the audience to remember that advice. As for the King's prayer at Agincourt, the outcome of the battle shows that God has not visited the usurper's sin upon the son – not, of course, therefore condoning the usurpation and Richard's murder, but rather recognizing the son's contrition. To see the King's prayer as a calculated piece of insurance, buying off divine punishment with chantries and masses, not only makes God mocked but also goes quite against the tone of the speech. In the Epilogue the loss of France and the civil wars are ascribed to the troubles of a realm ruled by a child, not to divine punishment.

The Prince's reformation is referred to several times. In Act 1 the bishops' reminiscences and the Dauphin's outdated taunt relate directly to his 'wilder days' and to his change of behaviour on succeeding to the crown; other references relate to one of the actions by which he displayed that change, the discarding of his former companions, particularly Falstaff.

Canterbury says that the reformation was the immediate effect of the succession and that it happened with miraculous suddenness, but in discussing it with Ely he concludes that, as miracles are ceased, the Prince must have been obscuring his contemplation under the veil of wildness. Both these points are consistent with the *Henry IV* plays. In the second scene of *1 Henry IV* the Prince has a soliloquy stating his intention of throwing off his loose behaviour when the time is ripe, and of indulging his idle companions only for a while. In the last act of *2 Henry IV* he allays the apprehensions of his brothers and the Lord Chief Justice by declaring his reformation. He has protested his loyalty to his father's crown, which may also imply his future shedding of loose behaviour, in a private interview in *1 Henry IV* (3.2), he has demonstrated it by his conduct at the battle of Shrewsbury, and he has protested it again in another private interview in *2 Henry IV* (4.3[5]), adding:

> if I do feign,
> O, let me in my present wildness die,
> And never live to show th'incredulous world
> The noble change that I have purposèd.

Thus the reformation of his private life has been foreseen by himself but by no one else in the plays,[1] and this has led to his being sometimes blamed for dissimulation. The accusation would have more force if he did not genuinely enjoy the tavern life when taking part in it, and if he did not make it clear often enough to Falstaff that the latter's expectations are unfounded. At the end of *2 Henry IV* he sententiously rebuffs and disclaims Falstaff, who has boisterously saluted him in his coronation procession, and forbids him to come near him in future. It is evidently to this rejection of Falstaff that the Hostess is referring when she declares that he is not long for this world: 'The King has killed his heart.' Nym and Pistol confirm her words, though Nym laconically admits that 'The King is a good king', as Pistol is also to declare, in his own florid style, on the eve of Agincourt. The rejection is not returned to in the scene after Falstaff's death, but at Agincourt it comes up again when Fluellen is praising the King by comparing him to Alexander the Great. Fluellen refers not to any heroic deed of Alexander's but to the well-known story of how in a drunken passion he killed his friend Clytus. Gower objects, 'Our king

---

1 Except Warwick, who gives the King a hint that the Prince is merely learning what to avoid by frequenting idle company (*2H4* 4.3[4].67–78); but in 5.2 Warwick is as pessimistic as the rest.

is not like him in that: he never killed any of his friends.'
Fluellen's retort is that he is not speaking literally but is
comparing Alexander's wrongful killing of Clytus with King
Henry's righteous rejection of Falstaff. In short, the comparison
is of a piece with his comparison of Macedon and Monmouth.
It can be argued that Gower's astonished objection, by an irony
of which he is unaware, forces upon the audience the reflection,
when Fluellen completes his analogy, that the King has indeed
killed this particular friend; and since from the Hostess's point
of view that is true, and Falstaff is beyond question dead, there
is bound to be a hint of sadness in the present reminder of
him, evoking the sadness of his reported death in the earlier
part of the play. Johnson's commentary note, 'This is the last
time that Falstaff can make sport', perhaps acknowledges this
hint of sadness, though he would probably have been surprised
to see the passage cited in moral criticism of the King.[1] That
two stars keep not their motion in one sphere was as true of
Falstaff and King Henry as it had been of Harry Percy
and the Prince of Wales, the rejection of Falstaff was the
predetermined end of *2 Henry IV* (there had been an equivalent
scene in *The Famous Victories*), and the manner in which it
occurs is to be placed rather to the credit of Shakespeare (who
makes a dramatic climax of it) than to the discredit of the
King.[2]

Neither the usurpation nor the reformation, then, as presented in the earlier plays of the series, reflects adversely on
the King in this one. Nor can it be fairly argued that by
removing him irrevocably from Eastcheap Shakespeare is

---

1   In fact there are two kinds of sport made here, the first by Fluellen's incongruous
    comparison and the second by his having to describe Falstaff because, he says, 'I
    have forgot his name'. Did some wag in the audience hereupon cry 'Oldcastle!'?
    The covert joke between actors and audience implies the latter's familiarity not
    only with the history plays themselves but with their recent theatrical history.
2   In *Henry V* the King never learns that Falstaff has died. In *1 Henry
    IV* 5.4.101–9 he had spoken Falstaff's epitaph over his supposedly dead body at
    Shrewsbury.

showing him as cut off from ordinary human nature, losing the common touch, wanting the natural touch. The chorus before Agincourt shows him cheerfully visiting all his host and calling them brothers, friends and countrymen, so that both mean and gentle behold 'A little touch of Harry in the night'. In his Saint Crispin's day speech he not only declares that they are all his brothers, which a cynic might say that he says to make them fight cheerfully, but warmly imagines the veteran remembering year by year 'with advantages' his part in the glorious battle. Such gleams of humour as this, and those in his Harfleur exhortation ('men of grosser blood') and his two replies to Montjoy ('Almost no better than so many French'; 'And my poor soldiers tell me yet ere night / They'll be in fresher robes'), show him as being at one with his men. In his dialogue with the soldiers he pays Williams the compliment of seriously arguing with him, and it is hard to imagine a production in which his parting joke about clipping French crowns is received without at least a flicker of a smile. The business of the gloves, though not begun as a joke, turns to one that revives an audience's memories of the Gadshill robbery in *1 Henry IV* or the tapster disguise in *2 Henry IV*, and at its conclusion the mutual respect of Williams and the King is evident: 'How canst thou make me satisfaction?' and 'It was our self thou didst abuse' actually invite the sturdy but not discourteous self-justification of Williams's replies. The 'ceremony' soliloquy on the burden of kingship, though perhaps over-elaborate, testifies to the King's human feelings: if he were nothing but a king by now he would not be capable of it.

His brothers, though nothing is done to distinguish them from each other except by name in this play, would be collectively remembered by the regular spectators because of the scene near the end of *2 Henry IV* where they are agreeably surprised by the new King's reformation. Their function in *Henry V*, to provide on-stage support for the central figure, is a continuation of the brotherly unity there established.[1] Brotherhood, literal and figurative, becomes a prominent theme (indeed, in the Agincourt scenes, the most prominent one) from the moment when, addressing Gloucester, the King says, 'We are in God's hand, brother, not in theirs.' In the last scene, with the return of peace, one somewhat comic consequence of the betrothal is that the Kings of France and England, who have begun by addressing each other with amicable politeness as brother, become respectively father and son.

At Agincourt all the royal army are brothers, and hardship and danger have helped to make them so, but it should not be therefore concluded that there was disunity earlier. Though Fluellen and Macmorris may not see eye to eye on military matters – the latter going so far as to threaten to cut off the former's head – they are both committed to the campaign. Pistol and his fellows are committed to their own profit (however incompetently, according to the Boy), and it is impossible to forget that they are Falstaff's soldiers, but that very fact marks them off as separate from the other troops. Whereas in the *Henry IV* plays much was said about soldiers pressed into their country's service (and about Falstaff's abuse of his commission in that respect), nothing of the kind is said in *Henry V*. If Bates, Court and Williams are conscripts they never mention the fact, unless it is implied when they talk of their duty as subjects (which is equally their duty if they are volunteers). In his dialogue with them, making the point that 'every subject's soul is his own', the King recognizes that no king can try out his cause, however spotless, with all unspotted

---

1   The most conspicuous of the nobles is Exeter, a new figure in the later histories (though included in *1 Henry VI*), who continually reminds an audience that the King is a young man by being his uncle. It is Exeter who discloses the tennis-balls, arrests the conspirators, confronts the French King and the Dauphin, enters Harfleur as its new governor, is reported to have captured the bridge and to have sentenced Bardolph, relates the deaths of York and Suffolk, announces the names of the captured French lords, and in the final scene recites in French and Latin the title that King Henry has acquired as the French King's proclaimed son and heir.

soldiers, and he specifies three kinds of guilty men who use the army as a refuge from justice. This admission is a welcome touch of moral realism. In his speech to the defenders of Harfleur, intimidating them into surrender, he talks as though every soldier let loose upon a conquered town is a monster of brutality. This speech uses hyperbole as a means to an end (the culminating comparison with the Slaughter of the Innocents cannot possibly be an unconscious admission that he himself is Herod-like), and though its horrors are a dreadful reminder of what some human beings have always been capable of doing to other ones[1] it does not describe the disciplined stage army standing at the speaker's side – though obviously no knowing sign must pass between him and them.

The campaign begins aggressively at Harfleur and ends defensively, albeit victoriously, at Agincourt. In terms of theme this development is not a progression from wrong to right, the justice of King Henry's claim and therefore of the war not being called in question, but it is a development that allows courage to be presented as a more complex quality than determined and energetic violence. Fluellen can mention after Agincourt how the King's ancestors fought a most brave battle in France, but there is no place now for the Black Prince as a lion's whelp foraging in his foemen's blood. In his Crispin speech the King is no longer urging his men to imitate tigers or to make their brows beetle like impending rocks over eyes like brass cannons. In the final scene Queen Isabel reminds King Henry that his own eyes have formerly 'borne in them / Against the French that met them in their bent / The fatal balls of murdering basilisks', but hopes that now quarrels are to be changed into love – a hope which he echoes.

France is not so absolutely and naturally the enemy of England as to make the hope of lasting peace and even of

---

1 'We read ... of children in Desmond's rebellion [in Munster, Ireland, 1579–83] being hoisted by the English soldiers on the point of their spears and whirled about in their agony' (Warner & Marten, 425).

brotherhood between the nations impossible ('That English may as French, French Englishmen, / Receive each other'), but of course the play presents its history from the English viewpoint, and patriotism is its constant theme. To voice patriotic feelings is one of the Chorus's chief functions:

> O England, model to thy inward greatness,
> Like little body with a mighty heart,
> What mightst thou do, that honour would thee do,
> Were all thy children kind and natural!

These lines (2.0.16–19) immediately precede the mention of the three conspirators, whose extermination ensures that all England's remaining children are indeed kind and natural, and that therefore there is nothing that she cannot accomplish. The account of the King's welcome at Dover and at London makes the audience witness patriotic fervour, while the account of the fleet's sailing to Harfleur makes them demonstrate it:

> Follow, follow!
> Grapple your minds to sternage of this navy,
> And leave your England as dead midnight still,
> Guarded with grandsires, babies and old women,
> Either past or not arrived to pith and puissance.
> For who is he, whose chin is but enriched
> With one appearing hair, that will not follow
> These culled and choice-drawn cavaliers to France?

England is to be left unguarded, not because the Chorus has forgotten that only a quarter of her soldiers were to be taken to France and that at the time of Agincourt there will be well over 10,000 still at home, but because all the men in the audience are to follow the King to Harfleur.[1] It is a flight of fancy suitable to the imaginative inventiveness that is such a feature of the Chorus's speeches. To seek out inconsistencies

---

1 This is the play's clearest indication that it is particularly likely to attract male spectators.

between what the Chorus says and what the stage action shows, as if they betrayed Shakespeare's concealed uneasiness over his story or his hero, or as if they were Shakespeare's deliberate insinuations that his story and his hero were not what they might seem, is surely misguided.

The Chorus is in the play to encourage the audience to be imaginative as well as patriotic, and any consideration of the style of *Henry V* must begin with his speeches. Full of phrases in the imperative mood (even the Epilogue ends with one), they demand attention and command obedience, however humble their professions: 'Piece out our imperfections with your thoughts.' Such is the force of their expression that the audience finds its work half done:

> Think, when we talk of horses, that you see them
> Printing their proud hoofs i'th' receiving earth.

In fact there is no description of the French cavalry charge at Agincourt (discrepancy collectors might make another memorandum here), but these lines from the Prologue manage to bring it into the play all the same, and the mettlesomeness and power of the warhorses are wonderfully suggested. They reappear in the Chorus's speech before Agincourt –

> Steed threatens steed, in high and boastful neighs
> Piercing the night's dull ear

– where it is naturally sounds and not sights that are noticed. The structure of this speech is as fine as the diction. 'Steed threatens steed' is paralleled by 'Fire answers fire' two lines earlier, both these phrases being themselves symmetrical, but further obvious patterning is avoided, and there is much variety in the shape of the phrases and the rhythm that they give to the verse. The first three lines –

> Now entertain conjecture of a time
> When creeping murmur and the poring dark
> Fills the wide vessel of the universe

– evoke an awful sense of comprehensive darkness. All the details that follow relate to the impending battle, until we reach the two lines

> The country cocks do crow, the clocks do toll,
> And the third hour of drowsy morning name

which, besides informing us of passing time, remind us that this dreadful battle is to take place in a peaceful setting that has never known the like. From this we move first to the French camp and then to the contrasted English one, where 'the gazing moon', now mentioned for the first time, sees the soldiers as 'so many horrid ghosts'. To each of them the visiting King imparts 'A largess universal, like the sun'. He is introduced by a circumlocution as 'The royal captain of this ruined band', but in the last line of the description he is named with engaging simplicity as 'Harry'. The remaining half-dozen lines expertly bring the speech back to the theatre, with a brisk concluding couplet to round it off. The speech describing the fleet's progress to Harfleur is equally fine, with every epithet a telling one:

> behold the threaden sails,
> Borne with th'invisible and creeping wind,
> Draw the huge bottoms through the furrowed sea,
> Breasting the lofty surge. O do but think
> You stand upon the rivage and behold
> A city on th'inconstant billows dancing,
> For so appears this fleet majestical,
> Holding due course to Harfleur.

The combination of weight and buoyancy in the ships, and the swell of the sea, are satisfyingly realistic, and throw into relief the fanciful image 'A city on th'inconstant billows dancing'. By contrast, the speech describing the King's return mentions no ships at all (the audience's winged thoughts transport him), but 'the deep-mouthed sea', outvoiced by the welcoming crowds on the beach, is personified as 'a mighty whiffler', another fanciful image, and one that leads naturally on to the processional entry into London.

Long speeches, not only by the Chorus and not only in verse, abound in *Henry V*. They suit the public, demonstrative nature of the play, as well as arising, for the most part, from situations in which argument and persuasion are expected. Because the play is to be above all else an exhibition of the King it is appropriate that Canterbury's account of his present perfections should be comprehensive in content and rhetorical in expression ('Hear him but reason in divinity', etc.). The argument of the Salic law speech came ready-made from Holinshed and required the minimum of alteration to make it metrical ('That *fair* Queen Isabel, his grandmother'), but the bees'-commonwealth speech goes well beyond mere enumeration of social offices, and the shift by way of the bee-soldiers' booty-laden return 'with merry march' (a vivid and consciously incongruous touch) to their emperor in his 'tent royal' allows the rest of the bee-society to be seen from his point of view: all is activity without haste ('The singing masons building roofs of gold'), and even the condemned drone is incapable of his own distress (consider how much better is 'The lazy yawning' than 'Th'unprofitable' would have been). Variations in pace and in intensity keep the long speeches full of life. The King's measured reply to the Dauphin's mocking message comes to its climax with the reiteration of the noun 'mock' as a verb:

> for many a thousand widows
> Shall this his mock mock out of their dear husbands,
> Mock mothers from their sons, mock castles down . . .

His denunciation of Scroop's fall from friendship to treason works up to a four-times-repeated 'Why, so didst thou', but just when this device of anaphora is on the verge of being over-indulged Shakespeare produces a different series of parallel phrases, such as Hamlet might have applied to Horatio, after which 'Such and so finely boulted didst thou seem' recalls 'Why, so didst thou' without (unthinkably) repeating it. Every one of the long rhetorical verse speeches shows this kind of poetic skill, and, as has been seen in the two Channel-crossing choruses, there are no repeats of effects already made. Rhetorical prose is used with equal judgement. Montjoy's first message to King Henry is in prose, not so that the French can be presented in an unfavourable light ('Thou dost thy office fairly' is the King's tribute to its delivery) but so that it does not diminish the effect of the King's verse reply. This is not the contrast between Brutus' prose speech in the market-place and Mark Antony's verse one, but it foreshadows that contrast.[1] The dialogue in which the King and Williams argue is one where long prose speeches are subtly differentiated, the two given to the King having a more obviously rhetorical structure, while the one given to Williams has a simple natural eloquence: 'when all those legs and arms and heads chopped off in a battle shall join together at the latter day and cry all "We died at such a place", some swearing...'.[2] The King's wooing of Katherine is a *tour de force*, and another, at the opposite extreme of sophistication, is the Hostess's account of Falstaff's death, with its merging of two alternative syntactical structures (''A made a finer end, and went away an it had been any christom child') as well as its repeated use of 'So' to begin sentences in its narrative, not to mention the speaker's characteristic blunders of diction ('Arthur's bosom', 'christom child') and of implication ('Now I, to comfort him, bid him 'a should not think of God').

---

1   The last two full lines of the King's reply, 'We would not seek a battle as we are, / Nor as we are, we say, we will not shun it', look forward to *Julius Caesar* too: 'If it were so, it was a grievous fault, / And grievously hath Caesar answered it' (*JC* 3.2.80–1), and 'Caesar did never wrong but with just cause, / Nor without cause will he be satisfied' (the putative original version of 3.1.47–8: see *Julius Caesar*, ed. Arthur Humphreys (Oxford, 1984), pp. 82–3).

2   The subject of the verb 'cry' is the implied resurrected soldiers, not the series of plural nouns; and the series of present participles beginning with 'swearing' relates to the actions of the soldiers at the time of their deaths, not at the Day of Judgement.

Henry V is at first sight, or in generalizing recollection, a simple play on a simple theme. In one sense this is true, far more true than that it is a play that sets its audience problems. In another sense it is a subtle play, as it cannot fail to be when it comes from Shakespeare in the middle of his career as actor-poet-playwright.

CRITICAL OPINIONS OF THE PLAY AND ITS HERO

'By far the most controversial of the histories, *Henry V* remains at the centre of a long-standing critical debate' (Berry, 255). 'Is it a celebration of national glory, with Henry a truly heroic warrior prince? Or is it a dark satire on warfare and the abuses of power, a prelude to the tragedies soon to follow? ... Between the antithetic views of the play as national epic, with a heroic king, or as anti-war satire, dominated by a self-interested hypocrite, several readings have tried to reconcile the possibilities in terms of tension or ambiguity' (Dutton, 360–1, 362). These quotations from two recent surveys summarize the history of the play's reception by twentieth-century critics who believe that Shakespeare's intentions in writing it are in some measure deducible from its plot, from its language, from its relationship to its sources, to other plays of its author's and to the political concerns of late sixteenth-century England, or from any combination of these. In the second half of the twentieth century more radical forms of criticism have arisen which challenge hitherto accepted views of 'the nature of language, the capacity of writing to express the operations of the writer's mind or to present "character", and indeed the nature of characters, of reading and of the written text'.[1] The effect of such critical theory, as applied to Shakespeare, may be either to make his intentions irrecoverable or to make them

---

1 Hawkes, 288. Hawkes gives a concise and sympathetic account of these critical movements.

irrelevant. Whether or not his intentions are directly discussed, the most useful modern criticism, of whatever kind, is likely to be that which continues to base itself on a close study of the whole play. In the following pages a full account of its critical history will not be attempted.[1] Instead, some of the chief critical issues will be raised and commented on.

Hazlitt's provocative essay in his *Characters of Shakespeare's Plays* (1817) makes a good starting-point. Emphatically political, it moves from a diatribe against Henry V to an attack on kings in general, including a highly topical allusion:

> The object of our late invasions and conquest of France was to restore the legitimate monarch, the descendant of Hugh Capet, to the throne: Henry V in his time made war on and deposed the descendant of this very Hugh Capet, on the plea that he was a usurper and illegitimate.

Hazlitt blames Henry V for claiming the French crown in order to strengthen his doubtful title to the English one, and blames Canterbury for the self-interested policy with which he supports the claim. These points had been made in A. W. Schlegel's lectures on dramatic art and literature, which Hazlitt had reviewed in their English translation in 1816, and which he quotes extensively in his preface; but Schlegel, who also noted the irony of history when the French marriage, intended to secure his conquests, failed to do so, did not use them to attack the hero but to show Shakespeare's inclusive view of events and motives. For Schlegel, Henry V was manifestly Shakespeare's favourite historical hero. Hazlitt too sees him as a favourite of Shakespeare and of the English nation, but 'we feel little love or admiration for him' (the 'we' is personal, not collective). 'How then do we like him? We like him in the

---

1 Besides the surveys already mentioned there is a detailed and comprehensive bibliography of work on all aspects of the play (e.g. sources, text, stage history, film) to 1980 (Candido & Forker 1983), the introduction to which is another survey. Collections of modern critical essays exist: Berman, Quinn, Bloom.

play. There he is a very amiable monster, a very splendid pageant.' He is like a panther or a young lion, and 'we take a very romantic, heroic, patriotic, and poetical delight' in his words and acts in the theatre, where no blood is really shed. All this is tinged with irony, but when Hazlitt begins quoting fine passages from this 'second-rate' play his tone changes, and he presently commends the hero's 'patient and modest' behaviour in adversity. Nevertheless, he does not much like him, and in the last paragraph of his essay on *Henry IV* he has given a further reason: 'The truth is, that we never could forgive the Prince's treatment of Falstaff' (Hazlitt, 169–70, 176, 167).

'The Rejection of Falstaff' – a phrase given everlasting currency as the title of A. C. Bradley's famous essay (1902, reprinted in 1909 in his *Oxford Lectures on Poetry*) – has dogged the steps of the King. Bradley is, in many ways, all that Hazlitt is not. Politically disinterested, temperate in expression, and scrupulous in argument, he examines the final scene of *2 Henry IV* in many aspects. His conclusion is that Shakespeare meant the dashing of Falstaff's enormous hopes as a moral and comic nemesis which spectators would accept without pain and resentment, but that he failed:

> We wish Henry a glorious reign and much joy of his crew of hypocritical politicians, lay and clerical; but our hearts go with Falstaff to the Fleet, or, if necessary, to Arthur's bosom or wheresomever he is.

Here, for a moment, Bradley does speak like Hazlitt; but his analysis of Henry's character, as prince and as king, has been in quite another manner. Maintaining that Shakespeare, particularly in his history plays, is not a partisan (Richard II's misrule and Bolingbroke's usurpation create, inevitably, 'an inextricable tangle of right and unright'), he argues that we are not entitled to expect the characters to be absolutely good or bad. Henry is 'deservedly a favourite' and in *Henry V* he 'is treated as a national hero' and given many fine qualities (which Bradley enumerates), but he is not Shakespeare's 'ideal man of action', still less his ideal man,[1] and this is not just because 'his nature is limited' but because his 'many fine traits' are accompanied by 'a few less pleasing', such as superstition (he tries to buy off divine vengeance) and politically minded disingenuousness (he knows that Canterbury wants the war but he invites him to justify it); nor does he show to anyone a strong affection such as Hamlet has for Horatio – 'We do not find this in *Henry V*, not even in the noble address to Lord Scroop' (Bradley, 260, 255, 256–7, 258).

Bradley does not confront the question whether this complex moral presentation of a national hero modifies the effect of *Henry V*, in which the Chorus presents him as absolutely admirable. Gerald Gould, however, writing in 1919, does confront it, declaring that neither Hazlitt nor Bradley goes far enough. '*Henry V* is a satire on monarchical government, on imperialism, on the baser kinds of "patriotism", and on war.' Henry's claim to the French crown can be shown to be unjustifiable, the origin of the war is confused by an 'extra-ordinary accumulation and contradiction of motives', and the war is waged with 'unscrupulous brutality' (the killing of the prisoners, again marked by 'the old hypocrisy, the continual confusion of motive'; the threats to Harfleur's inhabitants). Gould regards the whole play as covertly ironic, designed to succeed in the theatre by deceiving the original audience ('the groundlings'), but conveying a very different message to posterity (and presumably also to the judicious spectators at the Globe). His final, and in his opinion clinching, point is that Scroop's ingratitude to Henry is ironically juxtaposed with Henry's ingratitude to Falstaff (Quinn, 83, 89, 90, 91, 81, 94).

---

1   Bradley is here dissenting from the opinion of Edward Dowden (*Shakespeare: A Critical Study of his Mind and Art* (1875), quoted by Quinn, 43), who made the former claim while dissenting from that of G. G. Gervinus, who had made the latter one.

Gould's rejection of Henry has not established itself as orthodoxy, though equally hostile attitudes have appeared,[1] and critical ingenuity has added fresh detail to the case against the hero,[2] from time to time. Yet there has not been that general swing back to an uncomplicated reading of the play, based on the choruses, that might have been expected. Many critics have felt that *Henry V* requires strenuous effort, and that, while Gould's ironic reading of it excludes too much, it cannot be as straightforward as it seems. One of the most recent, Alexander Leggatt, declares that 'a full reception of the play demands both engagement and questioning' and that 'to a degree unusual even for him, Shakespeare is setting the material before us, leaving its contradictions intact, and inviting us to make of it what we can.'[3] This is in direct contrast to A. C. Sprague's judgement: 'The seriousness of the choruses is as remarkable as their eloquence. For Shakespeare in this most commemorative, most epic of the histories is taking sides. He is not in the least detached, nor even momentarily ironic.'[4]

Critics, as distinct from unprofessional readers and spectators, are expected to formulate their conclusions. Norman Rabkin has written:

> One way to deal with a play that provokes such conflicting responses is to try to find the truth somewhere between them. Another is to suggest that the

1 As in *After Agincourt*, a dramatic monologue written by Peter Mottley and read by Bob Hoskins on BBC Radio 3, 15 November 1988, the speaker being Pistol.

2 Bardolph is made to steal a pax, not a pyx as in Holinshed, 'to parallel Bardolph's crime with Henry's, which was to steal the *pax* or peace' (Babula, 53). Replying to Fluellen at 4.7.115, 'The King prays to God to keep him honest and breaks his word of honor to Williams' (Goddard, 1.256). The courtship scene uses the language barrier as 'a kind of figure, a paradigm, for his predicament, as he is now so separated from the rest of humanity that he cannot even talk to his wife' (Williamson, 334).

3 Leggatt, 124–5. Leggatt's chapter on *Henry V* is the fullest possible examination of the play along these lines and allows the reader to consider most of the points that former critics have made.

4 Quinn, 199, who reprints Sprague's chapter on *Henry V* from his *Shakespeare's Histories: Plays for the Stage* (1964).

73

author couldn't make up his mind which side he wanted to come down on and so left us a mess. A third is to interpret all the signals indicating one polar reading as intentional, and to interpret all other signals as irrepressible evidence that Shakespeare didn't believe what he was trying to say.

All these approaches he refuses, arguing that 'in *Henry V* Shakespeare creates a work whose ultimate power is precisely the fact that it points in two opposite directions, virtually daring us to choose one of the two opposed interpretations it requires of us'.[1] One may doubt, however, whether a reader, and still more a spectator, can preserve this state of moral suspension and still receive satisfaction: one cannot help thinking of the fabled ass starving between two equal heaps of hay. A. R. Humphreys takes a quite different view of the supposed contradictions:

> When *Henry V* is looked at closely, certain features complicate the impression of simple zest and conviction the unreflecting reader is likely to form. If these features are now to be discussed at some length, the reason is not that the play is radically uncertain in its aims; even with its ambiguities it remains powerful and assured. As Dr Johnson remarked in his *Life of Gray*, 'by the common sense of readers uncorrupted with literary prejudices, after all the refinements of subtlety and the dogmatism of learning, must finally be decided all claim to poetical honours'. Common sense long ago decided that the play's subject is unambiguous valour and that its spirit is expressed in Henry's Agincourt speech. It works splendidly – as

---

1 Rabkin, 279. His title, 'Rabbits, ducks and *Henry V*', refers to an image in silhouette which can be seen alternatively, but not simultaneously, as the head of a rabbit (facing one way, with ears) or of a duck (facing the other way, with a bill). In discussing the play Rabkin stresses 'the terrible subversiveness with which Shakespeare undermines the whole structure' (ibid., 288).

74

before observed – at a speed which prevents awkward questions, and it is charged with a rich and compelling emotion. Before Agincourt in particular it achieves a humanity and honesty, as well as a sense of great peril and noble courage, which live in the mind as its valid message.

He maintains that the inconsistencies have received undue attention because of the nature of the play, which 'is concerned with moral vindications of national interest and policy, and so undertakes to explain and to justify all that is done in the nation's name', and that 'it is because *Henry V* argues so much that flaws in the argument may seem significant'; Shakespeare's imagination 'was engaged at a brilliantly effective level for dramatic excitement; it was not engaged at the deeper levels of thoughtfulness of which he had already elsewhere shown himself capable' (Humphreys, 22–3, 31–2). This last comment is not, in the context, a severe criticism. Harley Granville-Barker, on the other hand, had regarded the play as 'a well-carpentered piece of work' but not a fully satisfying one: 'For behind the action, be the play farce or tragedy, there must be some spiritually significant idea, or it will hang lifeless. And this is what is lacking in *Henry V*' (Granville-Barker, 61). For him, as for Hazlitt and many others, *Henry V* is one of Shakespeare's second-rate plays. Perhaps, judged by the highest Shakespearean standards, it is. But to regard it, as modern criticism predominantly regards it, as a problematic play full of ambiguities and ironies surely does not make it a better one.

The critical debate which has just been briefly reviewed is concerned with *Henry V* chiefly as a work of art. Other critics have considered the ways in which it may reflect the political thought and the practical politics of its own time. The topical allusions to the Earl of Essex in Gower's mention of 'a beard of the General's cut' (3.6.75–6) and the Chorus's anticipation of his triumphant return from Ireland (5.0.29–35) have persuaded some that Shakespeare was as active a sympathizer with Essex as was Shakespeare's patron, the Earl of Southampton, to whom he had dedicated his two narrative poems. Richard Simpson (416–17) suggests that the dialogue of the four captains in 3.2 illustrates Essex's wish to see a union of the British Isles which James VI of Scotland's accession to the English throne after Elizabeth's death would create. This suggestion, though not compelling, is far more reasonable than some others that have been made, by Simpson and his successors, about this play and the three preceding histories. David Bevington has commented as follows:

> Extremists of the Essex persuasion would have us believe that Shakespeare wished to see the earl on the throne, and that Essex's military and pragmatic virtues are reflected not only in Bolingbroke but more especially in his son. A more temperate but still highly debatable interpretation is that Shakespeare sympathized with the earl and his platform, but feared the rashness of the passionate young nobleman and did not approve of the dangerous tendency beginning in 1599 towards insurrection.
>
> (Bevington, 18–19)

The matter has recently been reopened by Annabel Patterson, who regards the Act 5 chorus as Shakespeare's 'well-meant but ill-advised attempt at mediation' between Essex and Elizabeth. Their strained relations had been common knowledge from the summer of 1598, when she gave him a box on the ear during a quarrel as to who should lead the Irish campaign, whereupon he withdrew from court and expressed his resentment in a strongly worded letter to Lord Keeper Egerton and in an allegorical lyric ('It was a time when silly bees could speak') representing himself as a bee whose service to the hive is unrewarded. Patterson argues that the tense political situation following his return and imprisonment dictated not only the suppression of that chorus but also the drastic simplification of the play by heavy cutting, and that the result was the Quarto version, 'a Lancastrian history that would pass the closest inspection' (Patterson, 54, 46). Her demonstration of the effects of governmental control upon printed works in 1599 (particularly the suppression of John Hayward's *History of Henry IV*, dedicated to Essex) is valuable, but her well-argued case is open to certain objections. It does not explain such omissions from the Quarto as the opening scene or the King's 'Once more unto the breach' exhortation, which cannot be considered politically motivated (unless, in the latter case, by the fear that Henry would be taken as portraying Essex), nor does it explain why it was a faulty text compiled by memorial reconstruction that was printed in 1600, when one would have thought that the Lord Chamberlain's Men would have supplied an accurate text if they were anxious that their loyalty should be placed beyond doubt. Her assertion that the language of the Act 5 chorus is 'provocative' is also questionable.[1]

More general aspects of the play's Tudor historical context, as distinct from its particular application to Essex's career, have been studied by other critics. E. M. W. Tillyard's account of Shakespeare's purpose in the history plays, 'to dramatise the whole stretch of English history from the prosperity of Edward III, through the disasters that succeeded, to the establishment of civil peace under the Tudors', a purpose which Tillyard derives from Hall's chronicle, leads him to find the last play of the series, and the presentation of its hero, unsatisfactory. Henry could not be made 'the symbol of some great political principle', nor could his complex personality in the *Henry IV* plays be simplified into the perfect king and hearty 'good mixer' that tradition required (Tillyard, 304–6).

---

1 Patterson, 52. She extracts subversive ambiguity from 'How many would the peaceful city quit / To welcome him', from 'Bringing rebellion broached on his sword' and from 'With the plebeians swarming at their heels' ('Swarming, bees notoriously desert the hive under the leadership of another monarch'; they do not, but follow the queen once she has emerged).

Tillyard's general view of Shakespeare's history plays as embodiments of orthodox Tudor historical thought (particularly as regards order and divine providence as universal principles) has met with much opposition on the grounds both that the plays themselves deal with complex historical events and that sixteenth-century historical thought was not wholly Tudor-orthodox (Dutton, 341–5).

The most recent developments in this area have, in direct contrast to Tillyard, endeavoured to bring out the subversive element in *Henry V*. The critical movements known as new historicism and cultural materialism have both produced influential and forcefully expressed essays on the play.[1] Stephen Greenblatt's new historicist essay 'Invisible bullets: Renaissance authority and its subversion' juxtaposes the *Henry IV* and *Henry V* plays with Thomas Harriot's account of Virginia (1588: the invisible bullets of the title were the natives' interpretation of a smallpox epidemic as the vengeance upon them of the Christians' god) and Thomas Harman's exposure of the practices of rogues and vagabonds (1567). Greenblatt applies the moral and psychological implications of these two works to the plays. As regards *Henry V* he concludes:

> The play deftly registers every nuance of royal hypocrisy, ruthlessness, and bad faith – testing, in effect, the proposition that successful rule depends not upon sacredness but upon demonic violence – but it does so in the context of a celebration, a collective panegyric to 'This star of England', the charismatic leader who purges the commonwealth of its incorrigibles and forges the martial national state.

For instance, after Fluellen's damaging reference to 'Hal's symbolic killing of Falstaff', the King makes a triumphant

---

1 On these two movements and on the critical terminology that they employ, see the Introduction and the glossary of 'Key Concepts' in Wilson & Dutton.

entrance: 'This entrance, with its military "Alarum" followed by a royal "Flourish", is the perfect emblematic instance of a potential dissonance being absorbed into a charismatic celebration.'[1] Thus, according to Greenblatt, Elizabethan authority fosters the subversive in order to control it.

In their cultural materialist essay 'History and ideology, masculinity and miscegenation: the instance of *Henry V*', Alan Sinfield and Jonathan Dollimore invert Greenblatt's emphasis: 'even in this play, which is often assumed to be the one where Shakespeare is closest to state propaganda, the construction of ideology is complex – even as it consolidates, it betrays inherent instability.' Pointing to the conflicting attitudes in late Elizabethan England towards foreign war, they look beneath the national unity affirmed in *Henry V* and find that 'its obsessive preoccupation is insurrection', so that though 'systematically, antagonism is reworked as subordination or supportive alignment' (the co-operative multinational captains, the penitent traitors) it keeps breaking in. In his soliloquy on ceremony 'Henry speaks his fear of deceptive obedience – masking actual antagonism'; just before the battle 'the idea of idle and implicitly disaffected people at home is raised'. Whereas Elizabeth depended for her power on the support of a divided aristocracy, '*Henry V* was a powerful Elizabethan fantasy simply because nothing is allowed to compete with the authority of the king.' Whereas Ireland's subjugation was an intractable problem, 'the play offers a displaced, imaginary resolution' of it, namely the conquest of France. In the last two sections of the essay the play's treatment of masculinity and of the courtship scene is explored with similar scepticism as regards conventional views of gender and of sexuality.[2]

It is evident that the 'long-standing critical debate' referred to at the beginning of this section will continue, and also that

1 Greenblatt, 56, 58. A shorter version of the essay was published in 1981.
2 Sinfield, 114, 118, 119, 121, 125. The last two sections have been added to the essay as first published in 1985. Quotations are taken from the revised text.

it will continue to be linked with various forms of politics, just as it was when Hazlitt inaugurated it.

HENRY V IN PERFORMANCE

Everyone who has seen Sir Laurence Olivier's film *Henry V* (1944) will recall that it opens with a view of Elizabethan London from the air, the camera presently focusing on the Globe playhouse and then on an airborne playbill that comes to rest and announces a performance of *The History of King Henry the Fift* on the first of May 1600. We are taken inside the playhouse and are shown the audience assembling, the actors dressing, the flag being run up the flagpole and the trumpeter blowing a preliminary flourish. The performance then commences, the stage and the spectators remaining in view until early in Act 2 when the camera follows the Hostess's exit 'above' and takes us through a lighted casement to see Falstaff on his deathbed. The play now becomes wholly film – and who could fail to remember the Agincourt sequence, with the heavily armed French lords being hoisted on to their horses with pulleys, the horses' feet splashing through water afloat with green cresses and reflecting a cloudless sky, and then the releasing of a shower of English arrows, with their unforgettable sound, to the music of Sir William Walton? – and it continues as film until, just after the closing lines of dialogue have been spoken, we are returned to the Globe, where the Princess Katherine, played by a boy actor, is taking her bow hand-in-hand with the King.

Hardly anyone who sees this reconstruction of an Elizabethan performance is likely to take it for an exact copy of the reality (especially not the unrehearsed muddle into which Canterbury and Ely get with their bundle of documents), and Olivier clearly did not mean it to be taken as such. His purpose was artistic, not archaeological. But how it makes one wish that one could see exactly how the play was performed by the Lord

3 The charge of the French horsemen at Agincourt. *Henry V*, directed by Laurence Olivier, 1944

Chamberlain's Men at the Globe or (on 7 January 1605) at court by the King's Majesty's Players, as they had then become!

Richard Burbage, their leading tragedian, no doubt would play King Henry, and many of the minor roles would be doubled (as they still are). The women's roles would be taken by boys. The staging requirements are not elaborate. The walls and gates of Harfleur, needed for one scene only, could be sufficiently represented by the gallery over the stage and by the double doors below the gallery, normally curtained off but now exposed. The two flanking doors at the rear of the stage, available for all other exits and entrances, are put to ceremonial use in the final scene when the English and French courts meet for their peace negotiations. A royal throne of England is specified in the dialogue of 1.2, and a similar French throne is evidently required in 2.4 (another scene in which a foreign embassy is received), but there is no need for this French throne to reappear in 3.5, nor in the final scene, where its presence might be an embarrassment, since the French King does not preside, and since King Henry gains France only in reversion and not immediately. Scaling-ladders are brought in, but not used, in 3.1, and small pieces of ordnance ('chambers') provide an off-stage sound-effect at the end of the Act 3 chorus. The dress, and particularly the armour (see Fig. 1), was probably contemporary, like the speech and manners of the play.

Much of the later stage history of *Henry V* is the history of the progress, or alternatively the decline, from this simple staging to more and more elaborate theatrical effects in the eighteenth and nineteenth centuries. *Henry V* was not among the Shakespearean plays revived when the London theatres reopened after their closure in the middle years of the seventeenth century.[1] It returned to the stage in the 1730s and

---

1 When Pepys saw Betterton act in *Henry V* (on 13 August 1664 and again on 6 July 1668) the play was not by Shakespeare but by Roger Boyle, Earl of Orrery. It is a quite independent love-and-honour drama in heroic couplets in which

immediately established itself there, performances being particularly frequent during the wars with France in the century's middle and late years.[1] Changeable scenery, which by now affected the representation of any play of Shakespeare's, posed a particular problem in this one, where the Chorus insists that the audience must supply what the actors cannot. As expressions of mood the Chorus's speeches remained invaluable, but as statements of theatrical fact they became increasingly false. For the modern film director the problem is even more acute, but in the eighteenth century it was already felt, and though Garrick spoke the speeches in 1747 and 1748 they seem to have been often omitted.[2] They were certainly omitted from John Philip Kemble's version of 1789, a version that held the stage till Macready's last production of the play, in 1839, which restored them. Their restoration is somewhat curious, considering that this production of Macready's was more elaborately authentic as regards scenery and costume than hitherto (his own earlier productions, like Kemble's, having met with criticism in this respect); the explanation is probably that Macready, who also restored the Fool in *King Lear*, was trying to get back to Shakespeare in as many ways as possible. In his production a moving diorama by Clarkson Stanfield, who was by now a Royal Academician as well as Drury Lane's scene painter, showed the royal fleet sailing to Harfleur and

Betterton played not the King but Owen Tudor, here Katherine's other suitor who unselfishly renounces his hopes at its end. Aaron Hill's *Henry V* (1723) is also, in the main, an original work – a new fabric built on Shakespeare's foundation, as he described it. It includes passages from Shakespeare's play, particularly in its first and last acts, but its chief action is a romantic intrigue in which Scroop's niece Harriet, whom the King has in his younger days seduced and deserted, joins her uncle's conspiracy. This intrigue ends pathetically for Harriet, who after intending to stab the King is reconciled to him and stabs herself, but happily for Katherine, who discovers that King Henry is the very courtier with whom she formerly fell in love at first sight, then supposing his name to be Owen Tudor. (Extracts from Hill's play in Vickers, 373–97.)

1 For details, including cast-lists, see Van Lennep. Most modern editions of *Henry V* contain stage histories of the play.

2 As Cam[1] (l) notes, it is not clear what was done with them, for though they are omitted by Bell's acting version (1773) the cast lists of the period regularly assign the role of Chorus to one of the actors.

then the besieged town while the chorus to Act 3 was being spoken, and another showed the King's triumphal entry into London as a background to the Act 5 chorus. This made it seem as though the audience's imagination had worked visual miracles. The next step was Charles Kean's presentation in 1859 of the triumphal entry as a 'historical episode'. Drawing on a contemporary account of it reprinted in Sir Harris Nicolas's *The Battle of Agincourt* (1827), Kean reconstructed the gatehouse standing at the Southwark end of old London Bridge, from which girls dressed as white-robed angels let fall a shower of gold on the King as he rode by, while beside it the yards of a ship moored in the Thames provided standing room for cheering Londoners (see Fig. 4). This production, and its spectacular successors, naturally required long intervals for scene-changing, which in their turn required a return to more heavily cut texts than Macready's.

By the end of the nineteenth century this kind of theatrical splendour, though it might be perpetuated, could develop no further, and the time was ripe for a reaction against it. On 23 October 1901 a special matinée performance at the Memorial Theatre, Stratford-upon-Avon, directed by William Poel, presented the entire text in an 'Elizabethan' staging, namely a bare platform hung with tapestries and backed by a gallery. The predictable debate followed this innovation, some arguing that Shakespeare would have commended it as a return to the essentials of his art, others that he would have used the full resources of the nineteenth-century theatre if he had had them. Though Poel's production was somewhat austere, it revealed the advantages of continuous action, a principle which during the twentieth century has been everywhere adopted. The invention of motion pictures, accustoming audiences to continuous action, assisted the process.

The cinema, however, having at its command greater realism even than the nineteenth-century theatre, may deviate even further in that respect from the Elizabethan one. The fleet's

4 Henry V's triumphal reception into London: a 'historical episode' between Acts 4 and 5 of Charles Kean's production, Princess's Theatre, London, 1859. Watercolour by F. Lloyds, one of a series to the stage designs of William Telbin, 1859

sailing to France, the siege of Harfleur and above all the battle of Agincourt – no 'four or five most vile and ragged foils' here – are all within its power to show. And it is not only empowered to show them, it is obliged to do so, or to falsify its nature by self-denial. The result may be disharmony between these parts of the film and those parts that stay closest to the original play, especially in view of Shakespeare's emphasis on his stage and actors, and of his presentation of the King as the hero, the all-important figure, the role that asks for a virtuoso performance. Olivier's use of the Globe playhouse as the scene of his film's gradual beginning and of its rapid end confronted this difficulty and surmounted it by drawing attention to the play's theatrical nature, encouraging the audience to inhabit both worlds, of film and play, at the same time: we begin by watching a film of an Elizabethan performance (and are therefore aware that it is an Elizabethan performance seen through twentieth-century eyes), then we make a conscious transition from that to a cinematic realism (in which, with a willing suspension of disbelief, we participate while fully aware that we are enjoying a dramatic experience), and finally we are returned to the playhouse with its make-believe action performed by real actors. The directors of the other two film versions also portrayed the main action with cinematic realism while retaining the Chorus. David Giles (The BBC TV Shakespeare, 1979) explained that 'We're starting with the Chorus coming out of black into a stylized setting, then as scenes end we go in tight on him again, then when he turns what is behind him has changed' (BBC, 20). His Chorus, like Olivier's, was in 'period' costume. Kenneth Branagh began his 1989 version in an empty film studio, using a modern image instead of Olivier's Elizabethan one to suggest its theatrical dimension, of which the scarfed and overcoat-clad Chorus was a persistent reminder.[1]

---

1   A Chorus in jersey and mackintosh first appeared in 1960 at the Old Vic, London (Sprague & Trewin, 100).

This emphasis on the play as a performance has not been confined to the cinema. At Stratford-upon-Avon in 1975 Terry Hands began with all the actors dressed in rehearsal clothês: 'Only with the arrival of the French ambassador; arrayed in the panoply of his office, did the dry stems of the action begin to bud, bursting into full bloom with the unfolding of the great ceiling-cloth of the royal standard, which canopied the stage for the King's arrival at Southampton.'[1] The Chorus, who never assumed a theatrical costume, suddenly put this process into reverse when he took the part of Burgundy in the final scene and delivered the pathetic speech about the post-war condition of France. The effect was not only to reaffirm that the play was a piece of theatre but also to suggest that a modern (and, by implication, better) estimate of war was being uttered. There was a touch of Bertolt Brecht about this, though the play as a whole was done in a manner that engaged the audience's emotions in the usual way.

The deliberate and sustained use of anachronistic elements in a production is another method of drawing attention to the play as performance and to its debatable moral and political content. Michael Bogdanov's touring production (English Shakespeare Company, 1986–9) dressed its King and officer-lords, in Act 1 and thereafter, in nineteenth-century scarlet tunics; other lords in the court scene wore morning suits, the bishops were in cassocks with sashes, and the ambassador (Montjoy) wore a grey lounge suit. At Southampton the conspirators wore hats and overcoats, and Cambridge was shot in the leg while attempting to escape.[2] At the end of the scene, at 'No king of England, if not king of France!', a permanent metal bridge above the stage was suddenly thronged with

---

1 David, 194; the production is fully discussed by Beauman and by Taylor, *Moment*.
2 In Gregory Boyd's production (Great Lakes Shakespeare Festival, Cleveland, Ohio, 1983) 'Grey tried to flee and only Cambridge stood still, as the text implies all should. The scene peaked on Henry's disarming of Scroop, who had tried to knife him' (Liston, 103).

football-hooligan types, singing 'Here we go, here we go, here we go!' to the trio section of Sousa's 'Stars and Stripes Forever' and displaying a banner daubed with the words 'FUCK THE FROGS!'; combined effects of gunfire, thunderflashes and an orchestra playing Parry's 'Jerusalem' accompanied the general exit. The French court in 2.4 were all in white and cream, drinking champagne, the men at a table, the women around a picnic spread on a tablecloth upstage (through which Exeter walked on leaving); at the end of the scene the French King proposed Katherine's marriage, in mime, to her alarm and the Dauphin's rage. At Harfleur the English soldiers retiring from the breach crouched behind sandbags; they wore modern camouflage battledress and berets. The King delivered his ultimatum speech, in full, seated at a table upstage, at which he received the frock-coated Governor's surrender. For the battle of Agincourt the French wore sky-blue tunics and white trousers, with much gold braid. In 4.2 Grandpré's description of the English army's wretchedness was presented as a report which Montjoy had been typing, read aloud, and finally crumpled up. Pistol brutally kicked and punched his French prisoner and threw him on the supermarket trolley in which he had brought in his loot. The boys' bodies were brought in on an ammunition truck covered with a tarpaulin sheet. When told to 'fill this glove with crowns' for Williams, Exeter took a collection among the officers. '*Non nobis*' was mingled with 'The Stars and Stripes Forever'. The leek-eating scene took place on shipboard (a portable rail with a lifebelt). Pistol, who had been dressed successively in a flashy suit, a German helmet and swastika-daubed battledress tunic, and a singlet and trousers with a 'biker's' studded belt, was now wearing a French tunic looted from his dead prisoner. The final scene confronted the English red-coated officer-lords (who looked at their watches while Burgundy made his speech) with a French court in deep mourning. Katherine sat passively in a chair throughout the courtship. Elgar's march 'Pomp and Circumstance, Number 1' ('Land of Hope and Glory') and renewed gunfire brought the play to a close.

Watching this production, which, while often infuriating, was well performed and continually interesting, one was reminded how little stage business is demanded by the play's lines. Mention has just been made of the boys' bodies and of Pistol's dead prisoner. In the text the King's order to kill the prisoners is his response to the military threat presented by the French rally, but it is later interpreted by Gower as a reprisal for the killing of the boys and the burning and pillaging of the King's tent by 'the cowardly rascals that ran from the battle'. From this last phrase, which echoes Holinshed's fuller account, it is clear that Shakespeare did not intend the French nobles to be responsible, but in some productions the Boy is stabbed by the Dauphin or by the Constable, sometimes immediately after his last sentence – which is doubly regrettable, for that should leave us with a foreboding which is not proved true till later. We all like the Boy, and it is natural that directors should want to make more of his death than Shakespeare does in terms of stage action, though it is at least arguable that the passing reference ('there's not a boy left alive') is more truly moving than stage action that may be either shocking or sentimental (see Fig. 5). Sometimes the Boy's body is carried in Fluellen's arms (as in Glen Byam Shaw's Old Vic production of 1951), sometimes in the King's (as in Kenneth Branagh's film). Whether Shakespeare intended the prisoners to be killed on stage is more open to question. The Quarto does give Pistol his favourite phrase 'Couple gorge' after the order, but since other Quarto lines are evidently actors' gags there is little reason to give much weight to this one, and in the Folio the half-line that ends the scene, 'Give the word through', strongly suggests that the prisoners – who may be off stage already – are killed off stage. Their bodies would have to be dragged off if they were killed in the Elizabethan playhouse, but the modern stage can use a 'black-out' to cover

5 After Agincourt. *Henry V,* directed by Kenneth Branagh, 1989

their disappearance, or they can be left on stage till the end of the battle. The promptbook for Terry Hands's 1975 production, when the King is naming the field of Agincourt, has the stage direction 'Mon[tjoy] prays over L.F.'s [i.e. Le Fer's] body'. In this production Pistol killed Le Fer in immediate response to the order, but in Michael Bogdanov's he required persuasion from an officer who drew a gun on him. Pistol's voluntary or compulsory sacrifice of his promised 200 crowns thus becomes a prominent dramatic feature of Agincourt – but whether wisely or no let the spectator judge.

Bardolph's execution is another instance of the modern tendency to add substance to what Shakespeare leaves shadowy. In both the Quarto and the Folio texts Fluellen tells the King of it, and it is treated as having already taken place. In Hands's production, Exeter (who was on stage) gave a signal just before Fluellen's last sentence, a rising roll of drums was heard off stage, and everybody on stage looked at the King. In Bogdanov's, Bardolph was led across the overhead metal bridge to his execution, unseen by the King. In Adrian Noble's (Stratford-upon-Avon, 1984), the King was obliged to watch as Bardolph was brought in, forced to his knees and then garotted from behind (by, of all unsuitable people, Exeter), a thick trickle of blood emerging from his lowered face, and his kneeling unsupported body remaining in position during the whole dialogue with Montjoy. This, though unforgettable, was hardly forgivable. From Pistol's earlier speech and the Boy's later one it is positive that Bardolph was hanged (did Holinshed's 'strangled', meaning hanged, influence the director?), and one could not properly attend to the rest of the scene while registering with admiration the actor's almost unbelievable immobility. In Branagh's film, Bardolph arrives in a cart and is hanged from a tree in the presence of the King, who sheds a tear.[1] If Shakespeare had wanted a hanging his stage could

---

1 A flashback to the Eastcheap tavern shows Bardolph (not Falstaff as in *1 Henry IV* 1.2.60–1) saying to the Prince, 'Do not thou when thou art king hang a thief'

have given it him without difficulty: Pedringano, in Kyd's *Spanish Tragedy*, had been publicly executed in this way ten years before. But Shakespeare did not want it. Directors, to be fair to them, have more in view than mere stage effect. They intend Bardolph's execution to throw light on the King's state of mind.

In the early years of the twentieth century Sir Frank Benson played the King as a courageous, religious, energetic and uncomplicated young man. This will no longer do, unless he is to be supposed jingoistic and immature. Instead he is often presented as highly strung and emotionally vulnerable. The Southampton scene with the conspirators is particularly reveal-ing. His reproachful address to Scroop, a long and rhetorical speech on a well-filled stage, is very difficult to deliver other than formally: Fuseli's painting (see Fig. 6), though depicting the moment when the traitors' guilt is exposed, suggests the appropriate stance. But in the promptbook of Terry Hands's 1975 production the directions are 'Henry knocks Scroop to floor and kneels by him, face to face, grabs and drops him and grabs again, knocks him sprawling.' In Kenneth Branagh's film 'The king wrestles the disloyal Scroop on to a table-top in a violent yet intimate scene of reproach, at one moment tenderly caressing his brow while reciting the list of his treasons.'[1] Sensibility is expensively purchased by the loss of dignity.

The French King in Branagh's film (played by Paul Scofield) was a figure of tragic dignity – a much better way of presenting the character than the alternative tradition (see Sprague & Trewin, 100), in existence since the beginning of the twentieth century, of making him a senile and vacuous figure with occasional lucid intervals, though Harcourt Williams in the Olivier film gave pathos to that reading. It is a wrong reading in terms of Shakespeare's lines, despite its historical basis. Shakespeare found it stated by Holinshed that the French

---

1 Donaldson, 67. Branagh also 'wrestles Montjoy, who has come once too often for ransom, to the ground' (Donaldson, 66).

6 King Henry exposing the conspiracy of Cambridge, Scroop and Grey. One of nine oils by Henry Fuseli (1741–1825) for John Boydell's Shakespeare Gallery exhibition (1789–1802), later engraved for Boydell's illustrated edition of Shakespeare (1802)

King was subject to attacks of 'frenzy' during which the Dauphin acted as regent, but he made no use of the fact in his play. He did, however, follow Holinshed in making Burgundy a young man, whereas modern productions often make him an old one. In historical plays, history and drama may have rival claims. The history, too, may be of two kinds, the Elizabethan history that Shakespeare read and the modern history that is available to us. At Agincourt the battlefield became a sea of mud,[1] but Holinshed does not mention the fact. For the stage director this knowledge makes no difference, but for the film director it calls for a choice. In Olivier's film there was no mud, in Branagh's lots of it.[2]

Henry V has not only been reinterpreted by various directors; by some of them it has been rewritten, at least in part. At Stratford-upon-Avon in 1964, when it was included in the complete cycle of English histories directed by Peter Hall and John Barton, Cambridge's importance was magnified to draw attention to his dynastic challenge taken up by his son York in the *Henry VI* plays. He replaced Westmorland in 1.2 ('Shall we call in th'ambassador, my liege?' / 'Not yet, good Cambridge') and was the only conspirator at Southampton, the Act 2 chorus and the King's address to Scroop being adapted accordingly. Shakespeare's cryptic reference to his ulterior motive in taking the French bribe was amplified in two additional lines ('What 'twas, God knows, and thou and thine shall know it, / For God doth sanction what I did

---

1   Hibbert, 117. Keegan (78–116) reconstructs the battle in vivid detail and is very informative on the conditions of warfare involved.

2   The battle was handled quite differently in these two films. Of Olivier's Agincourt it has been said that 'It is all Hollywood, with a great charge of French horsemen taken from Griffith, an Eisenstein-like flight of arrows through the sky, and English soldiers dropping from branches to pull the French knights from their horses as in Errol Flynn's Robin Hood films' (Gurr, 52). Branagh's, which owes something to Orson Welles's battle of Shrewsbury in his Falstaff film *Chimes at Midnight* (1966), is literally down-to-earth, with 'heavy bodies splashing in the mud', mud which 'provides an almost ritual immersion from which Henry emerges not only victorious but in a kind of communion with his men, including the common men, that he has sought throughout the action' (Donaldson, 64).

intend'), and his expression of penitence was cut. (He was similarly impenitent, but more discreet, in Adrian Noble's production twenty years later.) At Bremen, also in 1964, Peter Zadek brought the quarrel between the disguised King and Williams to a tragic end instead of a comic one. Williams was mortally wounded in the battle and was brought into the King's presence. The King revealed to Williams that he had been his antagonist. Williams asked pardon and immediately died.[1] Such drastic adaptation has been rare. Cutting, transposition and the insertion of additional action have been frequent.

Even if we could go back in time and witness the original performance of *Henry V* we still could not reproduce it. It is obvious that every new production must spring from a re-examination of the script. One would not wish a sense of theatrical tradition, even if an unbroken one existed from Shakespeare's day, which it does not, to stifle the director's creativity. At the same time, surveying twentieth-century productions, one cannot help noticing the growth of powerful contemporary traditions, fashionable innovations which may interpose between a director and the script. 'Trust Shakespeare' may seem a facile question-begging maxim, but a director will do well to remember that many spectators will be seeing the play for the first time, and that many who are not will be coming to it from a recent reading of the text. Such spectators, one may feel, are entitled to witness a performance that is reasonably close to what that text demands.

TEXT

The text of this edition is based on that of the First Folio (1623; hereafter F or F1) for the reasons given on pages 18– 32 of this Introduction, namely that it shows signs of having

---

1 'The intention may have been to show two characters trapped in their social roles, but the effect was curiously moving, followed as it was by a sober Henry ordering the singing of the *Te Deum* and *Non nobis*' (Potter, 47).

been printed from Shakespeare's manuscript, whereas the first published text, that of the First Quarto (1600; hereafter Q or Q1), shows signs of having been memorially reconstructed from stage performances of the F text; Q's cuts and other alterations are such that it is unsafe to conclude that they reflect what was done to the play in these performances. Nevertheless, though F is evidently superior to Q, there are instances where the inferior text can be shown to give the better reading or to supply an omission in F. Before discussing such instances it is proper to give some details of the early history of the play's publication, since it is relevant to any attempt to establish the text of the play for a modern edition.

Q had certainly been published before 14 August 1600, when 'The historye of Henrye the vth wth the battell of Agencourt' was among several books 'formerlye printed' that were being transferred by copyright to Thomas Pavier.[1] Whether it had been published before 4 August is not known. On that date 'Henry the Fift: a booke' was listed, with three other 'books' (*As You Like It, Every Man in his Humour* and *Much Ado About Nothing*), as 'to be staied'. This entry is on a preliminary leaf of the third volume of the Stationers' Register and is now thought not to record a formal transaction but to be the clerk's memorandum to himself. Its meaning is doubtful. If it marked an attempt to prevent the publication of these four plays belonging to the Lord Chamberlain's Men that attempt had either already failed to prevent the publication of *Henry V* or would fail to do so within ten days – unless, as has recently been suggested, *2 Henry IV* and not *Henry V* is meant.[2] Another doubtful question is whether the transfer to

---

1   *TxC*, 375. Knowles (353–64) discusses the various interpretations of the facts given in this paragraph.
2   Peter Blayney, unpublished paper cited by Gurr, 220. Blayney suggests that the clerk noted the last three words of the title as printed in the 1600 quarto edition (first page of text): 'The second part of Henry the fourth, continuing to his death, and coronation of Henry the fift.' This argument requires the manuscript to have begun with that title.

Pavier of copyright in *Henry V* is connected with the 'staying entry'. Thomas Creede, who had printed Q for Millington and Busby, had in 1598 printed *The Famous Victories of Henry the fifth*, and though the title-pages show that this and *The Chronicle History of Henry the fift* are two different plays belonging to the Queen's Men and the Lord Chamberlain's Men respectively it might have escaped notice that the copyright of the former did not also apply to the latter; the transfer to Pavier may have been meant to conceal, or to remedy, an irregularity. The most probable explanation of the 'staying entry' is that the Lord Chamberlain's Men were laying claim to payment for any of these plays that should be printed; if so, they seem to have succeeded in the case of *Every Man in his Humour* and *Much Ado About Nothing*, both of which were duly registered, and subsequently published as 'good' quartos, in 1600, as was *2 Henry IV*. *As You Like It* was not registered until 1623, just before its publication in F, and no attempt was made to supersede the 'bad' quarto of *Henry V* by selling a better text and having it published, as seems to have been the case with *Romeo and Juliet* earlier and with *Hamlet* later.

Abbreviation, paraphrase and misplacement of lines or phrases have already been noted as characteristics of Q *Henry V*, as of other 'bad' quartos. To these should now be added auditory errors such as 'the function' for 'defunction' (1.2.58), 'Foraging' for 'Forage in' (1.2.110), 'England' for 'inland' (1.2.142), 'quit' for 'quick' (2.2.79), 'cophetua' for '*Caveto*' (2.3.51), 'approach' for 'reproach' (3.6.47), 'partition' for 'perdition' (3.6.97), 'raunsome' for 're-answer' (3.6.127–8, 'faire, return' for 'fairly. Turn' (3.6.138), 'lessoned' for 'lessened' (3.6.145), 'your heire' for 'your air' (3.6.150) and 'Doing his actiuitie' for 'Doing is activity' (3.7.99). Most of these errors involve more misunderstanding of the sense than an actor would be likely to display, and therefore, if shorthand is ruled out (as the many misplacements of passages require it to be), imply a process of dictation. There are similar auditory errors in words without an equivalent in F, such as 'while they a more frosty clymate' ('they a' for 'their': F's 'whiles a more frosty people', 3.5.24) and 'Vnmaskt his power for *France*' ('Vnmaskt' for 'Embarkt': F's 'went with his forces into France', 1.2.147).

A few phrases in the comic scenes of Q look like gags interpolated by the actors, though whether on stage or during the compilation of Q it is impossible to say. Examples are Pistol's 'Keepe fast thy buggle boe' substituted for his last speech in 2.3, his 'Couple gorge' at the end of 4.6, and his parting exchange with Fluellen in 3.6 in which he echoes his defiance of Nym in 2.1 and Fluellen ironically asks 'Captain *Gour*, cannot you hear it lighten & thunder?' Just before this exchange Fluellen repeats a phrase for effect: 'for look you, / Disciplines ought to be kept, they ought to be kept.' He also repeats his interlocutor's phrase, for effect, on two occasions: once in this scene, when he replies to Gower's 'I know him not' with 'Do you not know him, here comes the man', and once in 5.1, where he takes up Gower's 'Inough Captaine, you haue astonisht him' with 'Astonisht him, by Iesu, Ile beat his head / Foure dayes, and four nights'; 'and four nights' is a further gag. In the same scene he uses the vocative 'Antient *Pistoll*' six times to F's once; similarly, in 4.1, the disguised King addresses Pistol five times as 'sir', which he never does in the corresponding F scene.

The text of Q is printed as verse throughout, each new line beginning with a capital letter even in prose scenes and passages. Pistol's speeches usually preserve their strongly metrical form, a notable exception being his defiance of Nym, 2.1.47–54. Enough of the play's original verse survives to allow a line-by-line comparison with F, though in Q the lines are often wrongly divided. In about a score of places new verse has been improvised to substitute for verse lost by memorial failure: 'Whom like a caytiffe she did leade to *France*' (1.2.161); 'Your message and his present we accept' (1.2.261); 'And therefore

gaue our selues to barbarous licence' (1.2.271–2); 'What dost
thou push, thou prickeard cur of Iseland?' (2.1.42–3); 'And
Pistolls flashing firy cock is vp' (2.1.53–4); 'Will make vs
conquerors in the field of *France*' (2.2.16); 'Haue steeped their
galles in honey for your sake' (2.2.30); 'That hath so chased your
blood out of apparence' (2.2.75–6); 'And how his resolution
andswered him, / You then would say that *Harry* was not
wilde' (2.4.34–5); 'Although we did seeme dead, we did but
slumber' (3.6.118; prose in original); 'But could be well content,
without impeach' (3.6.140–1); 'And from this day, vnto the
generall doome' (4.3.58); 'Vnto these English, or else die with
fame' (after 4.5.18; an addition, in which 'fame' must be an
error for 'shame'); 'for hearing you, / I must conuert to teares'
(4.6.33–4; an improvised line, wrongly divided); 'We may haue
leaue to bury all our dead, / Which in the field lye spoyled
and troden on' (4.7.72, 74 82); 'With pardon vnto both your
mightines. / Let it not displease you if I demaund / What
rub or bar hath thus far hindred you, / To keepe you from
the gentle speech of peace?' (5.2.23–67); 'Nor this haue we so
nicely stood vpon, / But you faire brother may intreat the
same' (5.2.337–8; the first line adapts 5.2.94); 'This and what
else, / Your maiestie shall craue. / God that disposeth all, giue
you much ioy. / *Har.* Why then faire *Katherine*, / Come giue
me thy hand: / Our marriage will we present solemnise'
(5.2.342–52; the first and third lines wrongly divided).

In 1602 Pavier, who had acquired the copyright in 1600,
brought out another edition, the Second Quarto (Q2). It was
again printed by Creede, and is a line-for-line following of Q1,
with only such variants, mainly of spelling, as a compositor
might introduce.

The Third Quarto (Q3), as already stated, was published by
Pavier in 1619 with the false date 1608 ('Printed for *T.P.*
1608'). The unnamed printer was William Jaggard, who with
his son Isaac printed F in 1622–3, in which latter year the
elder Jaggard died. Q3, like Q2, was printed from a copy of

Q1, but unlike Q2 it shows clear signs of editorial preparation. Much of this editing is technical rather than critical. Q1's line divisions, when they are altered, are altered in order to avoid filling the measure or over-filling it and having to turn the extra words over or under, not in order to improve the versification. Towards the end of the play the text is deliberately extended by spacing out the existing stage directions and adding a new unnecessary one, '*He makes Ancient Pistoll bite of the Leeke*', in order to fill almost three leaves of the final gathering (G1–3), where Q1 had filled just over two of them (G1–2, the latter misnumbered G3); a few phrases are even added to the lines, presumably for the same reason.[1] Such editing as can be called critical is almost wholly based on conjecture. In the opening scene (corresponding to 1.2 in F), typical emendations are the additions (here given in square brackets) to Q1's 'Which salicke land as I [haue] said before' (1.2.52), 'Foraging [the] blood of French Nobilitie' (1.2.110), 'We will by Gods grace play [him] such a set' (1.2.263) and 'When we do rowse vs in [the] throne of *France*' (1.2.276), none of which is supported by the corresponding F passage. These and other conjectural emendations show that no independent text, such as the manuscript on which F was based, can have been consulted in making them. In fact there is only one occasion on which Q3 emends Q1 with a reading that is evidently more than conjectural, when Q1 has

> And Gentlemen in England now a bed,
> Shall thinke themselues accurst,
> And hold their manhood cheape,
> While any speake that fought with vs
> Vpon Saint Crispines day.

and Q3 has

> And Gentlemen in England now a bed,
> Shall thinke themselues accurst,

---

1 One page (F4') is reproduced in *TxC*, 42.

> They were not there, when any speakes
> That fought with vs vpon S. Crispines day.

It is obvious from versification and sense that F (4.3.64–7) gives the correct version of this passage, and that Q3's correct insertion is followed by an incorrect omission, but three explanations of Q3's reading are possible. Q3 may be following a copy of Q1, not now extant, in which a four-word insertion has wrongly been treated as a substitution (*TxC*, 381); Q3 may be wrongly treating as a substitution an insertion marked on the copy of Q1 from which it is being printed, in which latter case the insertion may be derived from knowledge of the passage as currently spoken on the stage (Greg, *Problem*, 133); or, again in the latter case, the insertion may be derived from an authoritative manuscript, perhaps that from which F was later printed (Gurr, 216). This third explanation is weakened by Q3's reliance elsewhere on conjectural emendation.

The text of *Henry V* in F occupies signatures h1–k2, the double-column pages being numbered 69–95.[1] It is thought to have been set by the two principal compositors employed on F, known as Compositor A and Compositor B; they divided the work on h and i between them, Compositor A then setting k2, k1^v and k1 (in that order) by himself.[2]

---

1 The pagination of the previous histories is 1–102 (the preceding comedies having been separately paginated). *Henry V* was the first of the histories to be printed, and the error in pagination was caused by miscalculation.

2 Typesetting normally began in the middle of the six-leaf gathering or quire, with one compositor setting forwards from the seventh page to the twelfth while the other set pages six to one in reverse order. In the following analysis (based on *TxC*, 148–9, 150) the page signature is given first (superscript ^{v} indicates verso, i.e. the back of the page, and a and b the two columns), then the compositor, and then the reference to the present edition. h3^v, B (2.1.114–2.2.113); h4a, B (2.2.114–80), h4b, A (2.2.181–2.3.53 (horse- /)); h3, B (2.0.18–2.1.113); h4^v, A (2.3.53 (/ leeches) to 2.4.112); h5, A (2.4.113–3.2.13); h2^v, A (1.2.202–2.0.17); h2, A (1.2.70–201); h5^v, A (3.2.14–3.3.2); h1^v, A (1.1.45–1.2.69); h6, A (3.3.3–3.5.12); h1, A (title to 1.1.44); h6^v, A (3.5.13–3.6.75 (trick)); i3^v, A (4.2.0–4.3.52); i4, A (4.3.53–4.4.44); i3, A (4.1.185–304); i4^v, B (4.4.45–4.7.22); i2^v, A (4.1.59–184); i5, B (4.7.23–145); i2, A (3.7.151–4.1.58); i5^v, A (4.7.146–4.8.90); i1^v, A (3.7.25–150); i6, A (4.8.91–5.1.37 (make)); i1, A (3.6.75 (up) to 3.7.24); i6^{v}a, B (5.1.37 (you) to 5.2.11), i6^{v}b, A (5.2.12–76); k2, A (5.2.329 to Epilogue 14); k1^v, A (5.2.206 (that) to 328); k1, A (5.2.77–206 (English)).

Their copy is thought to have been a manuscript in Shakespeare's own hand, his draft of the play, known as his foul papers. Stage directions and speech prefixes suggesting this have already been instanced (p. 24 above), and there are other instances of both (stage directions at 3.1.0.1, 4.3.0.1–2, 5.2.0.1; speech prefixes at 2.3.31, 5.2.112). Wilson has listed a number of spellings which he regards as characteristically Shakespearean (Cam[1], 111). Such misreading errors as occur strongly suggest that the copy was a manuscript in Elizabethan secretary hand, like that of Hand D, attributed to Shakespeare, in *Sir Thomas More*. One striking instance is the phrase (3.2.117) which F prints as 'ay, or goe to death' but which the context shows should have read (in the original spelling) 'ay ow god a death'. From the reproduction of minuscule letters (Fig. 7) it will be seen that w/r and d/e can be easily confused, and that one form of the letter 'a' can be misread as 'to'. All these features occur in the facsimile of Hand D reproduced in the *Textual Companion*, and so does the invariable spelling of 'God' as 'god'.[1]

It was said earlier (p. 24) that the only sign of editorial interference with Shakespeare's manuscript in preparing it for the press was the incorrect insertion of act divisions. Another form of interference has sometimes been alleged, the expurgation of oaths making use of holy names such as God, Christ and Jesus, particularly as Q is rather free in its use of them. But they are not scarce in F either, Fluellen uttering three in 3.2 before the arrival of Macmorris, who utters twice that number, and the King himself exclaiming 'God's will' and 'God's peace' in 4.3 when he is repudiating Westmorland's wish for reinforcements. In Q he greets Montjoy's arrival at the end of the battle with the angry 'Gods will what means

---

1 *TxC*, 11 (facsimile), 466–7 (transcript). Note particularly 'god' (ll. 102, 104–6, 135), the final 'e' of 'peace' (l. 109), the final 'de' of 'leade' (l. 121), the first letters of the two words 'rout who' (l. 116), and the first 'a' of 'a saies trewe' (l. 141).

7 Elizabethan handwriting, minuscules. Ronald B. McKerrow, *An Introduction to Bibliography for Literary Students* (Oxford, 1927)

8 Elizabethan handwriting, capitals. Ronald B. McKerrow, *An Introduction to Bibliography for Literary Students* (Oxford, 1927)

this?' where F has the ironical 'How now, what meanes this Herald?' (4.7.67, 'Herald' being vocative); here F's seems the better reading in view of Holinshed's account of his motivation ('to vnderstand what they would saie'). Pistol's 'by gaddes lugges' and Fluellen's 'Godes plud' in Q are consistent with their interpolated gags. There is little reason, then, to regard F as an expurgated text.

If Shakespeare's manuscript came straight to the compositors with hardly any editorial intervention, the only errors in F might be expected to be simple compositorial ones, such as the misreading of 'mare' as 'name' at 2.1.25 and the omission of a line of verse at 4.3.48, both of which can be corrected from Q. The situation is, however, complicated by the fact that Q3 had been printed in Jaggard's shop, one of its compositors perhaps being F's Compositor B (*TxC*, 376). A theory that F *Henry V* was printed not from manuscript copy but from marked-up and cut-up pages of Q3 and of Q2 has not found many adherents, but its proposer, Andrew S. Cairncross, pointed out two typographical features of F which persuasively indicate Q3's influence. First, at 2.1.41, set by Compositor B, Nym's interjection 'Pish' ('Push' in Quartos 1–3), with its speech prefix, is printed in the same line as the last line of the previous speech, as in Q3 but not in Q1 or Q2. Secondly, at 4.8.107, set by Compositor A, the King's line 'But five and twenty. O God, thy arm was here' is printed as two lines, the second being indented; this layout reflects the fact that Q1 had begun a new line at 'O God' and that both Q2 and Q3 had wrongly added the speech prefix *King* because Q1's omission of the King's previous speech prefix made it look as though Exeter had been speaking (Cairncross, 71). If one or two copies of Q3 were available to F's compositors, readings from them could enter the F text. This possibility allows an editor to doubt the accuracy of certain readings shared by F and the quartos, readings which would seem irrefutable if the possibility did not exist. Two notable cases are '*Enter Gouernour*' (3.3.43

SD: Q1, Q2, Q3, F) and 'Crispianus' (4.7.90: Q3, F), and there are others.

An editor, then, is under no compulsion to repress doubts when an improbable F reading is apparently confirmed by a reading in one of the quartos. Nor is an editor compelled to expect Compositors A and B always to behave according to their deduced characteristics.[1] It is an editor's responsibility, in trying to establish the text, to take into consideration as many aspects of textual transmission as possible and then to exercise personal judgement. This accounts for the variety of opinion that is seen when modern editions, including the present one, are compared with each other.

A comparison of Q1's and F's treatments of the same passage (4.6.4–38) will show what conclusions the present editor has drawn from them (Figs 9 and 10). In Q Exeter's speech is so much better reproduced than the King's two speeches that precede and follow it that it gives reasonable grounds for supposing, here at least, that the actor who played Exeter had supplied it, probably by dictation.[2] The hypothesis here proposed is that three sources of error may exist. Firstly, the actor may have originally learned his lines from the text that is preserved in F, but by the time he helped to compile Q he had become less than word-perfect in them (supposing that he had ever been so), while his grasp of other actors' lines had always been looser. Secondly, if he dictated the dialogue to another person, that person may have misheard some of the words. Thirdly, if manuscript copy prepared in this way was sometimes difficult to read, the compositor may have reproduced it inaccurately. Given the absence of objective evidence, such as a written statement by someone with personal knowledge

---

1   Walker, 'Principles', points out A's greater liability to misreading and B's greater liability to carelessness.

2   Irace, in a detailed analysis of the variations between Q and F in the lines they have in common, concludes that the actor playing Exeter, along with the actors who played Pistol and Gower and doubled some minor roles, memorially reconstructed and abridged the play.

of how Q's text was produced, this hypothesis is not susceptible of incontrovertible proof. What is argued is merely that it can be supported by a detailed comparison of the Q passage with the corresponding F one, the conclusion being that an attempt was made to reconstruct a text not radically different from that later printed in F.

In ll. 4–6, it is inferred, 'within this hour' and 'and fighting' are omitted through memorial failure, and 'all bleeding ore' is a substitution proceeding from l. 11 in Exeter's speech. In that line Q's 'hasted' must be the compositor's misreading of manuscript 'hagled', as 'honour dying' is of 'honour-owing' (l. 9). Another compositorial error is 'steept' for 'insteept' (l. 12), an omission caused either by 'in blood' in the same line or by mere carelessness like the omission of 'had' in l. 30. In l. 20 'them' for 'him' must be an auditory error, for the actor could hardly suppose that the dead Suffolk was included. In l. 17 'to rest' is a puzzling substitution. Authorial revision is out of the question, given the continuation of the speech in both texts, and an actor's substitution is barely more probable. Possibly the manuscript copy correctly read 'abrest', with an accidental gap after the first two letters, and the compositor made sense of 'ab' by changing it to 'to'; if the following line correctly began with 'As' it may have made no sense to him either, so he substituted 'And' (or this may have been mere carelessness again). In ll. 21–2 the actor has conflated two verse lines into one new one, as he has simplified and re-versified the King's ll. 33–4. But in ll. 25–7 it seems that he remembered the lines accurately as verse (though he substituted 'argument' for 'testament' and 'never-ending' for 'noble-ending') and that the compositor corrupted them through eyeskip from one 'and' ('and kissed') to another ('and so'), an inference that receives some slight support from the irrational full stop and capital letter after 'sealed', the capital letter possibly representing the start of another verse line. At the end of the passage the line giving the King's reason for ordering the prisoners to be killed

King. Liues he good Vnckle, twise I sawe him downe,
Twise vp againe:
From helmet to the spurre, all bleeding ore,

Exe. In which aray, braue souldier doth he lye,
Larding the plaines, and by his bloody side,
Yoake fellow to his honour dying wounds,
The noble Earle of *Suffolke* also lyes.
Suffolke first dyde, and *Yorke* all hasted ore,
Comes to him where in blood he lay steept,
And takes him by the beard, kisses the gashes
That bloodily did yane vpon his face,
And cryde aloud, tary deare cousin *Suffolke*:
My soule shall thine keep company in heauen:
Tary deare soule awhile, then flie to rest:
And in this glorious and well foughten field,
We kept togither in our chiualdry.
Vpon these words I came and cheerd them vp,
He tooke me by the hand, said deare my Lord,
Commend my seruice to my soueraigne:
So did he turne, and ouer *Suffolkes* necke
He threw his wounded arme, and so espoused to death,
With blood he sealed. An argument
Of neuer ending loue. The pretie and sweet matter of it,
Forst those waters from me, which I would haue stopt,
But I not so much of man in me,
But all my mother came into my eyes,
And gaue me vp to teares.

Kin. I blame you not: for hearing you,
I must conuert to teares.

Alarum soundes.

What new alarum is this?
Bid euery souldier kill his prisoner.

Pist. Couple gorge. *Exit omnes.*

9 The First Quarto (1600) version of *Henry V*, 4.6.4–38

108

King. Liues he good Vnckle: thrice within this houre
I faw him downe ; thrice vp againe, and fighting,
From Helmet to the fpurre, all blood he was.

   Exe. In which array (braue Soldier) doth he lye,
Larding the plaine : and by his bloody fide,
(Yoake-fellow to his honour-owing-wounds)
The Noble Earle of Suffolke alfo lyes.
Suffolke firft dyed, and Yorke all hagled ouer
Comes to him, where in gore he lay infteeped,
And takes him by the Beard, kiffes the gafhes
That bloodily did yawne vpon his face.
He cryes aloud; Tarry my Cofin Suffolke,
My foule fhall thine keepe company to heauen :
Tarry (fweet foule) for mine, then flye a-breft :
As in this glorious and well-foughten field
We kept together in our Chiualrie.
Vpon thefe words I came, and cheer'd him vp,
He fmil'd me in the face, raught me his hand,
And with a feeble gripe, fayes : Deere my Lord,
Commend my feruice to my Soueraigne,
So did he turne, and ouer Suffolkes necke
He threw his wounded arme, and kift his lippes,
And fo efpous'd to death, with blood he feal'd
A Teftament of Noble-ending-loue :
The prettie and fweet manner of it forc'd
Thofe waters from me, which I would haue ftop'd,
But I had not fo much of man in mee,
And all my mother came into mine eyes,
And gaue me vp to teares.

   King. I blame you not,
For hearing this, I muft perforce compound,
With mixtfull eyes, or they will iffue to.   *Alarum*
But hearke, what new alarum is this fame?
The French haue re-enforc'd their fcatter'd men :
Then euery fouldiour kill his Prifoners,
Giue the word through.   *Exit*

10 The First Folio (1623) version of *Henry V*, 4.6.4–38

109

is omitted, probably through memorial failure, and Pistol's 'Couple gorge' is thrust in as an exit-line gag. F appears to reproduce the passage with almost total accuracy (though in l. 15 several editors have preferred Q's reading), but 'mixtfull' is an evident misreading which will be discussed in the commentary.

The text of the present edition is a modernized one, and accordingly the spelling and punctuation of this F passage follow twentieth-century practice, for instance in the replacing of parentheses by commas, the introducing of quotation marks round York's reported speeches, and the deletion of the superfluous second hyphens in 'honour-owing-wounds' and 'Noble-ending-loue'. Though spelling is modernized, vocabulary is not, so not only is 'well-foughten' retained but also 'raught' (not 'reached'), 'gripe' (not 'grip') and 'alarum' (not 'alarm'). The spelling of '-ed' verb endings, according to the principles devised for the series, is uniformly given in modern form, as above, without indicating in the text whether or not a final syllable is to be pronounced; but in the commentary notes all pronounced endings are indicated when they diverge from normal late twentieth-century English standard pronunciation. The modernization of the French passages and the dialect passages has followed the same principles as that of the passages in standard sixteenth-century English: in the French passages archaic spelling has been silently adjusted but archaic grammar has been retained, and so has. incorrect grammar when it seems evident that this is what Shakespeare wrote, the commentary notes indicating what the correct modern grammar is; in the dialect passages accepted modern dialect forms are substituted where they exist (thus, in 3.2, Jamy's 'gud' becomes 'guid', his 'bath' becomes 'baith' and his 'de' becomes 'dae', but his 'ay' has been normalized as 'I'); eccentricities of pronunciation have been retained but have not been uniformly imposed, so that Fluellen, for instance, does not substitute p for b in every speech he makes. Proper names of places are modernized, so that 'Callice' becomes 'Calais', 'Harflew' becomes 'Harfleur' and 'Roan' becomes 'Rouen'. Similarly proper names of persons are normally modernized, so that 'Alanson' becomes 'Alençon' and 'Dolphin' becomes 'Dauphin'. An exception has been made in the case of 'Britaine' (Brittany), which is anglicized as 'Britain', not turned into 'Bretagne', which would ruin the versification at 2.4.4. As with the '-ed' verb endings, the commentary notes indicate the metrical value and, more tentatively, the pronunciation that Shakespeare probably expected these names to have. 'Fluellen' is another exception; logically it should no doubt be 'Llewelyn', but since one hardly ever hears this name pronounced in the Welsh manner outside Wales, and since Fluellen is one of the favourite characters in Shakespeare's plays, his name has been retained in that familiar form. Similarly Ancient Pistol has not had his familiar, if archaic, title modernized to 'Ensign'.

The textual notes record all verbal departures from the basic text, F (other than those involved in modernizing, though even in some of these cases noteworthy F spellings are recorded), all departures from its punctuation which affect the meaning, all alterations to its stage directions and speech prefixes, and all alterations to the lineation of its verse. Merely typographical errors, such as wrong letters and turned letters, are not recorded; examples are 'begia' for 'begin' (1.2.168) and 'theu' for 'then' (1.2.174). The text of Q1 differs so greatly from that of F that only those of its readings that are relevant to establishing the text or are notable for some other reason have been recorded. It is printed in full as Appendix 1. Readings from the later Quarto and Folio texts and from editions since the early eighteenth century have also been selectively recorded on the same principle.

THE LIFE OF
KING
HENRY THE
FIFTH

CHORUS

KING Henry the Fifth

Duke of CLARENCE
Duke of BEDFORD ⎫
Duke of GLOUCESTER ⎬ his brothers
Duke of EXETER, his uncle ⎭ 5
Duke of YORK
Earl of HUNTINGDON
Earl of SALISBURY
Earl of WARWICK 10
Earl of WESTMORLAND

Richard, Earl of CAMBRIDGE ⎫
Henry, Lord SCROOP of Masham ⎬ conspirators against the
Sir Thomas GREY ⎭ King

Archbishop of CANTERBURY 15
Bishop of ELY

Sir Thomas ERPINGHAM ⎫
Captain FLUELLEN ⎪
Captain GOWER ⎬ officers in the King's army
Captain JAMY ⎪ 20
Captain MACMORRIS ⎭

John BATES ⎫
Alexander COURT ⎬ soldiers in the King's army
Michael WILLIAMS ⎭

An English Herald 25

BARDOLPH ⎫
NYM ⎬ associates of Sir John
PISTOL ⎭ Falstaff
A BOY, Falstaff's page
Nell, HOSTESS of an Eastcheap tavern; formerly Mistress 30
  Quickly, now married to Pistol

114

Charles the Sixth, the FRENCH KING
QUEEN ISABEL, the French Queen
Louis the DAUPHIN, their son
Princess KATHERINE, their daughter   35
ALICE, a lady attending on Princess Katherine
Duke of BERRY
Duke of BOURBON
Duke of BRITAIN
Duke of BURGUNDY   40
Duke of ORLEANS
Charles Delabreth, the CONSTABLE of France
Earl of GRANDPRÉ
Lord RAMBURES
GOVERNOR of Harfleur   45
MONTJOY, the French herald
Two French Ambassadors to the King of England
Monsieur Le Fer, a FRENCH SOLDIER
A French Messenger
Attendants; Lords; Soldiers; Citizens of Harfleur   50

LIST OF ROLES No list of roles is given in F or Q, the first such list being in Rowe. The F text contains forty-nine roles, including four mute ones (Second Ambassador, Berry, Clarence, Huntingdon) and excluding one named at 4.2.0.1 but never speaking or addressed and therefore presumably abandoned (Beaumont). These can be distributed among eighteen actors, three of them boys, so as to provide extras to play the mute attendants, lords, soldiers and citizens of Harfleur required by the stage action. A doubling chart is given as Appendix 5; the number of lines for each actor is based on the length of his roles in F, measured in F lines of verse or prose, as recorded in Spevack 2 (1968), without taking note of the small number of speeches reassigned by editors. The Q text contains forty roles, including two mute ones (Second Bishop, Second

Ambassador). Like F it requires extras, which it specifies as 'Attendants' (twice) and 'others' (twice).

1 CHORUS The (male) presenter of the dramatic action, perhaps distinctively dressed (Prologue 33n.). The role has also been performed as Time (John Vandenhoff, Theatre Royal, Covent Garden, 1839), as Clio, the muse of history (Ellen Kean, Princess's Theatre, 1859), as an Elizabethan youth (acted by a woman: Sybil Thorndike, Lyric Theatre, Hammersmith, 1928; Gwen Ffrangcon-Davies, Theatre Royal, Drury Lane, 1938), and in various kinds of modern dress, civil and military.

2 KING The eldest son (1387–1422) of Henry IV. As Prince of Wales he is mentioned in *R2* and has a major role in *1H4* and *2H4*. His three campaigns in France (1415; 1417–20; 1421–2, when he died at Vincennes) are reduced to the first in *H5*.

3 CLARENCE Thomas (1388–1421), the second son of Henry IV. He has a minor role in *2H4* and a mute one (1.2, 5.2) in F *H5*; in Q *H5* he is substituted for Bedford. After the capture of Harfleur he returned to England ill and took no further part in the campaign, though Holinshed (3.553) says that he was at Agincourt. He was not at Troyes (5.2), though he took part in the abortive negotiations of 1419 (Holinshed, 3.569).

4 BEDFORD John (1389–1435), the third son of Henry IV. As Prince John of Lancaster he appears in *1H4* and *2H4*, and as Bedford in *H5* and *1H6*, in the latter play as Regent of France. He was Lieutenant of England throughout the Agincourt campaign. He was not at Troyes.

5 GLOUCESTER Humphrey (1391–1447), the fourth and youngest son of Henry IV. He has a minor role in *2H4* and major ones in *1H6* and *2H6*, where he is Protector of England. He was wounded at Agincourt (Holinshed, 3.555). He was not at Troyes, though he took part in the abortive negotiations of 1419 (Holinshed, 3.569).

6 EXETER Thomas Beaufort (d. 1427), illegitimate (later legitimated) son of John of Gaunt by Katherine Swynford, and half-brother of Henry IV. He was created Earl of Dorset in 1412 and Duke of Exeter in 1416; in Holinshed (3.546) he is created 'Earl of Exeter' in 1414 and is named as Duke of Exeter thereafter. Holinshed (3.553) wrongly says that he was at Agincourt and commanded the rearguard (see 3.3.51–6n., 52n., 3.6.5n.), but rightly says that he was at Troyes (3.572). He appears also in *1H6*.

7 YORK Edward (*c.* 1373–1415), eldest son of the Duke of York in *R2*, in which play he is called Aumerle. See 4.3.128 SDn.

8 HUNTINGDON John Holland (1395–1447); a mute role. See 5.2.85n.

9 SALISBURY Thomas de Montacute (1388–1428). See 4.3.0.2n., 10n. He was at Troyes (Holinshed, 3.572), but

is not reintroduced into 5.2 of *H5*.

10 WARWICK Richard de Beauchamp (1382–1439). He appears in the French scenes of *1H6*. During the Agincourt campaign he was not with the army but was Captain of Calais (Hibbert, 48); *DNB* (but not Holinshed) states that he was among those who returned with Clarence from Harfleur. He was not at Troyes, but he was twice sent to negotiate peace terms with the elder and the younger Burgundy in 1419 (Holinshed, 3.569, 572).

11 WESTMORLAND Ralph Neville (1364–1425). He appears among Henry IV's supporters in *1H4* and *2H4*. His participation in the Agincourt campaign and at Troyes is unhistorical, since he remained in England as a member of Bedford's council and warden of the Scottish marches.

12 CAMBRIDGE The younger brother (d. 1415) of the Duke of York. He had been created Earl of Cambridge in 1414. See 2.0.23n.

13 SCROOP (*c.* 1376–1415) On his relationship to other Scroops in Shakespeare's history plays see 2.0.24n. He had been made treasurer and Knight of the Garter through Prince Henry's influence in 1410; on Henry V's accession he was entrusted with diplomatic missions.

14 GREY (d. 1415) of Heton, Northumberland. See 2.0.25.

15 CANTERBURY Henry Chichele or Chicheley (*c.* 1362–1443)

16 ELY John Fordham (d. 1435). He was at Troyes (Holinshed, 3.572) but is not reintroduced to 5.2.

17 ERPINGHAM (1357–1428) See 4.1.13n.

18 FLUELLEN On the spelling of his name see p. 111 and note on 3.2.20 SD.

20 JAMY On the choice of his name see 3.2.76n.

26 BARDOLPH He appears also in *1H4*, *2H4* and *MW*, in all of which he is conspicuous for his red face, the result of heavy drinking. On his military rank see 2.1.0.1n.

27 NYM He appears also in *MW*.

28 PISTOL He appears also in *2H4* and *MW*. He should probably be bearded; see 3.6.76n. On his military rank and title see 2.1.0.1, 2.1.3.

29 BOY He appears also in *2H4* and *MW*, in the latter being named as Robin. A boy actor's role, requiring the ability to speak French.

30 HOSTESS She appears also in *1H4*, *2H4* and *MW*. See 2.1.19n. A boy actor's role.

32 FRENCH KING Charles VI (1368–1422). His periods of insanity are mentioned by Holinshed (3.547) but not in *H5*. He died two months after the death of Henry V.

33 QUEEN ISABEL Isabel (1370–1435), daughter of Stephen II of Bavaria. A boy actor's role.

34 DAUPHIN Louis (d. 1415), eldest son of Charles VI. On his early death (see 5.0.35–42n.) he was succeeded as Dauphin by his brother John (d. 1417); John was succeeded by Charles, later Charles VII, the Dauphin of *1H6*. The title is invariably spelled 'Dolphin' in Q and F, as in Holinshed: see 1.2.222n. The role requires the ability to speak French at 3.7.65–6.

35 KATHERINE (1401–37) After Henry V's death she secretly married Owen Tudor, a Welsh gentleman of her household, and their descendants were the Tudor royal family: see Appendix 4. A boy actor's role, requiring the ability to speak French.

36 ALICE Shakespeare is apparently in two minds about her age: see 5.2.118n. A boy actor's role, requiring the ability to speak French.

37 BERRY John (d. 1416), son of John II of France and uncle of Charles VI. A mute role.

38 BOURBON John (*c.* 1380–1433), mater-

nal uncle of Charles VI. After being made prisoner at Agincourt he was taken to England, where he died in captivity.

39 BRITAIN John de Montfort (d. 1442), Duke of Bretagne (Brittany: see 2.4.4n.).

40 BURGUNDY Philip (1396–1467), who succeeded his father John in 1419 (see 5.2.7n.). To be acted as a young man: see same note, and Introduction, p. 94. He appears also in *1H6*.

41 ORLEANS Charles (1391–1463), nephew of Charles VI. After being made prisoner at Agincourt he was taken to England, where he lived in captivity till ransomed in 1440.

42 CONSTABLE Charles d'Albret (d. 1415). For his title see 2.4.0.1n. For the spelling of his name in *H5* see 3.5.40n.

46 MONTJOY His name is titular, not personal: see 3.6.136–7n.

47 Ambassadors In *Famous Victories* the ambassador who brings the tennis-balls is the Archbishop of Bourges, but in Holinshed the two embassies are distinct (3.545, 547), and there is no sign that Shakespeare intended the First Ambassador to be clerically dressed. The Second Ambassador is a mute role.

48 FRENCH SOLDIER For his incongruous name, Le Fer, see 4.4.26n. He is sometimes played by a small actor, but the scene is equally (perhaps more) effective if he is the normal size.

49 Messenger In 2.4, 3.7 and 4.2 the part can be played by the same actor.

50 Attendants ... Harfleur All these minor parts can be doubled by members of the cast who are elsewhere taking individual roles.

THE LIFE OF
KING HENRY THE FIFTH

[PROLOGUE]   *Enter* CHORUS.

CHORUS

O for a muse of fire, that would ascend
The brightest heaven of invention,
A kingdom for a stage, princes to act,
And monarchs to behold the swelling scene!
Then should the warlike Harry, like himself,   5
Assume the port of Mars, and at his heels,
Leashed in like hounds, should famine, sword and
    fire

PROLOGUE 0.1 *Enter* CHORUS In F this speech is displayed between the play's title and the heading *Actus Primus. Scæna Prima*. Its text is printed in italic, in double column. 'Enter Prologue' is centred, within rules. (The Prologue of *H8* is displayed in the same manner.) The speaker identifies himself as 'Chorus' at l. 32. His later appearances are headed '*Enter Chorus*' (Acts 2, 3, 5) or '*Chorus*' (Act 4).

1 **a muse of fire** 'inspiration as brilliant and aspiring as the highest and brightest of the four elements' (Humphreys); *OED* muse *sb.*[1] 2

2 **invention** creative imagination (*OED* 4). It is pronounced as four syllables.

3–4 i.e. the power to re-create the very persons of history. *Princes (OED sb.* 1) is synonymous with *monarchs*: the rulers of England and France wage war while the other crowned heads of Europe (e.g. the Emperor, 5.0.38)

look on.

4 **swelling** majestic (*OED ppl. a.* 8). Cf. *Mac* 1.3.127–8, 'the swelling act / Of the imperial theme'.

5 **like himself** in his own heroic manner. Cf. *Tim* 1.2.0.5–6, '*Then comes, dropping after all, Apemantus, discontentedly, like himself.*'

6 **port** bearing, demeanour

7 **Leashed in** kept on the leash (*OED* leash *n.*, first example). Three was the usual number of hounds coupled in one leash.

famine, sword and fire the traditional instruments of war. Cf. *1H6* 4.2.11, 'Lean famine, quartering steel, and climbing fire'. In Holinshed (3.567) King Henry answers a deputation from Rouen, which he is besieging, by declaring that he is using the third and mildest of Bellona's three 'handmaidens', who are 'blood, fire, and famine'.

TITLE] *F (table of contents), F2 (heading);* The Life of Henry the Fift *F (heading and running titles);* The Chronicle Historie of *Henry* the fift: with his battell fought at *Agin Court* in *France*. Togither with Auncient *Pistoll. Q (heading)* PROLOGUE] *(*Enter Prologue*); speech not in Q* 0.1 CHORUS] *Capell; Prologue* F 1 SP] *Dyce; not in* F

119

Crouch for employment. But pardon, gentles all,
The flat unraised spirits that hath dared
On this unworthy scaffold to bring forth   10
So great an object. Can this cockpit hold
The vasty fields of France? Or may we cram
Within this wooden O the very casques
That did affright the air at Agincourt?
O pardon, since a crooked figure may   15
Attest in little place a million,
And let us, ciphers to this great account,
On your imaginary forces work.

---

8 gentles gentlemen and gentlewomen, especially as an audience (cf. 2.0.35 and *MND* 5.1.126), but also in more general use, e.g. *MW* 3.2.83, 'Will you go, gentles?'

9 flat unraised spirits 'dull, uninspired actors and playwright' (Walter); with word-play on the raising of supernatural spirits by incantations, as Taylor notes.
unraised unraisèd
hath A singular verb with a plural antecedent is common, especially after the relative pronoun *that* (Abbott, 247).

10 scaffold theatrical stage

11 cockpit i.e. circular playhouse; literally a small arena designed for cock-fighting

12 vasty vast, wide: 'a poetical form of the word' (Wright), apparently coined by Shakespeare, though not peculiar to him (*OED*), and also used at 2.2.123 and 2.4.105 and at *MV* 2.7.41 ('vasty wilds') and *1H4* 3.1.51 ('vasty deep')

13 wooden O another mock-derogatory synonym for the timber-built circular theatre, probably the Globe. See Introduction, pp. 3–5.
the very casques all those real helmets. Gurr makes a weak case for word-play on casque and cask.

14 affright the air Walter compares the Latin trope '*coelum territat armis*'

(affrights heaven with arms) listed in Susenbrotus, *Epitome Troporum* (1565), 17. Cf. *R3* 5.6.71 [3.341], 'Amaze the welkin with your broken staves!' (For the square brackets in Shakespeare references, see p. 406, 'Abbreviations and references'.)

15–16 a crooked ... million a nought or zero (a curved figure) standing in the humblest position (as the unit at the end of a row of figures) is able to signify a million (by converting 100,000 into 1,000,000); cf. *WT* 1.2.6–7, 'like a cipher, / Yet standing in rich place'. *Crooked*, elsewhere in Shakespeare implying 'decrepitude, deformity, or dishonesty', here reiterates 'the inadequacy of the human actor' (Taylor).

17 ciphers (1) noughts or zeros, (2) non-entities (*OED sb.* 2)
to ... account in comparison with this great sum total. *OED* explains that the F spelling 'Accompt' indicates etymology (Lat. *computare*, to count), not pronunciation. A secondary sense of *account*, i.e. story, is unlikely because Shakespeare nowhere else uses the word in that sense; *OED*'s first example of such use is in 1614.

18 imaginary forces powers of imagination (*OED* imaginary *a.* 2: first two examples from Shakespeare: *KJ* 4.2.265, *Son* 27.9). *Forces*, often used

---

8 all,] *F4;* all: *F*   13 casques] *(Caskes)*   17 account] *(Accompt)*

Suppose within the girdle of these walls
Are now confined two mighty monarchies,   20
Whose high upreared and abutting fronts
The perilous narrow ocean parts asunder.
Piece out our imperfections with your thoughts.
Into a thousand parts divide one man
And make imaginary puissance.   25
Think, when we talk of horses, that you see them
Printing their proud hoofs i'th' receiving earth.
For 'tis your thoughts that now must deck our kings,
Carry them here and there, jumping o'er times,
Turning th'accomplishment of many years   30
Into an hour-glass: for the which supply,
Admit me Chorus to this history,
Who prologue-like your humble patience pray,

by Shakespeare to mean armies, may
hint at that meaning here (cf. 25).

21–2 **Whose ... asunder** Geographically, the English Channel separates the facing cliffs of England and (less appropriately) France. Figuratively, the foreheads of England and France oppose each other across the English Channel: cf. *R2* 1.1.15–16, 'Face to face / And frowning brow to brow', and *Mac* 4.3.234, 'Front to front'.

21 **upreared** erected (uprearèd)
   abutting 'projecting towards; terminating upon or against; coming into contact, touching' (*OED*: first example)
   fronts foreheads (frequently in Shakespeare), and possibly also frontiers (*OED sb.* 7c: examples from 1589 and 1593). Not used elsewhere in this sense by Shakespeare, but here appropriate to *abutting*. Cf. abut *v.* 2 ('to end at, march with, border on, as contiguous lands or estates do').

22 **perilous narrow ocean** Shakespeare refers to Channel shipwrecks in *MV* 3.1.2–7 and *KJ* 5.3.11 (both on the Goodwin Sands).
   parts asunder 'An intensive

tautology, not recorded elsewhere' (Taylor)

23 **Piece out** extend, make go further (*OED* piece *v.* 6)

24 **Into ... man** turn each man into a thousand (paradoxically multiplying by dividing)

25 **puissance** armed force (*OED* 2). Shakespeare uses both three-syllable (here and at 2.2.191) and two-syllable pronunciation (3.0.21).

28 **deck** adorn

29 **Carry ... there** as at 5.0.8–9
   jumping o'er times as at 5.0.40–2

30–1 **Turning ... hour-glass** i.e. condensing the events completed in six years (1414–20) into mere hours. Cf. *RJ* Prologue 12, 'the two hours' traffic of our stage'. The verb may have been suggested by the idea of turning the hour-glass itself (cf. *WT* 4.1.16).

31 **for ... supply** to aid you in which. *Supply* is used in the sense 'reinforcement', as in the military contexts of *1H4* 4.3.3 ('looks he not for supply?' and *2H4* 1.3.28 ('Eating the air on promise of supply').

32 **Chorus** commentator

33 **prologue-like** in the manner (rather

21 high upreared] *Pope;* high, vp-reared *F*

Gently to hear, kindly to judge our play.   *Exit.*

[1.1]   *Enter the* Archbishop of CANTERBURY *and the* Bishop of
ELY.

CANTERBURY
My lord, I'll tell you, that self bill is urged

than in the costume) of a prologue-speaker, though there may have been a convention of prologue-speakers wearing a long black velvet cloak (mentioned by the Prologue in Heywood's *Four Prentices of London*, 1614, as one of the 'signs' of a Prologue) **humble** gentle: cf. *LLL* 5.3.622, 'This is not generous, not gentle, not humble', and Lodge, *Rosalynde* (Bullough, 2.211), 'Thy lips are kinde, and humble like the dove'. Not in *OED* in this sense, unless implied in *a.* 1, 'the opposite of proud'. Gurr regards the phrase as 'a striking inversion', with the sense 'humbly pray your patience'.

34 **hear** To hear, rather than see, a play is the usual Shakespearean expression: *MND* 5.1.81, *TS* Ind.1.91, 94, Ind.2.130.

1.1 Q omits this scene and begins with Exeter speaking 1.2.2, Canterbury and Ely being already in the King's presence.

0.1 Neither F nor Q indicates in SD or text that Canterbury is an archbishop, though Holinshed does (see 86–9n.).

1–21 Cf. Holinshed, 3.545: 'In the second yeare of his reigne, king Henrie called his high court of parlement, the last daie of Aprill in the towne of Leicester, in which parlement manie profitable lawes were concluded, and manie petitions mooued, were for that time deferred. Amongst which, one was, that a bill exhibited in the parlement holden at Westminster in the eleuenth yeare of king Henrie the fourth (which by

reason the king was then troubled with ciuill discord, came to none effect) might now with good deliberation be pondered, and brought to some good conclusion. The effect of which supplication was, that the temporall lands deuoutlie giuen, and disordinatlie spent by religious, and other spirituall persons, should be seized into the kings hands, sith the same might suffice to mainteine, to the honor of the king, and defense of the realme, fifteene earles, fifteene hundred knights, six thousand and two hundred esquiers, and a hundred almesse-houses, for reliefe onelie of the poore, impotent, and needie persons, and the king to haue cleerelie to his coffers twentie thousand pounds, with manie other prouisions and values of religious houses, which I passe ouer.

'This bill was much noted, and more feared among the religious sort, whom suerlie it touched verie neere, and therefore to find remedie against it, they determined to assaie all waies to put by and ouerthrow this bill: wherein they thought best to trie if they might mooue the kings mood with some sharpe inuention, that he should not regard the importunate petitions of the commons.'

1 **I'll tell you** not a reply to a question but an emphatic way of making a statement, equivalent to 'I'll tell you what'. Cf. 4.7.51.
self selfsame, very same
urged moved (in Parliament)

1.1] F *(Actus Primus. Scœna Prima.); scene not in Q*   0.1] *Rowe; Enter the two Bishops of Canterbury and Ely F*   1+ SP] *Rowe; Bish. Cant. F*

Which in th'eleventh year of the last king's reign
Was like and had indeed against us passed
But that the scambling and unquiet time
Did push it out of farther question.   5

ELY

But how, my lord, shall we resist it now?

CANTERBURY

It must be thought on. If it pass against us
We lose the better half of our possession:
For all the temporal lands which men devout
By testament have given to the Church   10
Would they strip from us, being valued thus:
As much as would maintain, to the King's honour,
Full fifteen earls and fifteen hundred knights,
Six thousand and two hundred good esquires,
And to relief of lazars and weak age,   15
Of indigent faint souls past corporal toil,
A hundred almshouses right well supplied,
And to the coffers of the King beside,
A thousand pounds by th' year. Thus runs the bill.

ELY

This would drink deep.

CANTERBURY   'Twould drink the cup and all.   20

2 **th'eleventh ... reign** 1410
3 **like** likely (to have passed)
4 **scambling** contentious (*OED ppl. a.*
1). To scamble is to struggle indecor-
ously or rapaciously to obtain something (*OED v.* 1). Shakespeare has
scambling or *scamble* four times
(this passage; 5.2.202; *KJ* 4.3.147;
MA 5.1.95), never 'scrambling' or
'scramble'.
   unquiet time Cf. Hall's chapter-
heading, 'The unquiet time of King
Henry the Fourth'.
5 **question** consideration
8 **our possession** what we possess
14 **esquires** gentlemen of rank immedi-

ately below knights (*OED* 2)
15 **to relief** for the relief. On the omission of 'the', see Abbott, 89, and cf.
Holinshed's phrase quoted in 1–21n.
   lazars poor and diseased persons
(from the proper name Lazarus, Luke
16:20), particularly lepers (*OED*)
   weak age weak old people
19 **A thousand ... year** the sum that
Holinshed's 20,000 pounds would
bring in at 5 per cent interest.
20–1 Canterbury's vigorous retort to
Ely's remark is surely meant to complete the line, leaving the half-line
'But what prevention?' as a rephrasing
of Ely's earlier question, l. 6.

4 scambling] *F*; scrambling *Oxf¹*   6+ SP] *Rowe; Bish.* Ely. *F*   15 age,] *Theobald;* age *F*
20–1] *as Cam; F lines* ... deepe. / ... all. / ... preuention? /

ELY

But what prevention?

CANTERBURY

The King is full of grace and fair regard.

ELY

And a true lover of the holy Church.

CANTERBURY

The courses of his youth promised it not.
The breath no sooner left his father's body   25
But that his wildness, mortified in him,
Seemed to die too; yea, at that very moment,
Consideration like an angel came
And whipped th'offending Adam out of him,
Leaving his body as a paradise   30
T'envelop and contain celestial spirits.
Never was such a sudden scholar made,
Never came reformation in a flood
With such a heady currence scouring faults,
Nor never Hydra-headed wilfulness   35

---

22 **grace ... regard** virtue and good intentions (*OED* regard *sb.* 4c, citing this passage and *JC* 3.1.226). The usual sense of *full of grace* makes this a more probable sense than 'favour and kind interest in us' (Moore Smith).

24 **courses** habits, behaviour

25–7 **The breath ... too** Cf. *2H4* 5.2.122–3: 'My father is gone wild into his grave, / For in his tomb lie my affections.'

26 **mortified** subdued by self-discipline

28 **Consideration** meditation

28–30 **like ... paradise** Cf. Genesis 3:23–4.

29 **th'offending Adam** i.e. the wickedness. St Paul (Romans 6:6) calls the unregenerate condition 'the old Adam'.

33 **reformation** moral amendment. Cf. *1H4* 1.2.210: 'My reformation, glitt'ring o'er my fault'.

33–4 **in a flood ... faults** alluding to the cleansing (*scouring*) of the Augean stables by Hercules, who diverted a river through them. In Shakespeare a *flood* is either a river (e.g. 1.2.45) or a sea (e.g. 5.0.10), often, as here, implying fullness.

34 **heady currence** impetuous flowing (*OED* currence: first example 1641). F2's emendation 'currant' (i.e. current) may be correct: cf. *1H4* 2.3.55, 'And all the currents [Qq 1–3; current F] of a heady fight'.

35 **Nor never** The double negative, for emphasis, is common (Abbott, 406).
Hydra-headed many-headed, multiplying. Another of Hercules' labours was to kill the Hydra, a monster with nine serpentine heads; whenever he cut off one, two more grew in its place, until his companion Iolaus thrust a burning torch into each fresh stump to sear it. Cf. *1H4* 5.4.24,

---

34 currence] *F (currance); currant F2*

So soon did lose his seat, and all at once,
As in this king.
ELY   We are blessed in the change.
CANTERBURY
Hear him but reason in divinity
And, all-admiring, with an inward wish
You would desire the King were made a prelate.   40
Hear him debate of commonwealth affairs,
You would say it hath been all in all his study.
List his discourse of war, and you shall hear
A fearful battle rendered you in music.
Turn him to any cause of policy,   45
The Gordian knot of it he will unloose,
Familiar as his garter, that when he speaks,
The air, a chartered libertine, is still,
And the mute wonder lurketh in men's ears

'Another king! They grow like Hydra's heads.'
36 **seat** throne
all at once (1) immediately (2) completely
37 **blessed** blessèd
38 **reason in divinity** Holinshed (3.544) records that in the first year of his reign King Henry attempted to convert the Lollard (Wycliffite) Sir John Oldcastle from his heretical opinions, a passage which may have suggested to Shakespeare the idea of the King as a theologian, though there is no allusion to it in the present context.
42 **all in all** entirely
43 **List** hear attentively
44 **fearful** frightful
rendered you in music i.e. 'narrated with moving eloquence' (Walter)
45 **cause of policy** political question
46 **Gordian knot** complexity. A proverbial phrase alluding to the knot, so intricate that none could undo it, tied by Gordius of Phrygia. Alexander the Great cut it with his sword.

47 **Familiar** 'as though it were as ordinary a thing to untie' (Moore Smith)
48 **a chartered libertine** one licensed to go his own way freely (*OED* libertine *sb.* 2c: first example). Cf. John 3:8 ('The wynde bloweth where it listeth'), *AYL* 2.7.47–9 ('I must have liberty / Withal, as large a charter as the wind, / To blow on whom I please') and the proverbial phrase 'free as air'. As Taylor notes, *libertine* is elsewhere opprobrious in Shakespeare; hence the passage suggests that the King converts the breeze from its waywardness.
49 **mute wonder** wonder, mute with attention. This must be the sense if *wonder* is Shakespeare's word; but ll. 49–50 are so consequent to l. 48 that Staunton's conjecture 'wand'rer' (cf. *MND* 2.1.43, 2.2.247) is attractive – more so than Wilson's conjecture 'wonderer', not used by Shakespeare elsewhere. Yet it would not be beyond Shakespeare to superimpose the personification Wonder upon the 'wand'ring air' (*R3* 1.4.39).

49 wonder] F; wand'rer *(Staunton)*; wonderer *(Cam¹)*

To steal his sweet and honeyed sentences.   50
So that the art and practic part of life
Must be the mistress to this theoric:
Which is a wonder how his grace should glean it,
Since his addiction was to courses vain,
His companies unlettered, rude, and shallow,   55
His hours filled up with riots, banquets, sports,
And never noted in him any study,
Any retirement, any sequestration
From open haunts and popularity.

ELY

The strawberry grows underneath the nettle,   60
And wholesome berries thrive and ripen best
Neighboured by fruit of baser quality.

---

50 **sentences** maxims (Lat. *sententiae*)
51–2 i.e. And so we must suppose that practical experience of life has taught him all this knowledge of abstract principles. (*OED* mistress *sb.* 7: authoress, creator or patroness of an art.) *Art* and *practic part* are used synonymously; *practic* and *theoric* are usually contrasted terms, as here, in Shakespeare's time.
53 **Which** i.e. 'how his grace should glean it': Abbott, 271, 'which' for 'which thing'
his grace his majesty. The terms are synonymous (cf. ll. 71, 75, 78, 83, 85), though in *1H4* 1.2.17–18 Falstaff uses word-play to distinguish them.
glean it learn it, pick it up. The word, now a dead metaphor, means to gather scattered grain by hand after corn has been reaped.
54 **addiction** inclination (without pejorative sense: *OED* 3, citing *Oth* 2.2.6)
courses vain foolish behaviour
55 'The kinds of society in which he mixed were illiterate, uncultured and empty-headed.'
56 **riots** revellings
57 **noted** was noted
58–9 **sequestration ... popularity** 'keeping aloof from places of common resort and from mixing with the

people' (Humphreys). Cf. *1H4* 3.2.68–9 (Henry IV speaking of Richard II): 'Grew a companion to the common streets, / Enfeoffed himself to popularity'.
60 **The strawberry ... nettle** The moralizing of the strawberry's habit of growth, creeping on the ground but untainted, was traditional: cf. Oxf[1]'s quotation from St Francis de Sales. The nettle is typically noxious in Shakespeare: cf. *R2* 3.2.18, *1H4* 1.3.238 and 2.4[3].9. In *R3* 3.4.31–4 the King gets the Bishop of Ely to send for some of the strawberries in his garden at Ely Place, Holborn, a fact which may relate to Ely's mention of the strawberry here, and even to Shakespeare's choice of Ely as the name of Canterbury's confidant, though Ely did take part in the peace negotiations (Holinshed, 3.572). Gurr, 67 and 1.1.8n., citing Cox (106–8), improbably states that Ely was chosen because 'the Elizabethan Bishop of Ely, Richard Cox, had fought to retain his episcopal property from 1558 until 1581, so strongly that after his death Elizabeth kept the see of Ely vacant for eighteen years, up to February 1599'.

And so the Prince obscured his contemplation
Under the veil of wildness, which, no doubt,
Grew like the summer grass, fastest by night,   65
Unseen, yet crescive in his faculty.

CANTERBURY
It must be so, for miracles are ceased,
And therefore we must needs admit the means
How things are perfected.

ELY   But my good lord,
How now for mitigation of this bill   70
Urged by the Commons? Doth his majesty
Incline to it, or no?

CANTERBURY   He seems indifferent,
Or rather swaying more upon our part
Than cherishing th'exhibitors against us.
For I have made an offer to his majesty,   75
Upon our spiritual convocation,
And in regard of causes now in hand
Which I have opened to his grace at large,
As touching France, to give a greater sum
Than ever at one time the clergy yet   80
Did to his predecessors part withal.

64 **which** i.e. his contemplation, l. 63
65–6 The simile derives from Horace, *Odes*, 1.12.45–6, 'crescit occulto velut arbor aevo / fama Marcelli' (the fame of Marcellus, like a tree, grows in the hidden time), the reference to grass deriving from Erasmus's paraphrase of Horace, which includes the phrase 'herba crescens' (growing grass): Baldwin, 2.501–3, cited in Oxf[1].
66 **crescive ... faculty** making growth, as it is in its nature to do; Shakespeare's only use of *crescive* (*OED* first example 1565), from Lat. *crescere*, to grow
67 **miracles are ceased** proverbial; cf. *AW* 2.3.1, 'They say miracles are past'
68 **means** natural causes

69 **perfected** with stress on the first syllable, *Tem* 1.2.79, *TGV* 1.3.23
69–71 **But ... Commons?** See 1–21n., second paragraph.
72 **indifferent** impartial
73 **swaying** inclining
74 **exhibitors** presenters of the bill
75–81 These lines, the substance of which is repeated at 1.2.132–5, correspond closely to the conclusion of Canterbury's oration in Parliament (Holinshed, 3.546: see 1.2.132–5n.).
76 **Upon** on the occasion of. Cf. 'in their spirituall conuocation' (Holinshed, 3.546).
77 **causes** matters of importance
78 **opened ... large** disclosed to the King in general terms. Cf. ll. 84–9.

66 crescive] *(cressiue)*

127

ELY

How did this offer seem received, my lord?

CANTERBURY

With good acceptance of his majesty,
Save that there was not time enough to hear,
As I perceived his grace would fain have done,   85
The severals and unhidden passages
Of his true titles to some certain dukedoms,
And generally to the crown and seat of France,
Derived from Edward, his great-grandfather.

ELY

What was th'impediment that broke this off?   90

CANTERBURY

The French ambassador upon that instant
Craved audience, and the hour I think is come
To give him hearing. Is it four o'clock?

ELY

It is.

CANTERBURY

Then go we in, to know his embassy,   95
Which I could with a ready guess declare

83 **of** by
84 **Save that** but for the fact that
85 **fain** gladly
86–9 Cf. Holinshed, 3.545 (immediately following the passage quoted in 1–21n.): 'Whereupon, on a daie in the parlement, Henrie Chichelie archbishop of Canturburie made a pithie oration, wherein he declared, how not onelie the duchies of Normandie and Aquitaine, with the counties of Aniou and Maine, and the countrie of Gascoigne, were by vndoubted title apperteining to the king, as to the lawfull and onelie heire of the same; but also the whole realme of France, as heire to his great grandfather king Edward the third.'
86–7 **The severals ... passages / Of** the particulars (*OED sb.* 3a) and the indisputable courses of argument (*OED* passage 2) relating to. In 1.2 the King desires to be satisfied as to the legitimacy of his claim, not as to his line of descent.
87 **some certain** The same redundancy is in *1H4* 4.3.81, 'Some certain edicts'.
88 The metre requires some elision, reducing *generally* to 'gen'rally' and *to the* to 'to th' '.
generally without exceptions
seat throne
89 **great-grandfather** grandfather's father. Holinshed (cf. 86–9n.) spells as two words, as does F, but in neither case is the meaning in doubt: cf. 1.2.103, 105, 146.
95 **embassy** message committed to him as ambassador (*OED* 2)

89 great-grandfather] *(great Grandfather)*

Before the Frenchman speak a word of it.

ELY

I'll wait upon you, and I long to hear it. *Exeunt.*

[1.2] *Enter the* KING, GLOUCESTER, BEDFORD, CLARENCE, WARWICK, WESTMORLAND *and* EXETER [*and Attendants*].

KING

Where is my gracious lord of Canterbury?

EXETER

Not here in presence.

KING   Send for him, good uncle.

[*Exit an Attendant.*]

WESTMORLAND

Shall we call in th'ambassador, my liege?

KING

Not yet, my cousin: we would be resolved,
Before we hear him, of some things of weight   5
That task our thoughts concerning us and France.

Enter the Archbishop of CANTERBURY *and the* Bishop of ELY.

97 **speak** shall speak (subjunctive: Abbott, 368)

1.2.0.1 GLOUCESTER F's '*Humfrey*' is elsewhere in the play always named and addressed as Gloucester. In *2H4* the King once addresses him as 'Humphrey, my son of Gloucester' (4.3[4].12), and he is frequently called Duke Humphrey as well as Gloucester in the *H6* plays.

0.2 *Attendants* needed at ll. 2, 222 and 298. Exeter should speak to one at l. 2; though Canterbury arrives immediately afterwards, his entry is presented as the consequence of the King's order.

1 **Where ... Canterbury?** King Henry has seated himself in his throne: cf. ll. 7, 35, 270, and Holinshed, 3.547, where he receives the French ambassadors 'sitting in his throne imperiall'.

2 **in presence** present. (Cf. 2.4.111 and *R2* 4.1.58, 'You were in presence then', i.e. at a private conversation.)

4 **my cousin** Westmorland had married, as his second wife, the only daughter of John of Gaunt (the King's grandfather) by his third wife Katharine Swynford. He was therefore Exeter's brother-in-law.

we The King consistently uses the plural pronoun, as suits the formality of the occasion, until l. 96 ('May I with right and conscience make this claim?'), and again thereafter except in ll. 274–80 and 291–4.

would be resolved wish to be satisfied

6 **task** seriously employ. Cf. 1. 310.

SD Canterbury and Ely bow to the

1.2] *Pope*   0.1–2] *F (subst.); Enter King* Henry, Exeter, 2. Bishops, Clarence, *and other Attendants. Q*   0.2 *and Attendants*] *Q (subst.)*   1–2] *F; not in Q*   2 SD] *Capell*   6 SD] *Rowe; Enter two Bishops. F*

CANTERBURY
> God and his angels guard your sacred throne
> And make you long become it!

KING   Sure, we thank you.
> My learned lord, we pray you to proceed
> And justly and religiously unfold   10
> Why the law Salic that they have in France
> Or should or should not bar us in our claim.
> And God forbid, my dear and faithful lord,
> That you should fashion, wrest or bow your reading
> Or nicely charge your understanding soul   15
> With opening titles miscreate, whose right
> Suits not in native colours with the truth.

King on entering his presence (Cam[1]).

10 **justly and religiously** with scrupulous exactness

11 **the law Salic** See ll. 39, 54, 91. The first syllable is pronounced like that of 'sailor'.

12 **our claim** King Henry's claim to the French throne was through his descent from Edward III, whose mother was Isabella, daughter of Philip IV of France (see Appendix 4). Edward III's claim is expounded in *E3*, 1.1.5–29, where it is stated that Philip IV's three sons succeeded him in turn, none of them leaving (male) issue, and that the French then proclaimed John, Count of Valois, as king, giving as their reason the necessity of having the crown descend through the male line, though their real motive was to exclude Edward III. (Actually it was John's father, Philip of Valois, who succeeded Philip IV's sons as Philip VI.) *E3* does not apply the term 'Salic law' to this exclusion of the female line. Wilson points out that neither Holinshed nor Shakespeare mentions Isabella, 'the peg upon which Henry's whole case hangs', though *Famous Victories* and Hall do. Indeed, *Famous Victories* mentions nothing else, the Salic law

included: 'Your right to the French Crowne of *France*, / Came by your great grandmother *Izabel*, / Wife to King *Edward* the third, / And sister to *Charles* the French king: / Now if the French king deny it, as likely inough he wil, / Then must you take your sword in hand, / And conquer the right' (scene ix: ll. 759–65; note the error of making Isabella Edward III's wife instead of his mother).

13 **faithful** religious. Cf. *R3* 1.4.4, 'a Christian faithful man'.

14 **fashion ... reading** misshape (*OED* fashion *v.* 4b), strain the sense of (*OED* wrest *v.* 5) or bend your interpretation

15 **nicely** by using sophistry
charge load (with guilt)
understanding conscious (of truth and falsehood)

16 **With ... miscreate** by putting forward falsely invented claims (of mine). *Miscreate*, first recorded in Spenser, *Faerie Queene*, 2.10.38, is a poetical coinage; cf. 4.5.16n. for other latinate participial adjectives.
whose right i.e. the right that they supposedly give the claimant

17 **Suits not** fails to match
native natural, true

15–17] *F; not in Q*

For God doth know how many now in health
Shall drop their blood in approbation
Of what your reverence shall incite us to.   20
Therefore take heed how you impawn our person,
How you awake our sleeping sword of war:
We charge you in the name of God take heed.
For never two such kingdoms did contend
Without much fall of blood, whose guiltless drops   25
Are every one a woe, a sore complaint
'Gainst him whose wrongs gives edge unto the
    swords
That makes such waste in brief mortality.
Under this conjuration speak, my lord,
For we will hear, note, and believe in heart   30
That what you speak is in your conscience washed
As pure as sin with baptism.

CANTERBURY
    Then hear me, gracious sovereign, and you peers

---

19 **approbation** putting to the test, i.e. by war. *Approbation* is pronounced as five syllables.

20 **your reverence** you (an honorific title)
    incite us to encourage me to do (i.e. to pursue my claim)

21 **impawn our person** pledge my life, put it at risk. *Impawn* (Shakespeare's coinage) is 'a metrical synonym for "pawn"' (Taylor). Cf. *embare*, l. 94.

22 **our** Q's 'the' may suggest that F's reading was wrongly caught from l. 21 ('our person'), but *our* is supported by 'your bloody flag', l. 101.

27 **wrongs** wrongdoings
    gives Third person plural in -s is frequent (Abbott, 333), as is relative pronoun followed by a singular verb though having a plural antecedent, e.g. *makes*, l. 28 (Abbott, 247).

28 **brief mortality** 'human life, which is short at the best' (Moore Smith)

29 **conjuration** solemn appeal

32 **sin** original sin, inherited at birth through Adam's disobedience
    with by

33–95 Cf. Holinshed, 3.545–6 (immediately following the passage quoted at 1.1.86–9n.): 'Herein did he much inueie against the surmised and false fained law Salike, which the Frenchmen alledge euer against the kings of England in barre of their iust title to the crowne of France. The verie words of that supposed law are these, *In terram Salicam mulieres ne succedant*, that is to saie, Into the Salike land let not women succeed. Which the French glossers expound to be the realme of France, and that this law was made by king Pharamond; whereas yet their owne authors affirme, that the land Salike is in Germanie, betweene the riuers of Elbe and Sala; and that when Charles

---

22 our] *F*; the *Q*   24–8] *F*; not in *Q*   27 wrongs gives] *F*; wrong giues *F2*; wrongs give *Malone*   27–8 swords / That makes] *F*; swords / That make *Rowe*; sword / That makes *Capell*

That owe your selves, your lives and services
To this imperial throne. There is no bar   35
To make against your highness' claim to France
But this which they produce from Pharamond:
In terram Salicam mulieres ne succedant,
'No woman shall succeed in Salic land':
Which Salic land the French unjustly gloze   40
To be the realm of France, and Pharamond
The founder of this law and female bar.
Yet their own authors faithfully affirm
That the land Salic is in Germany,

the great had ouercome the Saxons, he placed there certeine Frenchmen, which hauing in disdeine the dishonest maners of the Germane women, made a law, that the females should not succeed to any inheritance within that land, which at this daie is called Meisen, so that if this be true, this law was not made for the realme of France, nor the Frenchmen possessed the land Salike, till foure hundred and one and twentie yeares after the death of Pharamond, the supposed maker of this Salike law, for this Pharamond deceassed in the year 426, and Charles the great subdued the Saxons, and placed the Frenchmen in those parts beyond the riuer of Sala, in the yeare 805.

'Moreouer, it appeareth by their owne writers, that king Pepine, which deposed Childerike, claimed the crowne of France, as heire generall, for that he was descended of Blithild daughter to king Clothair the first: Hugh Capet also, who vsurped the crowne vpon Charles duke of Loraine, the sole heire male of the line and stocke of Charles the great, to make his title seeme true, and appeare good, though in deed it was starke naught, conueied himselfe as heire to the ladie Lingard, daughter to · king Charlemaine, sonne to Lewes the emperour, that was son to Charles the great.

King Lewes also the tenth otherwise called saint Lewes, being verie heire to the said vsurper Hugh Capet, could neuer be satisfied in his conscience how he might iustlie keepe and possesse the crowne of France, till he was persuaded and fullie instructed, that queene Isabell his grandmother was lineallie descended of the ladie Ermengard daughter and heire to the aboue named Charles duke of Loraine, by the which marriage, the bloud and line of Charles the great was againe vnited and restored to the crowne & scepter of France, so that more cleere than the sunne it openlie appeareth, that the title of king Pepin, the claime of Hugh Capet, the possession of Lewes, yea and the French kings to this daie, are deriued and conueied from the heire female, though they would vnder the colour of such a fained law, barre the kings and princes of this realme of England of their right and lawfull inheritance.'

35 **imperial** majestic (*OED* 5). Cf. Holinshed at 1n.
36 **To make** to be (i.e. that can be) made
37 **Pharamond** the legendary ancestor of the Frankish kings
40 **gloze** interpret, explain as by a gloss or comment
42 **female bar** bar against inheritance through the female line

38] *F; not in Q*   succedant] *F2; succedaul F*   40 gloze] *F, Q; gloss Oxf¹*

Between the floods of Sala and of Elbe, 45
Where Charles the Great, having subdued the
　　Saxons,
There left behind and settled certain French,
Who, holding in disdain the German women
For some dishonest manners of their life,
Established then this law, to wit, no female 50
Should be inheritrix in Salic land;
Which Salic (as I said, 'twixt Elbe and Sala)
Is at this day in Germany called Meissen.
Then doth it well appear the Salic law
Was not devised for the realm of France. 55
Nor did the French possess the Salic land
Until four hundred one-and-twenty years
After defunction of King Pharamond,

45 **floods** rivers
45, 52, 63 **Sala** The spelling is now Saale, but the pronunciation of Sala and Salic must preserve the relationship between the words.
45, 52 **Elbe** So in Holinshed (also the modern spelling); F's 'Elue' (i.e. Elve) follows Hall's spelling.
46 **Charles the Great** Charlemagne; see 65n.
47 **There** The redundancy after *Where* (l. 46) results from Shakespeare's now following Holinshed's expression after deviating from it just before.
　　settled synonymous with *did seat* (l. 62) and with Holinshed's repeated 'placed'
　　certain French Holinshed, 3.545, has the line-division at 'certeine French- / men', which may have influenced Shakespeare's diction.
49 **dishonest manners** unchaste conduct. Holinshed's first edition (1577) has 'vnhonest', after Hall.
50 **then** Oxf[1] prefers Q's 'there' because of its insistence 'that the law was established *in* and *for* the Salic land'; but F's *then* relates more closely to the

moral objection to the contemporary German women, and avoids further duplication after *Where* and *There* in ll. 46–7.
　　to wit namely
52 The repunctuation is necessary: Canterbury has already said where the Salic land is but not what is its present German name.
53 F's punctuation gives an ambiguous phrase (1) is at this day located in Germany and is called Meissen (2) is at this day called Meissen in the German language. Holinshed makes the intended sense clear.
55 **devised** devisèd
57 **four ... twenty** Hall's error, followed by Holinshed: comparing 805 and 426, Hall must have isolated 800 and 400, noticed a difference of 21 in the remaining figures, and added it to 400 instead of subtracting it. The error may be corrected by substituting 'Until three hundred nine and seventy years', but it will pass in the theatre.
58 **defunction** the decease. Cf. 'defunct and dead', 4.1.21.

45, 52 Elbe] *Capell;* Elue *F* 46 Great] *F;* fift *Q* 50 then] *F;* there *Q* 52] *this edn;* Which *Salike* (as I said) 'twixt Elue and Sala, *F* 53 Germany called] *Q;* Germanie, call'd *F* Meissen] *(Meisen)*

Idly supposed the founder of this law,
Who died within the year of our redemption   60
Four hundred twenty-six, and Charles the Great
Subdued the Saxons and did seat the French
Beyond the river Sala in the year
Eight hundred five. Besides, their writers say,
King Pepin, which deposed Childeric,   65
Did as heir general, being descended
Of Blithild, which was daughter to King Clothair,
Make claim and title to the crown of France.
Hugh Capet also, who usurped the crown
Of Charles the Duke of Lorraine, sole heir male   70
Of the true line and stock of Charles the Great,
To fine his title with some shows of truth,
Though in pure truth it was corrupt and naught,
Conveyed himself as heir to th' Lady Lingard,

59 **Idly** baselessly
60–1 **within ... twenty-six** in the year
426 AD (*Anno Domini*: in the year of
Our Lord, the Redeemer)
65 **Pepin** The reigns of the French kings
mentioned were as follows: Clothair I
(511–61); Childeric III (742–52);
Pepin (752–68); Charles the Great,
or Charlemagne (768–814); Louis I
(814–40); Charles II, or Charles the
Bald (843–77); Hugh Capet (987–96);
Louis IX (1226–70).
deposèd deposed
66 **heir general** heir at law: heir by
descent, whether through the male or
the female line
70, 83 **Lorraine** Shakespeare evidently
intended to stress the first syllable (cf.
E3, 1.1.52, 55), for at l. 70 he could
have followed Holinshed's phrasing
'Charles duke of Loraine, the sole
heire male' if he had intended to
stress the second.
72 *****fine** make beautiful (*OED v.³* 3). Cf.
1H4 5.1.74–5, 'To face the garment
of rebellion / With some fine colour',

with a similar opprobrious sense. F's
'find' has been interpreted as 'supply,
provide, furnish' (*OED v.* 18), but
'find with' is not a construction
recorded in *OED*, so 'find' is probably
the result of a *d/e* misreading.
shows illusory appearances (*OED sb.¹*
6)
74 **Conveyed ... heir** represented
himself as heir; Holinshed's
expression, probably without word-
play on 'convey' (= steal) as in *MW*
1.3.26
*****heir** Holinshed (following Hall) and
Q agree in this reading; F's reading
is probably caught from 'th' Lady'.
*****Lingard** Holinshed's spelling of
Luitgard. Shakespeare presumably
followed Holinshed, and a *d/e* misreading error resulted in F's '*Lingare*'.
Wilson concludes from Q's '*Inger*'
'that "Lingare" was spoken on the
stage'; but a final *d* may have dropped
out if dictation was involved in producing Q (see Introduction, p. 97).

60–8] F; *not in Q*   70–1] F; *not in Q*   72 fine] *Q; find F*   shows] *F (shewes); showe Q*   74
heir] *Q; th'Heire F*   Lingard] *Sisson (Cam¹); Lingare F; Inger Q*

Daughter to Charlemagne, who was the son   75
To Louis the Emperor, and Louis the son
Of Charles the Great. Also King Louis the Ninth,
Who was sole heir to the usurper Capet,
Could not keep quiet in his conscience,
Wearing the crown of France, till satisfied   80
That fair Queen Isabel, his grandmother,
Was lineal of the Lady Ermengard,
Daughter to Charles the foresaid Duke of Lorraine,
By the which marriage the line of Charles the Great
Was reunited to the crown of France.   85
So that, as clear as is the summer's sun,
King Pepin's title, and Hugh Capet's claim,
King Louis his satisfaction, all appear
To hold in right and title of the female.
So do the kings of France unto this day,   90
Howbeit they would hold up this Salic law
To bar your highness claiming from the female,
And rather choose to hide them in a net

75 **Charlemagne** Holinshed's error, following Hall, for Charles II. In the theatre the sobriquet 'Charles the Bald' might be substituted here, to rectify the confusion with 'Charles the Great' earlier. *Charlemagne* is pronounced as three syllables.

76, 77, 88 **Louis** monosyllabic in Shakespeare (*KJ*, *H5*, *3H6*: with one exception, *3H6* 3.3.169), and invariably spelled Lewes, as in Hall and Holinshed

77 *****Ninth** Holinshed wrongly has 'tenth' (and is followed by Shakespeare) where Hall correctly has 'ninth'.

79 **conscience** pronounced as three syllables

82 **lineal** directly descended
*****Ermengard** Holinshed's spelling. Cf. l. 74, Lingard, for F's *d/e* misreading error.

86 **as clear ... sun** 'As clear as the sun' (Tilley, S 969) is proverbial. Holinshed has 'so that more cleere than the sunne it openlie appeareth'. It is common for actors, fearing an uninvited laugh, to invite one by pausing – wrongly, since there is nothing obscure in Canterbury's evidence or in his presentation of it.

88 **satisfaction** Cf. *satisfied*, l. 80.
appear / To manifestly

89 **in right and title** by titular right (the figure of speech called hendiadys: cf. l. 164)

91 **Howbeit** though (which is Holinshed's word). See textual note for F's mispunctuation.
would wish to

92 **To bar ... female** to bar you from the throne, claiming it as you do through the female line

93 **hide them in a net** 'You dance in a

75 82] *F*; *not in Q*   75 Charlemagne] *(Charlemaine)*   76↑ Louis] *(Lewes)*   77 Ninth] *Pope*;
Tenth *F*   82 Ermengard] *Sisson (Cam¹)*; Ermengare *F*   84–5] *F*; *not in Q*   88 Louis] *F (Lewes)*;
Charles *Q*   90 1 day, / Howbeit they] *Q*; day. / Howbeit, they *F*

Than amply to embare their crooked titles
Usurped from you and your progenitors.   95

KING

May I with right and conscience make this claim?

CANTERBURY

The sin upon my head, dread sovereign:
For in the Book of Numbers is it writ,
'When the man dies, let the inheritance
Descend unto the daughter.' Gracious lord,   100
Stand for your own, unwind your bloody flag,
Look back into your mighty ancestors.
Go, my dread lord, to your great-grandsire's tomb,

net and think nobody sees you' (Tilley, N 130) is proverbial; sometimes 'dance naked', to add point to the desire of concealment (*OED* net *sb.*[1] 2b).

94 *embare make bare (Shakespeare's coinage: a metrical synonym for 'bare'; cf. 'impawn', l. 21). *OED* (Em-, *prefix*) explains that nearly all such English words exist in both em- and im- forms, and records 'Embared Breasts' in Alexander Niccholes, *A discourse of marriage and wiving*, 1615. The verb denoting self-exposure follows naturally from *net* (cf. l. 93n.), whereas F's 'imbarre', whether meaning 'bar in' (*OED v.* 1) or 'bar out' (*OED v.* 2), has no connection with it, is less appropriate to the adverb *amply* (openly), can be explained as a misreading of 'imbare', as can Q's meaningless 'imbace', and may have been influenced by 'barre' in l. 92.

98–101 Cf. Holinshed, 3.546 (immediately following the passage quoted in 33–95n.): 'The archbishop further alledged out of the booke of Numbers this saieng: When a man dieth without a sonne, let the inheritance descend to his daughter. At length, hauing said sufficientlie for the proofe

of the kings iust and lawfull title to the crowne of France, he exhorted him to aduance foorth his banner to fight for his right, to conquer his inheritance, to spare neither bloud, sword, nor fire, sith his warre was iust, his cause good, and his claime true.'

99–100 **When ... daughter** Numbers 27:8: 'If a man dye and haue no sonne, ye shall turne his inheritaunce vnto his daughter.' Holinshed paraphrases the text, and Shakespeare condenses the paraphrase to fit the metre, knowing that his audience will not misunderstand the passage as meaning that daughters are to inherit before sons. Q substitutes 'sonne' for 'man'.

101 **bloody** portending bloodshed (*OED a.* 5)

102 **into** unto. Cf. *AW* 1.3.253, *TN* 5.1.80, *Tem* 1.2.100.
     your mighty ancestors Perhaps echoing Hall (52): 'diminishe not your title, which your noble progenitors so highly haue estemed.' But, as the amplification in ll. 103–21 is Shakespeare's, this phrase may also be his own.

103 **great-grandsire** Edward III. For the details of the claim, see l. 12n.

94 embare] *Theobald (Warburton)* (*imbare*); imbarre *F*; imbace *Q1*; embrace *Q3*; unbare *Capell (Theobald)*; unbar *Ridley*   98 is it] *F, Q*; it is *Q3, F3*   99 man] *F*; sonne *Q*   102 into] *F*; unto *Capell*   103 great-grandsire's] (*great Grandsires*)

From whom you claim; invoke his warlike spirit,
And your great-uncle's, Edward the Black Prince,   105
Who on the French ground played a tragedy,
Making defeat on the full power of France,
Whiles his most mighty father on a hill
Stood smiling to behold his lion's whelp
Forage in blood of French nobility.   110
O noble English, that could entertain
With half their forces the full pride of France
And let another half stand laughing by,
All out of work and cold for action!

ELY

Awake remembrance of these valiant dead,   115
And with your puissant arm renew their feats.
You are their heir, you sit upon their throne,
The blood and courage that renowned them
Runs in your veins, and my thrice-puissant liege
Is in the very May-morn of his youth,   120
Ripe for exploits and mighty enterprises.

106 **played a tragedy** i.e. the battle of Cressy (Crécy), 1346. Though this was in the usual sense tragic from the French point of view, the theatrical metaphor represents the Black Prince as acting a hero's part. Cf. Marlowe, *1 Tamburlaine*, Prologue 7, 'View but his picture in this tragic glass' (when the play is to end with his triumph).

107 **Making defeat on** defeating (*on* = of)

108 **on a hill** He 'stood aloft on a windmill hill' (Holinshed, 3.372), refusing to intervene when the English were hard pressed because he wished his son to have the honour of the victory.

110 **Forage** glut himself; also applied to preying lions in *LLL* 4.1.90 (as noun) and *KJ* 5.1.59
in blood For the omission of 'the', cf. 1.1.15n.

111 **entertain** engage (*OED v.* 9c)

112 **half** 'actually two-thirds' (Wilson), as Holinshed, following Froissart, makes clear.
full pride full power; cf. l. 107

114 **cold for action** i.e. cold for want of activity; cf. *Mac* 1.5.33, 'almost dead for breath'

115 **these valiant dead** Edward III and the Black Prince; cf. l. 117

118 **renowned** renownèd

119 **thrice-puissant** most powerful. Cf. *1H4* 3.2.92, 'my thrice-gracious lord', and many similar expressions, including 'thrice-worthy', 4.4.60. Gurr suggests that Canterbury is referring specifically to 'the three points made in lines 117–19'.

120 **May-morn** bloom (proverbial: Dent, M 768.1). King Henry, born in August 1387, was not yet twenty-seven years old.

105 great-uncle's] *(*Great Vnckles*)* 115-35] *F; not in Q* 115 SP] *F3 (subst.); Bish. F* these] *F; those Oxf¹*

EXETER

    Your brother kings and monarchs of the earth
    Do all expect that you should rouse yourself
    As did the former lions of your blood.

WESTMORLAND

    They know your grace hath cause, and means,
        and might;   125
    So doth your highness. Never king of England
    Had nobles richer and more loyal subjects,
    Whose hearts have left their bodies here in England
    And lie pavilioned in the fields of France.

CANTERBURY

    O let their bodies follow, my dear liege,   130
    With blood and sword and fire to win your right;
    In aid whereof we of the spiritualty

123–4 **rouse ... blood** Cf. Marlowe, *1 Tamburlaine*, 1.2.52–4, 'As princely lions when they rouse themselves, / Stretching their paws, and threat'ning herds of beasts, / So in his armour looketh Tamburlaine.' The 'former lions' are Edward III and his son, the 'lion's whelp' of l. 109: alluding both to the lion as king of beasts and to the lions on the English royal coat of arms.

125–6 *****They ... highness** The most natural way to speak F's version of this passage is to pronounce 'your highness' as if it referred to a different person from 'your grace'. Since it does not, Capell argued that F's 'hath' (l. 126) should be stressed; but this underlines the redundancy and spoils the line's rhythm. Johnson's heightening of Theobald's repunctuation breaks up 'cause ... might', which is surely a unit (cf. *Ham* additional passage J.35 [4.4.45–6], 'Sith I have cause, and will, and strength, and means, / To do't'), and deprives *So* of its function. This edn's emendation assumes a compositor's substitution

of 'hath' for 'doth' (having just set 'hath' in l. 125), and gives the sense as 'They know, and you know too, that your cause is just,' etc.

125 **cause ... might** a just cause, wealth enough ('nobles richer', l. 127) and military strength enough ('more loyal subjects ... France', ll. 127–9)

129 **pavilioned** in military tents

131 **With ... fire** Cf. Holinshed, quoted in 98–101n.

132 **spiritualty** clergy. Shakespeare's and Holinshed's form of the word is more appropriate to the metre than the modern 'spirituality'.

132–5 **In aid ... ancestors** Cf. Holinshed, 3.546 (immediately following the passage quoted in 98–101n.): 'And to the intent his louing chapleins and obedient subiects of the spiritualtie might shew themselues willing and desirous to aid his maiestie, for the recouerie of his ancient right and true inheritance, the archbishop declared that in their spirituall conuocation, they had granted to his highnesse such a summe of monie, as neuer by no spirituall persons was to any prince

125 cause ... might;] *F;* cause, and means, and might, *Theobald;* cause; and means and might *Johnson*   126 doth] *this edn;* hath *F*   131 blood] *F3;* Bloods *F*

Will raise your highness such a mighty sum
As never did the clergy at one time
Bring in to any of your ancestors.   135

KING
We must not only arm t'invade the French,
But lay down our proportions to defend
Against the Scot, who will make road upon us
With all advantages.

before those daies giuen or aduanced.'
This is the offer which in 1.1.75–81
Canterbury says he has already made
to the King. The repetition is more
likely to be inadvertent than deliberate on Shakespeare's part.

136–77 Cf. Holinshed, 3.546 (immediately following the passages quoted in
132–5 n.): 'When the archbishop had
ended his prepared tale, Rafe Neuill
earle of Westmerland, and as then
lord Warden of the marches against
Scotland, vnderstanding that the king
vpon a couragious desire to recouer
his right in France, would suerlie take
the wars in hand, thought good to
mooue the king to begin first with
Scotland, and therevpon declared
how easie a matter it should be to
make a conquest there, and how greatlie the same should further his wished
purpose for the subduing of the Frenchmen, concluding the summe of his
tale with this old saieng: that *Who so
will France win, must with Scotland
first begin*. Manie matters he touched,
as well to shew how necessarie the
conquest of Scotland should be, as
also to prooue how iust a cause the
king had to attempt it, trusting to
persuade the king and all other to be
of his opinion.

'But after he had made an end, the
duke of Excester, vncle to the king, a
man well learned and wise, (who had
beene sent into Italie by his father,
intending that he should haue been
a preest) replied against the erle of
Westmerlands   oration,   affirming

rather that he which would Scotland
win, he with France must first begin.
For if the king might once compasse
the conquest of France, Scotland
could not long resist; so that conquere
France, and Scotland would soone
obeie. For where should the Scots
lerne policie and skill to defend themselues, if they had not their bringing
vp and training in France? If the
French pensions mainteined not the
Scotish nobilitie, in what case should
they be? Then take awaie France, and
the Scots will soone be tamed; France
being to Scotland the same that the
sap is to the tree, which being taken
awaie, the tree must needs die and
wither.'

136 SP In Hall and Holinshed it is
Westmorland who urges the subduing
of Scotland. Shakespeare makes the
King take an active part in the con-
sultation.

137 **lay ... proportions** estimate the
armed forces that we require
defend make defence (*OED v.* 4b)

138 **the Scot** i.e. the Scots (cf. ll. 144,
148, 170), not the King of Scots (l.
161)
make road invade. Cf. *Cor* 3.1.5–6,
'Ready when time shall prompt them
to make raid [roade F] / Upon's
again.' *Road* (*OED sb.* 2), current in
English between 1500 and 1650, has
the same etymology as Scottish 'raid'
which has now supplanted it.

139 **With all advantages** whenever
they have a favourable opportunity
(*OED* advantage *sb.* 4)

138 road] *F (roade), Q (rode); raid Oxf¹*

139

CANTERBURY

They of those marches, gracious sovereign, 140
Shall be a wall sufficient to defend
Our inland from the pilfering borderers.

KING

We do not mean the coursing snatchers only,
But fear the main intendment of the Scot,
Who hath been still a giddy neighbour to us. 145
For you shall read that my great-grandfather
Never went with his forces into France
But that the Scot on his unfurnished kingdom
Came pouring like the tide into a breach,

140–2 **They ... borderers** In Hall (56) Exeter urges the King to 'leue my lorde of Westmerlande and other graue capitaines of the Northe with a conuenient nombre to Defend the Marches if the subtill Scottes encouraged by the Frenchmen will any thyng attempt duryng your voyage and absence.' The Wardens of the Marches, i.e. the parts of England bordering upon Scotland (as here) and Wales, 'kept a military retinue and a quasi-regal authority there until the seventeenth century' (Gurr).

142 **Our inland** the interior part of our land, as opposed to its border regions (*OED sb.* 2); here particularly the prosperous rural areas lying south of the Scottish border. Q's 'your *England*' must be an auditory error which has in its turn affected the possessive pronoun.

143 **coursing snatchers** fast-riding robbers (*OED course v.* 5; snatcher 1). Oxf[1] and Cam[2] suggest an allusion to the coursing of hares with greyhounds, but this distracts from the sense by implying a chase and a fleeing quarry.

144 **main intendment** chief purpose, i.e. armed invasion

145 **still** constantly
   giddy 'light-headed, dizzy, dizzying, inconstant (without an exact parallel, though clearly within the range of accumulated senses)' (Taylor). Here probably somewhat jocular: cf. 'ill neighbourhood', l. 154.

146–54 These lines amplify an argument of Westmorland's in Hall (not in Holinshed): 'None of your progenitors euer passed the sea in iust quarell against the Frenche nacion, but the Scottishe people in their absence entered your realme spoyled your houses slewe your people and toke great praies innumerable, only to prouoke your auncestors for to returne from the inuadyng of Fraunce' (Hall, 54).

146–7, **that ... France** Q's 'Vnmaskt his power' has been admired (cf. Oxf[1]'s note), but Q's following word is 'for', which suggests that 'Vnmaskt' may be no more than an error for 'Embarkt' (cf. 3.0.5, 'Embark his royalty'). There is no warrant for conflating Q's and F's readings.

148 **unfurnished** unprovided with defence

149 **breach** i.e. in a sea-wall

142 Our inland] F *(Our in-land);* your *England Q;* Our England *Cam[2]* 145] F; *not in Q* 146–7 that ... France] F *(... great Grandfather ...); neuer my great grandfather / Vnmaskt his power for France Q;* that my great-grandfather / Never unmasked his power unto France *Oxf[1]*

With ample and brim fullness of his force,   150
Galling the gleaned land with hot assays,
Girding with grievous siege castles and towns,
That England, being empty of defence,
Hath shook and trembled at th'ill neighbourhood.

CANTERBURY

She hath been then more feared than harmed, my
    liege.   155
For hear her but exampled by herself:
When all her chivalry hath been in France
And she a mourning widow of her nobles,
She hath herself not only well defended
But taken and impounded as a stray   160
The King of Scots, whom she did send to France,
To fill King Edward's fame with prisoner kings
And make her chronicle as rich with praise

150 **ample ... fullness** full fullness to
  the brim. The tautology gives weight
  to the expression. This is the only
  recorded adjectival usage of the noun
  brim.
151 **Galling** wounding
  gleaned stripped of defenders
  (gleanèd). The image is of a cornfield
  after gleaning (see 1.1.53n.).
  hot assays fierce assaults
154 **th'ill neighbourhood** Cf. 4.1.6,
  'our bad neighbour', i.e. the enemy.
  Q's reading 'the brute [i.e. bruit]
  hereof' is less likely to be Shakespeare's revision than an unauthorized
  substitution recalled from *3H6*
  4.8[7].64, 'The bruit thereof will
  bring you many friends'.
155 **more ... harmed** proverbial ('More
  afraid than hurt', Tilley, A 55)
156 **exampled by herself** i.e. given an
  example by her own former conduct
157 **chivalry** mounted fighting men;
  here synonymous with *nobles*, l. 158
160 **impounded** put in the pound
  (parish pen for straying beasts)

161 **The King ... France** David II was
  captured at the battle of Neville's
  Cross, Durham, 17 October 1346,
  during Edward III's absence at the
  siege of Calais. That he was brought
  to Edward III at Calais is a fiction of
  E3, 5.1.63. Not in Holinshed, but cf.
  Exeter's speech in Hall (55): 'And
  where they haue inuaded, as I cannot
  deny but they haue dooen, what glory
  or what profite succeded of their
  entreprice, I report me to their pecu-
  lier histories.... Was not Malcol slain
  beside Tinmouth and King Dauid
  taken beside Durrham?'
163 ***her** England is the heroine of Canterbury's present narrative, and Holinshed's history is entitled *The first
  and second volumes of the Chronicles of
  England, Scotland, and Ireland.* Gurr,
  reading 'their' with F, interprets 'i.e.
  England's and Edward's'. Taylor,
  reading 'your' with Q, says that it
  draws attention to 'the implicit obli-
  gations and comparisons which the
  heroic past imposes on Henry'.

150–2] *F; not in Q*   154 th'ill neighbourhood] *F;* the brute hereof *Q;* the bruit thereof *Boswell*
156 herself:] *Theobald (subst.);* her selfe, *F*   163 And ... chronicle] *Capell (Johnson);* And make
their Chronicle *F;* Filling your Chronicles *Q*

As is the ooze and bottom of the sea
With sunken wrack and sumless treasuries.   165
WESTMORLAND
But there's a saying very old and true,
    If that you will France win,
    Then with Scotland first begin.
For once the eagle England being in prey,
To her unguarded nest the weasel Scot   170
Comes sneaking and so sucks her princely eggs,
Playing the mouse in absence of the cat,
To 'tame and havoc more than she can eat.
EXETER
It follows then the cat must stay at home;
Yet that is but a crushed necessity,   175
Since we have locks to safeguard necessaries

164–5 **As ... treasuries** Cf. Clarence's dream, *R3* 1.4.24–33.

164 **ooze and bottom** muddy bottom (hendiadys, cf. l. 89): cf. *R3* 1.4.32, 'the slimy bottom of the deep'

165 **wrack** wreckage
  sumless incalculable, impossible to reckon up (*OED*'s first example)
  treasuries treasures (*OED sb.* 5)

166 SP *WESTMORLAND F gives the speech to '*Bish. Ely*' and Q to '*Lord*'. Westmorland has the corresponding speech in Hall and Holinshed. (cf. ll. 136–77n.). Shakespeare need not have followed his sources – he had already transferred an observation of Westmorland's to the King (ll. 136–9, 146–54: cf. 146–54n.) and one of Exeter's to Canterbury (cf. 161n.) – but it is hard to explain why he should give this speech to Ely. 'Ely is present to second the Archbishop, not contradict him' (Taylor), and he does second him at ll. 115–21, a speech which reads like a continuation of Canterbury's. It also seems inappropriate that Ely should raise a point about strategy. F's '*Bish. Ely*' may

have prefaced another speech seconding Canterbury, which Shakespeare deleted, leaving visible the SP, which then got attached to the next speech. Q's '*Lord*' 'testifies that in the theatre the speech was given to a nobleman' (Taylor).

169 **in prey** in search of prey

172 Cf. the proverb 'When the cat's away the mice will play' (Tilley, C 175); but *Playing* here means 'acting like'. Cf. also *traps* and *petty thieves* (l. 177).

173 **'tame** broach, break into (*OED* tame *v.²*: aphetic form of 'attame'), here with reference to spoiling provisions by letting the air get to them. Cf. *TC* 4.1.64, 'The lees and dregs of a flat 'tamèd piece'.
  havoc destroy

174–83 **It ... music** In Hall and Holinshed Exeter replies to Westmorland's argument by inverting the old saying about France and Scotland: cf. ll. 136–77n.

175 **crushed** strained, forced (*OED* crush *v.* 2). Cf. *TN* 2.5.135, 'to crush this a little'.

---

166 SP] *Capell; Bish. Ely F; Lord. Q*   167–8] *Q; one line F*   173 'tame] *Cam¹ (Greg); tame F; spoyle Q; tear Rowe³*   175 crushed] *F (crush'd); curst Q*

And pretty traps to catch the petty thieves.
While that the armed hand doth fight abroad
Th'advisèd head defends itself at home.
For government, though high and low and lower   180
Put into parts, doth keep in one concent,
Congreeing in a full and natural close
Like music.
CANTERBURY   True. Therefore doth heaven divide
The state of man in diverse functions,
Setting endeavour in continual motion,   185
To which is fixed, as an aim or butt,
Obedience. For so work the honey-bees,
Creatures that by a rule in nature teach
The act of order to a peopled kingdom.
They have a king and officers of sorts,   190

177 **pretty** ingenious (*OED a.* 2b)
178 **armed** armèd
179 **advised** deliberate (advisèd)
180–3 **For ... music** Cicero, *De Republica* 2.69, is the ultimate source of this comparison between various levels of social classes and of musical tones combining to make up a harmony, as Theobald first showed.
181 **parts** the melodies assigned to the different voices or instruments in concerted music (*OED sb.* 10)
concent harmony (figurative): Lat. *concentus* (*OED sb.* 2)
182 **Congreeing** agreeing together (*OED* congree *v.*: the only listed occurrence). 'Shakespeare apparently coined the word out of *agreeing* and *congruing*' (Moore Smith).
full ... close A 'full close' is the technical term for a perfect cadence; *natural* relates to the human aspect of the analogy.
183 ***True*** 'True' opens a speech at 2.2.29 in F. F's omission of the word here may be due to inadvertence or to the mistaking of it for a false beginning of *Therefore*.

184 **state of man** human kingdom, body politic (*OED sb.* 29). Cf. the figurative use in *Mac* 1.3.140, 'Shakes so my single state of man'.
186–7 **To which ... Obedience** i.e. the object of which endeavour is obedience
186 **fixed** fixèd
butt target (as in archery)
187–204 **For so ... drone** The bees' commonwealth as a model for human beings is a traditional theme, found in Virgil's *Georgics* 4 and Pliny's *Natural History* 11. Elyot's *The Book of the Governor*, 1531, 1, and Lyly's *Euphues*, 1578 (1902), 2.45, may both have been English sources for Shakespeare's version.
189 **The act of order** order in practice, orderly behaviour
190 **king** Aristotle, and later scientists until Luis Mendez de Torres, 1586, believed the queen bee to be male; Charles Butler, *The Feminine Monarchy*, 1609, first published the facts in England (Taylor).
sorts various ranks

181 concent] *(consent)*   183 True. Therefore] *Q* *(*True: therefore*)*; Therefore *F*   185] *F; not in Q*   189 act] *F;* art *Pope*

Where some like magistrates correct at home,
Others like merchants venture trade abroad,
Others like soldiers, armed in their stings,
Make boot upon the summer's velvet buds,
Which pillage they with merry march bring home   195
To the tent-royal of their emperor,
Who busied in his majesty surveys
The singing masons building roofs of gold,
The civil citizens kneading up the honey,
The poor mechanic porters crowding in   200
Their heavy burdens at his narrow gate,
The sad-eyed justice, with his surly hum,
Delivering o'er to executors pale
The lazy yawning drone. I this infer,
That many things having full reference   205
To one consent may work contrariously,
As many arrows loosed several ways
Come to one mark,

191 **correct** enforce the laws
193 **armed in their stings** having their stings for weapons
   armed armèd
194 **Make boot upon** plunder, take booty from
197 ***majesty** F's anomalous plural, sometimes taken to mean 'kingly occupations', is more probably a compositor's error (repeated at 4.7.96–7) induced by the following word which made this word seem like a possessive; 'majesties, surveys' would be difficult to articulate.
199 **civil** orderly, well-mannered
   kneading up the honey i.e. moulding into shape the wax of the honeycomb. 'To *knead* gives an easy sense, though not physically true' (Johnson).
200 **mechanic** mechanical, i.e. performing manual labour
202 **sad-eyed** serious-looking: cf. *AYL*

2.7.153–5, 'the justice ... With eyes severe'
203 **executors** executioners. *Executors* is stressed on the first syllable.
   pale The adjective is probably chosen because pallor is associated with death. Since human executioners were usually masked and dressed in black, such parts of their faces as were visible would look pale by contrast.
205–6 **having ... consent** being wholly directed to a common purpose
206 **contrariously** by contrary (i.e. different) means
207 **loosed several ways** shot in different directions, i.e. shot from different positions towards one target
   loosed loosèd
208 **Come** F's sequence of verbs (*Come ... meet ... meet ... close*) preserves the leading idea of convergence, whereas Q's (*fly ... meet ... run ... close*) loses it.

192 venture] *(venter)*   197 majesty] *Q (maiestie)*; Maiesties *F*   199 kneading] *F*; lading *Q*   200 1] *F; not in Q*   204 I this] *F*; This I *Q*   205–6] *F; not in Q*   207–9] *as Capell; F lines ... seuer wayes / ... towne, / ; Q lines ... marke: / ... towne: /*   208 Come] *F*; flye *Q*

As many several ways meet in one town,
As many fresh streams meet in one salt sea, 210
As many lines close in the dial's centre.
So may a thousand actions once afoot
End in one purpose and be all well borne
Without defeat. Therefore to France, my liege.
Divide your happy England into four, 215
Whereof take you one quarter into France
And you withal shall make all Gallia shake.
If we with thrice such powers left at home
Cannot defend our own doors from the dog,
Let us be worried and our nation lose 220
The name of hardiness and policy.

KING
Call in the messengers sent from the Dauphin.
[Exeunt some Attendants.]

209 *several 'Q surely preserves the right metre; and *many* and *several*, first separate and then combined, surely also shows the poet's hand; while the F compositor would have a strong temptation to omit *several*, since to include it in the long line "Come to . . . one towne" would have overrun the column' (Wilson). Taylor, taking F's long line as a hexameter, says that 'Q's additional *several* adds nothing to the sense'. It is consistent, however, with the repetition of *ways* (a reading supported by Q), in the different sense of 'roads'.

211 **close** converge
dial's sun-dial's

213–14 **borne / Without defeat** sustained without being brought to nothing (*OED* defeat *sb.* 2: first example)

217 **all Gallia** all France. The synonym not only avoids repetition but evokes Caesar's conquests, the familiar opening statement of his *De Bello Gallico* being 'Gallia est omnis divisa

in partes tres' ('All Gaul is divided into three parts'). 'One quarter' is also contrasted with 'all Gallia'.

219 **the dog** Gurr persuasively identifies this as an echo of Psalm 22:20, 'Deliuer my soule from the sword: my darlyng from the power of the dogge' (Book of Common Prayer version). Canterbury's allusion implies that heaven helps those who help themselves.

220 **worried** savaged

221 **The name . . . policy** its reputation for boldness and statesmanship

222 **Dauphin** since 1349 the title of the King of France's eldest son, whose crest was a dolphin (Fr. *dauphin*). 'Dolphin', the invariable form of the title in F, Q, Hall, Holinshed and *Famous Victories*, indicates the contemporary pronunciation. 'Dauphin', the form that superseded it in English, is pronounced as if it were spelled 'Dawfin' (*OED*). The present Dauphin, Louis, died in December 1415. He was succeeded as Dauphin

209 several ways] *Q;* wayes *F* 212 afoot] *(a foote)* 213 End] *Q;* And *F* 214 defeat] *F;* defect *Q* 222+ Dauphin] *(Dolphin)* 222 SD] *Capell*

Now are we well resolved; and by God's help
And yours, the noble sinews of our power,
France being ours, we'll bend it to our awe   225
Or break it all to pieces. Or there we'll sit,
Ruling in large and ample empery
O'er France and all her almost kingly dukedoms,
Or lay these bones in an unworthy urn,
Tombless, with no remembrance over them.   230
Either our history shall with full mouth
Speak freely of our acts, or else our grave
Like Turkish mute shall have a tongueless mouth,
Not worshipped with a waxen epitaph.

Enter Ambassadors of France [*with Attendants carrying a tun*].

Now are we well prepared to know the pleasure   235

by his brother John (not mentioned in Holinshed), who died in 1417. John was succeeded by Charles (later Charles VII), who appears in *1H6*.

223 **well resolved** '(1) freed from doubt, (2) determined on action' (Gurr). The first sense is the leading one: cf. l. 4.

224 **sinews** i.e. chief source of strength

225 **France being ours** since France is mine (by right of inheritance)

225-6 **bend … pieces** i.e. as in the fable of the reed and the oak: the reed bowed to the wind, and was unharmed, but the oak resisted and was uprooted.

225 **our awe** reverential dread of me (i.e. as its king): *OED sb.* 2

227 **empery** sovereignty

228 **dukedoms** Cf. 1.1.86–9n.

229 **urn** grave (poetical: to avoid repetition of *grave* at l. 232)

230 **Tombless … them** without any monument or memorial inscription

231 **with full mouth** loudly (*OED* mouth *sb.* 3h)

232 **freely** largely, without stint

233 **Turkish mute** a tongueless Turkish

slave, so mutilated to ensure his secrecy

234 **Not … epitaph** 'without the honour even of a waxen epitaph, much less one of stone or brass' (Evans)

SD **Ambassadors** Gurr substitutes one ambassador and his attendants, but F and Q call for ambassadors, both in this SD and in the following dialogue (F consistently; Q inconsistently, substituting 'I' for 'we' in l. 240). In 1.1.91–7 and 1.2.3–6 only one ambassador is mentioned in F; Q's version of 1.2.3 (the only line relevant to the matter) is 'Shall I call in Thambassadors my Liege?' Holinshed also (3.545) has 'certeine ambassadors, that brought with them a barrell of Paris balles'. In *Famous Victories* only one ambassador, the Archbishop of Bourges, appears.

tun barrel; cf. preceding note. Hall (57) has 'a tunne of tennis balles'; *Famous Victories*, which twice uses Hall's phrase, also has 'a guilded Tunne' (scene ix: l. 830).

223] F; *not in Q* 226–30 Or there … them] F; *not in Q* 234 waxen] F; paper *Q* SD Ambassadors] F; *Thambassadors Q; Ambassador Cam²* with … tun] *Cam¹ (subst.)*

Of our fair cousin Dauphin; for we hear
Your greeting is from him, not from the King.

AMBASSADOR

May't please your majesty to give us leave
Freely to render what we have in charge,
Or shall we sparingly show you far off   240
The Dauphin's meaning and our embassy?

KING

We are no tyrant but a Christian king,
Unto whose grace our passion is as subject
As are our wretches fettered in our prisons:
Therefore with frank and with uncurbed plainness   245
Tell us the Dauphin's mind.

AMBASSADOR   Thus then, in few.

Your highness lately sending into France
Did claim some certain dukedoms in the right
Of your great predecessor King Edward the Third.
In answer of which claim the Prince our master   250

236 **fair cousin** Cf. 5.2.280 (the King addressing Burgundy).
239 **Freely** in freedom, i.e. with the privilege of our office
have in charge are ordered to say
240 **sparingly ... far off** discreetly and indirectly tell you; cf. *R3* 3.5.91, 'Yet touch this sparingly, as 'twere far off'
241 **embassy** message
243 **grace** (1) majesty, (2) gracious disposition
244 *****are** F's 'is', after 'our passion is as subject', creates the wrong expectation of another singular noun, and may have been wrongly introduced by a compositor who expected one. The passage thus differs from others (e.g. 1.0.9, 2.4.1) in which a singular verb precedes or follows a plural subject. Taylor notes that *are* and *our* were differently pronounced (so too at 4.1.8, where again they are juxtaposed).
245 **uncurbed** uncurbèd
246–97 See 2.4.129–33n. for the passage

in Holinshed on which these two passages in the play are based.
247–9 The *dukedoms* were not claimed, as here stated, before the tennis-balls embassy. Holinshed (3.546) reports that, after Canterbury's parliamentary speech, a French embassy was sent to England and then an English one, headed by Exeter, to France: it was then that 'the realme and crowne of France, with the entier duchies of Aquiteine, Normandie and Aniou, with the countries of Poictiou and Maine', were demanded, and an offer made by King Henry to marry the Princess Katherine 'and to indow hir with all the duchies and countries before rehearsed'. 'The Frenchmen being not a little abashed at these demands, thought not to make anie absolute answer in so weightie a cause, till they had further breathed'; and they accordingly returned a message promising to send ambassadors to England with their decision.

244 are] *Q;* is *F*   249 King Edward] *F, Q;* Edward *Pope*

Says that you savour too much of your youth
And bids you be advised. There's naught in France
That can be with a nimble galliard won;
You cannot revel into dukedoms there.
He therefore sends you, meeter for your spirit,   255
This tun of treasure, and in lieu of this
Desires you let the dukedoms that you claim
Hear no more of you. This the Dauphin speaks.

KING

What treasure, uncle?

EXETER   Tennis-balls, my liege.

KING

We are glad the Dauphin is so pleasant with us.   260
His present and your pains we thank you for.
When we have matched our rackets to these balls
We will in France, by God's grace, play a set
Shall strike his father's crown into the hazard.

251 **savour** taste (figurative)
252 **be advised** consider, reflect (*OED* advised *ppl. a.* 1). F's punctuation, the next word beginning with a capital letter, gives the colon after 'advised' the value of a full stop; otherwise the sense might be 'be informed that there's' etc. Q's reading ('He saith, theres nought in *France* that can be with a nimble / Galliard wonne' etc.) does not help decide the question. Cf. 3.6.158, 'Go, bid thy master well advise himself.'
253 **galliard** a lively dance
255 **meeter** more suitable
256 **in lieu of** in return for (the usual sense in Shakespeare)
257 **you let** either (1) that you let or (2) you to let (with the same sense)
260 **pleasant with us** merry at my expense. Cf. *Famous Victories* (scene ix: l. 846), 'My lord prince *Dolphin* is very pleansaunt [*read* pleasant] with me'.
262–7 **When … chases** a metaphorical threat of war in terms of royal or real tennis. The game is described in *Shakespeare's England*, 2.459–62. 'The oblong court was paved and enclosed by walls, the two shorter walls being pierced by holes or galleries called *hazards*. Netted string rackets were used to drive a leather ball stuffed with hair over a low net or rope halfway along the two longer walls. Points were scored when a ball was driven into a hazard or when it bounced twice (*chase*)' (Walter).
262 **our rackets** The plural noun suggests that he is speaking both of himself and of his countrymen at this moment.
263–4 **We … hazard** A *set* is a match consisting of a number of games. *France* and *crown* have sometimes been interpreted as allusions to the game (e.g. Ard²), but the primary sense, and probably the whole sense, is that King Henry will play a match in France that will win the French King's crown.

252 advised. There's] *F* (aduis'd: There's)*; advised, there's *Steevens*

Tell him he hath made a match with such a
   wrangler   265
That all the courts of France shall be disturbed
With chases. And we understand him well,
How he comes o'er us with our wilder days,
Not measuring what use we made of them.
We never valued this poor seat of England,   270
And therefore living hence did give ourself
To barbarous licence, as 'tis ever common
That men are merriest when they are from home.
But tell the Dauphin I will keep my state,
Be like a king and show my sail of greatness,   275
When I do rouse me in my throne of France.
For that have I laid by my majesty
And plodded like a man for working-days,

265 **made ... wrangler** taken on such a quarrelsome opponent

266–7 **all ... chases** (1) all the tennis courts of France shall resound with bouncing balls; (2) all the royal and ducal courts of France shall be disturbed with hunting (cf. 2.4.68), i.e. King Henry's warlike pursuit of his opponents

266 ***shall** Q's reading here is consistent with the correct use of *will* and *shall* illustrated throughout this long speech both in Q and (other than in this line) in F. At l. 296 *will* indicates simple futurity.

268 **comes o'er us with** taunts me with, i.e. assumes a superior attitude in respect of (*OED* come *v.* 43c)

270–3 **We ... home** The King admits that he irresponsibly neglected the court ('living hence') and did not recognize the true value of the English throne, but 'this poor seat' introduces the ironical idea that England is only the lesser part of his rightful inheritance, his 'throne of France' being the greater part.

274 **keep my state** (1) maintain my

dignity; (2) sit in my throne (cf. *Mac* 3.4.4, 'Our hostess keeps her state')

275 **show ... greatness** spread the sail of my greatness, display it in all its fullness. Dyce compares *3H6* 3.3.4–5, 'now Margaret / Must strike her sail and learn awhile to serve', as the opposite metaphor.

276 **rouse me** raise myself up. Cf. *2H4* 4.1.116, 'Being mounted and both roused in their seats'. The leonine image of ll. 123–4 is also recalled.

277 **For that** with that object
***have I ... majesty** i.e. in the past, as Prince of Wales (cf. *1H4* 1.2.194–200), and also in the present (with irony, as he is sitting in state to receive the ambassadors). Taylor points out that Q's inverted word-order is more metrical than F's and also that it avoids the undesirable ambiguity whereby *for that* can mean 'because'.

278 **like ... working-days** like a man made for working-days, i.e. a common working-man (mock-derogatory). Cf. *OED* working-day *a.* 1b, and *MA* 2.1.306–7, 'another [husband] for working days'.

266 shall] *Q; will F*   277 that have I] *Oxf¹; that I haue F; this haue we Q; this we haue Q3*
278 working-days] *(working dayes)*

But I will rise there with so full a glory
That I will dazzle all the eyes of France,   280
Yea, strike the Dauphin blind to look on us.
And tell the pleasant Prince this mock of his
Hath turned his balls to gun-stones, and his soul
Shall stand sore charged for the wasteful vengeance
That shall fly with them; for many a thousand
   widows   285
Shall this his mock mock out of their dear husbands,
Mock mothers from their sons, mock castles down,
And some are yet ungotten and unborn
That shall have cause to curse the Dauphin's scorn.
But this lies all within the will of God,   290
To whom I do appeal, and in whose name
Tell you the Dauphin I am coming on
To venge me as I may, and to put forth
My rightful hand in a well-hallowed cause.

279 **rise** i.e. like the sun
283 **Hath … gun-stones** Cf. Caxton's *Chronicle*, 1482 (Bullough, 4.352), where King Henry 'lete make tenys balles for the dolphyn in al the hast that they myght be made, and they were harde and grete gunne-stones for the Dolphyn to playe with-alle'. Cannon-balls were at first made of stone, and gun-stones was the usual word for them. Taylor suggests that *his balls* is a 'somewhat irrational' pun (i.e. his testicles); but *his balls* (i.e. these tennis-balls of his) is related to 'this mock of his', l. 282. (Nevertheless, in the theatre, 'these balls' is usually substituted.) In *Famous Victories* (scene ix: ll. 847–8), the King threatens that 'in steed of balles of leather, / We wil tosse him balles of brasse and yron'.
284 **charged** chargèd
   wasteful destructive
285 **fly with** F's reading (i.e. accompany) is preferable to Q's 'flye from', which has an additional inappropriate sense

(i.e. flee from).
   widows widows-to-be
288 **And** F's reading. Q's 'I' (= Ay) is repetitive, having already been substituted for F's 'Yea' in l. 281, there the more emphatic and appropriate word.
290–4, 298 Cf. Holinshed, 3.547, where the King says to the French ambassador the Archbishop of Bourges, 'In the meane time tell this to the vsurper your master, that within three moneths, I will enter into France, as into mine owne true and lawfull patrimonie, appointing to acquire the same, not with brag of words, but with deeds of men, and dint of sword, by the aid of God, in whome is my whole trust and confidence. Further matter at this present I impart not vnto you, sauing that with warrant you maie depart suerlie and safelie into your countrie, where I trust sooner to visit you, than you shall haue cause to bid me welcome.'
293 **as I may** to the utmost of my power

285 with] *F;* from *Q*   288 And] *F;* I *Q*

So get you hence in peace. And tell the Dauphin   295
His jest will savour but of shallow wit
When thousands weep more than did laugh at it. –
Convey them with safe conduct. – Fare you well.

Exeunt Ambassadors [and Attendants].

EXETER

This was a merry message.

KING

We hope to make the sender blush at it.   300
Therefore, my lords, omit no happy hour
That may give furtherance to our expedition,
For we have now no thought in us but France,
Save those to God that run before our business.
Therefore let our proportions for these wars   305
Be soon collected and all things thought upon
That may with reasonable swiftness add
More feathers to our wings, for, God before,
We'll chide this Dauphin at his father's door.
Therefore let every man now task his thought,   310
That this fair action may on foot be brought.

Flourish. Exeunt.

301 **omit ... hour** lose no favourable occasion
302 **expedition** expeditionary enterprise; perhaps with the secondary sense 'speed'; cf. 2.2.192
305 **proportions** requisite money and troops; cf. l. 137
307–8 **with ... wings** i.e. make us able to fly to France with the speed of thought; cf. *Ham* 1.5.29–30, 'with wings as swift / As meditation or the thoughts of love', and *TC* 2.2.42–4, 'if he do set / The very wings of reason to his heels, / And fly like chidden Mercury from Jove'. At 2.0.7 Mercury's winged heels are mentioned (cf. the *TC* passage, but implying flight towards battle, not away from it), but in the present passage

ordinary wings are suggested, as in the *Ham* passage.
308 **God before** God willing (cf. 3.6.155n.); not the oath 'Before God' (2.2.1, 5.2.143)
309 **at ... door** i.e. in France; with the suggestion that the Dauphin's mockery is puerile
310 **task** Cf. l. 6n.
311 i.e. in order that this operation, giving promise of success (*OED* fair *a.* 14), may be set afoot.
SD *Flourish fanfare of trumpets. Since other scenes with royal figures conclude with a flourish (2.2.194 SD) and a sennet (5.2.368 SD), editors rightly infer that F has misplaced the flourishes at the end of this scene and of 2.4.

298 SD *Ambassadors*] F; *Ambassador Cam²*; SD *not in Q* *and Attendants*] *Cam²* 301 4] F; *not in Q* 302 furtherance] *(furth'rance)* 306 8 and ... wings] F; *not in Q* 311 SD *Flourish. Exeunt*] *Dyce²*; *Exeunt* F; *Exeunt omnes* Q

[2.0]   *Enter* CHORUS.

CHORUS

Now all the youth of England are on fire,
And silken dalliance in the wardrobe lies.
Now thrive the armourers, and honour's thought
Reigns solely in the breast of every man.
They sell the pasture now to buy the horse,   5
Following the mirror of all Christian kings
With winged heels, as English Mercuries.
For now sits expectation in the air
And hides a sword from hilts unto the point
With crowns imperial, crowns and coronets,   10
Promised to Harry and his followers.
The French, advised by good intelligence
Of this most dreadful preparation,

2.0.1–11 Perhaps suggested by Hall's account of the reception of Exeter's speech (see 1.2.136–77n., 161n.) by the King, his brothers, 'and diuerse other lordes beynge yonge and lusty, desirous to win honor and profite in the realme of Fraunce. ... So that now all men cried warre, warre, Fraunce, Fraunce' (Hall, 55).

2 silken ... lies 'idle pastimes and luxurious garments are alike laid aside' (Walter). Cf. *E3*, 2.2.94, 'Away, loose silkes of wavering vanitie!' – where, however, the King is temporarily quelling his passion for the Countess of Salisbury.

6 mirror ... kings A *mirror* is a pattern or exemplar (*OED sb.* 5). King Henry is termed by Hall (113) 'the mirror of Christendome' and by Holinshed (3.583) 'a paterne in princehood, a lode-starre in honour, and mirrour of magnificence'. He calls himself 'a Christian king', 1.2.242.

7 With ... Mercuries Mercury, the messenger of Jove in classical mythology, was represented wearing winged sandals and a winged hat.

winged wingèd

9–10 And ... coronets A woodcut in the first (1577) edition of Holinshed shows Edward III holding a sword encircled by two crowns (of England and France). Shakespeare may have known this (though he used Holinshed's 1587 edition), and perhaps also that a heraldic device of Edward III was a sword encircled by three crowns.

9 hilts the two arms of the cross-piece guarding the user's hand; cf. 2.1.66

10 crowns imperial kings' or emperors' crowns (*OED*, first example 1542); cf. 4.1.258

11 and his followers Cf. Marlowe, *1 Tamburlaine*, where Tamburlaine's three chief followers acquire at his victory over Bajazeth the crowns of the latter's three 'contributory kings': 'Each man a crown? Why, kingly fought, i'faith!' (3.3.216). He crowns them at 4.4.115–18.

12 advised ... intelligence warned by trustworthy information

13 preparation (five syllables)

2.0] *Johnson; not in F*   0.1 *Enter* CHORUS] *Dyce; Flourish. Enter Chorus F; speech not in Q*   1 SP] *Johnson; not in F*

Shake in their fear, and with pale policy
Seek to divert the English purposes.   15
O England, model to thy inward greatness,
Like little body with a mighty heart,
What mightst thou do, that honour would thee do,
Were all thy children kind and natural!
But see, thy fault France hath in thee found out,   20
A nest of hollow bosoms, which he fills
With treacherous crowns; and three corrupted men,

14 **pale policy** i.e. intrigue dictated by
their fear
15 **divert** wrench awry (*OED v.* 4, citing
TC 1.3.98–101, 'frights, changes,
horrors / Divert and crack, rend and
deracinate / The unity and married
calm of states / Quite from their
fixture.')
16 **model ... greatness** 'visible form in
which dwells a mighty spirit' (Moore
Smith); 'a mould; something that
envelops closely': *OED sb.* 3, citing
this passage and *R2* 3.2.149–50
18 **that ... do** that honour (personified)
would wish you to do. (For omission
of 'to' before infinitive, see Abbott,
349.) Cf. Lodge, *Rosalynde* (Bullough,
3.168): 'but thou *Rosader* the youngest
in yeares, but the eldest in valour, art
a man of strength and darest doo what
honour allowes thee.'
19 **kind** 'having the feelings of kin, i.e.
here of Englishmen' (Deighton)
natural fulfilling the law of nature
20–30 Cf. Holinshed, 3.548: 'When king
Henrie had fullie furnished his nauie
with men, munition, & other prouisions, perceiuing that his capteines
misliked nothing so much as delaie,
determined [*sic:* 'he' omitted] his
souldiors to go a ship-boord and
awaie. But see the hap, the night
before the daie appointed for their
departure, he was crediblie informed,
that Richard earle of Cambridge
brother to Edward duke of Yorke, and
Henrie lord Scroope of Masham lord

treasuror, with Thomas Graie a
knight of Northumberland, being
confederat togither, had conspired his
death: wherefore he caused them to
be apprehended. ... These prisoners
vpon their examination, confessed,
that for a great summe of monie which
they had receiued of the French king,
they intended verelie either to haue
deliuered the king aliue into the hands
of his enimies, or else to haue mur-
thered him before he should arriue in
the duchie of Normandie.'
20 **But see** The exclamatory imperative
(addressed here to England personified) may derive from Holinshed's
phrase 'But see the hap' (cf. preceding
note).
21 **A nest ... bosoms** a breeding-place
of treachery, a set of traitors; cf. *WT*
2.3.82, 'A nest of traitors'. The latent
image is probably of a nest of vipers
(Gurr), though Shakespeare nowhere
uses that phrase.
hollow bosoms breasts empty of
loyalty. The verb *fills* introduces an
additional sense of *bosom* (*OED sb.*
3b), the clothes covering the chest,
'considered as receptacles for money
or valuables'.
he the French King (cf. *France* at
l. 20, and Holinshed at 20–30n.) At
the same time, ll. 20–7 suggest a
personified France as the opponent of
the personified England of ll. 16–19.
Contrast 'The French', ll. 12–15.
22 **treacherous crowns** gold coins

20 But ... fault] *F;* But see thy fault! *Capell*   out,] *F;* out *Capell*   22 crowns;] *Theobald;* Crownes,
F   men,] *Theobald;* men: *F*

One, Richard Earl of Cambridge, and the second,
Henry Lord Scroop of Masham, and the third,
Sir Thomas Grey, knight, of Northumberland,   25
Have, for the gilt of France, – O guilt indeed! –
Confirmed conspiracy with fearful France,
And by their hands this grace of kings must die,
If hell and treason hold their promises,
Ere he take ship for France, and in Southampton.   30
Linger your patience on and well digest

(contrast *crowns* at l. 10) inciting to
treachery

23 Richard ... Cambridge the younger
brother of the Duke of York. He was
created Earl of Cambridge in 1414.
By his marriage to Anne Mortimer,
the great-granddaughter of Edward
III's second son Lionel Duke of Clarence, he provided his son with a claim
to the throne. See Appendix 4.

24 Henry ... Masham The son of Sir
Stephen Scroop who announces to
Richard II the execution at Bristol of
Bushy, Green and the Earl of Wiltshire (*R2* 3.2.91–142). This Earl of
Wiltshire was Sir Stephen Scroop's
brother, and was a distant cousin (not
a brother, as in Holinshed and in *1H4*
1.3.265) of the Archbishop of York in
1H4 and *2H4*.
Masham This Yorkshire place-name
is pronounced (Mass'am) as though
spelled Massham (a spelling which
occurs twice in Q's version of 2.2).

25 Sir Thomas Grey of Heton, Northumberland. He was married to
Westmorland's daughter. His brother
Sir John Grey served with distinction
in King Henry's French campaigns
and was created Earl of Tankerville
and a Knight of the Garter in 1419.

26 gilt gold (*OED sb.*[1] 3); cf. *TC* 3.3.173,
'gilt o'er-dusted'. For the word-play
on *guilt*, cf. *2H4* 4.3.257 [5.129],

'England shall double gild his treble
guilt'.

27 Confirmed made strong, i.e. sworn
themselves to; cf. 2.2.90
fearful frightened; cf. l. 14

28 grace of kings king who does the
greatest honour to the title. Steevens
compares Chapman's *Iliad* (1598 edn)
1.322–3, 'With her [i.e. Chriseis] the
grace of kings, / Wise Ithacus,
ascended too' (Chapman's Homer,
1.518).

31–2 *Linger ... play The defective
metre of F's l. 32 indicates corruption.
In l. 31 'wee'l' may be an error for
'well': 'well digest / Th'abuse of distance' (i.e. willingly stomach (*OED v.*
6) the failure to observe the unity of
place) gives a more acceptable sense
than 'we'll ... distance' (i.e. 'we'll set
in order our changes of place, i.e. our
breach of the unity of place': Walter),
since Shakespeare's two other theatrical uses of *digest* (*TC* Prologue 28–
9, 'starting thence away / To what
may be digested in a play'; *Ham*
2.2.442, 'an excellent play, well
digested in the scenes') both involve
setting in order the material itself, not
its treatment. The imperative *Linger
... on* (i.e. prolong) leads to the parallel imperative *digest*. This editor conjectures that 'and weele' stood in the
copy at l. 32, helped to cause a mis-

28 die,] *F2;* dye. *F*   31–2 well ... distance, ... our play.] *this edn;* wee'l ... distance; force a play:
F; well ... distance, while we force a play. *Pope;* well ... distance. Force a play! *Kittredge;* we'll
... distance, force – perforce – a play. *Oxf*[1]

Th'abuse of distance, and we'll force our play.
The sum is paid, the traitors are agreed,
The King is set from London, and the scene
Is now transported, gentles, to Southampton.   35
There is the playhouse now, there must you sit,
And thence to France shall we convey you safe
And bring you back, charming the narrow seas
To give you gentle pass; for if we may,
We'll not offend one stomach with our play.   40
But till the King come forth and not till then
Unto Southampton do we shift our scene.   *Exit.*

reading error in l. 31 and was itself omitted from l. 32, and that in l. 32 the copy had 'our', which was corrupted into 'a' by the compositor, who was carrying the sound of the line in his head when setting it. Taylor defends his emendation by arguing that 'perforce' was omitted as a result of setting 'force' immediately before, and by pointing to the punning technique and apologetic tone as characteristic of the Chorus: 'To mirror history they must "perforce" pack the play with incidents.' He cites four other occurrences of 'force perforce'; in three of them the expression simply has its usual sense (by force, of necessity); in *MND* 3.1.133 it is used punningly, but with 'force' as a noun and not as a verb ('And thy fair virtue's force perforce doth move me'). Knight and others have suggested that Shakespeare intended to delete the two lines. In performance they had better be either omitted or emended.

32 **force** 'stuff, cram full; a culinary word, following close upon *digest*' (Wilson)

34 **is set from London** has set forth from London (*OED* set *v.* 108). Shakespeare, not having mentioned

in 1.1 or 1.2 that the tennis-balls incident took place at Kenilworth and the parliament at Leicester, allows it to be assumed that the action of Act 1 took place in London.

37 **safe** safely; the adverb applies both to 'convey you' and to 'bring you back'. The latter phrase is 'often a joke in the theatre: an afterthought, or anxious reassurance' (Taylor).

38 **charming** compelling by our magic art

39 **pass** passage

40 **offend one stomach** '(a) make any one seasick, (b) offend any one's taste' (Wilson)

41–2 This rhymed couplet, contradicting the sense of l. 35 and following the rhymed couplet ll. 39–40 that looks like the end of the Chorus's speech, may have been added by Shakespeare to allow for the insertion of 2.1. See Introduction, pp. 39–40.

41 **till ... forth** 'as if he had been going on to say "we do *not* shift", but the negative notion, being uppermost in his mind, thrusts itself in prematurely' (Evans). The line is 'a species of double negative' (Taylor, Oxf[1], 292). Hanmer's emendation is as good a normalization as any. A compositor's error is unlikely.

41 But till] *F;* But when *Hanmer*

[2.1]   *Enter* Corporal NYM *and* Lieutenant BARDOLPH
                    [, *meeting*].

BARDOLPH   Well met, Corporal Nym.
NYM   Good morrow, Lieutenant Bardolph.
BARDOLPH   What, are Ancient Pistol and you friends
yet?
NYM   For my part I care not. I say little; but when time   5
shall serve there shall be smiles; but that shall be as
it may. I dare not fight, but I will wink and hold out
mine iron. It is a simple one, but what though? It
will toast cheese, and it will endure cold as another

2.1 Location: the urgent entrances of the Boy (81 SD) and the Hostess (116.3) indicate that the scene takes place in the street not far from the tavern kept by the Hostess in *1H4* and *2H4*. This was in Eastcheap, a street just north of the Thames, near London Bridge. Cf. *1H4* 1.2.129, 189; 2.5.446 [4.426]; *Famous Victories* (scene i), l. 87, (scene ii), l. 162, 'the olde Tauerne in Eastcheape'.

0.1 **Corporal** NYM In *MW* 2.1.127 he tells Page 'My name is Corporal Nim'. It comes from the verb *nim*, to thieve, and is spelled Nym (Nymme twice in l. 110) throughout this scene and at 4.4.69, and Nim throughout 2.3 and 3.2, in F. In Q it is always Nim.
Lieutenant BARDOLPH At 3.2.2 Nym addresses Bardolph as *Corporal*, which was his rank in *2H4* 2.4.147. His rank in this scene may have been raised in order to give him a higher station than Pistol, who has a higher station than Nym. At l. 39 he calls Pistol *Lieutenant*, perhaps in flattery.

3 **Ancient** This is the invariable spelling of Pistol's title in F, except in Fluellen's speeches, where it is invariably 'Aunchient'. *Ancient* is also his title in Q, which has 'an Ensigne' only in its equivalent of 3.6.12.

Though *ancient* is a corruption of 'ensign' with the same sense, i.e. standard-bearer (*OED*), the traditional form is retained because it is Shakespeare's word: cf. F. Markham (1622) quoted in *OED* (ancient *sb.*^{2} 1), 'This Ensigne we corruptly call Antient'.

5 **I say little** i.e. I say nothing, I keep my intentions to myself
5–6 **when ... serve** when opportunity arises. Cf. Fluellen's 'when time is serve', 3.6.65.
6 **there ... smiles** Cf. *Oth* 4.1.121, 'They laugh that wins'.
6–7 **that ... may** proverbial (Tilley, T 202)
7 **I ... fight** ironical (i.e. 'You and Pistol perhaps think that I am a coward'). Nym goes on to imply that even if he were too cowardly to look on his sword he would still draw it in his quarrel with Pistol.
   wink close both eyes
8 **iron** sword
   what though? what of that?
9 **will toast cheese** is good enough to toast cheese. More irony (i.e. and good enough to kill Pistol). In *KJ* 4.3.99 the Bastard calls Salisbury's sword, contemptuously, 'your toasting-iron'.
   will endure cold 'i.e. does not mind being naked' (Wilson)

2.1] *Hanmer*   0.2 meeting] *Cam^1*   3 Ancient] *F (Ancient), Q (antient); Ensign Oxf^1*   9 will toast] *F*; will serue to toste *Q*

man's sword will, and there's an end.   10

BARDOLPH I will bestow a breakfast to make you
friends, and we'll be all three sworn brothers to
France. Let't be so, good Corporal Nym.

NYM Faith, I will live so long as I may, that's the
certain of it, and when I cannot live any longer, I   15
will do as I may. That is my rest, that is the
rendezvous of it.

BARDOLPH It is certain, Corporal, that he is married
to Nell Quickly, and certainly she did you wrong, for
you were troth-plight to her.   20

NYM I cannot tell. Things must be as they may. Men
may sleep, and they may have their throats about
them at that time, and some say knives have edges.
It must be as it may. Though patience be a tired
mare, yet she will plod. There must be conclusions.   25
Well, I cannot tell.

12 **sworn brothers** 'companions in arms
who took an oath according to the
rules of chivalry to share each other's
good and bad fortunes' (*OED* sworn
ppl. a. 1). At 3.2.44–5 the Boy modifies this: 'sworn brothers in filching'.
12–13 **to France** i.e. when we go to
France
13 **Let't** Taylor points out that this contraction appears also at *TS* 4.3.191
and at *WT* 2.2.56 and 5.3.73 (all verse
passages where metre requires the
contraction). In the present prose
passage *Let't* ends the line of type
in F, and the compositor may have
contracted *Let it* to save space, though
there is ample space for *it* in the
following line. The pronunciation is
exactly the same as *Let*.
14–17 **Faith ... rendezvous of it**
Nym's speech, continuing from his
preceding one, amounts to a rejection
of Bardolph's proposal.
16 **do as I may** proverbial: 'Men must
do as they may, not as they would'

(Tilley, M 554). It is an anticlimax because 'die' might be expected (and is
substituted by Dyce): Taylor notes that
in some modern stage performances
Nym therefore stutters on the 'd'.
rest reserved stake at the card game
primero, the game ending when that
is lost (*OED* rest *sb.* 6)
17 **rendezvous** retreat, refuge: *OED*,
first recorded in this sense in *1H4*
4.1.57, 'A rendezvous, a home to fly
unto'. Cf. 5.1.84.
19 **Nell Quickly** the Hostess of the
Eastcheap tavern in *1H4* (where she
is a married woman) and *2H4* (where
she is a widow). In *MW* she is the
unmarried housekeeper of Doctor
Caius, and Pistol resolves to make her
his 'prize' (2.2.133). Her first name
Nell (short for Helen or Eleanor) is
used only in *H5*.
20 **troth-plight** solemnly engaged to be
married
25 **yet ... plod** i.e. and get there (to the
satisfaction of my revenge) in the end

10 an end] *F;* the humor of it *Q*   13 Let't] *F;* Let it *Rowe*   16 do] *F, Q;* die *Dyce² (Mason)*
17 rendezvous] *F (rendeuous), Q (randeuous)*   25 mare] *Q;* name *F*

Enter PISTOL *and* HOSTESS.

BARDOLPH   Here comes Ancient Pistol and his wife.
Good Corporal, be patient here.

NYM   How now, mine host Pistol?

PISTOL
Base tyke, call'st thou me host?   30
Now by this hand I swear I scorn the term;
Nor shall my Nell keep lodgers.

HOSTESS   No, by my troth, not long. For we cannot
lodge and board a dozen or fourteen gentlewomen
that live honestly by the prick of their needles but it   35
will be thought we keep a bawdy-house straight.

                         [*Nym draws his sword.*]
O well-a-day, Lady, if he be not drawn! Now we

27–9 **Here ... host Pistol?** Q must be
right in making Nym, not Bardolph,
greet Pistol as 'mine host' (with a
provocative allusion to his acquiring
the tavern by marriage): if Bardolph
is the speaker, why does he not resent
Pistol's reply? But Q is wrong in
making Bardolph greet Pistol before
announcing his approach.

30 **tyke** low-bred dog (*OED* 1). Cf. the
insult 'Iceland dog', l. 42.

31 **by this hand** Pistol uses the same
oath in *2H4* 2.4.151. Q's reading is
more probably an actor's substitution
than (as Taylor suggests) Shakespeare's second thought.

32 **Nor ... lodgers** Pistol implies that,
far from being dependent on her
tavern for his support, he has the
means to support her without it.

35 **honestly** (1) respectably, (2) chastely.
Both meanings the Hostess intends
the former) underline the innuendo,
of which she is unconscious.
prick pricking (with further unconscious innuendo on *prick*, i.e. penis);

'live by their needles' would be the
normal expression

36 SD The drawing and sheathing of
swords in this scene has been variously prescribed by editors. F has no
SDs about it until 98 SD, and Q has
none until '*They drawe*' at Pistol's
'Therefore exhale' (l. 63), though it
is evident from Bardolph's ll. 39–40
that swords have been drawn before
this. The SDs of Oxf[1] are accepted
in this edn.

37 **Lady** by Our Lady
*drawn! Now Emendation is necessary because F's 'hewne' (without
additional 'down') has no precedent
in the sense 'cut down', and even if
it had it would be in too poetical a
style for the Hostess. Her phrase 'if
... drawn' is not a conditional clause
but means 'See, he has drawn his
sword!' For *drawn* in this sense, cf.
RJ 1.1.63, 67. F's error may have
been caused by the proximity of 'he':
cf. *MW* 3.3.157, where F has 'vncape'
for 'escape' (*MW*, ed. T. W. Craik,

26 SD HOSTESS] Q (*Hostes Quickly, his wife*); *Quickly* F   27–8] F; Godmorrow ancient *Pistoll.*
/ Here comes ancient *Pistoll*, I prithee *Nim* be quiet. Q   29 SP] Q; *not in* F   30–32] *verse* Q;
prose F   30 tyke] F; slaue Q; tick Oxf[1] (*Malone*)   31 this hand] F; gads lugges Q   36 SD]
Malone   37 O ... drawn! Now] *Theobald*; O welliday Lady, if he be not hewne now, F; O Lord
heeres Corporall *Nims*, now Q   drawn] *Theobald*; hewne F; here *Knight*

shall see wilful adultery and murder committed.

[*Pistol draws his sword.*]

BARDOLPH   Good Lieutenant, good Corporal, offer
nothing here.   40

NYM   Pish!

PISTOL

Pish for thee, Iceland dog, thou prick-eared cur of
Iceland!

HOSTESS   Good Corporal Nym, show thy valour and
put up your sword. [*Nym and Pistol sheathe their swords.*]

NYM [*to Pistol*]   Will you shog off? I would have you   45,
solus.

Oxford, 1989; Oxf has 'uncoop') because of 'vnkennell' in the preceding line. Ard²'s defence of Knight's emendation 'here', postulating that 'heere' was misread as 'hewne', is unconvincing because the Hostess already knows that Nym is present, a fact which suggests that Q's reading accidentally omits the word 'weapon' (with the usual unconscious innuendo, as in *RJ* 1.1.32, *2H4* 2.4.207) rather than adds a final s to a surname in the manner of the Welsh parson Evans in *MW* (in the Q text, but not the F one, of that play). Q's attaching of *now* to the phrase about wilful adultery and murder suggests that Theobald was right in emending F's punctuation as well as 'hewne': cf. the Hostess's words at *2H4* 2.4.206, 'So! Murder, I warrant now!'

38 **wilful … murder** The absurdity consists in transferring *wilful*, a usual epithet for *murder* (distinguishing it from manslaughter), to *adultery* (which presupposes the parties' intent), and in bringing in adultery at all, perhaps through the juxtaposition of the two sins in the Ten Commandments recited at the beginning of the Holy Communion service ('Thou shalt not do murther'; 'Thou shalt not committ adultery').

39 **Lieutenant** See l. 0.1n.
39–40 **offer nothing** attempt no violence
42 **Iceland dog** lap-dog from Iceland. William Harrison's *Description of England* (1577; reprinted in Holinshed, 1.231) mentions their 'sawcinesse and quarrelling'. They were also very long-haired (*OED* Iceland²: many examples), so Pistol may be reviling Nym's person as well as his personality.
prick-eared cur dog with pointed and erect ears. Harrison (see preceding note) includes 'sholts or curs dailie brought out of Iseland' among the 'currish kind, meet for manie toies: of which the whappet, or prickeared cur, is one'. The word *cur* is not necessarily derogatory, though Pistol's use of it is, here and at 4.4.1, 18.
43 **valour** The incongruous word suggests that the Hostess is thinking of 'discretion' which Shakespeare had associated with valour in two witty passages in *MND* (5.1.228–33) and *1H4* (5.4.118–20).
44 **SD** In view of Q's SD 'They drawe' at 63 SD, Nym had better respond to the Hostess's appeal (Pistol following his example) before he begins inviting Pistol to a private duel.
45 **shog off** go away (*OED* shog v. 3b):

38 SD] *Oxf¹*   42 Iceland] F *(*Island*)*, *Q* (Iseland)   44 SD] *Oxf¹*   45 SD] *this edn*

PISTOL

Solus, egregious dog? O viper vile!
The *solus* in thy most marvailous face,
The *solus* in thy teeth, and in thy throat,
And in thy hateful lungs, yea, in thy maw, perdy,   50
And, which is worse, within thy nasty mouth!
I do retort the *solus* in thy bowels,
For I can take, and Pistol's cock is up,
And flashing fire will follow.

NYM   I am not Barbason, you cannot conjure me. I have   55
an humour to knock you indifferently well. If you

i.e. come away to a place where we can fight undisturbed; cf. l. 58, 'If you would walk off'. Gurr wrongly assumes, like many actors, that Nym addresses the Hostess.

solus alone (a theatrical SD: *OED* solus *a.* 1). Pistol, not understanding the Latin word, takes it as an insult.

47 **egregious** outrageous (i.e. remarkable in a bad sense: *OED a.* 3). Pistol uses the word, again affectedly, at 4.4.11.

48–51 Cf. *Ham* 2.2.576–7, 'gives me the lie i'th' throat / As deep as to the lungs'.

48 **marvailous** marvellous, i.e. prodigious. The F spelling is not an unusual one (*OED*), but the word is to be accented on the second syllable as suits the metre.

50 **maw** stomach
perdy by God (Fr. *par Dieu*): archaic-poetical

51 **nasty** filthy (*OED a.* 1)

52 **I do ... bowels** Cf. *E3*, 1.1.89–90, where the Prince of Wales responds to Lorraine the French ambassador's defiance of his father: 'Defiance, French man? we rebound it backe, / Even to the bottom of thy masters throat.'

53 **take** take fire (*OED v.* 7f): alluding to his inflammable temper. The rest of the speech, and Nym's reply, plays on Pistol's name.

cock is up hammer, that falls and ignites the powder when the trigger is pulled, is raised ready for action. A pistol so prepared is said to be cocked. The phrase 'cock is up' is capable of a bawdy sense (penis is erect), which Q's over-elaborated version may reflect: 'And *Pistolls* flashing firy cock is vp'.

55 **Barbason** one of three 'names of fiends' mentioned by Ford in *MW* 2.2.88–9. It is apparently Shakespeare's variation on 'Marbas, alias Barbas' in Scot (378), whether through simple confusion with the name of 'one monsieur de Barbason, a Gascon', who fought hand to hand with King Henry in the mines at the siege of Harfleur (Holinshed, 3.577), or because Shakespeare deliberately invented the trisyllabic name in *MW* to match those of Amaimon and Lucifer.

conjure me control me with your big words. Scot, 378, says that Barbas 'appeareth in the form of a mighty lion, but at the commandment of a conjuror cometh up in the form of a man and answereth fully as touching anything which is hidden or secret'.

56 **humour** inclination
indifferently well pretty well (*OED* indifferently *adv.* 5)

47–54] *as Pope; prose F; Q (many variants) lines* ... throte, / ... within / ... solus in thy / ... talke, / ... vp. /   48 marvailous] *F(meruailous)*; marvellous *F3; not in Q*   51 nasty] *F (nastie)*; mesfull *Q*

grow foul with me, Pistol, I will scour you with my
rapier, as I may, in fair terms. If you would walk off,
I would prick your guts a little, in good terms, as I
may, and that's the humour of it.   60

PISTOL

O braggart vile and damned furious wight,
The grave doth gape, and doting death is near;
Therefore exhale.   [*Pistol and Nym draw their swords.*]

BARDOLPH [*Draws his sword.*]   Hear me, hear me what
I say. He that strikes the first stroke, I'll run him up   65
to the hilts, as I am a soldier.

PISTOL   An oath of mickle might, and fury shall abate.
                                    [*All sheathe their swords.*]
Give me thy fist, thy fore-foot to me give.
Thy spirits are most tall.

NYM   I will cut thy throat one time or other, in fair   70
terms, that is the humour of it.

---

57 **foul** abusive (*OED a.* 8); also, playing
on Pistol's name, clogged like a gun-
barrel (*OED a.* 6b, and 1674 example:
'The Body of it [i.e. a gun] is fowl
... by being too much heated')

57–8 **scour ... rapier** clean you by using
my rapier as a ramrod, i.e. run my
sword through or up you

58 **as I may** to the best of my ability
in fair terms in plain language (*OED
fair a.* 17), i.e. I tell you plainly. Nym
varies the phrase to 'in good terms',
l. 59, and repeats it at ll. 70–1.

60 **that's ... it** that's the way things are.
The word *humour* (originally meaning
moisture, then extended to all the four
physical and temperamental human
types, sanguine, choleric, phlegmatic
and melancholy) was in the late sixteenth century used in a variety of
colloquial senses, e.g. mood, fancy,
inclination. Chapman's *A Humorous
Day's Mirth* (1597) and Jonson's
Every Man in his Humour (1598) had
recently exploited the fashion. Nym's

use of the word is particularly
random.

61 **damned** damnèd
wight man (archaic-poetical)

62 **The grave doth gape** i.e. to swallow
you; cf. *2H4* 5.5.53; proverbial (Dent,
GG 2)
doting death amorous death (cf. *RJ*
5.3.103), i.e. longing to possess you

63 **exhale** draw your sword. A sense
peculiar to Pistol: elsewhere in Shakespeare the verb is transitive and is
used to denote the action of drawing
something forth, e.g. vapours from
the earth (by the sun, *LLL* 4.3.67) or
blood from a corpse (by Richard's
presence, *R3* 1.2.58).

67 **of mickle might** of much force;
archaic-poetical, e.g. Spenser, *Faerie
Queene*, 2.4.7

68 **fist** hand, i.e. to grasp mine
fore-foot hand (*OED* 1b: the only
example in this jocular sense)

69 **tall** valiant (*OED* 3)

---

61 braggart] F (*Braggard*), Q (*braggard*)   63 SD] Q (*They drawe.*)   64 SD] *Malone*   67 SD]
Cam¹   68–9] *verse Pope; prose F; not in Q*

PISTOL
> 'Couple a gorge'!
> That is the word. I thee defy again.
> O hound of Crete, think'st thou my spouse to get?
> No, to the spital go,   75
> And from the powdering-tub of infamy
> Fetch forth the lazar kite of Cressid's kind,
> Doll Tearsheet she by name, and her espouse.

72 **Couple a gorge** false French for 'cut the throat'. Taylor conjectures that the compositor should have set '*Coupe la gorge*' ·but made a transposition error; but cf. Q's reading, and 4.4.37, where F has 'cuppele gorge' and Q 'couple la gorge' (also adding 'Couple gorge' as a speech by Pistol after 4.6.37). Cf. a similar phrase in Marlowe's *Jew of Malta* 4.3.5, 'But, if I get him, *coupe de gorge* for that.' Pistol speaks no French words in *2H4* or *MW*.

73 **word** motto. Cf. *Ham* 1.5.111.
*thee defy Q's reading suggests that F's, which loses the stress of the verse, is an accidental transposition.

74 **hound of Crete** The phrase 'a hound of *Crete*' (in a merely descriptive sense) occurs in Golding's Ovid, 3.247, in a passage about Actaeon's hounds, which also has the line 'And shaggie Rugge with other twaine that had a Syre of *Crete*' (3.267). Wilson concludes from the latter line that Pistol is referring again to Nym's hair, but he may be simply indulging in picturesque abuse.
my spouse to get i.e. by killing me

75 **spital** 'A house or place for the reception of the indigent or diseased; charitable foundation for this purpose, esp. one chiefly occupied by persons of a low class or afflicted with foul diseases; a lazar-house' (*OED* spittle *sb.*[1] 1); often 'distinguished from *hos-*

pital, as being of a lower class than this' (*OED* 1b)

76 **powdering-tub** (literally) barrel for salting beef; (figuratively) tub in which patients were enclosed up to the neck to be treated for venereal disease by sweating and by fumigation with the powder of cinnabar, an ore of mercury, which was thrown on a hot plate or hot coals beneath the tub

77 **lazar** leper (here adjectival, i.e. diseased); cf. 1.1.15n.
kite ... kind i.e. prostitute. *Kite*, literally a bird of prey and carrion-eater, is figuratively 'a term of reproach or detestation' (*OED* sb. 2: cf. *KL* 1.4.241 [262], 'Detested kite! Thou liest'). Cressid (Cressida), who deserted Troilus for Diomede in Chaucer's *Troilus and Criseyde*, was afflicted with leprosy by the gods in Henryson's *Testament of Cresseid* (a sequel poem usually included in Chaucer's works), and went to 'the spittaill-hous'. The phrase 'kite of Cressid's kind' was already proverbial (Tilley, K 116) by Shakespeare's time. He probably took it from Barnabe Riche's *Rich his Farewell to the Military Profession* (1581: R2'), as Gurr points out, since Riche's book is the direct source of *TN*. Its alliteration would recommend it to Pistol.

78 **Doll Tearsheet she** Pistol's use of *she* is archaic-poetical (cf. *MW* 2.1.113, 'Like Sir Actaeon he'): many

I have and I will hold the quondam Quickly
For the only she; and *pauca*, there's enough.   80
Go to.

Enter the BOY.

BOY Mine host Pistol, you must come to my master,
and you, hostess. He is very sick and would to bed.
Good Bardolph, put thy face between his sheets and
do the office of a warming-pan. Faith, he's very ill.   85
BARDOLPH Away, you rogue!
HOSTESS By my troth, he'll yield the crow a pudding
one of these days. The King has killed his heart.
Good husband, come home presently.

[Exeunt Hostess and Boy.]

instances in *Sir Clyomon and Sir Clamydes* (anon., 1599), e.g. '*Clamydes* he', '*Neronis* she', E1'. Doll Tearsheet, referred to again as 'Doll' in Q and F 5.1.79, is Falstaff's whore in *2H4* 2.4 and 5.4; her surname means 'tearer of sheets'.

79–80 **I have ... she** Pistol echoes the marriage service ('to have and to hold'), and also uses *hold* to mean 'esteem' (*OED* hold *v.* 12).

79 **the quondam Quickly** her that was formerly Quickly. More alliteration. The Latin adverb is rare as an English adjective, but the anonymous *King Leir* (*c.* 1590, printed 1605), 1.1.33, has the phrase 'our *quondam* Queene' (Bullough, 7.338), and *OED* gives other examples.

80 **the only she** the unequalled woman (*OED* only *a.* 5), i.e. the paragon
pauca (Lat.) few [words]. In *MW* 1.1.123 the laconic Nym similarly uses the adjective elliptically. The implied Latin noun is *verba*, and the sense is the proverbial 'few words are best' (Tilley, W 798); cf. 4.1.66n.

82 **my master** i.e. Falstaff. The Boy is

his page, given him by Prince Henry, *2H4* 1.2.12–14.

83 ***you, hostess** Hanmer's emendation is confirmed by Q's paraphrase: 'Hostes you must come straight to my maister, / And you Host *Pistoll*.'

84 **thy face** Bardolph's red complexion, inflamed with drink (*1H4* 2.5.317–20), is a continual source of jokes in the English histories.

87 **he'll ... pudding** he'll become carrion, i.e. he'll die; proverbial (Tilley, C 860). The Hostess's next remark makes it clear that she means Falstaff, not the Boy. A *pudding* was minced meat etc., tied in a skin.

88 **killed his heart** been the death of him (i.e. by rejecting him after coming to the throne, *2H4* 5.5.41–71); proverbial (Dent, KK 2)

89 **presently** at once, i.e. as soon as you can
SD Capell's SD implies that the Boy waits to make sure that somebody comes back with him to Falstaff. Cam[1] inserts the SD '*The Boy runs off*' (too obediently?) after Bardolph's 'Away, you rogue!'

80–1 enough. / Go to] *Pope* (enough, go to.); enough to go to. *F*; enough too! / Go to. *Riv*; *verse Cam*   83 you, hostess] *Hanmer*; your Hostesse *F*   He ... bed] *F*; *not in Q*   85–6 Faith ... rogue] *F*; *not in Q*   88 The ... heart] *F*; *not in Q*   89 SD] *Capell*; Exit *F*

BARDOLPH   Come, shall I make you two friends? We   90
must to France together. Why the devil should we
keep knives to cut one another's throats?

PISTOL
Let floods o'erswell and fiends for food howl on!

NYM   You'll pay me the eight shillings I won of you at
betting?   95

PISTOL   Base is the slave that pays.

NYM   That now I will have; that's the humour of it.

PISTOL   As manhood shall compound: push home!

Pistol and Nym draw their swords.

BARDOLPH [*Draws his sword.*]   By this sword, he that
makes the first thrust, I'll kill him. By this sword, I   100
will.

PISTOL
Sword is an oath, and oaths must have their course.

[*He sheathes his sword.*]

BARDOLPH   Corporal Nym, an thou wilt be friends, be
friends. An thou wilt not, why then, be enemies with
me too. Prithee, put up.   105

---

92 **one another's** (emphatic) i.e. as distinct from Frenchmen's

93 **Let ... on** The floods are no doubt fiery ones (cf. *MM* 3.1.122), appropriate to the fiends who roar for their prey, i.e. Nym. That Pistol is referring to the war in France (as Taylor alternatively suggests) is improbable: the line looks more like a retort to Bardolph's proposal than an acceptance of it.

96 **Base ... pays** The expression is so characteristic of Pistol that its later proverbial use (Tilley, S 523, examples from 1619 and 1631) probably originated here.

98 **As ... compound** as valour shall settle the matter; i.e. that will depend on the result of our combat (*OED* compound *v.* 6b)

102 **Sword ... course** A soldier's oath's an oath that must be kept. Pistol's statement may imply either that Bardolph will have to kill one of them or that they are compelled to make peace to save Bardolph from having to do so. Since Bardolph now turns his persuasion to Nym, Oxf[1]'s SD seems to be right. Pistol's sword-sheathing will be amusing whether it is done with alacrity and relief or as the result of reflection. Oxf[1] and Cam[2] follow Joel H. Kaplan, *SQ*, 22 (1971): 399–400, in interpreting *Sword* as wordplay, i.e. 'sword (God's word); but no such oath exists, and Pistol is a ranter, not a quibbler.

105 **put up** Cf. l. 45.

93] *F; not in Q*   94 You'll ... the] *F;* I shal haue my *Q*   97 that's] *F;* and theres *Q*   98 SD] *F (Draw), Q (They draw.)*   99 SD] *Oxf[1]*   102 SD] *Oxf[1]*

NYM   I shall have my eight shillings?

PISTOL

A noble shalt thou have, and present pay,
And liquor likewise will I give to thee,
And friendship shall combine and brotherhood.
I'll live by Nym and Nym shall live by me.   110
Is not this just? For I shall sutler be
Unto the camp, and profits will accrue.
Give me thy hand.

NYM   I shall have my noble?

PISTOL   In cash, most justly paid.   115

NYM   Well, then, that's the humour of't.

> [*Nym and Bardolph sheathe their swords.*]
> [*Pistol and Nym shake hands.*]

Enter HOSTESS.

HOSTESS   As ever you come of women, come in quickly
to Sir John. Ah, poor heart, he is so shaked of a

---

106 *I ... shillings? Q's speech for
Nym, though probably wrong in
exactly repeating the wording of its
version of ll. 94–5, evidently preserves
the sense of a speech omitted from F,
without which Pistol's statement at ll.
107–8, which contradicts his earlier
one at l. 96, is unmotivated. Oxf¹'s
emendation is therefore adopted in
this edn.

107 noble 6s. 8d., one-third of a pound.
The *liquor* (l. 108) that Pistol promises
will either make up the balance of 1s.
4d. or mark their agreement.
   and present pay with immediate
payment

109 And friendship ... brotherhood
and friendship and brotherhood shall
unite us

110 I'll ... me I'll be supported by Nym,
and he'll be supported by me. Pistol
reiterates their brotherhood. Some
editors suggest that in the first half
of the line *by Nym* is a quibble, but
the quibble would be linguistically
strained ('by nim' would have to mean
'by thieving' but would actually mean
'by thieve'), and the second half of
the line refutes the suggestion because
there is no parallel quibble.

111 sutler seller of provisions

117 come of women were born of
women, i.e. have any natural feelings;
proverbial (Tilley, W 637). *Come* for
'came' is frequent in popular spoken
English: cf. *1H4* 2.5[4].183–4, 'And
unbound the rest; and then come in
the other.'

106] *Oxf¹; Nim*. I shall haue my eight shillings I wonne of you at beating? *Q; not in F*   107–12] *verse*
Q; prose F   112 profits] *F;* profit *Q*   113] *F; not in Q*   116 that's] *F2;* that *F;* theres *Q*   116.1]
Oxf¹   116.2] *Cam¹*   116.3] *F, Q; enter Hostess and Boy Cam²*   117 come of] *F;* came of *Q*   women]
F; men *Q*   117–18 come in ... of] *F;* come in, / Sir *Iohn* poore soule is so troubled / With *Q*   118
Ah,] *(Λ)*

burning quotidian tertian that it is most lamentable
to behold. Sweet men, come to him.   [*Exit.*]
NYM   The King hath run bad humours on the knight,   121
that's the even of it.

PISTOL
Nym, thou hast spoke the right;
His heart is fracted and corroborate.
NYM   The King is a good king, but it must be as it   125
may. He passes some humours and careers.

---

119 **quotidian tertian** 'The quotidian
and the tertian were intermittent
fevers, the paroxysm of the one recur-
ring every day, of the other every
other day' (*Shakespeare's England*,
1.435). Taylor quotes John Jones, *A
Dial for all Agues*, 1568, ch. 16, to
show that 'compound agues' could
exist and were especially dangerous
when 'the tertian and quotidian
interpolate be joined in one'; so the
Hostess's diagnosis may be quite
correct. But her habit is to misuse
words that she has picked up, so
earlier editors may be right in regarding 'quotidian tertian' as a contradiction in terms, and Shakespeare
may have so regarded it even if he
knew Jones's work.
120 SD **Exit* Oxf¹'s SD is preferable to
including the Hostess in the *Exeunt
omnes* of Q (l. 127 SD). Q reduces ll.
121–7 to l. 127. No exit for anyone is
given in F. It is natural for the Hostess
to wish to go straight back to Falstaff,
and Pistol's exit-line is more appropriate if she is no longer present.
Cam² reintroduces the Boy with the
Hostess at l. 116.3 so that the irony
of Pistol's 'we will live' (l. 127) may
embrace him as well as Nym and
Bardolph. But the Boy is Falstaff's
page, and having delivered his
message at ll. 82–3 he has no further
reason to leave his master unattended.
121 **run ... knight** treated the knight

badly. Editors who gloss 'run bad
humours' as 'vented his ill-humour'
give the word *humour* a more precise
sense than Nym habitually does: cf.
MW 1.3.71–2, 'I will run no base
humour. Here, take the humour-
letter' (i.e. I will do no base thing.
Here, take the letter-thing).
122 **that's ... it** that's the plain truth of
the matter. Cf. *Ham* 2.2.289, 'be even
and direct with me'.
123 **the right** the truth
124 **fracted and corroborate** Pistol,
emphatically confirming the Hostess's
statement 'The King has killed his
heart' (l. 88) as well as Nym's, uses
two latinisms. *Fracted* (Lat. *fractus*)
does mean 'broken' (cf. *Tim* 2.1.25,
'my reliance on his fracted dates'),
but *corroborate* (Lat. *robur*, 'strength')
means 'strengthened', not, as Pistol
perhaps supposes, 'in ruins', 'reduced
to rubble'. The verb is frequent in
medical contexts, e.g. Thomas Elyot,
The Castle of Health (1539 edn,
quoted in *OED v.* 2b), 'Olyves condite
in salte lykoure ... doth corroborate
the stomacke'. For the adjectival
form, cf. *miscreate*, 1.2.16.
126 **He ... careers** Nym adapts a recognized phrase in horsemanship, 'to pass
a career' (i.e. to make a short gallop at
full speed), to the present topic and to
his obsessive use of *humour*. The King
will run his own course and there is no
turning him from it.

119–20 quotidian ... him] *F*; tashan contigian feuer, tis wonderfull *Q*   120 SD] *Oxf¹*   121–6]
F; not in *Q*   123–4] *verse Capell; prose F*

PISTOL

Let us condole the knight, for, lambkins, we will
live. *[Exeunt.]*

[2.2] *Enter* EXETER, BEDFORD *and* WESTMORLAND.

BEDFORD

'Fore God, his grace is bold to trust these traitors.

EXETER

They shall be apprehended by and by.

WESTMORLAND

How smooth and even they do bear themselves,
As if allegiance in their bosoms sat,
Crowned with faith and constant loyalty!   5

BEDFORD

The King hath note of all that they intend,
By interception, which they dream not of.

EXETER

Nay, but the man that was his bedfellow,

127 **condole** express our sympathy with
(*OED v.* 5: not an eccentric use)
for . . . live i.e. for we, my lively lads,
are not going to die, as he is. 'Pistol
is in high spirits at the thought of
the campaign and its profits' (Verity).
Shakespeare's only other use of
lambkin is at *2H4* 5.3.117, where
Pistol tells Falstaff 'Sir John, thy
tender lambkin now is king.'
2.2 Location: at Southampton, but with
no further indication in the text of
place, e.g. a council chamber or a
quayside.
    Q reduces the speakers to two,
gives Gloucester a version of l. 1,
prints Exeter's reply as in F, omits
the speeches of Westmorland and
Bedford, reassigns Exeter's speech
(ll. 8–11) to Gloucester and adds an
explanatory comment by Exeter, 'O
the Lord of *Massham*.' Q never uses

the name Scroop in either SD, SP or
dialogue; whether because of censorship (Oxf[1], 16) or some other cause
remains conjectural.
2 **by and by** very soon
3 **even** calm
4–5 Walter points out the ironic echo of
2.0.21–2.
5 **Crowned** crownèd
constant firm
8–11 Cf. Holinshed, 3.548 (immediately
following 'apprehended' in 2.0.20–
30n.): 'The said lord Scroope was in
such fauour with the king, that he
admitted him sometime to be his bedfellow, in whose fidelitie the king
reposed such trust, that when anie
priuat or publike councell was in
hand, this lord had much in the determination of it. For he represented so
great grauitie in his countenance, such
modestie in behauiour, and so ver-

127 SD] *Q (Exeunt omnes.)*

2.2] *Pope*   0.1] *F; Enter Exeter and Gloster. Q*   1 SP] *F; Glost. Q*   3–7] *F; not in Q*   8 SP] *F;
Glost. Q*

167

Whom he hath dulled and cloyed with gracious
      favours,
That he should for a foreign purse so sell   10
His sovereign's life to death and treachery!

Sound trumpets. Enter the KING, SCROOP, CAMBRIDGE *and*
        GREY [*, Lords and Soldiers*].

KING

Now sits the wind fair, and we will aboard. –
My lord of Cambridge, and my kind lord of Masham,
And you, my gentle knight, give me your thoughts:
Think you not that the powers we bear with us   15
Will cut their passage through the force of France,
Doing the execution and the act
For which we have in head assembled them?

SCROOP

No doubt, my liege, if each man do his best.

KING

I doubt not that, since we are well persuaded   20
We carry not a heart with us from hence
That grows not in a fair consent with ours,
Nor leave not one behind that doth not wish
Success and conquest to attend on us.

CAMBRIDGE

Never was monarch better feared and loved   25

tuous zeale to all godlinesse in his
talke, that whatsoeuer he said was
thought for the most part necessarie
to be doone and followed. Also the
said sir Thomas Graie (as some write)
was of the kings priuie councell.'
(2.0.20–30n. proceeds at 'These
prisoners'.)
9 **dulled** i.e. whose appetite's sharp
    edge he has taken off (*OED v.* 4)
11.2 ***Lords and Soldiers*** F's call for
    trumpets (11.1), together with the

King's l. 12, indicates that the stage
is now to fill with the *lords* (l. 183)
and *dear countrymen* (l. 190: cf. 3.1.1)
who compose the army.
17 **the execution ... act** the action of
    destruction (*OED* execution *sb.* 5)
    (hendiadys)
18 **in head** as a military force (*OED*
    head *sb.* 30)
23 **Nor leave not** nor leave; cf. 1.1.35n.
25–6 **Never ... majesty** Cf. Holinshed
    3.583: 'This Henrie was a king, of life

11 treachery!] *F* (treachery.); trechery. / *Exe.* O the Lord of *Massham. Q*   11.2 *Enter ...* GREY]
F; Enter the King and three Lords. Q   Lords and Soldiers] *this edn; and Attendants Theobald; and*
Officers Cam²   13 of Masham] *F, Q; Masham Cam²*   17 18] *F; not in Q*   19, 36, 44 SP] *F;*
Masha. Q   20–4] *F; not in Q*

Than is your majĕsty; there's not, I think, a subject
That sits in heart-grief and uneasiness
Under the sweet shade of your government.

GREY

True: those that wcrc your father's enemies
Have steeped their galls in honey and do serve you   30
With hearts create of duty and of zeal.

KING

We therefore have great cause of thankfulness,
And shall forget the office of our hand
Sooner than quittance of desert and merit
According to their weight and worthiness.   35

without spot, a prince whome all men loued, and of none disdained, a capteine against whome fortune neuer frowned, nor mischance once spurned, whose people him so seuere a iusticer both loued and obeied [*sic*: read 'whose people him both loued and obeied, so seuere a iusticer'] (and so humane withall) that he left no offense vnpunished, nor freendship vnrewarded; a terrour to rebels, and suppressour of sedition, his vertues notable, his qualities most praiseworthie.'

26 **Than ... subject** As Taylor points out, this line would be easier to speak if it did not contain *I think*, which interrupts the phrase 'there's not a subject' (i.e. there's not a single subject) and thus makes it hard to give *a subject* the required sense. He suggests that Compositor B may have substituted 'a' for 'one'. It is possible that Shakespeare originally wrote the line as 'Than is your majesty. There's none, I think,' and then substituted 'not' for 'none', and 'a subject' for 'I think'; the compositor then treated 'a subject' as an addition instead of as a substitution. Alternatively *majesty* may end in two unstressed syllables preceding the caesura.

30 **galls** gall-bladders, traditionally regarded as the source of bitter feelings, especially those of resentment: cf. *Oth* 4.3.91. Gall (the bitter product of animal gall-bladders) and honey are proverbially contrasted as types of bitterness and sweetness.

31 **create ... zeal** either (1) created out of duty and zeal (i.e. as the components) or (2) created by duty and zeal (i.e. as the agents, half personified). In either case they are implied to be newly created. For the participial adjective form, cf. *miscreate*, 1.2.16.

33 **And shall ... hand** echoing Psalm 137:5, 'If I forget thee, O Hierusalem: let my ryght hande forget her cunning'

34 **quittance** requital

35 **According ... worthiness** i.e. in exact proportion: cf. 3.6.127
*their Though Q follows F's l. 33 with nonsense ('Sooner than reward and merit, / According to their cause and worthinesse') it may preserve the right word in *their*, which is appropriate after two nouns and before two others. Oxf[1] records four other confusions of *the* and *their* in F. F's reading, *the*, requires 'of them' to be understood.

26–8 there's ... government] *F; not in Q* 26 not ... subject] *F; not a subject Pope;* not, I think, one subject *Oxf[1]* 29 SP] *Q; Kni. F* 30–1 and ... zeal] *F;* for your sake *Q* 34] *F;* Sooner then reward and merit *Q; not in Q3* 35 their] *Q;* the *F*

SCROOP

So service shall with steeled sinews toil,
And labour shall refresh itself with hope
To do your grace incessant services.

KING

We judge no less. – Uncle of Exeter,
Enlarge the man committed yesterday   40
That railed against our person. We consider
It was excess of wine that set him on,
And on his more advice we pardon him.

SCROOP

That's mercy, but too much security.
Let him be punished, sovereign, lest example   45
Breed, by his sufferance, more of such a kind.

KING

O let us yet be merciful.

CAMBRIDGE

So may your highness, and yet punish too.

GREY

Sir,
You show great mercy if you give him life,   50
After the taste of much correction.

KING

Alas, your too much love and care of me

36 **steeled** as strong as steel (steelèd)
37 **hope** i.e. of due reward
40–83 'The incident here told is not historical. Perhaps it was suggested to Shakespeare by the parable of the Unmerciful Servant, Matthew 18:23–34' (Moore Smith). Richard Proudfoot (privately) compares the incident at *R3* 2.1.96–126.
40 **Enlarge** set free
   committed i.e. to prison
42 **excess of wine** Cf. 1 Peter 4:3. There is another allusion to 1 Peter at l. 122.
43 **on ... advice** 'on his return to more coolness of mind' (Johnson): *OED* advice *sb*. 4. Cf. *MV* 4.2.6–7, 'My

lord Bassanio upon more advice / Hath sent you here this ring.' Q, which reads identically, confirms that it is the drunkard's better consideration, not the King's, that causes the pardon to be granted.
44 **security** culpable absence of apprehension (*OED* 3): cf. 4.0.17, 'secure in soul'. The words 'too much' add strong emphasis to the statement.
46 **by his sufferance** by your tolerating him (i.e. his offence)
49–50 Grey's deferential *Sir* is additional to the full line of verse that follows (which Q, omitting the preceding *Sir*, gives as in F). Taylor (Oxf[1] 304),

39 We ... less] *F; not in Q*   43 his] *F, Q; our Collier[2]*   49–50 Sir, / You] *Dyce;* Sir, you *F;* You *Q*

Are heavy orisons 'gainst this poor wretch.
If little faults proceeding on distemper
Shall not be winked at, how shall we stretch our
    eye   55
When capital crimes, chewed, swallowed, and
    digested,
Appear before us? – We'll yet enlarge that man,
Though Cambridge, Scroop and Grey, in their dear
    care
And tender preservation of our person,
Would have him punished. And now to our French
    causes.   60
Who are the late commissioners?

CAMBRIDGE

I one, my lord;
Your highness bade me ask for it today.

SCROOP

So did you me, my liege.

accepting F's lineation, compares other 'lines with an extra initial stress', but all of these involve some elision to fit the metre, which F's line does not permit.

53 **heavy orisons** 'weighty petitions' (Moore Smith). The strict sense of *orisons* is 'prayers' (so on its four other appearances in Shakespeare), which may suggest that Portia's speech on mercy in *MV* 4.1 (especially ll. 197–9) was here in Shakespeare's mind.

54 **on distemper** from ill-health (here specifically intoxication: cf. *Ham* 3.2.288–9, *Oth* 1.1.100)

55 **winked at** encountered with closed eyes, i.e. ignored. To wink at faults is proverbial (Tilley, F 123).
    stretch open wide (enough)

56 **capital** (1) most serious (*OED a.* 4), (2) punishable by death (*OED a.* 2b)
    chewed ... digested i.e. deliberately, not impulsively, committed

58 **dear care** synonymous with *tender*

preservation (l. 59), so it is superfluous to interpret *dear* equivocally as (1) deeply felt, (2) dire, as modern editors do (Cam¹, Oxf¹, Cam²)

60 **causes** affairs

61 **late** lately (i.e. recently) appointed (*OED a.*¹ 6: first occurrence in this sense)
    commissioners persons entrusted by the King with an office. Shakespeare's only use of the word, though he mentions commissions of various kinds, e.g. *KJ* 3.3.11 (the Bastard is to raise money from monasteries) and *2H4* 4.1.160 (Prince John is to negotiate with the rebels). In *MM* 1.1.13, 47 the Duke hands Angelo and Escalus written commissions to rule in his absence. The present commissions, of unspecified import, are entirely Shakespeare's invention, as is the use the King makes of them.

63 **it** the letter of commission

58 Scroop and Grey,] *F; and the rest Q* 61–2] *as F; one line Oxf¹*   64, 78, 151 SP SCROOP] *F (Scro.); Mash. Q*   64–5] *as F; one line Oxf¹*

GREY

   And me, my royal sovereign.   65

KING [*Gives papers.*]

   Then, Richard Earl of Cambridge, there is yours;

   There yours, Lord Scroop of Masham; and, sir
      knight,

   Grey of Northumberland, this same is yours:

   Read them, and know I know your worthiness. –

   My lord of Westmorland and uncle Exeter,   70

   We will aboard tonight. – Why, how now, gentlemen!

   What see you in those papers, that you lose

   So much complexion? – Look ye how they change!

   Their cheeks are paper. – Why, what read you there,

   That hath so cowarded and chased your blood   75

   Out of appearance?

              [*Cambridge, Scroop and Grey fall upon their knees.*]

---

65 ***me** 'When Shakespeare had once made Scroop say, "So did you me," etc., it was altogether unlikely that he should fail to write in the next speech, "And me," etc.' (Dyce). Moore Smith, however, says that 'Grey chimes in with the first words used by Cambridge.' What perhaps happened was that Shakespeare wrote Cambridge's 'I one, my lord', completed a line of verse with 'And I, my royal sovereign', and then interpolated the two sentences that call for the delivery of the papers, accidentally letting the nominative pronoun stand in what had now become the final speech of the sequence. The pronoun was probably changed in performance. Q's version of the last two speeches is '*Mash.* So did you me my Soueraigne. / *Gray.* And me my Lord.'

66 SD The papers would be brought in by the King himself, buttoned up in his doublet or stuffed into his belt. Cam¹, locating the scene in a council chamber, adds the SD '*He takes up papers*' at l. 60.

69 **your worthiness** The expression is 'purposely ambiguous' (Deighton).

70 **Westmorland** stressed on the first syllable. It is invariably spelled 'Westmerland' in F and in Holinshed.

74 **paper** i.e. as white as paper

    read present tense; cf. *see*, l. 72

75 ***hath** The singular verb (as in Q) is the natural consequence of *what* in l. 74. F's plural verb may have resulted from the compositor's auditory error while carrying the line in his head. Cf. *Cor* 1.2.4–6, 'What ever have [F; hath F2] been thought on in this state / That could be brought to bodily act ere Rome / Had circumvention?' In both cases F's reading can be defended only as a verb governed by an implied plural noun, i.e. what things, what words. Also the plural pronoun *you* in l. 74 may have attracted a plural verb in l. 75.

76 **Out of appearance** into hiding

---

65 me] *Q;* I *F*   66 SD] *Capell (subst.)*   67 Lord Scroop] *F;* my Lord *Q*   67–8 and ... Northumberland] *F;* And sir *Thomas Gray* knight of *Northumberland Q*   70 My ... and] *F; not in Q*   75 hath] *Q;* haue *F*   76 appearance] *(apparance)*   76 SD] *Cam¹*

CAMBRIDGE   I do confess my fault
And do submit me to your highness' mercy.
GREY, SCROOP
To which we all appeal.
KING
The mercy that was quick in us but late
By your own counsel is suppressed and killed: 80
You must not dare, for shame, to talk of mercy,
For your own reasons turn into your bosoms
As dogs upon their masters, worrying you. –
See you, my princes and my noble peers,
These English monsters! My lord of Cambridge
    here,   85
You know how apt our love was to accord
To furnish him with all appertinents
Belonging to his honour; and this man
Hath for a few light crowns lightly conspired
And sworn unto the practices of France   90
To kill us here in Hampton. To the which

79 **quick** living
82 **reasons** arguments
83 **As ... masters** like Actaeon's
hounds, which tore their master to
pieces when Diana, whom he had
surprised bathing, transformed him
to a stag. Cf. 2.1.74n.
84 **See you** behold
85 **English monsters** 'The conspirators' treachery is the more "monstrous" in that they are *English*;
"monsters" (monstrosities) were commonly shown as exotic marvels'
(Humphreys).
86 **apt** ready
    accord agree
87–8 **appertinents / Belonging to**
things properly appertaining to.
Shakespeare's only use of *appertinents*.
88 **this man** F's reading, if correct,
makes the King speak with notable
self-control. Q's 'this vilde man' is
emotionally intense. Both readings

give a metrical line, and Q's text
(though mislined) otherwise reads as
F from *Belonging* to *in Hampton*. F's
compositor omitted a word in the
preceding line and may here have
omitted another (though a more
striking one). But Q's 'vilde' may be
an addition for metrical reasons, since
Q gives 'And this vilde man hath for
a fewe light crownes' as a line of
verse.
89 **light** of little physical weight: i.e.
constituting only a small temptation.
As applied to coins, *light* often carries
the derogatory sense 'counterfeit', as
in Falstaff's quibble 'your ill angel is
light', *2H4* 1.2.166. This second sense
may colour the expression here.
    lightly readily (*OED adv.* 4)
90 **practices** plots (*OED* 6c)
    France the French King. Cf. 2.0.20–
7.

86–8 our ... honour] *F;* we were to grace him, / In all things belonging to his honour *Q*
87 furnish him] *F2;* furnish *F*   88 this] *F;* this vilde *Q*

This knight, no less for bounty bound to us
Than Cambridge is, hath likewise sworn. – But oh,
What shall I say to thee, Lord Scroop, thou cruel,
Ingrateful, savage and inhuman creature,   95
Thou that didst bear the key of all my counsels,
That knewst the very bottom of my soul,
That almost mightst have coined me into gold
Wouldst thou have practised on me for thy use?
May it be possible that foreign hire   100
Could out of thee extract one spark of evil
That might annoy my finger? 'Tis so strange
That though the truth of it stands off as gross
As black on white, my eye will scarcely see it.
Treason and murder ever kept together,   105
As two yoke-devils sworn to either's purpose,
Working so grossly in a natural cause
That admiration did not whoop at them.
But thou, 'gainst all proportion, didst bring in
Wonder to wait on treason and on murder;   110
And whatsoever cunning fiend it was
That wrought upon thee so preposterously

96–7 **Thou that ... soul** Cf. Holinshed, 3.548 (quoted in ll. 8–11n.).
97 **bottom of my soul** proverbial (Dent, BB 16)
99 **Wouldst ... use** if you had worked upon me for your own profit. In conjunction with l. 98 *practised* suggests alchemical experiment.
102 **annoy** hurt (*OED v.* 4)
103 **stands ... gross** stands out as plainly
104 ***on** Maxwell's emendation is supported by the sense of Q's 'from'. F's 'and' probably resulted from the compositor's carrying the phrase in his head and assimilating it to the commonplace 'black and white', rather than from his misreading 'on' as 'and'.

will scarcely almost refuses to
105 **ever kept together** have always dwelt together (*OED* keep *v.* 55b)
106 **yoke-devils** devils working as 'yoke-fellows' (2.3.52, 4.6.9); Shakespeare's coinage to suit the present context **either's** each other's
107–8 'so evidently engaged in a purpose natural to them that they aroused no astonished outcry'
108 **admiration** wonder
whoop exclaim. Cf. *AYL* 3.2.188–9, 'out of all whooping' (past all power of exclamation).
109 **proportion** natural order of things (*OED sb.* 4)
110 **wait on** attend on
112 **preposterously** perversely (*OED* 2)

94 Lord Scroop] *F;* false man *Q* 95 inhuman] *(inhumane)* 98, 99 have] *F, Q3;* a *Q;* ha' *Oxf* 100–1 that ... evil] *F;* that out of thee / Should proceed one sparke *Q* 100 hire] *(hyer)* 103 of ... off] *F;* doth showe *Q* 104 on] *Cam¹* 1955 *(J. C. Maxwell);* and *F;* from *Q* 105–41] *F; not in Q* 106 yoke-devils] *(yoake diuels)* 107 a] *F2;* an *F* 108 whoop] *(hoope)*

Hath got the voice in hell for excellence.
All other devils that suggest by treasons
Do botch and bungle up damnation   115
With patches, colours and with forms being fetched
From glistering semblances of piety;
But he that tempered thee, bade thee stand up,
Gave thee no instance why thou shouldst do treason
Unless to dub thee with the name of traitor.   120
If that same demon that hath gulled thee thus
Should with his lion-gait walk the whole world,

113 **voice** vote, preference, i.e. supreme reputation (*OED sb.* 3b)
114 ***All** The sense of ll. 114–20 calls for Hanmer's emendation. The compositor's error is natural, as he had just set ': / And' (ll. 110–11). Q, omitting everything between l. 104 and the last four words of l. 142, is of no help here.
suggest by treasons If this phrase is correct, the sense must be 'tempt [people] by recommending [to them] treacherous acts': *suggest* (tempt) is here absolute or intransitive. Cf. *Oth* 2.3.343 (*OED v.* 7, first two examples). The difficulty lies in *by treasons*, which (granting the above sense) is still highly elliptical. Mason's conjecture (giving the sense 'tempt to treacherous acts') is attractive, because when *suggest* is used transitively *to* usually follows the direct object of the verb (*OED v.* 2).
115 **botch ... up** patch up and put together unskilfully. Both verbs were commonly followed, as here, by *up*.
damnation (four syllables)
116 **colours** (1) outward appearances (*OED sb.* 11), (2) shows of reason (*OED sb.* 12)
forms likenesses (*OED sb.* 2)
116–17 **being ... piety** which they have fetched from (speciously) shining

images of virtue. A *semblance* is 'An appearance or outward seeming *of* (something which is not actually there or of which the reality is different from its appearance)' (*OED* 4: first example).
118 **tempered** moulded like wax. Cf. *2H4* 4.2[3],125–6. 'I have him already tempering between my finger and my thumb'. But Johnson's conjecture *tempted* would be an easy emendation, and is attractive.
bade i.e. that bade. Otherwise *Gave* (l. 119) would be 'And gave'.
stand up stand boldly up (in opposition: *OED* stand *v.* 103n.). Cf. *JC* 2.1.167, 'We all stand up against the spirit of Caesar'. The phrase may also anticipate *dub* (l. 120), for *stand up* was a variant of 'arise' in the formula of conferring an honour: cf. *1H6* 3.8.25–6.
119 **instance** impelling motive (*OED sb.*2)
120 **dub ... traitor** dub yourself traitor; confer a traitor's title on yourself. To *dub* a person was to touch him on the shoulder with a sword as he knelt to be created a knight.
121 **gulled** fooled
122 **Should ... world** 'Be sober, & watch, for your aduersarie the deuyll, as a roaring Lion walketh about seking whom he may deuour' (1 Peter 5:8)

114 All] *Hanmer;* And *F* by treasons] *F;* by-treasons *Theobald;* to treasons *(Mason)* 116 being] *F;* are *conj. Oxf¹* 117 glistering] (glist'ring*)* 118 tempered] *F* (temper'd*);* tempted *(Johnson)* thee, bade] *F* (thee, bad*);* thee bade *Pope* 121 demon] *(Dæmon)* 122 lion-gait] *(*Lyon-gate*)*

He might return to vasty Tartar back
And tell the legions 'I can never win
A soul so easy as that Englishman's.'   125
O how hast thou with jealousy infected
The sweetness of affiance! Show men dutiful?
Why, so didst thou. Seem they grave and learned?
Why, so didst thou. Come they of noble family?
Why, so didst thou. Seem they religious?   130
Why, so didst thou. Or are they spare in diet,
Free from gross passion or of mirth or anger,
Constant in spirit, not swerving with the blood,
Garnished and decked in modest complement,
Not working with the eye without the ear,   135
And but in purged judgement trusting neither?
Such and so finely boulted didst thou seem:
And thus thy fall hath left a kind of blot
To mark the full-fraught man and best endued
With some suspicion. I will weep for thee,   140
For this revolt of thine, methinks, is like
Another fall of man. – Their faults are open.

123 **vasty** Cf. 1.0.12.
   Tartar hell (Tartarus, the deepest part of the classical mythological underworld). See l. 164n.
124 **legions** multitudes of devils. In Mark 5:8–9 the 'unclean spirit', asked his name, replies 'My name is legion: for we are many'.
125 **so easy as** as easily as I won
126 **jealousy** suspicion
127 **affiance** trust
127–37 **Show … seem** Cf. Holinshed, 3.548 (quoted in ll. 8–11n.)
128 Pope introduced 'or' before *Seem* to regularize the metre by analogy with l. 131, but in that line *or* introduces the final item of the series. Here the mid-line pause has syllabic value.
   learned learnèd
132 **or of** either of
133 **the blood** The blood was popularly

supposed to be the seat of the passions.
134 **complement** courtesy (*OED sb.* 8b)
135 **Not … ear** i.e. Scroop 'did not trust the air or look of any man till he had tried him by enquiry and conversation' (Johnson).
136 **but in** except in
   purged purified (purgèd)
137 **finely boulted** finely sifted (like flour), i.e. free from all faults
139 **full-fraught** (most) fully loaded (with virtues). 'Here the force of *best* retroacts on *full-fraught*, giving it the sense of the superlative' (Hudson).
   best endued most fully supplied
141 **revolt** act of disloyalty (*OED sb.* 1)
142 **fall of man** act of disobedience by Eve and Adam (Genesis 3)
   open manifest

128 Seem] *F; or seem Pope*   139 mark] *Theobald; make F*   the] *Pope; thee F*   endued] *F*
(*indued*); endowed *Oxf¹*   140 suspicion. I … thee,] *Pope; suspition, I … thee. F*

Arrest them to the answer of the law,
And God acquit them of their practices!
                    [*Cambridge, Scroop and Grey rise.*]
EXETER   I arrest thee of high treason, by the name of   145
Richard Earl of Cambridge.
I arrest thee of high treason, by the name of Henry
Lord Scroop of Masham.
I arrest thee of high treason, by the name of Thomas
Grey, knight, of Northumberland.   150

SCROOP

Our purposes God justly hath discovered,
And I repent my fault more than my death,
Which I beseech your highness to forgive,
Although my body pay the price of it.

CAMBRIDGE

For me, the gold of France did not seduce,   155

---

143 **to the ... law** so that they may be answerable to the law. In the play, as in Holinshed, they are summarily executed. In fact they were arrested on 20 July 1415 and found guilty by a Southampton jury on 2 August. Grey was thereupon executed, but Scroop and Cambridge claimed the privilege of trial by a court of peers. This took place at Southampton on 5 August, and they were executed on that day (*DNB*, 'Richard, Earl of Cambridge'; 'Scrope, Henry Le').

144 **acquit** release (i.e. from the guilt): *OED v.* 10

practices treacheries (*OED sb.* 6a)

151 **discovered** uncovered

155–7 **For me ... intended** Cf. Holinshed, 3.548 (immediately following the passage quoted in 183–94n.): 'Diuerse write that Richard earle of Cambridge did not conspire with the lord Scroope & Thomas Graie for the murthering of king Henrie to please the French king withall, but onelie to the intent to exalt to the crowne his

brother in law Edmund earle of March as heire to Lionell duke of Clarence: after the death of which earle of March, for diuerse secret impediments, not able to haue issue, the earle of Cambridge was sure that the crowne should come to him by his wife, and to his children, of hir begotten. And therefore (as was thought) he rather confessed himselfe for need of monie to be corrupted by the French king, than he would declare his inward mind, and open his veric intent and secret purpose, which if it were espied, he saw plainlie that the earle of March should haue tasted of the same cuppe that he had drunken, and what should haue come to his owne children he much doubted.' See Appendix 4 for the relationships and for the lines of descent from Edward III.

155 **For me** for my part, as for me
seduce i.e. with the implied object 'me'

---

144 SD] *this edn (Cam²)*   147 Henry] *Q; Thomas F*   148 Lord Scroop] *F;* Lord *Q*   Masham] *Q; Marsham F*   155–65] *F; not in Q*   155 seduce] *F;* seduce me *Keightley*

Although I did admit it as a motive
The sooner to effect what I intended.
But God be thanked for prevention,
Which I in sufferance heartily will rejoice,
Beseeching God and you to pardon me.   160
GREY
Never did faithful subject more rejoice
At the discovery of most dangerous treason
Than I do at this hour joy o'er myself,
Prevented from a damned enterprise.
My fault, but not my body, pardon, sovereign.   165
KING
God quit you in his mercy! Hear your sentence.

156 **motive** inciting cause (*OED sb.* 4b)
158 **thanked** thankèd
    prevention (four syllables)
159 ***Which ... rejoice** F's line is obviously corrupt. F2's insertion of *I* is accepted by all editors except Taylor, who says that it would require *rejoice* to mean 'enjoy' (but it might equally well require *Which* to mean 'as to which', as Abbott (272) points out with other examples), and who argues that *prevention* now takes on a second meaning in the sentence, i.e. 'the person prevented from committing the act'. Though his emendation is unconvincing, Taylor valuably points out that 'in 23 other uses in verse, Shakespeare never elides *heartily*, whereas *sufferance* can be readily elided.' This editor conjectures that the compositor has not only omitted *I* but has brought in *rejoice* by anticipation from l. 161 and substituted it for 'bless' (i.e. to praise or extol with grateful heart: *OED v.*[1] 5), a monosyllable that would restore to *heartily* its usual metrical value. But since there are other repeated words later in the scene ('We doubt not', ll. 185, 188; 'in our way', l. 187, 'on our way', l. 189) and at the beginning of the

next ('earn', ll. 3, 6) it would be unsafe to emend.
    sufferance suffering the penalty (*OED* 2b: first example)
164 **damned enterprise** Cf. *1 Troublesome Reign of John* (anon., 1591), F4, 'And let the black tormenters of deepe *Tartary* / Upbraide them with this damned enterprise.'
    damned damnèd
166 **quit** acquit. Cf. 144n.
166–82 Cf. Holinshed, 3.548 (immediately following the passage quoted in 2.0.20–30n.): 'When king Henrie had heard all things opened, which he desired to know, he caused all his nobilitie to come before his presence, before whome he caused to be brought the offendors also, and to them said. Hauing thus conspired the death and destruction of me, which am the head of the realme and gouernour of the people, it maie be (no doubt) but that you likewise haue sworne the confusion of all that are here with me, and also the desolation of your owne countrie. To what horror (O lord) for any true English hart to consider, that such an execrable iniquitie should euer so bewrap you, as for pleasing of a forren enimie to imbrue your

159 I ... heartily] *F2*; in sufferance heartily *F*; heartily in sufferance *Oxf*[1] will rejoice] *F*; rejoice for *Rowe*; will rejoice at *(Capell)*; will bless *(this edn)*

You have conspired against our royal person,
Joined with an enemy proclaimed and fixed,
And from his coffers
Received the golden earnest of our death;   170
Wherein you would have sold your king to slaughter,
His princes and his peers to servitude,
His subjects to oppression and contempt,
And his whole kingdom into desolation.
Touching our person seek we no revenge,   175
But we our kingdom's safety must so tender,
Whose ruin you have sought, that to her laws
We do deliver you. Get ye therefore hence,
Poor miserable wretches, to your death,
The taste whereof God of his mercy give   180
You patience to endure, and true repentance
Of all your dear offences! – Bear them hence.
        [Exeunt Cambridge, Scroop and Grey, guarded.]
Now, lords, for France; the enterprise whereof

hands in your bloud, and to ruine your owne natiue soile. Reuenge herein touching my person, though I seeke not; yet for the safegard of you my deere freends, & for due preseruation of all sorts, I am by office to cause example to be shewed. Get ye hence therefore ye poore miserable wretches to the receiuing of your iust reward, wherein Gods maiestie giue you grace of his mercie and repentance of your heinous offenses. And so immediatlie they were had to execution.'

168 *and fixed Taylor aptly compares *Cor* 2.3.250, 'fixèd enemy', and *LLL* 1.1.251–2, 'thy established proclaimed edict'. On metrical grounds Q's reading, resulting in a part-line in mid-speech, is preferable to F's, resulting in a line of six feet and an extra syllable. The compositor, who made evident errors in ll. 159 and 177, presumably made an eyeskip error over 'and fixed' and 'and from'.

170 **golden earnest** advance payment in gold

176 **tender** hold dear (*OED v.*[2] 3a)

178 *ye Q's reading is supported against F's 'you' by Holinshed, whose reiteration of the pronoun in that form may have caught Shakespeare's eye, as he was here following his source closely.

182 **dear** grievous (*OED* dear, dere *a.*-poetic. 2). Cf. *R2* 1.3.145, 'thy dear exile'.
Bear conduct, escort, 'carry' (*OED* carry *v.* 5): cf. *1H6* 5.5.4 ('Go, bear them hence – I will not hear them speak'), *1H4* 5.5.14 ('Bear Worcester to the death'). They have been on their feet since 144 SD.

168–70] *Oxf*[1]; Ioyn'd with an enemy proclaim'd, and from his Coffers, / Receyu'd the Golden Earnest of Our death *F*; Ioyned with an enemy proclaimed and fixed. / And from his coffers receiued the golden earnest of our death *Q*   171–4] *F; not in Q*   177 you have] *Q*; you *F*; you three *F2*   178 ye] *Q*; you *F, Q3*   182 dear offences] *F*; deeds amisse *Q*   SD] *Capell (subst.)*; Exit. *F*; Exeunt. *F2*; Exit three Lords. *Q*

Shall be to you as us, like glorious.
We doubt not of a fair and lucky war,   185
Since God so graciously hath brought to light
This dangerous treason lurking in our way
To hinder our beginnings. We doubt not now
But every rub is smoothed on our way.
Then forth, dear countrymen. Let us deliver   190
Our puissance into the hand of God,
Putting it straight in expedition.
Cheerly to sea; the signs of war advance.
No king of England, if not king of France!

Flourish. [*Exeunt.*]

183–94 Cf. Holinshed, 3.548 (immediately following the passage quoted in 166–82n.): 'This doone, the king calling his lords againe afore him, said in words few and with good grace. Of his enterprises he recounted the honor and glorie, whereof they with him were to be partakers, the great confidence he had in their noble minds, which could not but remember them of the famous feats that their ancestors aforetime in France had atchieued, whereof the due report for euer recorded remained yet in register. The great mercie of God that had so gratiouslie reuealed vnto him the treason at hand, whereby the true harts of those afore him made so eminent & apparant in his eie, as they might be right sure he would neuer forget it. The doubt of danger to be nothing in respect of the certeintie of honor that they should acquire, wherein himselfe (as they saw) in person would be lord and leader through Gods grace. To whose maiestie as cheeflie was knowne the equitie of his demand: euen so to his mercie did he onelie recommend the successe of his trauels. When the king had said, all the noble men kneeled downe, & promised faithfullie to serue him, dulie to obeie him, and rather to die than to suffer him to fall into the hands of his enimies.

'This doone, the king thought that suerlie all treason and conspiracie had beene vtterlie extinct: not suspecting the fire which was newlie kindled, and ceassed not to increase, till at length it burst out into such a flame, that catching the beames of his house and familie, his line and stocke was cleane consumed to ashes.'

184 **Shall ... glorious** shall be to you as it shall be to me, equally glorious

189 **rub** obstacle; literally, in the game of bowls, an unevenness in the ground **smoothed** smoothèd

191 **puissance** pronounced as three syllables. See 1.0.25.

192 **expedition** speedy motion (pronounced as five syllables)

193 **the signs ... advance** raise (*OED* advance *v*. 9) the banners (*OED* sign *sb*. 5b) of war. For this unusual Shakespearean sense of *advance*, cf. 5.2.348.

194 i.e. I will win France, or die in the attempt. Perhaps suggested by *Famous Victories* (scene xx: l. 1,489), 'What, not King of *France*? then nothing' (when the French King has said that he has considered King Henry's demands 'But cannot finde that you should be crowned / King of *France*').

184 like glorious] *F*; successiuely *Q*   186 so ... light] *F*; cut off *Q*   188–92] *F*; *not in Q*   189 on] *F*; in *F4*   194 SD *Exeunt.*] *Q (Exit omnes.)*

[2.3] *Enter* PISTOL, NYM, BARDOLPH, BOY *and* HOSTESS.

HOSTESS   Prithee, honey-sweet husband, let me bring
    thee to Staines.

PISTOL

No; for my manly heart doth earn.
Bardolph, be blithe. Nym, rouse thy vaunting veins.
Boy, bristle thy courage up;   5
For Falstaff he is dead, and we must earn therefore.

BARDOLPH   Would I were with him, wheresome'er he
    is, either in heaven or in hell!

HOSTESS   Nay, sure, he's not in hell; he's in Arthur's
    bosom, if ever man went to Arthur's bosom. 'A made   10
    a finer end, and went away an it had been any christom

2.3 Since Falstaff died at night (ll. 12–13) this scene takes place the day after 2.1.

1 Prithee I pray thee
honey-sweet The compound adjective occurs twice in *TC* 3.1.64, 138. Taylor, reading with F3, argues for 'two pleading vocatives'. In *Oth* 2.1.205 *honey* is used as a vocative.
bring accompany

2 Staines a town 17 miles west of London, where Pistol and the others will cross to the south side of the Thames on their way to Southampton (about 80 miles south-west of London)

3 earn grieve (*OED v.³* 2: cf. *JC* 2.2.129). Cf. 4.3.26. 'Apparently a variant of "yearn"' (*OED*).

4 rouse ... veins i.e. take heart (in Pistol's alliterative style). The literal sense of *vaunting* is boasting; *veins*, being plural, must mean the physical veins and not the mood (as in 'in the vein'). Cf. 3.1.7, 'conjure up the blood'.

5 bristle ... up Cf. *1H4* 1.1.97–8, 'and

bristle up / The crest of youth against your dignity'. Pistol's use of *bristle up* with an abstract noun is eccentric.

6 earn Cf. l. 3n. Pistol speaks with 'a forced cheerfulness' (Wilson). The sense of his speech is 'Because we must grieve inwardly, let us pull ourselves together and put a cheerful face on things', but he cannot resist a final tragic hexameter line. Taylor and Gurr take the sense to be the modern one, i.e. to gain by labour, but elsewhere in Shakespeare that is always a transitive verb.

7 wheresome'er wheresoever

9–10 Arthur's bosom The Hostess means 'Abraham's bosom'. Cf. Luke 16:22 (in the parable of Dives and Lazarus, where the former goes to hell and the latter to Abraham's bosom, i.e. heaven) and *R2* 4.1.94–5 [103–4], *R3* 4.3.38. There are allusions to King Arthur in *2H4* 2.4.32 and 3.2.277.

10 'A he; a colloquial form of the pronoun

11 a finer end The Hostess, in her emotion, leaves the rest of the sen-

---

2.3] *Pope* 0.1] *F; Enter Nim, Pistoll, Bardolfe, Hostes and a Boy. Q* 1 honey-sweet husband] *Theobald;* honey sweete Husband *F;* honey, sweet Husband *F3;* sweete heart *Q* 3–4] *verse Pope; prose F;* No fur, no fur *Q* 3 earn] *F (*erne*);* yern *F3;* yearn *Cam; not in Q* 5–6] *as Capell; prose F; Pope lines ... dead, / ... therefore. / ; not in Q* 7–9 Would ... in Arthur's] *F;* Well sir *Iohn* is gone. God be with him. / *Host.* I, he is in *Arthors Q* 11 finer] *F;* fine *Capell* an ... been] *F (*and it had been*);* as if it were *Q* any christom] *F (*any Christome*);* a crysombd *Q*

child. 'A parted even just between twelve and one, even
at the turning o'th' tide. For after I saw him fumble
with the sheets and play wi'th' flowers, and smile upon
his fingers' ends, I knew there was but one way; for   15
his nose was as sharp as a pen, and 'a babbled of green
fields. 'How now, Sir John?' quoth I, 'what, man! be o'
good cheer.' So 'a cried out 'God, God, God!' three or

tence to be understood. It might have
been 'than any christom child', since
that is the comparison that follows.
an as if

11–12 christom child i.e. innocent
baby. A 'chrisom child' was a child
newly christened; the term was specially applied (e.g. in bills of
mortality) to children who died within
a month of their birth. In pre-Refor-
mation England a child at baptism was
anointed with chrism (consecrated oil)
and a white cloth was put on its head.
Later the term for this, the chrisom-
cloth, was applied to the white
christening-robe in which the child
was wrapped, and in which it was
buried if it died within the month.
The Hostess's word *chrisom* also
evokes the senses 'Christian' and
'christened'.

12 even just exactly

13 at the ... tide i.e. when the tidal
Thames was at low water. The connection between death and ebbing
tide is a popular superstition.

13–16 fumble ... pen further traditional signs of approaching death,
as shown by the quotations from
Thomas Lupton (1578) and Peter
Lowe (1597) cited in Oxf[1]

14 *play wi'th' flowers i.e. with the
flowers strewn on the sheets to keep
the sick-room sweet

15 *fingers' ends fingertips. Q's and F's
'fingers' could be either a singular or
a plural possessive. F has three other
instances of 'fingers ends' (*LLL*
5.1.74, *TN* 1.3.75, *KJ* 3.4.168) and

none of 'fingers end', so Q's reading
is probably correct, and the sense
is that Falstaff smiled with infantile
pleasure at his fumbling fingers.

there ... way i.e. he was sure to die
(proverbial: Tilley, W 148)

16 *babbled of talked idly about. Cf.
'babble' (*sb.* and *v.*) in *TN* 4.2.99 ('thy
vain bibble-babble') and *MA* 3.3.34
('for the watch to babble and to talk').
As Taylor shows in his long note
(Oxf[1] 292–5) on F's 'and a Table of
greene fields', no convincing defence
of F has been proposed, whether
'Table' is taken to mean an article of
furniture or a picture; hence emendation is necessary, and involves
choosing between 'talkd' and 'babld'
as the word that stood in the compositor's copy. Whichever word it
was, it probably appeared in the form
just given (cf. l. 36, 'talk'd', and
4.1.71–2, 'tiddle tadle nor pibble ba-
/ble'), and in secretary hand either
word could be misread as 'table'.

16–17 green fields Wilson's suggestion,
that Falstaff was recollecting Psalm
23:2 ('He shal feede me in a greene
pasture') is more attractive than
Theobald's, that those suffering from
calenture (sunstroke) 'have their
heads run on green fields'. Falstaff
makes a number of scriptural allusions
in his speeches in *1H4, 2H4* and *MW*.
Leslie Hotson (*TLS*, 6 April 1956)
over-ingeniously maintained that 'a
Table of greene fields' meant 'a
picture of Grenville's' (i.e. Sir
Richard Grenville, *c.* 1541–91, naval

12 even ... even] *(*eu'n ... eu'n*)*   14 play wi'th'] *this edn;* play with *F;* talk of *Q*   15 fingers'
ends] *Q (*fingers ends*);* fin-/gers end *F;* finger's end *Theobald*   16–17 and ... fields] *F (*... Table
...*); not in Q*   16 babbled] *Theobald;* Table *F;* talked *(anon. in Theobald)*   17 be o'] *(*be a*)*

four times. Now I, to comfort him, bid him 'a should
not think of God; I hoped there was no need to trouble   20
himself with any such thoughts yet. So 'a bade me
lay more clothes on his feet. I put my hand into the
bed and felt them, and they were as cold as any
stone. Then I felt to his knees, and so up'ard and
up'ard, and all was as cold as any stone.   25

NYM   They say he cried out of sack.

HOSTESS   Ay, that 'a did.

BARDOLPH   And of women.

HOSTESS   Nay, that 'a did not.

BOY   Yes, that 'a did, and said they were devils incarnate.   30

commander, mortally wounded in the long fight of the Revenge against fifteen Spanish ships).

19–21 **Now I ... yet** Malone (quoted in Oxf[1]) cites a jest-book story (1595) turning on a similar unconscious impiety. The Hostess's phrase also unconsciously echoes Belzebub and Lucifer in Marlowe's *Doctor Faustus* 2.2.93–4, 'Thou shouldst not think on God.' 'Think of the devil'.

23 **felt them** Q's 'felt to them' is idiomatic (cf. Beaumont, *Knight of the Burning Pestle*, 3.2.68–70, 'make him put his fingers between his toes, and smell to them'), and may preserve the Hostess's expression, though it is not found elsewhere in Shakespeare. In that case 'felt to his knees' (l. 24) would mean 'felt his knees' rather than 'felt as far as his knees'.

23–4 **as cold ... stone** proverbial (Tilley, S 876)

24 **knees** Q's additional words may preserve a passage omitted from F through eyeskip from one *and* to another. On the other hand, Q may be labouring the point, and its additional words interrupt the sequence of actions which F represents as continuous.

up'ard F's 'vp-peer'd' probably arose from a misreading of 'vppard'; 'if the word were then spelt "vpard" the second time (the juxtaposed spelling variation being common enough), the compositor could hardly have misread it in the same way, and so normalized to "upward"' (Taylor).

25 **stone** 'unintentionally suggesting "testicle" (*sb.* 11)' (Taylor, who lists three of the many Shakespearean puns on the word, e.g. *MW* 1.4.107–9)

26 **They say** This may suggest that Nym was not at Falstaff's bedside, but Bardolph (whose l. 28 may either imply another 'They say' or be a witness's addition to the Hostess's l. 27) certainly was: see ll. 38–9. The dramatic purpose is rather to introduce the topics of sack and women than to picture the scene.

of sack against sack (a Spanish wine)

30 **Yes** an emphatic and contradictory affirmative (= Oh yes, he did)
devils incarnate devils in the flesh, i.e. in human form. The hyperbolical phrase, though current as early as 1395 (*OED*), had recently been memorably used by Lodge in *Wit's Misery, and the World's Madness: Discovering the Devils Incarnate of this Age* (1596),

24 knees] *F*; knees, and they were as cold as any stone *Q*   24–5 up'ard and up'ard] *Cam¹*; vp-peer'd, and vpward *F*; vpward, and vpward *Q*   28 SP] *F (Bard.); Boy. Q*   30 devils] *(Deules)*

HOSTESS   'A could never abide carnation, 'twas a colour he never liked.

BOY   'A said once the devil would have him about women.

HOSTESS   'A did in some sort, indeed, handle women;   35
but then he was rheumatic and talked of the Whore of Babylon.

BOY   Do you not remember 'a saw a flea stick upon Bardolph's nose and 'a said it was a black soul burning in hell-fire?   40

BARDOLPH   Well, the fuel is gone that maintained that fire; that's all the riches I got in his service.

NYM   Shall we shog? The King will be gone from Southampton.

a prose tract against the Seven Deadly Sins, *Deuils Incarnat* being the running headline of the volume.

31 **carnation** light rosy-pink colour (*OED*). In *MV* 2.1.24–5 Lancelot Gobbo makes the same verbal error: 'the very devil incarnation'.

33 **once** at one moment when he was on his deathbed (not on some earlier occasion). Cf. the reply.

35 **handle** discuss (with an unintentional sexual sense)

36 **rheumatic** literally, suffering from catarrh (called rheum: cf. 3.5.52). Since this cannot be the Hostess's intended sense, she probably uses it in mistake for 'lunatic', by which she means delirious. In *2H4* 2.4.54 she substitutes it for 'choleric'. (The word is stressed on the first syllable; cf. *MND* 2.1.105.)

36–7 **Whore of Babylon** the 'scarlet woman' of Revelation 17:4–5

39 **black** i.e. damned. In some Last Judgement plays in the mystery cycles the costume of white souls and black souls indicated their condition.

40 *hell-fire Q's word provides a more obvious cue for Bardolph's reply in F ('that fire'), but in Q Bardolph does not take the cue (see textual footnotes). F's word may derive from Q3, where 'Burning in hell?' is the conspicuous final line of sig. B4ᵛ. For the expression, cf. *1H4* 3.3.30–2, where Falstaff tells Bardolph, 'I never see thy face but I think upon hell-fire and Dives that lived in purple – for there he is in his robes, burning.' (Cf. ll. 9–10n.)

41 **fuel** i.e. liquor

42 **that's ... service** either (1) 'I got no other payment in his service but liquor' or (2) 'That red nose of mine' (pointing to it) 'is the only wealth I got in his service'. Cf. *1H4* 3.3.77–8 (Falstaff, of Bardolph), 'How, poor? Look upon his face. What call you rich? Let them coin his nose, let them coin his cheeks' – where the implied image is 'the red red gold' of many a ballad.

43 **shog** be going. Cf. 2.1.46.

31 SP] *Q (Host.); Woman. F*   33] *F; Nim.* Well he did cry out on women. *Q*   devil] *(Deule)*
36 rheumatic] *F (rumatique), Q (rumaticke)*   40 hell-fire] *Q (hell fire); hell Q3; Hell F*
41–2 Well ... fire;] *F;* Well, God be with him, *Q*

PISTOL

Come, let's away. – My love, give me thy lips.   45

[*Kisses her.*]

Look to my chattels and my moveables.
Let senses rule. The word is 'Pitch and pay'.
Trust none;
For oaths are straws, men's faiths are wafer-cakes,
And Holdfast is the only dog, my duck;   50
Therefore *Caveto* be thy counsellor.
Go, clear thy crystals. – Yoke-fellows in arms,
Let us to France, like horse-leeches, my boys,
To suck, to suck, the very blood to suck!

46 **Look ... moveables** i.e. Take care of my personal property. 'As the usual sense of chattel was "A movable possession: any possession or piece of property other than real estate" (*sb.* 4), a sense of legal or irrational redundancy may have been intended' (Taylor). In *TS* 3.3.102[2.226], Petruchio says of Katherine 'She is my goods, my chattels' (etc.), there may be an undercurrent of innuendo after 'My love, give me thy lips', running through to l. 59.

47 **Let senses rule** Pistol evidently means 'Keep your wits about you', but the phrase might mean 'Be guided by your sensual desires'.
word motto. Cf. 2.1.73.
Pitch and pay cash down, no credit (proverbial: Tilley, P 360)

49 **oaths** solemn promises (to pay up), synonymous with *faiths*
straws i.e. worthless (proverbial: Tilley, S 918)
wafer-cakes i.e. brittle (proverbial: Dent, W 1.1); literally, biscuit-like cakes as thin as wafers

50 **Holdfast ... dog** i.e. nothing is worth having but cash down. The ironical proverb 'Brag is a good dog' (Tilley, B 587) was current by 1580, but 'Brag is a good dog, but Holdfast is a better'

(Tilley, B 588) is not recorded before 1709 and may derive from this passage. The context suggests that Holdfast is chosen as the name of a metaphorical watchdog simply as an attribute (like Keeper or Towser) rather than as part of an elaborate pun on other senses of *holdfast* (staple, hook, clamp, bolt), *dog* (gripping device) and *brag* (large nail), as Hilda M. Hulme maintained (cited in Oxf[1]).
the only the best. Cf. 2.1.80n.
my duck my dear. *OED sb.*[1] 3 cites *MND* 5.1.276 ('O dainty duck, O dear!') as its first example.

51 *Caveto* Beware. Pistol personifies the imperative of Lat. *cavere*.

52 **crystals** eyes (figurative: *OED sb.* 4b, citing *VA* 963 as its first example, and this passage as its second). 'As clear as crystal' has been proverbial since *c.* 1300 (*OED* crystal *sb.* 2b), so Pistol's verb is somewhat paradoxical.
Yoke-fellows companions. Cf. 4.6.9; and 2.2.106, *yoke-devils*.

53 **horse-leeches** a large variety of leech (*OED* 2). The word was also used metaphorically of a rapacious person (*OED* 3), but Pistol's simile uses it literally.

54 Cf. 4.4.64, 'As I suck blood, I will show some mercy show', and note.

45–54] *verse Capell; prose F* 45 Come ... lips] *F; not in Q* SD] *Capell* 47 word] *Q; world F* 50 dog, my duck;] *Theobald; Dogge: My Ducke, F; dog my deare. Q* 51 *Caveto*] *F, cophetua Q* 52–5 Yoke-fellows ... say] *F; not in Q*

BOY   And that's but unwholesome food, they say.   55
PISTOL
   Touch her soft mouth, and march.
BARDOLPH   Farewell, hostess.   [*Kisses her.*]
NYM   I cannot kiss, that is the humour of it; but adieu.
PISTOL
   Let housewifery appear; keep close, I thee command.   59
HOSTESS   Farewell. Adieu.   *Exeunt.*

[2.4]   *Flourish. Enter the* FRENCH KING, *the* DAUPHIN, [*the*
   CONSTABLE *and*] *the* Dukes of BERRY *and* BRITAIN.

FRENCH KING
   Thus comes the English with full power upon us,

55 **And ... say** Wilson cites Andrew
Boorde's statement (*Dietary*, 1542, p.
276) that the blood of beasts and fowls
is hard to digest. The Boy may mean
this literally, or he may be commenting critically on Pistol's blood-
thirstiness, or he may be implying
that Frenchmen's blood is particularly
unwholesome.

56 **Touch ... march** Q's version of the
line, 'Touch her soft lips and part',
has become familiar as the title of a
movement from William Walton's
suite of music for Olivier's film *Henry
V* (1944).

58 **I cannot kiss** Nym still resents the
Hostess's marriage. The Boy, as well
as Bardolph, should probably kiss her
(or she him), so that Nym is the only
one who does not.

59 **housewifery** thrifty housekeeping
(pronounced 'hussif'ry')
   keep close stay within doors, i.e.
don't gad about. Q's quite different
reading, where 'buggle boe', as Taylor
points out, presumably means 'bugle-

bow', which Shirley (*The Gentleman
of Venice*, 1639, 1.1.60) uses as a
synonym for sexual parts, underlines
the second sense of F's expression,
with which cf. Jonson, *Every Man in
his Humour*, 4.4.48, where Cob bids
his wife Tib 'keep close thy door; I
ask no more'.

2.4 Both Holinshed and *Famous Victories*
supplied material for this scene. In
Holinshed (3.547), 'The Frenchmen hauing knowledge hereof [i.e.
of King Henry's preparations to
invade France], the Dolphin, who had
the gouernance of the realme, bicause
his father was fallen into his old
disease of frensie, sent for the dukes
of Berrie and Alanson, and all the
other lords of the councell of France:
by whose aduise it was determined,
that they should not onelie prepare a
sufficient armie to resist the king of
England, when so euer he arriued to
inuade France, but also to stuffe and
furnish the townes on the frontiers
and sea coasts with conuenient gar-

56 mouth, and march] *F*; lips and part *Q*   57 SD] *Capell*   58 that is] *F*; theres *Q*   59 Let ...
command] *F*; Keepe fast thy buggle boe *Q*   housewifery] *(Huswiferie)*

2.4] *Pope*   0.1-2] *F* (*Flourish. / Enter the French King, the Dolphin, the Dukes of Berry and
Britaine.*); *Enter King of France, Bourbon, Dolphin, and others. Q*   0.2 *the* CONSTABLE *and*]
Rowe   1+ SP] *(King.)*   1-14 Thus ... fields] *F*; Now you Lords of *Orleance*, / Of *Bourbon*, and
of *Berry*, / You see the King of England is not slack, / For he is footed on this land alreadie. *Q*

And more than carefully it us concerns
To answer royally in our defences.
Therefore the Dukes of Berry and of Britain,
Of Brabant and of Orleans, shall make forth,   5
And you, Prince Dauphin, with all swift dispatch,

risons of men: and further to send to the king of England a solemne ambassage, to make to him some offers according to the demands before rehearsed.' (For these demands see 1.2.247–9n.) The Archbishop of Bourges acts as ambassador, but does not succeed in getting King Henry to reduce his demands. King Henry prepares to sail for France from Southampton. 'And first princelie appointing to aduertise the French king of his comming, therefore dispatched Antelope his purseuant at armes with letters to him for restitution of that which he wrongfully withheld, contrarie to the lawes of God and man.' In *Famous Victories* (scene xi), ll. 963–1000, the French King, the Dauphin and the Constable await the Archbishop of Bourges's return. The French King has made preparations for defence, which the Constable approves; but the Dauphin says, 'Tut my Lord, although the King of England / Be yoong and wilde headed, yet neuer thinke he will be so / Unwise to make battell against the mightie King of *France*.' His father replies, 'Oh my sonne, although the King of England be / Yoong and wilde headed, yet neuer thinke but he is rulde / By his wise Councellors.'

0.1–2 F's inclusion of the Dukes of Berry and Britain is justified by l. 4. On Q's inclusion of Bourbon in the opening SD and in the French King's address to his nobles, and again in 3.5, see Introduction, p. 29.

CONSTABLE a principal officer in the royal household of France, having jurisdiction in matters of arms and chivalry; commander-in-chief of the army in the absence of the King (*OED* 2a)

1 **Thus ... us** This is often regarded as creating a comic-satiric effect after the end of 2.3; but if a throne is brought on stage – and one is required if the French King is to receive Exeter's message with due formality – there will be a short break in the action. The bringing in of a throne (heraldically decorated) establishes that the location is now France. See also note at l. 140 SD.

comes Cf. Prologue 9 for the singular verb.

2–3 **more ... defences** i.e. 'it is vitally important that we should put up a first-class defence' (Wilson)

4 **Berry** The English pronunciation (stressing the first syllable) is metrically appropriate.

Britain Brittany (which, with its two unstressed syllables, might be used on stage in a modern production, instead of *Britain* with its one unstressed syllable: 'Bretagne' is metrically impossible)

5 **Brabant** As in *LLL* 2.1.114–15, the English pronunciation, with the first syllable stressed and the final *t* sounded, is appropriate.

Orleans In this play regularly two syllables, the first stressed; English pronunciation. In *1H6* sometimes thus, sometimes three syllables (always so at line endings).

6 **swift dispatch** promptitude in settling the affair (*OED* dispatch *sb.* 5, glossing the phrase)

4 Berry] *F*; Berri *Cam*   Britain] *F* (Britaine); Bretagne *Capell*   5 Orleans] *F* (Orleance); Orléans *Oxf¹*   6+ Dauphin] (Dolphin)

To line and new repair our towns of war
With men of courage and with means defendant,
For England his approaches makes as fierce
As waters to the sucking of a gulf.   10
It fits us then to be as provident
As fear may teach us, out of late examples
Left by the fatal and neglected English
Upon our fields.

DAUPHIN   My most redoubted father,
It is most meet we arm us 'gainst the foe,   15
For peace itself should not so dull a kingdom,
Though war nor no known quarrel were in question,
But that defences, musters, preparations,
Should be maintained, assembled, and collected,
As were a war in expectation.   20
Therefore, I say, 'tis meet we all go forth
To view the sick and feeble parts of France.
And let us do it with no show of fear,
No, with no more than if we heard that England
Were busied with a Whitsun morris-dance.   25
For, my good liege, she is so idly kinged,

---

7 **line** reinforce (*OED v.*[1] 2: first example)
8 **defendant** defensive (*OED a.* and *sb.*[3]: sole example)
9 **England** the King of England
approaches hostile advance (*OED sb.* 2): plural here, as in *Tim* 5.2.49 [1.162] and *AC* 1.3.46; singular at 4.2.35
10 **gulf** whirlpool. Cf. 4.3.82.
12 **late examples** i.e. the French defeats at Crécy (1346) and Poitiers (1356); see l. 54n.
13 **fatal and neglected** fatally neglected (i.e. under-estimated by us, with fatal consequences)
14 **fields** battlefields
redoubted dreaded (complimentary and formal language), i.e. respected

19 **maintained ... collected** The verbs relate to the corresponding nouns.
20 **As ... expectation** as though a war were expected. *Expectation* is pronounced as five syllables.
24 **England** the nation, not (as at l. 9) its king. Cf. ll. 26–9.
25 **Whitsun morris-dance** Whit Sunday is the seventh Sunday after Easter, commemorating the descent of the Holy Spirit on the apostles at Pentecost (Acts 2) and beginning a week of celebrations. Morris-dancing (the name, cf. 'morisco', originated from the dancers' blackened faces, these making them look like Moors) was specially associated with Whitsun week and with May Day (1 May).
26 **idly** vainly, uselessly (*OED* 1)

14–22 My ... France] *F*; My gratious Lord, tis meet we all goe foorth, / And arme vs against the foe *Q*

Her sceptre so fantastically borne
By a vain, giddy, shallow, humorous youth,
That fear attends her not.

CONSTABLE   O peace, Prince Dauphin!
You are too much mistaken in this king.   30
Question your grace the late ambassadors,
With what great state he heard their embassy,
How well supplied with noble counsellors,
How modest in exception, and withal
How terrible in constant resolution,   35
And you shall find his vanities forespent
Were but the outside of the Roman Brutus,
Covering discretion with a coat of folly,
As gardeners do with ordure hide those roots
That shall first spring and be most delicate.   40

DAUPHIN

Well, 'tis not so, my lord High Constable;
But though we think it so, it is no matter.
In cases of defence 'tis best to weigh

27–8 **Her ... youth** Modern editors
(Taylor, Gurr) take this as equating
King Henry with the May King (and
Gurr as making him the consort of
England as May Queen); cf. Bris-
senden, 19–22. It need not be more
than a direct comment on King
Henry's supposed incapacity to wield
the royal sceptre of England.

28 **giddy** Cf. 1.2.145.
humorous capricious (*OED a.* 3)

29 **fear ... not** 'she has no terrors in her
train' (Wilson)

32 **embassy** ambassadorial message
(*OED* 2)

33 **noble** Taylor, reading 'aged' with Q,
defends this as 'much more pertinent
in rebuking the Dauphin's charges of
adolescent giddiness'. But in 1.2 none
of King Henry's council is evidently
aged; the Lord Chief Justice of *2H4*
(who perhaps lies behind Q's

adjective) is not present.

34 **in exception** in taking exception (i.e.
to the Dauphin's message); with reference to King Henry's subordination
of his revengeful purpose to the will
of God, 1.2.290–1

36 **vanities forespent** former frivolities
(*OED* forespent: spent previously)

37–8 **the outside ... folly** Lucius
Junius Brutus feigned mental incapacity (Lat. *brutus*, stupid: hence his
attributed name) as a safeguard when
plotting to expel the tyrant Tar-
quinius Superbus, the last king of
Rome. Cf. *Luc* 1.807–20, where the
same imagery of disguise occurs.

39 **ordure** dung

42 **though ... matter** i.e. though we
are wrong if we think it so, it is not
amiss to think it so

43 **weigh** estimate

29–30 O ... king.] *F;* O peace Prince *Dolphin,* you deceiue your selfe, *Q*   33 noble] *F;* aged
Q   34–64] *F;* And how his resolution andswerd him, / You then would say that *Harry* was
not wilde. / *King.* Well thinke we *Harry* strong: / And strongly arme vs to preuent the foe. *Q*

The enemy more mighty than he seems.
So the proportions of defence are filled,   45
Which, of a weak and niggardly projection,
Doth like a miser spoil his coat with scanting
A little cloth.
FRENCH KING   Think we King Harry strong;
And, princes, look you strongly arm to meet him.
The kindred of him hath been fleshed upon us,   50
And he is bred out of that bloody strain
That haunted us in our familiar paths.
Witness our too much memorable shame
When Cressy battle fatally was struck,
And all our princes captived, by the hand   55
Of that black name, Edward, Black Prince of Wales;

45 **So ... filled** 'In this way the forces necessary for defence are fully made up' (Moore Smith); cf. 1.2.305, *proportions*. F's punctuation of ll. 44–5 is ambiguous, allowing *So* to be understood as 'provided that'; but this would weaken the connection between l. 45 and ll. 46–8.

46 **Which ... projection** which defensive forces, being planned (*OED* projection *sb*. 3: first example) on a weak and penny-pinching scale. *Which* does double duty, meaning first 'the proportions of defence' and then the 'weak and niggardly projection'.

47 **scanting** sparing, saving

48 **Think we** let us think (taking up ll. 41–2)

50 **The kindred of him** his kindred. For this use of 'of him' (cf. l. 64), see Abbott, 225.
fleshed initiated in bloodshed (*OED* flesh *v*. 2). The literal sense of the verb (*OED v*. 1) is to reward a hawk or hound with a piece of the game killed in order to excite its eagerness for the chase.

51 **strain** race

52 **haunted** persistently followed (*OED*

haunt *v*. 4), pursued, molested (*OED* haunt *v*. 5). Cf. *1H4* 5.3.4, 'And I do haunt thee in the battle thus'. Some editors (Taylor, Gurr) call it a term from hunting, but *OED* gives no instances of such use.
familiar native (*OED a*. 1: pertaining to one's family or household)

53 **memorable** 'Used by Shakespeare only four times, all in this play' (Taylor): cf. l. 88, 4.7.103, 5.1.72

54 **Cressy** Crécy. The English pronunciation (F's 'Cressy') is appropriate, in a play written in English verse, for the name of this battle (cf. l. 12n.), a well-remembered one in English history; cf. the spelling and pronunciation of Agincourt (Fr. Azincourt).
struck fought. Cf. Holinshed, 3.551, 'where his great grandfather king Edward the third a little before had striken the battell of Cressie'.

55 **captived** taken captive. Shakespeare's only use of the verb, which is frequent in contemporary writers.

56 **Black Prince** He was so called from his black armour; his colouring was fair.

44 seems.] *Cam* (seems:); seemes, *F*   45 filled,] *Cam* (fill'd;); fill'd: *F*   54 Cressy] *F*; Crécy *Humphreys*

Whiles that his mountain sire, on mountain standing
Up in the air, crowned with the golden sun,
Saw his heroical seed, and smiled to see him,
Mangle the work of nature and deface   60
The patterns that by God and by French fathers
Had twenty years been made. This is a stem
Of that victorious stock, and let us fear
The native mightiness and fate of him.

Enter a Messenger.

MESSENGER
Ambassadors from Harry, King of England,   65
Do crave admittance to your majesty.
FRENCH KING
We'll give them present audience. Go and bring them.
                                        [*Exit Messenger.*]
You see this chase is hotly followed, friends.
DAUPHIN
Turn head and stop pursuit, for coward dogs

---

57 **mountain sire** F's adjectival use of *mountain*, though often doubted, can be easily defended as a metaphor meaning 'immovable as a mountain' (cf. *2H4* 4.1.186, 'Our peace shall stand as firm as rocky mountains'), since the point of the passage is that Edward III did not intervene (cf. 1.2.108–10). The repetition of the word is deliberate and is comparable with that of *black* in the preceding line.

58–62 **Up ... made** Some editors see an allusion to God the Father speaking from heaven (but not appearing) at the baptism of Jesus and declaring himself well pleased with his beloved son (Matthew 3:16–17; Mark 1:10–11; Luke 3:21–2). Taylor describes the allusion as 'blasphemous', and

Gurr interprets it pejoratively: 'Edward smiles on destruction, not loving creation.'

64 **The ... him** the inborn strength and the destiny (i.e. to be victorious) that he derives from such ancestors

67 **SD** The blunt command 'Go and bring them' is more appropriately addressed to the Messenger than to the 'Lords' who, in Capell's edn, here depart and return with Exeter. There is no need for the Messenger to re-enter, since Exeter has his own retinue (cf. 141n.).

68–71 **this chase ... them** 'Continues the metaphor begun with fleshed (l. 50)' (Wilson)

69 **Turn head** *OED* defines this phrase as 'to turn and face an enemy; to show a bold opposing front; the opposite

---

57 ¹mountain] *F;* mounting *Theobald;* mountant *Oxf¹* 65–7] *F; Con.* My Lord here is an Embassador / From the King of England. / *Kin.* Bid him come in. *Q* 67] *as Pope; F lines ...* audience. / ... them. / SD] *Oxf¹; Exeunt Mes. and certain Lords / Capell* 69–73] *F;* My gracious father, cut vp this English short, *Q*

Most spend their mouths when what they seem to
     threaten   70
Runs far before them. Good my sovereign,
Take up the English short and let them know
Of what a monarchy you are the head.
Self-love, my liege, is not so vile a sin
As self-neglecting.

Enter EXETER[, *with Attendants*].

FRENCH KING   From our brother England?   75
EXETER
From him, and thus he greets your majesty:
He wills you, in the name of God Almighty,
That you divest yourself and lay apart
The borrowed glories that by gift of heaven,
By law of nature and of nations, longs   80
To him and to his heirs, namely the crown
And all wide-stretched honours that pertain

of *turn tail*' (turn *v.* 57, citing *1H4*
3.2.102, 'Turns head against the lion's
armèd jaws').
69–71 coward ... them That cowardly
dogs bark loudest is proverbial (Tilley,
D 523).
70 spend their mouths cry, give
tongue. Cf. *VA* 692–5, where the
hounds 'spend their mouths' once
they have picked up the temporarily
lost scent.
72 Take ... short Make a quick and
decisive reply to the English (*OED*
short *adv.* 5b)
75 SD The plural *Ambassadors* and *them*
(ll. 65, 67) require Exeter to be
attended as befits his ambassadorial
dignity.
  ***brother England** Taylor (*TxC*)
convincingly argues that here and at
l. 114 F is wrongly influenced by Q3.
In 5.2 the forms *brother France* (l. 2)
and *brother England* (ll. 10, 12) occur,

and in the history plays such forms
are four times more frequent than the
alternative.
78 divest yourself dispossess yourself,
i.e. of the 'borrowed glories', l. 79
(*OED v.* 2b)
80 By ... nations The law of nature
is the body of commandments
implanted by nature in the human
mind (*OED* law *sb.*[1] 9c). The law of
nations is international law (*OED* law
sb.[1] 4c, which points out that the two
terms were often coupled, citing this
passage and *TC* 2.2.183–4). Cf. Holinshed (quoted at 2.4n.): 'contrarie to
the lawes of God and man'.
  longs appertains (*OED* long *v.*[2]: not
an abbreviated form of 'belongs',
though now often conventionally so
written)
82 wide-stretched far-spreading (stret-
chèd)

75 SD] *Oxf*[1] *(subst.); Enter Exeter F, Q; Re-enter Lords, with Exeter and Train / Capell*
brother] *Q;* brother of *F, Q3*   78 divest] *(deuest)*   80 longs] *F, Q;* 'long *Pope;* 'longs *Ard*[1]

By custom and the ordinance of times
Unto the crown of France. That you may know
'Tis no sinister nor no awkward claim,   85
Picked from the worm-holes of long-vanished days,
Nor from the dust of old oblivion raked,
He sends you this most memorable line,
In every branch truly demonstrative,
Willing you overlook this pedigree.   90
And when you find him evenly derived
From his most famed of famous ancestors,
Edward the Third, he bids you then resign
Your crown and kingdom indirectly held
From him the native and true challenger.   95
        [Gives the French King a paper.]

FRENCH KING
  Or else what follows?

EXETER
  Bloody constraint; for if you hide the crown

83 **By ... times** through the law ordained by long-established tradition

85 **sinister** (accented on second syllable) literally 'left-handed', i.e. irregular
awkward oblique (literally, turned the wrong way: *OED a.* 1): 'almost synonymous with *sinister*' (Wright)

88 **line** line of descent, i.e. family tree: synonymous with *pedigree*, l. 90. In Holinshed King Henry sends 'letters': cf. 2.4n.

90 **overlook** read over, examine (*OED v.* 3)

91 **evenly derived** directly descended (*OED* evenly *adv.* 2)

94 **indirectly** wrongfully (*OED* 1b)

95 **native** rightful. Cf. *R2* 3.2.25, 'her native king'.
challenger claimant
SD The most effective moment for the delivery of the document is at the end of the speech, after Exeter has finished stating its significance.

97 **Bloody constraint** compulsion by force of war. Cf. Holinshed, 3.548

(immediately following the passage quoted at 2.4n.): 'the king further declaring how sorie he was that he should be thus compelled for repeating of his right and iust title of inheritance, to make warre to the destruction of christian people, but sithens he had offered peace which could not be receiued, now for fault of iustice, he was forced to take armes. Neuertheless exhorted the French king in the bowels of Iesu Christ, to render him that which was his owne, whereby effusion of Christian bloud might be auoided.' But Shakespeare draws also on Holinshed's account of an earlier embassy (cf. 1.2.247-9n.), where after the words 'before rehearsed' there follows this passage (Holinshed 3.546): 'and if he would not so doo, then the king of England did expresse and signifie to him, that with the aid of God, and helpe of his people, he would recouer his right and inheritance wrongfullie with-

95 SD] *Theobald (opp. 89); not in F, Q*

Even in your heart, there will he rake for it.
Therefore in fierce tempest is he coming,
In thunder and in earthquake, like a Jove,   100
That if requiring fail, he will compel.
And bids you, in the bowels of the Lord,
Deliver up the crown and to take mercy
On the poor souls for whom this hungry war
Opens his vasty jaws; and on your head   105
Turning the widows' tears, the orphans' cries,

holden from him, with mortall warre, and dint of sword. This in effect dooth our English poet comprise in his report of the occasion, which Henrie the fift tooke to arrere battell against the French king: putting into the mouthes of the said king of Englands ambassadors an imagined speech, the conclusion whereof he maketh to be either restitution of that which the French had taken and deteined from the English, or else fier and sword.' The 'English poet' is Christopher Ocland, whose *Anglorum Praelia* (1580, in Latin hexameters), celebrating English battles from Edward III's reign onwards, was appointed by Elizabeth I's privy council to be read in all grammar schools. **if … crown** Shakespeare may be recalling Marlowe's *1 Tamburlaine* 2.4, a scene in which Mycetes the King of Persia tries to hide his crown in a hole during his battle with Tamburlaine.

98 *****heart** The emendation is necessary: Exeter is addressing the French King personally (cf. *head*, l. 105, where Q has 'heads'), who can therefore be hidden only in one place at a time. F's 'hearts' may come from Q (via Q3) or may be a misreading error. See 99n.

99–100 **Therefore … Jove** Gurr compares Isaiah 29:7: 'Thou [i.e. Jerusalem] shalt be visited of the Lorde of hoastes, with thunder, earthquake,

and with a great noyse, with storme and tempest' (visited = afflicted). The thunderbolt is the weapon of Jove, ruler of the gods.

99 **fierce** Q and F again agree, but 'fiery' is an attractive conjecture, supposing an easy misreading of 'fierie' (F's spelling at 4.1.250) as 'fierce'. Cf. *JC* 1.3.10, 'a tempest dropping fire'. The phrase 'fierce tempest' (not elsewhere in Shakespeare) is almost tautological. Moore Smith's statement that *fierce* is disyllabic is not confirmed by any other occurrence of the word in Shakespeare. On Q's and F's agreement, see Introduction, pp. 105–6.

101 **requiring** demanding authoritatively (*OED v.* 5a: cf. *Tem* 5.1.134–5, 'and require / My dukedom of thee')

102 **in … Lord** for the love of Christ (Philippians 1:8; *OED* bowel *sb.*[1] 3). Cf. Holinshed, 3.548 (quoted at l. 97n.), who uses the biblical phrase.

103 **to take** *To* is introduced for metrical reasons.

105 **vasty** Cf. Prologue 12; 2.2.123.

105–6 **and … Turning** Q omits 'And bids you … jaws' (ll. 102–5) and follows l. 101 with the line 'And on your heads turnes he the widowes teares'. Taylor, who regards Q's omission as an authorized cut, accepts 'turnes he' as preferable to F's 'Turning', which he finds 'extremely awkward'. It is true that F's syntax is irregular (cf. 103n.), but its sense is not doubtful, and 'Turning' makes

98 heart] *this edn*; hearts *F, Q*   99 fierce] *F, Q*; fiery *Dyce*[2] *(Walker)*   102–5 And … jaws] *F*; *not in Q*   102 And] *F*; He *Rowe*; A *(Oxf*[1]*)*   105 head] *F*; heads *Q*   106 Turning] *F*; turnes he *Q*

The dead men's blood, the pining maidens' groans,
For husbands, fathers and betrothed lovers
That shall be swallowed in this controversy.
This is his claim, his threatening, and my message –   110
Unless the Dauphin be in presence here,
To whom expressly I bring greeting too.

FRENCH KING
For us, we will consider of this further.
Tomorrow shall you bear our full intent
Back to our brother England.

DAUPHIN   For the Dauphin,   115
I stand here for him. What to him from England?

EXETER
Scorn and defiance, slight regard, contempt,

for a more fluent line than 'Turns he'
would. Shakespeare might have made
the syntax of *Turning* (parallel to
coming, l. 99) consistent by writing
'upon' instead of 'and on' in l. 105,
but this would have made *war*, the
nearest noun, seem to be related to
Turning. The conjunction *and* at ll.
102 and 105 holds the speech together
by introducing the several heads of
King Henry's message.

107 **The ... blood** Johnson notes that
this phrase, as placed, disturbs the
otherwise highly systematic structure whereby widows/husbands,
orphans/fathers, and maidens/lovers
are mutually related. Yet Q, though
substituting 'bones' for 'blood', confirms F's phrase order, and Shakespeare may have wished to increase
the pathos by making the widows'
tears and the orphans' cries more
prominent than the dead men's blood.
***pining** As Taylor says, 'The context
makes clear for what the maidens
pine'. F's reading is evidently wrong
(if 'privy' applied to *groans* it would
not precede *maidens*'), and Walter's

emendation 'prived' is unlikely
because Shakespeare never uses the
word elsewhere and *OED* gives no
instance of its being used in this
absolute sense ('priued of their liues',
cited by Walter, is a typical usage); it
is also less consistent with the
emotional tone of the passage.

108 **betrothed** betrothèd

112 **too** as well as to the French King.
Though Gurr defends F's 'to' by
pointing out that 'A double preposition is quite usual', F's reading at
4.6.34 ('or they will issue to': read
'too') strongly suggests that Q's *too* is
to be followed in a modern edition.

115–16 **For ... him** 'As for the
Dauphin, I represent him.' An ironical way of declaring that he is *in
presence* (l. 111). Sometimes in performance he corrects Exeter's pronunciation of Dauphin as Dolphin –
not a happy invention.

117–19 **Scorn ... at** F's punctuation.
Capell's treats 'Scorn and defiance'
as Exeter's reply to the Dauphin's
question. 'But this is to impede the
torrent of scorn that breaks from

107 pining] *Q;* priuy *F;* prived *Ard²* *(Warburton)*   110 threatening] *F* ('Threatning), *Q*
(threatning)   112 too] *F (*to*), Q*   113-15 For ... England] *F; not in Q (see 140–6)*   115 brother]
Q (at 140); brother of *F, Q3 (at 140)*   117 defiance,] *F, Q;* defiance; *Capell*   contempt,] *F, Q;*
contempt; *Oxf¹*

And anything that may not misbecome
The mighty sender, doth he prize you at.
Thus says my king: an if your father's highness   120
Do not, in grant of all demands at large,
Sweeten the bitter mock you sent his majesty,
He'll call you to so hot an answer for it
That caves and womby vaultages of France
Shall chide your trespass and return your mock   125
In second accent of his ordinance.

DAUPHIN

Say if my father render fair return
It is against my will, for I desire
Nothing but odds with England. To that end,
As matching to his youth and vanity,   130

Exeter's lips, and to mark a more precise syntactical arrangement than was in Shakespeare's mind' (Wilson).

120 **an if** if. Abbott (101, 102, 103) explains how 'and' (or 'an') was used in conditional clauses and how it became superseded by 'and if' (or 'an if'). F is ambiguous here, but most probably 'Thus says my king' relates to what follows and not to what precedes. Q, omitting l. 121, has to substitute 'Vnles' for F's 'and if'.

121 **at large** in full. *OED* large *adv.* 5e, 'at large'. Cf. *LLL* 1.1.153, 'So to the laws at large I write my name'.

123 ***for** 'There is no parallel for *answer of* in this sense (in reply to an insult or provocation, not a question)' (Taylor). F's 'of' was probably caused by anticipation ('of France', l. 124).

124 **womby vaultages** 'hollow recesses. Both words are apparently coinages' (Taylor)

125 **trespass** sin

126 **second accent** echo
ordinance ordnance, artillery

127 **Say** Say that. Wilson takes F's colon as indicating 'a significant pause', but a pause at this point would not be

natural, and the colon probably does no more than introduce the message.
render fair return make a conciliatory reply

129 **odds** quarrel, conflict
England the King of England. Cf. *his* (l. 130), *him* (l. 131).

129–33 **To that end ... Europe** Cf. Holinshed, 3.545: 'Whilest in the Lent season the king laie at Killingworth, there came to him from Charles [*read* Lewes] Dolphin of France certeine ambassadors, that brought with them a barrell of Paris balles, which from their maister they presented to him for a token that was taken in verie ill part, as sent in scorne, to signifie, that it was more meet for the king to passe the time with such childish exercise, than to attempt anie worthie exploit. Wherfore the K. wrote to him, that yer ought long, he would tosse him some London balles that perchance should shake the walles of the best court in France.'

130 **vanity** worthlessness, insignificance (*OED* 2). Cf. *vain*, l. 28.

120 king: an if] *F* (King: and if), *Dyce;* king. Vnles *Q;* king, and if *Cam²* 121] *F; not in Q* 123 for] *Q;* of *F* 127 Say] (Say:) 129–30] *as Rowe; F lines* ... England. / ... Vanitie, / ; And for that cause according to his youth *Q*

196

I did present him with the Paris-balls.

EXETER

He'll make your Paris Louvre shake for it,
Were it the mistress-court of mighty Europe.
And be assured you'll find a difference,
As we his subjects have in wonder found,   135
Between the promise of his greener days
And these he masters now. Now he weighs time
Even to the utmost grain. That you shall read
In your own losses, if he stay in France.

FRENCH KING

Tomorrow shall you know our mind at full.   140

Flourish.

EXETER

Dispatch us with all speed, lest that our king
Come here himself to question our delay,
For he is footed in this land already.

131 **Paris-balls** tennis-balls, so called because the game was brought to England from Paris

132 **Louvre** Pope first gave the French spelling, but the sense was always recognized, as F2's 'Loover' shows. This F2 spelling indicates the pronunciation, and there is no need to suppose word-play on 'lover'. Holinshed (3.578) refers to 'the castell of Louer'.

133 **mistress** principal

136 **greener days** unripe 'wilder days' (1.2.268)

137 **masters** is master of, possesses. Cf. *Son* 106.8, 'Even such a beauty as you master now'.

137–8 **weighs ... grain** i.e. makes the best use of his time; *grain* is here figurative for the smallest possible quantity (*OED sb.*[1] 9). Gurr suggests, with some probability, that Shakespeare has in mind the sand in an hour-glass.

140 SD *Flourish* Capell's note justifies

F's SD: 'the French king rises from his throne at that place, as dismissing the embassy; a matter worthy the noting, as it shews the boldness of Exeter, who will not be so dismiss'd.' Q fails to register this dramatic point – surprisingly, if Exeter was one of the reporters of the text: see Introduction, pp. 23, 106.

141 **our king** Gurr's interpretation, 'i.e. the king of England and of the French', heightens Exeter's boldness into insulting behaviour. More probably 'our king' and 'our delay' relate to *us*, i.e. himself and the other members of his embassy (cf. l. 75 SD).

142 **here** i.e. to the French court at Rouen

143 **is footed ... already** has already set foot (i.e. landed with his forces) in France. King Henry did not land until 14 August 1415 (by which time all negotiations were at an end). Taylor states that Exeter need not be

132 Louvre] *F, Q (Louer), F2 (Loover), Pope*   134 difference] *Q;* diff'rence *F*   136] *F; Betweene his yonger dayes Q*   140 6] *F; King.* Well for vs, you shall returne our answere backe / To our brother England. *Q*

FRENCH KING

You shall be soon dispatched with fair conditions.
A night is but small breath and little pause   145
To answer matters of this consequence.

                              [*Flourish.*] *Exeunt.*

[3.0]   *Enter* CHORUS.

CHORUS

Thus with imagined wing our swift scene flies
In motion of no less celerity
Than that of thought. Suppose that you have seen
The well-appointed King at Hampton pier

implying that the King has already
invaded under cover of negotiations,
as England possessed some territories
(notably Calais) in France. Shakespeare, however, is making free with
history for dramatic effect. Exeter,
who was present in 2.2, is at this
point supposed to have sailed with
the King at the end of that scene
and to have been dispatched on his
mission from the English camp before
Harfleur, to which he 'comes back'
(3.0.28). In *Famous Victories* (scene
xi), ll. 986–90, the returning French
ambassador tells the French King that
King Henry has threatened to be in
France before him, 'and so far as I
heare, / He hath kept promise, for
they say, he is alreadie landed / At
Kidcocks in *Normandie*, vpon the
Riuer of *Sene*, / And laid his siege to
the Garrison Towne of *Harflew*.' This
probably influenced Shakespeare's l.
143, especially as its facts derive from
Holinshed, 3.549: 'and tooke land at
Caur, commonlie called Kidcaux,
where the riuer of Saine runneth into

the sea, without resistance.'
145–6 Cf. Holinshed, 3.546 (on the
  demands made on King Henry's
  behalf by the English embassy after
  Canterbury's parliamentary speech:
  cf. 1.2.247–9n.): 'The Frenchmen
  being not a little abashed at these
  demands, thought not to make anie
  absolute answer in so weightie a cause,
  till they had further breathed.'
145 **breath** breathing-space. Cf. *R3*
  4.2.25–6: 'Give me some little breath,
  some pause, dear lord, / Before I
  positively speak in this.'
146 SD *Flourish* See note at 1.2.311 SD.
3.0 Shakespeare had announced King
  Henry's arrival in France at 2.4.143,
  but he could not forgo this picture of
  the fleet's progress to Harfleur.
1 **with imagined wing** on the wing
  of imagination. Cf. *MV* 3.4.52,
  'imagined speed', i.e. the speed of
  imagination.
2–3 **of no … thought** as swift as
  thought (proverbial: Tilley, T 240)
4 **well-appointed** well-equipped
  *Hampton F's 'Douer', whether due

145 breath] *(breathe)*   146 SD *Flourish. Exeunt.*] Dyce; *Exeunt. F*

3.0] *Pope; Actus Secundus. F*   0.1 *Enter* CHORUS] Dyce; *Flourish. Enter Chorus. F; speech not in
Q*   1 SP] *Johnson; not in F*   2   3] *verse Rowe; F lines … Thought. / … seene /*   4 Hampton]
Theobald; Douer *F*

Embark his royalty, and his brave fleet   5
With silken streamers the young Phoebus fanning.
Play with your fancies, and in them behold
Upon the hempen tackle ship-boys climbing;
Hear the shrill whistle which doth order give
To sounds confused; behold the threaden sails,   10
Borne with th'invisible and creeping wind,
Draw the huge bottoms through the furrowed sea,
Breasting the lofty surge. O do but think
You stand upon the rivage and behold
A city on th'inconstant billows dancing,   15
For so appears this fleet majestical,
Holding due course to Harfleur. Follow, follow!
Grapple your minds to sternage of this navy,

to 'the indolence of a transcriber or a compositor' (Theobald) or to 'Shakespeare's inadvertence' (Wilson), is grossly inconsistent with the many previous references to Southampton.

5 **his royalty** his royal person (*OED* royalty 1b)
  brave fine, making a gallant appearance

6 ***With ... fanning** fanning with its silken pennants the hot face of the rising sun. Rowe's emendation is supported not only by *Mac* 1.2.49–50 ('Where the Norwegian banners flout the sky / And fan our people cold') but by Williams's sarcastic remark about cooling the sun by fanning it, 4.1.197–9.

7 **Play ... fancies** indulge your imaginations

9 **whistle** i.e. the master's (*Tem* 1.1.6–7) or the boatswain's (*Per* Sc.15.114 [4.1.65])

9–10 **which ... confused** which (1) conveys orders to the sailors, (2) reveals that there is orderliness in the bustle of working the ships. The meaning is enlarged as l. 10 is added.

10 **threaden** made of thread, especially

of linen thread (*OED*). Shakespeare contrasts the apparent slightness of the sails with the weight and size of the ships that they move.

11 **Borne** carried forward (*OED* bear *v.*[1] 26)

12 **bottoms** vessels (*OED* sb. 7)
   furrowed i.e. ploughed with their keels

13 **Breasting ... surge** meeting the high swell of the sea with their bows (the first example of the verb in *OED*)

14 **rivage** shore. Shakespeare's only use of the word. Holinshed (3.557), recounting a French attack on Harfleur (after Agincourt), mentions 'the riuage and shore adioining to the towne'.

17 **Harfleur** the French port at the mouth of the Seine. 'Harflew', the invariable spelling of F and Q, indicates the pronunciation (accented on the first syllable).

18 **Grapple** fasten with grappling irons (figurative)
   sternage the sterns (a Shakespearean coinage, and the only recorded occurrence). For the omission of 'the', cf. 1.1.15.

6 fanning] *Rowe;* fayning *F*   17, 27 Harfleur] *(Harflew)*

And leave your England as dead midnight still,
Guarded with grandsires, babies and old women,   20
Either past or not arrived to pith and puissance.
For who is he, whose chin is but enriched
With one appearing hair, that will not follow
These culled and choice-drawn cavaliers to France?
Work, work your thoughts, and therein see a siege;   25
Behold the ordnance on their carriages,
With fatal mouths gaping on girded Harfleur.
Suppose th'ambassador from the French comes back,
Tells Harry that the King doth offer him
Katherine his daughter and with her, to dowry,   30
Some petty and unprofitable dukedoms.
The offer likes not; and the nimble gunner
With linstock now the devilish cannon touches,

Alarum, and chambers go off.

19 **as ... still** as quiet as midnight when nothing stirs (proverbial: Dent, M 919.1)
21 **pith and puissance** strength and power (*puissance*, two syllables)
22–3 **whose ... hair** For the humorous phrase, cf. *TC* 1.2.135–7: 'Pandarus. And she takes upon her to spy a white hair on his chin. / Cressida. Alas, poor chin! Many a wart is richer.'
24 **culled and choice-drawn** picked out and selected: like 'pith and puissance', l. 21, virtually synonymous **cavaliers** military gentlemen. The related 'cavaleros' is usually a jocular form of address in Shakespeare (used by Bottom to Cobweb in *MND*, and by the Host to Shallow and to Slender in *MW*); in *2H4* 5.3.60 Shallow uses it to mean military gentlemen like Bardolph.
25 **Work** set in action (*OED v.* 20)
26 **carriages** frames on which cannon are mounted
27 **With ... Harfleur** with their deadly open mouths turned towards encircled Harfleur. Cf. Holinshed, 3.549: 'he besieged it on euerie side'.
28 **th'ambassador ... back** the English

ambassador (Exeter, in 2.4) comes back from the French
29–31 **doth ... dukedoms** In Holinshed, 3.547, this offer is made by the French embassy, headed by the Archbishop of Bourges, which came to England when the King was known to be preparing to invade France in support of his claim (cf. 2.4n.): 'the archbishop of Burges made an eloquent and a long oration, dissuading warre, and praising peace; offering to the king of England a great summe of monie, with diuerse countries, being in verie deed but base and poore, as a dowrie with the lady Catharine in mariage, so that he would dissolue his armie, and dismisse his soldiers, which he had gathered and put in a readinesse.'
30 **to dowry** as dowry, i.e. the property that a woman brings to her husband at marriage
32 **likes not** is not pleasing **nimble gunner** 'Garrard, *Art of Warre*, 1591, p. 5, recommends the effectiveness of a "nimble discharge" ' (Walter).
33 **linstock** staff to hold the gunner's

26 ordnance] *F4*; Ordenance *F*

And down goes all before them. Still be kind,   34
And eke out our performance with your mind.   *Exit.*

[3.1]   *Alarum. [Enter Soldiers with] scaling-ladders at Harfleur.*
Enter the KING, EXETER, BEDFORD *and* GLOUCESTER.

KING
   Once more unto the breach, dear friends, once more,
   Or close the wall up with our English dead.
   In peace there's nothing so becomes a man
   As modest stillness and humility;
   But when the blast of war blows in our ears,   5
   Then imitate the action of the tiger:
   Stiffen the sinews, conjure up the blood,

lighted match
devilish Spenser devotes a whole stanza of *Faerie Queene* (1.7.13) to a simile drawn from the cannon, 'that diuelish yron Engin wrought / In deepest Hell, and framd by Furies skill'.
touches The gunner's match was applied to the touch-hole of the cannon, to ignite the gunpowder.
33 SD *Alarum* A military signal, made with either trumpets (e.g. *2H6* 5.3 [2].3) or drums (e.g. *R3* 4.4.149). The word derives from the Italian command *all'arme* (to arms). For spelling and pronunciation, cf. 4.6.35.
chambers small cannon without carriages (*OED sb.* 10b), 'being so called from the movable chamber containing the charge of powder which was let into the breech of the gun' (Wright). The SD refers to the theatre (which would have a few chambers for such military effects), not to the battlefield (where full-sized cannon were employed).
35 **eke out** supplement

3.1 Q has nothing corresponding to this scene.
0.1 F's SD, doubtless authorial, indicates that Harfleur is the location but not that its walls are to be represented or even imagined at this point. The action does not require them until the beginning of 3.3. See 34 SD and 3.2.142 SD.
1–2 **Once ... dead** The breach in Harfleur's walls has evidently been assailed at least once. The thought in ll. 1–2 is discontinuous: Johnson may be right in suggesting that an intervening line has been lost (e.g. 'And either enter in, and win the town').
1 **breach** Holinshed does not mention any breach. Wilson notes that *Gesta Henrici Quinti* 'describes the making of a breach in a bulwark specially erected to defend one of the gates and speaks of many assaults being launched upon it.'
5 **blast of war** i.e. the warlike trumpet's sound
6 **tiger** a creature proverbial for ferocity
7 ***conjure** Walter shows that this

35 eke] *(eech)*

3.1] *Hanmer*   0.1–2] *this edn; Enter the King, Exeter, Bedford, and Gloucester. / Alarum: Scaling Ladders at Harflew. F; scene not in Q*   0.1 *Enter Soldiers with*] *Theobald (subst.)*   1] *as Pope; F lines ... Breach, / ... more; /*   7 conjure] *Ard²; commune F; summon Rowe*

201

Disguise fair nature with hard-favoured rage.
Then lend the eye a terrible aspect;
Let it pry through the portage of the head   10
Like the brass cannon; let the brow o'erwhelm it
As fearfully as doth a galled rock
O'erhang and jutty his confounded base,
Swilled with the wild and wasteful ocean.
Now set the teeth and stretch the nostril wide,   15
Hold hard the breath and bend up every spirit
To his full height. On, on, you noble English,
Whose blood is fet from fathers of war-proof,

word, written 'coniure', could easily have been misread as 'comune' or 'comune' (whereas a misreading of 'summon' is unlikely), and that it is appropriate because Galenist physiological theory maintained that the blood contained the vital spirits, and because to conjure up spirits was a common expression (cf. 5.2.285–6, 'conjure [F coniure] up the spirit of love').

8 **nature** natural feeling (*OED sb.* 9e)
hard-favoured hard-featured, i.e. ugly-looking (contrasted with *fair*)

9 **aspect** appearance. *Aspect* is accented on the second syllable.

10 **portage** 'An abstract term for "portholes" (of a ship)' (Moore Smith); the word's only listed occurrence in this sense (*OED sb.*²)

11 **o'erwhelm** overhang so as to cover more or less (*OED v.* 2b: an extension peculiar to Shakespeare of the sense 'submerge completely', *OED v.* 2). Cf. *VA* 183, 'His louring brows o'erwhelming his fair sight'.

12–13 **As fearfully ... base** 'as dreadfully as the worn rock overhangs and projects beyond its ruined base' (Wilson): *galled* (gallèd)

13 **jutty** project beyond (*OED v.* 2: the only example in a transitive sense)

14 **Swilled ... ocean** washed (*OED* swill *v.* 1) by the wild and destructive sea. Some editors interpret *swilled* pri-

marily as 'greedily swallowed', citing *R3* 5.2.9, 'Swills your warm blood like wash'; but this verb, appropriate to Richard as 'boar', l. 7, is inappropriate to the ocean, which is itself liquid and is wearing away solid rock.
ocean pronounced as three syllables

16 **bend up** 'strain to the utmost' (Wilson). Cf. *Mac* 1.7.79–80, 'and bend up / Each corporal agent to this terrible feat' (*OED* bend *v.* 3: to bring into tension as with a string).

17 **his** its

17–25 **On, on ... to war** King Henry 'addresses the gentry first' (Wilson), then in ll. 25–30 the yeomen.

17 ***noble** 'F by eyeskip sets the ending of the next word. F2 normalizes the mistake' (Gurr). Taylor, who regards F2's emendation as more easily explaining F's error, says that it 'implies (characteristically) that *all* the English are noble.' But this implication is the objection to it: it involves the King in a pedantic distinction – all are noble, but some are more noble than others, and in another sense of the word. For 'noble English' in this sense of 'English nobles', cf. *KJ* 5.4.10, 'Fly, noble English, you are bought and sold.'

18 **fet** fetched, derived
of war-proof of valour tried in war (*OED* war-proof *sb.*: only example as substantive); *proof* is the proved or

15 nostril] (Nosthrill)   17 noble] *Malone;* Noblish *F;* Noblest *F2*

Fathers that like so many Alexanders
Have in these parts from morn till even fought,   20
And sheathed their swords for lack of argument.
Dishonour not your mothers; now attest
That those whom you called fathers did beget you.
Be copy now to men of grosser blood
And teach them how to war. And you, good yeomen,   25
Whose limbs were made in England, show us here
The mettle of your pasture; let us swear
That you are worth your breeding – which I doubt
    not,
For there is none of you so mean and base

tested strength of armour or arms (*OED sb.* 10)

19 **Alexanders** Alexander the Great, who sighed for more worlds to conquer

21 **argument** subject of contention (*OED* 5b), i.e. opponents with whom to fight

24 **Be copy ... blood** be an example now to men (i.e. your opponents) whose blood is less fine (not being derived from such valiant fathers). Coming after ll. 22–3 this can bear the further sense 'those French bastards'. Gurr takes 'men of grosser blood' to refer to 'the yeomen whom Henry turns to in the next line', but it is surely too uncomplimentary, and deprives 'And teach them how to war' of its contemptuous edge. Shakespeare may be drawing on King Henry's speech before Agincourt (Holinshed, 3.553): 'calling his capteins and soldiers about him, he made to them a right graue oration, moouing them to plaie the men, whereby to obteine a glorious victorie, as there was hope certeine they should, the rather if they would but remember the iust cause for which they fought, and whome they should incounter, such faint-harted people as

their ancestors had so often ouercome.'

25 **yeomen** strictly, farmer freeholders; here applied in a complimentary way to the rest of the soldiers (cf. l. 29, which admits that some of them are of very low social position)

26–8 **Whose ... breeding** a somewhat jocular metaphor from the breeding and grazing of farm animals; bulls and rams, conspicuous for strength and courage, are no doubt implied. At ll. 31–2 the simile 'like greyhounds' raises the imagery to a higher level, in lines that are probably addressed to all the soldiers.

26 **us** As again in l. 27, this seems to be the royal plural rather than referring to the aristocracy of king and nobles. With *I* (l. 28) the King relaxes into informality.

27 **The mettle ... pasture** the quality of your rearing: *OED* metal *sb.* 1f ('stuff' of which one is made), pasture *sb.* 2 (food)

28 **worth your breeding** worthy of your parentage (*OED* worth *a.* 7b; breeding *vbl. sb.* 1b). The usual Shakespearean sense of *breeding* is now superimposed on that in ll. 26–8.

29 **mean and base** of low social position (*mean* and *base* are here synonymous).

24 men] *F4; me F*   26 limbs] *(Lyms)*   27 mettle] *(mettell)*

That hath not noble lustre in your eyes.   30
I see you stand like greyhounds in the slips,
Straining upon the start. The game's afoot.
Follow your spirit, and upon this charge
Cry 'God for Harry! England and Saint George!'
                    [*Exeunt.*] *Alarum, and chambers go off.*

[3.2]   *Enter* NYM, BARDOLPH, PISTOL *and* BOY.

BARDOLPH   On, on, on, on, on, to the breach, to the
     breach!
NYM   Pray thee, Corporal, stay; the knocks are too hot,
     and for mine own part I have not a case of lives. The

The King would not at this moment use *base* in an opprobrious sense. The adjective *noble* in l. 30 gets its force from this juxtaposition. Cf. 4.3.62–3.

31 **in the slips** held in leashes ready to be loosed upon a hare. *OED* slip *sb.*[3]: 'A leash for a dog, etc., so contrived that the animal can readily be released: esp. one used for a couple of greyhounds in coursing, by which they can be let go simultaneously.'

32 **upon the start** while waiting for the hare to be dislodged from cover. Cf. *1H4* 1.3.195–6, 'O, the blood more stirs / To rouse a lion than to start a hare!'
     The game's afoot Your quarry flies before you. Cf. *1H4* 1.3.272, 'Before the game is afoot thou still lett'st slip.'

33 **Follow your spirit** let your body follow your eager spirit. Cf. 1.2.128–30.
     charge onset (*OED sb.* 18)

34 **God ... George** i.e. 'God for Harry's cause! Saint George for England's victory!' Cf. *R3* 5.5.224 [3.270], 'God and Saint George! Richmond and victory!'
     SD Oxf[1]'s interpretation (that the

soldiers leave, with their scaling-ladders, through the side door opposite to the one at which they entered) is preferable to Cam[2]'s (that they scale the balcony of the tiring-house and pull the ladders up after them) because the latter action 'always implies (in other scenes of this type) entrance into and conquest of the city' (Taylor). The military sound-effects are better placed between the *Exeunt* and the next scene than before the *Exeunt*, where Oxf[1] and Cam[2] place them.

3.2.0.1 Bardolph and his fellows enter upon an empty stage as the noise of battle subsides (for it cannot be meant to be kept up through the dialogue), thus creating a comic anti-climax.

1–2 **On ... breach** Cf. 3.1.1 and 3.1.17.

3 **knocks** Cf. 2.1.56 ('to knock you'), Nym again being the speaker

4 **a case of lives** more lives than one, a set of lives (*OED* case *sb.*[2] 7b, this figurative sense deriving from either *sb.*[2] 7, a chest with its proper contents, or *sb.*[2] 8, a pair, e.g. of pistols or rapiers)

32 Straining] *Rowe;* Straying *F*   34 Harry! England and] *Delius;* Harry, England, and *F;* Harry! England! and *Theobald*   SD *Exeunt.*] *Theobald (subst.)*

3.2] *Hanmer*   1–11] *F; Nim.* Before God here is hote seruice. / *Pist.* Tis hot indeed, blowes go and come, / Gods vassals drop and die. / *Nim.* Tis honor, and theres the humor of it. *Q*

humour of it is too hot, that is the very plain-song of 5
it.

PISTOL

The plain-song is most just, for humours do abound.
Knocks go and come, God's vassals drop and die,
            And sword and shield
            In bloody field 10
            Doth win immortal fame.

BOY   Would I were in an alehouse in London! I would
give all my fame for a pot of ale and safety.

PISTOL   And I.
            If wishes would prevail with me 15
            My purpose should not fail with me,
            But thither would I hie.

BOY   As duly –
            But not as truly –
            As bird doth sing on bough. 20

Enter FLUELLEN.

FLUELLEN [*Beats them.*]
Up to the breach, you dogs! Avaunt, you cullions!

4–5 **The humour of it** i.e. this business

5 **plain-song** simple melody, as contrasted with descant (*OED* 2): here figuratively for the plain truth

7 **The ... abound** 'You are right to call it the plain truth (that the knocks are too hot), for there are plenty of things happening.' Pistol, like Nym, uses *humours* in an imprecise sense, rather than applying its precise sense to particular things, e.g. gunpowder smoke, blood, emotions or fantastical behaviour.

8 **God's vassals** 'Pistol's bombast for "men"' (Deighton)

9–11, 15–20 Johnson and several later editors describe these lyrical lines (wrongly printed as prose in F) as fragments of song, and some direct them all to be sung. More probably they are extempore verse: the Boy's 'But not as truly' is clearly a topical interpolation into a proverbial phrase. Dyce justly remarks that Pistol is 'too dignified' to sing.

18 **duly** properly (i.e. to Pistol's cowardice)

19 **truly** honestly

20 **As ... bough** Cf. the proverbial 'as blithe as bird on bough' (Tilley B 359).

SD FLUELLEN an anglicized spelling of Llewelyn (cf. Floyd for Lloyd) that prevents incorrect pronunciation

21 **Up ... cullions** F and Q differ con-

7–11] *verse Johnson; prose F.* 12 in an alehouse] *F; not in Q* 13 fame ... safety] *F; honor for a pot of Ale Q* 14–17] *verse Johnson; prose F* 15–16 with ... with me] *F; I would not stay Q* 17 hie] *(high)* 18–20] *verse Ridley; prose F; not in Q* 20 SD] *F; Enter Fluellen and beates them in. Q; Enter Llewellyn. Cam²* 21 SD] *Q (subst.)* 21] *verse Pope; prose F; Godes plud vp to the*

PISTOL

Be merciful, great duke, to men of mould!
Abate thy rage, abate thy manly rage,
Abate thy rage, great duke!
Good bawcock, bate thy rage! Use lenity, sweet
    chuck!   25

NYM   These be good humours! Your honour runs bad
    humours!   [*Exeunt all but Boy.*]

BOY   As young as I am, I have observed these three swa-
    shers. I am boy to them all three, but all they three,

spicuously here. Several editors, including Capell, have followed Q. Oxf¹ conflates F and Q, Taylor maintaining that Q's 'Godes plud' and 'breaches' indicate an authorized revision 'with the intention of making Fluellen's first appearance funnier and more characteristic'; but the conflation is unsatisfactory, destroying the blank verse while retaining its poetical diction. Q's 'breaches' is typical of its mechanical application of plural forms to Fluellen's nouns.
Avaunt (1) go forward (Fr. *avant*), (2) be off
cullions rascals (*OED* 2); originally, testicles (*OED* 1)
22 **duke** i.e. captain (Lat. *dux*, leader: *OED*'s last example 1591)
    men of mould men made of earth, i.e. mortal men (*OED* mould *sb.*¹ 4b)
25 **bawcock** fine fellow (Fr. *beau coq*). Cf. 4.1.44.
    lenity mildness. Cf. 3.6.111.
    chuck chick; a term of endearment used seven other times by Shakespeare
26–7 ***These ... bad humours** Capell's emendation of F's 'wins' to 'runs' is supported by Nym's use elsewhere of 'humour' or 'humours' as the direct

object of 'run' (2.1.121; *MW* 1.1.153–4, 1.3.71: in this last example, 'I will run no base humour', the expression is used just as in the present speech, without any indirect object such as 'on the knight' at 2.1.121). A misreading would be easy. No satisfactory interpretation of F's 'Your honour wins bad humours' has been proposed: see Taylor's discussion. Taylor suggests that Nym is gleeful until Fluellen begins to beat him too, but if that had been the point one would expect it to be preserved in some form in Q, whereas Q transfers to Nym a portion of Pistol's speech 'Abate thy rage sweete knight, / Abate thy rage') and proceeds straight to the Boy's soliloquy. Fluellen, needless to say, does not strike the Boy, but he may strike such of the others as he can conveniently reach: cf. Q's SD at l. 20.
27 SD It is probable that Shakespeare originally brought Gower on at this point to call Fluellen back as he was driving out Pistol and the rest. See note at 53 SD.
28–9 **swashers** blustering braggarts (*OED*)
29 **boy** servant

breaches / You rascals, will you not vp to the breaches? *Q; God's plud! Up to the breaches, you dogs! Avaunt, you cullions! Oxf¹* 22–5] *verse Pope (omitting 24); prose F; Oxf¹ lines ... mould. / ... manly rage. / ... bate / ... chuck. / ; Nim. Abate thy rage sweete knight, / Abate thy rage. Q* 26 runs] *Rann (Capell);* wins F   27 SD] *Capell (subst.); Exit. F; Exit Nim, Bardolfe, Pistoll, and the Boy. Q (at 53 SD)*   28–53] *F; Boy.* Well I would I were once from them: / They would haue me as familiar / With mens pockets, as their gloues, and their / Handkerchers, they

though they would serve me, could not be man to me,   30
for indeéd three such antics do not amount to a man.
For Bardolph, he is white-livered and red-faced, by
the means whereof 'a faces it out but fights not. For
Pistol, he hath a killing tongue and a quiet sword, by
the means whereof 'a breaks words and keeps whole   35
weapons. For Nym, he hath heard that men of few
words are the best men, and therefore he scorns to say
his prayers lest 'a should be thought a coward: but his
few bad words are matched with as few good deeds, for
'a never broke any man's head but his own, and   40
that was against a post when he was drunk. They will
steal anything, and call it purchase. Bardolph stole a
lute-case, bore it twelve leagues, and sold it for three-
halfpence. Nym and Bardolph are sworn brothers in
filching, and in Calais they stole a fire-shovel. I knew   45
by that piece of service the men would carry coals.

30 **man to me** more of a man than I am
(quibbling on *man* in the sense of
'serving-man')
31 **antics** buffoons
32 **white-livered** cowardly; having no
blood in the liver, the liver being
supposed the seat of courage
red-faced literally so (cf. 2.1.84–5),
and by implication choleric in appearance. Cf. *1H4* 2.5.322–8 [4.307–13].
33 **faces it out** carries a quarrel through
with effrontery, brazens it out (*OED*
face *v.* 3b): here with a quibble on
face
35 **breaks words** exchanges (hostile)
words (*OED* break *v.* 3). The word-
play on 'breaks swords' reinforces the
satirical meaning.
35–6 **keeps whole weapons** preserves
weapons in one piece. Cf. *MW*
3.1.71–2, 'Let them keep their limbs
whole, and hack our English'. *Whole*

attaches itself to *keeps*, not to *weapons*.
36–7 **men of ... men** proverbial; cf.
2.1.80n. *Best* here means bravest,
most manly.
40 **broke ... head** gave anyone's head a
blow that made it bleed
42 **anything** i.e. however valueless
purchase plunder (*OED sb.* 8). Cf.
1H4 2.1.92.
44 **sworn brothers** Cf. 2.1.12. 'The
irony is made more apparent by a
pause after *brothers*' (Taylor).
45 **Calais** like 'Dover' in F at 3.0.4,
presumably a slip by Shakespeare, but
one that will pass in the theatre
46 **piece of service** conspicuous military
exploit (ironical). Cf. l. 116, 3.6.3.
carry coals endure insults without
retaliation (proverbial: Tilley, C 464;
and cf. *RJ* 1.1.1); here quibbling on
the literal sense

will steale any thing. / *Bardolfe* stole a Lute case, carryed it three mile, / And sold it for three
hapence. / *Nim* stole a fier shouell. / I knew by that, they meant to carry coales: / Well, if they
will not leaue me, / I meane to leaue them. *Q*   31 antics] *(Antiques)*   42 anything] *(any
thing)*   45 Calais] *(Callice)*

They would have me as familiar with men's pockets as
their gloves or their handkerchiefs, which makes much
against my manhood if I should take from another's
pocket to put into mine, for it is plain pocketing up of   50
wrongs. I must leave them and seek some better
service; their villainy goes against my weak stomach,
and therefore I must cast it up.   *Exit.*

Enter GOWER [*and* FLUELLEN, *meeting*].

GOWER   Captain Fluellen, you must come presently to

47–8 as familiar ... handkerchiefs i.e.
go into men's pockets (to pick them)
as often as their gloves or handkerchiefs do (to be kept safe)

48–9 makes ... manhood strongly
argues against (*OED* make *v.*[1] 76)
my courage (cf. 2.1.98); here with a
quibble on 'man' as contrasted with
'boy'

50–1 pocketing ... wrongs enduring
injuries without retaliation (proverbial: Tilley, I 70); quibbling on a
nonce literal sense, i.e. putting wrongfully acquired goods in my pocket

51–2 I must ... service The Boy means
this literally, but it is poignantly pro-
phetic if Shakespeare added this soliloquy after he had decided that the
Boy was to be killed while guarding
the luggage (4.4.73–6, 4.7.1–7).

52 goes ... stomach For the quibble,
cf. *AYL* 3.2.20–1 (Touchstone on the
shepherd's life), 'but as there is no
more plenty in it, it goes much against
my stomach'. The Boy's adjective
weak emphasizes the quibble on the
usual sense of 'against my stomach',
i.e. against my inclination (cf. 4.3.35,
'he which hath no stomach to this
fight').

53 cast it up (1) abandon it (*OED* cast
v. 83h), (2) vomit it up (*OED* cast *v.*
83b)

SD Enter ... meeting See 27 SDn.
Oxf[1] here begins a new scene, 3.3.

Taylor argues that as Fluellen must
be supposed to go off stage at 27 SD,
and the Boy has an *Exit* at the end
of his soliloquy, 'the stage is briefly
cleared'; 'Time may have passed, the
place may have changed.' But if
Shakespeare interpolated the Boy's
soliloquy while writing the scene it is
probable that he envisaged the time
and place continuing. It is to be noted
that Q, as well as F, has the SD *Enter
Gower* instead of one that calls for
Fluellen as well as Gower to enter.
There is no absolute necessity to clear
the stage. Gower can enter as the
Boy is leaving, look about him for
Fluellen, call out 'Captain Fluellen!'
and then, when Fluellen re-enters
(from the door at which he had earlier
made his exit), continue 'You must
come presently to the mines.' Cf. *MW*
4.2.97, where Mistress Page makes
her exit just before Mistress Ford re-
enters with the servants, the scene
obviously continuing.

SD GOWER Taylor convincingly
argues that this captain is the 'Master
Gower' of *2H4* 2.1, from 'the overlapping characters in the two plays,
this Gower's knowledge of Falstaff
and Pistol, his similar equanimity of
character, and the fact that these two
are the only two Gowers to appear in
plays before 1600'.

54 presently at once

---

48 handkerchiefs] *(*Hand-kerchers*)*   53 SD Enter ... FLUELLEN] *Theobald (Enter Gower, and
Fluellen.); Enter Gower F, Q; Re-enter Fluellen; to him Gower / Capell   meeting*] *Oxf*[1]

the mines; the Duke of Gloucester would speak with   55
you.

FLUELLEN   To the mines? Tell you the Duke it is not
so good to come to the mines; for, look you, the
mines is not according to the disciplines of the wars;
the concavities of it is not sufficient; for, look you,   60
th'athversary, you may discuss unto the Duke, look
you, is digt himself four yard under the countermines.

---

55 **mines** Cf. Holinshed, 3.550: 'And
dailie was the towne assaulted: for the
duke of Glocecester [*sic*], to whome
the order of the siege was committed,
made three mines vnder the ground,
and approching to the wals with his
engins and ordinance, would not
suffer them within to take anie rest.
For although they with their coun-
termining somwhat disappointed the
Englishmen, & came to fight with
them hand to hand within the mines,
so that they went no further forward
with that worke, yet they were so
inclosed on ech side, as well by water
as land, that succour they saw could
none come to them.'

57 **To the mines?** This repeated phrase
instantly establishes both Fluellen's
nationality (if a rising intonation is
given to *mines*) and his positiveness.

59 **disciplines ... wars** military science
*wars Fluellen uses the phrase 'the
true disciplines of the wars' at l. 72;
at ll. 131–2 and 141 he uses the phrase
'the disciplines of war'; at 4.1.68–9
he speaks of 'the true and anchient
prerogatifs and laws of the wars', and
at 4.1.73 of 'the ceremonies of the
wars'. It seems therefore that he uses
the definite article with the plural
wars and no article with the singular
war. This justifies Dyce's emendation,
particularly as the line ('is not according to the disciplines of the Warre;
the con-') is very cramped in F, and

the last letter of 'Warres' may have
been omitted to save space. Cf. l. 98n.

60 **concavities** Fluellen's characteristic
plural, for *concavity*, hollowness.
From the rest of the speech it appears
that he means the depth.

61 **athversary** adversary: Fluellen's distinctive pronunciation (cf. 3.6.92, 97).
Holinshed (3.549) uses the word, in
the plural, when describing the siege
of Harfleur (the French 'dooing what
damage they could to their
aduersaries') and on two other
occasions, but his usual word is 'enimies'. Only Fluellen uses the word in
Shakespeare's play.
discuss declare (*OED v.* 5; last
example 1632). Shakespeare's use of
it is limited to *MW* (1.3.87, 4.5.2)
and *H5* (other instances 4.1.37, 4.4.5,
29) always implying eccentricity in
the speaker.

62 **is digt ... countermines** i.e. has
dug countermines four yards under
them. Fluellen means 'has dug
himself under the mines to a depth
of four yards', but since this digging
has created countermines he
irrationally substitutes that word for
'mines' in his excitement. Q confirms
that this is the sense.
digt digged (with Welsh pronunciation). Shakespeare always uses
this form, never 'dug'.
yard yards

---

59 wars] *Dyce*; Warre *F*   62 is ... countermines] *F*; is digd / Himselfe fiue yardes vnder the
countermines *Q*; is digt himself, four yard under them, countermines *(Moore Smith)*; is digt
himself, four yard under, the countermines *Oxf¹*

By Cheshu, I think 'a will plow up all, if there is not
better directions.

GOWER   The Duke of Gloucester, to whom the order   65
of the siege is given, is altogether directed by an
Irishman, a very valiant gentleman, i'faith.

FLUELLEN   It is Captain Macmorris, is it not?

GOWER   I think it be.

FLUELLEN   By Cheshu, he is an ass, as any is in the   70
world. I will verify as much in his beard. He has no
more directions in the true disciplines of the wars,
look you, of the Roman disciplines, than is a puppy-
dog.

63 **Cheshu** Jesu
   plow up blow up
64 **directions** (with Fluellen's plural)
   management: cf. ll. 72, 80, 101. At
   this point Q's version of the scene
   ends, without marking an exit for
   Fluellen and Gower, and its version
   of 3.3 begins.
65–6 **The Duke ... given** This is from
   Holinshed; cf. 55n.
66–7 **an Irishman** Macmorris is not historical, but Holinshed (3.565–6)
   reports the arrival of 'the lord of
   Kilmaine in Ireland, with a band of
   sixteene hundred Irishmen, in maile,
   with darts and skains after the maner
   of their countrie' to assist at the siege
   of Rouen in 1418.
68 **Macmorris** For 'Mac' as a prefix
   characteristic of Irish names, see *OED*
   mack *sb.*[3] J. Le Gay Brereton, *MLR*,
   12 (1917): 350, notes a reference in
   Gabriel Harvey's letter-book to an
   unnamed author's satirical songs
   against the wild Irish, in particular
   one 'Mack Morrise', and conjectures
   that this may have been a common
   ethnic nickname.
70–1 *****as any is ... world** F's 'as in the
   world' is not characteristic either of

Shakespeare's usage elsewhere
(contrast *TC* 1.2.37–8: 'Hector's a
gallant man. / *Alexander.* As may be
in the world, lady') or of Fluellen's
(contrast 4.8.10–11). Eyeskip could
easily account for any of the errors
postulated in the recorded emendations.
71 **verify** maintain to be true
   in his beard Fluellen's version of 'to
   his face'; to beard is to oppose openly,
   to affront (*OED v.* 3)
73 **Roman disciplines** Fluellen is
   endorsing the views of the math-
   ematician Leonard Digges, whose
   Stratioticos (completed by his son
   Thomas and published 1579;
   reprinted 1590 by Richard Field,
   Shakespeare's fellow Stratfordian who
   published *VA*, 1593) commends 'the
   ancient Roman discipline for the
   wars', as Hotson (118) first showed.
   His views were reiterated by his
   grandson Dudley Digges, *Four Para-
   doxes*, 1604 (quoted in Ard[2]).
   than is than has. Cf. 3.6.9–10 ('He
   is not ... any hurt'), 4.7.147–8 and
   MW 4.1.76 (Evans, speaking of
   William Page), 'He is a good sprag
   memory.'

65–140] *F; not in Q* 67 Irishman] *(Irish / man)* 68+ SP FLUELLEN] *Rowe; Welch. F*   70 as
any is] *this edn; as F; as is Theobald; as any (Walker)*

Enter MACMORRIS *and* JAMY.

GOWER   Here 'a comes, and the Scots captain, Captain   75
Jamy, with him.

FLUELLEN   Captain Jamy is a marvellous falorous
gentleman, that is certain, and of great expedition and
knowledge in th'anchient wars, upon my particular
knowledge of his directions. By Cheshu, he will main-   80
tain his argument as well as any military man in the
world, in the disciplines of the pristine wars of the
Romans.

JAMY   I say guid day, Captain Fluellen.

FLUELLEN   God-den to your worship, good Captain   85
James.

GOWER   How now, Captain Macmorris, have you quit
the mines? Have the pioneers given o'er?

76 **Jamy** This familiar form of the fore-
name James is not a characteristic
Scottish surname, though Jamieson
is common. See l. 86n. Gurr aptly
suggests that the personal participation of James I of Scotland in
King Henry's French campaign of
1420–1 (Holinshed, 3.577, 580) led
to Shakespeare's choice of the name,
though Holinshed both times refers
only to his title ('the yoong king of
Scots'), naming him as James only
when reporting his capture at sea in
1406 (3.531–2). Alternatively, James
VI of Scotland (later James I of
England) may have been in Shakespeare's mind when naming the Scot.
77 **falorous** valorous
78 **expedition** quickness of action or wit
(*OED* 5, 5b). Fluellen's habit is to pair
together words of similar meaning
(cf. 4.7.147–8, 'Gower ... is good
knowledge and literature in the
wars'), and Wright suggests 'a
blunder between "experience" and
"erudition"', but such blunders are

not characteristic of Fluellen, whose
vocabulary is pedantic rather than
loose.
84–8 Jamy greets Fluellen, who replies,
while Gower greets Macmorris. This
exchange of courtesies postpones the
confrontation between Fluellen and
Macmorris.
84 **say** This seems to have an idiomatic
sense (not recorded in *OED*) of 'bid',
i.e. 'wish [you]'.
guid Where accepted conventions
now exist for representing Scottish
pronunciation they are followed in
this edn, the F spelling being given
in the textual footnotes.
85 **God-den** Good even (a greeting used
at any time after midday: *OED*, which
gives this and other forms under
'Good even')
86 **James** See l. 76n. Though James is a
common surname, Fluellen must be
politely (and pedantically) adapting
Jamy's name.
88 **pioneers** soldiers employed in digging trenches etc.; sappers

74 SD] F *(Enter Makmorrice, and Captaine Iamy.)*   79 ancient] *(aunchiant)*   84+ SP JAMY]
Rowe; Scot. F   84 guid day] *(gudday)*   85 God-den] *F (Godden); Good-e'en Oxf¹; Goodden
Cam²*   88 pioneers] *(Pioners)*

MACMORRIS   By Chrish, la, 'tish ill done; the work ish
          give over, the trompet sound the retreat. By my hand   90
          I swear, and my father's soul, the work ish ill done;
          it ish give over. I would have blowed up the town,
          so Chrish save me, la, in an hour. Oh, 'tish ill done,
          'tish ill done; by my hand, 'tish ill done!
FLUELLEN   Captain Macmorris, I beseech you now, will   95
          you vouchsafe me, look you, a few disputatior.s with
          you as partly touching or concerning the disciplines
          of the wars, the Roman wars, in the way of argument,
          look you, and friendly communication? Partly to satisfy
          my opinion, and partly for the satisfaction, look you,   100
          of my mind, as touching the direction of the military
          discipline, that is the point.
JAMY   It sall be vara guid, guid feith, guid captains
          baith, and I sall quit you, with guid leave, as I may
          pick occasion; that sall I, marry.   105
MACMORRIS   It is no time to discourse, so Chrish save
          me. The day is hot, and the weather, and the wars, and
          the King, and the Dukes. It is no time to discourse, the
          town is besieched, and the trumpet call us to the breach,

89 **la** an interjection used to intensify
either oaths, as here, or substitutes
for oaths, such as 'indeed'. Cf. *2H4*
2.1.156–7, where the Hostess says 'so
God saue me law' (Q) and 'in good
earnest la' (F).

93 **in an hour** in one hour more

96 **vouchsafe** grant. The other occurrences of the F spelling in Shakespeare show that this is not a dialect
form.

98 ***the wars** The immediately following
phrase 'the Roman wars', together
with the cramping of the line ('the
Warre, the Roman Warres, in the way
of Argument,') in F, justifies Collier's
emendation; cf. 59n.

99 **communication** conversation (*OED*
4)

99–101 **Partly ... mind** Fluellen's pedantic style is shown in this distinction
without a difference (cf. the synonymous 'touching or concerning', l.
97) and in the elegant variation of 'to
satisfy' and 'for the satisfaction ...
of'.

103–5 *guid* (F 'gud') occurs four times
in this short speech to display Jamy's
accent.

104 **quit ... leave** repay you (for my
pleasure in hearing you, by giving you
my own observations), with your kind
permission

109 ***besieched, and** Johnson's punctuation, taking *and* as a conjunction,
recognizes that ' 'Tis shame for us all'
(ll. 110–11) anticipates the reiteration
and amplification of the idea in ' 'tis

89+ SP MACMORRIS] *Rowe; Irish. F*   89+] la *(Law)*   96 vouchsafe] *(voutsafe)*   98 the wars]
Collier²; the Warre F   103 vara] *(vary)* guid] *(gud)*   104 baith] *(bath)* guid leave] *(gud leue)*
109 besieched, and] *Johnson (subst.); beseech'd: and F; beseech'd: an Ridley* breach] *(breech)*

and we talk, and, be Chrish, do nothing. 'Tis   110
shame for us all, so God sa' me, 'tis shame to stand
still, it is shame, by my hand; and there is throats to
be cut, and works to be done, and there ish nothing
done, so Chrish sa' me, la!

JAMY   By the mess, ere these eyes of mine take them-   115
selves to slumber I'll dae guid service, or I'll lig i'th'
grund for it. I owe God a death, and I'll pay't as
valorously as I may, that sall I surely do, that is the
breff and the long. Marry, I wad full fain heard some

shame to stand still' (ll. 111–12).
Ridley, strictly observing F's punctuation, interprets *and* as 'an' (if), an
unlikely reading in view of the nine-
fold occurrence of the conjunction
and in this exasperated speech. *Call*
(l. 109) is not subjunctive but indicative (cf. *sound*, l. 90) – which invalid-
ates a possible argument in favour of
'an'. Cam^1, Oxf^1 and Cam^2 all follow
Ridley.

113 **works** If F is correct, this must
mean 'tasks', 'pieces of work' (with
done it cannot mean 'siegeworks'). But
the compositor may have been influenced by the plural *throats* to make
work plural too, in Fluellen's manner.
To use the plural for the singular is
not characteristic of Macmorris.

115 **mess** mass

116–17 **lig i'th' grund** lie in the ground

117 **I owe God a death* In *TLS*, 29
February 1980, p. 236, this editor
pointed out that F's version of this
phrase does not connect either with
what goes before ('lig i'th' grund') or
with what follows ('and I'll pay't'),
that the proverbial phrase (Tilley, G
237) is found in *1H4* 5.1.126 and *2H4*
3.2.233, and that 'ay ow god a death'
could easily assume F's form by misreading (see Introduction, p. 102).
Taylor, to explain the misreading

process as he sees it, reads *Got* for
God; but that pronunciation is used
by stage Welsh, not Scottish, speakers, and the frequent use of *guid* (F
'gud') in Jamy's lines shows that he
pronounces the final consonant rather
emphatically than otherwise.

118 **surely** F's spelling ('suerly') possibly
indicates Jamy's pronunciation. Holinshed's usual (somewhat archaic)
spelling is 'suerlie', and this may have
caught Shakespeare's attention.

118–19 **the breff and the long** 'the long
and the short of it', i.e. my last word
on the matter (proverbial: Tilley, L
419). Shakespeare probably intended
the substitution of *breff* for the usual
'short' to characterize the speaker.

119 **wad ... heard** would very gladly
have heard. The ellipsis of 'have' in
such expressions is found in both
English and Scottish colloquial usage
in the period (Oxf^1 refers to articles
confirming this). But there are no
exactly comparable instances in
Shakespeare, and a *d/e* misreading
error is not impossible, in which case
Jamy's speech can be understood as
meaning that there will be plenty of
time for fighting even if they discuss
military matters now; he need not
have accepted Macmorris's opinion as
final.

110 nothing. 'Tis] *Capell (subst.);* nothing, tis *F*   111 all, so] *Alexander;* all: so *F*   113 works]
F (Workes); work *(this edn)*   114 Chrish] *Theobald;* Christ *F*   115 mess] *(Mes)*   116 I'll dae]
*F (*ayle de); aile do *Theobald;* I'll dee *Cam^2*   117 I owe ... death] *this edn (Craik);* ay, or goe to
death *F;* Ay owe Got a death *Oxf^1*   118 surely] *(suerly)*   119 heard] *F;* hear *Cam (Walker)*

question 'tween you twa.   120
FLUELLEN   Captain Macmorris, I think, look you,
under your correction, there is not many of your
nation –
MACMORRIS   Of my nation? What ish my nation? Ish
a villain, and a bastard, and a knave, and a rascal?   125
What ish my nation? Who talks of my nation?
FLUELLEN   Look you, if you take the matter otherwise
than is meant, Captain Macmorris, peradventure I
shall think you do not use me with that affability as
in discretion you ought to use me, look you, being as   130
good a man as yourself, both in the disciplines of
war, and in the derivation of my birth, and in other
particularities.
MACMORRIS   I do not know you so good a man as
myself. So Chrish save me, I will cut off your head.   135
GOWER   Gentlemen both, you will mistake each other.

120 **question** discussion (*OED sb.* 1)
   twa two (Scots dialect)
122 **under your correction** Fluellen
   combines 'under correction' and 'by
   your leave'
   not many i.e. (presumably) in the
   King's army
124–5 **Ish a … rascal?** i.e. 'Am I, being
   an Irishman, a villain, and a bastard,
   and a knave, and a rascal, in your
   opinion?' F's 'Ish' may be an error
   for 'Ish't ('isht' in copy) caused by the
   frequency with which the compositor
   had been setting *ish*, especially as he
   did not recognize the sentence as a
   question.
128 **Captain Macmorris** All the captains except Macmorris address each
   other by title and name (Macmorris
   uses neither).
   peradventure 'Much less common
   than *perhaps*, this may have sounded
   somewhat pedantic or affected'
   (Taylor). In Fluellen's mouth it cer-

tainly does, as in Evans's (*MW* 1.1.40,
70), but Taylor's list of Shakespeare's
characters who use it is not complete,
omitting e.g. King Henry at 4.1.161.
129–30 **you do … ought to use me**
   'you do not treat me with that affability with which, if you are wise, you
   ought to treat me'. The five syllables
   of *affability* are one of Shakespeare's
   many gifts to the actor playing Fluellen, like the six syllables of *particularities* (l. 133), where 'particulars'
   would be normal.
136 **you will mistake** you will misunderstand. Whether *you will* means
   'you are determined to' or 'you are
   going to' (the latter 'an amusing
   understatement' according to Taylor),
   it seems a doubtful reading. The
   former interpretation gives the actor
   a difficult line to speak (he will have
   to emphasize the *will*, which may
   make him sound as aggressive as
   Fluellen and Macmorris are); the

120 twa] *(tway)*   123 nation –] *Pope;* Nation. F   124–6 Ish … ²nation?] *F;* What ish my nation?
Who talks of my nation, ish a villain, and a bastard, and a knave, and a rascal. *Knight*   124 Ish]
F; Ish't *(this edn)*   125 rascal?] *Rowe;* Rascall. F   136 you will] *F;* you still *(Walker);* you *(this
edn)*

JAMY   Ah, that's a foul fault.   *A parley [is sounded]*.

GOWER   The town sounds a parley.

FLUELLEN   Captain Macmorris, when there is more
   better opportunity to be required, look you, I will be   140
   so bold as to tell you I know the disciplines of war,
   and there is an end.   [*Exeunt.*]

[3.3]   [*The* GOVERNOR *and others upon the walls.*] *Enter the*
   KING *and all his train before the gates.*

second makes him more obtuse than
his other remarks warrant. Possibly
will has been accidentally repeated
from the line above. The speech reads
like a line of blank verse: was that, or
was it not, what Shakespeare
intended?

137 SD *parley* trumpet-call, inviting the
enemy to an informal conference,
under truce, about terms of surrender
etc.

139–40 **more better** The doubled comparative, usually for emphasis, is
common in the period: Abbott 11.

140 **required** obtained (i.e. asked and
granted): Fluellen's eccentric usage

142 SD **Exeunt* Rowe's emendation of
F's *'Exit'* is justified because both F's
compositors (perhaps expanding '*Ex*'
in the copy) occasionally set *Exit* for
Exeunt (A at 3.2.27 SD, 3.2.142 SD,
3.4.56 SD, 4.1.83 SD, 4.1.226 SD; B
at 2.2.182 SD, 4.5.23 SD, 4.6.38 SD);
only three of these errors were corrected in F2 (2.2.182 SD, 3.4.56 SD,
4.1.226 SD). The implied action is as
follows. A parley is sounded off stage,
and the four captains leave the stage
(Fluellen perhaps making his exit
first, having delivered his parting
shot) on their way to the walls, which
are at this point still considered as
being off stage. 3.3 then begins with
the appearance of the French above,
the upper level now representing the
walls; when they are in position, and

the location is thus established, King
Henry and his army (including the
four captains) enter on the main stage.
Cam[1] substitutes '*They stand aside*' for
F's '*Exit*', but marks a new scene as
beginning here. Oxf[1], which continues the scene, retains F's '*Exit*' and
applies it to Fluellen alone, 'the exit
of Fluellen defusing the quarrel, and
the others joining Henry's army as it
marches on stage'. This is surely
wrong, for Fluellen would hardly be
absent at the parley, and his absence
would be conspicuous if the other
three captains remained on stage.
Cam[2] reverts to the staging implied
by F and accepted in this edn.

3.3.0.1 **The ... walls* Capell's addition.
Neither Q nor F marks an entry for
any inhabitants of Harfleur until the
end of the King's speech, when both
have the SD '*Enter Gouernour*', which
the Governor's speech may have
seemed to require. In this edn it is
supposed that F incorporated it from
Q3, and that F's '*Enter the King and
all his Traine before the Gates*' is authorial and implies in its last three words
the presence (above) of the defenders
who have just asked for a parley. (If
the Governor had begun the scene
with a speech, no doubt an authorial
SD would have marked his entry.)
Cf. *1H6* 4.2 for the staging of a parley
before the walls of a besieged town.

0.2 *train* army (cf. 4.6.0.1). Cf. *2H4*

137 Ah,] *(A,)*   SD *is sounded*] *Rowe (subst.)*   142 SD] *Rowe; Exit. F; they stand aside. Cam[1]*

3.3] *Hanmer*   0.1] *Capell (subst.)*   0.2] *F; Enter the King and his Lords alarum. Q*

KING

> How yet resolves the Governor of the town?
> This is the latest parle we will admit.
> Therefore to our best mercy give yourselves,
> Or like to men proud of destruction
> Defy us to our worst; for, as I am a soldier,   5
> A name that in my thoughts becomes me best,
> If I begin the battery once again,
> I will not leave the half-achieved Harfleur
> Till in her ashes she lie buried.
> The gates of mercy shall be all shut up,   10
> And the fleshed soldier, rough and hard of heart,
> In liberty of bloody hand shall range
> With conscience wide as hell, mowing like grass

4.1.319–20 [2.93–4], 'let our trains / March by us'. The SDs of Marlowe's *2 Tamburlaine* frequently include '*and their train*' and '*and his train*'. It can be assumed that the other lords are present with Exeter, who is addressed at l. 51: cf. Q's SD.

1–43 Holinshed has nothing corresponding to the King's speech. Q has only ll. 1–10 and 42–3.

1 **How ... town?** Though this could be an enquiry about an absent person, it is more probably a formal address to one who is present. Cf. *KJ* 2.1.481–2, 'Why answer not the double majesties / This friendly treaty of our threatened town?'

2 **latest** ultimate
we the royal plural: cf. ll. 3, 5 (*us*), 24, 54–8. Elsewhere in the speech the King uses the singular pronoun.

3 **our best mercy** our gentle mercy. Cf. 'thy soft mercy', l. 48.

4 **proud of destruction** glorying in ruin. *Destruction* is four syllables.

5 **to our worst** to do our worst

7 **battery** bombardment (*OED* 3)

8 **half-achieved** half-conquered (achievèd)

9 **Till ... buried** i.e. till the ashes of the buildings bury the ground on which they stood. The majority of domestic buildings were made with wooden frames.
buried burièd

10 **The gates ... shut up** i.e. My heart shall be impenetrable to merciful impressions. Cf. *MA* 4.1.105 (Claudio to Hero), 'for thee I'll lock up all the gates of love', and Marlowe, *1 Tamburlaine*, 5.1.53–4, 'And through the eyes and ears of Tamburlaine / Convey events of mercy to his heart.'

11 **fleshed** Cf. 2.4.50n., and (for the implied image of 'the wild dog') *2H4* 4.5.131–3 [3.259–61] and *R3* 4.3.6, 'fleshed villains, bloody dogs'.

12 **liberty ... hand** with unrestrained freedom to spill blood
range roam (*OED v.*[1] 7a)

13 **wide as hell** 'stretched wide enough to sanction hellish deeds' (Walter). Cf. also 2.2.123, 'vasty Tartar', and the traditional image, in pictorial art

2 parle we will] *F;* parley weele *Q*   7 battery] *(*batt'rie*)*   8+ Harfleur] *(*Harflew*)*   10 shall be] *F;* are *Q*   11–41] *F; not in Q*

Your fresh fair virgins and your flowering infants.
What is it then to me if impious war,   15
Arrayed in flames like to the prince of fiends,
Do with his smirched complexion all fell feats
Enlinked to waste and desolation?
What is't to me, when you yourselves are cause,
If your pure maidens fall into the hand   20
Of hot and forcing violation?
What rein can hold licentious wickedness
When down the hill he holds his fierce career?
We may as bootless spend our vain command
Upon th'enraged soldiers in their spoil   25
As send precepts to the leviathan
To come ashore. Therefore, you men of Harfleur,
Take pity of your town and of your people
Whiles yet my soldiers are in my command,

and theatrical representation, of hell as a monstrous animal head with gaping jaws.
mowing like grass i.e. cutting down in multitudes

15 **impious war** wicked war. Not *bellum impium*, i.e. civil war (Ard², Cam²), for the King is describing war's invariable nature, not discussing the political nature of this particular campaign.

16 **Arrayed** clothed
the prince of fiends Lucifer. Cf. Marlowe, *Doctor Faustus*, 1.4.66, 'How comes it then that he is prince of devils?'

17 **with ... complexion** a phrase directly related to 'impious war', but also appropriate to 'the prince of fiends' and 'the fleshed soldier'
fell feats ruthless acts

18 **Enlinked** joined like links in a chain: Shakespeare's only use of the word
waste and desolation devastation and destruction (synonymous)

desolation (five syllables)

19 **are cause** are to blame for it

21 **hot ... violation** lustful and violent rape. *Violation* is pronounced as five syllables.

22 **hold** rein in (of a horse), restrain

23 **holds ... career** maintains his furious gallop

24 **bootless** uselessly (adjective for adverb)

25 **enraged** enragèd
in their spoil once they have begun sacking the town

26–7 **As send ... ashore** Cf. Job 40:25: 'Canst thou drawe out Leuiathan with an hooke?' The biblical leviathan, an unspecified huge sea-creature, was usually identified as the whale. Cf. Shakespeare's other references to it, *TGV* 3.2.77–80 and *MND* 2.1.173 4.

26 **precepts** writs of summons (*OED sb.* 4). *Precepts* is accented on the second syllable.

28 **of** on

14 flowering] (flowring) 23 career] (Carriere) 26 7] *as Rowe; F lines ... ashore. / ... Harflew, /*

Whiles yet the cool and temperate wind of grace   30
O'erblows the filthy and contagious clouds
Of heady murder, spoil and villainy.
If not, why, in a moment look to see
The blind and bloody soldier with foul hand
Defile the locks of your shrill-shrieking daughters,   35
Your fathers taken by the silver beards,
And their most reverend heads dashed to the walls,
Your naked infants spitted upon pikes,
Whiles the mad mothers with their howls confused
Do break the clouds, as did the wives of Jewry   40
At Herod's bloody-hunting slaughtermen.
What say you? Will you yield and this avoid?
Or, guilty in defence, be thus destroyed?

31 **O'erblows** blows away (*OED v.*[1] 1)
filthy and contagious dark and full of infection. Cf. *1H4* 1.2.195, 199–200, where 'base contagious clouds' is synonymous with 'foul and ugly mists / Of vapours.'
clouds 'Suggesting specifically the smoke of cannonfire and burning cities' (Taylor), though in the figurative context they are storm-clouds.

32 ***heady** violent: cf. 1.1.34. F's error probably arose from the compositor's 'mental conflation of *heady* and *deadly*' (Taylor), and F2's from a compositor's mistaking a deletion sign for an instruction to insert a *d*.

33 **look** expect

34 **blind and bloody** indiscriminately slaughtering
foul 'literal and figurative' (Taylor)

35 **Defile ... daughters** i.e. by dragging them by the hair

38 **spitted** transfixed (as on a spit for roasting)

39 **confused** mingled discordantly together

40 **break the clouds** i.e. split the sky

with noise; also, perhaps, ascend to pitying heaven: cf. *RJ* 3.5.196–7, 'Is there no pity sitting in the clouds / That sees into the bottom of my grief?'

40–1 **as did ... slaughtermen** Herod ordered his soldiers to kill all the children in and about Bethlehem who were under two years old, in the hope that Jesus would thus be killed (Matthew 2:16–18). The mystery plays on this topic always included the mothers' lamentations, and Shakespeare, who refers to the ranting of Herod in such plays, may have these stage representations in mind.

40 **Jewry** Judaea (here Bethlehem)

41 **bloody-hunting** hunting for the children to spill their blood
slaughtermen butchers

43 **guilty in defence** 'guilty of the slaughter caused by your foolhardy persistence in a hopeless defence' (Taylor, who comments that it is 'surely intended to sound paradoxical')

32 heady] *F2* (headdy); *headly F* 35 Defile] *Rowe*[3]; Desire *F* shrill-shrieking] (shrill-shriking) 43–4 destroyed? / GOVERNOR] *Capell;* destroy'd. / *Enter Gouernour.* / *Gouer. F, Q*

GOVERNOR

Our expectation hath this day an end.
The Dauphin, whom of succours we entreated,   45
Returns us that his powers are yet not ready
To raise so great a siege. Therefore, dread King,
We yield our town and lives to thy soft mercy.
Enter our gates, dispose of us and ours,
For we no longer are defensible.   50

KING

Open your gates.   *[Exit Governor.]*

44–50 Cf. Holinshed, 3.550: having granted Harfleur a five-day truce, after which if no rescue came the town was to be yielded, 'The king neuerthelesse was after content to grant a respit vpon certeine conditions, that the capteins within might haue time to send to the French king for succour (as before ye haue heard) least he intending greater exploits, might lose time in such small matters. When this composition was agreed vpon, the lord Baqueuill was sent vnto the French king, to declare in what point the towne stood. To whome the Dolphin answered, that the kings power was not yet assembled, in such number as was conuenient to raise so great a siege. This answer being brought vnto the capteins within the towne, they rendered it vp to the king of England, after that the third daie was expired, which was on the daie of saint Maurice being the seuen and thirtith daie after the siege was first laid. The souldiors were ransomed, and the towne sacked, to the great gaine of the Englishmen.'

45 **succours** help. This was the original form of the word, from medieval Lat. *succursus* by way of Old French *socours* (cf. Fr. *secours*). By the thirteenth century this form was sometimes regarded as plural, and *succour* came into existence. Both forms persisted,

and both are used by Holinshed and by Shakespeare.

47 **raise** end, i.e. by forcing the enemy to remove (*OED v.*[1] 28)
*dread 'The Folio's *great* is probably due to dittography; repetition here weakens the adjective's force, and *dread* is more appropriate to the Henry we have just heard' (Taylor). The adjective's sense was not restricted to 'terrible' (*OED ppl. a.* 1); in the sense 'awful, revered' (*OED ppl. a.* 2) it is twice applied to the King by Canterbury, 1.2.97, 103, and frequently to Shakespeare's other rulers.

48 **thy** The second person singular pronoun is used reverentially, as though addressing God.

50 **defensible** able to defend (the town) (*OED a.* 1b). Cf. *2H4* 2.3.37–8, 'Where nothing but the sound of Hotspur's name / Did seem defensible'.

51 SD *Exit Governor* 'Open your gates' is the signal for general movement 'above', and the Governor's exit is better placed here than left till the end of the scene. Unlike the Mayor of York in a somewhat comparably staged scene (*3H6* 4.8[7].27–39), he is not shown emerging from the gates and yielding up the keys, and Taylor's suggestion that he should do so, and might be addressed by the King at ll. 57–8, is inappropriate. If the King

44 Dauphin] *(Dolphin)*   succours] *F;* succour *Q*   47 dread] *Q;* great *F*   51–8] *F; not in Q*
51 SD] *Alexander*

Come, uncle Exeter,
Go you and enter Harfleur; there remain
And fortify it strongly 'gainst the French.
Use mercy to them all. For us, dear uncle,
The winter coming on and sickness growing   55
Upon our soldiers, we will retire to Calais.
Tonight in Harfleur will we be your guest;
Tomorrow for the march are we addressed.

Flourish, and enter the town.

addressed him he would address him
by his office, and in any case that
office now belongs to Exeter.

51-6 **Come ... Calais** Cf. Holinshed,
3.550: 'All this doone, the king or-
deined capteine to the towne his vncle
the duke of Excester, who established
his lieutenant there, one sir Iohn Fastolfe, with fifteene hundred men, or
(as some haue) two thousand and
thirtie six knights. ... King Henrie,
after the winning of Harflue, determined to haue proceeded further in
the winning of other townes and for-
tresses: but bicause the dead time of
the winter approched, it was determined by aduise of his councell, that
he should in all conuenient speed
set forward, and march through the
countrie towards Calis by land, least
his returne as then homewards should
of slanderous toongs be named a
running awaie: and yet that iournie
was adiudged perillous, by reason that
the number of his people was much
minished by the flix and other feuers,
which sore vexed and brought to
death aboue fifteene hundred persons
of the armie: and this was the cause
that his returne was the sooner
appointed and concluded.' He entered
Harflue, made an offering at the
church of St Martin, and repaired the
fortifications.

52 **there remain** Shakespeare's suppression of Holinshed's reference to
Exeter's deputy Fastolfe (cf. preceding note) involves him in an incon-

sistency when Exeter continues to
take part in the campaign. Fastolfe
was unmentionable for two reasons:
(1) he was disgraced as a coward in
the French campaign of *1H6* (3.5.63–
8 [2.103–8], 4.1.9–47), (2) his name
had been adapted into Falstaff's when
the latter ceased to be Oldcastle.

54 **Use ... all** addressed still to Exeter,
not 'to the whole of the onstage army',
as Taylor speculates. In fact Harfleur
was sacked (cf. 44–50n.), though
without atrocities, and Holinshed
reports (3.550) that all the inhabitants
were expelled and the town repopu-
lated with English subjects who were
given free housing: for details see
Hibbert, 70–1.

55 **sickness** i.e. dysentery and other
fevers. Cf. 51–6n.

56 **retire** Taylor suggests that Shakespeare still had in mind the idea that
King Henry had come to Harfleur by
way of Calais (cf. 3.0.4, 3.2.45). On
the other hand, with Holinshed's 'set
forward' before him, he may have
meant 'fall back upon Calais' (the port
being English territory at the time)
rather than 'retrace our route back to
Calais'.

58 **Tomorrow** Shakespeare thus begins
to create the sense of urgency required
for the march to Calais. In fact (cf.
51–6n.) the King did not leave Harfleur, which yielded on 22 September,
till 7 October.

addressed prepared (*OED v.* 3)

54 all. For] *Pope;* all for *F*   uncle,] *Pope;* Vnckle. *F*   56 Calais] *(Calis)*

[3.4]   *Enter* KATHERINE *and* [ALICE,] *an old Gentlewoman.*

KATHERINE   *Alice, tu as été en Angleterre, et tu bien parles le langage.*

ALICE   *Un peu, madame.*

KATHERINE   *Je te prie m'enseigner; il faut que j'apprenne à parler. Comment appelez-vous la main en anglais?*   5

ALICE   *La main, elle est appelée* de hand.

KATHERINE   De hand. *Et les doigts?*

ALICE   *Les doigts? Ma foi, j'oublie les doigts, mais je me*

3.4.0.1 KATHERINE Born 27 October 1401, she was just short of fifteen years old at the time of Agincourt. Though she twice addresses Alice by name, Katherine is not identified in the dialogue except as Alice's social superior. The recent mention (3.0.29–31) of the marriage offer would help spectators to identify her, particularly if they had heard the epilogue of *2H4* where her appearance was promised. She may have worn a coronet to make her identity clear.

an old Gentlewoman By the final scene, where King Henry addresses Alice as 'fair one' (5.2.118), Shakespeare may have decided that Alice should not be old. In the present scene he may have intended Alice's visit to England to have taken place some time ago, so that her English is now rusty.

1–56 The French is translated in the footnotes, keeping as close as possible to the original and to Shakespeare's English usage as reflected in it.

1–6 'Alice, you have been in England, and you speak the language well.' 'A little, my lady.' 'I pray you to teach me; I must learn to speak [it]. What do you call the hand in English?' 'The hand, it is called *de hand*.'

1–2 *bien parles* F's word-order is consistent with contemporary usage. C. F. de Vaugelas, *Remarques sur la langue françoise*, 1647, p. 461, states that provided the adverb is close to the verb it can be either before or behind it (Z. P. Zaddy, privately).

4 **Je ... m'enseigner* F's reading, interpreted by Capell (who added a comma after *prie*) and by later editors as an imperative plural, is a compositor's error (*z* for *r*, easy in secretary hand) for an infinitive. The omission of *de* is consistent with sixteenth-century usage. Cf. 4.4.40–1, '*je vous supplie ... me pardonner*' (Z. P. Zaddy, privately). Every occurrence of *pray* (1.2.9; 4.8.65; 5.0.3) is similarly followed by an infinitive.

4–5 *il faut ... parler* Shakespeare is preparing for the courtship dialogue in 5.2.

7–14 '*De hand*. And the fingers?' 'The fingers? [By] my faith, I forget the fingers, but I shall remember. The fingers, I think they are called *de fingres*; yes, *de fingres*.' 'The hand, *de hand*; the fingers, *de fingres*. I think I am a good pupil. I have acquired two words of English quickly. What do you call the nails?' 'The nails, we call them *de nails*.'

3.4] *Capell*   0.1] *F; Enter* Katherine, Allice. *Q*   1–2 *bien parles*] *F* (*bien parlas*); *parlois bien F2; parte fort bon Q*   2 *le langage*] *F* (*le Language*); Angloys *Q*   3 *Un*] *Rowe; En F*   4 *prie m'enseigner*] *F2; prie m'ensigniez F; prie de m'enseigner / Pope; prie, m'enseignez / Capell*   *j'apprenne*] *F2* (*ie apprene*); *ie apprend F*   5 *parler*] *F2; parlen F*   *Comment*] *F2; Comient F*   *appelez-vous*] (*appelle vous*)   7 *Et*] *Theobald; Alice. E F*   8 SP ALICE] *Theobald; Kat. F*   *les doigts*] *F2* (*le doyt*); *e doyt F*

souviendrai. Les doigts, je pense qu'ils sont appelés de
fingres; *oui,* de fingres.　　　　　　　　　　　　　　10

KATHERINE　*La main,* de hand; *les doigts,* de fingres. *Je
pense que je suis le bon écolier. J'ai gagné deux mots
d'anglais vitement. Comment appelez-vous les ongles?*

ALICE　*Les ongles, nous les appelons* de nails.

KATHERINE　De nails. *Écoutez; dites-moi si je parle bien:*　15
de hand, de fingres, *et* de nails.

ALICE　*C'est bien dit, madame; il est fort bon anglais.*

KATHERINE　*Dites-moi l'anglais pour le bras.*

ALICE　De arm, *madame.*

KATHERINE　*Et le coude?*　　　　　　　　　　　　　20

ALICE　D'elbow.

KATHERINE　D'elbow. *Je m'en fais la répétition de tous
les mots que vous m'avez appris dès à présent.*

ALICE　*Il est trop difficile, madame, comme je pense.*

KATHERINE　*Excusez-moi, Alice. Écoutez:* d'hand, de　25
fingres, de nails, de arm, de bilbow.

---

14 **nails** Actors often give the word a
French pronunciation by treating the
ai as two consecutive French vowels
(naïls, as in naïve), which is amusing,
though the text gives no warrant for
it. The second *e* in F's '*Maylees*' (l.
40) is merely a compositor's error. F's
spelling elsewhere, '*Nayles*', is usual:
cf. F's spelling at 4.4.71.

15–21 '*De nails.* Listen; tell me if I speak
well [i.e. pronounce correctly]: *de
hand, de fingres,* and *de nails.*' 'That is
well said, my lady; it is very good
English.' 'Tell me the English for the
arm.' '*De arm,* my lady.' 'And the
elbow?' '*D'elbow.*'

19 **arm** Q has 'arma' throughout its
version of the scene. F has '*Arme*',
except at l. 26 where it has '*Arma*'
(corrected to '*Arme*' in F2), which

Oxf[1] takes as confirmation of the Q
reading, but which may have been
introduced accidentally (cf. l. 45,
'*roba*' for '*robe*'). It is not this word
but the next one that Katherine pronounces incorrectly.

22–33 '*D'elbow.* I am going to repeat all
the words that you have taught me
up to the present.' 'It is too difficult,
my lady, as I think.' 'Pardon me,
Alice. Listen: *d'hand, de fingres, de
nails, de arm, de bilbow.*' '*D'elbow*, my
lady.' 'O Lord God, I am forgetting!
D'elbow. What do you call the neck?'
'*De nick,* my lady.' '*De nick.* And the
chin?' '*De chin.*' '*De sin.* The neck, *de
nick.* The chin, *de sin.*'

25 *Excusez-moi* i.e. No, you are wrong

26 ***fingres** F's '*Fingre*' must be a compositor's error, though one that is

---

9 *souviendrai*] F2 *(souviendray); souemeray* F　*sont*] Capell; *ont* F　10 *oui*] Rowe; *ou* F　11 SP
KATHERINE] Theobald; *Alice* F　de fingres] Capell *(*de fingers); *le Fingres* F　12 *le bon écolier.
J'ai*] Theobald *(subst.); le bon escholier. / Kath. I'ay* F; *la bonne écolière. J'ai* Oxf[1]　*gagné*]
(gaynie)　13 *les*] F2; *le* F　14 *Les*] F2; *Le* F　*nous les*] Cam; *les* F　nails] F *(Nayles);* naïlès
Cam[1]　15, 25 *Écoutez*] *(escoute)*　19, 42, 53 arm] F *(Arme);* arma Q　20 *le coude*] F2; *de coudee*
F　22 *répétition*] F2; *repiticio* F　23 *appris*] Steevens; *apprins* F　26, 40, 53 fingres] Cam; *Fingre*
F　26 arm] F2 *(Arme); Arma* F; arma Q

ALICE   D'elbow, *madame.*

KATHERINE   *O Seigneur Dieu, je m'en oublie!* D'elbow.
Comment appelez-vous le col?

ALICE   De nick, *madame.*   30

KATHERINE   De nick. *Et le menton?*

ALICE   De chin.

KATHERINE   De sin. *Le col,* de nick; *le menton,* de sin.

ALICE   *Oui. Sauf votre honneur, en vérité, vous prononcez
les mots aussi droit que les natifs d'Angleterre.*   35

KATHERINE   *Je ne doute point d'apprendre, par la grâce
de Dieu, et en peu de temps.*

ALICE   *N'avez-vous déjà oublié ce que je vous ai enseigné?*

KATHERINE   *Non, je le réciterai à vous promptement:*
d'hand, de fingres, de mails, –   40

persisted in (ll. 40, 53).

bilbow The mispronunciation produces an English word, *bilbo,* meaning (1) a sword (originally a sword made in Bilbao, Spain), (2) an iron bar equipped with two sliding fetters for a prisoner's ankles (hence usually plural, *bilboes*). The word occurs in both senses in Shakespeare: *MW* 1.1.148, 3.5.92 (sense 1), *Ham* 5.2.6 (sense 2, plural).

30 **nick** It is arguable that Alice should pronounce *neck* correctly, since she can pronounce *chin*, and since she flatteringly praises Katherine's mispronunciation of both words; but Shakespeare may have wished to indicate a French accent (cf. *fingres*). F2 corrects both speakers' pronunciation to *neck,* and Q invariably gives the word as *neck. Nick* and *sin* (l. 33) are English words, like *bilbo* (l. 26). Oxf[1]'s use of *OED* to support alleged wordplay on *nick* is unconvincing: *sb.*[1] 1b (1562 quotation) means an anal fissure, not the vulva, and *sb.*[1] 5 means not simply 'pun' but any verbal correspondence (the sense being derived

from the corresponding notches on a pair of tallies).

34–45 'Yes. Saving your reverence, in truth, you pronounce the words as right as the natives of England.' 'I have no doubt at all that I shall learn [English], by the grace of God, and in little time.' 'Have you not already forgotten what I have taught you?' 'No, I shall repeat it to you promptly: *d'hand, de fingres, de mails –*' '*De nails,* my lady.' '*De nails, de arm, de ilbow –*' 'Saving your reverence, *d'elbow.*' 'So I say, *d'elbow – de nick,* and *de sin.* What do you call the foot and the gown?'

38 **N'avez-vous* Oxf[1] retains F's *y,* interpreting it as *there,* 'often used idiomatically, especially in questions', but producing no instances of sixteenth-century or modern use.

39 **Non, je le* This edn's emendation assumes that F's '*Nome ie*' resulted from the misreading of '*Non ie le*' in the copy. This emendation provides *réciterai* with the direct object *le,* i.e. what Alice has already taught Katherine.

30+ nick] *F (Nick); Neck F2;* neck *Q*   38 N'avez-vous] *Riv (subst.); N'aue vos y F; N'avez vous pas F2; déjà] Theobald; desia F*   39 Non, je le] *this edn; Nome ie F; Nomme, ie F2; Non, je Rowe; Non, et je Oxf[1]; Nenni, je (Oxf[1])*   40 mails] *Capell; Maylees F;* mailès *Cam[1]*

ALICE   De nails, *madame.*

KATHERINE   De nails, de arm, de ilbow –

ALICE   *Sauf votre honneur,* d'elbow.

KATHERINE   *Ainsi dis-je,* d'elbow – de nick, *et* de sin.
Comment appelez-vous le pied et la robe?   45

ALICE   De foot, *madame, et* de coun.

KATHERINE   De foot, *et* de coun? *O Seigneur Dieu, ils sont
les mots de son mauvais, corruptible, gros, et impudique,
et non pour les dames d'honneur d'user. Je ne voudrais
prononcer ces mots devant les seigneurs de France*   50
pour tout le monde. Foh! De foot *et* de coun! *Néanmoins, je réciterai une autre fois ma leçon ensemble:*
d'hand, de fingres, de nails, d'arm, d'elbow, de nick,
de sin, de foot, de coun.

ALICE   *Excellent, madame!*   55

KATHERINE   *C'est assez pour une fois. Allons-nous à dîner.*

                                        Exeunt.

---

43 *honneur For F's misreading *honeus*, confusing *r* and terminal *s*, cf. 5.2.188 (F *melieus*) and 251 (F *grandeus*): Oxf[1] adds examples from *Ham.*

45 *le pied* Though F2 turns F's *les pied* into *les pieds*, a too obvious (mis-) correction, Alice's translation and Katherine's objection to the word require the singular form. Oxf[1], accepting F2's reading and comparing *'les main'* at 4.4.57, supposes that Alice mistranslates.

46–56 '*De foot*, my lady, and *de coun*.' '*De foot*, and *de coun*? O Lord God, they are words of evil sound, corrupting, gross, and immodest, and not for ladies of honour to use. I would not pronounce these words before the lords of France for all the world. Fie! *De foot* and *de coun*! None the less, I shall repeat, one other time, my lesson all together: *d'hand, de fingres, de nails,* *d'arm, d'elbow, de nick, de sin, de foot, de coun.*' 'Excellent, my lady.' 'That is enough for one time. Let us go to dinner.'

46 *coun F's spelling *Count* may have originated in Shakespeare's (or the compositor's) wish to make the joke clear to English audiences (or readers) more familiar with the English word *cunt* than with the French word *con*. That Alice adds a final *t* is improbable. (The English vulgar pronunciation of 'gown' as 'gownd' is not recorded before the eighteenth century.) Q, in which the word also occurs four times, always spells it 'con'.

47 **foot** Katherine's comments imply the word's resemblance to Fr. *foutre* (to fuck), used dismissively as a noun ('a foutre') by Pistol in *2H4* 5.3.100, 116.

---

43 *Sauf*] *Rowe; Sans* F; *Sar* F4   *honneur*] F2; *honeus* F   44 *dis-je*] F2; *de ie* F   45 *le pied*] Q (*le peid); les pied* F; *les pieds* F2   *la robe*] Q (*le robe); de roba* F   46+ De ... de ...] *Capell; Le ... le ...* F   46+ coun] *Cam; Count* F; con Q; *cown* Oxf[1]   47 *ils*] Cam[1]; *il* F; *ce* F2   51–2 *Néanmoins*] F2 (*neant moins); neant moys* F   56.1 *Exeunt.*] F2; *Exit.* F; *Exit omnes.* Q

[3.5] *Enter the* KING *of France, the* DAUPHIN, *[the* Duke of BRITAIN,] *the* CONSTABLE *of France and others.*

FRENCH KING
'Tis certain he hath passed the river Somme.
CONSTABLE
An if he be not fought withal, my lord,
Let us not live in France; let us quit all
And give our vineyards to a barbarous people.
DAUPHIN
O Dieu vivant! Shall a few sprays of us, 5
The emptying of our fathers' luxury,
Our scions, put in wild and savage stock,
Spirt up so suddenly into the clouds

3.5.0.1 DAUPHIN 'The Dauphin was probably not present, but Shakespeare follows Hall and Holinshed in mistaking Louis King of Sicily, Charles VI's cousin, for the Dauphin' (Bullough, 4.360). Cf. ll. 1–4n.
0.2 BRITAIN See 1–4n. and 2.4.0.1–2n.
1–4 Cf. Holinshed, 3.552: 'The French king being at Rone, and hearing that king Henrie was passed the riuer of Some, was much displeased therewith, and assembling his councell to the number of fiue and thirtie, asked their aduise what was to be doone. There was amongst these fiue and thirtie, his sonne the Dolphin, calling himself king of Sicill; the dukes of Berrie and Britaine, the earle of Pontieu the kings yoongest sonne, and other high estates. At length thirtie of them agreed, that the Englishmen should not depart vnfought withall, and fiue were of a contrarie opinion, but the greater number ruled the matter: and so Montioy king at armes was sent to the king of England to defie him as the enimie of France, and to tell him that he should shortlie

haue battell.'
1 **passed … Somme** i.e. on his march towards Calais (cf. 3.3.51–6). The Somme lies a little over halfway between Harfleur and Calais. The ensuing dialogue (1–49) represents the march as a conquering progress, rather than a tactical withdrawal, after the capture of Harfleur.
2 *An if if. F's ambiguous 'And' is probably equivalent to *An* (= if) rather than a conjunction. Cf. 2.4.120 and n.
5 *O Dieu vivant* O living God
sprays shoots. Cf. l. 7, *scions*.
6 **The … luxury** the seed emptied out by our ancestors (i.e. the Norman invaders of England in 1066) in their lechery
7 **scions** shoots used for grafting. Cf. l. 5, *sprays*.
put … stock Grafting, e.g. of roses, usually consists in inserting a shoot of a cultivated shrub into the rooted stem of a wild (*wild and savage*) one. Cf. *WT* 4.4.92–3, 'we marry / A gentler scion to the wildest stock'.
8 **Spirt** sprout

3.5] *Capell* 0.1–2] *F; Enter King of* France *Lord Constable, the Dolphin, and* Burbon. *Q* 0.1+ DAUPHIN] *(Dolphin)* 0.1 the Duke of BRITAIN] *Cam¹* 2–4] *F; not in Q* 2 An] *this edn (anon. in Cam);* And *F* 7–8] *F; not in Q* 7 scions] *(Svens)*

And overlook their grafters?

BRITAIN

Normans, but bastard Normans, Norman bastards!   10
Mort de ma vie, if they march along
Unfought withal, but I will sell my dukedom
To buy a slobbery and a dirty farm
In that nook-shotten isle of Albion.

CONSTABLE

Dieu de batailles, where have they this mettle?   15
Is not their climate foggy, raw and dull,
On whom, as in despite, the sun looks pale,
Killing their fruit with frowns? Can sodden water,

9 **overlook** overtop, rise above (*OED v.* 1b)

grafters '(a) those who have done the grafting (b) original trees from which the shoot for grafting was taken' (Taylor). The latter sense completes the metaphor, but the former sense is present too, with an implication of retribution.

10 **but** no more than

11 ***Mort de ma vie*** 'Death of my life' (a common French oath). Taylor notes that since the compositor correctly set *Dieu* in l. 5 and three times in 3.4 it is unlikely that he would substitute *du* if *Dieu* stood in the copy. Q's 'mor du' here (in an unfinished phrase) corresponds in its use of *du* for *de* to its equivalent of 3.4.25–6 ('du cin', i.e. 'de sin', anticipated from 3.4.33) and to its equivalent of 4.5.3 ('Mor du ma vie'). In its equivalent of l. 5 it replaces *O Dieu vivant* with 'Mordeu ma via'.

vie pronounced as two syllables

12 **Unfought withal** This is from Holinshed: cf. 1–4n.

but I will sell if I will not (dependent on the oath, i.e. Let me die if I do not)

13 **a ... and a** For the repetition of the indefinite article with the second adjective, cf. 4.1.196 ('a poor and a

private displeasure') and 4.3.86 ('a peaceful and a sweet retire').

slobbery disagreeably wet, slimy or dirty (*OED*): 'slobber' is mud or slime. The first of many derogatory references by the French to the English climate.

14 **nook-shotten** 'running out into corners or angles' (*OED*: examples show that it was applied to any irregular shape), i.e. misshapen

Albion the island composed of England, Scotland and Wales, so called from its white cliffs fronting the Channel ·

15 *Dieu de batailles* 'God of battles' (*batailles* is three syllables)

where whence

mettle ardent or spirited temperament (*OED sb.* 3); so too at l. 29.

16 **raw** combining cold and damp

17 **On whom** The antecedent is *they*, l. 15.

as in despite as if with ill-will (*OED sb.* 4). Comparable expressions in Shakespeare refer to the moon (*MND* 2.1.104, 'Pale in her anger'; *R2* 2.4.10, 'The pale-faced moon looks bloody on the earth'). The sun is here pictured as appearing moonlike through the mists.

18 **sodden** boiled

10 SP BRITAIN] *F (Brit.); Bur. Q* 11 *Mort ... vie*] *F2; Mort du ma vie F;* mor du *Q;* Mort Dieu! ma vie! *Cam¹ (Greg)* 13 slobbery] *(slobbry)*

A drench for sur-reined jades, their barley-broth,
Decoct their cold blood to such valiant heat?   20
And shall our quick blood, spirited with wine,
Seem frosty? O, for honour of our land,
Let us not hang like roping icicles
Upon our houses' thatch, whiles a more frosty people
Sweat drops of gallant youth in our rich fields!   25
Poor we may call them in their native lords.

DAUPHIN
By faith and honour,
Our madams mock at us and plainly say

19 **drench** medicinal draught, especially
for horses (cf. *1H4* 2.4.107–8, 'Give
my roan horse a drench'), usually of
bran or malt mixed with hot water
and called a mash
   sur-reined overridden, overworked
(*OED*: probably from 'sur', over, and
'reined' *ppl. a.*). It may be a Shakespearean coinage, being *OED*'s first
example, and *OED*'s only other one,
by Marston (*Jack Drum's Enter-
tainment*, 1601), 'A surreinde Iaded
wit, but a rubbes on', may derive
from it.
   jades horses (derogatory)
   barley-broth strong ale (*OED* barley,
B,2 (special combinations): first
example 1593). Here contemptuous,
though not in the 1593 example.
20 **Decoct** boil up (*OED v.* 3b)
21 **quick** full of life (contrasted with
cold, l. 20)
   spirited made more lively (*OED*
spirit *v.* 1: first example)
22 **for honour** Cf. 1.1.15, 'to relief'.
23 **roping** hanging down like ropes.
Probably an echo of Golding's Ovid,
1.137, 'Then isycles hung roping
down.' Cf. 'down-roping', 4.2.47.
24 **houses' thatch** The presence of both
these words makes the line a hexameter, unusual in a pentameter
context. Either word would suffice for

the sense, and Shakespeare may have
substituted one for the other and
failed to cancel the original word.
Nevertheless, Q's corrupt reading
'houses tops' shows that *houses' thatch*
was still in the text as performed in
the theatre.
25 **Sweat ... fields** 'be gallantly ready
to shed their youthful blood to
manure our already fertile fields'
26 **Poor ... lords** 'Rather should we call
them poor because they have bred
such poor-spirited masters' (Walter)
   *we may F has evidently omitted
something, and F2's emendation is
satisfactory; F's omission can be explained as due to the attraction of the
verb *call* to the pronoun *we*.
27 **By faith and honour** Shakespeare
nowhere else has *by faith*, though he
frequently has *by my faith*, including
3.7.110, where the speaker, as here, is
a Frenchman. There appears to be no
metrical reason for the absence of *my*
from this half-line, and eyeskip from
by to *my* could easily have caused its
omission. Alternatively the asseveration may have been 'My faith and
honour' (cf. '*Ma foi*', 3.4.8), which
would be stronger rhythmically.
28 **madams** ladies, i.e. wives (cf.
'bastard warriors', l. 31)

23 icicles] *(Isyckles)*   24 houses' thatch] *F;* houses tops *Q*   25–60 in our ... ransom] *F; not in
Q*   26 Poor we may] *F2;* Poore we *F;* Poor may we *Keightley;* Poor must we *(Cam¹);* Lest poor
we *Humphreys*   27 By faith] *F;* My faith *(this edn)*

Our mettle is bred out, and they will give
Their bodies to the lust of English youth,   30
To new-store France with bastard warriors.
BRITAIN
They bid us to the English dancing-schools
And teach lavoltas high and swift corantos,
Saying our grace is only in our heels,
And that we are most lofty runaways.   35
FRENCH KING
Where is Montjoy the herald? Speed him hence:
Let him greet England with our sharp defiance.
Up, princes, and with spirit of honour edged
More sharper than your swords hie to the field.
Charles Delabreth, High Constable of France,   40

29 **bred out** exhausted, degenerated (*OED* breed *v.* III, recording no other examples than this and *Tim* 1.1.254–5, 'The strain of man's bred out / Into baboon and monkey')

32–5 **They ... runaways** This passage can be read either as partly direct speech and partly reported speech (so Oxf[1]) or as reported speech throughout (so this edn), when the verb *go* is to be understood after *bid*: cf. *Cor* 4.2.1, 'Bid them all home.' At 4.1.27 'Desire them all to my pavilion' similarly implies the verb of motion.

33 **lavoltas ... corantos** The *lavolta* (Ital. *la volta*, the turn) was a dance in 3/4 time consisting of a body-turn in two steps followed by a high leap. The *coranto* (Ital. *coranta*, from Fr. *courante*, running) was a dance in 2/4 time with a rapid running step. The point of the sarcasm is the reference to turning and running.

34 **grace** (1) accomplishment, (2) attractiveness
heels (1) kicked up in dancing, (2) shown in running away

35 **most lofty runaways** pre-eminent in running away

36–7 **Where ... defiance** From Holinshed: cf. 1–4n.

37 **England** the King of England
sharp fierce

38 **Up, princes** Shakespeare cannot have expected all these nobles to be present in this scene. It is a case of the audience's having to piece out imperfections with thoughts.

38–9 **with ... swords** 'with honourable courage sharper-edged than your swords'. For the double comparative, cf. 'more better', 3.2.139–40.

40–5 **Charles ... Charolais** Most of these names are taken from Holinshed's list of the principal nobles who were killed at Agincourt (Holinshed, 3.555: cf. 4.8.81–101n.), and are given in almost the same order. The exceptions are Berry (see 1–4n.), Burgundy (mentioned by Holinshed as being brother to two of the slain nobles, and also, in Holinshed's account of the present incident, as forbidding his son Philip Earl of Charolais to take part in the battle) and Charolais. These three may have been included for metrical reasons.

40 **Delabreth** F's spelling, no doubt Shakespeare's, is from Holinshed, who refers to the Constable as

32 SP] *F (Brit.); Bour. Theobald*   32–3 to ... corantos] *F; 'To ... corantos' Steevens[2]*
33 corantos] *(Carranto's)*   39 hie] *(high)*   40 Delabreth] *F; De-la-bret Capell*

You Dukes of Orleans, Bourbon and of Berry,
Alençon, Brabant, Bar and Burgundy,
Jaques Chatillon, Rambures, Vaudemont,
Beaumont, Grandpré, Roussi and Fauconbridge,
Foix, Lestrelles, Boucicault and Charolais,   45
High dukes, great princes, barons, lords and knights,
For your great seats now quit you of great shames.
Bar Harry England, that sweeps through our land
With pennons painted in the blood of Harfleur.
Rush on his host as doth the melted snow   50
Upon the valleys, whose low vassal seat

'Charles lord de la Breth high constable of France' (3.555). The modern French form is d'Albret (variant d'Alberet).

41 **Bourbon** John, Duke of Bourbon, was the maternal uncle of the French King. Theobald substituted him for 'Britaine' in the opening SD and in 10 SP and 32 SP, probably because he appears in Q and because the French King addresses him and others here. At 2.4.0.1 Theobald had substituted Burgundy for F's 'Berry and Britaine'.

42 **Alençon** F spells 'Alanson', as in Holinshed (stressed on second syllable)

43 **Jaques ... Vaudemont** *Jaques* (so spelled by Holinshed and also elsewhere by Shakespeare, e.g. *AYL*) was undoubtedly meant to be spoken as two syllables with English pronunciation (Jay-quees), and *Chatillon* as three syllables (pronounced Shatillion). *Rambures* is probably, as at 4.8.95, accented on the second syllable; if it were transposed with *Vaudemont* (trisyllabic and accented on the first syllable) the metre would be improved.

44 **Fauconbridge** Holinshed spells this

name (modern Fr. Fauquembergues) indifferently 'Fauconbridge' and 'Fauconberge' (3.554, 555); in F it is spelled 'Faulconbridge' here and 'Fauconbridge' at 4.8.100.

45 *Foix Capell's normalization of Holinshed's 'Fois' (3.555), misprinted in F as 'Loys'
Lestrelles Oxf[1]'s emendation of F's 'Lestrale', which is nearer to the name than Holinshed's 'Lestrake' (3.555), though it may have arisen from a misreading of copy if Shakespeare followed Holinshed's spelling

47 **For ... seats** for the sake of your great estates (i.e. those from which you derive your noble titles)
quit you rid yourselves

48 **Bar** set a barrier before, i.e. prevent him in his progress (*OED v.* 4)

49 **pennons** long narrow flags, pointed at the end, attached to the heads of lances

50 **host** army

51 **vassal seat** subjected situation (*OED* seat *sb.* 18: cf. *Mac* 1.6.1). A vassal is one who is subject to his feudal overlord. Cf. *TC* 1.2.2–3, 'Up to the eastern tower, / Whose height commands as subject all the vale.'

41 Orleans] *(Orleance)* Bourbon] *(Burbon)* 42 Alençon] *(Alanson)* Burgundy] *(Burgonie)* 43 Jaques] *F (Iaques);* Jacques *Cam[2]* Chatillon] *(Chattillion)* Vaudemont] *F2; Vandemont F* 44 Beaumont] *(Beumont)* Grandpré] *(Grand Pree)* Fauconbridge] *F (Faulconbridge);* Fauconberg / *Capell* 45 Foix] *Capell; Loys F* Lestrelles] *Oxf[1];* Lestrale *F;* Lestrake *Cam[1]* Boucicault] *(Bouciquall)* Charolais] *(Charaloyes)* 46 knights] *Pope[2] (Theobald 1726);* Kings *F* 49 pennons] *(*Penons*)* Harfleur] *(*Harflew*)*

The Alps doth spit and void his rheum upon.
Go down upon him, you have power enough,
And in a captive chariot into Rouen
Bring him our prisoner.
CONSTABLE   This becomes the great.   55
Sorry am I his numbers are so few,
His soldiers sick and famished in their march,
For I am sure when he shall see our army
He'll drop his heart into the sink of fear
And for achievement offer us his ransom.   60
FRENCH KING
Therefore, Lord Constable, haste on Montjoy,
And let him say to England that we send
To know what willing ransom he will give. –
Prince Dauphin, you shall stay with us in Rouen.

52 **The Alps ... upon** i.e. in snow-slips.
As Steevens first pointed out, the
metaphor originated in a line of verse
by the Latin poet Furius Bibaculus,
'Iuppiter hibernas cana niue conspuit
Alpes' ('Jupiter spits upon the wintry
Alps with white snow'), which Horace
parodied by substituting 'Furius' for
'Iuppiter' (*Satires*, 2.5, 41). Shakespeare, who presumably knew the line
in Horace's version, adapts it to his
own context. For *void his rheum*
(discharge his phlegm), cf. *MV*
1.3.116, 'You, that did void your
rheum upon my beard'. Elsewhere in
Shakespeare the Alps are plural (*KJ*
1.1.202, *R2* 1.1.64, *AC* 1.4.66).

54 **captive chariot** chariot devised for
parading a captive enemy. (If the
words had been accidentally transposed, as has sometimes been suggested, *our prisoner*, l. 55, would be
superfluous.) Holinshed, 3.553, mentions this chariot when reporting the
vainglorious behaviour of the French
immediately before the battle of Agincourt: 'The noble men had deuised a
chariot, wherein they might tri-

umphantlie conueie the king captiue
to the citie of Paris' (not, as here, to
Rouen).
Rouen See preceding note. The F
spelling 'Roan', here and at l. 64 (cf.
Q, '*Rone*'), indicates the pronunciation and the monosyllabic
metrical value of the name.

55 **This ... great** This kingly resolution
befits your greatness.

59 **sink** cesspit (*OED sb.* 1a); in the
context suggesting a military latrine

60 **for achievement** for a finish, to
bring the matter to an end (*OED sb.*
1, not necessarily implying successful
completion of an action: cf. Fr.
achèvement). A more natural sense
than 'instead of achieving a victory
over us' (Malone), 'before we capture
him' (Staunton, emending to *and,
'fore achievement*: followed by Oxf[1]),
or 'by way of, or instead of, battle
honours' (Gurr, invoking the heraldic
sense of *achievement*, i.e. full coat of
arms with its outer adornments).

61 **haste on** dispatch with speed. Cf. l.
36.

64–6 **Prince ... us** 'The Dolphin sore

54 captive chariot] *F;* chariot, captive *Cam[1] (Daniel)*   Rouen] *(Roan)*   60 for] *F;* fore *Oxf[1]*
('fore Staunton)   64 Rouen] *(Roan)*

DAUPHIN

  Not so, I do beseech your majesty.   65

FRENCH KING

  Be patient, for you shall remain with us. –
  Now forth, Lord Constable and princes all,
  And quickly bring us word of England's fall.   *Exeunt.*

[3.6] *Enter the English and Welsh Captains* GOWER *and*
        FLUELLEN[, *meeting*].

GOWER How now, Captain Fluellen, come you from
  the bridge?
FLUELLEN I assure you there is very excellent services
  committed at the bridge.
GOWER Is the Duke of Exeter safe?   5
FLUELLEN The Duke of Exeter is as magnanimous as

desired to haue been at the battell, but he was prohibited by his father: likewise Philip earle of Charolois would gladlie haue beene there, if his father the duke of Burgognie would haue suffered him' (Holinshed, 3.552, after reporting King Henry's reply to Montjoy and the assembling of the French army). Cf. 40–5n. and (for the Dauphin at Agincourt) Introduction, p. 29. In *Famous Victories* the scene ends with a dialogue of thirteen lines between the Dauphin, who asks his father to 'bestow, / Some part of the battell on me', and the French King, who refuses, saying 'I tell thee my sonne, / Although I should get the victory, and thou lose thy life, / I should thinke my selfe quite conquered, / And the English men to haue the victorie.' (scene xi: ll. 1,018–24).

68 **England's fall** King Henry's defeat
3.6.2 **bridge** Cf. Holinshed, 3.552 (immediately following the passage quoted in 3.5.64–6n.): 'The king of

England hearing that the Frenchmen approched, and that there was an other riuer for him to passe with his armie by a bridge, and doubting least if the same bridge should be broken, it would be greatlie to his hinderance, appointed certeine capteins with their bands, to go thither with all speed before him, and to take possession thereof, and so to keepe it, till his comming thither.' This bridge was over the River Ternoise at Blangy, but Holinshed does not say so, and hence neither does Shakespeare.

3 **services** military action: cf. l. 70 (here with Fluellen's characteristic plural)
4 **committed** performed. Fluellen's verb would be appropriate to offences, rather than to services.
5 **Duke of Exeter** Exeter was not in fact present at this skirmish (though Holinshed does not say that he was not), nor at Agincourt (though Holinshed says that he was and commanded the rearguard, 3.553). 'He is presumably needed here so that Pistol

66–8] *F; King.* Well, I say it shalbe so. *Q*

3.6] *Capell* 0.1] *F (Enter Captaines, English and Welch, Gower and Fluellen.); Enter* Gower. *Q meeting*] *Capell* 3 I assure you] *F; By Iesus Q* 6 7 as magnanimous ... and] *F; not in Q*

Agamemnon, and a man that I love and honour with
my soul, and my heart, and my duty, and my life, and
my living, and my uttermost power. He is not, God be
praised and blessed, any hurt in the world, but   10
keeps the bridge most valiantly, with excellent discipline. There is an ancient lieutenant there at the
pridge, I think in my very conscience he is as valiant a
man as Mark Antony, and he is a man of no estimation
in the world, but I did see him do as gallant service –   15
GOWER   What do you call him?

can ask Llewellyn [Fluellen] to plead
with him for Bardolph's life' (Gurr).
7 **Agamemnon** Agamemnon is probably mentioned because his name
  sounds well in Fluellen's mouth, and
  because, as Taylor notes, it echoes the
  vowels and consonants of *magnanimous*.
8–9 **and my life ... living** a Fluellen-
  like distinction without a difference.
  Q spoils the effect by implying too
  clearly the usual material sense of
  living, i.e. income ('and my life, /
  And my lands and my liuings').
9 **He is not** he has not. Cf. 3.2.73n.
10 **world** Q has 'worell' here, and consistently in Fluellen's speeches in 4.1,
  4.7 and 4.8 (whether or not there is a
  corresponding word in F). F has
  'World' everywhere except at 4.7.24
  and 112 (in a page set by Compositor
  B), where it has 'Orld'. Though
  Fluellen will obviously pronounce the
  word in his own way, Oxf[1] persuasively regards the latter spellings as
  'compositorial sophistication'. Cam[2]
  employs its own version of Q's spelling, 'woreld', but not consistently.
12 **ancient lieutenant** Since Fluellen
  uses many eccentric expressions it
  would be unsafe to emend, but Q's
  reading suggests that in performance

one word was used and not the other.
Wilson states that F's reading is not
an error because *ancient* was 'the equivalent of sub-lieutenant in modern
times and already recognized as such';
this may support the use of the two
titles interchangeably but hardly in
combination. Shakespeare may have
originally written *lieutenant* and then
substituted *ancient* when he reached
l. 17 and decided that Fluellen was
frequently to use *Anchient* in the vocative.
14 **Mark Antony** Shakespeare's next
  play was probably *Julius Caesar*. He
  had not referred to Mark Antony in
  any previous play. The comparison
  reflects Fluellen's reading in the
  Roman wars.
14–15 **no ... world** no social standing
  whatsoever (*OED* estimation 2b)
15 **as gallant service** – an unfinished
  sentence, implying some such conclusion as 'as you shall see in a summer's day', and therefore much more
  characteristic of Fluellen than Q's
  unqualified 'gallant seruice'. F's
  punctuation is not unusual in such
  circumstances. Editors who retain it
  presumably understand Fluellen to
  mean 'as Mark Antony'.

8 life] *Q;* liue *F*   10–11 but ... valiantly] *F;* He is maintain the bridge very gallantly *Q*   12
anchient lieutenant] *F (*aunchient Lieutenant*);* Ensigne *Q;* auchient *Dyce*   12–13 there ...
conscience] *F;* There, I do not know how you call him, but by Iesus I think *Q*   14 Antony] *F
(Anthony); Anthonie,* he doth maintain the bridge most gallantly *Q*   15 as gallant service –] *this
edn (Walker);* as gallant seruice. *F;* gallant seruice. *Q*   16 What] *F;* How *Q*

FLUELLEN   He is called Anchient Pistol.
GOWER   I know him not.

Enter PISTOL.

FLUELLEN   Here is the man.
PISTOL
Captain, I thee beseech to do me favours.   20
The Duke of Exeter doth love thee well.
FLUELLEN   Ay, I praise God, and I have merited some
love at his hands.
PISTOL
Bardolph, a soldier firm and sound of heart,
Of buxom valour, hath, by cruel fate   25
And giddy Fortune's furious fickle wheel,
That goddess blind

17 **He ... Pistol** 'The surprise of the identification is surely intended as comic' (Taylor)

25 ***Of** F (which prints the speech, like Pistol's others, as prose) probably caught the preceding 'and' from the beginning of the line below (assuming that Shakespeare wrote out Pistol's speech as verse). In Q's version of ll. 24–6 ('*Bardolfe* a souldier, one of buxsome valour, / Hath by furious fate / And giddy Fortunes fickle wheele') 'one', which might be supposed to be either a corruption of F's 'and' or the correct reading corrupted into 'and' by F, is more probably due to the compiler's attempt to reconstruct a line of verse.

buxom The only other occurrence in Shakespeare is in Gower's prologue in *Per* (l. 23), 'So buxom, blithe, and full of face'. *OED* gives the present passage under *a*. 3 ('Blithe, gladsome, bright, lively, gay'). Shakespeare may have recalled Lodge's *Rosalynde* (Bullough, 2.194–5), where, in the

incident dramatized in *AYL* 2.6, Adam Spencer moralizes on Fortune's inconstancy, which now threatens his companion with starvation: 'Oh *Rosader*, thou art in the flower of thine age, and in the pride of thy yeares, buxsome and full of May.'

26 **giddy** Cf. 1.2.145, 2.4.28.
wheel the wheel, turned by Fortune, by which mortal persons were raised up and cast down

27–8 **That ... stone** Q gives these words as one line, but it is unlikely that Shakespeare intended a 'fourteener' here; more probably he either conceived the lines from the first as editors usually arrange them or originally wrote 'And giddy Fortune's wheel, that goddess blind' and then threw in two alliterative adjectives to heighten Pistol's style and match those in the following line. For the alliterative style parodied, cf. *Locrine* (anon., 1595) 5.4.175–6, 'see where he murdred lies / By luckesse lot and froward frowning fate'.

18 SD] *F; Enter Ancient* Pistoll. *Q*   20–1] *verse Q; prose F*   24 6] *verse Pope; prose F*   25 Of]
Capell; and of F; one of Q   27–8] *verse Capell; prose F*

That stands upon the rolling restless stone –
FLUELLEN   By your patience, Ancient Pistol. Fortune
is painted blind, with a muffler afore her eyes, to signify   30
to you that Fortune is blind; and she is painted also
with a wheel, to signify to you, which is the moral of
it, that she is turning, and inconstant, and mutability,
and variation; and her foot, look you, is fixed upon a
spherical stone, which rolls, and rolls, and rolls. In good   35
truth, the poet makes a most excellent description of
it: Fortune is an excellent moral.
PISTOL
Fortune is Bardolph's foe, and frowns on him,
For he hath stolen a pax,

28 **rolling restless** probably Shakespeare's conscious echo, as Steevens pointed out, of Gascoigne's *Jocasta* (1566, printed 1573) 4. Chorus, 'O blisful concord, bredde in sacred brest / Of him that guides the restlesse rolling sky' (*Works* 1.305). Cf. Kyd, *Spanish Tragedy*, 1.3.23–30, 'Fortune is blind ... What help can be expected at her hands, / Whose foot is standing on a rolling stone / And mind more mutable than fickle winds?'
29 **By your patience** i.e. forgive me (for interrupting you)
30 **painted blind** represented as blindfolded. Cf. *MND* 1.1.235, 'And therefore is winged Cupid painted blind.' **muffler** blindfolding bandage (*OED* 1b). In the final dumb-show of *Jocasta* (see 28n.) Fortune is introduced 'muffled with a white laune about hir eyes' (*Works* 1.308).
33–4 **mutability, and variation** Fluellen is recollecting Virgil, *Aeneid* 4.569, 'varium et mutabile semper / Femina' (woman is always a fickle and changeable thing).
34 **fixed** standing firmly
36 **the poet** Fluellen's praise of some particular poet is humorous because this *description* of Fortune is so thor-

oughly traditional.
37 **moral** symbolical figure (*OED sb.* 3)
38 **Fortune ... him** 'Fortune my foe, why dost thou frown on me?' is the first line of a popular song, with a popular tune named after its first three words. Cf. *MW* 3.3.60.
39–40 **For he ... must** 'a be Cf. Holinshed, 3.552: 'Yet in this great necessitie, the poore people of the countrie were not spoiled, nor anie thing taken of them without paiment, nor anie outrage or offense doone by the Englishmen, except one, which was, that a souldiour tooke a pix out of a church, for which he was apprehended, & the king not once remooued till the box was restored, and the offendor strangled.'
39 **pax** 'A tablet of gold, silver, ivory, glass, or other material, round or quadrangular, with a projecting handle behind, bearing a representation of the Crucifixion or other sacred subject, which was kissed by the celebrating priest at Mass, and passed to the other officiating clergy and then to the congregation to be kissed; an osculatory' (*OED*): Lat. *pax*, peace; the kiss of peace in Christian ritual. In Hall and Holinshed it

28 stone –] *Rowe;* Stone. *F*   30 her] *Q;* his *F*   38] *verse Q; prose F*   39–40] *verse Oxf¹; prose F; Q lines 39–41* ... be: / ... dogs, /   39 stolen] *(stolne)*   39, 44 pax] *F (*Pax), *Q (*packs); pix *Theobald*

And hanged must 'a be, a damned death!   40
Let gallows gape for dog, let man go free,
And let not hemp his windpipe suffocate!
But Exeter hath given the doom of death
For pax of little price.
Therefore go speak – the Duke will hear thy voice –   45
And let not Bardolph's vital thread be cut
With edge of penny cord and vile reproach.
Speak, Captain, for his life, and I will thee requite.

FLUELLEN   Anchient Pistol, I do partly understand
   your meaning.   50
PISTOL   Why then, rejoice therefor.
FLUELLEN   Certainly, Anchient, it is not a thing to rejoice
   at; for if, look you, he were my brother, I would desire
   the Duke to use his good pleasure and put him
   to execution; for discipline ought to be used.   55

---

is a pix (a box, usually of precious
metal, in which the consecrated
wafers were kept) that is stolen, and
in Hall (but not in Holinshed) the
soldier eats the consecrated wafers.
40 **hanged** hangèd
   damned execrable (damnèd)
41 **Let ... dog** Dogs were sometimes
   destroyed by hanging (though not on
   a *gallows*). For *gape* cf. 2.1.62 (with
   similar alliteration)
43 **doom** verdict
46 **vital thread** thread of life, as spun,
   measured and cut by the Fates
47 **With edge ... reproach** The word
   edge inappropriately pursues the
   metaphor of l. 46. For the incongruity, cf. *MV* 2.2.158–9, 'and to be
   in peril of my life with the edge of a
   featherbed'.
48 **requite** repay. Pistol may display
   some concrete bribe (Taylor), but this
   would over-emphasize the point, and

would be inconsistent with the mod-
eration of Fluellen's response.
49–50 **I do ... meaning** The word
   partly, typical of Fluellen's deliberation of speech, is also unconsciously apt, in view of Pistol's
   bombast.
51 **Why then, rejoice therefor** Malone
   aptly compares Marlowe, *The Mas-
   sacre at Paris*, 22.150, 'The Guise is
   slain, and I rejoice therefor.' Pistol's
   similar expression in *2H4* 5.3.109,
   'Why then, lament therefor', shows
   that it is idiosyncratic and theatrical.
   Therefor (= thereat) is accented on
   the second syllable.
55 **execution** Q's 'executions' is a typical
   mechanical 'Welsh plural' of that text
   and of *MW*, Q (1602), seen also in
   what follows: 'for look you, / Disciplines ought to be kept, they ought
   to be kept' (where the repetition is an
   evident actors' gag).

41–2] *as Pope; prose F; Q lines* ... dogs, / ... windpipe stop. /   43–4] *verse Q; prose F*   44 little]
F; pettie *Q*   47 penny cord] *(*Penny-Cord*)*   51 therefor] *Oxf¹;* therefore *F, Q*   55 execution]
F; executions *Q*   for ... used] *F;* for look you, / Disciplines ought to be kept, they ought to be
kept *Q*

PISTOL

Die and be damned, and *fico* for thy friendship!

FLUELLEN　It is well.

PISTOL　The fig of Spain!　　　　　　　　　*Exit.*

FLUELLEN　Very good.

GOWER　Why, this is an arrant counterfeit rascal, I　60
remember him now – a bawd, a cutpurse.

FLUELLEN　I'll assure you 'a uttered as prave words at
the pridge as you shall see in a summer's day. But it is
very well; what he has spoke to me, that is well, I
warrant you, when time is serve.　　　　　　　　65

GOWER　Why, 'tis a gull, a fool, a rogue, that now and
then goes to the wars to grace himself at his return
into London under the form of a soldier. And such
fellows are perfect in the great commanders' names,
and they will learn you by rote where services were　70
done, at such and such a sconce, at such a breach, at

---

56 *fico* (Ital.) fig. *OED sb.*[2]: 'A contemptuous gesture which consisted in
thrusting the thumb between two of
the closed fingers or into the mouth.
Also *fig of Spain*, and *To give (a
person) the fig.*' For the spelling cf
MW 1.3.26–7, 'a fico for the phrase'
(F).

58 **The fig of Spain** Cf. preceding note
and *2H4* 5.3.119–20, 'When Pistol
lies, do this, and fig me, / Like the
bragging Spaniard.'

59 **Very good** Q's two additional speeches
(adopted by Oxf[1]) are clearly more
actors' gags, the former influenced by
2.1.48–52.

60 **Why ... rascal** an indirect criticism
of Fluellen's expressed admiration for
Pistol, which Fluellen as indirectly
acknowledges; more subtle than the

directly critical expostulation in Q
(adopted by Oxf[1]).
arrant notorious

61 **cutpurse** thief who cuts purses to
steal their contents

63 **as you ... day** proverbial (Tilley, S
967), a summer's day being long in
comparison with a winter's day. The
incongruity of *words* and *see* is typical
of Fluellen's usage, and of Shakespeare's humour; cf. *MND* 3.1.85, 'he
goes but to see a noise that he heard'.
Cf. 4.8.23.

66 **gull** synonymous with *fool* (*OED sb.*[3]
1)

69 **perfect** word-perfect. Cf. l. 70, 'learn
you by rote' (*you* being redundant:
see Abbott, 220).

71 **sconce** small fort or earthwork

---

56 *fico*] *Collier; Figo F;* figa *Q*　57 60 It ... rascal,] *F;* That is good. / *Pist.* The figge of *Spaine*
within thy Iawe. / *Flew.* That is very well. / *Pist.* I say the fig within thy bowels and thy durty
maw. / *Exit Pistoll.* / *Fle.* Captain *Gour,* cannot you hear it lighten & thunder? / *Gour.* Why is
this the Ancient you told me of? *Q*　62 I'll ... you] *F;* By Iesus *Q*　69 perfect] *F* (perfit). *Q*

such a convoy; who came off bravely, who was shot,
who disgraced, what terms the enemy stood on. And
this they con perfectly in the phrase of war, which
they trick up with new-tuned oaths; and what a beard   75
of the General's cut and a horrid suit of the camp
will do among foaming bottles and ale-washed wits is
wonderful to be thought on. But you must learn to
know such slanders of the age, or else you may be
marvellously mistook.   80

FLUELLEN   I tell you what, Captain Gower: I do perceive
he is not the man that he would gladly make show to
the world he is. If I find a hole in his coat, I will tell
him my mind.   [*Drum within.*]
Hark you, the King is coming, and I must speak with   85
him from the pridge.

72 **convoy** military operation involving
an armed escort
came off acquitted himself
73 **what terms ... on** To stand on terms
is 'to insist upon conditions' (*OED*
term *sb*. 8b. 6). Cf. 5.2.94, 'When
articles too nicely urged be stood on.'
74 **con** memorize
phrase particular language (*OED sb.*
1)
75 **trick up** adorn
new-tuned newly devised (*OED*
tuned *ppl. a.*: e.g. (1579) 'straunge
doctrine and new tuned opinions'),
i.e. in the latest style
76 **of the General's cut** trimmed in
the General's fashion. Cf. 5.0.30, 'the
General of our gracious Empress', i.e.
the Earl of Essex (see Introduction,
p. 1). F. S. Le Comte, *Shakespeare
Association Bulletin*, 23 (1948), 17–19,
notes the probable allusion to the full
beard that Essex took to wearing after
the Cadiz expedition of 1596, hence
known as his 'Cadiz beard', and
quotes a reference to such a beard in
Everard Guilpin's *Skialetheia*, 1598,

'his face, / Furr'd with Cads-beard'.
'This passage clearly implies that
Pistol had such a beard, in the original
performances' (Taylor).
horrid frightful (*OED a.* 2). Cf.
4.0.28, 4.1.268, and Shakespeare's
thirteen other uses of the word.
suit ... camp military dress. Q's
'shout' probably derives from the
phonetic spelling of *suit* as 'shoot' in
the copy.
77 **foaming ... wits** In *2H4* 2.4.127,
Doll Tearsheet abuses Pistol as 'you
bottle-ale rascal'.
79 **slanders ... age** persons who bring
disgrace on the present time (*OED*
slander *sb.* 3d): cf. *R2* 1.1.113, 'this
slander of his blood'.
82–3 **would ... he is** pretends to be
83 **find ... coat** have the chance to
expose him (proverbial: Tilley, H 522)
85–6 **speak ... pridge** i.e. give him the
news from the bridge. Fluellen's
expression ludicrously suggests that
he will retire to a distance before
addressing the King.

74 perfectly] F (perfitly), Q   76 suit] F (Sute); shout Q   83–4 I will ... mind] F; I shall tell
him a litle of my desires Q   84 SD] *Capell (subst.)*

Drum and Colours. Enter the KING *[and* GLOUCESTER*] and his poor Soldiers.*

God pless your majesty!

KING
How now, Fluellen, cam'st thou from the bridge?

FLUELLEN   Ay, so please your majesty. The Duke of
Exeter has very gallantly maintained the pridge; the   90
French is gone off, look you, and there is gallant and
most prave passages. Marry, th'athversary was have
possession of the pridge, but he is enforced to retire,
and the Duke of Exeter is master of the pridge. I can
tell your majesty, the Duke is a prave man.   95

KING   What men have you lost, Fluellen?

FLUELLEN   The perdition of th'athversary hath been
very great, reasonable great. Marry, for my part, I think
the Duke hath lost never a man, but one that is like
to be executed for robbing a church, one Bardolph, if   100
your majesty know the man. His face is all bubuncles,

86.1 GLOUCESTER He speaks at l. 167.
86.1–2 *his poor Soldiers* (cf. l. 144 and
3.5.57) his soldiers, looking the worse
for their hardships
89–94 **The Duke ... pridge** Cf. Holinshed, 3.552 (immediately following
the passage quoted in 3.6.2n.): 'Those
that were sent, finding the Frenchmen
busie to breake downe their bridge,
assailed them so vigorouslie, that they
discomfited them, and tooke and slue
them; and so the bridge was preserued
till the king came, and passed the
riuer by the same with his whole
armie.'
92 **passages** passages of arms, hand-to-
hand combats (*OED* 13c)
athversary Cf. 3.2.61n.
97 **perdition** losses. The primary sense
is 'utter destruction' (*OED* 1). *OED*
gives three examples of 'affected or
rhetorical use' to mean 'loss, dim-
inution, lessening' (1b), all from

Shakespeare: this passage; *Ham*,
Addition N.7 [5.2.112–13] ('Sir, his
definement suffers no perdition in
you'); and *Tem* 1.2.30 ('No, not so
much perdition as an hair'). The
eccentricity of Fluellen's diction is
emphasized by the proximity *of lost*
at ll. 96 and 99.
99–100 **is like to be** is likely to be.
Fluellen's expression is sometimes
taken to mean that the King could
still save Bardolph if he chose, but
more probably it reflects his recollection of Pistol's appeal; by the end
of his speech he has decided that the
execution will have taken place.
100–1 **if ... man** Fluellen, of course,
does not expect the King to know
Bardolph personally (hence the dramatic irony), but supposes that Bardolph's unusual appearance may have
caught his attention.
101 ***bubuncles** the plural of Fluellen's

86 SD *Drum ...* KING [...] *and ... Soldiers*] as *F; Enter King,* Clarence, Gloster *and others*
Q   GLOUCESTER] *Q*   88 cam'st thou] *F;* come you *Q;* com'st thou *Oxf¹*   89–95 The Duke ...
man] *F;* There is excellent seruice at the bridge *Q*   101 bubuncles] *Oxf¹;* bubukles *F;* not in *Q*

and whelks, and knobs, and flames o' fire, and his lips
blows at his nose, and it is like a coal of fire, sometimes
plue and sometimes red; but his nose is executed, and
his fire's out.   105

KING   We would have all such offenders so cut off; and
we give express charge that in our marches through
the country there be nothing compelled from the
villages, nothing taken but paid for, none of the French
upbraided or abused in disdainful language; for when   110
lenity and cruelty play for a kingdom, the gentler
gamester is the soonest winner.

conflation of *bubo* (Lat. = abscess)
and *carbuncle* (an inflamed tumour of
the skin). The spelling 'charbucle'
was obsolete by the sixteenth century,
and the F spellings elsewhere (*KL*
2.2.397 [2.4.223], 'Carbuncle'; *AC*
4.9[8].28, 'Carbunkled') suggest that
F's omission of the *n* here is an error.
Oxf¹'s reading (adopted here) should
therefore be considered as an emendation, not as a modernization.
101–2 **His face ... fire** Cf. Chaucer's
portrait of the Summoner (*Canterbury
Tales*, General Prologue, 624–33),
who has a 'fyr-reed' face and has
'whelkes white' (white-headed
pimples) and 'knobbes' on his cheeks.
103 **blows** blow, as bellows blowing air
at a *coal* to inflame it
104–5 **but ... out** Fluellen means 'but
he is executed, nose and all, and his
nose's fire's out'. His ludicrous
expression led Wilson to misinterpret
it as meaning that Bardolph's nose
had been 'slit, as he stood in the
pillory, before being hanged', a notion
unsupported by the context or by
Holinshed. Ard², Oxf¹ and Cam² per-
petuate the mistake, as does Kenneth
Branagh's film (see Branagh, 71).
105 **his fire** its fire. See 5.2.40n.
106 **We ... cut off** Perhaps to be spoken
as a line of verse ('We would' being

equivalent in metrical value to
'We'd'). For *cut off*, cf. *R3* 1.4.213–
14, 'He [i.e. God] needs no indirect
or lawless course / To cut off those
that have offended him.'
106–12 **and we ... winner** Cf. Holinshed, 3.549: 'At his first comming
on land, he caused proclamation to be
made, that no person should be so
hardie on paine of death, either to
take anie thing out of anie church that
belonged to the same, or to hurt or
doo anie violence either to priests,
women, or anie such as should be
found without weapon or armor, and
not readie to make resistance; also
that no man should renew anie quarell
or strife, whereby anie fraie might
arise to the disquieting of the armie.'
Cf. also Holinshed, 3.552 (immediately after the passage quoted at 39–
40n.): 'The people of the countries
thereabout, hearing of such zeale in
him, to the maintenance of iustice,
ministred to his armie victuals, and
other necessaries, although by open
proclamation so to do they were prohibited.'
108 **compelled** extorted (*OED* 2a)
110 **upbraided** reproached
111 **lenity** Cf. 3.2.25n.
112 **gamester** player

102 o' fire] F *(a fire); afire Cam¹ (anon. in Cam)*   106–7 off ... that] F; off, / And we here giue
expresse commaundment, / That *Q*; off, and we here give express charge that *Oxf¹*   111 lenity]
*Q (*lenitie*); Leuitie F*

239

Tucket. Enter MONTJOY.

MONTJOY   You know me by my habit.

KING

Well then, I know thee: what shall I know of thee?

MONTJOY   My master's mind.   115

KING   Unfold it.

MONTJOY   Thus says my king: 'Say thou to Harry of
England, though we seemed dead, we did but sleep.
Advantage is a better soldier than rashness. Tell him
we could have rebuked him at Harfleur, but that we   120
thought not good to bruise an injury till it were full
ripe. Now we speak upon our cue, and our voice is
imperial. England shall repent his folly, see his weak-
ness, and admire our sufferance. Bid him therefore

112 SD *Tucket* a flourish on a trumpet
(*OED sb.*[1])

113 **You ... habit** Walter calls this 'a
particularly insolent greeting' and
Humphreys 'a terse, discourteous
opening, which Henry answers in the
same vein'. The exchange is certainly
terse, but 'Thou dost thy office fairly'
(l. 138) does not suggest that the King
thinks Montjoy personally at fault.
habit costume, i.e. the tabard
(sleeveless coat) bearing the French
King's coat of arms

117–34 **Say ... pronounced** Taylor suggests that Montjoy may read this from
a scroll, but this would make him
seem to be reading out a message
addressed to himself, not delivering a
message from the French King. The
speech needs to be delivered with
some force.

119 **Advantage** favouring circumstance
(*OED sb.* 5), i.e. the patience to wait
for it. Cf. the personifications here
with those of lenity and cruelty as
gamesters, ll. 110–12.

120 **rebuked** checked (*OED v.* 1)

but that except that, but for the fact
that

121–2 **bruise ... ripe** squeeze out a boil
till it had come to a head. Rather than
using *injury* in a concrete sense for 'a
bodily wound or sore' (*OED* 3b, this
passage only), Shakespeare is substituting the abstract noun (*OED* 3,
an instance of harm sustained) for the
concrete sore or boil implied in the
metaphor.

122 **speak ... cue** cf. (in a similar serious
context) *Oth* 1.2.84–5. 'This phrase
our author learned among players,
and has imparted it to kings'
(Johnson).

123 **imperial** kingly
England the King of England

124 **admire our sufferance** wonder at
our (earlier) forbearance

124–5 **Bid him ... ransom** There is no
mention of ransom at the corresponding interview in Holinshed.
See 3.5.1–4n., and ll. 138–65 below.
When Holinshed's ransom interview
is reached, Shakespeare makes
Montjoy state that he comes 'once

112 SD MONTJOY] *F (Mountioy); French Herauld Q*   115–17 My ... king] *prose F; verse line
Oxf*[1]   119–22 Tell ... ripe] *F; not in Q*   120 Harfleur] *(Harflew)*   122 our cue] *F (our Q.), Q
(our kue)*   124–7 Bid ... digested] *F; not in Q*

consider of his ransom,, which must proportion the   125
losses we have borne, the subjects we have lost, the
disgrace we have digested, which in weight to re-
answer, his pettiness would bow under. For our losses,
his exchequer is too poor; for th'effusion of our blood,
the muster of his kingdom too faint a number; and for   130
our disgrace, his own person kneeling at our feet but a
weak and worthless satisfaction. To this add defiance,
and tell him, for conclusion, he hath betrayed his followers, whose condemnation is pronounced.' So far
my king and master, so much my office.   135

KING

What is thy name? I know thy quality.

MONTJOY

Montjoy.

KING

Thou dost thy office fairly. Turn thee back,
And tell thy king I do not seek him now,
But could be willing to march on to Calais   140
Without impeachment; for, to say the sooth,

more' about it, 4.3.79.

125 **proportion** be in proportion to
(*OED v.* 3: first occurrence)

127 **digested** passively endured. Cf.
2.0.31–2n.

127–8 **which ... under** i.e. which
to repay in full measure would be
too much for his small resources.
For *weight*, cf. 2.2.35. The image
is of a weak person carrying too heavy
a load.

130 **muster** roll-call, i.e. whole popu-
lation
faint feeble, i.e. insignificant

133 **betrayed** led to their destruction

136–7 **What ... Montjoy.** 'Montjoy is
not a name, as Shakespeare implies,
but the title of the chief herald of
France (in fact, a *quality*), borrowed
from "Montjoy St Denis!" the French
King's war-cry' (Wilson)

138 **fairly** handsomely, in the proper
manner

138–65 **Turn ... master** Holinshed
(3.552: immediately following the
passage quoted at 3.5.1–4n.) is echoed
in ll. 139–41 and 155–61: 'King
Henrie aduisedlie answered: Mine
intent is to doo as it pleaseth God: I
will not seeke your maister at this
time; but if he or his seeke me, I will
meet with them, God willing. If anie
of your nation attempt once to stop
me in my iournie now towards Calis,
at their ieopardie be it; and yet wish
I not anie of you so vnaduised, as to
be the occasion that I die your tawnie
ground with your red blood.'

141 **impeachment** hindrance (*OED sb.*
1: two instances in this military connection, dated 1596 and 1601). The
word, from Old French *empeschement*,

128–9 For ... poor] *F; not in Q*   133–4 and tell ... pronounced] *F; not in Q*   138 dost]
(doo'st)   140 Calais] *(Callice)*   141 the] *F, Q; thee (Oxf¹)*

Though 'tis no wisdom to confess so much
Unto an enemy of craft and vantage,
My people are with sickness much enfeebled,
My numbers lessened, and those few I have   145
Almost no better than so many French;
Who when they were in health, I tell thee, herald,
I thought upon one pair of English legs
Did march three Frenchmen. Yet forgive me, God,
That I do brag thus! This your air of France   150
Hath blown that vice in me. I must repent.
Go therefore, tell thy master here I am.
My ransom is this frail and worthless trunk,
My army but a weak and sickly guard.
Yet, God before, tell him we will come on,   155
Though France himself and such another neighbour
Stand in our way. [*Gives a purse.*]
                        There's for thy labour, Montjoy.
Go, bid thy master well advise himself.
If we may pass, we will; if we be hindered,
We shall your tawny ground with your red blood   160

was current from the fifteenth
century.
say the sooth tell the truth. Q and
F agree in this common phrase (*OED*
sooth *sb.* 5b). Taylor's conjecture 'say
thee sooth' would confuse the sense
of ll. 142–3, where it is of the French
King, not of Montjoy, that King
Henry is speaking.
143 **of craft and vantage** who is
cunning and has a military advantage
147 **Who** i.e. 'those few I have', l. 145.
The construction, putting the relative
Who before the conjunction *when*, is
a latinate one.
148–9 **upon ... Frenchmen** i.e. were
each of them equal as a fighter to
three Frenchmen
150–1 **This your air ... me** Frenchmen,
like Spaniards, were often regarded
by Englishmen as braggarts. *Your*
refers to the Frenchmen collectively

(cf. l. 160). Henry consistently uses
thou to Montjoy. The same distinction
is made in 4.3 and 4.7.
150 **air** Q's 'heire', in which Taylor and
Gurr see a punning reference to the
Dauphin, is merely one of that text's
many auditory errors: cf., at l. 145,
Q's 'My Army lessoned'.
151 **blown ... me** puffed me up with
that vice (of proudly bragging). Cf.
1H4 4.2.49 (Prince Henry to Falstaff)
'How now, blown Jack?'
153 **trunk** body. The adjectives *frail* and
worthless limit the sense, and make
word-play on a trunk of treasure
improbable.
155 **God before** Holinshed's 'God willing' (cf. 138–65n.)
157 **There's ... labour** 'When he had
thus answered the herald, he gaue
him a princelie reward, and licence to
depart' (Holinshed, 3.552).

150 air] *F* (ayre)*;* heire *Q*   157 SD] *this edn; Giving a chain. / Collier²*   159 hindered] *(hindred)*

Discolour. And so, Montjoy, fare you well.
The sum of all our answer is but this:
We would not seek a battle as we are,
Nor as we are, we say, we will not shun it:
So tell your master. 165

MONTJOY

I shall deliver so. Thanks to your highness. [*Exit.*]

GLOUCESTER

I hope they will not come upon us now.

KING

We are in God's hand, brother, not in theirs. –
March to the bridge. – It now draws toward night.
Beyond the river we'll encamp ourselves, 170
And on tomorrow bid them march away. *Exeunt.*

[3.7] *Enter the* CONSTABLE of France, *the* Lord RAMBURES,
ORLEANS [*and the*] DAUPHIN, *with others.*

CONSTABLE Tut, I have the best armour of the world.
Would it were day!

ORLEANS You have an excellent armour; but let my
horse have his due.

---

166 **Thanks ... highness** Wilson adds
the SD '*He bows low and departs*'.
The courtesy that he shows here, in
contrast to his terse greeting, suggests
that the King has gained his respect
by his bearing, not merely by his gift.

171 **And ... away** And tomorrow (i.e.
when tomorrow dawns) give them the
order to march away (towards Calais).
Q and F both give the line in this
form. MacD. P. Jackson's conjecture
(*N&Q* 13 (1966): 133–4, see textual
notes) is rendered improbable by the
fact that the King has just given the
order 'March to the bridge', l. 169.

3.7.0.2 DAUPHIN F-includes him in this
scene and in 4.2 and 4.5. Q, which
lacks an equivalent of 4.2, substitutes
Bourbon here and in 4.5. Oxf[1] and
Cam[2] adopt this substitution. See
Introduction, pp. 29–32.

with others Perhaps these super-
numeraries are visualized by Shakespeare as passing to and fro at the
beginning of the scene to suggest the
bustle of preparation. There is no
indication in the dialogue that any
other listeners are present.

1 **armour** suit of armour. Cf. *2H4*
4.3.161 [5.30], 'a rich armour'.

166 SD] *Rowe* 169–70] *F;* To night we will encampe beyond the bridge *Q* 171 tomorrow bid]
F, Q (to morrow bid); tomorrow. Bid *Cam*[2] (*Jackson*)

3.7] *Hanmer* 0.1–2] *F; Enter* Burbon, Constable, Orleance, Gebon. *Q* RAMBURES]
(*Rambures*) ORLEANS] (*Orleance*) 0.2↑ DAUPHIN] (*Dolphin*)

CONSTABLE It is the best horse of Europe. 5
ORLEANS Will it never be morning?
DAUPHIN My lord of Orleans and my lord High Constable, you talk of horse and armour?
ORLEANS You are as well provided of both as any prince in the world. 10
DAUPHIN What a long night is this! I will not change my horse with any that treads but on four pasterns. Ch'ha! He bounds from the earth as if his entrails were hairs – *le cheval volant*, the Pegasus, *qui a les narines de feu!* When I bestride him, I soar, I am a hawk. He 15 trots the air. The earth sings when he touches it; the

9–10 **You ... world** Here and at l. 19 Orleans seems to be prompting the Dauphin's boasts with covert irony, like one who has heard them before. If so, his later defence of the Dauphin must also be coloured with irony (ll. 93–109).

12 **pasterns** feet. The pastern is the part of the foot between the fetlock and the hoof.

Ch'ha! Perhaps a noise imitating the snorting of a horse. Cf. (in Geneva Bible) Job 39:25 (of the horse), 'He saith among the trumpets, Ha, ha.' Other explanations are (1) a sound made by a French rider to encourage his horse (*Shakespeare's England* 2.423) and (2) an exclamation of triumph, delight, etc. (with various emendations). All this horse dialogue may spring from *Famous Victories* (scene xiii) ll. 1,102–4, when the French are throwing dice for the English (cf. 4.0.18–19): 'Faith, me wil tro at the Earle of *Northumberland* / And my Lord a *Willowby*, with his great horse, / Snorting, farting, oh braue horse.' Another probable source is a dialogue on horsemanship in John Eliot's *Ortho-epia Gallica*, 1593, dis-

cussed by J. W. Lever (Lever, 79–90).

13–14 **as if ... hairs** i.e. as if his body weighed nothing at all. Less probably, as if he were a bouncing tennis-ball stuffed with hair. Less probably still, as if his entrails were *hares* (Oxf[1]) – Lever's suggestion (87–8) because hares are described as depicted, with flying horses (*chevaux volants*) and other creatures, on an apothecary's boxes in Eliot's *Ortho-epia Gallica* (cf. l. 12n.); but cf. Eliot's phrase, of a horse, 'he is as light as a feather' (Lever, 86).

14 **Pegasus** the winged horse of classical mythology

14–15 *qui a ... feu* who has fiery nostrils. Cf. 'a fiery Pegasus', *1H4* 4.1.110 (Vernon, praising Prince Henry's horsemanship). F's *ches* cannot represent *chez*, which never means 'with' in this possessive sense. Capell's emendation *qui a* is consistent with F's *Che* for *Qui* at 4.1.35.

16 **The earth ... it** i.e. Trotting the air, and only seldom touching the earth, he produces a musical sound when he does so.

5–6] *F; not in Q* 7–18] *F; Burbon.* Now you talke of a horse, I haue a steed like the / Palfrey of the sun nothing but pure ayre and fire, / And hath none of this dull element of earth within him. *Q* 8 armour?] *F; armour – Theobald* 12 pasterns] *F2; postures F* Ch'ha!] *F (ch'ha.); ça ha! / Theobald;* Ha, ha! *Capell;* Ah ha! *Oxf[1]* 14 hairs] *F (hayres); hares Oxf[1] (Lever) qui a] Capell; ches F; qu'il a / Rowe; chez / Theobald*

basest horn of his hoof is more musical than the pipe
of Hermes.

ORLEANS   He's of the colour of the nutmeg.

DAUPHIN   And of the heat of the ginger. It is a beast for   20
Perseus; he is pure air and fire, and the dull elements
of earth and water never appear in him but only in
patient stillness while his rider mounts him. He is
indeed a horse, and all other jades you may call beasts.

CONSTABLE   Indeed, my lord, it is a most absolute and   25
excellent horse.

DAUPHIN   It is the prince of palfreys; his neigh is like the
bidding of a monarch, and his countenance enforces
homage.

ORLEANS   No more, cousin.   30

DAUPHIN   Nay, the man hath no wit that cannot, from
the rising of the lark to the lodging of the lamb, vary

---

17 **basest horn** meanest horny substance, possibly with a pun on *horn*,
the musical instrument, in conjunction with *pipe*. A pun on *base*
(bass, as distinct from treble) is a
more remote possibility.

17–18 **pipe of Hermes** Hermes (in
Shakespeare's other references called
Mercury) charmed the hundred-eyed
Argus asleep by the music of his
'merrie Pipe' (Golding's Ovid, 1.843–
56).

19 **He's ... nutmeg** Walter cites the
first page of Thomas Blundeville's *Art
of Riding*, 1560: 'A horse for the most
part is coloured according as he is
complexioned.... Again he is complexioned according as he doth participate more or less of any of the
four elements.' The reddish-brown
nutmeg and the hot *ginger* (l. 20),
both spices, are appropriate to a horse
wholly composed of 'air and fire' (l.
21). Both are mentioned, among other
apothecaries' goods, by J. Eliot (see l.
12n.).

21 **Perseus** Though in classical mythology it was Bellerophon who rode
on Pegasus in killing the Chimaera,
Renaissance poets often transferred
the incident to Perseus' rescue of
Andromeda from the sea-monster,
e.g. Spenser, *Ruins of Time*, 646–9.

26 **horse** Actors often pause before the
word to show that the Constable is
speaking ironically; but the same
point can be made less obtrusively.

27 **prince of palfreys** i.e. king of horses.
A palfrey is properly an easy-going
horse for riding, not a war-horse, but
the words alliterate pompously.

31–2 **from the ... lamb** all day long.
To rise with the lark and go to bed
with the lamb was proverbial (Tilley,
R 186). In these speeches there is
some parody of Lyly's stylistic man-
nerisms – parallelism, antithesis,
word-play and alliteration.

32 **vary** express in varied terms, as in
academic rhetoric. Cf. *LLL* 4.2.8–9,
'the epithets are sweetly varied, like a
scholar at the least.'

20–34 It is   sea] *F; not in Q*

deserved praise on my palfrey. It is a theme as fluent
as the sea. Turn the sands into eloquent tongues and
my horse is argument for them all. 'Tis a subject for   35
a sovereign to reason on, and for a sovereign's sovereign to ride on, and for the world, familiar to us
and unknown, to lay apart their particular functions
and wonder at him. I once writ a sonnet in his praise
and began thus: 'Wonder of nature!'   40

ORLEANS   I have heard a sonnet begin so to one's mistress.

DAUPHIN   Then did they imitate that which I composed
to my courser, for my horse is my mistress.

ORLEANS   Your mistress bears well.   45

DAUPHIN   Me well, which is the prescript praise and
perfection of a good and particular mistress.

CONSTABLE   Nay, for methought yesterday your mistress shrewdly shook your back.

33–4 **as fluent ... sea** i.e. as full-
flowing, as copious, as the sea; Shakespeare's only use of the adjective
34 **the sands** traditionally innumerable:
OED 2a
35 **argument** subject-matter
35–6 **a subject ... reason on** a subject
fit for a king to discourse of. There
seems to be word-play on *subject* (one
who owes service to a king) and on
'sovereign reason' (the reason, as
having the right of rule over other
faculties, *Ham* 3.1.160).
37 **the world** all peoples
38 **lay ... functions** lay aside their
proper business
40 **nature!** Editors commonly add a
dash, as if the Dauphin, about to
repeat his whole sonnet, is interrupted
by Orleans, but by quoting its first
three words he has made his point.
43–4 **Then ... mistress** Perhaps suggested by *E3*, 2.1.95–8, where the

King is commanding his confidant
Lodowick to write a love-letter full of
admiring terms: '*Lod.* Write I to a
woman? / *King.* What bewtie els
could triumph over me, / Or who
but women doe our love layes greet?
/ What, thinkest thou I did bid thee
praise a horse?'
45 **bears well** carries her rider well
46 **prescript** prescribed
47 **particular** i.e. as opposed to common
48 **Nay, for** If F's reading is correct, the
sense is 'I deny that your horse bears
you well, for ...' On the other hand,
Q's 'Ma foy' ('[by] my faith') is appropriate to the positive tone of the
speech, and, as Q is not conspicuous
for its French, may be the right
reading. Cf. '*ma foy*' in F at 3.4.8.
49 **shrewdly** severely (*OED* 5)
shook your back i.e. jolted you in
the saddle. The retort carries sexual
innuendo.

35–9 'Tis ... him] *F; not in Q*   39 him. I] *F2;* him, I *F*   40 'Wonder of nature!'] *F (* Wonder
of Nature.*); Wonder of nature, – Capell*   45–7 Your ... mistress] *F; not in Q*   46 prescript] *F;*
prescribed *Oxf¹*   48–9] *F; Con.* Ma foy the other day, me thought / Your mistresse shooke you
shrewdly. *Q*

DAUPHIN   So perhaps did yours.   50
CONSTABLE   Mine was not bridled.
DAUPHIN   O then belike she was old and gentle, and you
   rode like a kern of Ireland, your French hose off and in
   your strait strossers.
CONSTABLE   You have good judgement in horse-   55
   manship.
DAUPHIN   Be warned by me then: they that ride so,
   and ride not warily, fall into foul bogs. I had rather
   have my horse to my mistress.
CONSTABLE   I had as lief have my mistress a jade.   60
DAUPHIN   I tell thee, Constable, my mistress wears his
   own hair.
CONSTABLE   I could make as true a boast as that if I had
   a sow to my mistress.
DAUPHIN   *'Le chien est retourné à son propre vomissement, et*   65

---

51 **not bridled** i.e. not a horse, but a
   woman
53 **kern of Ireland** Irish peasant; originally (*OED*) an Irish foot-soldier,
   then by extension a member of the
   class from which such soldiers were
   recruited.
54 **strait strossers** narrow, skin-tight
   trousers; here implying the skin itself,
   i.e. bare legs
55–6 **horsemanship** riding (with sexual
   innuendo). Actors often pronounce
   this as 'whoresmanship', but probably
   no such word-play was intended,
   since no such word existed and since
   the sexual sense is clear without labouring the joke.
58 **foul bogs** (1) literally (Irish bogs), (2)
   figuratively (filthy, perhaps diseased,
   women). Cf. *CE* 3.2.118–21, 'In what
   part of her body stands Ireland?'
   'Marry, sir, in her buttocks. I found
   it out by the bogs.' *OED* bog *sb.*[4], a
   privy, is not recorded till 1789 but is
   probably at least as old as the six-

teenth century.
60 **I had ... jade** jade (*OED sb.*[1]) is a
   contemptuous term for either a horse
   (*OED* 1: cf. l. 24) or a woman (*OED*
   2). This retort to the Dauphin's last
   statement may mean either (1) I'd as
   gladly copulate with a horse, or (2)
   I'd as gladly have as my mistress a
   worthless woman. The first alternative is by far the more effective; cf.
   also ll. 63–6.
61–2 **wears ... hair** i.e. implying that
   the Constable's mistress does not. Cf.
   MV 3.2.92–6, denouncing 'supposed
   fairness' that decks itself with false
   hair, and *Tim* 4.3.144–6, where the
   wearers of false hair are prostitutes
   who have lost most of their own, it is
   implied, through syphilis.
65–6 *Le chien ... bourbier* 2 Peter 2:22
   (referring to backsliders from religion
   to worldliness): 'The dogge is tourned
   to his owne vomite againe, and the
   sowe that was wasshed, is turned
   againe to her wallowyng in the myre.'

50–62] *F; Bur.* I bearing me. I tell thee Lord Constable, / My mistresse weares her owne haire.
Q   60 lief] *(liue)*   61 his] *F;* her *Q*   63 had] *F;* had had *Q*   65–6 'Le ... bourbier.'] *F; not in*
Q   65 *vomissement*] *F2; vemissement F   et*] *Rowe; est F*

247

la truie lavée au bourbier.' Thou mak'st use of anything.

CONSTABLE   Yet do I not use my horse for my mistress,
or any such proverb so little kin to the purpose.

RAMBURES   My Lord Constable, the armour that I saw
in your tent tonight, are those stars or suns upon it?   70

CONSTABLE   Stars, my lord.

DAUPHIN'   Some of them will fall tomorrow, I hope.

CONSTABLE   And yet my sky shall not want.

DAUPHIN   That may be, for you bear a many superflu-
ously, and 'twere more honour some were away.   75

CONSTABLE   Even as your horse bears your praises,
who would trot as well were some of your brags dismounted.

DAUPHIN   Would I were able to load him with his desert!
Will it never be day? I will trot tomorrow a mile, and   80
my way shall be paved with English faces.

CONSTABLE   I will not say so, for fear I should be faced
out of my way. But I would it were morning, for I
would fain be about the ears of the English.

The French is as in Huguenot Bibles printed in 1540, 1551 and 1556 (Gurr).

68 **so little ... purpose** so irrelevant

70 **stars or suns** i.e. ornamental features in such a form, not part of the wearer's heraldic arms. Cf. Sidney, *Astrophel and Stella*, sonnet 104, 'If I but stars upon my armour beare'; Sidney's heraldic device was an inverted lance-head, and his crest a porcupine.

72 **fall** i.e. be knocked off in the battle; alluding to falling, or shooting, stars

73 **And yet ... want** i.e. and yet my suit of armour shall not lack stars. Possibly with a metaphorical implication of undiminished honour; cf. 'more honour' in the rejoinder.

74 **a many** a great number; '*a* was frequently inserted before a numerical adjective, for the purpose of indi-

cating that the objects enumerated are regarded collectively as *one*' (Abbott, 87: cf. a few, a score)

77–8 **dismounted** taken off his back

79 **his desert** what he deserves

80–1 **I will ... faces** i.e. I will kill so many Englishmen tomorrow that their bodies will cover a mile. Cf. *LLL* 4.3.276–7, 'if the streets were paved with thine eyes', and Chapman's Homer, *Iliad*, 8.336–7, 'For some prowd Troyans shall be sure to nourish dogs and foules, / And pave the shore with fat and flesh, depriv'd of lives and soules.'

82–3 **faced ... way** outfaced (cf. 3.2.33, 'faces it out'), i.e. intimidated, from my course

84 **about ... English** beating the English about the heads. Cf. *RJ* 3.1.79–80.

66 *truie*] *Rowe; leuye F*   68–79 or any ... desert] *F; not in Q*   83–4 But ... English] *F; not in Q*

RAMBURES   Who will go to hazard with me for twenty   85
  prisoners?

CONSTABLE   You must first go yourself to hazard ere
  you have them.

DAUPHIN   'Tis midnight; I'll go arm myself.   *Exit.*

ORLEANS   The Dauphin longs for morning.   90

RAMBURES   He longs to eat the English.

CONSTABLE   I think he will eat all he kills.

ORLEANS   By the white hand of my lady, he's a gallant
  prince.

CONSTABLE   Swear by her foot, that she may tread out   95
  the oath.

ORLEANS   He is simply the most active gentleman of
  France.

CONSTABLE   Doing is activity, and he will still be doing.

ORLEANS   He never did harm that I heard of.   100

CONSTABLE   Nor will do none tomorrow; he will keep
  that good name still.

ORLEANS   I know him to be valiant.

CONSTABLE   I was told that by one that knows him
  better than you.   105

ORLEANS   What's he?

CONSTABLE   Marry, he told me so himself, and he said
  he cared not who knew it.

---

85 **go to hazard** play at hazard (a dice game, *OED sb.* 1). Cf. 4.0.17–19n.

85–6 **for twenty prisoners** i.e. for their ransom-money

87 **go ... hazard** put yourself at risk

92 **I think ... kills** i.e. I don't think he will kill any: cf. *MA* 1.1.40–3. A proverbial type of joke (Dent, A 192.2, and cf. *KJ* 1.1.233–5).

95 **tread out** rub out with her foot. The image is of treading out either fire (*3H6* 4.9[8].7, 'A little fire is quickly trodden out') or, more basely, spittle on the ground.

97 **active** 'Abounding in action; ener-getic, lively, agile, nimble' (*OED a.* 5). Cf. *2H4* 4.2[3].20–1 (Falstaff), 'An I had but a belly of any indifferency, I were simply the most active fellow in Europe.'

99 **Doing ... doing** *Doing* here is often taken to mean 'copulating' (e.g. Oxf[1], Cam[2] and R. D. Eagleson's revised edn of Onions, 1986), but there is nothing in the dialogue to support this view of the Dauphin's character. More probably 'he will still be doing' means that he is always (ineffectually) busy: cf. *MA* 1.1.110, 'I wonder that you will still be talking'.

85–8] *F; after 108 Q*   90 SP ORLEANS] *F; Gebon. Q*   Dauphin] *F (Dolphin); Duke of* Burbon *Q*   93–6] *F; not in Q*   97 He is] *F; Well the Duke of* Burbon, is *Q (after 120)*

ORLEANS   He needs not, it is no hidden virtue in him.

CONSTABLE   By my faith, sir, but it is: never anybody   110
saw it but his lackey. 'Tis a hooded valour, and when
it appears it will bate.

ORLEANS   'Ill will never said well.'

CONSTABLE   I will cap that proverb with 'There is
flattery in friendship.'   115

ORLEANS   And I will take up that with 'Give the devil
his due.'

CONSTABLE   Well placed: there stands your friend for
the devil. Have at the very eye of that proverb with
'A pox of the devil.'   120

ORLEANS   You are the better at proverbs by how much
'A fool's bolt is soon shot.'

CONSTABLE   You have shot over.

ORLEANS   'Tis not the first time you were overshot.

110–11 **never ... lackey** i.e. 'He has beaten no body yet but his foot-boy' (Johnson) – 'who would not resist him' (Moore Smith).

111–12 **a hooded ... bate** satirical references to falconry. A falcon is kept hooded till it is flown at game, and when it is unhooded it bates (i.e. flutters its wings: *OED v.*[1] 2) before flying from the wrist. The Dauphin's valour is well muffled, and when it does appear it will *bate* (lose heart: *OED v.*[2] 2c).

113 **Ill ... well** proverbial (Tilley, I 41)

114 **cap** follow up with another, by way of a contest (*OED v.* 6)

114–15 **There ... friendship** proverbial (Dent, F 349.1)

116–17 **Give ... due** proverbial (Tilley, D 273). Cf. *1H4* 1.2.117–18, 'he was never yet a breaker of proverbs; he will give the devil his due.'

118 **Well placed** i.e. your friend has been given his proper position. Cf. *1H4* 4.3.95–7, 'his kinsman March – / Who is, if every owner were well placed, / Indeed his king.'

119 **the very eye** not certainly explained. The bull's-eye of a target is not recorded before the nineteenth century, but some such sense would be appropriate here; or perhaps the eye as the tenderest part (a common idea in Shakespeare) is meant.

120 **A pox ... devil** proverbial (Dent, *PLED*, P 536.11); for 'a pox of' as a curse, cf. *Tem* 1.1.39.

121–2 **You ... shot** 'You are as much better at proverbs than I am as a fool is readier with his replies than a wise man.' The proverb (Tilley, F 515) means that a fool does not take careful aim before shooting his arrow (*bolt*).

123 **shot over** shot over the target. The Constable will not allow that Orleans's proverb follows in the sequence.

124 **were overshot** were wide of the mark, have overshot yourself (*OED* overshoot *v.* 3b: cf. *LLL* 1.1.140, 'So study evermore is overshot'). Perhaps with word-play on overshot as (1) intoxicated (*OED ppl. a.* 3, example from 1605) and (2) outshot, excelled in shooting.

109–12] *F; not in Q*   111 lackey] *(Lacquey)*   120 pox] *F;* Iogge *Q*   121–4] *F; not in Q*

Enter a Messenger.

MESSENGER   My lord High Constable, the English lie   125
within fifteen hundred paces of your tents.

CONSTABLE   Who hath measured the ground?

MESSENGER   The Lord Grandpré.

CONSTABLE   A valiant and most expert gentleman.

[*Exit Messenger.*]

Would it were day! Alas, poor Harry of England! He   130
longs not for the dawning as we do.

ORLEANS   What a wretched and peevish fellow is this
King of England, to mope with his fat-brained followers so far out of his knowledge!

CONSTABLE   If the English had any apprehension they   135
would run away.

ORLEANS   That they lack, for if their heads had any
intellectual armour they could never wear such heavy
headpieces.

RAMBURES   That island of England breeds very valiant   140
creatures: their mastiffs are of unmatchable courage.

125–9 **My lord ... gentleman** Holinshed (3.552) says that the French
host 'was incamped not past two
hundred and fiftie pases distant from
the English' and (3.554) that when
the armies confronted each other for
battle they were 'not distant in sunder
past three bow shoots'. Why Shakespeare altered this is not clear. The
Constable's question (l. 127) is usually
spoken ironically, as though he doubts
the accuracy of the Messenger's statement, but his comment on Grandpré
(for whom cf. 4.2.37–54) makes the
latter a reliable source of information.
Q gives the Messenger's speech as
'My Lords, the English lye within a
hundred / Paces of your Tent.'

132 **peevish** The word has many sixteenth-century senses (*OED*, which
notes the difficulty of establishing an

exact one in many contexts): foolish,
mad, obstinate are all possible senses
here.

133 **mope** wander aimlessly (*OED v.* 1)
fat-brained thick-witted, stupid. Cf.
1H4 1.2.2, 'fat-witted'.

134 **so far ... knowledge** i.e. so much
further than he would have gone if
he had known what was good for
him; cf. the Constable's next speech.
Alternatively, 'leaving his wits so far
behind him' (Moore Smith).

135 **apprehension** understanding (*OED*
8)

137–8 **if ... armour** i.e. if their skulls
were not so thick as to leave no room
for brains (*intellectual armour*)

141 **their mastiffs** Harrison's 'Description of England' (in Holinshed,
1.230–1) includes a description of the
strength and courage of the mastiff.

126 fifteen hundred] *F;* a hundred *Q*   128 Grandpré] *(Grandpree)*   129 SD] *Oxf¹*   130–56] *F;*
not in Q

251

ORLEANS   Foolish curs, that run winking into the mouth
of a Russian bear and have their heads crushed like
rotten apples. You may as well say that's a valiant
flea that dare eat his breakfast on the lip of a lion.   145

CONSTABLE   Just, just; and the men do sympathize with
the mastiffs in robustious and rough coming on,
leaving their wits with their wives. And then give
them great meals of beef and iron and steel, they will
eat like wolves and fight like devils.   150

ORLEANS   Ay, but these English are shrewdly out of beef.

CONSTABLE   Then shall we find tomorrow they have
only stomachs to eat and none to fight. Now is it time
to arm; come, shall we about it?

ORLEANS
It is now two o'clock; but, let me see, by ten   155

142 **winking** with closed eyes (cf. 2.1.7),
i.e. blindly, rashly
143 **Russian bear** i.e. in a bear-baiting
ring
145 **eat his breakfast on** i.e. suck blood
from
146 **Just, just** True, true; 'exactly so'
(Moore Smith, citing *MM* 3.1.65–6,
'Perpetual durance?' 'Ay, just, perpetual durance.')
sympathize with agree in nature
with, resemble
147 **robustious** violent, boisterous
(*OED* 2)
coming on hostile advancing (*OED*
come *v.* 62a)
148–53 **give ... to fight** The Constable's
oration in Hall (66) (not in Holinshed)
includes the following: 'For you must
vnderstand, that kepe an Englishman
one moneth from his warme bed, fat
befe and stale [i.e. strong] drynke,
and let him that season tast colde and
suffre hunger, you then shall se his
courage abated, his bodye waxe leane
and bare, and euer desirous to returne
into his owne countrey.' *Famous Victories* (scene xiii: ll. 1,135–7) echoes

this. In *E3*, 3.3.158–62 the French
King similarly says that King
Edward's soldiers are incapable of
fight if you 'scant them of their chines
of beefe / And take awaie their
downie featherbedes'. Cf. also *1H6*
1.2.9–12.
148–9 **give them ... steel** The parallel
phrases that end the sentence indicate
that the iron and steel are in their
hands as weapons; but the sentence's
structure suggests that the iron and
steel are part of the *great meals*.
151 **shrewdly out of** sorely (cf. l. 49)
short of
153 **only ... fight** only appetites for food
(*OED* stomach *sb*. 5), not inclinations
(5b) for fighting
153 **Now** If this word is emphasized it
is a hit at the Dauphin, who went
to arm himself at midnight (l. 89);
otherwise – perhaps preferably – it is
a simple statement of fact, leading to
the end of the scene.
155 **It is ... ten** The metre calls for
some elision ('*Tis*, with stresses on
now and *clock* in the first part of the
line).

144 say that's] *F* (say, that's); say, 'That's *Oxf¹*   145 lion.] *F* (*Lyon.*); lion.' *Oxf¹*   155-6] *F*;
Come, come away: / The Sun is hie, and we weare out the day. *Q*

We shall have each a hundred Englishmen.   *Exeunt.*

[4.0]   *Enter* CHORUS.

CHORUS

Now entertain conjecture of a time
When creeping murmur and the poring dark
Fills the wide vessel of the universe.
From camp to camp through the foul womb of night
The hum of either army stilly sounds,   5
That the fixed sentinels almost receive
The secret whispers of each other's watch.
Fire answers fire, and through their paly flames
Each battle sees the other's umbered face.
Steed threatens steed, in high and boastful neighs   10
Piercing the night's dull ear; and from the tents
The armourers accomplishing the knights,

by ten 'They [i.e. the Frenchmen]
rested themselues, waiting for the
bloudie blast of the terrible trumpet,
till the houre betweene nine and ten
of the clocke of the same daie'
(Holinshed, 3.553); *by ten* may imply
that they will win the battle within
the hour, or it may be used merely
for the sake of the rhyme.
4.0.1 entertain conjecture of imagine
2 poring eye-straining (transferred
   epithet: *OED* pore *v.* 1, to search into
   something by gazing)
3 Fills The verb 'is singular, as the
   "creeping murmur and the poring
   dark" form but one idea' (Wright).
4–9 From ... face Holinshed (3.552)
   states that the English halted at 'a
   little village, where they were refreshed with meat and drinke somewhat more plentiouslie than they had
   been diuerse daies before. Order was
   taken by commandement from the
   king after the armie was first set in

battell araie, that no noise or clamour
should be made in the host; so that
in marching foorth to this village,
euerie man kept himselfe quiet; but
at their comming into the village, fiers
were made to giue light on euerie
side, as there likewise were in the
French host, which was incamped
not past two hundred and fiftie pases
distant from the English.'
4 foul womb dark cavern (figurative)
5 stilly quietly
6 That so that. Cf. ll. 41, 45.
8 paly pale. Cf. *2H6* 3.2.141, 'his paly
   lips'.
9 battle army
   umbered darkened as if stained with
   umber, a brown earth used as a
   pigment (cf. *AYL* 1.3.111)
12 accomplishing completing the
   arming of (by 'closing rivets up', i.e.
   riveting some parts of the armour to
   others, e.g. the helmet to the cuirass):
   OED accomplish 4

156 Englishmen] *F4;* English men *F*

4.0] *Pope; Actus Tertius F*   0.1 *Enter] Rowe; speech not in Q*   1 SP] *Johnson; not in F*   6 sentinels]
(Centinels)

With busy hammers closing rivets up,
Give dreadful note of preparation.
The country cocks do crow, the clocks do toll,   15
And the third hour of drowsy morning name.
Proud of their numbers and secure in soul,
The confident and over-lusty French
Do the low-rated English play at dice,
And chide the cripple tardy-gaited night   20
Who like a foul and ugly witch doth limp
So tediously away. The poor condemned English,
Like sacrifices, by their watchful fires
Sit patiently and inly ruminate
The morning's danger; and their gesture sad,   25
Investing lank-lean cheeks and war-worn coats,

14 **note** sound
   preparation pronounced as five syllables
17–19 **Proud ... dice** Cf. Holinshed, 3.552: 'They were lodged euen in the waie by the which the Englishmen must needs passe towards Calis, and all that night after their comming thither, made great cheare and were verie merrie, pleasant, and full of game.' Next day, just before the battle, 'The Frenchmen in the meane while, as though they had been sure of victorie, made great triumph, for the capteins had determined before, how to diuide the spoile, and the soldiers the night before had plaied the Englishmen at dice' (3.553).
17 **secure** over-confident (*OED a.* 1)
18 **over-lusty** arrogant, over-confident (*OED*; cf. examples 1583, 1587, and lusty *a.* 6)
19 **play** play for (cf. 17–19n. and 3.7.85)
20 **cripple** lame (*OED* cripple *a.*)
   tardy-gaited slow-paced
21–2 **Who ... away** Cf. *TC* 4.2.14–15: 'Beshrew the witch! With venomous

wights she stays / As tediously as hell'.
22 **condemned** doomed to destruction (condemnèd)
23 **Like sacrifices** as passively as animals ready for sacrificial slaughter. Contrast *1H4* 4.1.114, where Hotspur says of Prince Henry and his comrades, who are approaching in martial splendour, 'They come like sacrifices in their trim' (i.e. like beasts decked out for sacrifice on the altar of Bellona, goddess of war).
   by ... fires wakeful beside their fires (transferred epithet; *OED* watchful 1)
24 **inly** inwardly
   ruminate turn over and over in mind, meditate deeply upon (*OED* 1); here, though not elsewhere in Shakespeare, figuratively associated with literal chewing of the cud (*OED* ruminate 3). Cf. *sacrifices*, l. 23.
25 **gesture sad** melancholy bearing (*OED* gesture *sb.* 1; sad *a.* 5c)
26 **Investing** enveloping or surrounding like clothing (*OED ppl. a.*: antedates first example 1646)

15 toll,] *Steevens² (Tyrwhitt)*; towle: *F*   16 name.] *Steevens² (Tyrwhitt)*; nam'd, *F*   20 cripple tardy-gaited] *(creeple-tardy-gated)*   26 lank-lean] *F*; lank lean *Oxf¹*

Presenteth them unto the gazing moon
So many horrid ghosts. O now, who will behold
The royal captain of this ruined band
Walking from watch to watch, from tent to tent, 30
Let him cry 'Praise and glory on his head!'
For forth he goes and visits all his host,
Bids them good morrow with a modest smile,
And calls them brothers, friends and countrymen.
Upon his royal face there is no note 35
How dread an army hath enrounded him,
Nor doth he dedicate one jot of colour
Unto the weary and all-watchèd night,
But freshly looks and overbears attaint
With cheerful semblance and sweet majesty, 40
That every wretch, pining and pale before,
Beholding him plucks comfort from his looks.

lank-lean shrunken, hollow (*OED* lank *a.* 1) with leanness

27 ***Presenteth** Oxf[1] defends F's 'Presented' as contrasting 'the mood of the English soldiers before and after Henry visits them', but the fact that the present tense is consistently used in this Chorus and in all the others is decisively in favour of Hanmer's emendation. 'Presented them' would be an error easily made by a compositor carrying 'Presenteth them' in his head.
the gazing moon Wilson compares *Ham* 1.4.34[53] (of the Ghost), 'Revisitst thus the glimpses of the moon'.

28 **horrid** horrible. Cf. *Ham* 1.4.36[55], 'So horridly to shake our disposition', and preceding note.

28–47 **O now ... night** There is no mention of this action in Hall or Holinshed.

28 **who will behold** whoever consents to see; either in imagination (cf. l. 1) or represented on the stage (cf. l.

46, 'as may unworthiness define', and 48n.)

30 **watch** group of guards (*OED sb.* 12). Cf. l. 1.

32 **host** army

33 **modest** not harsh or domineering (*OED a.* 1), i.e. affable

35 **note** sign (*OED sb.*[2] 7)

36 **enrounded** encircled (Shakespeare's only use of the verb). The statement, not literally true, emphasizes the numerical superiority of the French.

37 **dedicate** sacrifice
jot least bit

38 **all-watched** all passed in wakefulness (watchèd)

39 **overbears** subdues
attaint weariness. *OED sb.* 7 notes it as a unique usage, derived either from the obsolete adjectival use to mean 'overcome with weariness' (*OED ppl. a.* 3: last example 1485) or from *OED sb.* 6, 'stain', i.e. 'any stain upon his freshness'.

40 **semblance** appearance (without any suggestion of false appearance): *OED* 1

A largess universal, like the sun,
His liberal eye doth give to every one,
Thawing cold fear, that mean and gentle all   45
Behold, as may unworthiness define,
A little touch of Harry in the night.
And so our scene must to the battle fly,
Where – oh for pity! – we shall much disgrace
With four or five most vile and ragged foils   50
Right ill-disposed in brawl ridiculous
The name of Agincourt. Yet sit and see,
Minding true things by what their mockeries be.   *Exit.*

[4.1]   *Enter the* KING *and* GLOUCESTER[, *meeting*] BEDFORD.

KING
    Gloucester, 'tis true that we are in great danger;
    The greater therefore should our courage be. –

43–4 **A largess ... every one** Quintilian, *Institutio*, 1.2.14 ('ut sol universis idem lucis caloris largitur': 'as the sun abundantly gives the same light and warmth to all men'), has been suggested as a source of Shakespeare's expression of this familiar idea, but the resemblance may be coincidental, as *universal* and *largess* occur elsewhere in Shakespeare.
44 **liberal** generous
    every one every single one of them
45 **that** so that
    mean and gentle i.e. the lower and higher ranks of the army
46 **as ... define** either (1) as my unworthy self may describe [it] or (2) as our unworthy selves may present [it] (*OED* define *v*. 6: describe). Cf. 48n.
47 **touch** trace (*OED sb*. 19), i.e. glimpse. Cf. *H8* 5.1.12–13, 'give your friend / Some touch of your late business'.
48 **And so** and then. This suggests that

the King's tour of the camp will first be presented.
50 **four ... foils** Shakespeare echoes Sidney's criticism of stage conventions: 'While in the meane time two Armies flie in, represented with foure swords & bucklers, and then what hard hart will not receive it [i.e. the stage] for a pitched field' (*Defence of Poesy*, printed 1595: Sidney, 3.38).
    ragged beggarly
    foils light fencing weapons
51 **Right ill-disposed** very unskilfully handled (*OED* dispose *v*. 2)
53 **Minding** calling to mind
    mockeries imitations (*OED sb*. 2); here with the additional sense (*OED sb*. 1b) 'A subject or occasion of derision; a person, thing, or action that deserves or occasions ridicule'
4.1.0.1 In ll. 1–3 it appears that the King enters with Gloucester, speaking to him, and then meets Bedford.

46 define,] *F2;* define. *F*   47 night.] *Rowe;* Night, *F*   53 mockeries] *(*Mock'ries*)*

4.1] *Hanmer*   0.1] *this edn; Enter the King, Bedford, and Gloucester. F; not in Q*   1–34] *F; not in Q*

Good morrow, brother Bedford. God Almighty!
There is some soul of goodness in things evil,
Would men observingly distil it out: 5
For our bad neighbour makes us early stirrers,
Which is both healthful and good husbandry.
Besides, they are our outward consciences
And preachers to us all, admonishing
That we should dress us fairly for our end.   10
Thus may we gather honey from the weed
And make a moral of the devil himself.

Enter ERPINGHAM.

Good morrow, old Sir Thomas Erpingham.
A good soft pillow for that good white head

---

3 **God Almighty** This, rather than being a mere oath, is a lightly spoken expression of thanks to God for so arranging matters that ll. 4–12 are true.

4–5 **There ... out** 'Playful rather than profoundly serious, as the context shows; yet there is deep feeling in the words' (Wilson)

4 **some soul of goodness** something essentially good, i.e. concealed beneath the outward form. Cf. *Ham* 2.2.91–2, 'since brevity is the soul of wit, / And tediousness the limbs and outward flourishes'.

5 **observingly** observantly

6 **bad neighbour** 'i.e. likely to be up to his tricks while we sleep' (Wilson). Taylor cites the two proverbs, 'He that has a good neighbour has a good morrow' and 'He that has an ill neighbour has oftentimes an ill morning' (Tilley, N 106, N 107).
early stirrers a common expression (Dent, SS 23). Cf. *R3* 3.2.33, 'you are early stirring'.

7 **good husbandry** i.e. a good way of living. *Husbandry* (*OED* 1: The administration and management of a household; domestic economy) was used figuratively for management in general (*OED* 1b), and the phrases 'good husbandry' and 'ill husbandry' were in common use (*OED* 4a).

8 **they** i.e. the enemy
outward consciences external admonishers, as our consciences are our internal ones

10 **dress us** prepare ourselves

11 **gather ... weed** i.e. like the proverbial bee (Tilley, B 205)

12 **make a moral of** draw a moral lesson from (*OED* moral *sb.* 2)

13 **old** Erpingham was fifty-eight years old at the time. Holinshed (3.554) writes that when the King, having posted his archers to await a signal, advanced with his other forces, 'These made somewhat forward, before whome there went an old knight sir Thomas Erpingham (a man of great experience in the warre) with a warder in his hand; and when he cast up his warder, all the armie shouted, but that was a signe to the archers in the meadow, which therwith shot wholie altogither at the vauward of the Frenchmen.'

---

3 Good morrow] *F3;* God morrow *F*

Were better than a churlish turf of France.   15
ERPINGHAM
    Not so, my liege, this lodging likes me better,
    Since I may say 'Now lie I like a king.'
KING
    'Tis good for men to love their present pains
    Upon example: so the spirit is eased,
    And when the mind is quickened, out of doubt   20
    The organs, though defunct and dead before,
    Break up their drowsy grave and newly move
    With casted slough and fresh legerity.
    Lend me thy cloak, Sir Thomas. – Brothers both,
    Commend me to the princes in our camp;   25
    Do my good morrow to them, and anon
    Desire them all to my pavilion.
GLOUCESTER
    We shall, my liege.
ERPINGHAM
    Shall I attend your grace?
KING   No, my good knight;
    Go with my brothers to my lords of England.   30

---

16 **likes** pleases. Cf. 4.3.77.
17 **like a king** i.e. richly. The common
    expression is humorously used in its
    literal sense. Gurr perversely suggests
    that there is also word-play on *lie* (tell
    a lie), 'given Henry's perversion of
    the proverb about ill neighbours'.
19 **Upon example** by taking others'
    good conduct as an object of imitation
    (*OED* example *sb.* 6). Moore Smith
    records a suggestion that ll. 18–23
    might be spoken aside, but the
    passage is rather too long for that and
    it also leaves Erpingham's jest without
    an appreciative reply. To moralize to
    his friends is quite in the King's style;
    cf. ll. 1–12.
20 **out of doubt** without doubt, cer-
    tainly. Cf. l. 109.

21 **organs** bodily organs
    defunct ... dead The words are
    synonymous: cf. *defunction*, 1.2.58.
22 **Break ... grave** arise from (literally,
    break open from within) their grave-
    like sleep
    newly again
23 **With ... legerity** having cast their
    slough (i.e. old snake-skin: cf. *TN*
    2.5.143–4, 'cast thy humble slough,
    and appear fresh') and acquired fresh-
    ness and nimbleness. There is 'a kind
    of zeugma' (Deighton) in the two
    different uses of *with*. This is Shake-
    speare's only use of *casted* and *legerity*.
26 **anon** shortly. The informal and con-
    tinuing nature of the dialogue makes
    it unlikely that Shakespeare intended
    the rhyme with *pavilion* (l. 27).

---

19 example:] *Pope (subst.)*; example, *F*   28] *F; Capell adds SD Exeunt Gloucester and Bedford.*

I and my bosom must debate awhile,
And then I would no other company.

ERPINGHAM
The Lord in heaven bless thee, noble Harry!
Exeunt [all but the King].
KING   God-a-mercy, old heart, thou speak'st cheerfully.

Enter PISTOL.

PISTOL   Che vous là?   35
KING   A friend.
PISTOL
Discuss unto me, art thou officer,
Or art thou base, common and popular?
KING   I am a gentleman of a company.

31 **debate** engage in discussion (*OED v.* 4b)
32 **then** i.e. while I am communing with my soul
would would have, desire. Cf. 5.2.68.
33 SD F's placing of the SD makes the King's l. 34 an apostrophe, spoken as Erpingham goes, rather than a direct address. This seems appropriate, as it then forms a bridge between Erpingham's exit and Pistol's entrance. It is not, as Gurr supposes, 'a soliloquising comment indicating that Henry himself is not cheerful'. If F placed the SD (the one word *Exeunt*) after l. 34 it would wrongly indicate that the King too left the stage. At l. 28 Gloucester and Bedford must make a move to depart, but in view of l. 30 it is better for them to turn back as Erpingham speaks than to make an exit which leaves Erpingham to catch up with them off stage.
34 **God-a-mercy** I thank thee: literally, 'God have mercy [on thee].' 'Used in response to a respectful salutation or a wish, usually expressed by an inferior, for a person's welfare'

(Onions 1986, comparing *Ham* 2.2.173).
SD Q (see textual footnotes) begins the scene here, omitting the King's borrowing of Erpingham's cloak.
35 **Che vous là?** Pistol's rendering of the conventional challenge '*Qui va là?*' ('Who goes there?'), to which the King returns the conventional answer (cf. ll. 91–3). The French phrase was familiar enough to be used in English contexts (Lever 1953: 81), which makes a compositorial misreading unlikely. Taylor takes *Che* to be 'a legitimate spelling of *Qui*', comparing '*Che la?*' in F *1H6* 3.2.13; but it is possible that '*Che*' there represents '*Qui est*', pronounced as Italian *Chi è* (cf. Kyd, *Spanish Tragedy*, 3.2.94, '*Che le Ieron!*', which may represent Italian '*Chi è là? Jeron!*', since Lorenzo's Page enters in response).
37 **Discuss** See 3.2.61n.
38 **base, common and popular** i.e. one of the common soldiers (synonymous)
39 **gentleman of a company** gentleman volunteer serving in the ranks. In *1H4* 4.2.25 Falstaff's 'ragged regi-

33 SD] *Cam; after 34 Oxf¹; Exeunt F; Exit Erpingham / Capell* 34 SD] *F; Enter the King disguised, to him Pistoll. Q* 35] *F (Che vous la?); Ke ve la? Q; Qui va là? Rowe; Qui vous là? Oxf¹* 37–8] *verse Q; prose F* 39 I am] *F; No sir, I am Q*

PISTOL   Trail'st thou the puissant pike?   40
KING   Even so. What are you?
PISTOL   As good a gentleman as the Emperor.
KING   Then you are a better than the King.
PISTOL

The King's a bawcock and a heart of gold,
A lad of life, an imp of Fame,   45
Of parents good, of fist most valiant.
I kiss his dirty shoe, and from heart-string

ment' includes 'gentlemen of companies'.

40 **Trail'st ... pike** To trail a pike was to hold it just below the head so that the butt trailed on the ground (the usual method of carrying it when not on the march). In Shakespeare's time the infantry consisted of pikemen and musketeers.

41 **you** The King consistently uses the polite *you*, Pistol the familiar *thou*.

42 **As good ... Emperor** proverbial (Dent, G 63.1)
Emperor Holy Roman Emperor

43 **a better** a better man, i.e. one higher in rank. This line should perhaps be made verse by inserting (or restoring) a one-syllable exclamation like 'Why' or 'O' before it. It is a reply to a verse line from Pistol, and another one from Pistol follows it. Q prefixes 'O', but omits 'a'.

44 **bawcock** See 3.2.25n.
heart of gold a common term of endearment (*OED* heart *sb.* 14). Cf. *1H4* 2.5[4].280–1, 'Gallants, lads, boys, hearts of gold, all the titles of good fellowship come to you!'

45 **lad of life** lively lad (Pistol's alliterative expression is unique). Cf. *1H4* 2.5[4].11–12, 'a Corinthian, a lad of mettle, a good boy.'
imp of Fame 'child of Renown' (Wilson). Pistol has used the same expression in saluting the newly

crowned Henry V, *2H4* 5.5.42. The word *imp* (a shoot, a scion) is used affectedly here, as it is by Armado and Holofernes with reference to Mote [Moth], *LLL* 1.2.5, 5.2.582. Shakespeare's only use of *of fame* in the sense 'famous' is in *TN* 3.3.23–4, 'the memorials and the things of fame / That do renown this city'. His only other personification of Fame is in *MA* 2.1.200–1, 'I have played the part of Lady Fame' (i.e. of Report). F's general use of capitals for nouns leaves it doubtful whether a personification is intended, but Wilson's interpretation seems to give the better sense.

46 **Of parents good** Q and F agree in this phrase, an inept parallel to 'of fist most valiant'. Pistol's meaning – if he has one – may be 'he is no bastard'. There is no comparable phrase in Shakespeare.

47 **I ... shoe** an affected and grotesque expression of adoration, more comparable to Armado's courtly 'I do adore thy sweet grace's slipper' (*LLL* 5.2.659) than to Caliban's servile 'let me lick thy shoe' (*Tem* 3.2.23). Cf. Pistol's expression in *2H4* 2.4.183, 'Sweet knight, I kiss thy neaf', where 'Courtliness collapses into the plebeian, *neaf* being dialectal for "fist"' (*2H4*, ed. A. R. Humphreys, Arden Shakespeare, London, 1966).
heart-string The word occurs three

41 so] *F*; so sir *Q*   43] *F*; O then thou art better then the King? *Q*   44–8] *verse Q*; *prose F*   44 bawcock] *F*; bago *Q*   45 imp of Fame] *F* (Impe of Fame); impe of fame *Q*   47 heart-string] *F* (heart-/ string); my hart strings *Q*

I love the lovely bully. What is thy name?

KING   Harry le Roy.

PISTOL   Le Roy?   50

A Cornish name: art thou of Cornish crew?

KING   No, I am a Welshman.

PISTOL   Know'st thou Fluellen?

KING   Yes.

PISTOL

Tell him I'll knock his leek about his pate   55
Upon Saint Davy's day.

KING   Do not you wear your dagger in your cap that
day, lest he knock that about yours.

PISTOL   Art thou his friend?

KING   And his kinsman too.   60

other times (in the plural) in Shake-speare, in *TGV* 4.2.60 (in prose, but the context calls for a stress on 'heart'), in *R3* 4.4.296 [365] ('Harp on it still shall I, till heart-strings break') and in *Oth* 3.3.265 ('Though that her jesses were my dear heart-strings'). It could apparently be stressed on either syllable – unless in *Oth* 'dear' is to be given two syllables. Q's reading 'my hart strings' stresses 'heart' and gives the line a feminine ending. F's reading, if correct in the singular, is probably meant to be in Pistol's distinctive style.

48 **bully** fine fellow (a familiar term of endearment: *OED sb.*[1] 1). Always in the vocative on its eighteen other appearances in Shakespeare.

49 **Harry le Roy** i.e. Harry the King (cf. 4.3.53). Pistol's obtuse and confident response improves the humour of the deception. Though 'roy' and 'moy' are Shakespearean spellings of the French words *roi* and *moi*, the false-true name must have been given an English pronunciation.

51 **A Cornish name** Pistol is evidently unaware of the proverb 'By Tre, Pol, and Pen, you shall know the Cornish men' (*ODEP*, 669).
crew set, crowd (usually derogatory in Shakespeare, e.g. *MND* 3.2.9, 'A crew of patches', *R2* 5.3.136, 'that consorted crew')

52 **Welshman** He was born at Mon-mouth; see 4.7.11. Cf. 4.7.104, 'For I am Welsh, you know, good country-man.'

55–6 **I'll ... day** St David is the patron saint of Wales, and his day is 1 March; for the leek, cf. 4.7.96–102.

57–8 **Do ... yours** Shakespeare refers to the use of a dagger to beat an opponent's head in *RJ* 4.4.143–4 [5.114–15] and (by implication) in *TN* 4.1.25–8. Daggers often had wooden handles (called dudgeons), so one would make a serviceable cudgel. It appears that Pistol is wearing his in his cap, as brooches and favours were worn (*LLL* 5.2.612, *2H4* 1.2.15).

60 **And ... too** He is being humorously provocative.

49 Harry le Roy] *F (Harry le Roy); Harry* le Roy *Q*; Harry *le roi Oxf¹* 50–1] *verse this edn; prose F; Q lines ... Cornish man: / ... crew? / 51 name] F; man Q 52 No] F; No sir Q 54 Yes] F; I sir, he is my kinsman Q 55–6] verse Pope; prose F; not in Q 56 Saint] (S.) 57–8] F; not in Q 60 And ... too] F; I sir Q*

PISTOL   The *fico* for thee`then!
KING   I thank you. God be with you!
PISTOL   My name is Pistol called.   *Exit.*
KING   It sorts well with your fierceness.

Enter FLUELLEN *and* GOWER[, *separately*].

GOWER   Captain Fluellen!   65
FLUELLEN   'So! In the name of Jesu Christ, speak fewer.
It is the greatest admiration in the universal world
when the true and ancient prerogatifs and laws of the
wars is not kept. If you would take the pains but to
examine the wars of Pompey the Great you shall   70

61 *fico* Having given Fluellen the *fico* at
3.6.56, Pistol now inevitably gives it
to his kinsman.
63 **My name ... called** Cf. 'My name
is Harry Percy' (Hotspur, confronting
Prince Henry at Shrewsbury, *1H4*
5.4.60).
SD 'God be with you' (l. 62) probably indicates that Pistol is moving
towards an exit after delivering his
broadside; l. 64 is ironically shouted
after his departing figure.
64 **sorts** fits
SD Gower can either meet Fluellen
or follow him, which is preferable,
since neither of them will then meet
Pistol going out.
66 **'So!** An abbreviation of the oath
'Godso!', as F's apostrophe indicates.
Cf. *MW* 3.1.38, 39, where F gives two
greetings as ' 'Saue you' and ' 'Plesse
you'.
speak fewer don't talk so much. Cf.
Lily's *Short Introduction of Grammar*,
1549, C7, '*Vir sapit, qui pauca loquitur*,
That manne is wyse, that speaketh
fewe.' Cf. 2.1.80, *pauca*. Shakespeare
has several allusions to this, the only
Latin grammar prescribed for school
use, e.g. *MW* 4.1 (where William

Page's Latin test is wholly based on
it), *MA* 4.1.21–2 ('some [inter-
jections] be of laughing, as "ah, ha,
he!"'), and *TN* 2.3.2 ('and *diluculo
surgere*, thou knowest'). Gower has
uttered two words, and Fluellen proceeds to wax eloquent. Gower
responds tactfully by assuming the
military reason for keeping quiet. Q's
'lewer' is more probably a foul-case
error for 'fewer' than one for 'lower',
and Q3's 'lower' is an emendation of
Q's reading.
67 **admiration** wonder (here derogatory)
the universal world the whole
world: a common expression (*OED*
universal *a.* 8a: cf. *RJ* 3.2.94, 'the
universal earth', where Juliet is the
speaker), perhaps devalued by
emphatic indiscriminate use (*RJ*
2.3[4].196, 'in the versal world',
where the Nurse is the speaker).
Fluellen uses it again at 4.8.10–11.
68 **prerogatifs** prerogatives, privileges
(Fluellen's eccentric usage: he means
principles)
70 **Pompey the Great** Gneius Pom-
peius (106–48 BC), the triumvir. Sulla
bestowed on him the surname

61 The *fico*] *Collier;* The *Figo* F; Figa *Q*   62] F; *not in Q*   63 SD] F; *opp.* 64 *Oxf¹*   64
fierceness.] F *(fiercenesse. / Manet King.); fiercenesse. / Pist.* Pistoll is my name. / *Exit* Pistoll.
Q   SD *Enter ...* GOWER] F; *Enter Gower and Flewellen Q   separately*] *Oxf¹ (subst.)*   66 'So!] F
(*'So,); not in Q*   fewer] F; lewer *Q;* lower *Q3*   70 Pompey the Great] F; the Romanes *Q*

find, I warrant you, that there is no tiddle-taddle nor
pibble-pabble in Pompey's camp. I warrant you, you
shall find the ceremonies of the wars, and the cares
of it, and the forms of it, and the sobriety of it, and
the modesty of it, to be otherwise.   75

GOWER   Why, the enemy is loud; you hear him all
night.

FLUELLEN   If the enemy is an ass and a fool and a
prating coxcomb, is it meet, think you, that we should
also, look you, be an ass and a fool and a prating   80
coxcomb, in your own conscience now?

GOWER   I will speak lower.

FLUELLEN   I pray you and beseech you that you will.
                                     [*Exeunt Gower and Fluellen.*]

KING

Though it appear a little out of fashion,
There is much care and valour in this Welshman.   85

Enter three Soldiers, JOHN BATES, ALEXANDER COURT *and*
MICHAEL WILLIAMS.

COURT   Brother John Bates, is not that the morning
which breaks yonder?

Magnus (the great) in consequence of
victories gained by the time he was
twenty-five years old. Everything
continued to go well with his campaigns till he was forty-five years old.
He was finally defeated by Julius
Caesar at Pharsalus and treacherously
murdered when he fled to Egypt. In
LLL 5.1 and 5.2 he is among the
Nine Worthies.

71 **tiddle-taddle** tittle-tattle (an intensive reduplication of 'tattle', as
'bibble-babble' is of 'babble'), foolish
chatter

79 **coxcomb** fool (*OED* 3)

81 **in … now** i.e. I ask you, on your
conscience

83 SD They must go out together, as
Gower has still something to say to
Fluellen.

84-5 A rhyming couplet, despite the
inadequacy of the rhyme.

71 tiddle-taddle] *F* (tiddle tadle); tittle tattle *Q*   72 pibble-pabble] *Theobald;* pibble ba-/ble *F;*
bible bable *Q*.   72 in Pompey's camp] *F;* there *Q*   78 If] *F;* Godes sollud, if *Q* 82 lower] *F, Q
Q3*   83 SD] *Q (Exit Gower, and Flewellen.); Exit. F*   85] *F;* Yet theres much care in this.
Q   SD] *F; Enter three Souldiers. Q*   86–133] *F;* 1.*Soul.* Is not that the morning yonder? / 2.*Soul.*
I we see the beginning, / God knowes whether we shall see the end or no. / 3.*Soul.* Well I thinke
the king could wish himselfe / Vp to the necke in the middle of the Thames, / And so I would
he were, at all aduentures, and I with him. / *Kin.* Now masters god morrow, what cheare? / 3.*S.*
I faith small cheer some of vs is like to haue, / Ere this day ende. / *Kin.* Why fear nothing man,

BATES I think it be; but we have no great cause to
desire the approach of day.

WILLIAMS We see yonder the beginning of the day,   90
but I think we shall never see the end of it. – Who
goes there?

KING A friend.

WILLIAMS Under what captain serve you?

KING Under Sir Thomas Erpingham.   95

WILLIAMS A good old commander and a most kind
gentleman. I pray you, what thinks he of our estate?

KING Even as men wrecked upon a sand, that look to
be washed off the next tide.

BATES He hath not told his thought to the King?   100

KING No, nor it is not meet he should. For though I
speak it to you, I think the King is but a man, as I am:
the violet smells to him as it doth to me; the element
shows to him as it doth to me; all his senses have but
human conditions; his ceremonies laid by, in his   105
nakedness he appears but a man; and though his
affections are higher mounted than ours, yet when they
stoop they stoop with the like wing. Therefore when
he sees reason of fears as we do, his fears, out of doubt,
be of the same relish as ours are. Yet, in reason, no man   110

95 *Thomas Cf. ll. 13, 24. F's '*Iohn*'
must be a compositor's error, probably through misunderstanding the
abbreviation 'Tho.' (Walter).
97 **estate** condition
98 **Even as men** i.e. our estate is even
as that of men
sand sandbank
101–2 **though ... to you** in the proverbial sense 'Though I say it, that
should not say it' (Tilley, S 114), i.e.
though I am no better than one of
the King's poor subjects. The phrase
also draws attention to the dramatic
irony in the next phrase.

103–4 **element shows** sky appears
105 **conditions** characteristics (*OED* 13)
ceremonies external accessories or
symbols of state (*OED* 4)
107 **affections** emotions (*OED* 2)
107–8 **are ... wing** soar higher than
ours, yet when they swoop down-
wards, they do so in the same fashion
(metaphor from falconry)
109 **reason of fears** reason to fear
110 **of the same relish** of the same
taste, i.e. the same nature
110–11 **in reason ... fear** it is only
reasonable that nobody (e.g.
Erpingham) should communicate any

the king is frolike. / 2.*S*. he may be, for he hath no such cause as we / *Kin.* Nay say not so, he
is a man as we are. / The Violet smels to him as to vs: / Therefore if he see reasons, he feares
as we do. *Q* 95 Thomas] *Pope* (*Theobald 1726*); *Iohn F* 98 wrecked] (*wrackt*) 105 human]
(*humane*)

should possess him with any appearance of fear,
lest he, by showing it, should dishearten his army.

BATES   He may show what outward courage he will,
but I believe, as cold a night as 'tis, he could wish
himself in Thames up to the neck; and so I would   115
he were, and I by him, at all adventures, so we were
quit here.

KING   By my troth, I will speak my conscience of the
King. I think he would not wish himself anywhere
but where he is.   120

BATES   Then I would he were here alone; so should he
be sure to be ransomed, and a many poor men's lives
saved.

KING   I dare say you love him not so ill to wish him
here alone, howsoever you speak this to feel other   125
men's minds. Methinks I could not die anywhere so
contented as in the King's company, his cause being
just and his quarrel honourable.

WILLIAMS   That's more than we know.

BATES   Ay, or more than we should seek after, for we   130
know enough if we know we are the King's subjects. If
his cause be wrong, our obedience to the King wipes
the crime of it out of us.

WILLIAMS   But if the cause be not good, the King himself
hath a heavy reckoning to make when all those legs   135

sign of (his own) fear to him (i.e. the
King). *OED possess, v.* 8. Cf. l. 287.
116 **at all adventures** at all risks, whatever the consequences (*OED* adven-
ture *sb.* 3c, for the phrase)
so ... here if only we were well out
of this
118 **speak my conscience** speak my
mind, express my conviction (*OED*
conscience *sb.* 2c, for the phrase)
122 **a many** See 3.7.74n.
125–6 **feel ... minds** test other men's
opinions

128 **his quarrel honourable** (synonymous with 'his cause being just'; *OED*
quarrel *sb.*³ 2c; cf. *KJ* 5.7.91, 'his
cause and quarrel')
130 SP Capell conjectured that the
speaker should be Court (who has no
speech after his first, ll. 86–7) because
Bates has been grumbling; but the
readiness with which the speech takes
up Williams's and turns it seems
appropriate enough to Bates.
133 **us** (emphatic)

124 ill to] *(*ill, to)*   125 alone, howsoever] *Collier;* alone: howsoever *F*   126 minds. Methinks]
Rowe; minds, me thinks *F*   135–6 legs ... battle] *F;* soules / Whose bodies shall be slaughtered
here, *Q*

265

and arms and heads chopped off in a battle shall join
together at the latter day and cry all 'We died at
such a place', some swearing, some crying for a
surgeon, some upon their wives left poor behind them,
some upon the debts they owe, some upon their chil-   140
dren rawly left. I am afeard there are few die well that
die in a battle, for how can they charitably dispose of
anything when blood is their argument? Now if these
men do not die well ĩt will be a black matter for the
King, that led them to it, who to disobey were against   145
all proportion of subjection.

KING   So if a son that is by his father sent about
merchandise do sinfully miscarry upon the sea, the
imputation of his wickedness, by your rule, should be
imposed upon his father that sent him; or if a servant,   150
under his master's command transporting a sum of
money, be assailed by robbers and die in many irreconciled iniquities, you may call the business of the
master the author of the servant's damnation. But this

136–7 **join together** i.e. to make whole
  bodies
137 **at the latter day** at the last day
  (the Day of Judgement): Job 19:25
  and cry all i.e. they (those resurrected bodies) shall all cry
139 **upon** about
141 **rawly left** left at an immature age
  (cf. 'left poor behind them', l. 139).
  Cf. *R2* 2.3.41–2, 'my service, / Such
  as it is, being tender, raw, and young'.
  die well die a Christian death
142–3 **charitably ... anything** settle
  anything with Christian charity
142 **dispose of** in the legal sense, make
  a bestowal or conveyance by deed or
  will (*OED v.* 8): here with particular
  reference to their souls, the bequeath-
  ing of which to God was usually

included in the first sentence of a last
will and testament
143 **blood ... argument** bloodshed is
  their theme (*OED* argument 6)
145 **who** i.e. whom (Abbott, 274)
145–6 **against ... subjection** altogether
  contrary to the proper relationship of
  king and subject
148 **sinfully miscarry** die in his sins.
  Q's attempted paraphrase 'fall into
  any leaud [i.e. lewd] action' shows a
  misunderstanding of the sense, which
  the whole passage (ll. 147–58) makes
  clear.
149 **imputation of** accusation of responsibility for (*OED* 1)
152–3 **irreconciled** unreconciled (to
  God)

138–41 some crying ... left] *F;* Some their wiues rawly left: / Some leauing their children poore
behind them. *Q*   141–3 I am ... argument] *F; not in Q*   142 in a] *F;* in *F2*   143–6 Now ...
subjection] *F;* Now if his cause be bad, I think it will be a greeuous matter to him. *Q*   145 who]
F; whom *F2*   148 do ... sea] *F;* fall into any leaud action *Q*   152–3 be assailed ... iniquities]
F; by any meanes miscarry *Q*

is not so: the King is not bound to answer the particular   155
endings of his soldiers, the father of his son, nor the
master of his servant; for they purpose not their death
when they purpose their services. Besides, there is no
king, be his cause never so spotless, if it come to the
arbitrement of swords, can try it out with all unspotted   160
soldiers. Some, peradventure, have on them the guilt of
premeditated and contrived murder, some of beguiling
virgins with the broken seals of perjury, some, making
the wars their bulwark, that have before gored the
gentle bosom of peace with pillage and robbery. Now   165
if these men have defeated the law and outrun native
punishment, though they can outstrip men, they have
no wings to fly from God. War is his beadle, war is his
vengeance; so that here men are punished for before

155 **bound to answer** compelled to answer for; liable for
157 **death** 'Symmetry seems to require Q's *deaths* to match *services*' (Taylor). But F's singular *death* is defensible if each particular case is now under consideration, for reference to one person's *services* is not uncommon in Shakespeare (e.g. *KJ* 5.7.104, 'I do bequeath my faithful services'). Also, in the preceding part of the sentence in Q, the sequence 'seruants', 'sonne', 'subiects', being predominantly plural, attracts another plural noun.
158 **when they purpose** The force of F's reading (contrast Oxf[1]'s emendation) consists in retaining the same verb while employing two contrasted nouns.
159–60 **the arbitrement of swords** decision by battle
160 **try it out** put it to the test (i.e. of battle)
   with all unspotted only with sinless.

The following examples show that this (not 'with entirely sinless') is the sense.
163 **the broken ... perjury** i.e. solemn promises, as binding as if they were authenticated by the impression of a seal on wax, which have been broken by perjury. (*OED* perjury *sb.*[1] b, the violation of a promise made on oath.)
164 **bulwark** rampart, i.e. security
166–7 **native punishment** the punishment due to them at home. Cf. 4.3.96, 'native graves'.
168 **no wings ... God** perhaps suggested by phrases in Psalm 139:7–10 ('Whyther can I goe from thy spirite: or whyther can I flee away from thy face? If I take the winges of the morning: and go to dwell in the uttermost part of the sea'), though the theme there is the omnipotence, not the retributive intent, of God
   beadle parish officer, who whipped offenders (*OED* 4)
169–70 **before breach** breach (i.e.

157 death] *F*; deaths *Q*   158 purpose] *F*; craue *Q*; propose *Oxf[1]*   158–61 Besides ... soldiers] *F*; *not in Q*   163–5 some ... robbery] *F*; *not in Q*   169–75 so that ... visited] *F*; *not in Q*   169–70 before breach] *F*; before-breach *Capell*

breach of the King's laws in now the King's quarrel.　170
Where they feared the death they have borne life away,
and where they would be safe they perish. Then if
they die unprovided, no more is the King guilty of their
damnation than he was before guilty of those impieties
for the which they are now visited. Every subject's　175
duty is the King's, but every subject's soul is his
own. Therefore should every soldier in the wars
do as every sick man in his bed, wash every mote out
of his conscience; and dying so, death is to him
advantage; or not dying, the time was blessedly lost　180
wherein such preparation was gained; and in him that
escapes, it were not sin to think that, making God so
free an offer, he let him outlive that day to see his
greatness and to teach others how they should prepare.

WILLIAMS　'Tis certain, every man that dies ill, the ill　185
upon his own head; the King is not to answer it.

breaking) that they have committed
before this time

170 **now ... quarrel** the King's present
quarrel. This adverbial compound is
'a mere construction for the occasion'
to correspond antithetically to 'before
breach' (Abbott, 429).

171 **the death** the death penalty. Cf. *CE*
1.1.146 ('adjudged to the death'), *R2*
3.1.29 ('Condemns you to the death').
borne life away got away with their
lives

173 **unprovided** spiritually unprepared

175 **visited** punished

178 **mote** spot, blemish (*OED sb.*[1] 2),
particularly on a garment

179–80 **death ... advantage** Philippians 1:21, 'For Christe is to me
lyfe, and death is to me aduantage'

180 **lost** spent, wasted (paradoxically,
with *blessedly*; antithetically, with
gained)

182–3 **making ... offer** i.e. so unre-

servedly giving himself to God, by
confessing his sins

185–8 **'Tis certain ... for him** Q combines F's two speeches into one
speech by '*3. Lord*' (i.e. third soldier,
corresponding to Bates in F), an
arrangement followed by Taylor, who
regards it as important that Williams
(= Q's second soldier) does not
assent to the King's argument. But
these are manifestly two speeches,
the second capping the first. Q has
accidentally omitted the SP before
the second, and has transposed the
intended full stop after 'head' with
the intended comma after 'me'.

185 **dies ill** dies badly, i.e. *unprovided* (l.
173)

185–6 **the ill ... head** let him take the
blame for the evil he suffers. For the
expression, cf. 1.2.97, 'The sin upon
my head'.

178 mote] *F* (Moth), *Q* (moath)　181–4 and in ... prepare] *F; not in Q*　185–8] *F; 3.Lord.*
Yfaith he saies true; / Euery mans fault on his owne head, / I would not haue the king answere
for me. / Yet I intend to fight lustily for him. *Q*　185 SP WILLIAMS] *F; Bates Oxf*[1]　185–6 ill
upon] *F;* ill is upon *F4;* fault on *Q;* fault is on *Q3*

BATES   I do not desire he should answer for me, and
yet I determine to fight lustily for him.

KING   I myself heard the King say he would not be
ransomed.   190

WILLIAMS   Ay, he said so to make us fight cheerfully; but
when our throats are cut he may be ransomed and
we ne'er the wiser.

KING   If I live to see it, I will never trust his word after.

WILLIAMS   You pay him then! That's a perilous shot out   195
of an elder-gun that a poor and a private displeasure
can do against a monarch. You may as well go about
to turn the sun to ice with fanning in his face with a
peacock's feather. You'll never trust his word after!
Come, 'tis a foolish saying.   200

KING   Your reproof is something too round; I should be
angry with you if the time were convenient.

WILLIAMS   Let it be a quarrel between us, if you live.

KING   I embrace it.

WILLIAMS   How shall I know thee again?   205

KING   Give me any gage of thine and I will wear it in my

187–8 **I do not ... him** The balanced
construction of this sentence ('do not
desire' / 'determine'; 'answer for me'
/ 'fight lustily for him') rules out
Taylor's secondary interpretation of
'I do not desire he should answer for
me' as 'I don't desire to die'.
189–90 **would ... ransomed** Cf.
3.6.153 and (for Shakespeare's anticipation of the incident in Holinshed)
3.6.124–5n.
195 **You pay him then!** 'Well, *you* pay
him out then, if he breaks it!'
(Wilson): *OED* pay *v.* 3b (= punish)
195–6 **perilous ... elder-gun** An elder-
gun is a pop-gun made by removing
the soft pith from a straight stick of an
elder tree. According to Nashe (3.62.9–
10) it shoots pellets of chewed paper.
For the construction cf. 3.7.144–5.

Perilous is used sarcastically.
196 **a poor and a private** i.e. of a mere
commoner; cf. ll. 234 (*private men*),
235 (*privates*). For the repetition of *a*,
cf. 3.5.13, 4.3.86.
197–8 **go about to** try to
198 **fanning in his face** i.e. fanning air
towards his distant face. Cf. 3.0.6.
198–9 **a peacock's feather** Fans were
often made of brightly coloured
feathers (*Shakespeare's England*,
2.97–8); but one feather does not even
make a fan.
201 **round** plain-spoken (*OED a.* 13c)
205 **thee** Williams and the King use the
second person singular pronoun,
aggressively, from this point.
206 **gage** pledge (of your readiness to
fight me)
      I will wear it The gloves are not

187 SP] *F; not in Oxf¹*   195–200] *F; 2.Sol.* Mas youle pay him then, tis a great displeasure /
That an elder gun, can do against a cannon, / Or a subiect against a monarke. / Youle nere take
his word again, your a nasse goe. *Q*

bonnet. Then if ever thou dar'st acknowledge it I
will make it my quarrel.

WILLIAMS Here's my glove. Give me another of thine.

KING There.   [*They exchange gloves.*]

WILLIAMS This will I also wear in my cap. If ever   211
thou come to me and say after tomorrow 'This is my
glove', by this hand I will take thee a box on the ear.

KING If ever I live to see it I will challenge it.

WILLIAMS Thou dar'st as well be hanged.   215

KING Well, I will do it, though I take thee in the King's
company.

WILLIAMS Keep thy word. Fare thee well.

BATES Be friends, you English fools, be friends! We
have French quarrels enough, if you could tell how   220
to reckon.

KING Indeed, the French may lay twenty French

---

fixed into the takers' caps at this
point. The King is usually hooded (in
Erpingham's cloak) in this scene, the
better to disguise himself (and to
remind the audience that he is
disguised); he can dispose of the glove
by sticking it into his belt after the
soldiers have gone.

207 **bonnet** A less frequent word in
Shakespeare than *cap* (l. 211), but
synonymously used here for a piece
of headgear. Both are distinguished
from a hat by the latter's having a
hard brim and a crown.

208 **make it my quarrel** treat your
claim to your glove as a challenge
which I am bound to take up

212 **after tomorrow** i.e. after tomorrow's battle. The time is still between
night and morning.

213 **take thee a box** give thee a blow

216 **take thee** find thee

218 **Fare thee well** At this point the
soldiers begin to move towards an
exit, allowing the King's humorous
final speech to be thrown across some

distance to them. Cf. 226 SD.

219–21 **Be friends ... reckon** Cf. Bardolph's remonstrance to Nym and
Pistol, 2.1.90–93.

220 **quarrels** Cf. l. 203. Gurr, because
the French used crossbows, proposes
a secondary sense, 'crossbow arrows'
(*OED sb.*² 1), surely inappropriate to
the context and to Bates's direct style.

220–1 **if ... reckon** if only you knew
how to count

222 **lay** bet
twenty i.e. because the French are –
hyperbolically – twenty times the
English in number

222–3 **French crowns** (1) French *écus*
(gold coins), (2) French heads. As
Taylor shows, Shakespeare sometimes
uses 'French crown' to mean a head
made bald by syphilis (*MND* 1.2.90,
MM 1.2.50 and possibly *AW* 2.2.21);
but the instances of 'French crown'
as the coin (without innuendo: *LLL*
3.1.138, *2H4* 3.2.219) allow the
present expression to be read in a
double rather than in a triple sense.

---

210 SD] *Capell (subst.)*   220 enough] *F (enow), Q (anow), Q3 (enow)*   222-4 Indeed ... but]
F; not in Q

crowns to one they will beat us, for they bear them
on their shoulders, but it is no English treason to cut
French crowns, and tomorrow the King himself will   225
be a clipper.   *Exeunt Soldiers.*
Upon the King! 'Let us our lives, our souls,
Our debts, our careful wives,
Our children and our sins lay on the King!'
We must bear all. O hard condition,   230
Twin-born with greatness, subject to the breath
Of every fool whose sense no more can feel
But his own wringing! What infinite heart's ease

224–6 **it is ... clipper** To mutilate current coin of the realm by fraudulently paring the edges (*OED* clip *v.*² 4) was a capital offence coming under the law of treason. The wit lies in (1) distinguishing, in this sense, between English and French coin, (2) playing on *crowns*, (3) playing on *clip*, which also meant to cut the hair off, to poll (*OED* clip *v.*² 2).

226 **clipper** (1) clipper of coin (*OED sb.* 1), (2) barber (*OED sb.* 1b), both jocularly incongruous with *King*. He will, of course, be cutting off French heads.

SD F's SD '*Exit Souldiers*', misplaced at the end of Bates's last speech, 'may indicate that Henry's last speech was an afterthought or a late insertion' (Gurr) – or, perhaps more probably, that the SD stood opposite the King's last words to the soldiers, and the compositor, not foreseeing that there would be enough space for it after *clipper*, was avoiding interrupting the King's speech (which the soliloquy continues) with the SD.

227–34 **Upon ... enjoy** F's lineation of this passage has been generally regarded as incorrect. Shakespeare may originally have written 'Upon the King! / Our lives, our souls,

our debts, our careful wives, / Our children, and our sins, upon the King!', and then decided to make the sense even clearer by introducing *let us* and substituting *lay on* for *upon*. Alternatively, he may have heard 'Upon ... wives' as two overlapping lines of verse, with 'our lives, our souls' common to both.

228 **careful** full of care: either (1) full of grief (if they are widowed: *OED a.* 1) or (2) full of anxiety (*OED a.* 2)

230 **We** I, the King (royal plural); also, in view of the theme of the speech, kings in general
condition pronounced as four syllables

231 **Twin-born** born at the same birth. The first example of the word listed in *OED*.
breath speech (*OED sb.* 9). Cf. *MA* 5.1.255–6, 'Art thou the slave that with thy breath hast killed / Mine innocent child?' (with the same implication of injurious breath).

232–3 **every ... wringing** Cf. Nashe, *Summer's Last Will and Testament* (acted 1592, printed 1600) ll. 1,671–2: 'A foole conceits no further then he sees; / He hath no scense of ought but what he feeles' (Nashe, 3.285–6).

233 **his own wringing** what pinches

226 SD] *F (opp. 221: Exit Souldiers.); Exit the souldiers. / Enter the King, Gloster, Epingam, and Attendants. Q* 227–85] *F; not in Q* 230–4] *as Cam; F lines* ... all. / ... Greatnesse, / ... sence / ... wringing. / ... neglect, / ... enioy? / 233 heart's ease] *(hearts-ease)*

Must kings neglect that private men enjoy!
And what have kings that privates have not too,   235
Save ceremony, save general ceremony?
And what art thou, thou idol ceremony?
What kind of god art thou, that suffer'st more
Of mortal griefs than do thy worshippers?
What are thy rents, what are thy comings-in?   240
O ceremony, show me but thy worth!
What is thy soul, O adoration?
Art thou aught else but place, degree and form,
Creating awe and fear in other men,
Wherein thou art less happy, being feared,   245
Than they in fearing?
What drink'st thou oft, instead of homage sweet,
But poisoned flattery? O be sick, great greatness,

him. Cf. the proverb 'I know best where my shoe wrings me' (*OED* wring *v.* 4b).

234 **neglect** forgo, do without
private men men who are not rulers (synonymous with *privates*, l. 235)

236 **ceremony** ceremonial display, pomp, state (*OED* 3d), and the universal respect and regard that accompany it (*OED* 3c: cf. l. 237, 'thou idol ceremony').

238 **thou, that suffer'st** Here begins the ambiguous use of *thou* to mean sometimes *ceremony* and sometimes *greatness*. For the latter sense, cf. 'thy worshippers' (l. 239), 'thou art less happy' (l. 245), 'drink'st thou' (l. 247), 'Think'st thou' (l. 250), 'Canst thou' (l. 253).

240 **comings-in** income, revenues

242 ***What ... adoration?*** 'What is thine essence (*OED sb.* 7), O adoration?' Johnson's emendation takes *adoration* as synonymous with *ceremony* (cf. 236n.), and l. 242 as substantially reiterating l. 241. For the style, cf. 1 Corinthians 15:55, 'O death where is thy styng? O hell

where is thy victorie?' F's treatment of *What* as exclamatory is a natural but wrong inference from the rhetorical style of the soliloquy, and if *O* were represented in the compositor's copy as *o* a (mis)correction into *of* would be easy. The interpretation of F's reading as 'What, is thy essence merely adoration?' suffers from the absence of any word corresponding to 'merely'. Knight's emendation, aiming at the sense 'What is the real nature or essence of the adoration paid thee?' with a transferred possessive pronoun (cf. *Ham* 3.2.324–5, 'your cause of distemper'), gives rather the sense 'What is the essence of thy adoration?' (as though the adoration were given, not received). Metrically *adoration* has five syllables.

243 **place, degree and form** eminence of position (virtually synonymous). *OED* form *sb.* 6, a degree of rank, eminence. Cf. *MM* 2.4.12–14, 'O place, O form, / How often dost thou with thy case, thy habit, / Wrench awe from fools.'

248 **poisoned** poisonous

240 comings-in] *(*Commings in*)* 242 What ... adoration?] *Johnson;* What is thy soul of adoration? *Knight* What is] *Theobald;* What? is F soul, O] *Johnson;* Soule of F; toll, O *Theobald (Warburton)* adoration] *F2;* Odoration F

And bid thy ceremony give thee cure!
Think'st thou the fiery fever will go out   250
With titles blown from adulation?
Will it give place to flexure and low bending?
Canst thou, when thou command'st the beggar's
    knee,
Command the health of it? No, thou proud dream
That play'st so subtly with a king's repose,   255
I am a king that find thee, and I know
'Tis not the balm, the sceptre and the ball,
The sword, the mace, the crown imperial,
The intertissued robe of gold and pearl,
The farced title running 'fore the king,   260
The throne he sits on, nor the tide of pomp
That beats upon the high shore of this world,
No, not all these, thrice-gorgeous ceremony,
Not all these, laid in bed majestical,
Can sleep so soundly as the wretched slave,   265

250–1 **go out ... adulation** be extinguished (blown out) by titles which are breathed forth by flattery. *Adulation* has five syllables .

252 **give ... bending** retreat before knee-bending and body-bowing

253–4 **Canst ... of it?** 'Can you, when you claim as your right the homage of the beggar who kneels to you, equally claim as your right the health which that beggar's knee enjoys?' Lines 248–52 show that this is the meaning (not 'Can you ... order it to be healthy?').

254 **No** Not an answer to the two rhetorical questions just asked, but an interjection introducing the next statement. Cf. 'No, not all these' (l. 263).
    thou proud dream i.e. ceremony (cf. l. 263)

255 **subtly** craftily

256 **I am ... find thee** I, who have

found you out, am a king (*I* is emphatic). *OED* find *v.* 8: cf. *Oth* 2.1.247–8, 'A pestilent complete knave, and the woman hath found him already.'

257 **balm** consecrated oil with which a king is anointed at his coronation
    ball orb of sovereignty

259 **intertissued ... pearl** robe interwoven with gold thread and seed pearls

260 **The farced ... king** the stuffed (i.e. bombastic) title preceding the king's personal name, e.g. 'his most gracious majesty'
    farced farcèd

261 **tide of pomp** full-flowing pomp. The image here and in l. 262 is of the high tide pounding against cliffs.

264 **majestical** Cf. 3.0.16.

265 **wretched slave** here synonymous: cf. *wretch* (l. 275), *slave* (l. 278); synonymous also with *peasant* (l. 281).

250 Think'st] *Rowe;* Thinks *F*   255 subtly] *(subtilly)*   repose,] *Capell;* Repose. *F*   258 mace]
*(*Mase*)*   259 intertissued] *(*enter-tissued*)*

Who with a body filled and vacant mind
Gets him to rest, crammed with distressful bread:
Never sees horrid night, the child of hell,
But like a lackey from the rise to set
Sweats in the eye of Phoebus, and all night   270
Sleeps in Elysium; next day after dawn
Doth rise and help Hyperion to his horse,
And follows so the ever-running year
With profitable labour to his grave.
And but for ceremony such a wretch,   275
Winding up days with toil and nights with sleep,
Had the fore-hand and vantage of a king.
The slave, a member of the country's peace,
Enjoys it, but in gross brain little wots

All three words have a range of application, from the merely descriptive to the contemptuous. Cf. 4.4.24, 38.

267 **distressful bread** food (*OED* bread *sb.*[1] 4) gained by hard toil. The phrase is found only here, perhaps alluding to the penalty of Adam: Genesis 3:17–19, 'in sorowe shalt thou eat of it all the dayes of thy lyfe.... In the sweatte of thy face shalt thou eate thy breade, tyll thou be turned agayne into the grounde.' Cf. *Sweats* (l. 270).

268 **horrid ... hell** Shakespeare often associates night and hell (e.g. *Luc* 764, *LLL* 4.3.252, *Oth* 1.3.395).

269–72 Shakespeare bases this simile on a recollection of the hero's lines in *Tit* 5.2.53–7, 'And when thy car is loaden with their heads / I will dismount, and by thy wagon wheel / Trot like a servile footman all day long, / Even from Hyperion's rising in the east / Until his very downfall in the sea.'

269 **lackey** footman: here one who runs beside a chariot

from ... set i.e. of the sun

270 **in the ... Phoebus** in the light and heat of the sun (Phoebus, the sun-god)

271 **in Elysium** i.e. in perfect contentment (literally in the abode of the blessed after death)

after dawn as soon as day has broken; before sunrise

272 **help ... horse** i.e. set to work by sunrise (literally, help harness the sun-god's horses to his chariot). Shakespeare, here as always (cf. 269–72n.), makes Hyperion synonymous with Phoebus, though in Greek mythology he is a Titan and the father of Helios the sun-god, who came to be identified with Apollo (Phoebus).

274 **profitable** useful (*OED* 1)

to his grave till he dies. Cf. *3H6* 2.5.38–40.

276 **Winding up** wrapping up, i.e. filling (*OED* wind *v.*[1] 22b, wind up)

277 **fore-hand** position in front of or above (*OED sb.* 1: here synonymous with *vantage*). The hyphen (from F) indicates that *hand* is to be given some metrical stress.

vantage advantage

278 **member of** sharer in (*OED sb.* 4c)

peace civil order

279 **gross** dull

wots knows

269 lackey] (Lacquey)   271 Elysium] *(Elizium)*   272 Hyperion] F2 *(Hiperion); Hiperio* F

What watch the King keeps to maintain the peace, 280
Whose hours the peasant best advantages.

Enter ERPINGHAM.

ERPINGHAM
My lord, your nobles, jealous of your absence,
Seek through your camp to find you.
KING   Good old knight,
Collect them all together at my tent.
I'll be before thee.
ERPINGHAM   I shall do't, my lord.   *Exit.*
KING [*Kneels.*]
O God of battles, steel my soldiers' hearts;   286
Possess them not with fear. Take from them now
The sense of reckoning, if th'opposed numbers

280 **watch** wakefulness, vigil (*OED sb.* 1)
281 **Whose ... advantages** Whose hours (i.e. the king's hours of wakeful meditation to maintain the peace) most benefit the peasant. Shakespeare often uses the verb *advantage* thus (*OED v.* 4), e.g. *TGV* 3.2.42, *TN* 4.2.114, *JC* 3.1.244; he never uses it in the sense 'to take advantage of', and *OED* recognizes no such sense. The form of the verb here is either an example of third person plural in *-s* (Abbott, 333) or influenced by the proximity of the singular noun *peasant*.
282 **jealous of** anxious about
285 SD The King may here return the cloak to Erpingham, who can take it off stage.
286 SD The long prayer requires him to kneel, and his kneeling prepares the audience for his prayer.

286-7 **steel ... fear** Cf. *2H6* 3.1.331-2, 'Now, York, or never, steel thy fearful thoughts, / And change misdoubt to resolution.'
287-9 **Possess ... from them** Hall (67) makes the King exhort his soldiers before the battle, 'let not their multitude feare your heartes, nor their great nombre abate your courage.'
288 **reckoning** counting, computation (*OED sb.* 1)
*if F's *of*, consistent with its mispunctuation after *numbers*, is universally agreed to be wrong. Modern editors are divided between *if* and *or* (and its synonym *ere*). *If* has been attacked on the grounds that 'if the soldiers had already lost heart it would be too late to take away their ability to count' (Taylor), an objection already refuted by Steevens ('when they could no more count their enemies, they could no longer fear them'). *Or/ere* is

281 SD] *F; Enter the King, Gloster, Epingam, and Attendants. Q (at 226 SD); Enter to the King, Glocester, Epingham, and Attendants. Q3 (at 226 SD)*   283-5] *as Pope; F lines ... you. / ... together / ... thee. / ... Lord.*   286 SD] *Irving & Marshall*   287 Possess ... fear] *F; not in Q*   288 reckoning] *(reckning)*   288-9 if ... them] *F (of ... numbers: ...); That the apposed multitudes which stand before them, / May not appall their courage Q   if] Steevens² (Tyrwhitt), of F; lest Theobald; or Moore Smith (anon. in Cam); ere Oxf¹   numbers / Pluck] Theobald; numbers: / Pluck F*

> Pluck their hearts from them. Not today, O Lord,
> O not today, think not upon the fault   290
> My father made in compassing the crown.
> I Richard's body have interred new,
> And on it have bestowed more contrite tears
> Than from it issued forced drops of blood.
> Five hundred poor I have in yearly pay,   295

open to two objections: the soldiers are already well aware how heavily they are outnumbered, and 'or th'opposed numbers / Pluck' is ambiguous (it might mean '*otherwise* the opposed numbers *will* pluck their hearts from them', which casts too much doubt on their courage). Q's paraphrase 'That the apposed multitudes which stand before them, / May not appall their courage' could equally well be an attempt to reproduce either version. F's *of* may have resulted from (1) a misreading of *if* (Ard²: the most likely explanation, and more likely than a misreading of *or* as *of*), (2) dittography after *of reckoning* (Oxf¹), (3) a normalization of *a*, itself a misreading of Shakespeare's *or* (Cam¹).
opposed opposèd

291 **compassing** obtaining (*OED* compass *v.* 11b)

292 **I Richard's ... new** Richard II, deposed by Henry V's father and murdered in Pomfret Castle by Sir Pierce of Exton (*R2* 5.4, 5.5), lay in state in St Paul's Cathedral for three days. His successor, now Henry IV, attended a funeral service for him in Westminster Abbey, after which his body 'was commanded to be had vnto Langlie, there to be buried in the church of the friers preachers ... none of the nobles nor anie of the commons (to accompt of) being present' (Holinshed, 3.517). At the beginning of his account of Henry V's reign (3.543) Holinshed reports that the

King 'caused the bodie of king Richard to be remooued with all funerall dignitie conuenient for his estate from Langlie to Westminster where he was honorablie interred with queene Anne his first wife, in a solemne toome erected and set up at the charges of this king.' 'Langlie' is King's Langley, Herts.
interred interrèd

294 **forced** forcèd

295–9 **Five hundred ... soul** Not derived from Hall or Holinshed but from Robert Fabyan's *Chronicle* (1516), ed. H. Ellis (1811), p. 589: 'For asmoche as he knewe well that his fader had laboured the meanes to depose the noble prynce Richarde the Seconde, and after was consentyng to his deth, for which offence his said fader had sent to Rome, of that great cryme to be assayled [i.e. assoiled, absolved], and was by the pope enioyned, that lyke as he had beraft hym of his naturall and bodely lyfe for euer in this world, that so, by contynuel prayer & suffragies of the churche, he shuld cause his soule to lyue perpetually in the celestyall worlde: Whiche penaunce, for that his fader by his lyfe dyd nat perfourme, this goostly [i.e. spiritual] knyght in most habundaunt maner perfourmed it: for first he buyldyd .iii. houses of relygyon, as the Charterhous of monkes called Shene, the house of close nunnes called Syon, and the thirde was an house of

295 Five ... I have] *F*; A hundred men haue I *Q*

Who twice a day their withered hands hold up
Toward heaven to pardon blood; and I have built
Two chantries, where the sad and solemn priests
Sing still for Richard's soul. More will I do,
Though all that I can do is nothing worth,   300
Since that my penitence comes after all,
Imploring pardon.
GLOUCESTER [*within*]   My liege!

Obseruauntes buyldyd vpon that other syde of Thamys, & after let fall by hym for the skyll [i.e. reason] that foloweth [i.e. that its French friars had political objections to his wars]. ... And ouer this great acte of founding of thise .ii. religious houses, he ordeyned at Westminster to brenne perpetuelly without extinccyon .iiii. tapers of waxe vpon the sepulture of kyng Richarde; & ouer yt he ordeyned ther, to be contynued for euer, one day in the weke, a solempne dirige to be songe, & vpon the morowe a masse; after which masse endid, certayn money to be gyuen, as before is expresyd, with other thynges in the begynnyng of this kynges reign.' Shakespeare converts the religious houses into chantries, and applies to them the performance of dirges and masses at Westminster.

297 **blood** i.e. Richard's murder

297–9 F's mislining suggests that this passage, from a source other than Shakespeare's usual ones, was a marginal addition to his manuscript, in which 'Toward heaven to pardon blood; more will I do' may have been the original form of l. 297.

298 **chantries** A chantry is a chapel endowed for the maintenance of one or more priests to sing masses for the souls of the founders or others specified by them.

sad and solemn synonymous. In Shakespearean usage each word includes the modern meaning of the other.

299 **still** perpetually

299–302 **More ... pardon** As Taylor shows (Oxf[1], Appendix B, 295–301), this passage is capable of various interpretations depending on what sense is given to *all* (l. 301): (1) all that I have done, (2) all that I can do, (3) all that has happened. Taylor's interpretation of Shakespeare's purpose is excellent: 'Shakespeare wanted an idea which would allow Henry to think himself inadequate, but permit the audience not to think so.' But his emendation of *all* to *ill* in l. 301 is neither necessary nor desirable: if ill did not precede penitence there would be no point in the penitence. More probably *all* is correct and the vagueness intentional. The King is so distressed by his father's sin (for what's done cannot be undone) that he might well say 'my penitence comes all too late', but to say so would be to deny the possibility of pardon; 'my penitence comes after all' seems to be a toned-down form of this idea, not clear-cut enough to run into theological difficulty.

302 SD *within* This emendation (1) explains why the King recognizes Gloucester by his voice and not by

296 Who ... day] *F;* Which euery day *Q*   297–9] *as Pope; F lines* ... blood: / ... Chauntries, / ... still / ... doe: 298–9 chantries ... More] *F;* two chanceries, more *Q*   300–302 Though ... pardon] *F;* Tho all that I can do, is all too litle *Q*   301 all] *F;* ill *Oxf[1]*   302 SD *within*] *this edn Rises*] *Irving & Marshall*

KING [*Rises.*]   My brother Gloucester's voice?

Enter GLOUCESTER.

I know thy errand, I will go with thee.
The day, my friends and all things stay for me.   *Exeunt.*

[**4.2**]   *Enter the* DAUPHIN, ORLEANS [*and*] RAMBURES.

ORLEANS
The sun doth gild our armour; up, my lords!

---

his appearance (it was not too dark for him to recognize Erpingham at 281 SD), (2) allows him to end his prayer, and rise to his feet, without seeming to be embarrassed by another person's entrance. Q and F concur in specifying that Gloucester enters before speaking, but cf. the SD '*Enter Gouernour*' and its placing just before his speech at 3.3.45 (discussed at 3.3.0.1n.); here, as there, Q3 may have contaminated F, or F's SD may have been inserted because it was not recognized that Gloucester was speaking within. Probably Shakespeare's manuscript did not mark Gloucester's entry.

302–3 **voice? / I* It is to be noted that if Gloucester's 'My liege!' is treated as extra-metrical -- indeed, as an off-stage sound-effect – the last two words of the King's prayer and his comment 'My brother Gloucester's voice?' make up a line of verse. F3 must be right in deleting the *I* which follows in F's l. 302, where it is an anticipation of the *I* that begins l. 303

(perhaps first having been carelessly written in the wrong place by Shakespeare). To read *Ay* (as F's compositor evidently did, spelling it *I* as usual) is possible only if the phrase is delivered as 'Ay, / I know thy errand' (which blunts the impact of the final couplet): to make the King ask a question and answer it himself, or to make Gloucester answer it, is preposterous.

304 **friends* F's 'friend' is an obvious error, as the word is not a vocative, though perhaps the compositor mistook it for one.

4.2 Q has no equivalent of this scene.

0.1 F's Beaumont (mentioned at 3.5.44 and 4.8.101) does not speak in the present scene nor reappear in 4.5, by which scene Shakespeare has decided that Bourbon shall be the other French lord. (He had perhaps noticed that there was a Beaumont on the English side too, mentioned by Holinshed (3.553) as serving in the vaward under York: 4.3.129–31n.)

1 **up** to horse (cf. l. 2)

302-3 voice? / I] *F3,* voyce? I: / I *F;* voice? / *Gloucester.* Ay. / *King.* I *(anon. in Cam)*   302 SD *Enter* GLOUCESTER] *this edn; F after* pardon *302; Q after* litle *300*   303] *F; Glost.* My lord, the Army stayes vpon your presence. / *King.* Stay *Gloster* stay, and I will go with thee, *Q*   304 friends] *Q;* friend *F*   SD] *F; not in Q*

4.2] *Capell*   0.1 DAUPHIN] *F (Dolphin); Bourbon Oxf¹*   ORLEANS] *(Orleance)* and RAMBURES] *Oxf¹ (subst.); Rambures, and Beaumont F; Rambures, and others / Capell; scene not in Q*   1 armour; up] *F2 (Armour, up); Armour vp F*

DAUPHIN   *Monte à cheval!* My horse, *varlet laquais*, ha!
ORLEANS   O brave spirit!
DAUPHIN   *Via, les eaux et terre!*
ORLEANS   *Rien puis? L'air et feu?*   5
DAUPHIN

      Cieux, cousin Orleans!

Enter CONSTABLE.

Now, my lord Constable!

2 *Monte à cheval!* To horse! The *monte à cheval* (together with its alternatives, *à cheval* and the Italianized variants *monte a caval* and *a caval*) was a trumpet signal used with cavalry troops. The Dauphin seems therefore to be calling for this signal to be sounded (Z. P. Zaddy, privately).
varlet laquais rascal lackey. F's italics indicate that the words are French, as does the spelling of '*Verlot*' and possibly of '*Lacquay*': the present compositor, A, spells the English word as 'Lacquey' at 3.7.111 and its plural as 'Lacquies' at l. 25 below; Compositor B spells its plural as 'Lackies' at 4.4.74. As there seems to be no reason why the Dauphin should use two synonymous terms of office for one servant, and as he is in the habit of beating his lackey (3.7.111), the first word is here taken to be a term of abuse corresponding to the abusive sense of English 'varlet' (*OED* 2b). Randle Cotgrave, *Dictionary*, 1611, lists both *Valet* and *Varlet* as French words, defining the latter as 'A groome, etc. as in *Valet*; also a younker, stripling, youth'. He gives *Lacquay* and *Lacquais* as variant forms of *Laquay* ('a lackey, footboy, footman').
4–6 **Via ... Orleans* The meaning of this dialogue is debatable. *Via* must be the Italian interjection, common in Shakespeare (*MW* 2.2.149, *LLL* 5.1.142, 5.2.112, *MV* 2.2.9), meaning either 'Come on!' (*OED int.* 1) or 'Be off!' (*OED int.* 2, where the example from Jonson shows that *Via* can be used with a vocative, as perhaps here if the base elements water and earth are being apostrophized). It cannot be the latinate preposition meaning 'by way of' (first *OED* instance 1779). F's *Rien puis* ('nothing after that') seems as satisfactory as Capell's emendation *Rien plus* ('nothing more'). F's *Cein* may stand either for *Cieux* ('heavens', 'skies') or for *Rien* ('nothing'). So alternative translations of the dialogue might be (1) 'Away [over] waters and land!' 'Nothing afterwards [to cross]? [Not] air and fire [also]?' '[Yes,] the heavens [themselves], cousin Orleans!' (2) 'Away, waters and earth [from our constitutions]!' 'Nothing afterwards [but] air and fire?' 'Nothing, cousin Orleans!'
4 *et terre* sixteenth-century French does not require the definite article here or before *feu* (l. 5).
6 One line of verse. F's SD filled up the space, so that '*Now*' had to begin a new line.

2+ SP DAUPHIN] *F (Dolph.); Bourbon Oxf¹*   2 *Monte à*] *this edn (Z. P. Zaddy); Monte F; Montez / Theobald; Montez à / Steevens*   *varlet laquais*] *this edn; Verlot Lacquay F; Valet Lacquay F2;* varlot lackey *Riv*   4 *Via, les eaux*] *Theobald (subst.); via les ewes F et terre*] *F (& terre); et la terre / Rowe*   5 *Rien puis? L'air*] *Malone; Rien puis le air F; Rien plus? l'air / Capell et feu*] *F (& feu); et le feu / Rowe*   6] *as Cam¹; F lines ... Orleance. / ... Constable? Cieux*] *Munro (Cam¹); Cein F; Cien F3; Ciel / Theobald; Rien (this edn)*

CONSTABLE

Hark, how our steeds for present service neigh!

DAUPHIN

Mount them and make incision in their hides,
That their hot blood may spin in English eyes
And dout them with superfluous courage, ha!   10

RAMBURES

What, will you have them weep our horses' blood?
How shall we then behold their natural tears?

Enter Messenger.

MESSENGER

The English are embattled, you French peers.

                                                              [*Exit.*]

CONSTABLE

To horse, you gallant princes, straight to horse!
Do but behold yon poor and starved band,   15

7 **Hark ... neigh** A livelier expression
than a mere statement would be, but
not one necessitating off-stage sounds
(as some editors believe).
8 **make incision** i.e. with spurs; figuratively used, as in medical contexts
(cf. *R2* 1.1.154–7)
9 **spin** spurt (*OED v.* 8)
10 **dout them** extinguish them, i.e.
blind them (the eyes); a coalesced
form of *do out* (*OED*)
superfluous courage the liveliness
(*OED* courage *sb.* 3) of which the
horses have a superabundance. Blood,
the vital fluid (*OED sb.* 5), was
regarded as the seat of passion, mettle,
high temper, etc.; cf. 3.1.7.
13 **embattled** arranged in battle forma-
tion. Cf. Holinshed, 3.553: 'king
Henrie also ... perceiuing a plot of
ground verie strong & meet for his
purpose, ... thought good there to
imbattell his host'.
15–23 **Do but ... them** Cf. Hall (66):
'And on the otherside is a smal hand-
full of pore Englishmen ... whiche by

reson that their vitaill is consumed &
spent, are by daily famyn sore
wekened, consumed & almost without
spirites: for their force is clerly abated
and their strength vtterly decaied, so
that or the battailes shall ioyne they
shalbe for very feblenes vanquished &
ouercom, and in stede of men ye shall
fight with shadowes. ... Therefore
nowe it is no mastery to vanquishe
and ouerthrowe them, beyng both
wery & weake, for by reason of feblenes and faintnes their weapones shal
fal out of their handes when they
profer to strike, so that ye may no
easilier kyll a poore shepe then
destroye them beyng alredy sicke &
hungerstaruen.' Holinshed (3.553)
merely states that 'the constable made
vnto the capteins and other men of
warre a pithie oration, exhorting and
encouraging them to doo valiantlie,
with manie comfortable words and
sensible reasons.'
15 **behold** i.e. come within sight of
starved starvèd

10 dout] *Rowe³*; doubt *F*   13 SD] *this edn*   15 yon] *(yond)*

And your fair show shall suck away their souls,
Leaving them but the shales and husks of men.
There is not work enough for all our hands,
Scarce blood enough in all their sickly veins
To give each naked curtle-axe a stain   20
That our French gallants shall today draw out
And sheathe for lack of sport. Let us but blow on
⸴ them,
The vapour of our valour will o'erturn them.
'Tis positive 'gainst all exceptions, lords,
That our superfluous lackeys and our peasants   25
Who in unnecessary action swarm
About our squares of battle were enough
To purge this field of such a hilding foe,
Though we upon this mountain's basis by
Took stand for idle speculation: 30
But that our honours must not. What's to say?
A very little little let us do,
And all is done. Then let the trumpets sound
The tucket sonance and the note to mount,

17 **shales and husks** synonymous: *OED* shale *sb.* 2, the husk or outer covering of a nut; the pod of peas, beans, etc.
20 **curtle-axe** a corruption of cutlass (Fr. *coutelas*): a short broadsword for cutting rather than thrusting
22 **sheathe … sport** Cf. 3.1.21.
24 **exceptions** objections
25 **superfluous** i.e. of whom we have more than enough
27 **squares of battle** square formations of troops (*OED sb.* 9)
28 **hilding** contemptible: *OED sb.* 3 (attributive, passing into adjectival, use: it is not known whether the substantive was originally applied to human beings or to beasts)
29–30 **Though … speculation** Cf. 2.4.57–9.
29 **this mountain's basis by** this nearby mountain's foot
30 **idle speculation** inactive onlooking. *Speculation* is five syllables.
31 **But that … not** but that (i.e. looking on) is what our dignities must not (let us do)
   What's to say? What remains to be said?
32–3 **A very … done** Cf. Hall (66), 'which pray is surely yours if euery man strike but one stroke'.
33–4 **sound … mount** sound a sonorous tucket and give the signal to mount. The *tucket*, a trumpet-call used at 3.6.112 SD and 4.3.78 SD to signal Montjoy's approach, was also the name of the third signal to cavalry (the others being to saddle, to mount and to charge), meaning to march; if that particular sense is included here,

17 shales] *F;* shells *Oxf¹*   20 curtle-axe] *(Curtleax)*   24 'gainst] *F2;* against *F*   25 lackeys] *(Lacquies)*   27 enough] *(enow)*   30 speculation:] *F;* speculation, *Oxf¹*   34 sonance] *Johnson;* Sonuance *F*

For our approach shall so much dare the field   35
That England shall couch down in fear and yield.

Enter GRANDPRÉ.

GRANDPRÉ

Why do you stay so long, my lords of France?
Yon island carrions, desperate of their bones,
Ill-favouredly become the morning field.
Their ragged curtains poorly are let loose,   40
And our air shakes them passing scornfully.
Big Mars seems bankrupt in their beggared host
And faintly through a rusty beaver peeps.
The horsemen sit like fixed candlesticks

the second and third signals are named in reverse order (Jorgensen, 22). *Sonance* (*OED*'s first example) is from Ital. *sonanza*, defined in John Florio's dictionary *A World of Words*, 1598, as 'a sound, a resounding, a noise, a ringing'.

35 **dare the field** dazzle the battlefield. To *dare* larks (*OED v.*² 5) is 'to fascinate and daze them, in order to catch them'. *OED*'s examples show that the word was applied both to bird-catchers' devices (e.g. stuffed or imitation birds of prey, bits of looking-glass) and to the hovering of living birds of prey. What is unusual here is that it is *the field*, not the enemy, that is to be dared, and so the reference is probably to the glittering armour (cf. l. 1) of the French.

36 **England** King Henry
couch cower (*OED v.*¹ 17)
SD GRANDPRÉ Taylor points out that, 'as he is not here identified in the dialogue, an audience has no opportunity to make the connection' with the reference to him at 3.7.128–9.

38 **island** Shakespeare's adjectival use (cf. *TC* 3.1.151) antedates *OED*'s first example.

carrions i.e. living carcases
desperate ... **bones** i.e. without hope of saving their lives

39 **Ill-favouredly** ... **field** ill befit (i.e. disgrace) the battlefield now that day has dawned

40 **Their** ... **loose** Their ragged banners, being displayed, make a poor show. The word *curtains* in this sense (*OED sb.*¹ 1d, a piece of hanging fabric) is unique, and is probably related to *morning* (l. 39), when bed-curtains are opened.

41 **passing** exceedingly

42 **Big Mars** the mighty god of war (*OED* big *a.* 1). Cf. Chapman's Homer, *Iliad*, 7.182, 'the hugely figur'd Mars'.

43 **faintly** faint-heartedly (*OED* 2), feebly (*OED* 3)
beaver strictly, the part of a close helmet that 'protected the lower portion of the face, as the visor did the rest except the forehead' (*Shakespeare's England*, 1.130), but here meaning the visor (cf. *Ham* 1.2.228, 'he wore his beaver up')

44 **fixed** fixèd

44–5 **sit** ... **hand** i.e. they seem like inanimate objects. Steevens compares

36 SD 37 SP GRANDPRÉ] *(Graundpree./Grandpree.)*   38 Yon island] *(*Yond Iland*)*   42 bankrupt]
*(*banqu'rout*)*

With torch-staves in their hand, and their poor jades 45
Lob down their heads, drooping the hides and hips,
The gum down-roping from their pale-dead eyes,
And in their palled dull mouths the gimmaled bit
Lies foul with chewed grass, still and motionless.
And their executors, the knavish crows, 50
Fly o'er them all, impatient for their hour.

Webster, *The White Devil*, 3.1.67–70, 'I saw him at last tilting, he showed, like a pewter candlestick fashioned like a man in armour, holding a tilting-staff in his hand, little bigger than a candle of twelve i'th' pound.' Cf. Fig. 1, p. 4.

45 **in their hand** in hand. Oxf[1] emends to *hands* because of the adjacent plurals; but it needs to be made clear that it is the candlestick-soldiers, not the real ones, who hold the torch-staves.

46 **Lob** hang heavily (*OED v.* 2): synonymous with *droop*
drooping F2's emendation is supported by other passages combining *droop* and *hang the head* in *VA* 666 and *2H6* 1.2.1-2. The horses' skins (cf. 1. 8 for the plural *hides*) are hanging loosely about them, and their hindquarters are sagging with weariness.

47 **gum** sticky moisture secreted by the eye (*OED sb.*[2] 4: a unique Shakespearean use). *Ham* 2.2.201, 'their [old men's] eyes purging plum-tree gum', shows the implied metaphor in the present passage.
down-roping falling in long strings. Cf. 3.5.23, 'roping icicles'.
pale-dead dead-pale, as colourless as if they were dead

48 ***palled** enfeebled, weakened (*OED ppl. a.*[1] 1): cf. *AC* 2.7.80, 'I'll never follow thy palled [F paul'd] fortunes more'. The context supports the

emendation, a repetition of *pale* is unlikely, and 'misreading of pald or pauld as pale would be easy' (Taylor).
dull lacking physical feeling (*OED a.* 2)
gimmaled made with gimmals or joints (*OED*, which gives this example and one from *E3*, 1.2.29, 'Nor lay aside their Iacks of Gymould mayle')

49 **still and motionless** completely motionless (synonymous)

50–1 **And ... hour** Moore Smith compares *E3*, 4.5.49–51, where the French King says that a flock of ravens are hovering 'for the carcases / Of those poor English, that are markt to die'. In fact the King is speaking with feigned confidence, knowing by a prophecy that the ravens portend the defeat of the French. Shakespeare may have recalled the incident, or the King's retort to the French Herald in *Famous Victories* (scene xiv: l. 1,200), 'Rather shall my bodie lie dead in the field, to feed crowes.'

50 **executors** i.e. 'who are to have the disposal of what they shall leave, their hides and flesh' (Johnson). The legal term, quite distinct from *executors* at 1.2.203 (and stressed in the modern way on the second syllable), is used with morbid wit.
knavish rascally (*OED a.* 3)

51 **them all, impatient** F's unambiguous punctuation makes good sense. Rowe's emendation, really

45 hand] *F;* hands *Oxf[1]* 46 drooping] *F2;* dropping *F* hides] *F;* hide *F2* 47 down-roping] *(*downe roping*)* pale-dead] *F;* pale dead *Oxf[1]* 48 palled dull] *Hudson;* pale dull *F;* palled *Capell* gimmaled] *Delius;* Iymold *F;* gimmal *Johnson* 49 chewed grass] *(*chaw'd-grasse*)* 51 them all, impatient] *F;* them, all impatient *Rowe;* them all impatient *Oxf[1]*

Description cannot suit itself in words
To demonstrate the life of such a battle
In life so lifeless as it shows itself.

CONSTABLE

They have said their prayers, and they stay for
    death.   55

DAUPHIN

Shall we go send them dinners and fresh suits
And give their fasting horses provender,
And after fight with them?

CONSTABLE

I stay but for my guidon. To the field!
I will the banner from a trumpet take   60
And use it for my haste. Come, come away!
The sun is high and we outwear the day.   *Exeunt.*

calling for a hyphen (cf. 4.0.38, *all-watched*), gives the sense 'wholly impatient' and over-stresses the crows' point of view.

their hour i.e. the hour of their death. Cf. *JC* 5.5.20, 'I know my hour is come.'

52 **suit** *clothe*
53 **demonstrate the life of** depict exactly as it is, paint it to the life
    battle army
54 **In life so lifeless** so lifelessly living (paradoxical)
55 **They have** elided ('They've'), *prayers* being disyllabic
56–8 **Shall ... them?** 'a scornful mock-proposal' arising from the speaker's impatience (Gurr)
59 ***guidon** a flag or pennant, broad at the end next to the staff and pointed at the other (*OED*, with several sixteenth-century examples, including Hall and Holinshed). Holinshed (3.554) confirms the emendation: 'When the messenger was come backe

to the French host, the men of warre put on their helmets, and caused their trumpets to blow to the battell' (cf. ll. 33–4). 'They thought themselues so sure of victorie, that diuerse of the noble men made such hast towards the battell, that they left manie of their seruants and men of warre behind them, and some of them would not once staie for their standards: as amongst other the duke of Brabant, when his standard was not come, caused a baner to be taken from a trumpet and fastened to a speare, the which he commanded to be borne before him in steed of his standard.'

60 **banner** *OED* (banner *sb.*[1] 4) explains that this is a banderole (*OED* 2b: 'A small ornamental streamer, e.g. that attached to the lance of a knight').
    trumpet trumpeter
61 **Come, come away** come, make haste (*OED* away *adv.* 1)
62 **outwear** wear out, waste

54 lifeless] (*liuelesse*)   55] *as Pope; F lines* ... prayers, / ... death.   59–60] *as Rowe; F lines* ... Guard: on / ... take   59 guidon] *Rann;* Guard: on *F*

[4.3] *Enter* GLOUCESTER, BEDFORD, EXETER, ERPINGHAM
with all his host, SALISBURY *and* WESTMORLAND.

GLOUCESTER
Where is the King?
BEDFORD
The King himself is rode to view their battle.
WESTMORLAND
Of fighting men they have full threescore thousand.

4.3.0.1–2 F's version of the SD suggests
that Salisbury and Westmorland were
added to it by Shakespeare while
writing the dialogue. Taylor, regarding *his* as an error for *the*, asks 'Why
should Erpingham's host be specified?' Perhaps the answer is that the
King had bidden Erpingham assemble
the nobles at his tent (4.1.284), and
that until he appears Shakespeare
regards Erpingham as having charge
of the army. Erpingham has no
speeches in the present scene. For
the possessive pronoun in a SD, cf.
3.3.0.1–2, 3.6.86 SD.
0.2 SALISBURY Thomas de Montacute
(1388–1428), son of the Salisbury of
R2, served at Agincourt. He appears
also in *1H6*: cf. l. 10n.
   WESTMORLAND Cf. 1.2.0n. Westmorland (1364–1425), who was fifty-
one years old at the time of Agincourt,
was in England as joint-warden of the
marches (cf. 1.2.140n.). Gurr suggests, with some probability, that
Shakespeare introduces him here so
that the King can address him as
cousin (as he did at 1.2.4) at ll. 19,
30, 73.
1 **Where is the King?** At 4.1.303 the
King declared that he would
accompany Gloucester, so Gloucester's question, though it may pass
in the theatre without notice, is an
inconsistent one. To give the question
to Bedford, and the reply to Gloucester, would not mend matters, since

it might draw the audience's attention
to the King's unexplained change of
plan. The probable purpose of ll. 1–
2 is (1) to bring in a mention of the
fearful odds (l. 5), and (2) to allow the
King's entrance to impinge dramatically on Westmorland's speech
(ll. 16–18).
2 **The King ... battle** Cf. Holinshed,
3.552 (immediately preceding the
passage quoted at 4.0.4–9n.). The
Duke of York, who led the vaward of
the army, learned that a great army
of Frenchmen was at hand: 'The duke
declared to the king what he had
heard, and the king therevpon,
without all feare or trouble of mind,
caused the battell which he led himselfe to staie, and incontinentlie rode
foorth to view his aduersaries, and
that doone, returned to his people,
and with cheerfull countenance
caused them to be put in order of
battell.' (In margin: 'King Henrie
rideth foorth to take view of the
French armie.')
   battle army
3 **Of fighting ... thousand** Cf. Holinshed (3.552): 'hauing in their armie
(as some write) to the number of
threescore thousand horssemen,
besides footmen, wagoners, and
other.' (In margin: 'The number of
the French men three score thousand.
Enguerant.': i.e. Enguerrand de Mon-
strelet, *c.* 1400–53, French chron-
icler.)

4.3] *Capell* 0.1–2] *F; Enter* Clarence, Gloster, Exeter, and Salisburie. *Q* 0.2 *host,*]
(Hoast:) WESTMORLAND] *F (Westmorland); Warwick Oxf¹* 1–2] *F; not in Q* 2 SP] *F;*
Clarence Oxf¹ 3 SP] *F; War. Q*

EXETER

There's five to one; besides, they all are fresh.

SALISBURY

God's arm strike with us! 'Tis a fearful odds.   5
God bye you, princes all; I'll to my charge.
If we no more meet till we meet in heaven,
Then joyfully, my noble lord of Bedford,
My dear lord Gloucester, and my good lord Exeter,
And my kind kinsman, warriors all, adieu.   10

BEDFORD

Farewell, good Salisbury, and good luck go with
    thee.

EXETER

Farewell, kind lord. Fight valiantly today.
And yet I do thee wrong to mind thee of it,
For thou art framed of the firm truth of valour.

[*Exit Salisbury.*]

4 **There's five to one** That's five to
one. Contrast Holinshed (3.553):
'Thus the Frenchmen being ordered
vnder their standards and banners,
made a great shew: for suerlie they
were esteemed in number six times
as manie or more, than was the whole
companie of the Englishmen, with
wagoners, pages and all.' (In margin:
'The French esteemed six to one
English.')

5 **a fearful odds** *Odds* is often, as here,
singular: cf. *R2* 3.4.90, 'with that
odds'.

6 **God bye you** In an edition exclus-
ively for readers *God be wi' you* would
be the form that most clearly expressed the sense. The F spelling,
however, indicates the pronunciation
and is therefore retained, in Moore
Smith's modified spelling: as he notes,
'to change it into *God be wi' you*
entails an unjustifiable alteration in
the rhythm of the lines.' It would
.be virtually impossible to pronounce

b'wi' as a monosyllable. If the phrase
should seem to a modern audience to
mean 'God buy (i.e. purchase) you,
princes all', the misapprehension is
not serious. The punctuation at 5.1.67
makes it clear that 'Goodbye, you
princes all' is at all costs to be avoided.

10 **my kind kinsman** addressed to
Westmorland, one of whose sons was
married to Salisbury's only daughter.
Shakespeare would know this from
Hall's account (145) of Salisbury's
death at the siege of Orleans, which
had been his source for *1H6* 1.6 [1.4]:
'leuyng behind him, an onely daughter named Alice, maried to Richarde
Neuell, sonne to Raufe earle of
Westmerland, of whom hereafter
shalbe made mencion.'

13–14 **And yet ... valour** misplaced in
F: 'a marginal addition in the manuscript, the position of which the compositor mistook' (Greg, 'Principles',
143)

14 **framed ... valour** composed of the

6 bye] *Moore Smith;* buy' *F;* be wi' *Rowe*   8 my ... Bedford] *F;* Braue *Clarence Q;* my
noble Lord of Clarence *Oxf¹*   11 SP] *F; Clarence Oxf¹; speech not in Q*   12 SP] *F; Clar. Q*
13–14] *placed as Q; after 11 F*   14 SD] *Rowe*

BEDFORD

He is as full of valour as of kindness,   15
Princely in both.

Enter the KING.

WESTMORLAND   O that we now had here
But one ten thousand of those men in England
That do no work today!
KING   What's he that wishes so?
My cousin Westmorland? No, my fair cousin:
If we are marked to die, we are enough   20

firmest and most constant valour. Taylor compares Chapman's Homer, *Iliad*, ll. 364–5: 'He that affects renowne in warre must like a rocke be fixt, / Wound or be wounded: valour's truth puts no respect betwixt.'

SD Salisbury's exit, not marked in F or Q, can be placed either here or after l. 12 (in which case ll. 13–14 are apostrophe, not direct address). Both arrangements seem equally acceptable.

15 **kindness** tenderness. Cf. *TN* 2.1.35–8, quoted at 4.6.31n.

16–18 **O that ... today** Cf. Holinshed (3.553): 'It is said, that as he heard one of his host vtter his wish to another thus: I would to God there were with vs now, so manie good soldiers as are at this houre within England! the king answered: I would not wish a man more here than I haue, we are indeed in comparison to the enimies but a few, but if God of his clemencie doo fauour vs, and our iust cause (as I trust he will) we shall speed well inough.' According to the *Gesta Henrici Quinti* (Williams, 47) the speaker was Sir Walter Hungerford, and his wish was that the King could have another ten thousand of the best English archers ('decem milia

de melioribus sagittariis Angliae'). Shakespeare may have obtained his figure from this source, or he may have invented it as a round number. Gurr, giving no reason, interprets 'But one ten thousand' as 'A fraction: one in ten thousand'. For the expression *but one*, cf. *Cor* 4.1.65–7, 'If I could shake off but one seven years / From these old arms and legs'.

18 **What's he** who is it (Abbott, 254, *what* for *who*)

20–2 **If we ... honour** In Holinshed (3.553, continuing after the passage quoted at 16–18n.) the King, trusting in God's merciful favour, hopes to gain the victory; 'And if so be that for our offenses sakes we shall be deliuered into the hands of our enimies, the lesse number we be, the lesse damage shall the realme of England susteine.' This and the word *few* (cf. 16–18n. and l. 60) are Shakespeare's only debts to the speech, which proceeds to argue that if they had more men they might trust too much in their own strength and irreligiously ascribe to it the victory if God gave it them.

20 **marked to die** destined to die (*OED* mark *v.* 6). For this phrase in *E3*, see 4.2.50–1n.

15 SP] F; *Clarence Oxf¹; speech not in Q*   16 SP] F; *War. Q*   18–19 What's ... Westmorland?] F; Whose that, that wishes so, my Cousen *Warwick? Q*   19–30 No ... England] F; *not in Q*   20 enough] *(enow)*

To do our country loss, and if to live,
The fewer men, the greater share of honour.
God's will, I pray thee wish not one man more.
By Jove, I am not covetous for gold,
Nor care I who doth feed upon my cost;   25
It earns me not if men my garments wear:
Such outward things dwell not in my desires.
But if it be a sin to covet honour
I am the most offending soul alive.
No, faith, my coz, wish not a man from England.   30
God's peace, I would not lose so great an honour
As one man more, methinks, would share from me,
For the best hope I have. O do not wish one more!

23 **God's will** This oath (again at l. 74) occurs four other times in Shakespeare: *RJ* 3.3.76 (Friar Lawrence), *Oth* 2.3.151, 155 (Iago: in Quarto 1622; see l. 24n.), *H8* 2.3.12 (Anne Boleyn).

24–7 **By ... desires** Perhaps suggested by Holinshed (3.583, summing up Henry V's qualities): 'Wantonnesse of life and thirst in auarice had he quite quenched in him; ... For bountifulnesse and liberalitie, no man more free, gentle, and franke, in bestowing rewards to all persons, according to their deserts: for his saieng was, that he neuer desired monie to keepe, but to giue and spend.'

24 **By Jove** not elsewhere in the English histories, but not rare in Shakespeare (e.g. *LLL* 5.2.494, 'By Jove, I always took three threes for nine'). Expurgation of *By God* has been suggested, but improbably in view of the proximity of *God's will* (l. 23) for which the expurgated F text of *Oth* substituted 'Alas' and 'Fie, fie' on its two occurrences.

covetous Here and at l. 28, cf. the Tenth Commandment, Exodus 20:17:

'Thou shalt not couet thy neyghbours house ... or whatsoeuer thy neyghbour hath.'

25 **upon my cost** at my expense

26 **earns** grieves. Cf. 2.3.3n.

30 **faith** indeed
   coz cousin (familiar form)

31 **God's peace** Here only in Shakespeare. Not peace as opposed to war, but the order of the universe under God's rule: cf. peace, 4.1.278n.

32 **share from me** take away from me. Shakespeare's only other use of *share from*, *TC* 1.3.360, 'What glory our Achilles shares from Hector' (i.e. in single combat), shows that the King is speaking metaphorically, *share* being *OED v.*[1] (a variant of *shear*), cut off; cf. Spenser, *Faerie Queene*, 5.5.9, 'Halfe of her shield he shared quite away'. *OED* share *v.*[2] 4d (*to share from:* to gain at the expense of) creates a special definition for these two Shakespearean examples. But the usual sense of *share* also lingers in the mind after l. 22.

33 **the best hope I have** i.e. my hope of salvation

26 earns] *(yernes)*   30, 73 coz] *(Couze)*

Rather proclaim it, Westmorland, through my host,
That he which hath no stomach to this fight,   35
Let him depart; his passport shall be made
And crowns for convoy put into his purse.
We would not die in that man's company
That fears his fellowship to die with us.
This day is called the feast of Crispian.   40
He that outlives this day and comes safe home
Will stand a-tiptoe when this day is named

34–6 Rather ... depart The source is the account in Hall (253) and Holinshed (3.664) of Edward IV's action before the battle of Towton: 'King Edward, perceiuing the courage of his trustie friend the earle of Warwike, made proclamation, that all men which were afraid to fight should depart: and, to all those that tarried the battell, he promised great rewards' (Holinshed: cf. *3H6* 2.3.49–53).

35–6 That ... depart Abbott (267) points out that 'That he which' could mean 'That man who', but thinks (no doubt correctly) that '*which* is here used for *that*, and there is a confusion of constructions'.

35 stomach to appetite for. Cf. 3.7.153n.

36 passport letter of authorization (to pass through the country and take ship): *OED sb.*[1] 1.

37 for convoy to pay for his journey

38 We like *us* (l. 39), the royal plural

39 fears ... to die fears to die in fellowship. Cf. 4.8.102, 'Here was a royal fellowship of death.'

40 This day ... Crispian Cf. Holinshed, 3.553: 'The daie following was the fiue and twentith of October in the yeare 1415, being then fridaie, and the feast of Crispine and Crispinian, a daie faire and fortunate to the English, but most sorrowfull and vnluckie to the French.' Crispin and Crispinian, whose history is largely legendary and not traced beyond the eighth century, are said to have been two brothers, of noble family, who left Rome and settled at Soissons (Noviodunum, Augusta Suessionum) in France, where they supported themselves by shoemaking (hence later becoming the patron saints of shoemakers), made many converts to Christianity, and were martyred by decapitation *c*. 287–300.

Crispian an adaptation (*Crispianus* in Q3 and F at 4.7.90) of the name Crispinian. It occurs in Thomas Deloney's *The Gentle Craft* (Part I, 1597; Part II, 1598; earliest surviving editions 1627, 1639). Part I, chs 5–9, includes an elaborate fiction in which Crispianus and his younger brother Crispine are Kentish princes who take refuge from the Roman Emperor's tyranny with a shoemaker in Faversham and become his apprentices. Crispine secretly marries the Emperor's daughter, and Crispianus (conscripted for wars in Gaul) secures as a reward for his bravery the Emperor's acquiescence in the marriage. Presumably poetical considerations dictated Shakespeare's combination of the two saints' names into *Crispin Crispian* (l. 57).

42 stand a-tiptoe stand on tiptoe (Abbott, 24: adverbs with prefix *a-* before nouns), i.e. feel exalted

---

34 Westmorland ... host] *F;* presently through our campe *Q*   42 a-tiptoe] *(a tip-toe)*

And rouse him at the name of Crispian.
He that shall see this day and live old age
Will yearly on the vigil feast his neighbours,   45
And say 'Tomorrow is Saint Crispian.'
Then will he strip his sleeve and show his scars,
And say 'These wounds I had on Crispin's day.'
Old men forget; yet all shall be forgot
But he'll remember, with advantages,   50
What feats he did that day. Then shall our names,
Familiar in his mouth as household words,
Harry the King, Bedford and Exeter,
Warwick and Talbot, Salisbury and Gloucester,

44 **He ... age** F's *live old age* is an
elliptical expression for 'live to old
age' or 'live out old age': *OED* live
v.[1] 9f, 'quasi-*trans. To live out*: to
complete (a term of life)'. Cf. *R3*
1.3.210, 'That none of you may live
his natural age.' For such expressions,
in which a preposition is omitted, see
Abbott, 198 (after verbs of motion),
200 (after quasi-transitive verbs) and
202 (in adverbial expressions of time,
e.g. *R3* 4.4.118, 'Forbear to sleep
the nights, and fast the days'). It is
therefore not necessary to suppose
with Keightley that F has omitted a
preposition, or with Pope that it has
transposed two verbs. Q's reading,
which at first sight reinforces Pope's
emendation, is a substitution for F's
half-remembered l. 41, which appears
in its fully remembered form at the
place corresponding to F's l. 44.
45 **vigil** the evening before the feast-day
48 **And say ... day* Q preserves this
line, accidentally omitted in F. F's
colon at the end of l. 47 may indicate
that something was to follow, and
the omission would be an easy error
because l. 46 had also begun with the
words *And say.*
49–50 **all ... remember** i.e. he'll forget

everything else rather than not
remember; whatever else he may
forget, he'll remember
50 **with advantages** with additions; cf.
Oth 4.3.84, 'as many to th' vantage'
(i.e. as many in addition). An indul-
gently humorous touch: the veteran
will embroider his war story.
52 **his mouth** Though his neighbours
would know the names too, he is the
speaker and they the listeners. Q's
their mouths results from its inadvertent rearrangement of the passage:
'Then shall we in their flowing bowles
/ Be newly remembred. *Harry* the
King, / *Bedford* and *Exeter, Clarence*
and *Gloster*, / *Warwick* and *Yorke*. /
Familiar in their mouthes as hushold
words.'
household words 'words or sayings
in familiar use': *OED* household 6
(*attrib.* passing into *adj.*) c, 'familiar,
intimate, homely', and 8 (*special
combs.*), this example. The phrase,
originating here, has become proverbial, e.g. as the title of the weekly
periodical started by Dickens in 1849.
54 **Warwick** He was not at Agincourt
(see List of Roles 10n.), but his prominence in the French wars of *1H6*,
like Talbot's (see following note), may

44] *F; He that outliues this day, and sees old age* Q *(transposed with 41);* He that shall live this
day, and see old age *Pope*   old age] *F;* to old-age *Keightley;* t'old age *Oxf[1]*   48] *Q; not in F*   49–
50 forgot / But] *Cam (subst.);* forgot: / But *F*   52 his mouth] *F;* their mouthes *Q*   53–4] *F;
Harry* the King, / *Bedford* and *Exeter, Clarence* and *Gloster*, / *Warwick* and *Yorke. Q*

Be in their flowing cups freshly remembered. 55
This story shall the good man teach his son,
And Crispin Crispian shall ne'er go by
From this day to the ending of the world
But we in it shall be remembered,
We few, we happy few, we band of brothers. 60
For he today that sheds his blood with me
Shall be my brother; be he ne'er so vile,
This day shall gentle his condition.
And gentlemen in England now abed
Shall think themselves accursed they were not here, 65
And hold their manhoods cheap whiles any speaks
That fought with us upon Saint Crispin's day.

Enter SALISBURY.

SALISBURY
My sovereign lord, bestow yourself with speed.

have led to the combination of their names in this line.

Talbot John Talbot, first Earl of Shrewsbury (?1388–1453), the military hero of *1H6* (and for that reason probably named in the list here, as a figure well known to Shakespeare's audience) did not in fact take part in the French wars till 1419; from 1414 he was lieutenant of Ireland.

55 **flowing** brimming (*OED ppl. a.* 6: the fundamental sense is 'rising like the tide')

56 **the good man** i.e. every good man. Though *goodman* has particular senses such as 'householder' (*OED* 2) and 'yeoman' (*OED* 4) there is little reason to suppose word-play here.

59 **remembered** rememberèd (at l. 55 it has the usual three syllables). Rowe restored the metrical value, which is lost in F and Q, both printing 'remembred', as they do in l. 55.

62 **vile** of small account (*OED a.* 5): cf. 63n. and 3.1.29, *mean and base* (whence Q's 'base' here). When Shakespeare uses *vile* and *base* synonymously together it is the context that determines the meaning (*TGV* 4.1.71, 'such vile, base practices'; *MND* 1.1.232–3, 'Things base and vile, holding no quantity, / Love can transpose to form and dignity'), and the context here rules out a derogatory sense, though Taylor argues that the King 'probably means that his soldiers can redeem past misconduct by fighting gloriously now'.

63 **gentle his condition** ennoble his rank (figuratively, not literally: hence the antithesis with *gentlemen*, l. 64). *Condition* is four syllables.

68 **bestow yourself** act (*OED bestow v.* 5c); cf. *TGV* 3.1.87. Here the sense is 'prepare for battle'.

57–8] *F;* And from this day, vnto the generall doome: *Q*   59 remembered] *Rowe;* remembred *F, Q*   62 vile] *F;* base *Q*   64 abed] *(a bed)*   65–6 accursed ... cheap] *F;* accurst, / And hold their manhood cheape *Q;* accurst, / They were not there *Q3*   67 SD] *F; not in Q*   68 SP] *F; Glost. Q*   68–70] *F;* My gracious Lord, / The French is in the field. *Q*

The French are bravely in their battles set
And will with all expedience charge on us.   70

KING

All things are ready, if our minds be so.

WESTMORLAND

Perish the man whose mind is backward now!

KING

Thou dost not wish more help from England, coz?

WESTMORLAND

God's will, my liege, would you and I alone,
Without more help, could fight this royal battle!   75

KING

Why, now thou hast unwished five thousand men,
Which likes me better than to wish us one.
You know your places. God be with you all!

Tucket. Enter MONTJOY.

MONTJOY

Once more I come to know of thee, King Harry,
If for thy ransom thou wilt now compound,   80
Before thy most assured overthrow:

69 **bravely ... set** handsomely drawn
up in their battle formations
70 **expedience** expedition, speed
74 **God's will** Westmorland enthusi-
astically repeats the King's oath, l. 23.
77 **likes** pleases. Cf. 4.1.16.
78 SD *Tucket* See note at 3.6.112 SD.
As Gurr observes, comparing 4.2.33–
4, 'The trumpet-call for the charge
might have been expected.' Montjoy's
mission is in fact an inconsistent
sequel to 4.2.59–62. It is introduced
for the sake of the King's rejoinder.
79–128 **Once more ... ransom** Cf.
Holinshed, 3.553 (immediately preceding the passage quoted at
4.2.59n.): 'Here we may not forget
how the French thus in their iolitie,
sent an herald to king Henrie, to

inquire what ransome he would offer.
Whereunto he answered, that within
two or three houres he hoped it would
so happen, that the Frenchmen
should be glad to common rather with
the Englishmen for their ransoms,
than the English to take thought for
their deliuerance, promising for his
owne part, that his dead carcasse
should rather be a prize to the Frenchmen, than that his liuing bodie should
paie anie ransome.'
80 **thou** 'The French Herald addresses
Henry as *thou*, not for discourtesy,
but in the "high style" appropriate
between heralds and monarchs'
(Abbott, 235). Cf. 4.7.70.
compound make terms (*OED v.* 10)
81 **assured** assurèd

72, 74 SP] *F; War. Q*   80–8] *F;* What thou wilt giue for raunsome? *Q*

For certainly thou art so near the gulf
Thou needs must be englutted. Besides, in mercy,
The Constable desires thee thou wilt mind
Thy followers of repentance, that their souls   85
May make a peaceful and a sweet retire
From off these fields where, wretches, their poor
    bodies
Must lie and fester.

KING   Who hath sent thee now?

MONTJOY
The Constable of France.

KING
I pray thee bear my former answer back: 90
Bid them achieve me and then sell my bones.
Good God, why should they mock poor fellows thus?
The man that once did sell the lion's skin
While the beast lived, was killed with hunting him.
A many of our bodies shall no doubt   95
Find native graves, upon the which, I trust,
Shall witness live in brass of this day's work.
And those that leave their valiant bones in France,
Dying like men, though buried in your dunghills,
They shall be famed, for there the sun shall greet
    them,   100
And draw their honours reeking up to heaven,

82 **gulf** whirlpool. Cf. 2.4.10.
83 **englutted** swallowed up
84 **mind** remind
86 **retire** retreat (in the military sense:
    OED sb. 3)
91 **achieve** win (*OED v.* 5b). As he
    immediately explains, he does not
    intend to be taken alive. Cf. also ll.
    122–5.
93–4 **The man ... him** Alluding to the
    proverb (Tilley, B 132) 'To sell the
    bear's skin before the beast is caught',
    itself derived from one of Aesop's
    fables. King Henry substitutes the
    lion for the bear because of its rank
    as king of beasts and its appearance

in England's royal coat of arms.
95 **A many** See 3.7.74n.
96 **native graves** graves in our native
    England; i.e. they will 'outlive this
    day' (l. 41)
97 **in brass** (1) written on brazen tablets
    covering the tombstones, (2) imper-
    ishably, cf. *Son* 64.4, 'brass eternal',
    MM 5.1.9–13
100–1 **the sun ... heaven** 'The sun
    exhales their honour (the fiery
    element in them; cf. Prologue 1) like
    vapour upwards' (Wilson), while its
    heat causes their dead bodies to
    decompose.

96–8] *F*; Finde graues within your realme of *France*: *Q*

Leaving their earthly parts to choke your clime,
The smell whereof shall breed a plague in France.
Mark then abounding valour in our English,
That being dead, like to the bullets crazing,   105
Break out into a second course of mischief,
Killing in relapse of mortality.
Let me speak proudly. Tell the Constable
We are but warriors for the working-day;
Our gayness and our gilt are all besmirched   110
With rainy marching in the painful field.
There's not a piece of feather in our host
(Good argument, I hope, we will not fly),

102 **clime** region, i.e. France (l. 103):
OED sb. 2

104 **abounding** abundant. Q reading
'abundant', recognizes only this sense.
Theobald emended to 'a bounding'
(i.e. a rebounding), and most later
editors allege word-play because of
the simile in l. 105. But such word-
play is improbable: Shakespeare uses
'bounding' only of a steed (*1H4*
2.4[3].49), and when he means
'rebound' he uses that word (*AC*
5.2.103).

105 **the bullets crazing** the bullets
when they shatter (*OED* craze *v.* 1c).
The context (ll. 104–7) makes *crazing*
more appropriate than F2's *grazing*
(ricocheting, *OED* graze *v.*² 2) because
it implies the destruction, not merely
the deflection, of the bullets. Both
senses of *bullet* (cannon-ball, *OED*
*sb.*¹ 2; musket-ball, *OED sb.*¹ 3) were
current and are found in Shakespeare
(*KJ* 2.1.227; *LLL* 3.1.62); the former
is the more probable here, a stone
cannon-ball being more likely to
shatter than a leaden bullet.

107 **relapse of mortality** 'the falling-
back or returning of the mortal body
to its original dust' (Hudson). The
phrase corresponds to 'being dead' (l.
105), as *Killing* corresponds to 'Break

out into a second course of mischief'
(l. 106). Though *OED* does not record
this sense of *relapse* before 1876 (*sb.*¹
4), it is one that the Latin derivation
of the word naturally supports. The
alternative interpretation, 'a fatal
relapse', is less probable, adding a
metaphor to the simile that the
passage already contains. *Relapse* is
stressed on the first syllable.

108 **Let ... proudly** i.e. 'It becomes me
to speak proudly (in the circumstances)'. Not 'leave this jesting'
(Wilson), as he continues to jest in
what follows.

109 **but ... working-day** soldiers fit
only for working-days, i.e. ordinary-
looking men (mock-derogatory, cf.
1.2.278), not dressed in our holiday
or Sunday clothes

110 **gayness** gay appearance, brightness
of colour (*OED* 2)

111 **rainy ... field** Cf. Holinshed, 3.552:
'dailie it rained, and nightlie it
freesed' during the march towards
Calais. The epithets *rainy* and *painful*
are transferred, to give the sense
'marching in the rain through a
difficult country'.

112 **feather** ornamental plume

113 **fly** flee (with word-play on flying
with wings)

104 abounding] *F*; abundant *Q*; a bounding *Theobald*   105 bullets] *F*, *Q*; bullet's *Hanmer*   crazing] *F*, *Q (*crasing*); grasing *F2*   108–11 Tell ... field] *F*; *not in Q*   109 working-day]
(*working day*)

And time hath worn us into slovenry.
But by the mass, our hearts are in the trim,   115
And my poor soldiers tell me yet ere night
They'll be in fresher robes, or they will pluck
The gay new coats o'er the French soldiers' heads
And turn them out of service. If they do this,
As, if God please, they shall, my ransom then   120
Will soon be levied. Herald, save thou thy labour:
Come thou no more for ransom, gentle herald.
They shall have none, I swear, but these my joints,
Which if they have as I will leave 'em them
Shall yield them little, tell the Constable.   125

MONTJOY
I shall, King Harry. And so fare thee well:

114 **time** i.e. day-by-day hardship
slovenry untidiness, dirtiness (common *c.* 1600, but only here in Shakespeare)
115 **by the mass** Cf. 3.2.115.
hearts i.e. as the seat of courage (*OED sb.* 11). The word is stressed, to bring out the contrast with *gayness* and *gilt* in l. 110.
in the trim (1) ready for action (*OED* trim *sb.* 1, the state of being fully rigged: cf. *CE* 4.1.90, 'The ship is in her trim'), (2) finely dressed (*OED sb.* 3b: cf. *1H4* 4.1.114, 'in their trim')
116–19 **And ... service** The obvious sense is that the soldiers will pillage their slain enemies, the *fresher robes* being the same as the *gay new coats*. Only the word *or* (*OED conj.²* 4: otherwise) has created problems. The emendations *for* or *as*, besides assuming that Q and F are both wrong in reading *or*, make the King speak pedantically: the *or* of Q and F has the force, after a boast, of the colloquial 'or they'll know the reason why', after which *they will ... service* states what they actually propose to

do. Wilson's interpretation, that the soldiers expect to get heavenly robes if they do not kill the French, is contrary to the jesting tone.
116 **my poor soldiers** Cf. 3.6.86.2. The speech being a public one, with the army present, the King here, in effect, brings them into the dialogue by putting jocularly defiant words into their mouths. His jest calls for a warm response from this on-stage audience.
117–19 **pluck ... service** Cf. *STM*, 4.1.348, 'Go one, and pull his coat over his ears' (More, dismissing a dishonest servant in the usual formula).
120 **if God please** Cf. 1.2.290.
120–1 **my ransom ... levied** i.e. because the English will have a fine spoil from the French
123 **joints** limbs (the usual Shakespearean sense)
124 **as I ... them** i.e. hacked bare of flesh (cf. *Mac* 5.3.33, 'I'll fight till from my bones my flesh be hacked') and therefore valueless as *joints* in the culinary sense (e.g. *2H4* 5.1.23, 'a joint of mutton')

117 or] *F, Q*: for *Hanmer*; as *Oxf¹*   118 the] *F*; your *Q*   121] *as Pope*; *F lines* ... leuyed / labour: 124 'em] *(vm)*   125 little, tell] *F, Q*; little. Tell *Johnson*   126 8] *F*; *Her.* I shall deliuer so. *Q*

Thou never shalt hear herald any more.   *Exit.*

KING

I fear thou wilt once more come again for a ransom.

Enter YORK.

YORK

My lord, most humbly on my knee I beg
The leading of the vaward.   130

KING

Take it, brave York. – Now, soldiers, march away,
And how thou pleasest, God, dispose the day!   *Exeunt.*

---

127 **Thou ... more** a forecast of King Henry's death in the battle, which the King affects to understand as a promise not to trouble him again

128 **I fear ... ransom** Some editors regard this as prose, others (some emending) as verse. The fact that this is a verse scene makes verse much more probable. As it stands, the line is best read as a pentameter, with elisions at *thou wilt* and *for a*. The tautology of 'once more come again' seems authorial: cf. 4.5.11 ('once more back again') and 5.0.42 ('Harry's back return again'). For the meaning see 127n.; some have suggested that the King expects Montjoy to have to come again about the ransom of his own countrymen (cf. his answer in Holinshed, quoted at 79–128n.), but at 4.7.70–82 this idea is never mentioned, and the expression 'come for a ransom' would not be appropriate to it. Gurr (uniquely) gives the line as an aside, 'revealing doubts that Henry will not admit to his soldiers'. SD YORK Edward 'Plantagenet', more correctly Edward of Norwich (?1373–1415), who succeeded his father as Duke of York in 1402 and who was killed at Agincourt (cf.

4.6.11–32), is the Duke of Aumerle (i.e. Albemarle) of *R2*, after which he has dropped out of Shakespeare's history plays (*1H4*, *2H4*) till now. The audience is not reminded of the connection between his present and his past.

129–31 **My lord ... York** Cf. Holinshed, 3.553: 'he appointed a vaward, of the which he made capteine Edward duke of Yorke, who of an haultie courage had desired that office, and with him were the lords Beaumont, Willoughbie, and Fanhope, and this battell was all of archers.'

130 **vaward** This form of the word now current as 'vanguard' (the foremost part of an army) is invariably found in Shakespeare, both in F and the Quartos, and is therefore retained. Holinshed gives it variously as 'vaward' and 'vauntgard'. Its opposite (modern 'rearguard') is always 'rearward' in Shakespeare, whether used literally or figuratively.

132 **dispose the day** bestow the victory. *OED* dispose *v.* 4; day *sb.* 10 (and cf. 4.7.83–5). Cf. *KJ* 2.1.393, 'To whom in favour she [i.e. Fortune] shall give the day.'

---

127 SD] *F, Q (Exit Herauld.); opp. 128 Oxf¹*   128 thou wilt] *F;* thou'lt *Theobald*   come ... ransom] *F;* come again for ransom *Theobald;* come for a ransom *Oxf¹ (Cam)*   128 SD] *F; not in Q*   130 vaward] *F, Q;* vanguard *Oxf¹*   131–2] *as Pope; F lines ... Yorke. / ... away, / ... day. /*

[4.4] *Alarum. Excursions. Enter* PISTOL, FRENCH SOLDIER
[*and*] BOY.

PISTOL   Yield, cur!

FRENCH SOLDIER   *Je pense que vous êtes le gentilhomme
de bonne qualité.*

PISTOL

Qualité? 'Caleno custore me'!

Art thou a gentleman? What is thy name? Discuss.   5

FRENCH SOLDIER   *O Seigneur Dieu!*

PISTOL

O Signieur Dew should be a gentleman. –

4.4.0.1 *Alarum* Cf. 3.0.33 SD.
Excursions The military sense of this
word (*OED* 3: An issuing forth against
an army; a sally, sortie, raid) became
a theatrical term for a stage skirmish:
cf. *1H6* 3.2, 3, 4, 5 [3.2] for several
examples. Cf. 4.0.48–53, where it is
foretold that the battle will be thus
conventionally represented.

0.1–2 *Enter ... and* BOY In Q, 4.5 precedes this scene. Taylor suggests that
the transposition was due to casting
problems and that Clarence and
Montjoy doubled the Boy and Pistol
(Clarence is Q's substitution for
Bedford in 4.3). Both he and Walter
see some dramatic merit in the transposition, Walter objecting to the battle's opening with Pistol's capture of
the Frenchman, an event which
cannot occur until the French are in
flight. On the other hand, if 4.5
directly followed 4.3 (even allowing
for *excursions*) the battle might seem
to be lost and won as soon as it was
begun. Pistol's comic scene suspends
the serious business.

2–3 *Je ... qualité* 'I think that you are
a gentleman of good quality' (i.e. of
high rank); cf. 40–2n.

4 **Qualité ... me* Pistol repeats the
French Soldier's last word uncom-
prehendingly (no doubt with bad
pronunciation) and then speaks the
Irish refrain of a popular song (which
the sound of the word has brought to
mind), meaning that both are equally
unintelligible to him. Not a reply;
rather an exclamation. Malone (note
in Boswell) first pointed out the
allusion to the song, which is printed
in Clement Robinson's *A Handful of
Pleasant Delights*, 1584, as 'A Sonet
of a Louer in the praise of his lady.
To Calen o Custore me: sung at euerie
lines end.' The refrain represents the
Irish words 'cailin og a' stor' (young
maiden, my treasure).

5 **Discuss** Cf. 3.2.61n.

6 *O Seigneur Dieu!* 'O Lord God!'

7 *O ... gentleman* 'O, Signieur Dew
presumably is a gentleman' (*OED*
shall *v.* 18b): cf. *RJ* 1.5.53, 'This, by
his voice, should be a Montague.'
Pistol takes the exclamation as a reply
to his question. The mistake
resembles the one that he makes over
'Harry le Roy', 4.1.49. Walter asks,
'As Pistol is content with Signieur
Dew as the name of his prisoner, why

4.4] *Capell*   0.1–2] *F; Enter Pistoll, the French man, and the Boy. Q (transposes this scene and
4.5)*   1–11] *F; Pist. Eyld cur, eyld cur. Q (see 38–9)*   3 *bonne*] *F2 (bonc); bon F*   4 *Qualité?*]
Oxf¹; Qualtitie F; Quality F4; Cality! Alexander; Calitie! Humphreys   'Caleno custore me'!] *Boswell;
calmie custure me F*   5] *verse Humphreys; prose F*   7–11] *verse Pope; prose F*

Perpend my words, O Signieur Dew, and mark:
O Signieur Dew, thou diest on point of fox,
Except, O Signieur, thou do give to me   10
Egregious ransom.

FRENCH SOLDIER   *O prenez miséricorde! Ayez pitié de moi!*

PISTOL

Moy shall not serve, I will have forty moys,
Or I will fetch thy rim out at thy throat
In drops of crimson blood.   15

should he again ask for his name in ll. 23–4?', and Taylor (Oxf[1] 16) infers that ll. 2–11 are an abandoned first draft of the scene's opening, Shakespeare anticipating censorship of the profanity. But Q's substitution, for ll. 37–9, of 'Onye ma foy couple la gorge. / Vnlesse thou giue to me egregious raunsome, dye. / One poynt of a foxe' shows that the passage remained in the acted version.

8 **Perpend** weigh mentally, consider. Synonymous here with *mark*. This is the only transitive use of the word in Shakespeare. The other uses are absolute: *MW* 2.1.110 (Pistol), *AYL* 3.2.65 (Touchstone), *TN* 5.1.296 (Feste), *Ham* 2.2.106 (Polonius). All these plays belong to the period immediately following his humorous allusion to Preston's *Cambyses* (*1H4* 2.5[4].390), a play in which *perpend* is used in both ways: 'My sapient words, I say, perpend' (l. 5); 'My queen, perpend. What I pronounce, I will not violate' (l. 1,018).

9 **fox** sword. *OED sb.* 6 suggests that the figure of a wolf on some foreign sword-blades was mistaken for that of a fox. Webster, *The White Devil*, 5.6.234–5 ('O what blade is't? / A Toledo, or an English fox?'), indicates that such swords might be made in England, but not that a fox was a broadsword as distinct from a rapier,

as Gifford (Jonson, *Works*, 1816, 4.429) states, for the point of Webster's lines is that the two swords are visually indistinguishable.

11 **Egregious** remarkably great (*OED a.* 2b). Cf. 2.1.47.

12 *O . . . moi* 'O, take mercy! Have pity on me!' For the pronunciation of *moi*, cf. *R2* 5.3.117–18, where it rhymes with 'destroy'.

13 **Moy** Pistol, ignorantly confident as usual, assumes that this is the name of a coin. This explanation (*OED sb.*[3]) is more probable than that he means a moidore (Johnson; but the Portuguese coin was not current in England till the eighteenth century), a bushel (Walter, Taylor: *OED sb.*[2]; but the sense requires a definition in terms of something other than measurement), or a half (Gurr: i.e. moiety, interpreting F's 'a Tonne of Moyes', l. 22, as 'a tun of moys', a 'box of half-coins').

forty many. *Forty* is often used indefinitely; cf. *Cor* 3.1.241–2, 'On fair ground / I could beat forty of them.'

14 **rim** the 'rim of the belly', i.e. the membrane lining the abdomen and covering the bowels; the peritoneum (*OED* rim *sb.*[2] 2). Pistol extravagantly threatens to put his fist down the Frenchman's throat and pull his insides out.

12 *miséricorde*] F2; *miserecordie* F   *pitié*] F2; *pitez* F · 13] *verse* Q; *prose* F   14–22] F; *not in* Q   14–15] *verse Johnson; prose* F   14 Or] *Hanmer (Theobald);* for F

FRENCH SOLDIER   *Est-il impossible d'échapper la force de ton bras?*

PISTOL

Brass, cur?
Thou damned and luxurious mountain goat,
Offer'st me brass?   20

FRENCH SOLDIER   *O pardonnez-moi!*

PISTOL

Say'st thou me so? Is that a ton of moys?
Come hither, boy;
Ask me this slave in French what is his name.

BOY   *Écoutez. Comment êtes-vous appelé?*   25

FRENCH SOLDIER   *Monsieur le Fer.*

BOY   He says his name is Master Fer.

16–17 *Est-il ... bras?* 'Is it impossible to escape the strength of your arm?'

18 **Brass** The final *s* of *bras* (l. 17) was sounded in sixteenth-century French.

19 **damned** damnèd
luxurious lecherous (*OED* 1)
mountain goat Pistol's abuse here seems related to other instances of it: at 5.1.36 he is said to have called Fluellen 'mountain-squire', and in *MW* 1.1.147, he calls Sir Hugh Evans 'thou mountain-foreigner'. Mountains are less appropriate to Frenchmen than to Welshmen, but they are appropriate to goats (cf. *1H4* 3.1.37, 'The goats ran from the mountains'), and goats are often associated with lechery (in Spenser, *Faerie Queene*, 1.4.24, Luxury rides 'Vpon a bearded goat', and cf. *Oth* 3.3.408, 'as prime as goats'). In some stage productions the French Soldier has a goatish beard.

21 *O pardonnez-moi!* 'O spare me!' This is a more probable sense (cf. ll. 41, 51) than 'Oh, I beg your pardon' (Gurr).

22 **ton** (Pistol's misinterpretation of the second syllable of *pardonnez*) a measure of weight (variable; now 2,240 lb in England). Cam² reads *tun*, as at 1.2.256, but this is improbable, as the same compositor (A) spelled 'Tun' at 1.2.256 and 'Tonne' here.

24 **slave** wretch, villain, peasant (cf. l. 38). Cf. 4.1.265n.

25 BOY 'Although in productions the Boy's French is usually halting and mispronounced, there is no evidence of this in the text' (Taylor). A contrast between his fluent French and Pistol's bad French improves the humour of the scene.
Écoutez ... appelé? 'Listen; what are you called?'

26 *le Fer* (Fr.) Iron, steel: an incongruous enough name for a soldier who yields to Pistol. Shakespeare gives a rather similar name to Cordelia's general in *KL* (Q version), scene 17.9 [4.3.9], 'The Maréchal of France, Monsieur La Far.'

27, 28 **Master Fer** Q confirms that F's abbreviation M. stands for Master

18 20] *verse Capell; prose F; Oxf¹ lines*   goat, / ... brass?   21 *pardonnez-moi*] *(perdoune moy)*   22] *verse Pope; prose F*   23–4] *this edn; prose F; Pope lines* ... French / ... name. /   25 *Écoutez*] *(Escoute)*   27 Master] *F* (M), *Q* (Master)

299

PISTOL   Master Fer? I'll fer him, and firk him, and
ferret him. Discuss the same in French unto him.

BOY   I do not know the French for fer, and ferret and   30
firk.

PISTOL
Bid him prepare, for I will cut his throat.

FRENCH SOLDIER   *Que dit-il, monsieur?*

BOY   *Il me commande à vous dire que vous faites vous prêt,*
car ce soldat ici est disposé tout à cette heure de couper   35
votre gorge.

PISTOL
Owy, cuppele gorge, permafoy,
Peasant, unless thou give me crowns, brave crowns;
Or mangled shalt thou be by this my sword.

FRENCH SOLDIER   *O je vous supplie pour l'amour de*   40
Dieu me pardonner! Je suis le gentilhomme de bonne

and not for Monsieur. The Boy also
translates 'le Fer' into 'Fer' (with
English pronunciation, as is clear
from Pistol's rejoinder, for which the
translating of the name gives the cue).
28 **I'll fer him** Cf. similar meaningless
threatening repetitions in *1H4* 2.2.88–
9 ('You are grand-jurors, are ye? We'll
jure ye, faith') and *MW* 4.2.168, 170
('Come, Mother Prat ...'; 'I'll prat
her!').
   firk beat (*OED v.* 4); sometimes used
with overtones of 'fuck' in Dekker's
Shoemaker's Holiday (1.232; 7.44;
13.28) and perhaps here.
29 **ferret** worry, as a ferret worries a
rabbit (*OED v.* 3a: this passage); alternatively, search thoroughly (*OED v.*
3d), cf. 14n.
   Discuss Cf. l. 5 and 3.2.61n.
33–6 *Que ... gorge* 'What does he say,
sir?' 'He commands me to tell you
that you [are to] make yourself ready,

for this soldier here is disposed, this
very hour, to cut your throat.'
37 **Owy ... permafoy** 'Yes, cut the
throat, by my faith.' Cf. 2.1.72n.
Taylor argues for the normalization
of the spelling, but F2, which has
overhauled the French in this scene,
does not alter it here – probably,
however, ignoring it because it is not
in italics.
38 **Peasant** Cf. l. 24n.
40–3 *O, je ... écus* 'O, I beseech you,
for the love of God, to spare me! I
am a gentleman of a good house: save
my life, and I will give you two
hundred crowns.'
41 *le gentilhomme* The Boy's translation
a gentleman (l. 45) seems to support
F2's emendation – and probably
caused it; but cf. l. 2, which suggests
that F preserves Shakespeare's
wording here.

28 Master] (M.)   34 *faites vous*] F (*faite vous*); *vous teniez* F2   35 *à cette heure*] (*asture*)   *couper*]
F2; *couppes* F   37–9] verse Cam; prose F   37] F; *Oui, couper la gorge, par ma foi* Dyce²   38–9]
F; *Vnlesse thou giue to me egregious raunsome, dye. / One poynt of a foxe.* Q   41 *Dieu me*]
(*Dieu: ma*) *le gentilhomme*] F (*le Gentilhome*); *Gentil-home* F2; *vn gentelhome* Q   *bonne*] F2; *bon* F

*maison: gardez ma vie, et je vous donnerai deux cents
écus.*

PISTOL   What are his words?

BOY   He prays you to save his life: he is a gentleman of   45
a good house, and for his ransom hc will give you
two hundred crowns.

PISTOL
Tell him
My fury shall abate, and I the crowns will take.

FRENCH SOLDIER   *Petit monsieur, que dit-il?*   50

BOY   *Encore qu'il.est contre son jurement de pardonner
aucun prisonnier, néanmoins, pour les écus que vous lui
ici promettez, il est content à vous donner la liberté, le
franchisement.*

FRENCH SOLDIER [*to Pistol*]   *Sur mes genoux je vous*   55
donne mille remerciements, et je m'estime heureux que j'ai

---

46 **house** family
49 **My fury ... take** 'one magnificent
line, suiting the speaker' (Capell,
Notes). Cf. other hexameters of Pistol's, 2.1.67, 2.3.59. Q, which omits
'Tell him' (l. 48), reinforces Capell's
lineation.
50–8 *Petit ... Angleterre* 'Little sir,
what says he?' 'Although it is contrary
·to his vow to spare any prisoner,
nevertheless, for the crowns that you
here promise him, he is content to
give you liberty, enfranchisement.'
'On my knees I give you a thousand
thanks, and I esteem myself happy
that I have fallen into the hands of a
knight, as I think, the most brave,
valiant and most distinguished lord of
England.'
51–2 *Encore ... prisonnier* The Boy
invents a justification of Pistol's *fury*
(l. 49).
52–3 **lui ici promettez* Taylor rightly

states that something in the copy must
have produced F's 'layt a'. Perhaps
ici is more likely than *ci* to have been
misread as *ta* (the *ci* being taken for
a), after which faulty word-spacing
may have occurred.
55 *Sur mes genoux* Oxf[1] adds the SD
'kneeling to Pistol'. This is warranted
by the opening words of the speech,
but may mislead readers into thinking
that the French Soldier has been
standing till now. More probably he
has been lying or crouching on the
ground in terror, and here rises to
his knees, perhaps clasping those of
Pistol. Cf. Holinshed, quoted at
4.5.6n.: 'manie on their knees desired
to haue their liues saued.'
56 7 **j'ai tombé* F's misreading may
represent *je ai tombé* (Sisson), though
at 3.4.12 F has *I'ay*. The correct form
is *je suis tombé*.

42–3 *deux cents écus*] F *(deux cent escus)*; Cinquante ocios *Q*   47 two hundred crowns] *F*;
500 crownes *Q*   48–9] as Capell *(Notes)*; prose *F*; *Johnson lines ... I / ... take.*   50–63] *F*; not in
Q   52 *prisonnier*] *F2*; *prisonner F   néanmoins*] *F2 (neant-moins)*; *neant-mons F*   52–3 *lui ici
promettez*] *this edn (Oxf[1])*; *layt a promets F*; *luy promettez F2*; *l'avez promis / Theobald*; *lui ci
promettez Oxf[1]*; *l'ayez promis Cam[2]*   55 SD] *this edn* *je*] *F2*; *se F*   56 *remerciements*] *F2
(remerciement)*; *remercious F*   56–7 *j'ai tombé*] *Sisson*; *Ie intombe F*; *ie ne tombe F2*; *je suis tombé /
Theobald*

tombé entre les mains d'un chevalier, comme je pense, le
plus brave, vaillant et très distingué seigneur d'Angleterre.
PISTOL   Expound unto me, boy.
BOY   He gives you upon his knees a thousand thanks,   60
and he esteems himself happy that he hath fallen into
the hands of one, as he thinks, the most brave,
valorous and thrice-worthy *seigneur* of England.
PISTOL
As I suck blood, I will some mercy show.
Follow me.   65
BOY   *Suivez-vous le grand capitaine.*
                    [*Exeunt Pistol and French Soldier.*]
I did never know so full a voice issue from so empty
a heart; but the saying is true, 'The empty vessel
makes the greatest sound.' Bardolph and Nym had
ten times more valour than this roaring devil i'th' old   70
play, that every vice may pare his nails with a wooden

57 **comme je pense* Cf. *as he thinks* (l.
62) and *comme je pense* at 3.4.24.
58 *très* i.e. *most* (literally *very*). Because
the Boy translates F's *tres distinie* as
thrice-worthy (l. 63), Taylor reads
treis-distingué, regarding *treis* as
Shakespearean French for *thrice*; but
since Shakespeare often uses *thrice* to
form an adjective's superlative (e.g.
1.2.119, 'my thrice-puissant liege';
1H4 3.2.92, 'my thrice-gracious lord')
there is no good reason for changing
the text.
64 **As ... show** Cf. the horse-leech
simile, 2.3.53–4; but Pistol probably
has a grander notion in mind: cf.
Lyly, *Endymion*, 3.2.26–31 (Tellus to
Corsites), 'I marvel, Corsites, that you
being a captain, who should sound
nothing but terror and suck nothing
but blood, can find in your heart to
talk such smooth words, for that it
agreeth not with your calling to use

words so soft as that of love.'
66 *Suivez-vous ... capitaine* 'Follow
the great captain'
67–8 **so empty a heart** a heart so empty
of courage
68–9 **The empty ... sound** proverbial
(Tilley, V 36)
70–2 **this ... dagger** i.e. 'this fellow,
roaring like the Devil in one of the
old-fashioned plays, but so cowardly
that every clown can give him a tows-
ing'. Here and in *TN* 4.2.129–34,
Shakespeare alludes to the paring of
the Devil's claws by the Vice, the
chief tempter and chief comedian of
the sixteenth-century moral inter-
ludes, e.g. Ulpian Fulwell's *Like Will
to Like*, 1568, where he fights his
companions (but not the Devil) with
his dagger, and finally rides away on
the Devil's back (but does not pare
his nails). The nail-paring, though
not to be found in any extant play,

57 mains] F2; main F   comme je] Oxf¹ (Capell); Ie F   pense] F2; peuse F   58 très distingué]
Capell; tres distinie F; tres destiné F2; treis-distingué Oxf¹   64] verse Pope; prose F   As] F; And as
Q   66 Suivez-vous] Capell; Saaue vous F; Suivez /. Rowe   capitaine.] F3 (Capitain!); Capitaine?
F   SD] Pope, Exit omnes. Q   67–76] F; not in Q   71 every vice] this edn; euerie one F

dagger, and they are both hanged, and so would this
be if he durst steal anything adventurously. I must
stay with the lackeys with the luggage of our camp;
the French might have a good prey of us if he knew   75
of it, for there is none to guard it but boys.

Exit.

[**4.5**]   *Enter* CONSTABLE, ORLEANS, BOURBON, [*the*]
                DAUPHIN *and* RAMBURES.

CONSTABLE   *O diable!*

ORLEANS   *O Seigneur! Le jour est perdu, tout est perdu!*

DAUPHIN

Mort de ma vie, all is confounded, all!
Mortal reproach and everlasting shame

was either familiar to Shakespeare's
audiences or readily imaginable by
them.
71 *that ... nails* whose nails every vice
may pare
every vice The wooden dagger, or
dagger of lath (*TN* 4.2.129, *1H4*
2.5[4].136–7), is the Vice's peculiar
appurtenance, and the point of the
Boy's remark is not that Pistol is
worsted by all opponents but that he
is worsted by the most contemptible
ones. Cf. *Oth* 5.2.250–1, 'I am not
valiant neither, / But every puny
whipster gets my sword.' A misreading of *vice* as *one* was (and still
is) easy.
72 **both hanged** 'The only exit Nym
has' (Wilson)
73–6 **I must ... boys** Cf. the Holinshed
passage quoted at 4.7.5–8n., and its
conclusion quoted at 4.6.35–8.
74 **lackeys** footmen (*OED sb.* 1) i.e. the
young personal servants of the nobles
in the army (cf. 4.2.25), not camp-

followers in a derogatory sense (*OED
sb*. 2, cited by Taylor). See 4.6.35–8n.
luggage baggage (cf. 4.7.1)
75 **the French** i.e. the enemy. Cf. the
singular pronoun in 'if he knew of it',
and 4.1.76.
have ... us get a good spoil from us.
The Boy does not contemplate the
possibility of being killed.
75–6 **knew of it** understood the situation
4.5.1 *O diable!* 'O the devil!'
2 *O Seigneur ... perdu!* 'O Lord
[God]! The day is lost, all is lost!'
3 *Mort de ma vie!* 'Death of my life!'
See 3.5.11n.
4 *Mortal reproach* This line must
originally have been a full line of
verse to follow l. 3. *Mortal* (this edn's
conjecture) is often used for 'deadly'
by Shakespeare; the reconstituted line
brings together a disgrace that will kill
them and a shame that will eternally
blacken their reputations. *Mortal*
might be overlooked by a compositor
who had set *Mor Dieu* in l. 3.

4.5] *Capell*   0.1–2] *F*; *Enter the four French Lords. Q (transposes this scene and 4.4); Enter the
Constable, the Dukes of Orléans and Bourbon, and Lord Rambures Oxf¹*   1] *F*; *Ge*. O diabello. *Q*   2]
F; *Bur*. O Iour dei houte all is gone, all is lost. *Q   Seigneur*] *F2 (signeur)*; sigueur *F   ¹perdu*]
Rowe; perdia *F   ²perdu*] *Rowe*; perdie *F*   3 SP] *F*; *Con. Q*; *Bourbon Oxf¹   Mort de*] *Q (*Mor
du*); Mor Dieu *F*   3–10 all is ... shame] *F*; *not in Q*   4 Mortal reproach] *this edn*; Reproach, *F*;
Reproach, reproach, *(Capell)*

Sits mocking in our plumes. *O méchante Fortune!*   5
                                   A short alarum.

Do not run away.
CONSTABLE   Why, all our ranks are broke.
DAUPHIN

   O perdurable shame! Let's stab ourselves.
Be these the wretches that we played at dice for?
ORLEANS

Is this the king we sent to for his ransom?
BOURBON

Shame, and eternal shame, nothing but shame!   10
Let us die instant. Once more back again,
And he that will not follow Bourbon now,

5–6 F's mislineation is caused by the SD: cf. 4.2.6n.
5 **Sits** See Prologue 9n.
   in our plumes 'At once mocking their fine feathers (cf. 4.3.112) and disdaining them from above' (Wilson)
   O méchante Fortune! 'O wicked Fortune!'
6 **Do not run away** Taylor regards this as addressed to Rambures, but more probably it is addressed to other French soldiers (perhaps passing over the stage) whose flight is indicated by the '*short alarum*'. Cf. Holinshed, 3.554: 'In conclusion, the king minding to make an end of that daies iornie, caused his horssemen to fetch a compasse about, and to ioine with him against the rereward of the Frenchmen, in the which was the greatest number of people. When the Frenchmen perceiued his intent, they were suddenlie amazed and ran awaie like sheepe, without order or arraie. Which when the king perceiued, he incouraged his men, and followed so quickelie vpon the enimies, that they ran hither and thither, casting awaie their armour:

manie on their knees desired to haue their liues saued.'
Why an exclamation, here of despair
7 **perdurable** everlasting (stressed on the first syllable, like the adverb 'perdurably' in *MM* 3.1.114)
11 ***instant** Like l. 4 this line is imperfect in F. See textual notes for conjectural restorations. Theobald's is adopted here because the adverbial use of *instant* occurs in *Ham* 1.5.94, and because the metre (*Let us* as two syllables) is consistent with every other occurrence of *let us* in the F texts of this play, *1H4*, *2H4* and *JC* (in the last two of which the elided form *Let's* also occurs in other places, and is duly indicated in F). If Shakespeare failed to join up 'in' and 'stant' the compositor may have lost his concentration and omitted the latter part of the word. Q's opening line of this speech ('A plague of order, once more to the field') is against the reading 'In once more' (Riv), and so is Gurr's defence of that reading, i.e. that the preposition 'means both going "in" to battle again, and exiting into the tiring house' (Cam²).

5–6] *verse Capell; F lines* ... Plumes. / ... away. /   11 die instant. Once] *Theobald;* dye in once *F;* flye in once *F2;* die in honour! Once *Knight;* die in harness: once *Cam¹;* die in arms: once *Ard² (Mason);* die! In once *Riv*

Let him go home and with his cap in hand
Like a base pandar hold the chamber-door
Whilst by a slave no gentler than my dog   15
His fairest daughter is contaminated.

CONSTABLE

Disorder, that hath spoiled us, friend us now!
Let us on heaps go offer up our lives.

ORLEANS

We are enough yet living in the field
To smother up the English in our throngs   20
If any order might be thought upon.

13 *home Q's word is more appropriate to ll. 13–16 than F's, and a misreading would be easy.

14 pandar Shakespeare has this word, as noun or verb, in seven other plays, and it is hard to see why he should use Q's 'leno' (Lat. pimp, pandar) on this occasion. Taylor, citing two occurrences of 'leno' in Nashe (2.291, 3.113) and one in Chettle's *Kind-Heart's Dream* (1592: E3) as the only English ones, describes it as 'a rare Latinate word most unlikely to have been intruded by a reporter' and regards *pandar* as Compositor B's substitution. But a sixteenth-century schoolboy might meet *leno* in Plautus or in Cicero and remember it, and perhaps the reporter was showing off his vocabulary.

hold ... door i.e. stand outside the bedroom door to ensure the brothel customer's privacy after admitting him. Cf. *Oth* 4.2.29–32.

15 *by a slave F's reading 'a base slaue' has been corrupted by the preceding l. 14. For *slave*, cf. 4.1.265n.
no gentler no better born

16 contaminated There is no compelling reason for departing from F's

reading. Q's reading may be a corruption of either 'contaminate' or 'contaminated'. Shakespeare has both words elsewhere. In *CE* 2.2.135–6 ('And that this body, consecrate to thee, / By ruffian lust should be contaminate'), which may have influenced Capell (see textual footnotes), the form of 'consecrate' probably dictated that of 'contaminate'. Yet *H5* has enough latinate participial adjectives (e.g. 1.2.16, miscreate; 2.1.124, corroborate; 2.2.31, create) to make Capell's emendation attractive.

17 spoiled ruined
friend befriend (i.e. in hastening our deaths)

18 on heaps in heaps. Cf. 5.2.39.

20 throngs F's word (there is no corresponding expression in Q), though satisfactory in itself, associates somewhat awkwardly with *throng* in l. 22 (the rhyme-word, and therefore obviously correct), meaning the crowd of combatants on both sides. It may be an accidental anticipation. A possible emendation is 'troops', whether in the military sense (*OED sb.* 1a) or in the more general sense of crowds (*OED sb.* 1b).

13 home] *Q*; hence *F* 14 pandar] *F*; leno *Q* 15 by a] *Q*; a base *F* 16 contaminated] *F*; contamurackc *Q*; contaminate *Capell* 18 on] *F*, in *Q* lives.] *F*, liues / Vnto these English, or else die with fame. *Q* 19 SP] *F*; Con. *Q* (placing this speech before Bourbon's 10–16) enough] *F* (enow), *Q* (inough) 20 throngs] *F*, troops (this edn)

BOURBON

The devil take order now! I'll to the throng.
Let life be short, else shame will be too long.   *Exeunt.*

[**4.6**] *Alarum. Enter the* KING *and his train, with Prisoners.*

KING

Well have we done, thrice-valiant countrymen,
But all's not done: yet keep the French the field.
                              [*Exeunt Soldiers and Prisoners.*]

                              [*Enter* EXETER.]

EXETER

The Duke of York commends him to your majesty.

KING

Lives he, good uncle? Thrice within this hour
I saw him down, thrice up again and fighting;   5
From helmet to the spur all blood he was.

EXETER

In which array, brave soldier, doth he lie,
Larding the plain; and by his bloody side,

4.6.0.1 *Prisoners* Cf. Holinshed, 3.554 (immediately following the passage quoted at 4.5.6n.): 'In the meane season, while the battell thus continued, and that the Englishmen had taken a great number of prisoners, certeine Frenchmen on horssebacke ... entred vpon the kings campe'. The passage is quoted in full at 4.7.5–8n.

2.1 The SD is appropriate because (1) the King has just commended his soldiers and indicated that they have more work to do, (2) Exeter's dialogue with the King (ll. 3–34) is better without a passive stage audience, and

(3) the King's order (l. 37), which is to be relayed to his soldiers, implies their absence at this moment.

2.2 'It makes more sense for Exeter to enter shortly after the others (and presumably from a different direction) than for him to stand there silent before delivering his news' (Taylor).

3 **commends him to** sends his greetings to

8 **Larding** enriching (*OED v.* 2), i.e. with his blood. A serious treatment of the idea used humorously in *1H4* 2.3.16–18 [2.104–5], 'Oldcastle [Falstaff] sweats to death, / And lards the lean earth as he walks along.'

22–3] *F; (no SP)* Come, come along, / Lets dye with honour, our shame doth last too long. *Q*   23 SD] *Q (Exit omnes.); Exit. F*

4.6] *Capell*   0.1] *F; Enter the King and his Nobles,* Pistoll. *Q*   1] *F;* What the French retire? *Q*   2.1] *this edn*   2.2] *Oxf[1]*

Yoke-fellow to his honour-owing wounds,
The noble Earl of Suffolk also lies.   10
Suffolk first died, and York, all haggled over,
Comes to him, where in gore he lay insteeped,
And takes him by the beard, kisses the gashes
That bloodily did yawn upon his face.
He cries aloud 'Tarry, my cousin Suffolk!   15
My soul shall thine keep company to heaven.
Tarry, sweet soul, for mine, then fly abreast,
As in this glorious and well-foughten field
We kept together in our chivalry.'
Upon these words I came and cheered him up;   20
He smiled me in the face, raught me his hand,
And with a feeble gripe says 'Dear my lord,
Commend my service to my sovereign.'

9 **Yoke-fellow** See 2.3.52n.
honour-owing honour-possessing (*OED* owe *v.* 1), i.e. honourable

11–27 **Suffolk . . . love** 'A variation upon the death of the Talbots in *1H6* 4.7' (Wilson). The incident is Shakespeare's invention.

11 **all haggled over** hacked all over (*OED* haggle *v.* 1)

12 **insteeped** immersed (*OED*'s first example)

14 **yawn** gape. Cf. *1H4* 1.3.96, 'Those mouthèd wounds'.

14–15 **face. / He** Objections raised against this F reading rest on two points: (1) the absence of an 'and' between 'takes him by the beard' and 'kisses the gashes'; (2) the existence of the alternative Q reading. The first point is not compelling: the conjunction can be easily understood from the sequence of clauses. The Q reading, though its 'And' creates a satisfactory sequence ('takes . . . kisses . . . And cryes': 'cryde' is obviously an error), makes ll. 11–19 a long sentence

in which the 'And' of l. 13 and that of l. 15 give the actor no natural pause. Taylor believes that the actor 'is here speaking a revised text', but some of the other variants suggest substitutions by the actor himself, e.g. 'deare cousin *Suffolke*' (l. 15), 'deare soule' (l. 17), 'He tooke me by the hand, said deare my Lord' (replacing ll. 21–2), and 'An argument / Of neuer ending loue' (replacing l. 27).

18 **foughten** 'Shakespeare's only use of this older form of the past participle (presumably for the metre's sake, like the redundant "in" of the neologism "insteeped", l. 12)' (Taylor)

19 **chivalry** bravery in battle

20 **cheered him up** encouraged him. Cf. *3H6* 1.1.6, 'Cheered up the drooping army'.

21 **me in the face** in my face
raught reached

22 **gripe** Shakespeare's invariable form of the word

23 **Commend my service** give my obedient greetings

9 honour-owing wounds] *F4*; honour-owing-wounds *F*; honour dying wounds *Q*   14–15 face. / He cries] *F*; face, / And cryde *Q*   15 my] *F*; deare *Q*   16 thine keep] *F, Q*; keep thine (*Walker*)   21 2] *F*; He tooke me by the hand, said deare my Lord, *Q*   22 gripe] *F*; grip *Oxf¹*

So did he turn, and over Suffolk's neck
He threw his wounded arm and kissed his lips,   25
And so, espoused to death, with blood he sealed
A testament of noble-ending love.
The pretty and sweet manner of it forced
Those waters from me which I would have stopped,
But I had not so much of man in me,   30
And all my mother came into mine eyes
And gave me up to tears.

KING   I blame you not,
For hearing this I must perforce compound
With my full eyes, or they will issue too.   *Alarum.*

24 **So** then (Abbott, 66, citing *MND* 1.1.244–5). Here the sense is 'so saying', 'having said this'.

26 **espoused to death** united (figuratively, by marriage) to Death, i.e. dying at that moment. For the metaphor, cf. *Luc* 20–1, 'That kings might be espousèd to more fame, / But king nor peer to such a peerless dame.'

26–7 **with blood ... love** i.e. with this last kiss he confirmed his love for his cousin Suffolk, a love ending with noble death on the battlefield. The only Shakespearean sense of *testament* is a will disposing of one's property after death: here York has figuratively bequeathed his love to his already dead cousin. Taylor and Gurr overelaborate the imagery, talking of 'the blood of a bride's broken maidenhead-seal' (Oxf[1]), etc.

29 **waters** i.e. tears.

31 **all my mother** i.e. all my tenderness. Cf. *TN* 2.1.35–8, 'My bosom is full of kindness, and I am yet so near the manners of my mother that upon the least occasion more mine eyes will tell tales of me.'

32 **gave me up** surrendered me

33–4 **compound / With** come to terms with (*OED v.* 12) (figurative). He must wipe his eyes, otherwise they will overflow with tears.

34 *****my full** F's 'mixtfull', though elaborately defended by Taylor, has long been generally doubted, and Warburton's emendation 'mistful', i.e. full of mist, is now doubted too. Gurr emends to 'wilful' (i.e. governed by the will, which rebels against the reason). The absence of any such word as 'my' or 'these' before any of these adjectives, making the King speak like Pistol, tells against them. Shakespeare twice has 'Mine eyes are full of tears' (*2H6* 2.3.17, *R2* 4.1.234[244]). In the present context it is unnecessary to state what the eyes are full of, and if *my* is stressed, as the verse demands, *my full eyes* follows naturally from ll. 31–2. A misreading of 'my full' as 'mixtfull' is not improbable: *x* and *y* often resemble each other in secretary hand, and the adjacent word *compound* may have influenced the compositor in its substantive sense, i.e. a mixture.

issue shed tears (*OED v.* 7b: 'To shed tears; to discharge', citing one other instance, 1680, of this absolute use: '... a little hole ... that doth sometimes issue'). Elsewhere in Shake-

27 noble-ending love] *Rowe;* Noble-ending-loue *F;* neuer ending loue *Q*   33–4 I ... too] *F (... mixtfull ...);* I must conuert to teares *Q*   34 my full] *this edn;* mixtfull *F;* mistful *Theobald (Warburton);* wilful *Cam*[2]   too] *(to)*

But hark, what new alarum is this same?   35
The French have reinforced their scattered men.
Then every soldier kill his prisoners!
Give the word through.   *Exeunt.*

[4.7]   *Enter* FLUELLEN *and* GOWER.

FLUELLEN   Kill the poys and the luggage! 'Tis expressly
against the law of arms. 'Tis as arrant a piece of

speare the intransitive verb *issue* means 'come forth', an obviously inappropriate sense here.

SD *Alarum* See 3.0.33 SD.

35–8 **But hark … through** Holinshed, 3.554, immediately after the paragraph referred to at 4.6.0.1 and quoted at 4.7.5–8n., continues: 'But when the outcrie of the lackies and boies, which run awaie for feare of the Frenchmen thus spoiling the campe, came to the kings eares, he doubting least his enimies should gather togither againe, and begin a new field; and mistrusting further that the prisoners would be an aid to his enimies, or the verie enimies to their takers in deed if they were suffered to liue, contrarie to his accustomed gentlenes, commanded by sound of trumpet, that euerie man (vpon paine of death) should incontinentlie slaie his prisoner.' Wilson (Cam[1] xxxvi–xxxvii) points out that Shakespeare has here linked together incidents not linked together by Holinshed, i.e. the attack on 'the boys and the luggage' (4.7.1) and the desperate rally led by Bourbon (4.5.12–23). In Holinshed it is the former, misunderstood by King Henry as the sign of an enemy rally, that prompts his order to kill the prisoners; here it is the 'alarum', actually signalling Bourbon's rally, that

prompts it. But Wilson's inference that Bourbon's rally is identical with the attack on the boys is wrong: Gower's reference to 'the cowardly rascals that ran from the battle' (4.7.5–6) identifies a quite different group of Frenchmen (see 4.7.5–8n.), and Bourbon was courageously returning 'to the throng' (4.5.22). Taylor (see textual notes 37–8) argues that the urgency of the situation requires the prisoners of the opening SD to be killed 'in front of the audience. Some of the bodies could be dragged off now, others removed in the next scene.' But 'Give the word through' implies that the killing happens off stage, as does Q's version of l. 37 ('Bid euerie souldier kill his prisoner'). See also l. 2.1n. For Q's addition of the phrase 'Couple gorge' for Pistol (see textual note to 37–8), see Introduction, p. 98.

4.7.1 **Kill … luggage** i.e. 'Kill the boys and plunder the luggage.' Fluellen, with characteristic passion, speaks as though the luggage was killed – an effectively serio-comic zeugma, as editors (none of whom has suggested a textual error) have recognized.

2 **arrant** Cf. 3.6.60n. This word now becomes one of Fluellen's favourite ones: cf. l. 139 and 4.8.10, 35.

36] *F; not in Q*   37–8 prisoners … through.]' *F; prisoner. / Pist.* Couple gorge. *Q.;* prisoners. / *The soldiers kill their prisoners. /* Give the word through. / *Pistol.* Coup' la gorge. *Oxf[1]*   38 SD] *Q (Exit omnes.); Exit. F*

4.7] *Capell; Actus Quartus F*   0.1] *F, Q (Enter Flewellen, and Captaine Gower)*   1 Kill] *F;* Godes plud kil *Q*

knavery, mark you now, as can be offert, in your
conscience now, is it not?

GOWER 'Tis certain there's not a boy left alive, and the 5
cowardly rascals that ran from the battle ha' done
this slaughter. Besides, they have burned and carried
away all that was in the King's tent, wherefore the
King most worthily hath caused every soldier to cut
his prisoner's throat. O, 'tis a gallant king! 10

5–8 **'Tis certain ... tent** Cf. 4.6.0.1n.
Holinshed clearly states which
Frenchmen were responsible for the
outrage (3.554): 'In the meane season
while the battell thus continued, and
that the Englishmen had taken a great
number of prisoners, certeine Frenchmen on horssebacke, whereof were
capteins Robinet of Borneuill, Rifflart
of Clamas, Isambert of Agincourt, and
other men of armes, to the number
of six hundred horssemen, which
were the first that fled, hearing that
the English tents & pauilions were a
good waie distant from the armie,
without anie sufficient gard to defend
the same, either vpon a couetous
meaning to gaine by the spoile, or
vpon a desire to be reuenged, entred
vpon the kings campe, and there
spoiled the hails [i.e. hales, pavilions],
robbed the tents, brake vp chests, and
caried awaie caskets, and slue such
seruants as they found to make anie
resistance. For which treason and has-
kardie [i.e. baseness] in thus leauing
their campe at the verie point of fight,
for winning of spoile where [*sic*: read
where were] none to defend it, verie
manie were after committed to prison,
and had lost their liues, if the Dolphin
had longer liued.' At 3.556 Holinshed,
reporting the Dauphin's death, reiterates that this 'happened well for
Robinet of Bourneuill, and his fellowes, as ye haue heard before, for
his death was their life, & his life

would haue beene their death.'

8–10 **wherefore ... throat** The most
natural interpretation of this passage
is that the King (according to Gower)
has ordered the killing of the prisoners in retaliation for the outrage.
Taylor, attempting to make Gower's
statement conform to the fact that
the order was a defensive measure,
interprets it as 'given the barbarity of
the subsequent French conduct, the
king *has* quite justifiably *caused* the
death of his prisoners', an interpretation that could be conveyed if *worthily* were heavily stressed by the
speaker; even so, however, the sense
would be ambiguous, for *worthily*
(*OED adv.* 3, cited by Taylor:
'According to desert or merit; as one
(or it) is deserving or worthy; deservedly, justly, rightly') often implies
punishment, as in 'worthily deposed',
R2 4.1.217[227]. At any rate, Q's
version is unambiguous: 'Wherevpon
the king caused euery prisoners /
Throat to be cut. O he is a worthy
king.' (Note, however, that in Q the
adjective *worthy*, substituted for F's
gallant, is derived from the omitted
adverbial phrase *most worthily*, and
therefore the variant reading probably
originated with the actor and not with
the author.)

10 **gallant** excellent (*OED a.* 4: 'A
general epithet of admiration or
praise'). Cf. Holinshed's marginal
comment quoted at 55–64n.

3 offert, in] *Capell (subst.);* offert in *F;* desired / In the worell now, in *Q*   5 'Tis certain there's]
F ('Tis certaine, there's*);* 'Tis certain. There's *Cam²*   9 most ... hath] *F; not in Q*   10 gallant]
F; worthy *Q*

FLUELLEN Ay, he was porn at Monmouth, Captain
Gower. What call you the town's name where Alexander the Pig was born?

GOWER Alexander the Great.

FLUELLEN Why, I pray you, is not pig great? The pig, 15
or the great, or the mighty, or the huge, or the
magnanimous, are all one reckonings, save the phrase
is a little variations.

GOWER I think Alexander the Great was born in
Macedon: his father was called Philip of Macedon, as 20
I take it.

FLUELLEN I think it is in Macedon where Alexander is
porn. I tell you, Captain, if you look in the maps of the
world, I warrant you shall find, in the comparisons
between Macedon and Monmouth, that the situations, 25

11 **Monmouth** the county town of Mon-
mouthshire (now in Gwent), near the
borders of Wales and England, situated where the river Monnow flows
into the river Wye.

12–13 **Alexander** Alexander the Great
(Alexander III, 356–323 BC; reigned
336–323 BC), son of Philip II

14 **the Great** Cf. *LLL* 5.2.544–6, where
Dumain corrects Costard's 'Pompey
surnamed the Big'. Costard, unlike
Fluellen, placidly admits the error.

16 **huge** Cf. *LLL* 5.2.678–9, 'Greater
than great – great, great, great
Pompey, Pompey the Huge!'

17 **are ... reckonings** all amount to the
same thing

17–18 **the phrase ... variations** the
wording is slightly different

19–20 **in Macedon** in Macedonia, a
region situated in the north of modern
Greece. The distinction made
between *in* (ll. 19, 22, 26) and *at* (ll.
11, 27, 28, 52) shows that neither
Gower nor Fluellen mistakes it for a
town.

22 **it is in Macedon** Taylor suggests

that Q's 'indeed' represents 'e'en' in
F's copy, and emends accordingly;
but *indeed* is a word characteristic of
Fluellen's part in Q (cf. 'I, I think it
is Sir Iohn *Falstaffe* indeed' for 'That
is he', l. 51), perhaps influenced by
Sir Hugh Evans's language in *MW*
(e.g. *MW* 4.2.179: 'I think the 'oman
is a witch indeed'). F's reading is
easier to speak than Oxf[1]'s, whether
is is stressed or not: if it is, Fluellen
acknowledges Gower's information; if
it is not, he affects not to have heard
him and to have remembered the fact
for himself.

24 **world** See 3.6.10n.
*shall F's 'sall' is presumably a com-
positor's error, since the word is *shall*
in its nine other appearances in Fluellen's part (three of them in passages
set by the present compositor, B:
5.1.62, 63, 66). In F Fluellen says
'silling' for 'shilling' at 4.8.73 (set by
Compositor A), but this hardly gives
grounds for retaining one exceptional
'sall' here, particularly as 'silling' may
have been imported from Q3.

11–12 Monmouth ... What] *F (Monmouth* Captaine *Gower:* What*); Monmorth.* / Captain *Gower*,
what *Q* 22 is in Macedon] *F;* was *Macedon* indeed *Q;* is e'en Macedon *Oxf[1]* 24 world] *Oxf[1];*
Orld *F;* worell *Q* shall] *Q;* sall *F*

look you, is both alike. There is a river in Macedon, and there is also moreover a river at Monmouth. It is called Wye at Monmouth, but it is out of my prains what is the name of the other river; but 'tis all one, 'tis alike as my fingers is to my fingers, and there is 30 salmons in both. If you mark Alexander's life well, Harry of Monmouth's life is come after it indifferent well, for there is figures in all things. Alexander, God knows, and you know, in his rages, and his furies, and his wraths, and his cholers, and his moods, and his 35 displeasures, and his indignations, and also being a little intoxicate in his prains, did in his ales and his angers, look you, kill his best friend Clytus.

30 **as my ... my fingers** Fluellen's stage-Welsh habit of turning singular nouns into plural ones leaves it somewhat doubtful whether he here means (1) all the fingers of each hand and of the other or (2) any one finger of one hand and the corresponding finger of the other hand. The former is by far the more likely (with appropriate gesture).

31–49 **If you ... name** Fluellen's comparison is Shakespeare's parody of *comparatio*, a rhetorical exercise in which two famous persons are compared in respect of their origins, achievements, etc. Baldwin (2.336–8) gives an account of it. In his concurrent reading for *JC* Shakespeare would find Alexander's life paralleled with Caesar's by Plutarch (Bullough 5.13).

32–3 **is come ... well** has resembled it pretty closely

33 **figures** i.e. comparisons (cf. l. 43); here alluding particularly to the prefiguring of one person or event by another (*OED* figure *sb*. 12: a type or emblem). Thus e.g. Isaac in the Old Testament is a 'type' of Christ in the New Testament, and Abraham's sacrifice is a 'type' of the Crucifixion.

34–6 **his rages ... indignations** a list of virtually synonymous words, comically throwing into relief the phrase 'and also being a little intoxicate in his prains'

36–7 ***a little ... prains** an echo of Preston's *Cambyses*, l. 527, where Cambyses, about to show the steadiness of his hand by shooting the son of his counsellor Praxaspes, who has been reproving his drunkenness, says 'For I must drink to make my brain somewhat intoxicate'. Cf. 4.4.8n. F's 'intoxicates' is a compositor's error caused by the proximity of many plural nouns (Richard Proudfoot, privately).

37–8 **in his ales ... angers** a summary of the content of ll. 34–7, employing alliteration, reverse patterning (the list of furious passions having preceded the mention of drunkenness) and zeugma

38 **Clytus** Alexander's friend and general. The occasion (328 BC, when Alexander was twenty-eight years old – King Henry's age at Agincourt, though he was only twenty-six when he became king and discarded Falstaff) was a banquet at Maracanda (Samarcand) at which, both being

GOWER   Our king is not like him in that: he never killed
    any of his friends.   40
FLUELLEN   It is not well done, mark you now, to take
    the tales out of my mouth ere it is made an end and
    finished. I speak but in the figures and comparisons of
    it. As Alexander killed his friend Clytus, being in his
    ales and his cups, so also Harry Monmouth, being in   45
    his right wits and his good judgements, turned away
    the fat knight with the great-belly doublet: he was
    full of jests, and gipes, and knaveries, and mocks; I
    have forgot his name.
GOWER   Sir John Falstaff.   50

heated with wine, they disagreed as
to whether Alexander had outdone
his father Philip. Fluellen echoes the
homily 'Against gluttony and drunkenness' (*Certain sermons or homilies*,
1547, enlarged 1563: for weekly use
in parish churches): 'The great Alexander after that he had conquered the
whole worlde, was himself ouercome
by drunkennesse, insomuch that,
being drunken, he slewe his faithful
freende Clitus, whereof when he was
sober, he was so much ashamed, that
for anguish of heart he wished death'
(1582 edn, Ii 1'). Lodge, *Wit's Misery*
(see 2.3.30n.) also refers to the incident in similar terms.
41–2 **take … mouth** proverbial (Tilley,
    T 50)
42 *made an end Q is to be preferred
    because (1) F's *made* does not
    adequately convey the sense *finished*;
    (2) compositor's eyeskip in F, induced
    by 'an end and', is very probable; (3)
    Q's 'made an end' (for 'made an end
    of' or 'brought to an end') is typical
    of Fluellen's eccentric language.
44–7 **As … doublet** In this 'as … so
    …' formula Shakespeare may be par-
    odying *Palladis Tamia: Wit's Treasury*
    (1598) by Francis Meres, which con-
    tains (pp. 279–89) 'a comparatiue dis-
    course of our English poets with the

Greek, Latin, and Italian poets',
including 'As *Plautus* and *Seneca* are
accounted the best for Comedy and
Tragedy among the Latines: so
Shakespeare among the English is the
most excellent in both kinds for the
stage'.
44–5 **being … cups** The stylistic par-
    allelism extends to idiomatic cor-
    rectness and incorrectness, *cups* and
    right wits (correct plurals) balancing
    each other, as do *ales* and *good judge-
    ments* (incorrect plurals).
45 **Harry Monmouth** Harry of Mon-
    mouth (cf. *1H4* 5.4.58). Cf. 'Harry
    England', 3.5.48.
47 **great-belly doublet** The lower part
    of the doublet, a close-fitting garment
    for the upper part of the body, was
    called its belly, and could be either
    'great' (padded) or 'thin' (not
    padded). Fluellen is alluding to Fal-
    staff's actual belly as well as (or rather
    than) to the fashion of his doublet.
48 **gipes** gibes
48–9 **I have forgot his name** 'Probably
    a joking allusion to the name having
    had to be changed (from Oldcastle
    to Falstaff)' (Taylor). Cf. a similar
    allusion in *MW* 3.2.16–21, where
    Mistress Page emphatically declares –
    twice – that she can never remember
    it.

42 made an end] *Q;* made *F*   47 great-belly] *(great belly)*

FLUELLEN   That is he. I'll tell you, there is good men porn at Monmouth.

GOWER   Here comes his majesty.

Alarum. Enter KING HARRY [*with*] BOURBON [*as his prisoner,* WARWICK, GLOUCESTER, EXETER, *a Herald and others,*] *with Prisoners. Flourish.*

KING

I was not angry since I came to France
Until this instant. Take a trumpet, herald;   55
Ride thou unto the horsemen on yon hill.

53 SD In F's SD the words '*and Burbon*' must have been added by Shakespeare as an afterthought, on reflecting that Bourbon was to be included in the list of prisoners (4.8.78), whereas his speech at 4.5.22–3 had suggested that he would die in a last desperate charge. The presence of the army was implied in the SD as originally written: '*Enter King Harry with prisoners.*' The '*Flourish*' (cf. 3.3.58 SD) helps to establish that the King is upon the verge of victory.

54–5 **I was ... instant** The King has just learned of the attack on his tents.

55–64 **Take ... so** Cf. Holinshed, 3.555: 'Some write, that the king perceiuing his enimies in one part to assemble togither, as though they meant to giue a new battell for preseruation of the prisoners, sent to them an herald, commanding them either to depart out of his sight, or else to come forward at once, and giue battell: promising herewith, that if they did offer to fight againe, not onelie those prisoners which his people alreadie had taken; but also so manie of them as in this new conflict, which they thus attempted, should fall into his hands, should die the death without redemption.' (In margin: 'A right wise and valiant challenge of the king.')

'The Frenchmen fearing the sentence of so terrible a decree, without further delaie parted out of the field.' Holinshed does not make clear the order of events hereabouts. After the passage quoted at 4.6.35–8n. he describes the killing of the prisoners, and then begins a new paragraph as follows: 'When this lamentable slaughter was ended, the Englishmen disposed themselues in order of battell, readie to abide a new field, and also to inuade, and newlie set on their enimies, with great force they assailed the earles of Marle and Fauconbridge, and the lords of Louraie, and of Thine, with six hundred men of armes, who had all that daie kept togither, but now slaine and beaten downe out of hand.' Then follows the sentence quoted at the beginning of this note, from which it appears that what 'Some write' is an alternative account of the killing of the prisoners, who are meant by 'the prisoners' and 'those prisoners which his people alreadie had taken'. Shakespeare's ll. 62–4 have to refer to a new group of prisoners, including Bourbon, who have been taken since the killing of the prisoners ordered at 4.6.37.

55 **trumpet** trumpeter (*OED sb.* 4), to announce the herald's approach

53.1–3] *this edn; Alarum. Enter King Harry and Burbon with prisoners. Flourish.* F; *Enter King and the Lords. Q*   53.2 WARWICK ... *others*] *Capell (subst.)*   56 yon] *(yond)*

If they will fight with us bid them come down,
Or void the field: they do offend our sight.
If they'll do neither, we will come to them
And make them skirr away as swift as stones   60
Enforced from the old Assyrian slings.
Besides, we'll cut the throats of those we have,
And not a man of them that we shall take
Shall taste our mercy. Go and tell them so.

Enter MONTJOY.

EXETER

Here comes the herald of the French, my liege.   65
GLOUCESTER

His eyes are humbler than they used to be.
KING

How now, what means this, herald? Know'st thou not
That I have fined these bones of mine for ransom?
Com'st thou again for ransom?

---

60 **skirr** run hastily (away), flee (*OED v.*
1); also here, cf. the simile, *v.* 2 ('To
move, run, fly, sail, etc., rapidly or
with great impetus')
60–1 **as swift … slings** probably
derived from Marlowe's translation of
Lucan's *Pharsalia* (Book I: not published till 1600, but entered in Stationers' Register 1593), ll. 230–2:
'This said, the restless general
through the dark, / Swifter than
bullets thrown from Spanish slings, /
Or darts which Parthians backward
shoot, march'd on.' Shakespeare,
perhaps thinking an allusion even to
ancient Spaniards inappropriate in
this patriotic play, substituted Assy-
rians who 'trust in shield, and spear,
and bow, and sling' (Judith 9:7:
Geneva Bible). He had used *Assyrian*
as a burlesque grandiose epithet in
2H4 5.3.102.

61 **Enforced** (Enforcèd) forcibly thrown
(*OED v.* 7)
64 **Go … so** There is no need for the
herald to obey this order, because
Montjoy's arrival alters the situation.
For further evidence that the herald
remains on stage, see 115n.
SD *Enter* MONTJOY Shakespeare's
alteration to Holinshed, who reports
(3.555) that Montjoy came on the
following morning. The French had
responded to King Henry's message
(55–64n.) by quitting the field, whereupon, 'about foure of the clocke in
the after noone', he gave thanks to
God for the victory (cf. 4.8.114–27n.).
68 **fined** paid (*OED v.²* 1 (*transitive*),
this example and one of 1297; *v.²* 3
(*intransitive*), with the same sense, has
several sixteenth-century examples).
The sense here is 'undertaken to pay':
cf. 4.3.123.

---

60 skirr] *(sker)*   63 a man … take] *F*; one aliue *Q*   64] *F; Capell adds SD Exeunt a Herald, and
Others.*   SD] *F; Enter the Herauld. Q*   65–6] *F; not in Q*   67 this, herald] *Boswell;* this Herald
F; this *Q*   69] *F; not in Q*

MONTJOY   No, great King:
I come to thee for charitable licence   70
That we may wander o'er this bloody field
To look our dead and then to bury them;
To sort our nobles from our common men.
For many of our princes – woe the while! –
Lie drowned and soaked in mercenary blood;   75

70–90 **I come ... Crispian** Cf. Holinshed, 3.555: 'In the morning, Montioie king at armes and foure other French heralds came to the K, to know the number of prisoners, and to desire buriall for the dead. Before he made them answer (to vnderstand what they would saie) he demanded of them whie they made to him that request, considering that he knew not whether the victorie was his or theirs? When Mountioie by true and iust confession had cleered that doubt to the high praise of the king, he desired of Montioie to vnderstand the name of the castell neere adioining: when they had told him that it was called Agincourt, he said, Then shall this conflict be called the battell of Agincourt. He feasted the French officers of arms that daie, and granted them their request, which busilie sought through the field for such as were slaine. But the Englishmen suffered them not to go alone, for they searched with them, & found manie hurt, but not in ieopardie of their liues, whom they tooke prisoners, and brought them to their tents. When the king of England had well refreshed himselfe, and his souldiers, that had taken the spoile of such as were slaine, he with his prisoners in good order returned to his towne of Calis.'

70 **charitable licence** permission inspired by Christian charity (love towards fellow creatures)

72 ***look** seek out (*OED* v. 6d): four times in this sense in Shakespeare

(*MW* 4.2.73, *AYL* 2.5.30, *AW* 3.6.107, *KL* 3.3.14). F's *book* (*OED* v. 2: 'To enter in a book; to record, register') occurs only once more, at *2H4* 4.2[3].45, where Falstaff says of his capture of Coleville 'Let it be booked with the rest of this day's deeds'. Holinshed's phrases 'busilie sought through the field' and 'searched with them' (see 70–90n.) support Collier's emendation, and Q's much abbreviated version of Montjoy's speech gives no reason to think that writing down names was mentioned in the original: 'I come great king for charitable fauour, / To sort our Nobles from our common men, / We may haue leaue to bury all our dead, / Which in the field lye spoyled and troden on.' The error would be easy: cf. Beaumont and Fletcher, *The Maid's Tragedy*, 5.3.113, where uncorrected Q1 has 'bookes' and corrected Q1 and Q2 have 'lookes'.

74 **princes** synonymous with *nobles*, l. 73

woe the while alas

75 **mercenary blood** In ll. 73–7 the distinction between *our nobles* and *our common men* is carried on in *our princes* and *blood of princes* contrasted with *mercenary blood* and *our vulgar*. Moore Smith must therefore be right in interpreting the mercenaries as native French soldiers serving for pay. Taylor and Gurr take them to be hired soldiers serving a foreign power. See also 4.8.89.

69+ SP MONTJOY] *Rowe; Her.* F   71–2] *F; not in Q*   72 look] *Collier²; booke* F   74–82 For ... bodies] *F; not in Q*

So do our vulgar drench their peasant limbs
In blood of princes; and their wounded steeds
Fret fetlock-deep in gore and with wild rage
Yerk out their armed heels at their dead masters,
Killing them twice. O give us leave, great King,   80
To view the field in safety and dispose
Of their dead bodies.

KING   I tell thee truly, herald,
I know not if the day be ours or no,
For yet a many of your horsemen peer
And gallop o'er the field.

MONTJOY   The day is yours.   85

KING

Praised be God, and not our strength, for it!
What is this castle called that stands hard by?

MONTJOY   They call it Agincourt.

KING

Then call we this the field of Agincourt,
Fought on the day of Crispin Crispian.   90

76 **vulgar** common people
   peasant Cf. 4.1.265n.
77 ***and their** F's 'and with' is caught
   from l. 78. If Malone's emendation is
   right, the similarly placed *their* in l.
   76 may have helped to cause the
   compositor's error. Taylor, emending
   to *our*, cites *our* in ll. 72, 73, 74 and
   76 and points to the ambiguity of
   Malone's *their* after l. 76 ('their
   peasant limbs'); on the other hand, if
   'So do . . . princes' (ll. 76–7) is spoken
   as a parenthesis, the ambiguity is
   more apparent than real, and 'their
   dead bodies' (l. 82) tells more in
   Malone's favour than in Taylor's,
   whose *our* is somewhat incongruous
   when applied to steeds after it has
   been four times applied to two different ranks of Frenchmen. Gurr reads
   while the, which may be right, since
   F's *and with* may not have kept either

of the original words: cf. 4.5.14, where
a base replaces *by a*.
78 **Fret** chafe
79 **Yerk out** lash out (*OED* yerk v. 5).
   The modern sense of 'jerk' (a word
   virtually synonymous in the sixteenth
   century) is less strong.
   armed i.e. iron-shod (armèd)
83 **day** victory. Cf. 4.3.132.
   be ours i.e. belongs to the English
   (not the royal plural); cf. *our strength*,
   l. 86.
84 **a many** See 3.7.74n.
   peer show themselves (*OED* v.² 3).
   See *OED*'s headnote on this verb,
   concluding 'In several of the Shakespearean uses of *peer* it is difficult
   to determine whether the things are
   thought of as looking out, or as just
   appearing'.
86 **Praised** Praisèd
90 ***Crispin Crispian** '*Crispianus* appears

77 and their] *Malone;* and with *F,* while their *Theobald;* and the *Capell;* and our *Oxf¹;* while the
Cam²   79 Yerk] *F (Yerke);* Jerk *Oxf¹*   90 Crispin Crispian] *Wordsworth;* Crispin Crispianus *F;*
Cryspin, Cryspin *Q;* Crispin, Crispianus *Q3*

FLUELLEN   Your grandfather of famous memory, an't
please your majesty, and your great-uncle Edward
the Plack Prince of Wales, as I have read in the
chronicles, fought a most prave pattle here in France.

KING   They did, Fluellen.   95

FLUELLEN   Your majesty says very true. If your majesty
is remembered of it, the Welshmen did good service
in a garden where leeks did grow, wearing leeks in
their Monmouth caps, which your majesty know to
this hour is an honourable badge of the service; and I   100
do believe your majesty takes no scorn to wear the
leek upon Saint Tavy's day.

nowhere else in Shakespeare's play;
Crispian is used 4 times, once in the
collocation *Crispin Crispian* (4.3.57)'
(*TxC*, 381–2). Taylor suggests that
F's reading was influenced by Q3's,
and that Q3's was a speculative correction of Q's, which was obviously
corrupt.

91 **Your grandfather** i.e. Edward III,
King Henry's great-grandfather (and
so correctly called at 1.1.89, 1.2.146).
Fluellen must know this, as he correctly calls the Black Prince the
King's great-uncle. However, the fact
that Q as well as F has *grandfather*
suggests that it is what Shakespeare
wrote and what the actor spoke. *OED*
recognizes that in Scottish usage both
grandfather and grandsire mean
great-grandfather, but does not
warrant any inference that this was so
in Welsh usage.

96–7 *majesty is For F's error, cf.
1.2.197.

97–8 **the Welshmen … grow** 'For the
fact of service done by Welshmen in
a garden of leeks, Fluellen remains
our only authority' (Evans). Fluellen's
statement is unintentionally comic
because what it suggests is that they
ate the leeks. Cf. *MA* 1.1.46–9, where
Beatrice interprets Benedick's 'good

service … in these wars' as valiant
eating.

99 **Monmouth caps** variously defined,
by *OED* (Monmouth, *Hist.*, 1) as 'a
flat round cap formerly worn by soldiers and sailors' and by Linthicum
(1936: 226) as 'a round, brimless cap
with a high tapering crown, worn
by sailors and soldiers'. They were
originally made at Monmouth.
During the sixteenth and seventeenth
centuries the industry was fostered by
legislation.
know Here *your majesty* is equivalent
to *you*; hence the form of the verb.
Contrast *says* (l. 96), *is* (ll. 97, 113),
but cf. *MW* 1.4.141–2, 'Have not your
worship a wart above your eye?'

100 **an honourable badge of** a badge
worn in honour of

101–2 **your majesty … day** 'Nor did
he [the Earl of Essex] fail to wear a
leek on St David's day, but besides
would upon all occasions vindicate
the Welsh inhabitants, and own them
for his countrymen, as Queen Elizabeth usually was wont, upon the first
of March' (Francis Osborne (1593–
1659), *Works*, 8th edn, 1682, p. 610;
quotation communicated to Cam[1] by
Moore Smith).

91 grandfather] *F* (Grandfather*)*; great-grandfather *(this edn)*   92 great-uncle] *(great Vncle)*
96–7 majesty is] *Dyce*[2] *(Keightley)*; Maiesties is *F*   99 know] *F*; knows *Pope*   102 Saint] *(S.)*

KING

I wear it for a memorable honour,

For I am Welsh, you know, good countryman.

FLUELLEN   All the water in Wye cannot wash your   105
majesty's Welsh plood out of your pody, I can tell
you that. God pless it and preserve it, as long as it
pleases his grace, and his majesty too!

KING   Thanks, good my countryman.

FLUELLEN   By Jeshu, I am your majesty's countryman,   110
I care not who know it. I will confess it to all the
world: I need not to be ashamed of your majesty,
praised be God, so long as your majesty is an honest
man.

KING

God keep me so!

Enter WILLIAMS.

Our herald go with him: 115
Bring me just notice of the numbers dead

105 **Wye** See 11n.
107–8 **as long ... too** as long as it
pleases him to do so. Fluellen's patriotism pushes him to the verge of
incoherence: *his grace* is probably connected with the idea 'by God's grace'
(cf. l. 161, 'an't please God of his
grace'), but the royal title 'his grace'
jostles with it, and brings in *his
majesty* as an amplification. Shakespeare uses 'grace' and 'majesty'
together, with comic word-play, in
1H4 1.2.17–18. Q loses the point,
printing 'God keep it, and preserue
it, / To his graces will and pleasure.'
111 **know** possibly plural and indicative,
possibly singular and subjunctive. Q
and F agree in this reading.
115 SD Williams's entry is delayed till
now in order to make him conspicuous to the audience, and to the
King, thereby setting in motion the
next part of the play. Some editors
(e.g. Cam, Ard¹, Cam¹) omit, implying, and in Cam¹ stating, that Williams enters among the '*others*' at 53
SD.
*herald The King has addressed one
herald at l. 55, Exeter calls Montjoy
'the herald of the French' at l. 65,
and at 4.8.73 SD F has '*Enter
Herauld*' and the King asks 'Now,
herald, are the dead numbered?' This
suggests that each stage army has one
herald, and therefore that Q, not F,
should be followed here. In Holinshed
(see 70–90n.) 'foure other French heralds' come with Montjoy, and an
unspecified number of 'Englishmen'
go with them to search among the
slain.
116 **just notice** accurate information

109 countryman] *Q*; Countrymen *F*   112 world] *Oxf¹*; Orld *F*   115 God] *Q*; Good *F*   SD] *F*;
not in Q   herald] *Q*; Heralds *F*

On both our parts.

        [Exeunt Montjoy, Gower and the English Herald.]

        Call yonder fellow hither.

EXETER   Soldier, you must come to the King.

KING   Soldier, why wear'st thou that glove in thy cap?

WILLIAMS   An't please your majesty, 'tis the gage of   120
one that I should fight withal, if he be alive.

KING   An Englishman?

WILLIAMS   An't please your majesty, a rascal that swaggered with me last night, who if 'a live and ever dare to
challenge this glove, I have sworn to take him a box   125
o'th' ear; or if I can see my glove in his cap, which he
swore as he was a soldier he would wear if 'a lived,
I will strike it out soundly.

KING   What think you, Captain Fluellen, is it fit this
soldier keep his oath?   130

FLUELLEN   He is a craven and a villain else, an't please
your majesty, in my conscience.

KING   It may be his enemy is a gentleman of great sort,
quite from the answer of his degree.

---

117 SD Gower needs to be off stage by
l. 147, and this is 'the only natural
opportunity for an unobtrusive exit'
by him (Taylor).

120 **gage** pledge

121 **should** ought to (Abbott, 323), i.e.
am to, have agreed to. Cf. *MW*
3.1.64–5 (of Evans, as Caius's presumed opponent in a duel), 'I warrant
you, he's the man should fight with
him.'

122 **An Englishman** a man in the
English army, i.e. a friend as distinct
from an enemy. The question probably carries a hint of displeasure,
which accounts for Williams's defensive further definition, *a rascal* (which,
in its turn, improves the dramatic
irony).

124 ***if 'a live** F's reading is evidently
wrong because it leaves *dare* without a
subject. The compositor was probably
influenced by 'if he be alive' (l. 121),
which he had just previously set. Cf.
his similar error at l. 127. Capell's
emendation is consistent with 'if you
live' at 4.1.203.

125 **take** strike (*OED v.* 5b). Cf. 4.1.213.

127 ***if 'a lived** See 124n.

131 **craven** acknowledged coward (*OED
sb.* 1)

133 **sort** rank (*OED sb.*² 2)

134 **quite … degree** far removed from
(*OED* from 8b; Abbott, 158) the obligation to accept a challenge from one
of Williams's rank; i.e. obliged by
his own rank not to accept such a
challenge. For *answer* in this sense,
cf. *RJ* 2.3[4].6–11. The expression in
the present passage is so elliptical that
it may have been affected by eyeskip
(see textual notes).

---

117 SD] *Craig & Bevington; Exit Heralds Q*   120, 123] An't *(And't)*   124 'a live] *Capell;* aliue
F   127 'a lived] *Oxf¹;* aliue *F*   131 an't] *(and't)*   134 quite … degree] *F; not in Q*   of his] *F;*
of one of his *(this edn)*

FLUELLEN   Though he be as good a gentleman as the   135
devil is, as Lucifer and Belzebub himself, it is necessary, look your grace, that he keep his vow and his
oath. If he be perjured, see you now, his reputation
is as arrant a villain and a jack-sauce as ever his black
shoe trod upon God's ground and his earth, in my   140
conscience, la!

KING   Then keep thy vow, sirrah, when thou meet'st
the fellow.

WILLIAMS   So I will, my liege, as I live.

KING   Who serv'st thou under?   145

WILLIAMS   Under Captain Gower, my liege.

FLUELLEN   Gower is a good captain, and is good knowledge and literature in the wars.

135–6 **as good ... devil is** Editors cite
KL 3.4.134 ('The Prince of Darkness
is a gentleman', spoken by Edgar as
madman) and Dent (D 240.1) for the
'traditional' nature of this idea, but it
may originate here as one of Fluellen's
fantastic observations.   Marlowe's
Doctor Faustus 2.2.90 ('I am Lucifer,
/ And this [i.e. Belzebub] is my companion prince in hell') may lie behind
it.

136 **Belzebub** This is the usual form of
the name in Shakespeare's time, and
it is so spelled in F *TN* 5.1.282 and
F *Mac* 2.3.3 (both plays exist only
in F), its only other occurrences in
Shakespeare (as here, in prose). In
Doctor Faustus (cf. 135–6n.) the metre
invariably requires this form (1.4.56;
2.1.5, 12).

137–8 **his vow ... oath** The synonyms
are typical of Fluellen; cf. 'God's
ground and his earth', l. 140.

138–9 **his reputation is** i.e. he will be
reputed

139 **jack-sauce** saucy or impudent
fellow (*OED* jack *sb.*[1] 35: first example
c. 1550)

139–40 **as ever ... earth** as ever existed.
Cf. the proverbial 'as good a man as
ever trod on shoe leather' (Tilley, M
66, one example being 'as puts his
foot in a black shoe', 1598). Shakespeare gives the proverb as 'As proper
men as ever trod upon neat's leather'
(*JC* 1.1.25; cf. *Tem* 2.2.69, 'any
emperor that ever trod upon neat's
leather').

142 **sirrah** sir (a form of address used to
inferiors)

145 **Who** whom (Abbott, 274). Cf.
4.1.145.

148 *literature learning (*OED* sb.* 1).
Cf. Q's reading, 'Captaine *Gower* is
a good Captaine / And hath good
littrature in the warres.' To use *is* for
has is typical of Fluellen (cf. 3.2.73n.),
and so is his habit of duplicating
nouns. If F's 'literatured' were right
(and *OED* does not list the verb)
it would require a preceding *is* (in
standard usage), which would conflict
with Fluellen's idiosyncratic *is* before
good knowledge. A misreading of final
e as final *d* would be easy.

135 gentleman] *(*Ientleman*)*   136 Belzebub] *F, Q;* Beelzebub *Oxf*[1]   139 jack-sauce] *F (*Iacke sawce*);* Jack Sauce *Cam*[2]   141 la] *(*law*)*   148 literature] *Q (*hath good littrature*);* literatured *F*

KING   Call him hither to me, soldier.

WILLIAMS   I will, my liege.   *Exit.*

KING   Here, Fluellen, wear thou this favour for me and   151
stick it in thy cap. When Alençon and myself were
down together I plucked this glove from his helm. If
any man challenge this he is a friend to Alençon and
an enemy to our person. If thou encounter any such,   155
apprehend him, an thou dost me love.

FLUELLEN   Your grace does me as great honours as can
be desired in the hearts of his subjects. I would fain see
the man that has but two legs that shall find himself
aggriefed at this glove, that is all; I would fain but see   160
it once, an't please God of his grace that I might.

151 **favour** decoration worn as a sign of
goodwill or as a party-badge (*OED sb.*
7b). By this circumlocution Fluellen's
failure to associate the two gloves is
made somewhat more plausible.

152–3 **When Alençon ... together** In
order to explain the King's possession
of the glove, Shakespeare adapts Holinshed's account, converting the fight
with Alençon to a hand-to-hand
struggle. Holinshed (3.554) writes:
'The king that daie shewed himselfe
a valiant knight, albeit almost felled
by the duke of Alanson; yet with
plaine strength he slue two of the
dukes companie, and felled the duke
himselfe; whome when he would haue
yelded, the kings gard (contrarie to
his mind) slue out of hand.' (*Sic*:
probably the first comma and first
semicolon should be transposed.)

153 **helm** helmet

157 **does** F's spelling 'doo's' does not
indicate a pronunciation peculiar to
Fluellen but 'is an indifferent variant.
Henry three times has *doo'st* (Taylor)
honours Fluellen's idiosyncratic
plural; cf. *hearts, subjects.*

159 **the man ... legs** i.e. the man,

whoever he might be. Cf. *1H4*
2.5[4].187–9, 'If there were not two-
or three-and-fifty upon poor old Jack,
then am I no two-legged creature',
and *Tem* 2.2.60–3, 'As proper a man
as ever went on four legs cannot make
him give ground.'

160–1 *I ... once** The position of *but* in
F, which obscures Fluellen's rhetoric
without making any comic point, is
probably a transposition error. Q's
version of this part of the speech is 'I
would see that man now that should
chalenge this gloue: / And it please
God of his grace, I would but see
him, / That is all.'

161 *that I might** Taylor, noting that
F's sentence is incomplete and that
'the incompleteness is neither characteristic nor dramatic', suggests that
might has been substituted for Q's
'would'; but this is improbable in view
of the fact that the compositor had
already twice set *would* in the speech,
and Taylor's repunctuation is drastic.
This edn conjectures that F's final
word *see* was set in error because
the word had occurred immediately
above.

152, 154 Alençon] *(Alanson)*   157 does] *(doo's)*   160 all; I would fain but] *this edn (Dyce);* all;
but I would faine *F*   161 once, an't] *F (once, and);* once. An't *Oxf¹*   that I might.] *this edn;*
that I might see. *F;* that I might see it. *Capell;* that I would see. *Oxf¹*

KING Know'st thou Gower?

FLUELLEN He is my dear friend, an't please you.

KING Pray thee go seek him and bring him to my tent. 164

FLUELLEN I will fetch him. *Exit.*

KING

My lord of Warwick and my brother Gloucester,
Follow Fluellen closely at the heels.
The glove which I have given him for a favour
May haply purchase him a box o'th' ear;
It is the soldier's. I by bargain should 170
Wear it myself. Follow, good cousin Warwick.
If that the soldier strike him – as I judge
By his blunt bearing he will keep his word –
Some sudden mischief may arise of it,
For I do know Fluellen valiant 175
And, touched with choler, hot as gunpowder,
And quickly will return an injury.
Follow, and see there be no harm between them. –
Go you with me, uncle of Exeter. *Exeunt.*

162–4 Know'st ... tent These three speeches, like the two previous ones, are not meant for close scrutiny: their function is to set up the confrontation between Williams and Fluellen. 'Know'st thou Gower?' is perhaps best taken as following up Fluellen's testimonial (ll. 147–8), i.e. 'You know Gower pretty well, I suppose?', thus prompting Fluellen's reply and his first speech in 4.8. The instruction 'bring him to my tent' may seem to add something to the instruction just given to Williams.

169 haply by chance

174 mischief harm, i.e. bloodshed

175 valiant pronounced as three syllables

176 touched being touched. The implied metaphor is that of applying fire to the gunpowder in a cannon.

Cf. 3.0.33.

177 And ... injury and the sort of man who will quickly return a blow. The expression, though elliptical, is clear because it follows other descriptive phrases that might have been introduced by 'Fluellen is'.

179 This line might mean that the King is taking Exeter somewhere else, but 4.8 shows that it does not. The King would not wish to miss the fun. SD Though Warwick and Gloucester are to be moving towards an exit before the King and Exeter make their move, all four should follow Fluellen smartly; cf. their arrival in 4.8.19 SD, 23 SD. The other soldiers and prisoners who entered with the King and Exeter at 53 SD can then make their exit.

163 an't] *(and)* 166] *F; not in Q* 172 him –] *Capell (subst.);* him, *F* 173 word –] *Capell (subst.);* word; *F* 176 And, touched] *Theobald;* And toucht *F* 179 SD] *F; not in Q*

[4.8]   *Enter* GOWER *and* WILLIAMS.

WILLIAMS   I warrant it is to knight you, Captain.

Enter FLUELLEN.

FLUELLEN   God's will and his pleasure, Captain, I
    beseech you now, come apace to the King: there is
    more good toward you, peradventure, than is in your
    knowledge to dream of.   5

WILLIAMS   Sir, know you this glove?

FLUELLEN   Know the glove? I know the glove is a
    glove.

WILLIAMS   I know this, and thus I challenge it.

                                              Strikes him.

FLUELLEN   'Sblood, an arrant traitor as any's in the   10
    universal world, or in France, or in England!

GOWER   How now, sir, you villain!

WILLIAMS   Do you think I'll be forsworn?

FLUELLEN   Stand away, Captain Gower: I will give
    treason his payment into plows, I warrant you.   15

WILLIAMS   I am no traitor.

4.8.1 to knight you Holinshed does not
record any conferring of knighthoods
immediately after Agincourt, but
earlier in the campaign he states that
the King knighted several captains
(3.551).

4 peradventure Cf. 3.2.128n.

6 this glove i.e. the glove in Williams's
cap. At l. 9 *this* is the glove in Fluellen's cap.

9 SD *Strikes him* i.e. hits him a box
on the ear according to his promise.
At l. 27 Fluellen accuses him of striking the glove, which is therefore to
be pictured as hanging down beside
the ear – unless Fluellen is sup-
pressing the fact that he has had a
box on the ear; cf. 4.7.125–6.

10 'Sblood God's blood. Gurr, reading
'God's blood', says that 'the F
expression looks like censorship of an
oath'. But F's way of censoring oaths
was to expunge them entirely, as in
1H4 1.2, where the Quartos have 'by
the Lord', 'I would to God',
''Sblood', and ''Zounds' (these two
abbreviated forms being normal
oaths), and F omits them all.

12 villain i.e. for striking an officer, not
for being (according to Fluellen's
accusation) a traitor

15 into plows in the form of blows.
Fluellen's unidiomatic preposition
stresses the conversion from one currency into another.

4.8] *Capell*   0.1] *F; Enter Gower, Flewellen, and the Souldier. Q*   1] *F; not in Q*   9 SD] *F. Q (He strikes him.)*   10 'Sblood] *F ('Sblud); Gode plut, and his Q*   10–13 an arrant ... forsworn] *F; not in Q*   10 any's] *(anyes)*   16–21 I am ... Warwick] *F; not in Q*

FLUELLEN   That's a lie in thy throat.

[Enter Soldiers.]

I charge you in his majesty's name apprehend him,
he's a friend of the Duke Alençon's.

Enter WARWICK *and* GLOUCESTER.

WARWICK   How now, how now, what's the matter?   20
FLUELLEN   My lord of Warwick, here is, praised be
God for it, a most contagious treason come to light,
look you, as you shall desire in a summer's day.

Enter [the] KING *and* EXETER.

Here is his majesty.
KING   How now, what's the matter?   25
FLUELLEN   My liege, here is a villain and a traitor that,
look your grace, has struck the glove which your
majesty is take out of the helmet of Alençon.
WILLIAMS   My liege, this was my glove, here is the

---

17 **That's ... throat** That's a downright
lie. The common formula (Tilley, T
268), frequent in Shakespeare, refers
less directly to the deliberateness of
the lie (as editors often allege) than
to the depth of indignation with
which the speaker hurls it back at its
originator. Cf. *Ham* 2.2.576–7, 'gives
me the lie i'th' throat / As deep as to
the lungs', and Pistol's retorting of
the *'solus'*, 2.1.48–52.

18 **I charge ... him** This is not
addressed particularly to Gower, 'as
Williams's captain' (Gurr) or because
'Williams somehow immobilizes
Fluellen' (Taylor), but to the crowd
that has by now gathered (17 SD), a
crowd necessary to heighten the comic
effect of the explanations to follow

and also to represent the whole
English army by ll. 75–127.

22 **contagious** pestilential, i.e. socially
injurious (*OED a.* 7)

23 **as you ... day** See 3.6.63n. Fluellen's
present idiosyncrasy is the omission
of 'to see', thus making treason an
inappropriately desirable thing. Cf.
MW 3.3.209–11 (Evans to Ford),
'Your wife is as honest a 'omans as I
will desires among five thousand, and
five hundred too.'

25 **How now, what's the matter?** 'Five
words surprisingly memorable in performance' (Taylor), particularly as
they echo l. 20 and so draw attention
to themselves. In Oxf (later than
Oxf[1]) Taylor reads 'what is' with Q,
thus making the speech metrical.

---

17 SD] *this edn*   19 SD] *F; Enter the King, Warwicke, Clarence, and Exeter. Q*   23 desire] *F;*
desire to see *Q*   SD] *F (opp. 24), Q (see 19 SD)*   25 what's] *F, Q3;* what is *Q*

fellow of it; and he that I gave it to in change promised 30
to wear it in his cap; I promised to strike him if he
did. I met this man with my glove in his cap, and I
have been as good as my word.

FLUELLEN   Your majesty hear now, saving your majesty's manhood, what an arrant, rascally, beggarly, 35
lousy knave it is. I hope your majesty is pear me
testimony, and witness, and avouchment that this is
the glove of Alençon that your majesty is give me, in
your conscience now.

KING   Give me thy glove, soldier. Look, here is the 40
fellow of it.
'Twas I indeed thou promised'st to strike,
And thou hast given me most bitter terms.

FLUELLEN   An't please your majesty, let his neck answer
for it, if there is any martial law in the world. 45

KING
How canst thou make me satisfaction?

WILLIAMS   All offences, my lord, come from the heart:

30 **change** exchange
33 **as good as my word** proverbial (Tilley, M 184)
34 **hear** Cf. 4.7.99n.
34-5 **saving ... manhood** The usual apologetic formula for mentioning a disagreeable subject is 'saving your reverence' (e.g. *MV* 2.2.23-4). Fluellen's formula recalls the Hostess's 'saving your manhoods' (to Fang and Snare), *2H4* 2.1.27, where, as here, a compliment to the hearer's courage is implied.
37 ***and avouchment** Q's version of this passage ('And your Maiestie will beare me witnes, and testimony, / And auouchments, that this is the gloue.') strongly suggests that F's compositor has wrongly inserted 'will', perhaps influenced by the first three letters of 'witnesse' which he had just set. Fluellen nowhere else

uses a noun in mistake for a verb, whereas to multiply nouns is thoroughly in his style.
40 **thy glove** i.e. the glove in your cap
40-1 **here ... of it** The dramatic point is most clearly made if the King draws off from his own hand the glove that he now shows Williams.
42 **promised'st** Gurr rejects this verbal form as 'a recurrent feature of Compositor A's work' and reads *promised*, but though Shakespeare often has 'you promised' he nowhere has 'thou promised', nor 'thou promised'st' apart from this passage. The pronoun *thou* is of course essential.
43 **terms** words, language
46 **satisfaction** amends (pronounced as five syllables)
47 **offences** i.e. actions that deserve to be called offences

32 this man] *F;* that Gentleman *Q*   36-8 I hope ... glove] *F; after 28 Q*   37 avouchment] *Wordsworth;* will auouchment *F;* auouchments *Q*   40-1] *prose Pope; F lines ... Souldier; / ... it. / ; Q lines ... gloue. Looke you, / ... it. /*   44 An't] *(And)*   45 martial] *(Marshall)*

never came any from mine that might offend your
majesty.

KING   It was our self thou didst abuse.   50

WILLIAMS   Your majesty came not like your self: you
appeared to me but as a common man – witness the
night, your garments, your lowliness; and what your
highness suffered under that shape, I beseech you take
it for your own fault and not mine, for had you been as   55
I took you for, I made no offence; therefore I beseech
your highness pardon me.   [*Kneels.*]

KING   [*Raises him.*]
Here, uncle Exeter, fill this glove with crowns
And give it to this fellow. – Keep it, fellow,
And wear it for an honour in thy cap   60
Till I do challenge it. – Give him the crowns. –
And Captain, you must needs be friends with him.

FLUELLEN   By this day and this light, the fellow has
mettle enough in his belly. – Hold, there is twelve
pence for you, and I pray you to serve God, and keep   65
you out of prawls and prabbles, and quarrels and
dissensions, and I warrant you it is the better for
you.

---

50 **It was ... abuse** Since the King is
now (ll. 42–3, 46) speaking verse, it
is curious that this verse line
(supposing it to be one) is metrically
defective. The phrase 'our royal self'
(cf. *KJ* 3.1.158[232], *R3* 3.1.63) would
be appropriate to the tone here, and
is not disproved by Williams's reply,
for 'Your majesty came not like your
royal self' (quoting the phrase back
in a prose sentence) would smack of
insolence.

53 **garments** i.e. Erpingham's cloak,
concealing the other garments
lowliness (apparent) low social rank

58 **this glove** i.e. the glove (the King's
own) that Williams handed him, l. 40.
Gurr, pointing out that 'Henry has
both gloves', wryly comments, 'One

glove filled with crowns is presumably
enough payment for Williams's vic-
timisation in Henry's game.' But the
King must retain his other glove if
his jest about challenging this glove
some day is to have any point.

59 **fellow** The King has referred to Williams as *yonder fellow* at 4.7.117, and
since then has addressed him three
times as *soldier* and once as *sirrah*.
In the present context of geniality
(especially the jest at ll. 60–1) *fellow*
is evidently an affable form of address.

64–5 **twelve pence** a shilling coin (cf.
l. 73). Fluellen, with characteristic
pedantry, states its value.

66 **prawls and prabbles** brawls and
brabbles (petty quarrels)

---

50 our] *F;* our royal *(this edn); speech not in Q*   56 I made] *F;* I had made *Q*   57 SD] *Cam²*   58
SD] *this edn*   64–5 twelve pence] *F (*twelue-pence*);* a shilling *Q;* a silling *Q³*

WILLIAMS   I will none of your money.

FLUELLEN   It is with a good will. I can tell you, it will   70
serve you to mend your shoes. Come, wherefore should
you be so pashful? Your shoes is not so good. 'Tis a
good shilling, I warrant you, or I will change it.

Enter Herald.

KING   Now, herald, are the dead numbered?

HERALD
Here is the number of the slaughtered French.   75

[*Gives the King a paper.*]

KING
What prisoners of good sort are taken, uncle?

EXETER
Charles, Duke of Orleans, nephew to the King;
John, Duke of Bourbon, and Lord Boucicault.
Of other lords and barons, knights and squires,
Full fifteen hundred, besides common men.   80

KING
This note doth tell me of ten thousand French

---

69 **I will ... money** Williams not
unnaturally resents Fluellen's advice
as to his future conduct. Fluellen's
conciliatory reply, and the fact that
'silence normally gives consent to a
direction implied in the dialogue'
(Taylor), make it clear that Williams
takes the shilling.

73 ***shilling** F's 'silling' is presumably
influenced by Q3.

76 **What ... uncle?** Exeter, who entered
with the King and some French prisoners at 4.7.53 SD, speaks from his
own knowledge. The herald's concern
has been only with French and
English losses.

good sort high rank. Cf. 4.7.133.

77–80 **Charles ... men** Cf. Holinshed,
3.555: 'There were taken prisoners,
Charles duke of Orleance nephue to

the French king, John duke of
Burbon, the lord Bouciqualt one of
the marshals of France (he after died
in England) with a number of other
lords, knights, and esquiers, at the
least fifteene hundred, besides the
common people.'

81 **This note** Moore Smith compares
E3, 3.5.95–6, 'Heere is a note, my
gratious Lord, of those / That in this
conflict of our foes were slaine.'

81–101 **This note ... Lestrelles** Cf.
Holinshed, 3.555 (immediately following the passage quoted in the preceding note): 'There were slaine in all
of the French part to the number
of ten thousand men, whereof were
princes and noble men bearing baners
one hundred twentie and six; to these,
of knights, esquiers, and gentlemen,

---

69 money] *F; money sir, not* I *Q*   73 shilling] *Q; silling F, Q3*   SD] *F; not in Q*   74–5] *F; not
in Q*   75 SD] *Capell (subst.)*   77 Orleans] *(Orleance)*   78 Bourbon] *(Burbon)* Boucicault]
(Bouchiquald)   81 SP] *F; not in Q*

That in the field lie slain. Of princes in this number
And nobles bearing banners, there lie dead
One hundred twenty-six. Added to these,
Of knights, esquires and gallant gentlemen,   85
Eight thousand and four hundred, of the which
Five hundred were but yesterday dubbed knights.
So that in these ten thousand they have lost
There are but sixteen hundred mercenaries;
The rest are princes, barons, lords, knights, squires   90
And gentlemen of blood and quality.
The names of those their nobles that lie dead:
Charles Delabreth, High Constable of France;
Jaques of Chatillon, Admiral of France;
The Master of the Crossbows, Lord Rambures;   95

so manie as made vp the number of eight thousand and foure hundred (of the which fiue hundred were dubbed knights the night before the battell) so as of the meaner sort, not past sixteene hundred. Amongst those of the nobilitie that were slaine, these were the cheefest, Charles lord de la Breth high constable of France, Jaques of Chatilon lord of Dampier admerall of France, the lord Rambures master of the crossebowes, sir Guischard Dolphin great master of France, John duke of Alanson, Anthonic duke of Brabant brother to the duke of Burgognie, Edward duke of Bar, the earle of Nevers an other brother to the duke of Burgognie, with the erles of Marle, Vaudemont, Beaumont, Grandpree, Roussie, Fauconberge, Fois and Lestrake, beside a great number of lords and barons of name.'

83 **bearing banners** entitled to bring their vassals to the field under their own banner, i.e. all ranks of nobles down to a knight banneret
89 **mercenaries** Cf. 4.7.75n. Gurr states that these two references to mer-

cenaries in the French army 'are both additions to the lists in Holinshed'. This means only that the word is not in Holinshed. The figures, which are identical, make it clear that Holinshed's 'of the meaner sort, not past sixteene hundred' corresponds to Shakespeare's 'but sixteen hundred mercenaries'; which, in conjunction with 4.7.73–7, shows that Shakespeare does not imagine a French army wholly composed of French nobles and hired foreign common soldiers, but equates the *mercenaries* with *our vulgar* (4.7.76).

92 **The names** For the forms of the names, see notes to 3.5.40–5.
94 **Jaques of** This is the reading of F, Q and Holinshed. It is presumably authorial, though it requires *Jaques* to be monosyllabic (pronounced Jakes: without, of course, any intended word-play on 'jakes', a privy), in contrast to 3.5.43 where it has two syllables. The discrepancy may be due to Shakespeare's inadvertence in transcribing from Holinshed. In performance it might be well to emend: see textual notes.

83–91 there ... quality] *F; not in Q*   93 Delabreth] *F; de le Brute Q; De-la-bret Capell*   94 Jaques of] *F, Q*; Jacques of *Cam²*; Jaques *(this edn)*   Chatillon] *F (Chatilion), Q (Chattillian)*

Great Master of France, the brave Sir Guichard
   Dauphin;
John, Duke of Alençon; Anthony, Duke of Brabant,
The brother to the Duke of Burgundy;
And Edward, Duke of Bar: of lusty earls,
Grandpré and Roussi, Fauconbridge and Foix,   100
Beaumont and Marle, Vaudemont and Lestrelles.
Here was a royal fellowship of death.
Where is the number of our English dead?
               [*Herald gives him another paper.*]
Edward the Duke of York; the Earl of Suffolk;
Sir Richard Keighley; Davy Gam, esquire;   105
None else of name, and of all other men
But five-and-twenty. O God, thy arm was here;
And not to us but to thy arm alone
Ascribe we all. When, without stratagem,

96 **Great Master** grand master, the chief officer of the royal household (*OED* great *a.* 12f; *OED* grand master 1)
98 **the Duke of Burgundy** i.e. the father (mentioned at 3.5.42) of the Duke of Burgundy who appears in 5.2
104–7 **Edward … five-and-twenty** Cf. Holinshed, 3.555 (immediately following the passage quoted in 81–101n.): 'Of Englishmen, there died at this battell, Edward duke [of] Yorke, the earle of Suffolke, sir Richard Kikelie, and Dauie Gamme esquier, and of all other not aboue fiue and twentie persons, as some doo report; but other writers of greater credit affirme, that there were slaine about fiue or six hundred persons. *Titus Livius* saith, that there were slaine of Englishmen, beside the duke of Yorke, and the earle of Suffolke, an

hundred persons at the first incounter.'
105 ***Keighley** This name, spelled 'Kikely' in Hall and Holinshed, and 'Ketly' in F, is given in older records as 'Kyghley', i.e. modern Keighley, a town in Yorkshire, pronounced 'Keithley'.
Davy Gam Davydd ap Llewelyn of Brecon. ' "Gam" is a nickname meaning "squinting", which, like other Welsh nicknames, became equivalent to a surname' (*DNB*).
106 **name** notable family
109 **stratagem** 'usually, an artifice or trick designed to outwit or surprise the enemy' (*OED* 1). As Gurr points out, Shakespeare never refers to King Henry's pitching of sharpened stakes before his archers to defend them against the French cavalry, described

96 Great Master] *F;* hie Maister *Q* Guichard Dauphin] *F (Guichard Dolphin); Gwigzard, Dolphin Q* 97 Alençon] *(Alanson)* 99 lusty earls] *F; Nobelle Charillas Q* 100 Grandpré] *(Grandpree)* Foix] *(Foyes)* 101 Beaumont and Marle] *F; Gerard* and *Verton Q* Vaudemont] *F2; Vandemont F; Vandemant Q* Lestrelles] *Oxf¹; Lestrale F;* Lestra *Q;* Lestrake *Cam¹* 102 Here] *F, Q; King.* Heeres *Q3* 103 SD] *Capell (subst.)* 104 Edward] *F, Q; Exe. Edward Q3* 105 Keighley] *Oxf¹;* Ketly *F, Q;* Kikely *Cam¹* 107] *verse Capell; F, Q line* … twentie. / … heere. twenty. O] *Capell;* twentie. / O *(indented) F;* twentie. / O *Q;* twenty. / *King.* O *Q3*

But in plain shock and even play of battle,   110
Was ever known so great and little loss
On one part and on th'other? Take it, God,
For it is none but thine.
EXETER   'Tis wonderful.
KING

Come, go we in procession to the village,
And be it death proclaimed through our host   115
To boast of this, or take that praise from God
Which is his only.
FLUELLEN   Is it not lawful, an't please your majesty, to
tell how many is killed?
KING

Yes, Captain, but with this acknowledgement,   120
That God fought for us.
FLUELLEN   Yes, in my conscience, he did us great good.
KING

Do we all holy rites.

by Holinshed 3.553 (margin) as 'a politike inuention'. In the context of the next line it is probable that by *stratagem* Shakespeare meant something more like the Trojan Horse.

110 **plain ... play** direct collision and straightforward contest

114–27 **Come ... happy men** Based, with alterations, on Holinshed (3.555: see note at 4.7.64 SD): 'And so about foure of the clocke in the after noone, the king when he saw no apperance of enimies, caused the retreit to be blowen; and gathering his armie togither, gaue thanks to almightie God for so happie a victorie, causing his prelats and chapleins to sing this psalme: *In exitu Israel de Aegypto*, and commanded euerie man to kneele downe on the ground at this verse: *Non nobis Domine, non nobis, sed nomini tuo da gloriam*. Which doone, he caused *Te Deum*, with certeine

anthems to be soong, giuing laud and praise to God, without boasting of his owne force or anie humane power. That night he and his people tooke rest, and refreshed themselues with such victuals as they found in the French campe, but lodged in the same village where he laie the night before.' (There follows the passage quoted at 4.7.70–90n.)

114 **village** Maisoncelles (not named in Holinshed)

115 **proclaimed** proclaimèd

118–22 **Is it not ... great good** This piece of dialogue is probably Shakespeare's afterthought: the two half-lines 'Which is his only' (117) and 'Do we all holy rites' (123) between them make a line of verse, the thought being likewise continuous.

122 ***in my conscience** See textual notes. 'Fluellen gets this idiom right six times elsewhere' (Taylor).

111 loss] Q *(losse,);* losse? F   112 other?] Q *(other.);* other, F   114 we] F2; me F   to the village] F; through the camp Q   115 through our host] F; to any man Q   118 not lawful, an't] F *(not lawfull and);* lawful, and it Q   122 in my] Q; my F   123] F; *not in* Q   rites] *(Rights)*

Let there be sung *Non nobis* and *Te Deum*,
The dead with charity enclosed in clay,   125
And then to Calais, and to England then,
Where ne'er from France arrived more happy men.

Exeunt.

[5.0]   *Enter* CHORUS.

CHORUS

Vouchsafe to those that have not read the story
That I may prompt them; and of such as have,
I humbly pray them to admit th'excuse
Of time, of numbers and due course of things
Which cannot in their huge and proper life   5
Be here presented. Now we bear the King
Toward Calais: grant him there; there seen,

124 *Non nobis* and *Te Deum* The
opening words of Psalm 115, Book of
Common Prayer ('Not vnto vs (O
Lord) not vnto vs, but vnto thy name
geue the prayse: for thy louyng mercy,
and for thy truethes sake') and the
canticle *Te Deum laudamus* ('We praise
thee, O God: we knowledge thee to be
the Lord'). Noble (80–1) points out
that in the Vulgate '*In exitu Israel*'
(Psalm 114 in the English Bible and
Prayer Book) continues, after verse 8,
with '*Non nobis, Domine*'. This was no
doubt clear to Shakespeare from
Holinshed (cf. 114–27n.), but he chose
to adapt Holinshed's statement in
order to make a line of verse which
would be effective in itself and
immediately comprehensible to his
audience (for the opening Latin words
were prefixed to the psalm and the
canticle in the Prayer Book, and the
canticle was in use at Morning Prayer
throughout the year).
125 **The dead . . . clay** the dead given
Christian burial. Holinshed (3.555)

relates that the French buried 5,800
corpses in three pits. He also relates
(3.556) that the King returned from
Calais to Dover 'hauing with him the
dead bodies of the duke of Yorke, and
the earle of Suffolke, and caused the
duke to be buried at his colledge of
Fodringhey (Fotheringhay], and the
earle at new Elme.'
127 **happy** (1) fortunate (*OED a, 2*), (2)
highly contented (*OED a.* 4)
5.0.2 **prompt** them i.e. tell them what
comes next (a suitably theatrical
expression)
of such as with regard to those who
(Abbott, 173)
3–6 **admit . . . presented** accept the
short time and few actors at our
disposal as our excuse for omitting the
next events, in reality too grand for us
to be able to present them (i.e. the
King's reception at Dover and
London)
7 **Toward . . . seen** F's line is suspect,
but is defensible by the argument
that Shakespeare meant to create a

126 Calais] *(Callice)*

5.0] F *(Actus Quintus)*   1 SP] *Johnson; not in F; speech not in Q*   7 Calais] *(Callice)*   there seen]
F; And there being seene *F2*

Heave him away upon your winged thoughts
Athwart the sea. Behold, the English beach
Pales in the flood with men, with wives and boys,   10
Whose shouts and claps outvoice the deep-mouthed
     sea,
Which like a mighty whiffler 'fore the King
Seems to prepare his way. So let him land,
And solemnly see him set on to London.
So swift a pace hath thought that even now   15
You may imagine him upon Blackheath,

somewhat comic effect, by using two strong caesuras in place of syllables, in order to enact the abrupt whisking-away of the King from Agincourt to Calais and from Calais to Dover. Alternatively, Shakespeare may have accidentally written a short line through momentarily imagining that the lineation was 'Now we bear / The King toward Calais'. The suggestion (Abbott, 480) that *there* is twice consecutively given the value of two syllables is improbable. F2's emendation implies a compositor's error (omission of alternate words) that is hard to credit.

8 **winged** wingèd
9 **beach** pebbled shore (*OED sb.* 1)
10 **Pales in** fences in (*OED*); a pale is a fence composed of pales (stakes)
   flood sea
   ***with men ... boys** F's line is obviously defective; F2's addition *with* not only restores the metre but introduces a quibble (i.e. 'with men – or rather with wives and boys'); *wives and boys* are women and boys in general (cf. *Cor* 4.4.5–6, 'Lest that thy wives with spits and boys with stones / In puny battle slay me'), not the wives and sons of the soldiers. A compositor's error could be easily caused by the identical first two letters of *with* and *wives*. Emendations that insert *maids* reduce the sense to a catalogue, and

Oxf¹'s juxtaposes *men* and *maids* in an unintentional antithesis.
11 **claps** hand-claps, applause (*OED*'s first example)
   outvoice shout down, make a louder sound than (*OED*'s first example)
   deep-mouthed having a deep or sonorous voice (especially used of dogs: *OED* gives an example from a sale notice of hounds, 1692, and cf. *TS* Ind. 1.16, 'the deep-mouthed brach'). Cf. *KJ* 5.2.173, 'the deep-mouthed thunder'. Here contrasted with the shrill voices of the women and boys.
12 **whiffler** 'one of a body of attendants armed with javelin, battleaxe, sword, or staff, and wearing a chain, employed to keep the way clear for a procession' (*OED*). The only occurrence in Shakespeare. Cf. *Sir Clyomon and Sir Clamydes* (1599) G2ᵛ: '*Enter Shift like a Wiffler.*'
14 **solemnly ... London** see him march forward ceremonially towards London
16 **Blackheath** a large common immediately south of Greenwich, and just outside the City of London. Cf. Holinshed, 3.556: 'The mayor of London, and the aldermen, apparelled in orient grained scarlet, and foure hundred commoners clad in beautifull murrie, well mounted, and trimlie horssed, with rich collars, & great chaines, met the king on Blackheath, reioising at his returne: and the clergie of

10 flood with] *Pope;* flood; with *F;* flood, with *F2*   with wives] *F2;* Wiues *F;* wives, maids *Stone* (*Brinsley M. Nicholson*); maids, wives *Oxf¹*

Where that his lords desire him to have borne
His bruised helmet and his bended sword
Before him through the city. He forbids it,
Being free from vainness and self-glorious pride,   20
Giving full trophy, signal and ostent
Quite from himself to God. But now behold,
In the quick forge and working-house of thought,
How London doth pour out her citizens.
The Mayor and all his brethren in best sort,   25
Like to the senators of th'antique Rome

London, with rich crosses, sumptuous copes, and massie censers, receiued him at saint Thomas of Waterings with solemne procession.'

17–22 Where ... God Cf. Holinshed, 3.556 (immediately following the passage quoted in 5.0.16n.): 'The king like a graue and sober personage, and as one remembring from whom all victories are sent, seemed little to regard such vaine pompe and shewes as were in triumphant sort deuised for his welcomming home from so prosperous a iournie, in so much that he would not suffer his helmet to be caried with him, whereby might haue appeared to the people the blowes and dints that were to be seene in the same; neither would he suffer any ditties to be made and soong by minstrels of his glorious victorie, for that he would wholie haue the praise and thanks altogither giuen to God.'

17 Where that where (Abbott, 287). The context, with its immediately preceding mention of Blackheath, makes this sense more probable than 'whereas', though F's punctuation (a colon after 'Black-Heath' and a colon after 'Citie') allows either interpretation.

have borne cause to be carried

18 bruised dented (bruisèd)

bended bent: 'a reversion, probably for metrical reasons, to the older form

of the past participle' (Taylor). The word was also probably chosen for its alliteration with *bruised*, since it is not likely that a sword of quality, however vigorously used, would become bent, though it would show hacks.

20 vainness personal vanity or conceit (*OED* b)

self-glorious self-glorifying (*OED*'s first example, and the only Shakespearean occurrence)

21 trophy token: cf. 5.1.72. Originally (*OED sb.* 1) a triumphal monument; here used metaphorically for an emblem hung up as a tribute: cf. *JC* 1.1.68–9 ('Let no images / Be hung with Caesar's trophies') and 1.2.285–6 ('for pulling scarves off Caesar's images').

signal and ostent 'symbol and external show of victory' (Wright). The three words *trophy, signal* and *ostent* are virtually synonymous.

23 In the ... thought in imagination, with its rapid and lively shaping power. Cf. *2H4* 4.2[3].96–7, where Falstaff declares that sack makes the brain 'apprehensive, quick, forgetive, full of nimble, fiery, and delectable shapes'. *Working-house* (workshop) is here synonymous with *forge*.

25 brethren fellow aldermen

in best sort in their civic finery

26 antique ancient

26–8 Like to ... Caesar in Shakespeare

17 Where that] *Pope;* Where, that *F*   him to] *Pope;* him, to *F*   21 trophy] *(*Trophee*)*   24 citizens.] *Pope;* Citizens, *F*

334

With the plebeians swarming at their heels,
Go forth and fetch their conquering Caesar in;
As, by a lower but as loving likelihood,
Were now the General of our gracious Empress,   30
As in good time he may, from Ireland coming,
Bringing rebellion broached on his sword,
How many would the peaceful city quit

may have already planned to begin *Julius Caesar* with Caesar's triumphal return to Rome after his victory over Pompey's sons (*JC* 1.1, in which the plebeians are conspicuous). Caesar had, of course, been awarded triumphs for his former victories. The disaffection expressed by the tribunes in *JC* 1.1 does not reflect adversely on King Henry here, as the circumstances are different.

27 **swarming** i.e. in multitudes. This is a usual figurative sense in Shakespeare (cf. 4.2.26), and is therefore unlikely to imply the migration of bees from an overcrowded hive. See Introduction, p. 77, for the discussion of a recent political reading of this passage.

29 **by ... likelihood** by a less glorious but no less loving similitude (*OED* likelihood 1: not elsewhere in this sense in Shakespeare, who may have used it here because its more usual sense, probability, is suggested by l. 31, 'As in good time he may')

*as loving 'F's repetition of *by* is meaningless and grammatically intrusive' (Taylor). This edn postulates that the compositor, noticing that one of the first two words of the line was repeated later in it, here set down the wrong one. The line, which has been emended in various ways, contains more syllables than usual. It can be regarded as a line of six metrical feet (Oxf¹, Cam²), but if so it would be the only one in all the

choruses, and more probably Shakespeare intended it to have the usual five feet with two extra syllables at the end (not unusual in his verse). Elsewhere *likelihood*, when it ends a line, carries two metrical stresses, on the first and last syllables.

30 **the General** Robert Devereux, Earl of Essex, who had left England on 27 March 1599 to suppress Tyrone's rebellion in Ireland. He returned unsuccessful on 28 September. See Introduction, pp. 1–2.

our gracious Empress Elizabeth I. Cf. Spenser, dedication of *Faerie Queene* (2nd edn, 1596): 'To the most high, mightie, and magnificent Empresse renowmed for pietie, vertue, and all gratious gouernment Elizabeth by the grace of God Queene of England, Fraunce and Ireland and of Virginia, Defender of the Faith, &c.'

31 **in good time** in a happy hour, propitiously

he may may he. In exclamatory expressions of wish 'The subject normally follows *may*, but examples are found in the older language in which this is not so' (*OED* may *v.*¹ 8b, citing Marlowe, *1 Tamburlaine*, 1.1.170–1, 'And Jove may never let me longer live / Than I may seek to gratify your love'; cf. also Spenser, *Epithalamion*, 418–23, where there are three examples).

32 **broached** spitted (*OED* *v.*¹ 3b) (broachèd)

28 conquering] *(*Conqu'ring*)*   29 as loving] *this edn:* by louing *F;* loving *Rowe;* high-loving *Oxf¹;* behoving *(Proudfoot)*

335

> To welcome him! Much more, and much more cause,
> Did they this Harry. Now in London place him.   35
> As yet the lamentation of the French
> Invites the King of England's stay at home.
> The Emperor's coming in behalf of France,
> To order peace between them [

34 **and much more cause** and (there was) much more cause (Abbott, 202). The phrase is used to exalt Henry V's achievement, not to belittle Essex's prospective success.

35 **Did they** did they welcome

35–42 ***Now ... France** The interpretation of this passage has been affected by the question whether or not something has been lost between *them* and *and omit* (ll. 39–40 in this edn). 'Now in London place him', as F's full stop shows, is a complete sentence, not connected with 'As yet ... at home'. F's further punctuation (a colon after *home* and another colon after *between them*) gives no grounds for supposing that 'As yet ... between them' is a long parenthesis and that the sentence is constructed round two imperatives addressed to the audience, namely *place him* and *omit*. 'The audience can hardly *omit* action – as the actors and author clearly can' (Taylor, Oxf¹ 302), and another reason for rejecting the parenthesis is that it would require 'The Emperor's coming' (i.e. the coming of the Emperor: cf. Holinshed, 3.558, 'by reason of the emperours coming') either to mean 'The Emperor is coming' or to serve as a second object of *Invites* (without the conjunction 'and'). Capell, who first noticed the gap in the text, and Taylor propose different ways of filling it (see textual notes). It was Wilson who suggested that 'a reference to the Dauphin's death, which is needed by his absence from 5.2, might follow l. 37.' Holinshed mentions it on the same page as the Emperor's visit (3.556), just after reporting the appointment of successors to the Constable and Rambures: 'Shortlie after, either for melancholie that he had for the losse at Agincourt, or by some hidden disease Lewes Dolphin of Viennois, heire apparant to the French king, departed this life without issue.' In performance, a practical alternative to adopting Capell's or Taylor's conjectural restoration might be to rephrase the passage as 'To order peace between them, we omit, / And all th'occurrences ...'; this is not offered, however, as an emendation, since Capell's explanation of the textual difficulty is accepted in this edn.

36 **As yet** for the present: *OED* as 34a (with adverbs of time)

38–9 **The Emperor's ... them** The Holy Roman Emperor Sigismund came to England on 1 May 1416. Cf. Holinshed (3.556): 'In this fourth yeare of king Henries reigne, the emperour Sigismund, coosine germane to king Henrie, came into England, to the intent that he might make an attonement betweene king Henrie and the French king.' After being installed as a Knight of the Garter, 'the emperour tarried still, and assaied all maner of meanes to persuade the king to a peace with the Frenchmen', but a skirmish near Rouen and a French siege of Harfleur made King Henry refuse to consider it.

39 **order** arrange (*OED v.* 2)

39–40 them [/] and] *Oxf¹;* them: and *F;* them: – But these now / We pass in silence over; and *(Capell);* them, and the death / O'th' Dauphin, leap we over, and *(Oxf¹)*

] and omit   40
All the occurrences, whatever chanced,
Till Harry's back return again to France.
There must we bring him; and myself have played
The interim, by remembering you 'tis past.
Then brook abridgement and your eyes advance   45
After your thoughts straight back again to France. *Exit.*

[5.1]   *Enter* FLUELLEN *and* GOWER.

GOWER   Nay, that's right. But why wear you your leek
    today? Saint Davy's day is past.
FLUELLEN   There is occasions and causes why and
    wherefore in all things. I will tell you ass my friend,
    Captain Gower. The rascally, scald, beggarly, lousy,   5

40 **omit** pass over, neglect (*OED v.* 2).
This is the usual sense in Shakespeare
(cf. 1.2.301 and *2H4* 4.3[4].27,
'Therefore omit him not, blunt not
his love'). In the present context, as
in *Per* sc. 10[3.0].42 ('Omit we all
their dole and woe'), the fundamental
sense 'to leave out, not to insert or
include' (*OED v.* 1) may also be
present.
41-2 **All ... France** 'Primarily, the
further English invasions and campaigns of 1416-19, and several abortive negotiations' (Taylor). As Holinshed reports, King Henry was in
France (contrary to the implication
here that he returned only for the
meeting in 5.2) for most of this time,
capturing Caen in 1417 and Rouen
(after a six months' siege) in January
1419, and meeting the French near
Meulan on the Seine for the abortive
negotiations of May 1419. The meeting dramatized in 5.2 took place in
May 1420.
42 **back return again** Cf. *1 Troublesome
Reign*, 1591, B1', 'And at my Fathers
back returne agen'.
43-4 **and myself ... past** humorous. By

reminding (*remembering*) the audience
that the events of the intervening time
have been skipped over, the Chorus
has certainly not acted them – nor, in
all probability, would the audience
have wished to see them acted.
5.1.1-2 **Nay ... today?** If Fluellen has
just been justifying the tradition of
wearing the leek, Gower will stress
today; if, on the other hand, Fluellen
has just been talking of something
else, Gower will stress *leek*.
3 **There is ... causes** Cf. *MW* 3.1.45,
'There is reasons and causes for it'
(Sir Hugh Evans, explaining why he
is equipped for a duel).
3-4 **why and wherefore** synonymous
and proverbial (Tilley, W 332)
4 **ass my friend** Fluellen's pronunciation of *as* makes him unintentionally insult Gower. Cf. the
covert insult of Maria's reply to Sir
Andrew's 'And your horse now would
make him an ass.' 'Ass I doubt not.'
(*TN* 2.3.162-4, where *Ass* may either
repeat his word or play upon *As*).
5 **scald** '"Scurvy", mean, paltry, contemptible' (*OED a.*[1] 2 *fig.*). The literal
sense (*OED a.*[1] 1) is 'affected with the

5.1] *Hanmer*   0.1] F, *Q (Enter Gower, and Flewellen.)* 1 Nay ... right] *F; not in Q*
2 Saint] *(S.)* 3-5 There ... Gower] *F; There is occasion Captaine Gower. / Looke you why,
and wherefore Q* 4 ass] *(asse)*

337

pragging knave Pistol, which you and yourself and
all the world know to be no petter than a fellow, look
you now, of no merits, he is come to me and prings
me pread and salt yesterday, look you, and bid me
eat my leek. It was in a place where I could not breed   10
no contention with him, but I will be so bold as to
wear it in my cap till I see him once again, and then
I will tell him a little piece of my desires.

Enter PISTOL.

GOWER   Why, here he comes, swelling like a turkey-
cock.   15
FLUELLEN   'Tis no matter for his swellings nor his
turkey-cocks. – God pless you, Anchient Pistol, you
scurvy, lousy knave, God pless you!
PISTOL
Ha, art thou bedlam? Dost thou thirst, base Trojan,

"scall"; scabby', particularly in the
head.
lousy infested with lice (*OED* 1),
hence contemptible (*OED* 2 *fig.*)
6 **you and yourself** an extreme case
of Fluellen's tautological rhetoric. Cf.
Evans, enumerating the peacemakers
between Falstaff and Shallow, *MW*
1.1.128–9, 'and there is myself, fid-
elicet myself.'
8 **merits** one of Fluellen's idiosyncratic
plurals. Cf. *desires*, l. 13.
9 **yesterday** i.e. St David's day, 1
March. Cf. l. 2.
bid i.e. is bid (= bade). Cf. *is come*
(= came).
11 **contention** Pope, influenced by Q's
'discentions', made this into an idiosyncratic plural; but since F's line of
text is not unusually close-set, and
since Q is inclined to overdo the
idiosyncratic plurals (like *MW* Q
1602), it is safer not to tamper with
the F reading.

11–12 **be so bold ... wear** take the
liberty of wearing
14-15 **swelling ... turkey-cock** puffed
up with self-importance and aggres-
siveness: proverbial (Tilley, T 612)
17 **God pless you** Fluellen, in exag-
gerated politeness, uses the respectful
you to Pistol, who uses the dis-
respectful *thou* to him, throughout
this dialogue in which Fluellen has
the upper hand.
19 **bedlam** mad: a common figurative
and attributive use of 'Bedlam', i.e.
the Hospital of St Mary of Bethlehem, a London asylum for lunatics,
situated just outside Bishopsgate
base Trojan This expression,
repeated at l. 32, is interpreted by
Cam[1] ('cant term for dissolute
fellow'), followed by Oxf[1], in a more
particular sense than is justified. Cf.
the epithets at *2H4* 5.3.102, 'O base
Assyrian knight' (Falstaff to Pistol),
MW 1.3.19, 'O base Hungarian wight'

9 bid] *F;* bids *Q;* is bid *(this edn)*   11 contention] *F;* discentions *Q;* contentions *Pope*
17 Anchient] *(aunchient)*   19] *as Pope; prose F; Q lines ...* bedlem? / ·... Troyan, /   19, 31
Trojan] *F (Troian);* Troyan *Q*

To have me fold up Parca's fatal web?   20
Hence! I am qualmish at the smell of leek.

FLUELLEN   I peseech you heartily, scurvy, lousy knave,
at my desires, and my requests, and my petitions, to
eat, look you, this leek. Because, look you, you do not
love it, nor your affections and your appetites and your   25
digestions does not agree with it, I would desire you
to eat it.

PISTOL   Not for Cadwallader and all his goats.

FLUELLEN   (*Strikes him* [*with a cudgel*].)   There is one
goat for you. Will you be so good, scald knave, as eat   30
it?

PISTOL   Base Trojan, thou shalt die.

(Pistol to Bardolph), *MW* 1.3.83, 'Base Phrygian Turk' (Pistol apostrophizing Falstaff).

20 **fold ... web** i.e. put an end to your life. The Parcae are the three Fates in classical mythology, imagined as respectively spinning, drawing and cutting the thread of every human life. At *2H4* 2.4.196 Pistol knows that they are 'the Sisters Three' and invokes Atropos the third of them. Here, by a linguistic error, he reduces them to one, *Parca*. His allusion to 'folding up' their 'web' (piece of woven cloth) is also peculiar to him, though in *AW* 4.3.74–5 ('The web of our life is of a mingled yarn, good and ill together') the image occurs again.

21 **qualmish** affected with a feeling of nausea
   smell of leek i.e. either the leek in Fluellen's cap or (more insultingly) his breath

28 **Cadwallader** 'Cadwallader, the last British king, defended Wales against the Saxons in the middle of the seventh century ... He is the subject of a poem in Blenerhasset's *Mirror for Magistrates*, Pt 2 (1578)' (Moore Smith).

goats associated with Wales. Cf. *1H4* 3.1.37, *MW* 5.5.136.

29 SD *Strikes him* F places the SD to the right of the speech, as usual; cf. 4.8.9 SD where the blow follows the speech. Here the blow precedes or accompanies the speech. F provides no further directions for Fluellen's actions, and none for Pistol's. Pope's direction at l. 35 is the only other blow that is positively required by the dialogue. Other SDs are at editors' and directors' discretion. Fluellen might use his dagger's handle as a cudgel so as not to come on stage too obviously armed (cf. 4.1.57–8n.), though ll. 65–7 imply that he has used a cudgel (staff, club).

29–30 **one goat** Fluellen's retort to 'all his goats' (with the prospect of more to follow). Taylor's suggestion that he means 'goad' is untenable because it destroys the repartee and virtually makes Fluellen pun on his own mannerism of pronunciation.

32 **thou shalt die** Wilson adds the SD '*draws his sword*', but it is unlikely that Pistol's resistance goes further than laying his hand upon it, if so far.

20–1] *verse Q; prose F*   26 digestions] *(disgestions)*   does] *(doo's)*   29 SD *Strikes him*] *F (you. Strikes him.* / Will*); He strikes him. Q*   with a cudgel] *Cam²*

FLUELLEN   You say very true, scald knave, when God's
   will is. I will desire you to live in the meantime and
   eat your victuals. [*Strikes him.*] Come, there is sauce   35
   for it. You called me yesterday mountain-squire, but
   I will make you today a squire of low degree. I pray
   you, fall to; if you can mock a leek you can eat a
   leek.
GOWER   Enough, Captain, you have astonished him.   40
FLUELLEN   I say I will make him eat some part of my
   leek, or I will peat his pate four days. – Bite, I pray

33–4 **when God's will is** Cf. *Mucedorus*
(1598) 2.4.72–9, where the King is
addressing the disguised hero:
'Shepheard, whereas it was my sentence, thou shouldst die, / So shall
my sentence stand, for thou shalt
die. / Se[*gasto*: the hero's accuser].
Thankes to your maiestie. / *King*. But
soft, *Segasto*, not for this offence. – /
Long maist thou liue, and when the
sisters shall decree / To cut in twaine
the twisted thread of life, / Then let
him die: for this I set thee free: /
And for thy valour I will honour
thee.' The allusion to the Fates, as
well as the interpretation of 'thou
shalt die', suggests that Shakespeare
had this passage in mind.
35 **victuals** pronounced 'vittles'
35–6 **sauce for it** i.e. to sharpen your
appetite
36 **mountain-squire** In this compound
(cf. 'mountain-foreigner', *MW*
1.1.147: Pistol to Evans) *squire* is more
likely to be a term of contempt (*OED
sb*. 1d: cf. *MA* 1.3.48, 'A proper
squire', and *Oth* 4.2.149, 'some such
squire he was') than to mean a country
gentleman (*OED sb*. 5), though some
editors interpret the compound noun
as 'landlord of barren land' (Oxf[1]).
37 **squire of low degree** The title of a
medieval romance in couplets (before
1500: its story is summarized in
CHEL, 1.315). Nashe uses the phrase

ironically in *Pierce Penniless* (1592:
Works, 1.169). Fluellen, knocking
Pistol down or threatening to do so,
makes a quibbling contrast with
mountain-squire.
38 **fall to** begin eating (*OED* fall *v*. 66e):
with the courtesy (here ironical) of
host to guest; cf. *AYL* 2.7.172. Pistol
has still not begun to eat when Fluellen replies to Gower at l. 41.
40 **astonished** stunned (*OED v*. 1).
Gower's *Enough* may indicate either
that Fluellen has just struck Pistol
again or that he is threatening to do
so.
41–2 **I say ... days** Taylor here follows
F's word-order while admitting variants from Q, commenting (Oxf[1], 317)
'Whether the variants here arise from
revision behind Q or censorship in F
is impossible to tell, though in either
case Q seems to me clearly superior',
attributing the censorship of 'By Jesu'
to Compositor B, and pointing out
that Fluellen nowhere else says *I say*.
On the other hand, Fluellen is here
reiterating his determination that
Pistol shall begin eating (cf. *fall to*, l.
38), and so *I say* is appropriate; and
Q's opening repetition 'Astonisht
him' is so evidently an actor's gag
that it throws doubt on the following
oath. As for Q's addition 'and four
nights', which Taylor thinks 'entirely
typical of Fluellen', that also may be

33–4 You ... is.] *F; I, I know I shall dye, Q*   35 SD] *Pope*   35–9 Come ... leek] *F; not in
Q*   41–2 I say ... days] *F; Astonisht him, by Iesu, Ile beate his head / Foure days, and foure
nights, but Ile / Make him eate some part of my Leeke Q*   42–4 Bite ... coxcomb] *F; not in Q*

you; it is good for your green wound and your ploody
coxcomb.

PISTOL   Must I bite?   45

FLUELLEN   Yes, certainly, and out of doubt and out of
question too, and ambiguities.

PISTOL   By this leek, I will most horribly revenge –

[*Fluellen threatens him.*]

I eat and eat – I swear –

FLUELLEN   Eat, I pray you. Will you have some more   50
sauce to your leek? There is not enough leek to swear
by.

PISTOL   Quiet thy cudgel, thou dost see I eat.

FLUELLEN   Much good do you, scald knave, heartily.
Nay, pray you, throw none away; the skin is good for   55
your broken coxcomb. When you take occasions to see
leeks hereafter, I pray you mock at 'em, that is all.

PISTOL   Good.

FLUELLEN   Ay, leeks is good. Hold you, there is a groat
to heal your pate.   60

an actor's gag (cf. Q3's further
addition of 'too'); if eyeskip had
occurred in F the omitted words
would have been 'days and four'.

43 **green** fresh (*OED a.* 10a)

44 **coxcomb** head (*OED* 2)

48–9 **By this leek ... swear** 'Some
threat by Fluellen seems necessary to
account for the about-face between
revenge and *I eat*; and since there is
no reason to *swear* that he is doing
what Fluellen can see him doing
(eating), *I swear* looks like an interrupted resumption of histrionics,
perhaps when Fluellen lowers his
cudgel or partly turns away' (Taylor).

48 **By this leek** Cf. *MV* 2.1.24, 'By this
scimitar'.

54 **Much ... you** The expression is

paralleled in Middleton's *No Wit, No
Help like a Woman's* and in Middleton
and Rowley's *Wit at Several Weapons*
(*TxC*, 382–3).

55–6 **the skin ... coxcomb** i.e. (when
eaten, cf. ll. 43–4) by encouraging
new skin to grow over the wound, by
a sort of sympathetic magic

58 **Good** 'Very well' (Wilson): 'OK'
would be a modern equivalent. Pistol
grudgingly concedes defeat. Fluellen's response is benignly obtuse,
stemming from his own appreciation
of leeks.

59 **Hold you** here, take this
groat coin worth four pence. At
4.8.64–5 he gave Williams a shilling –
which he gives Pistol here in Q's
version of the scene.

48–56 By ... coxcomb] *F; not in Q*   48–9] *Riv;* By this Leeke, I will most horribly reuenge I
eate and eate I sweare. *F*   48 SD] *Oxf¹*   49 eat and eat] *F;* eat and eke *Rann (Johnson);* eat, and
yet *Kittredge*   54 do you] *F;* do it you *Wordsworth*   56–7 When ... all] *F;* Antient *Pistoll*, if you
see Leekes an other time, / Mock at them, that is all: God bwy you *Q (after 68)*   59, 61, 64
groat] *F;* shilling *Q*

PISTOL   Me a groat?

FLUELLEN   Yes, verily and in truth, you shall take it, or
I have another leek in my pocket which you shall eat.

PISTOL   I take thy groat in earnest of revenge.

FLUELLEN   If I owe you anything, I will pay you in   65
cudgels: you shall be a woodmonger, and buy nothing
of me but cudgels. God bye you, and keep you, and
heal your pate.   *Exit.*

PISTOL   All hell shall stir for this.

GOWER   Go, go, you are a counterfeit cowardly knave.   70
Will you mock at an ancient tradition, begun upon an
honourable respect and worn as a memorable trophy of
predeceased valour, and dare not avouch in your
deeds any of your words? I have seen you gleeking and
galling at this gentleman twice or thrice. You thought   75
because he could not speak English in the native garb

---

61 **Me a groat?** Pistol is indignant. At
4.4.42–3 his French prisoner offered
him 200 crowns.

62 **verily ... truth** Fluellen's asseveration (typically tautological) has the
function of an oath (cf. the dialogue
about *verily* in *WT* 1.2.45–57).

63 **another leek** 'In performance,
invariably shown to be of monstrous
size' (Taylor). The comic effect is
subtler if Fluellen does not produce
it.

64 **in ... revenge** as an advance payment
towards my revenge, the balance to
be paid later – when, Pistol implies,
he will make Fluellen pay (figuratively) for making him eat the leek.
Cf. Fluellen's reply.

67 **God ... keep you** A mock-benediction. Cf. Marlowe, *Doctor Faustus*,
1.2.27–8 (echoing Numbers 6:24–6),
'And so the Lord bless you, preserve
you and keep you, my dear brethren'
(Wagner to the Scholars). For *God
bye you*, cf. 4.3.6n.

69 **All hell ... this** Thomson (106) compares Juno's 'Flectere si nequeo
superos, Acheronta movebo' ('If I
cannot bend the powers above, I will
stir up the powers below': Virgil,
Aeneid, 7.312). Cf. Pistol's 'Rouse up
Revenge from ebon den with fell
Alecto's snake', *2H4* 5.5.37, and
Aeneid, 7.323–53.

70–80 Gower's speech is absent from Q,
which does not include him in Fluellen's exit.

71 *begun Capell's emendation is the
usual Shakespearean form.

71–2 **upon ... respect** 'for an honourable reason' (Wilson)

72 **memorable** to be kept in memory
trophy token. Cf. 5.0.21n.

73 **predeceased valour** the bravery of
bygone days. Cf. Fluellen's speech at
4.7.96–102.

74–5 **gleeking and galling** scoffing
hurtfully. A compound verb, making a
unique use of the elsewhere transitive
gall (harass, chafe: *OED v.*[1] 6b).

76 **garb** manner (*OED sb.*[2] 3)

---

67 bye] *F (*Bu'y)*; bwy *Q*; be wi' *Rowe;* b'wi' *Cam*   68 SD *Exit*] *F; Exit Flewellen. Q*   69–80]
F; not in Q   71 begun] *Capell;* began *F*   72 trophy] *(*Trophee)

he could not therefore handle an English cudgel.
You find it otherwise, and henceforth let a Welsh correction teach you a good English condition. Fare ye
well.   *Exit.*

PISTOL

Doth Fortune play the huswife with me now?   81
News have I that my Nell is dead i'th' spital
Of malady of France,
And there my rendezvous is quite cut off.
Old I do wax, and from my weary limbs   85

---

79 **condition** disposition (*OED sb.* 11)
81 **play ... me** jilt me. *Huswife*
(pronounced 'hussif') was a common
pronunciation of 'housewife'. The
word (cf. 'merchant') could be used
in a familiar or derogatory sense (*OED
sb.* 2), becoming 'hussy' (*OED sb.* 3:
first instance 1647). Q's 'huswye' is
'huswyfe' with the *f* omitted. Cf. *AC*
4.16[15].46 ('the false hussy [F
Huswife] Fortune'), the references to
Fortune as a strumpet in *Ham* 2.2.238
and 496, and Dent, F 603.1.
82 ***my Nell** Johnson's emendation is
on the grounds that Pistol calls the
Hostess *my Nell* at 2.1.32 and speaks
of his *rendezvous* at l. 84 below. Shakespeare cannot have meant Doll Tearsheet, whom Pistol contemptuously
describes as being in the spital at
2.1.75–8: Gurr's explanation that
'Pistol, as the sole survivor of the
Eastcheap company, thought he had
acquired Falstaff's Doll as well as the
Hostess, and now knows she is gone
too' is unpersuasive. Nor is it likely
that Pistol is referring to the Hostess
as 'my doll' (i.e. my mistress: *OED
sb.*[1] 1: recorded from 1560), because
in *2H4* and *H5* Doll is always the
personal name of Doll Tearsheet. The
agreement of F and Q in reading
'Doll' may result either from F's compositor's consulting Q3 or from his

independent emending of *Nell* in his
copy because he had set 2.1 and
associated Doll with the spital (an
association which may also explain
Q's reading: 'Well *France* farwell,
newes haue I certainly / That Doll is
sicke. One mallydie of *France*').
83 **Of ... France** i.e. of syphilis, commonly known as the French disease
(*OED* French *a.* 6: example from J.
Sylvester, 1598). To omit the definite
article is in Pistol's histrionic style
(cf. 4.4.9, 'on point of fox'), and to
insert the indefinite article (F) is an
error because syphilis is not one of
several French diseases. Q's 'One' (=
On: cf. Q's spelling at 4.4.9, 'One
poynt of a foxe'), i.e. of, supports
Pope's emendation. J. C. Maxwell (in
Cam[1], 1955 edn) explains F's reading
by conjecturing that Shakespeare
wrote *a* (meaning *o*'), and that the
compositor, mistaking it for the
indefinite article, added *of.*
84 **my ... off** i.e. her death has 'deprived
him of a home' (Johnson)
85 **wax** grow
  limbs Pistol means his body in
general. It was his *pate* that Fluellen
beat (l. 42). In Q's version of the
passage ('Is honour cudgeld from my
warlike lines?') 'lines' is an easy error
for 'lims' (= limbs), though Q3
printed it as 'loynes'.

81] *verse Q; prose F* Doth] *(Doeth)* huswife] *F;* huswye *Q;* hussy *Oxf*[1] 82–8] *verse Capell;
prose F; verse (many variants) Q* 82 Nell] *Capell (Johnson); Doll F; Doll Q* 83 Of] *Pope; of a
F;* One *Q*

Honour is cudgelled. Well, bawd I'll turn,
And something lean to cutpurse of quick hand.
To England will I steal, and there I'll steal;
And patches will I get unto these cudgelled scars,
And swear I got them in the Gallia wars.   *Exit.*

[5.2]   *Enter at one door* KING HENRY, EXETER,
BEDFORD, WARWICK *and other Lords* [(GLOUCESTER,
WESTMORLAND, CLARENCE *and* HUNTINGDON)]. *At another,*
QUEEN ISABEL, *the* [FRENCH] KING, [KATHERINE, ALICE,]
the Duke of BURGUNDY, *and other French.*

86 **cudgelled** F's disyllabic form of the word, as opposed to Collier's tri-syllabic one, is allowable because the pause after this word corresponds to a metrical stress. Q also has the disyllabic form, though the verse is rewritten (cf. preceding note).

87 **something lean to** be somewhat inclined to become. Cf. *MV* 2.1.15–16, 'for indeed my father did something smack, something grow to; he had a kind of taste.'
  cutpurse ... hand a deft-handed cutpurse. In *MW* (2.1.18–19) Falstaff, repudiating Pistol, bids him take up this trade: 'a short knife and a throng'. Cf. Gower's 'a bawd, a cutpurse', 3.6.61.

88 **steal** The word-play (steal away; thieve) had been recently used in Dogberry's instructions to the watch, *MA* 3.3.57.

89 **And ... scars** Since the following line of the rhymed couplet is a pentameter, one would expect this line to be a pentameter too, not a hexameter. With some slurring it can be delivered

as such. On the other hand Q may preserve its correct form, if F's 'cudg-eld' was either recalled by the compositor from l. 86 or imperfectly deleted by Shakespeare if he revised 'And patches get unto these cudgelled scars' into 'And patches will I get unto these scars'.

90 **Gallia** So in Q and F. Shakespeare's only adjectival use of the noun: at *1H6* 5.6[4].139 and *Cym* 1.6.67 he has 'Gallian'. Cf. 'all Gallia', 1.2.217n.: Pistol's Gallic Wars, unlike Caesar's, have ended ingloriously.

5.2 Holinshed (3.572) reports how the French King and the Duke of Burgundy sent ambassadors to King Henry 'to moue him to peace', and that he, 'minding not to be reputed for a destroier of the countrie, which he coueted to preserue, or for a causer of christian bloud still to be spilt in his quarell', entered into negotiations. 'Now was the French king and his queene with their daughter Katharine at Trois in Champaigne gouerned and ordered by them, which

86 cudgelled] *F (*Cudgeld*); cudgellèd *Collier (subst.)* 89 these cudgelled] *F (*these cudgeld*);
these *Q* 90 swear] *Q;* swore *F*

5.2] *Hanmer* 0.1–5] *as F; Enter at one doore, the King of* England *and his Lords. And at the other
doore, the King of* France, *Queene* Katherine, *the Duke of* Burbon, *and others. Q* 0.2 GLOUCESTER]
Malone WESTMORLAND] *Capell* 0.3 CLARENCE] *Herford* HUNTINGDON] *Humphreys* 0.4
FRENCH] *Q (subst.)* KATHERINE] *Q* ALICE] *Capell* 0.5 BURGUNDY] *(Bourgongne)*

KING

Peace to this meeting, wherefore we are met.
Unto our brother France and to our sister
Health and fair time of day; joy and good wishes
To our most fair and princely cousin Katherine;
And, as a branch and member of this royalty,   5
By whom this great assembly is contrived,
We do salute you, Duke of Burgundy;
And, princes French and peers, health to you all.

FRENCH KING

Right joyous are we to behold your face,
Most worthy brother England; fairly met.   10

so much fauoured the duke of Burgognie, that they would not for anie
earthlie good, once hinder or pull
backe one iot of such articles as the
same duke should seeke to preferre.'
Accordingly a truce was declared,
King Henry's ambassadors were
received at Troyes, and it was agreed
that he should come himself, marry
Katharine, inherit the crown of
France after the French King's death
and be regent of France in the meantime. He came to Troyes on 20 May
1420, 'and there the king of England,
and the ladie Katharine were
affianced. After this, the two kings
and their councell assembled togither
diuerse daies, wherein the first concluded agreement was in diuerse
points altered and brought to a cer-
teinetie, according to the effect aboue
mentioned.' The marriage took place
on 2 June 1420 (3 June according to
Holinshed, 3.573).

0.1 The SD has been made consistent
with ll. 83–5.

1 **Peace ... met** 'Peace, for which we
are here met, be to this meeting'
(Johnson)

2 **brother** fellow monarch (*OED sb.* 6).
Cf. the courteous use of *sister* to

Queen Isabel and *cousin* to Katherine
and Burgundy.

3 **fair time of day** Cf. *LLL* 5.2.339,
'All hail, sweet madam, and fair time
of day!'

5 **royalty** body of royal persons (*OED
sb.* 4)

6 **By whom** refers to *you,* l. 7

7 **Duke of Burgundy** Holinshed
(3.560) records that in 1419 John,
Duke of Burgundy (see 4.8.98n.) was
treacherously murdered by assassins
acting for the Dauphin, i.e. Charles,
who had succeeded his brothers Louis
(see 5.0.35–42n.) and John in the title.
John of Burgundy was succeeded by
his son Philip (see 3.5.40–5n.). This
Burgundy should be played as a
young man, in view of the frankness
of his mirth in ll. 288–308, and his
being addressed as 'fair cousin' (l.
280). He was then twenty-four years
old, and King Henry thirty-three
years old.

9–10 **Right ... England** Capell's interpretation of F's punctuation is supported by the sense of Q's version:
'Brother of *England*, right ioyous are
we to behold / Your face, so are we
Princes English euery one.'

6] *F; not in Q* 7 Burgundy] *(Burgogne)* 8] *F; not in Q* 9+ SP] *Rowe; Fra.,* France. *F (except
316)* 9 face,] *F;* face; *Theobald* 10 England;] *Capell;* England, *F* met.] *Theobald (*met!*);* met,
F

So are you, princes English, every one.

QUEEN

So happy be the issue, brother England,
Of this good day and of this gracious meeting,
As we are now glad to behold your eyes,
Your eyes which hitherto have borne in them   15
Against the French that met them in their bent
The fatal balls of murdering basilisks.
The venom of such looks we fairly hope
Have lost their quality, and that this day
Shall change all griefs and quarrels into love.   20

KING

To cry amen to that, thus we appear.

QUEEN

You English princes all, I do salute you.

---

11 **So ... one** F's punctuation indicates
that the sense is 'So are all you
English princes' rather than 'So are
you, all you English princes' (which
would require an unmetrical stress on
you). Cf. 'You English princes all', l.
22. In Q's version (see 9–10n.) the
omission of 'fairly met' has necessi-
tated a change of pronoun.

12 **issue** outcome
*England Wilson suggests that F's
'Ireland' was Shakespeare's error
caused by his 'preoccupation with
Irish affairs', Walter that the manuscript spelling was 'Ingland' (a spelling twice found in the portion of
STM attributed to Shakespeare,
2.4.93, 151).

13 **gracious** happy, fortunate, prosperous (*OED a.* 7)

14 **behold your eyes** see you in person;
cf. *TC* 1.3.219, 'Do a fair message to
his kingly eyes' (Q; ears F), and *Ham*
4.7.43–4 (Hamlet's letter), 'Tomorrow shall I beg leave to see your
kingly eyes'. In the rest of the passage
eyes is used particularly, not in this

general complimentary sense equivalent to 'face'.

16 **bent** 'line of (a) sight, (b) fire'
(Wilson): *OED sb.*[2] 6a, 8

17 **balls** eyeballs (cf. *venom*, l. 18), with
word-play on cannon-balls (cf. word-
play on *basilisks*). The eyeball is
treated as a component of the eye, as
at *MV* 3.2.117.
basilisks (1) fabulous serpents (Gk
basiliskos, a serpent with a crown-like
crest on its head: Gk *basileus*, king)
whose eyes were death-dealing; (2)
large cannon, named after the serpent

18 **fairly** respectfully (*OED adv.* 2)

19 **Have ... quality** The plurals arise
from the sense 'We fairly hope *that*
such venomous looks'; cf. the construction in 'and that this day / Shall
change ...', where Gurr improbably
takes *that* to mean 'the loss of venom'
and to be the subject of *Shall*.
quality nature (*OED sb.* 8), i.e.
deadly nature

21 **cry amen** say 'so be it', i.e. assent:
cf. ll. 362–3

11] *Rowe;* So are you Princes (English) euery one *F*   12–22] *F; not in Q*   12 England] *F2;*
Ireland *F*   15–16] *as F2; F lines ... borne / ... bent,*   21+ SP] *Rowe (K. Hen.); Eng., England.*
F

BURGUNDY

My duty to you both, on equal love,
Great Kings of France and England. That I have
    laboured
With all my wits, my pains and strong endeavours,   25
To bring your most imperial majesties
Unto this bar and royal interview
Your mightiness on both parts best can witness.
Since then my office hath so far prevailed
That face to face and royal eye to eye   30
You have congreeted, let it not disgrace me
If I demand before this royal view
What rub or what impediment there is
Why that the naked, poor and mangled peace,
Dear nurse of arts, plenties and joyful births,   35
Should not in this best garden of the world,

23 **on** from
24–8 **That ... witness** Holinshed (cf. first note on this scene) mentions Burgundy's part in negotiating a settlement, but without this Shakespearean emphasis.
27 **bar** court (*OED sb.*[1] 23: an extension of *sb.*[1] 22, the barrier separating the judge's seat from the rest of the court of law), i.e. place of meeting to agree terms of peace
   interview face-to-face meeting (the basic sense: *OED sb.* 1)
28 **mightiness** mightinesses. For the dropping of the final syllable of words in which the singular ends in -*s*, see Abbott, 471.
   on both parts 'Burgundy makes his speech from centre stage' (Gurr)
29 **Since then** since therefore; not 'since that time' (as Gurr takes it)
30 **face ... eye** The expression, here applied to a peaceful meeting, suggests also their former warlike relationship. Cf. *R2* 1.1.15–16, 'Face

to face / And frowning brow to brow'.
31 **congreeted** greeted each other. *OED*'s first example: perhaps a Shakespearean coinage. Cf. *Congreeing*, 1.2.182.
   disgrace misbecome
32 **demand** enquire
33 **rub** obstacle: cf. 2.2.189. Synonymous with *impediment*, and with *let* (l. 65)
34, 65 **peace** Peace is personified throughout this speech. Contrast ll. 68, 70, 75.
35 **nurse** nourisher (*OED sb.*[1] 1d: the literal sense behind this figurative one is a woman who suckles a child)
   plenties 'things that constitute "plenty"; the necessaries and comforts of life' (*OED* plenty *sb.* 3b)
36 **this ... world** Cf. Epilogue 7, 'the world's best garden'. Shakespeare may have derived the expression from John Florio's proverb in *Second Fruits*, 1591, '*La Lombardia è il giardino del mondo*', which he adapted in *TS* 1.1.3–4.

23–67] *F;* With pardon vnto both your mightines. / Let it not displease you, if I demaund / What rub or bar hath thus far hindred you, / To keepe you from the gentle speech of peace? *Q* 23 love,] *Pope;* loue. *F* 24 England.] *Pope;* England: *F* 31 congreeted, let] *F (*congreeted: let*);* congreeted. Let *Cam*[2]

347

Our fertile France, put up her lovely visage?
Alas, she hath from France too long been chased,
And all her husbandry doth lie on heaps,
Corrupting in it own fertility.   40
Her vine, the merry cheerer of the heart,
Unpruned dies; her hedges even-pleached,
Like prisoners wildly overgrown with hair,
Put forth disordered twigs; her fallow leas
The darnel, hemlock and rank fumitory   45
Doth root upon, while that the coulter rusts
That should deracinate such savagery.
The even mead, that erst brought sweetly forth
The freckled cowslip, burnet and green clover,

37 **put up** lift up, i.e. show

39 **on** in: cf. 4.5.18

40 **it** Three forms of the possessive case neuter were in use: *his* (the most frequent in Shakespeare), *it* (less frequent) and *its* (rare).

41–54 **Her vine ... hedges** Perhaps reflecting the aspects of farming dealt with in the four books of Virgil's *Georgics*: crops in Book 1, vines in Book 2, pastures in Book 3 and hedges (related to bee-keeping) in Book 4 (J. H. Betts, *N&Q*, 25 (1978): 134–6). Alternatively, the list may be spontaneous, the first item, vines, being specially appropriate to France, and the others such as the English countryside would suggest.

41 **the merry ... heart** Cf. Psalms 104:15, 'wine that maketh glad the heart of man'. Also proverbial: 'Good wine makes a merry heart' (Tilley, W 460).

42 **Unpruned** Unprunèd
dies In view of ll. 39–40 there is no need to emend to 'lies' (Warburton's conjecture, because 'neglect of pruning does not kill the vine', etc.)
hedges even-pleached evenly interwoven hedges. To pleach or plash is to weave living boughs to make a

fence. Oxf[1] reads 'even-plashed' here, but since a plash is a puddle in *TS* 1.1.23 it is better to retain F's 'pleached' (as in *MA* 1.2.8, 3.1.7 and *AC* 4.15[14].73).

44 **fallow leas** arable fields (*OED* fallow *a.*[2] c, 'fit for tillage'; lea *sb.*[1]). Cf. l. 54.

45–6 **The darnel ... upon** Cf. *KL* 4.3[4].3–6, 'Crowned with rank fumitor and furrow-weeds, / With burdocks, hemlock, nettles, cuckooflowers, / Darnel, and all the idle weeds that grow / In our sustaining corn.' *Doth* is 'singular, as agreeing with the last, or because the three words form only one notion' (Moore Smith).

45 **darnel** rye-grass
rank over-abundant

46 **coulter** iron blade fixed in front of the ploughshare

47 **deracinate** uproot (cf. *TC* 1.3.99). *OED*'s first example of this latinate word.
savagery wild vegetation (*OED* sb. 4: the only citation in this sense)

48 **even mead** level meadow
erst formerly

49 **freckled** spotted. Cf. *MND* 2.1.11–13.
burnet the lesser or salad burnet, a

42 dies] *F;* lies *Theobald (Warburton)* even-pleached] *F (*euen pleach'd*);* even-plashed *Oxf[1]*
45 fumitory] *(*Femetary*)*

Wanting the scythe, all uncorrected, rank,   50
Conceives by idleness, and nothing teems
But hateful docks, rough thistles, kecksies, burrs,
Losing both beauty and utility.
And as our vineyards, fallows, meads and hedges,
Defective in their natures, grow to wildness,   55
Even so our houses and our selves and children
Have lost, or do not learn for want of time,
The sciences that should become our country,
But grow like savages, as soldiers will

low-growing plant with crimson flowers and leaf-stalks. Shakespeare's only reference to it.

50 *all uncorrected utterly uncultivated. F's 'withall' may have originated in a misreading of 'cyth [scythe] all' as 'wyth all' (J. Jowett in *TxC*, 383).

51 Conceives by idleness grows fruitful by lying idle; possibly with a sexual metaphor, i.e. 'idleness fathers the weeds' (Wilson). That idleness is the mother of vice was proverbial (Tilley, I 13).
nothing teems gives birth to nothing (*OED* teem *v.*[1] 1). The end of the sentence (l. 53) confirms this transitive sense – the only Shakespearean one, though Taylor gives 'nothing abounds' as an alternative sense, and Gurr gives 'flourishes' as the only sense of *teems*.

52 kecksies kexes, i.e. dry hollow stems, especially of such large umbelliferous plants as wild chervil. *OED*'s first example of kecksy (next in 1800; found also in dialect dictionaries, so unlikely to be a Shakespearean coinage), probably a singular noun formed by taking the plural kexes as kexies.

54 *And as Capell's emendation, together with the substitution of a comma for F's full stop at the end of

l. 55. F's punctuation shows that the compositor mistook Burgundy's recapitulation for a continuation, and that he consciously or unconsciously emended *as* to *all*. Taylor's defence of F's 'And all' (he accepts Capell's repunctuation of l. 55) as meaning 'If all' is unconvincing: he produces no example of *An* (= if) in the sense 'just as'.
fallows arable lands (*OED sb.* 1)

55 Defective ... natures being by nature degenerate (i.e. as a result of the Fall of Man). Cf. l. 62, *unnatural*.
grow proceed. The literal sense is also present.

56 houses households
our selves Since *our* applies to both *selves* and *children*, F's reading is preferable to the modern combination *ourselves*, which leaves *children* without a possessive.

58 sciences knowledges, i.e. skills, arts
become adorn, grace

59–62 But grow ... unnatural There is a double construction here: 'But grow like savages' has a self-contained sense, i.e. 'but become like savages'; 'But grow [...] / To swearing' has the sense 'but proceed to swearing'. In view of the fact that 'as soldiers will ... blood' is a parenthesis, 'like savages' cannot be treated as another parenthesis.

50 scythe] *(Sythe)* all] *Rowe³;* withall *F*   52 kecksies] *(Keksyes)*   54 And as] *Capell (R. Roderick);* And all *F;* An all *Oxf¹*   55 natures] *F;* nurtures *Theobald (Warburton)*   wildness,] *Capell (subst.);* wildnesse. *F*   56 our selves] *F;* ourselves *Johnson*

That nothing do but meditate on blood,   60
To swearing and stern looks, diffused attire,
And everything that seems unnatural.
Which to reduce into our former favour
You are assembled; and my speech entreats
That I may know the let why gentle peace   65
Should not expel these inconveniences
And bless us with her former qualities.

KING

If, Duke of Burgundy, you would the peace
Whose want gives growth to th'imperfections
Which you have cited, you must buy that peace   70
With full accord to all our just demands,
Whose tenors and particular effects
You have, enscheduled briefly, in your hands.

BURGUNDY

The King hath heard them, to the which as yet
There is no answer made.

KING   Well then, the peace   75
Which you before so urged lies in his answer.

FRENCH KING

I have but with a cursitory eye

60 **nothing ... blood** think of nothing but bloodshed.
61 **diffused** disorderly, disordered (*OED ppl. a.* 1)
63 **reduce** lead back, restore
  our former favour 'the comeliness or decency which formerly prevailed among us' (Deighton): *OED* favour *sb.* 9: appearance, aspect, look.
65 **let** hindrance
66 **inconveniences** harms, mischiefs (*OED sb.* 3). Cf. *1H6* 1.5[4].14, 'To intercept this inconvenience', the only other Shakespearean occurrence.
68 **would** desire. Cf. 4.1.32.
69 **imperfections** (five syllables)
72–3 **Whose ... hands** 'Whose general purport as well as their particular applications you have in your hands, briefly written out for you' (Moore Smith)
72 **tenors** The *tenor* of something written or spoken is the course of meaning which continues through it (*OED sb.* 1: F's 'Tenures' is a variant form of the word).
73 **enscheduled** listed in a schedule (*OED*'s only example). A schedule is a slip or scroll of paper containing writing: cf. *2H4* 4.1.166–7, *MV* 2.9.54.
77 *****cursitory** cursory. *OED*'s first example is from 1632, 'but it derives easily from *cursitor* (= courier,

61 diffused] *(defus'd)*   68 Burgundy] *(Burgonie)*   68–70 you ... must] *F; you wold haue peace, / You must Q*   71–3] *F; According as we haue drawne our articles. Q*   72 tenors] *(Tenures)*   74–6] *F; not in Q*   75–6] *as Pope; F lines ... made. / ... vrg'd /*   77 cursitory] *Cam¹; curselarie F; cursenary Q; cursorary Q3*

O'er-glanced the articles. Pleaseth your grace
To appoint some of your council presently
To sit with us once more, with better heed   80
To re-survey them, we will suddenly
Pass our accept and peremptory answer.

KING

Brother, we shall. – Go, uncle Exeter,
And brother Clarence, and you, brother Gloucester,
Warwick and Huntingdon, go with the King,   85
And take with you free power to ratify,
Augment or alter, as your wisdoms best
Shall see advantageable for our dignity,
Anything in or out of our demands,

running messenger: *sb.* 2, 1571 +)'
(Taylor, who points out that 'Q1's
cursenary could easily arise from compositorial error, *n* and *t* adjoining in
the type case').
78 **articles** items listed in the schedule,
i.e. conditions of peace
Pleaseth if it please. The indicative,
rather than subjunctive, form is used
here, probably for metrical reasons.
Cf. *CE* 4.1.12.
79 **presently** at this present time; cf.
3.2.54
81 **suddenly** in a very short time. Cf.
1H4 1.3.288, 'When time is ripe,
which will be suddenly'.
82 **Pass ... answer** formally give the
answer that we (i.e. I) have adopted
as final
Pass pronounce (*OED v.* 52)
accept accepted (*OED ppl. a.*, last
example)
peremptory final (*OED* 1b); stressed
on the first syllable
85 **Huntingdon** a non-speaking part.
John Holland (1395–1447), son of the
Earl of Huntingdon who was executed
after the Abbot of Westminster's

abortive plot to assassinate Henry IV
and restore Richard II (and whose
part in the plot is mentioned by Holinshed, but not by Shakespeare in
R2), was restored to his father's title
after distinguishing himself at Agincourt, and took part in King Henry's
second French campaign. He appears
in no other of Shakespeare's history
plays. Taylor suggests that he may
have been prominent in earlier plays
on Henry V's reign, as he is in *Sir
John Oldcastle* (later in 1599), and
hence familiar to the audience; on the
other hand, Shakespeare may simply
have noted his name in Holinshed
and remembered it when he wanted
to enlarge the list of persons here
addressed. Though his name is
usually omitted in editions and cast
lists, the more persons leave the stage
the better. The audience will not
recognize individuals and notice
Bedford's omission from ll. 83–5.

88 **advantageable** advantageous. Recorded by *OED* from 1548 to 1657, but
used only here by Shakespeare, who
twice elsewhere has *advantageous*.

81 re-survey] *F2;* re-saruey *F*   82 Pass ... and] *F;* Pass, or accept, and *Theobald (Warburton);*
returne our *Q*   83–98] *F;* Go Lords, and sit with them, / And bring vs answere backe. / Yet
leaue our cousen *Katherine* here behind. / *France.* Withall our hearts. *Q*   84 Clarence] *F;* Bedford
Cam²   85 Warwick and] *F;* Westmorland, *Cam²*   Huntingdon] *Capell;* Huntington *F*

And we'll consign thereto. – Will you, fair sister,   90
Go with the princes, or stay here with us?

QUEEN

Our gracious brother, I will go with them.
Haply a woman's voice may do some good
When articles too nicely urged be stood on.

KING

Yet leave our cousin Katherine here with us: 95
She is our capital demand, comprised
Within the fore-rank of our articles.

QUEEN

She hath good leave.

Exeunt all but King and Katherine [and Alice].

KING   Fair Katherine, and most fair,
Will you vouchsafe to teach a soldier terms
Such as will enter at a lady's ear   100
And plead his love-suit to her gentle heart?

KATHERINE   Your majesty shall mock at me; I cannot
speak your England.

KING   O fair Katherine, if you will love me soundly

---

90 **consign** subscribe, assent (*OED v.* 5: peculiar to Shakespeare in this intransitive sense 'consign to'). Cf. l. 296.
94 **When ... stood on** 'i.e. When men get to quarrelling about straws' (Wilson). For *stood on*, cf. 3.6.73.
nicely with insistence on detail, strictly (*OED adv.* 5a)
96 **capital** chief
97 **fore-rank** front row. Cf. Holinshed, 3.573: '1. First, it is accorded betweene our father and vs, that forsomuch as by the bond of matrimonie made for the good of the peace between vs and our most deere beloued Katharine, daughter of our said father, & of our most deere mother Isabell his wife; the same Charles and Isabell beene made our father and mother: therefore them as

our father and moother we shall haue and worship, as it fitteth and seemeth so worthie a prince and princesse to be worshipped, principallie before all other temporall persons of the world.'
98–277 There is a comparable wooing scene in *Famous Victories*.
98 **Fair Katherine** Cf. *2H4* Epilogue 26–7: 'and make you merry with fair Catherine of France'. Cf. also *Famous Victories* (scene xviii: l. 1,361), 'How now faire Ladie *Katheren* of *France*'.
102 **shall mock** At l. 169 F has 'sould' for 'should' and at l. 247 'sall' for 'shall' in Katherine's speeches, but (as with Fluellen's) there is no need to print her pronunciation as consistently unorthodox. The point here is the unidiomatic tense of the verb.

---

93 Haply] *F2 (*Happely*);* Happily *F*   98 SD] *Q (Exit King and the Lords. Manet* Hrry*, Katherine, and the Gentlewoman.); Exeunt omnes . / Manet King and Katherine. F*   98–137 Fair ... strength.] *F;* Now *Kate*, you haue a blunt wooer here / Left with you. *Q*

with your French heart I will be glad to hear you   105
confess it brokenly with your English tongue. Do you
like me, Kate?

KATHERINE   *Pardonnez-moi*, I cannot tell vat is 'like
me'.

KING   An angel is like you, Kate, and you are like an   110
angel.

KATHERINE   *Que dit-il, que je suis semblable à les anges?*

ALICE   *Oui, vraiment, sauf votre grâce, ainsi dit-il.*

KING   I said so, dear Katherine, and I must not blush
to affirm it.   115

KATHERINE   *O bon Dieu, les langues des hommes sont
pleines de tromperies!*

KING   What says she, fair one? That the tongues of men
are full of deceits?

ALICE   *Oui*, dat de tongues of de mans is be full of   120
deceits: dat is de Princess.

---

107 **Kate** The familiar and abbreviated
form of *Katherine* indicates the informal style of King Henry's courtship.
Hotspur in *1H4* likewise calls Lady
Percy *Kate*: her name in Holinshed
is Elianor (inaccurately: it was really
Elizabeth). Shakespeare's apparent
fondness for *Kate* in such dialogues
may have originated in *TS*. That *Kate*
is also 'a name associated with pro-
miscuous women' (Taylor, giving
examples) is irrelevant.

108 *Pardonnez-moi* 'Excuse me' (for not
understanding)
vat Here, and at ll. 177 and 260, F
has 'wat'. In *MW* Doctor Caius nine
times has *vat* in the F text of his part.

112–13 *Que ... dit-il* 'What does he say,
that I am like the angels?' 'Yes, truly,
save your grace, he says so.'

114 **I said so** i.e. those were my words

116–17 *O ... tromperies* 'O good God,
the tongues of men are full of deceits!'

118 **fair one** 'This may be flattery, or
Shakespeare may have forgotten that

Alice is "an old gentlewoman" [3.4.0]'
(Taylor). The latter is the more likely
explanation: otherwise the address
may seem ironical rather than flattering. At l. 258 the King calls Alice
'Madam my interpreter'. If Alice is
played as an old gentlewoman,
'madam' may be appropriately substituted in this speech. Editors before
Capell perhaps regard this 'Lady' as
a different person from Alice, but if
so they do not list her among the
characters.

120 *tongues F's 'tongeus' has been
defended (Oxf[1]) as representing a
foreign speaker's attempt to pronounce the final redundant vowels,
and as an unlikely technical error for
Compositor A to make; but since it
is hard to see how 'tongeus' would
actually be pronounced, and there is
ample linguistic eccentricity in the
speech without it, F2's emendation is
accepted here.

121 **dat is de Princess** This statement,

---

108 *Pardonnez-moi] (Pardonne moy)* vat] *(wat)*   113+ SP ALICE] *Capell; Lady F, Q (259,*
265)   113, 265 *vraiment] (verayment)*   117 *pleines] Pope; plein F*   120 tongues] *F2; tongeus F*
121 is de Princess] *F; is de Princess say Keightley; is say de Princess (Oxf[1])*

KING   The Princess is the better Englishwoman. I'faith,
Kate, my wooing is fit for thy understanding. I am
glad thou canst speak no better English, for if thou
couldst thou wouldst find me such a plain king that   125
thou wouldst think I had sold my farm to buy my
crown. I know no ways to mince it in love but directly
to say 'I love you.' Then if you urge me farther than
to say 'Do you in faith?', I wear out my suit. Give
me your answer, i'faith do, and so clap hands and a   130
bargain. How say you, lady?

KATHERINE   *Sauf votre honneur*, me understand vell.

as given in F, is sometimes delivered
as though it meant 'It is just like
the Princess to say that'; but this
anticipates the King's reply, so it is
better if it is simply given as an
affirmative statement (in which case,
the verb *say* – after *is* rather than after
Princess – may have been accidentally
omitted).

122 **the better Englishwoman** the
more an Englishwoman (i.e. for dis-
trusting flattery)

123 **thy** At this point the King first
uses the more familiar second person
singular pronoun, which hereafter
predominates, though *you* is still used
on occasion.

127 **mince it** *OED* (mince *v.* 4d) gives
this passage as an example of the
sense 'moderate (one's language)', but
v. 6 ('to walk in an affected manner')
is far more probably the (figurative)
sense: cf. Hotspur's disdain of
'mincing poetry', *1H4* 3.1.130.

127–8 **but ... say** This phrase involves
a change of construction, as if the
sentence began 'I know no other ways
to declare my love'.

128–9 **than to say** than by saying

129 **I ... suit** word-play: (1) I exhaust
my courtship, (2) I wear out my
clothes. Cf. the same word-play on
suit as petition/coat in *AYL* 2.5.43–
4.

130–1 **clap ... bargain** a proverbial

phrase for agreeing a transaction
(Dent, H 109.1). Cf. *WT* 1.2.105–6,
'open thy white hand / And clap
thyself my love.'

132 **me understand vell** Keightley's
conjecture that a negative is omitted
in F is attractive and probably right:
'*Sauf votre honneur*' is deferential and
apologetic (cf. l. 187, and 3.4.34, 43).
If F is right, Katherine's statement
must imply some reservation, i.e. 'I
understand your proposal, but I need
time to think it over.' If Keightley is
right, she is postponing her acceptance by taking refuge in her limited
understanding of English. Taylor
comments on F's reading 'This is
probably intended as Catherine's
error; her actual incomprehension
when confronted by Henry's hand is
easily communicable on stage'; but
the omission of a negative is not a
linguistic error. Gurr's suggestion that
there is 'a concealed pun on the
French "*entendre*", (1) to understand,
(2) to agree, make a bargain', is unconvincing, for his second sense is the
reflexive verb *s'entendre*.

*vell Consistency with *vat* (cf. 108n.)
justifies Capell's emendation. In F
MW Doctor Caius twice uses the
form *vell* (1.4.73, 2.3.87) and once,
presumably by an oversight, the form
well (2.3.7).

132 vell] *Capell;* well *F;* not well *Keightley*

KING   Marry, if you would put me to verses or to dance
for your sake, Kate, why, you undid me: for the one I
have neither words nor measure, and for the other I   135
have no strength in measure, yet a reasonable measure
in strength. If I could win a lady at leapfrog, or by
vaulting into my saddle with my armour on my back,
under the correction of bragging be it spoken, I should
quickly leap into a wife. Or if I might buffet for my   140
love or bound my horse for her favours, I could lay
on like a butcher and sit like a jackanapes, never off.
But before God, Kate, I cannot look greenly nor
gasp out my eloquence, nor I have no cunning in
protestation, only downright oaths, which I never use   145

134 **you undid me** you would ruin me
(i.e. as a suitor): the subjunctive mood
(Abbott, 361)
135 **neither ... measure** neither poetic
language nor metre (*OED* measure *sb*.
16)
136 **no strength in measure** no ability
in the dance (*OED* measure *sb*. 20)
136–7 **a reasonable ... strength** a
reasonable amount of physical
strength
137–42 **If ... never off** Cf. Holinshed,
3.583: 'In strength and nimbleness of
bodie from his youth few to him
comparable, for in wrestling, leaping,
and running, no man well able to
compare.'
137 **leapfrog** a game in which the
players vault over each other's bent
backs. The equivocal sexual sense of
leap, as of *vault* (*OED* v.² 1b), is
delayed until the phrase 'leap into a
wife'.
138 **vaulting ... back** Cf. *1H4* 4.1.105–
11, where Vernon praises Prince
Henry for this feat.
139 **under ... spoken** i.e. though I say
it that should not
140 **leap ... wife** word-play: (1) gain a
wife by my leaping, (2) possess a wife
sexually, copulate with her (*OED* leap

v. 9); cf. 'leaping-houses', *1H4* 1.2.9
buffet box: 'To deal blows, fight,
contend, struggle' (*OED* v. 2, citing
this passage)
140–1 **for my love** to win my beloved
141 **bound my horse** make my horse
bound (*OED* bound v.² 3)
favours goodwill, favour (*OED* sb. 1,
citing *TN* 1.4.7 as an instance of
plural form with singular sense)
141–2 **lay on** deal blows vigorously
(*OED* lay v. 55b)
142 **like a butcher** i.e. felling a beast
with his pole-axe
sit ... off stick to my horse as firmly
as a performing monkey trained to
be carried on a horse's back. Wilson
cites the popular name for a species
of flower, jackanapes-on-horseback
(*OED* jackanapes *sb*. 5: from 1577) as
evidence that the allusion would be
understood.
143 **look greenly** gaze at you like a
lovesick youth. In Shakespeare *green*
is often associated with sickness (e.g.
TN 2.4.113, *Mac* 1.7.37) and with
immaturity (cf. 2.4.136, 'his greener
days').
144–5 **cunning in protestation** skill in
solemnly affirming my love

137–40 If ... wife.] *F*; If I could win thee at leapfrog, / Or with vawting with my armour on
my backe, / Into my saddle, / Without brag be it spoken, / Ide make compare with any. *Q*
142 jackanapes] *(*Iack an Apes*)*

till urged, nor never break for urging. If thou canst
love a fellow of this temper, Kate, whose face is not
worth sunburning, that never looks in his glass for love
of anything he sees there, let thine eye be thy cook. I
speak to thee plain soldier. If thou canst love me for   150
this, take me; if not, to say to thee that I shall die is
true; but for thy love, by the Lord, no; yet I love thee
too. And while thou liv'st, dear Kate, take a fellow of
plain and uncoined constancy, for he perforce must do
thee right, because he hath not the gift to woo in other   155
places; for these fellows of infinite tongue, that can
rhyme themselves into ladies' favours, they do always
reason themselves out again. What, a speaker is but a
prater, a rhyme is but a ballad. A good leg will fall, a
straight back will stoop, a black beard will turn white,   160
a curled pate will grow bald, a fair face will wither, a
full eye will wax hollow; but a good heart, Kate, is the
sun and the moon, or rather the sun and not the moon,

146 **for urging** however much I may be
urged (by others) to do so
147 **temper** condition
147–8 **not worth sunburning** not fair-
complexioned enough for the sun to
be able to spoil. Cf. 'sun-burnt', *MA*
2.1.299, *TC* 1.3.279.
149 **be thy cook** 'i.e. dress the dish for
you' (Wilson)
150 **plain soldier** plainly, in a soldier's
fashion. Other instances of *speak* with
a noun used adverbially include *MW*
3.2.62 ('he speaks holiday') and *AYL*
3.2.209–10 ('Speak sad brow and true
maid').
150–1 **If ... this** Cf. ll. 146–7, 'If thou
canst love a fellow of this temper'.
Taylor improbably multiplies meanings: 'i.e. my plainness (behavioural
or facial); perhaps pointing to his
face'.
153 **while thou liv'st** a common
expression of advice, e.g. *1H4* 3.1.59
154 **uncoined** i.e. in its natural state.
The implied contrast is between
bullion and minted coin. There is no
need to extend the metaphor to the
rest of the sentence as most modern
editors do, e.g. 'not being current
he cannot be spent anywhere else'
(Gurr).
157 **rhyme** Cf. l. 133, 'put me to verses'.
'Neither rhyme nor reason' (cf. ll.
157–8) is proverbial (Tilley, R 98).
158 **What** an exclamation, here equivalent to 'when all is said and done'
158–9 **a speaker ... prater** an orator
(commendatory) is merely a talker
(derogatory)
159 **ballad** i.e. a popular, and therefore
despised, type of poem
fall waste away (*OED v.* 14)
162 **wax** grow, become (*OED v.* 9). The
usual opposition to 'wane', especially
of the moon (*v.* 6), leads on to the
remainder of the sentence.
162–3 **the sun and the moon** i.e. everything that gives light to the world,
i.e. makes life worth living

152 Lord] *F (*L.*), Q (*Lord*)   160 straight] *(strait)*

for it shines bright and never changes, but keeps his
course truly. If thou would have such a one, take me;   165
and take me, take a soldier; take a soldier, take a king.
And what sayst thou then to my love? Speak, my
fair, and fairly, I pray thee.

KATHERINE   Is it possible dat I sould love de enemy of
France?   170

KING   No, it is not possible you should love the enemy
of France, Kate: but in loving me you should love
the friend of France; for I love France so well that I
will not part with a village of it; I will have it all
mine: and Kate, when France is mine, and I am   175
yours, then yours is France, and you are mine.

KATHERINE   I cannot tell vat is dat.

KING   No, Kate? I will tell thee in French, which I am
sure will hang upon my tongue like a new-married
wife about her husband's neck, hardly to be shook off.   180

---

164 **his** its
166 **and take ... king** 'and in taking me
you take a soldier, and in taking a
soldier you take a king'. The sense of
the first part of this statement is clear,
that of the second part less clear. It
may mean that a soldier is by definition a king among men (*OED* king
sb. 6), but if so it associates awkwardly
with the fact that the speaker is literally a king. Shakespeare may be
echoing a piece of Hall's rhetoric
(112): 'This capitaine was a shepherde
whom his flocke loued and louyngly
obeyed. This shepherd was such a
iusticiary that no offence was vnpunished nor friendship vnrewarded.
This iusticiary was so feared, that all
rebellion was banished and sedicion
suppressed.'
168 **fairly** propitiously. Cf. l. 10, 'fairly
met'.
169–70 **Is it ... France?** Cf. *Famous
Victories* (scene xviii: ll. 1,384–6), 'But

tell me, canst thou loue the king of
England? / *Kate.* How should I loue
him, that hath dealt so hardly / With
my father', and (scene xx: ll. 1,536–
7): 'How saist thou *Kate*, canst thou
loue the King of England? / *Kate.*
How should I loue thee, which is my
fathers enemy?'
de enemy of France Taylor discusses whether F's spellings 'ennemie' and 'Fraunce' indicate that the
words are intended as French ones.
Since the words are essentially the
same in both languages, and since
Katherine undoubtedly says everything with a French accent, the question is not one of practical importance. The article 'de' (= the)
implies that Katherine means to speak
English, as does Q's reading 'de
enemie de *France*' (¹de = the; ²de =
of).
172 **you should** you would (i.e. you
would be loving)

169–70 de ... France] *F (de ennemie of Fraunce)*; de *ennemi* of France *Oxf¹*   177 vat] *(wat)*

357

Je, quand j'ai le possession de France, et quand vous avez
le possession de moi – let me see, what then? Saint Denis
be my speed! – *donc votre est France, et vous êtes mienne.*
It is as easy for me, Kate, to conquer the kingdom as to
speak so much more French. I shall never move thee   185
in French, unless it be to laugh at me.

KATHERINE   *Sauf votre honneur, le français que vous*
parlez, il est meilleur que l'anglais lequel je parle.

KING   No, faith, is't not, Kate; but thy speaking of my
tongue, and I thine, most truly-falsely, must needs   190
be granted to be much at one. But Kate, dost thou
understand thus much English? 'Canst thou love me?'

KATHERINE   I cannot tell.

KING   Can any of your neighbours tell, Kate? I'll ask
them. Come, I know thou lovest me, and at night,   195

181–3 *Je . . . mienne* 'I, when I have the possession of France, and when you have the possession of me [. . .], then yours is France, and you are mine.' In F's version the first words mean 'I when on the possession', and in Fuzier's version (see 181n.) 'I when [I] am the possessor'.

181 ***Je, quand j'ai le possession** The symmetry of ll. 175–6 ('when France . . . are mine') strongly suggests that the French version should be equally symmetrical and therefore that F's *possession* is right: contrast Jean Fuzier's emendation (*SQ*, 32 (1981): 97–100: see textual notes). A misreading of *Jay* as *sur* is possible (cf. *se* for *Je* at 4.4.55), though not as easy as a misreading of *suis*. A comic point can be made by halting after the pronoun *Je* at the very beginning of the sentence, and this may have been Shakespeare's intention. The incorrect gender (*le*) may also be meant as the speaker's 'false French', especially as it occurs twice. Q's version is too free to be helpful.

182 **Saint Denis** the patron saint of France

183 **be my speed** help me (a common expression: Dent, SS 17)

184 **the kingdom** i.e. all France, as distinct from Harfleur, captured in his first campaign (3.3), and most of Normandy, captured in his second (omitted, cf. 5.0.41–2n.)

187–8 **Sauf . . . parle** 'Saving your honour, the French that you speak, it is better than the English the which I speak.'

190 **and I thine** i.e. and my speaking of thine
     truly-falsely sincerely and incorrectly (with word-play on both words)

191 **much at one** much in agreement, i.e. much alike

193 **I cannot tell** Katherine's reply, and the King's rejoinder, show that 'Canst thou love me?' has been put to her as a direct question, not as a four-word English phrase.

194 **Can . . . tell** 'A jocular way of saying, "If you can't, no one else can"' (Deighton)

---

181 *Je . . . possession*] *this edn; Ie quand sur le possession* F; *quand j'ay le possession* Pope; *Je quand suis le possesseur* Oxf¹ *(J. Fuzier)*   187–8 *que . . . est*] *(ques vous parlez, il* &)   188 *meilleur*] *Rowe (melieur); melieus* F   *lequel*] *(le quel)*   190 truly-falsely] *(truely falsely)*

when you come into your closet, you'll question this
gentlewoman about me; and I know, Kate, you will to
her dispraise those parts in me that you love with your
heart: but, good Kate, mock me mercifully, the rather,
gentle Princess, because I love thee cruelly. If ever thou   200
be'st mine, Kate, as I have a saving faith within me
tells me thou shalt, I get thee with scambling, and thou
must therefore needs prove a good soldier-breeder.
Shall not thou and I, between Saint Denis and Saint
George, compound a boy, half French, half English,   205
that shall go to Constantinople and take the Turk by
the beard? Shall we not? What sayst thou, my fair
flower-de-luce?

KATHERINE   I do not know dat.

KING   No, 'tis hereafter to know, but now to promise: 210
do but now promise, Kate, you will endeavour for your
French part of such a boy, and for my English moiety
take the word of a king and a bachelor. How answer
you, *la plus belle Katherine du monde, mon très cher et
divin déesse?*   215

196 **closet** private room (*OED sb.* 1), not
necessarily a bedroom
200 **cruelly** extremely (*OED* 4): 'to make
a contrast to *mercifully*' (Moore
Smith)
201 **a saving faith** a faith sufficient to
salvation (*OED* saving *ppl. a.* 2); here
used humorously
202 **I get** I shall have got
scambling struggling, i.e. fighting a
war
204 **between** by the combined help of
(*OED* 13)
206-7 **shall ... beard** 'To drive the
Turk from Constantinople was, pro-
fessedly, the dearest wish of all sixteenth-century Christian princes.
That the Turk did not capture it until
1453, 31 years after Henry's death,
made no odds to Shakespeare, even if
he knew it. That the "boy" turned
out to be Henry VI was the point he
desired to suggest' (Wilson).

208 **flower-de-luce** fleur-de-lys (lily
flower), the arms of France being
golden lilies on a blue field. The
English form of the word was standard (e.g. *WT* 4.4.127). 'An actor
might prefer to modernize, as the
anglicized form now sounds like a
blunder' (Taylor).
212 **moiety** half
213 **bachelor** (young) unmarried man
214-15 *la plus ... déesse* 'the most fair
Katherine of the world, my very dear
and divine goddess'. This is the only
occasion when *la* appears in F's text
of the play: elsewhere always *le* irre-
spective of gender.
mon ... déesse Since F has *ma foy*
(3.4.8; *may foy*, 5.2.250-1), *ma lecon*
(3.4.52) and *ma vie* (3.5.11, 4.4.42,
4.5.3), there is evidently false French
in *mon*, and the false agreement of
the masculine adjective *divin* would
be audible in speech.

202 scambling] *F*; scrambling *Oxf¹*   214-15 *très cher et divin*] *(trescher & deuin)*

KATHERINE   Your majesty 'ave *fausse* French enough
to deceive de most *sage demoiselle* dat is *en France*.
KING   Now fie upon my false French! By mine honour,
in true English, I love thee, Kate: by which honour I
dare not swear thou lovest me, yet my blood begins to   220
flatter me that thou dost, notwithstanding the poor and
untempering effect of my visage. Now beshrew my
father's ambition! He was thinking of civil wars when
he got me: therefore was I created with a stubborn
outside, with an aspect of iron, that when I come to   225
woo ladies I fright them. But in faith, Kate, the elder
I wax the better I shall appear. My comfort is that old
age, that ill layer-up of beauty, can do no more spoil
upon my face. Thou hast me, if thou hast me, at the
worst; and thou shalt wear me, if thou wear me, better   230
and better. And therefore tell me, most fair Katherine,
will you have me? Put off your maiden blushes, avouch
the thoughts of your heart with the looks of an empress,
take me by the hand, and say 'Harry of England, I am

216 *fausse* (1) incorrect, (2) insincere: cf.
true (l. 219) and the word-play in
truly-falsely (l. 190). Oxf¹'s *faux*,
though correct as to gender, is too far
from the sound of English *false* to be
a satisfactory emendation.
217 *sage demoiselle* prudent young lady.
The English word 'sage' occurs only
four times in Shakespeare, always
associated with the wisdom of age.
The sense here is surely the French
one. F prints the whole sentence
without italicizing any words.
220 **blood** passion
222 **untempering** 'without power to
soften or melt a lady's heart' (Moore
Smith, comparing *tempered*, 2.2.118)
222–4 **Now ... got me** This makes
Henry IV's ambition precede his
usurpation by a dozen years, and is
presumably King Henry's humorous
fantasy.
222 **beshrew** cursed be (a light

imprecation)
225 **aspect** appearance. Cf. 3.1.9.
225–6 **that ... fright them** In *MV*
2.1.8–9 Portia's suitor Morocco – recommending himself – says 'I tell thee,
lady, this aspect of mine / Hath feared
the valiant.'
226 **elder** older
228 **that ill ... beauty** i.e. which
reduces beauty to wrinkles. Cf. *2H4*
5.1.76–7, 'you shall see him laugh till
his face be like a wet cloak ill laid up'
(i.e. put away without being dried
first). The imagery is carried on in
wear me, l. 230.
228–9 **do no more spoil upon** cause no
more damage to (*OED* spoil *sb.* 7c)
230 **wear me** 'an allusion to the use of
the word in regard to clothes, as well
as to the proverb "win me and wear
me" (*MA* 5.1.81), where "wear me"
meant originally "enjoy me" ' (Moore
Smith)

216 majesty 'ave *fausse*] F (*Maiestee aue* fause); *majesté* 'ave *faux* Oxf¹   217 *sage demoiselle*] (sage
Damoiseil)   218 French! By] (French: by)   221 dost] (doo'st)

thine': which word thou shalt no sooner bless mine ear   235
withal but I will tell thee aloud 'England is thine,
Ireland is thine, France is thine, and Henry Plantagenet
is thine', who, though I speak it before his face, if he
be not fellow with the best king, thou shalt find the
best king of good fellows. Come, your answer in broken   240
music, for thy voice is music and thy English broken.
Therefore, queen of all, Katherine, break thy mind
to me in broken English: wilt thou have me?

KATHERINE   Dat is as it sall please *le roi mon père.*

KING   Nay, it will please him well, Kate; it shall please   245
him, Kate.

KATHERINE   Den it sall also content me.

KING   Upon that I kiss your hand, and I call you my
Queen.

KATHERINE   *Laissez, mon seigneur, laissez, laissez! Ma*   250

237 **Plantagenet** the name of the
dynasty to which Henry V belonged
239 **fellow with** equal to
240 **king of good fellows** A *good fellow*
is 'a convivial person, a reveller' (*OED
sb.* 1), and the allusion is to the King's
wild young days (cf. *1H4* 2.5[4].280–
1, 'Gallants, lads, boys, hearts of gold,
all the titles of good fellowship come
to you!'). Walter and later editors cite
the proverb 'The king of good fellows
is appointed for the queen of beggars'
(Tilley, K 66: current by 1565), but
despite Walter's comment 'The
French, of course, were begging for
peace' it is hard to see any relevance
in the proverb, which presumably
connects roistering with the beggary
to which it traditionally leads. More
probably the point lies in the quibbling on *king* and *fellow.*
240–1 **broken music** music arranged in
parts for a number of voices or instruments (*OED* broken *a.* 16). Cf. *AYL*
1.2.131–2 and *TC* 3.1.49–51 for
similar quibbles; there is further

word-play in 'break [= tell] thy mind
to me', l. 242–3.
242 **of all** i.e. of England, Ireland,
France and Henry Plantagenet
244 *****sall** Assuming that *sall* in Katherine's next speech is Shakespeare's
spelling, it is reasonable to suppose
that the compositor accidentally set
'shall' here, seeing the word coming
in the King's reply.
*****le roi mon père** 'the king my father'.
F's italicizing of the phrase shows that
all the words, including the article
misprinted as *de*, were meant to be
French. (For the error, cf. F's '*de
roba*', 3.4.45.)
245 **shall** The verb here has the force of
'must', as contrasted with the simple
future tense of *will.*
250–4 *****Laissez ... seigneur** 'Let be, my
lord, let be, let be! [By] my faith, I
do not at all wish you to abase your
greatness in kissing the hand of one
[who is] your lordship's unworthy
servant; excuse me, I beg you, my
most mighty lord.' F's '*nostre*

240 good fellows] *(Good-fellowes)*   244 sall] *Cam;* shall *F   le roi] Theobald; de Roy F;* the King
Q; de king *Q3*   247 sall] *F;* shall *Rowe*   250–1 *laissez! Ma foi, je] Theobald (subst.); laisse, may
foy: Ie F*

361

foi, je ne veux point que vous abaissiez votre grandeur
en baisant la main d'une de votre seigneurie indigne
serviteur. Excusez-moi, je vous supplie, mon très-puissant
seigneur.

KING   Then I will kiss your lips, Kate.   255

KATHERINE   *Les dames et demoiselles pour être baisées*
    devant leurs noces, il n'est pas la coutume de France.

KING   Madam my interpreter, what says she?

ALICE   Dat it is not be de fashion *pour les* ladies of France –
    I cannot tell vat is *baiser en* English.   260

Seigneur' is an error, not a parenthetic oath: contrast 3.4.28, 47, l. 116 above, and '*Ma foi*' in this speech.

251 *abaissiez F's *abbaisse* (= *abaissez*) need not represent an indicative (as Taylor regards it as doing), for 'although *-iez* eventually ousted *-ez* as the second person plural ending in the present subjunctive, *-ez* continued to be used in the sixteenth century and even into the seventeenth' (Z. P. Zaddy, privately, citing K. Nyrop, *Grammaire historique de la langue française* (Copenhagen, 1899–1930), 2.110).

256–7 *Les dames ... France* 'For ladies and young ladies to be kissed before their marriages, it is not the custom of France.' The preposition would now be *avant*, but *devant* (now restricted to place) was still used of time.

259 **fashion** Taylor argues for Fr. *façon*, spelled 'fachon', because 'Compositor A rarely omits letters' and set 'fashon' here; but he must have omitted one (as he did at l. 359 setting 'Pation'), for Alice is translating Katherine's *coutume*, as the article 'de' (= the) confirms.

*les **ladies** In 3.4, F normally uses *le*

for Fr. *les* and only once for the French mispronunciation of English 'the' as 'de' (3.4.11), so it is more likely that F's 'le' here represents *les* (Alice dropping into French with *pour*, and resuming her translation with the noun, not with the article) than that it is an error for 'de' caused by the attraction of the first letter of 'Ladies'.

260 **I cannot ... *baiser*** Comparison with *MW* 3.2.16–21, where Mistress Page emphatically declares that she can never remember Falstaff's name (see 4.7.48–9n.) suggests that there is a special linguistic reason for Alice's ignorance, particularly as the King has just used the word *kiss* twice. The colloquial sense of *baiser*, as a euphemism meaning 'to copulate with', already existed in the sixteenth century (Z. P. Zaddy, privately, citing G. Matoré, *Le Vocabulaire et la société du XVIe siècle* (Paris, 1988), p. 340, with an instance from Marot, 1496–1564). If this is the reason, Alice's complimenting the King on his translation may be humorously intended (by Shakespeare, not by herself). On the other hand, Katherine has obvi-

251 abaissiez] *Rowe; abbaisse* F   grandeur] *F2; grandeus* F   252–3 d'une ... serviteur] *Cam; d'une nostre Seigneur indignie seruiteur* F; *d'une vostre indigne serviteur / Pope; d'une, notre Seigneur, indigne serviteur / Munro*   253 serviteur ... je] *Theobald (subst.); seruiteur excuse moy. Ie* F   253 très-puissant] F; *treis-puissant* Oxf¹   257 leurs ... coutume] *(leur nopcese il net pas le costume)*   259 de fashion ... ladies] *Theobald; de fashon pour le Ladies* F; *de fashion pour de ladies Capell; de façon pour les ladies* Oxf¹   260 vat] *(wat)*   baiser] *(buisse)*

KING To kiss.

ALICE Your majesty *entend* bettre *que moi.*

KING It is not a fashion for the maids in France to kiss
before they are married, would she say?

ALICE *Oui, vraiment.* 265

KING O Kate, nice customs curtsy to great kings. Dear
Kate, you and I cannot be confined within the weak
list of a country's fashion. We are the makers of
manners, Kate, and the liberty that follows our places
stops the mouth of all find-faults, as I will do yours 270
for upholding the nice fashion of your country in
denying me a kiss: therefore patiently, and yielding –
[*Kisses her.*] You have witchcraft in your lips, Kate:
there is more eloquence in a sugar touch of them than
in the tongues of the French Council, and they should 275

ously used the word in the sense in
which the King translates it, so his
readiness to kiss her may be the whole
point of the dialogue.

en **Anglish** Alice presumably pronounces 'English' as a blend of the
French and the English words. F
consistently has *Anglois* elsewhere in
this scene and in 3.4, so a compositor's
mistake is improbable. At l. 103
Katherine says 'England' when she
means 'English'.

262 **Your ... *moi*** 'Your majesty under-
stands better than I'

*entend **bettre** F's *entendre* (the
infinitive) is an error caused by 'compositorial assimilation to the following
"bettre" ' (*TxC*, 383). Cam²'s reading,
'*entends* bettre', overlooks the fact that
Alice would not use the familiar
second person singular form of the
verb in speaking to the King. The
spelling 'bettre' (italicized, like the
rest of the phrase, in F) indicates a
French pronunciation.

265 *Oui, vraiment* 'Yes, truly'

266 **O Kate ... kings** A line of blank

verse, befitting the proverbial-sound-
ing sentiment.

nice unimportant, trivial (*OED a.*
10b: both examples from Shakespeare, *RJ* 5.2.18, *JC* 4.2.60[3.8]);
contrasted with *great*

268 **list** limit, boundary: *OED* list *sb.*¹
8, citing this passage; but the sense
'barrier', *sb.*¹ 9, is no doubt also
present in view of *weak.*

269 **follows our places** accompanies
our social position

270 **stops the mouth** silences. For the
quibble cf. *MA* 5.4.97, 'Peace: I will
stop your mouth.'

271 **for upholding** to prevent its
upholding. Cf. *TC* 1.2.264–5, 'I can
watch you for telling how I took the
blow.'

274–7 **there ... monarchs** Cf. *Famous
Victories* (scene xviii: ll. 1,368–9), 'For
none in the world could sooner haue
made me debate [i.e. rebate] it / If it
were possible', and (ll. 1,402–3),
'That none in the world could sooner
haue perswaded me to / It then thou.'

262 *entend* bettre] *Oxf*; *entendre bettre* F   266 curtsy] *(cursie)*   272 yielding –] *this edn*; yeelding.
F   273 SD] *Rowe (subst.); not in* F

sooner persuade Harry of England than a general
petition of monarchs. Here comes your father.

Enter the French Power *and the* English Lords.

BURGUNDY
God save your majesty! My royal cousin,
Teach you our Princess English?

KING   I would have her learn, my fair cousin, how   280
perfectly I love her, and that is good English.

BURGUNDY   Is she not apt?

KING   Our tongue is rough, coz, and my condition is
not smooth, so that having neither the voice nor the
heart of flattery about me I cannot so conjure up the   285
spirit of love in her that he will appear in his true
likeness.

BURGUNDY   Pardon the frankness of my mirth if I
answer you for that. If you would conjure in her, you
must make a circle; if conjure up love in her in his   290
true likeness, he must appear naked and blind. Can

---

276 **persuade** i.e. to offer favourable
terms of peace

278–9 **God ... English?** The diction,
and the sudden filling of the stage,
support Capell's treatment of this
speech as verse. King Henry's prose
reply establishes his continued control
of the situation.

280 **my fair cousin** See 7n. above.

281 **good English** Cf. *'fausse'*, 216n.

282 **Is she not apt?** 'She is quick to
learn, is she not?'

283 **Our tongue** The language of us
Englishmen. (Not the royal plural, as
the rest of the speech shows.)
condition disposition; related to
heart, l. 285

284 **smooth** plausible, bland, insinu-
ating, flattering (*OED a.* 6b)

285–7 **so conjure ... likeness** i.e.
'arouse in her a feeling of love for me
that matches mine for her'. Cf. *TN*

1.1.9, 'O spirit of love, how quick and
fresh art thou'. Since *spirit* also means
a supernatural being, the image is that
of raising such a spirit by magic. Cf.
Mercutio's formula, *RJ* 2.1.17–21, 'I
conjure thee ... That in thy likeness
thou appear to us.'

288 **frankness** freedom (in language and
thought). He is about to indulge in
an audacious elaboration of King
Henry's expression. Cf. ll. 288–90
with Mercutio's sexual jesting in *RJ*
2.1.23–6.

290 **make a circle** (1) draw around
yourself a magic circle, such as con-
jurors use, (2) open her vagina

291 **naked and blind** (1) like Cupid,
who is represented naked and with
blindfolded eyes, (2) in the form of
the penis, *blind* because in the dark
of the vagina

---

277 SD] *F; Enter the King of France, and the Lordes. Q*   278–323] *F; not in Q*   278–9] *verse
Capell; prose F*   278 majesty! My] *Pope; Maiestie, my F*   283 coz] *(Coze)*

you blame her then, being a maid yet rosed over with
the virgin crimson of modesty, if she deny the
appearance of a naked blind boy in her naked seeing
self? It were, my lord, a hard condition for a maid to   295
consign to.

KING   Yet they do wink and yield, as love is blind and
enforces.

BURGUNDY   They are then excused, my lord, when
they see not what they do.   300

KING   Then good my lord, teach your cousin to consent
winking.

BURGUNDY   I will wink on her to consent, my lord, if
you will teach her to know my meaning. For maids
well summered and warm kept are like flies at Bar-   305
tholomew-tide, blind, though they have their eyes;
and then they will endure handling, which before
would not abide looking on.

KING   This moral ties me over to time and a hot
summer; and so I shall catch the fly, your cousin, in   310
the latter end, and she must be blind too.

BURGUNDY   As love is, my lord, before that it loves.

293 **deny** refuse
294 **seeing** as opposed to *blind*: alluding
to the popular expression referred to
in Middleton and Rowley, *The
Changeling*, 3.3.74–5, 'for a woman,
they say, has an eye more than a man'
295 **hard condition** (1) severe require-
ment, (2) tumescent state (of the
penis)
296 **consign** assent; cf. 90n.
297 **wink** close both eyes. Cf. l. 302,
winking.
298 **enforces** (1) exerts his power
(referring to Cupid), (2) forces its way
in (referring to the penis)
303 **wink on her** give her a signal by
winking my eye (in the modern sense)
304 **teach . . . meaning** make her ready
(by arousing her sexual feelings) to
understand what I mean
305 **well . . . kept** well fed and well off:

OED summer *v.*[1] 2 (first example),
provide with summer pasture; warm
a. 8, rich, affluent (cf. *1H4* 4.2.18,
'such a commodity of warm slaves as
had as lief hear the devil as a drum')
305–6 **Bartholomew-tide** St Bar-
tholomew's day (*tide* = time), 24
August
306 **blind . . . eyes** 'i.e. so sluggish that
they might as well be blind' (Taylor)
309 **This moral** the lesson to be drawn
from this comparison (*OED* moral *sb.*
2). Cf. *R2* 4.1.280[290], 'Mark, silent
King, the moral of this sport.'
ties me over to confines me to (*OED*
tie *v.* 5: no instance of 'tie over'
given), obliges me to wait for
310–11 **in the latter end** (1) in the later
part of summer, (2) in the lower part
of her body
312 **As love is** The proverb 'Love is

311 too] *(to)*   312 before that] *Oxf*[1]; before F

365

KING   It is so: and you may some of you thank love for
   my blindness, who cannot see many a fair French
   city for one fair French maid that stands in my way.   315
FRENCH KING   Yes, my lord, you see them perspectively, the cities turned into a maid; for they are
   all girdled with maiden walls that no war hath entered.
KING   Shall Kate be my wife?
FRENCH KING   So please you.   320
KING   I am content, so the maiden cities you talk of
   may wait on her: so the maid that stood in the way
   for my wish shall show me the way to my will.
FRENCH KING
   We have consented to all terms of reason.

blind' (Tilley, L 506), i.e. blind to reason, to the defects of the beloved, etc., is often referred to, and usually played upon, by Shakespeare (e.g. *TGV* 2.1.65–7, *RJ* 2.1.32–3, 3.2.9–10). At l. 291 it is love (i.e. Love, Cupid) who is blind; here it is the love in the heart of the lover.

*before that it loves in front of that which it loves, i.e. 'blind in the presence of the beloved' (Taylor, who points out that 'If *that* (= 'that which') were abbreviated *y* in the manuscript' it could easily be overlooked). Alternatively, the compositor may have misunderstood *before that* as meaning simply 'before' (as in the more common 'ere that'), especially since *before* had been used in that sense at l. 307. Gurr, who retains F's reading, misunderstands the proverb, commenting 'A cryptic play on the proverbial blindness of love until the loved object is seen'.

316 Yes yes, you *can* see them (emphatic-contradictory)

316–17 perspectively i.e. in another form than their natural one. The sense here is 'symbolically'. The word *perspective* is variously used by Shakespeare to mean (1) a picture that reveals its subject only when looked at ob-

liquely (*OED sb.* 4b), *R2* 2.2.18–20; (2) a distorting eye-glass (*sb.* 2), *AW* 5.3.48.

321–2 so ... on her 'provided she brings the cities with her' (Wilson). For *so* in this sense, cf. *RJ* 3.5.18. At l. 322 *so* means 'thereby'.

322–3 the maid ... will 'The sense seems to be that though Katherine had stood in the way of his wish to capture these cities, she will show him the way to accomplish his great determination to be King of France, of which the wish was but a part' (Moore Smith). But there must also be word-play on *wish* and *will*. Gurr glosses *my will* '(1) my sexual desire, (2) what my son may inherit.' The latter sense can be confidently dismissed (cf. Slender's fatuous reply to 'What is your will?', *MW* 3.4.55–7), and the former sense is insufficiently specific, *will* being elsewhere in Shakespearean innuendo the penis (*MW* 1.1.213–14, 'can you carry your good will to the maid?'; *MA* 5.4.28–30, 'But for my will, my will is your good will / May stand with ours this day to be conjoined / In the state of honourable marriage'). The remark is perhaps best delivered as a half-aside to Burgundy.

324 all terms of reason all reasonable

318 no war hath] *this edn*; Warre hath *F*; war hath` never *Rowe*; war hath not *Capell*   319–39 SP]
Rowe (K. Hen.); England F   323 for] *F*; of *(Heath)*

366

KING

Is't so, my lords of England?   325

WESTMORLAND

The King hath granted every article:
His daughter first, and in the sequel all,
According to their firm proposed natures.

EXETER   Only he hath not yet subscribed this, where
your majesty demands that the King of France,   330
having any occasion to write for matter of grant, shall
name your highness in this form and with this
addition: [*Reads.*] in French, *Notre très cher fils Henri,
roi d'Angleterre, héritier de France*; and thus in Latin,
Praeclarissimus filius noster Henricus, rex Angliae et   335
haeres Franciae.

terms. The French King implies his
consent to King Henry's stipulation,
ll. 321–23. There may be an echo of
the diction of *Famous Victories* (scene
xviii: ll. 1,364–5), 'My father sent me
to know if you will debate [*read*
rebate] any of these / Unreasonable
demands which you require' and (ll.
1,381–2) 'I would not vouchsafe so
much as one looke, / Untill you had
related [*read* rebated] all these vn-
reasonable demands'.

327 *and ... all* The word *sequel* occurs
nine other times in Shakespeare,
always with the definite article (e.g.
TN 2.5.126–7, 'there is no con-
sonancy in the sequel') except in *Ham*
3.2.316, 'but is there no sequel'.
Hence this edn's emendation of the
evidently defective line.

328 *According ... natures* 'According
to the nature of each as firmly proposed to him' (Moore Smith)
proposed proposèd

329 **subscribed** agreed to (subscribèd)

329–36 **where ... *Franciae*** Cf. Holinshed, 3.575: '25. Also that our said

father, during his life, shall name,
call, and write us in French in this
maner: *Nostre treschier filz Henry roy
d'Engleterre heretere de France*. And in
Latine in this maner: *Praeclarissimus
filius noster Henricus rex Angliae &
haeres Franciae.*'

331 **for ... grant** 'i.e. a deed conferring
lands or titles' (Wilson)

333–4 'Our very dear son Henry, King
of England, heir of France'

334–5 *Praeclarissimus* 'most renowned'.
'In Hall (ed. i [1548]) "prae-
charissimus"; misspelled "praeclarissimus" in ed. ii [1550], whence
Holinshed took it and so passed it
on to Shakespeare' (Wilson). Hall's
original reading follows that of the
treaty itself (Malone, citing Rymer,
Foedera (1704–35), 9.895, 901).
Shakespeare was no doubt transcribing without much thought here,
but he had enough Latin to understand *praeclarissimus* – though possibly not enough to emend it to
praecarissimus ('most dear': a non-
classical word), even with the French

326 SP] *F (West.); Warwick Oxf¹*   327 in the sequel all] *this edn;* in sequele, all *F*; then in
sequele, all *F2;* so in sequel all *Oxf¹*   332 addition:] *Oxf¹;* addition, *F;* addition *Q*   333 SD] *Munro
(subst.)*   French,] *F (French:);* French. *Q   très cher*] *(trescher)*   334 héritier] *(Heretier)*   334–5
Praeclarissimus] *F; Preclarissimus Q; Praecarissimus / Wordsworth (Warburton.)* 335 *haeres*] *(Heres)*

FRENCH KING

Nor this I have not, brother, so denied
But your request shall make me let it pass.

KING

I pray you then, in love and dear alliance,
Let that one article rank with the rest,   340
And thereupon give me your daughter.

FRENCH KING

Take her, fair son, and from her blood raise up
Issue to me, that the contending kingdoms
Of France and England, whose very shores look pale
With envy of each other's happiness,   345
May cease their hatred, and this dear conjunction
Plant neighbourhood and Christian-like accord
In their sweet bosoms, that never war advance
His bleeding sword 'twixt England and fair France.

LORDS

Amen.   350

KING

Now welcome, Kate, and bear me witness all
That here I kiss her as my sovereign queen.

> [*Kisses her.*] *Flourish.*

to help him – and may be supposed,
like Holinshed, to have accepted it as
appropriate.

341 **And ... daughter** See textual notes
for this edn's conjecture. It is unlikely
that Shakespeare meant the line to be
metrically incomplete, or to have a
long caesura after *thereupon*, or to give
daughter the metrical value of three
syllables. To address the French King
as *father* here, after the French King's
brother (l. 337), would be quite in
King Henry's manner, and would
prompt the reply 'Take her, fair son'
(l. 342). Q's version makes no use of
either expression.

344 **look pale** i.e. alluding to the chalk
cliffs

346–9 **and this ... France** Cf. Holinshed, 3.575: '29. Also that there
shall be from henceforward for euer-
more, peace and tranquillitie, & good
accord, and common affection, and
stable friendship betweene the said
realmes, and their subiects before
said.'

346 **dear conjunction** 'solemn union'
(Moore Smith): *OED* dear *a*. 4b, 'precious in import or significance'; all
examples from Shakespeare

347 **neighbourhood** friendly relations.
Contrast 'ill neighbourhood', 1.2.154.

352 **sovereign queen** The adjective
both intensifies the noun (*OED* sovereign *a*. 5, 'having supreme rank
or power') and is complimentary to

341] *F; And withall, / Your daughter* Katherine *in mariage. Q*   daughter] *F; daughter, father
(this edn)*   350 SP] *F; All. Capell*   352 SD *Kisses her*] *this edn*

QUEEN

God, the best maker of all marriages,
Combine your hearts in one, your realms in one!
As man and wife, being two, are one in love,   355
So be there 'twixt your kingdoms such a spousal
That never may ill office or fell jealousy,
Which troubles oft the bed of blessed marriage,
Thrust in between the paction of these kingdoms
To make divorce of their incorporate league;   360
That English may as French, French Englishmen,
Receive each other. God speak this amen.

ALL

Amen.

KING

Prepare we for our marriage; on which day,
My lord of Burgundy, we'll take your oath,   365
And all the peers', for surety of our leagues.

Katherine's personal qualities (*OED a.* 2, 'excelling').

SD Q here has 'Why then faire *Katherine*, / Come giue me thy hand:'

353 **God ... marriages** Cf. the words of the marriage service, 'Whom God hath joined together let no man put asunder', and the proverb 'Marriages are made in heaven' (Tilley, M 688).

356 **spousal** marriage

357–62 **That ... other** Cf. Holinshed, 3.575: '28. Also that henceforward, perpetuallie, shall be still rest, and that in all maner of wise, dissentions, hates, rancors, enuies and wars, betweene the same realmes of France and England, and the people of the same realmes, drawing to accord of the same peace, may ceasse and be broken.'

357 **ill office** disservice (*OED* office *sb.* 1)

fell deadly (*OED a.* 2)

359 **Thrust in** intrude

paction contract (*OED*)

360 **incorporate** united in one body

362 **Receive** accept

God ... amen God grant it. Cf. *R3* 5.5.41, 'That she [i.e. peace] may long live here, God say "Amen".'

364–6 **on which ... leagues** Cf. Holinshed, 3.572 (immediately following the passage quoted in the first note to 5.2): 'When this great matter was finished, the kings sware for their parts to obserue all the couenants of this league and agreement. Likewise the duke of Burgognie and a great number of other princes and nobles which were present, receiued an oth, the tenor whereof (as the duke of Burgundie vttered it in solemne words) thus insueth' (i.e. to obey King Henry as regent and as the French King's successor). In *Famous Victories* (scene xx: ll. 1,511–29) King Henry insists 'That all your Nobles must be sworne to be true to me', and on the French King's orders Burgundy is the first to take the oath upon King Henry's sword, after which King Henry says, 'Come Prince *Dolphin*, you must sweare too' and likewise '*He kisseth the sword*'.

359 paction] *Theobald;* Pation *F; speech not in Q*

Then shall I swear to Kate, and you to me,
And may our oaths well kept and prosperous be!

Sennet. Exeunt.

[EPILOGUE]   *Enter* CHORUS.

CHORUS

Thus far, with rough and all-unable pen,
Our bending author hath pursued the story,
In little room confining mighty men,
Mangling by starts the full course of their glory.
      Small time, but in that small most greatly lived   5

---

368 SD *Sennet* 'A set of notes on the trumpet or cornet, ordered in the stage-directions of Elizabethan plays, apparently as a signal for the ceremonial entrance or exit of a body of players' (*OED*, with many examples, including Dekker, *Satiromastix*, 1602, 'Trumpets sound a florish, and then a sennate', which shows that 'sennet' and 'flourish' were distinct from each other).

EPILOGUE The form is that of a regular Shakespearean sonnet of three quatrains and a couplet. Cf. the prologues to Acts 1 and 2 of *RJ*.

1 **all-unable** wholly inadequate to the task

2 **Our ... story** Cf. *2H4* Epilogue 25–6, 'our humble author will continue the story'.
    bending bowing, i.e. humble. Steevens compares the prologue to the play in *Ham* 3.2.143, 'Here stooping to your clemency'.

3 **room** space

4 **Mangling ... glory** i.e. misrepresenting their glorious series of achievements through the fragmentary nature of this play
    by starts 'intermittently, not continuously or with sustained effort' (*OED* start *sb.*[2] 4b)

course (1) regular order, cf. 5.0.4, (2) sun-like progress, cf. *Son* 59.6, 'Even of five hundred courses of the sun'

5 **Small time** King Henry died in 1422, aged thirty-five. Two passages in Holinshed are relevant. First, 3.581: 'This year [i.e. 1421], at Windsore, on the daie of saint Nicholas, in December, the queene was deliuered of a sonne named Henrie; ... The king, being certified hereof, as he laie at seige before Meaux, gaue God thanks; in that it had pleased his diuine prouidence to send him a sonne, which might succeed in his crowne and scepter. But, when he heard reported the place of his natiuitie, were it that he [was] warned by some prophesie, or had some foreknowledge, or else iudged himselfe of his sonnes fortune, he said vnto the lord Fitz Hugh, his trustie chamberleine, these words: My lord, I Henrie, borne at Monmouth, shall small time reigne, & much get; and Henrie, borne at Windsore, shall long reigne, and all loose; but, as God will, so be it.' Second, 3.584: 'Thus ended this puissant prince his most noble and fortunate reigne, whose life (saith Hall) though cruell Atropos abbreuiated; yet neither fire, malice nor

---

368 prosperous] *(prosp'rous)*

EPILOGUE] *Collier*[2] *(Enter Chorus, as Epilogue)*   1 SP] *Dyce; not in F; speech not in Q*

This star of England. Fortune made his sword
By which the world's best garden he achieved,
And of it left his son imperial lord.
    Henry the Sixth, in infant bands crowned King
Of France and England, did this king succeed,   10
Whose state so many had the managing
That they lost France and made his England bleed,
    Which oft our stage hath shown; and for their
        sake
In your fair minds let this acceptance take.   [*Exit.*]

fretting time shall appall his honour, or blot out the glorie of him that in so small time had doone so manie and roiall acts.'

6 **This star of England** Cf. Holinshed, 3.584: 'for conclusion, a maiestie was he that both liued & died a paterne in princehood, a lode-starre in honour, and mirrour of magnificence.' **Fortune ... sword** Fortune (personified as a goddess) forged his sword. Cf. Holinshed, 3.583: 'This Henrie was a king, of life without spot, a prince whome all men loued, and of none disdained, a capteine against whome fortune neuer frowned, nor mischance once spurned.'

7 **the ... garden** France. Cf. 5.2.36.

9 **infant bands** the strips of linen in which babies were wrapped; 'swathing-clouts' (*Ham* 2.2.385). He was nine months old when his father died.

11 **Whose ... managing** Of whose government (*OED* state *sb*. 29) so many had the control. The omission of 'of' is not unusual: cf. *WT* 4.4.139, 'for the ord'ring your affairs'.

12–13 **That ... shown** The three parts of *H6* had begun with English reverses in France immediately after Henry V's death, and had proceeded to the loss of France and to the Wars of the Roses.

13 **for their sake** in consideration of the pleasure that they [i.e. the *H6* plays] have given you

14 **let ... take** let this play find favour

9 Sixth] *(Sixt)*   14 SD] *Capell*

APPENDICES

THE FIRST QUARTO (1600)

The First Quarto (1600) of *Henry V*, reproduced in reduced photographic facsimile from the British Library's copy (press-mark C.12.g.22) by kind permission.

This copy is reproduced full-size as *Henry the Fifth. 1600. Shakespeare Quarto Facsimiles, No. 9*, ed. W. W. Greg (Oxford, 1957). Another copy, in the Henry E. Huntington Library, San Marino, California, is reproduced full-size in *Shakespeare's Plays in Quarto*, ed. Michael J. B. Allen and Kenneth Muir (Berkeley, Los Angeles and London, 1981). A reprint of the First Quarto's text is edited by Graham Holderness and Bryan Loughrey (Hemel Hempstead, 1993) in their series 'Shakespearean Originals: First Editions'.

The top-of-page references indicate the corresponding act, scene and line reference in the present edition, and the corresponding through line numbers (TLN) in *The First Folio of Shakespeare: The Norton Facsimile*, prepared by Charlton Hinman (New York, London, Sydney and Toronto, 1968).

THE
CRONICLE
History of Henry the fift,

With his battell fought at *Agin Court* in
France. Togither with *Auntient*
Pistoll.

As it hath bene sundry times playd by the Right honorable
the Lord Chamberlaine his seruants.

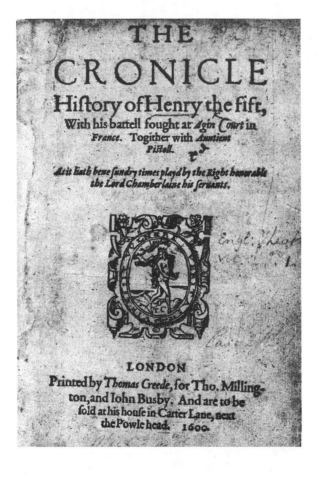

LONDON

Printed by *Thomas Creede*, for Tho. Millington, and Iohn Busby. And are to be
sold at his house in Carter Lane, next
the Powle head. 1600.

The Chronicle Historie

of *Henry* the fift: with his battel fought
at *Agin Court* in *France*. Togither with
Auncient *Pistoll.*

Enter King Henry, Exeter, 2. Bishop, Clarence and other
Attendants.

Exeter.

SHall I call in Thambassadors my Liege?
King. Not yet my Cosin till we be resolude
Of some: serious matters touching vs and *Fran-*
Bi. God and his Angels guard your sacred throne,
King. Shure we thanke you. My learned Lord I pray
Why the Lawe *Salike* which they haue in *France,*
Or should or should not, stop vs in our claime:
And God forbid my wise and learned Lord,
That you should fashion, frame, or wrest the same,
For God doth know how many now in health,
Shall drop their blood in approbation,
Of what your reuerence shall incite vs too,
Therefore take heed how you impawne our person,
How you awake the sleeping sword of warre:
We charge you in the name of God take heed.
After this coniuration, speake my Lord;
And we will iudge, note, and beleeue in heart,
That what you speake, is washt as pure
As sin in baptisme.

A 2

The Chronicle Historie

Then heare me gracious soueraigne, and you peeres,
Which owe your liues, your faith and seruices
To this imperiall throne.
There is no bar to stay your highnesse claime to France
But one, which they produce from Pharamond,
No female shall succeed in salicke land,
Which salicke land the French vniustly gloze
To be the realme of France:
And Pharamond the founder of this law and female barre,
Yet their owne writers faithfully affirme
That the land salicke lyes in Germanie,
Betweene the floods of Sabeck and of Elme,
Where Charles the fift hauing subdude the Saxons,
There left behind, and setled certaine French,
Who holding in disdaine the Germaine women
For some dishonest maners of their liues,
Establisht there this lawe. To wit,
No female shall succeed in salicke land,
Which salicke land as I said before,
Is at this time in Germanie called Mesene,
Thus doth it well appeare the salicke lawe
Was not deuised for the realme of France,
Nor did the French possesse the salicke land,
Vntill 400. and one yeeres,
After the fine stor of king Pharamond,
Godly supposed the founder of this lawe,
Hugh Capet also that vsurpt the crowne,
To fine his title with some showe of truth,
When in pure truth it was corrupt and naught,
Conuaid himselfe as heire to the Lady Inger,
Daughter to Charles, the forsaid Duke of Loraine,
So that as cleare as is the sommers Sun,
King Pippins title and Hugh Capets claime,
King Charles his satisfaction all appeares,
To bold in right and rule of the female:
So do the Lords of France vntill this day,
Howbeit they would hold vp this salicke lawe

To

To bar your highnesse claiming from the female,
And rather choose to hide them in a net,
Then amply to imbace their crooked causes,
Vsurpt from you and your progenitors.   (claime
King. May we with right & conscience make this
Bish. The sin vpon my head dread soueraigne.
For in the booke of Numbers is it writ,
When the sonne dies, let the inheritance
Descend vnto the daughter.
Noble Lord stand for your owne,
Vnwinde your bloudy flagge,
Go my dread Lord to your great grandsirs graue,
From whom you clayme:
And your great Vncle Edward the blacke Prince,
Whom the French ground playd a Tragedy,
Making defeat on the full power of France,
Whiles his most mightie father on a hull
Stood smiling to behold his Lyons whelpe,
Foraging blood of French Nobilitie.
O Noble English, that could entertaine
With halfe their Forces the full power of France,
And let an other halfe stand laughing by,
All out of worke, and cold for action.
King. We must not onely arme vs against the French,
But lay downe our proportion for the Scot,
Who will make rode vpon vs with all aduantages.
Bish. The Marches gracious soueraigne, shalbe sufficient
To guard vs, Engl. from the pilfering bordrers.
King. We do not meane the couring snatchers onely,
But feare the maine entendment of the Scot,
For you shall read, neuer my great grandfather
Vnmaskt his power for France,
But that the Scots, his vnfurnisht Kingdome,
Came pouring like the Tide into a breach,
That England being empty of defence,
Hath shooke and trembled at the brute thereof.
Bish. She hath bin then more feard then hurt my Lords,

For

A 3

The Chronicle Historie

For heauen her selfe hath exemplified by her selfe,
When all her chiualry hath bene in France,
And shee a mourning widow of her Nobles,
She hath her selfe not only well defended,
But taken and impounded as a stray, the king of Scots,
Whom like a caytiffe she did leade to France,
Filling your Chronicles as rich with praise
As is the owse and bottome of the sea
With sunken wrack and shiplesse treasure.

Lord. There is a saying very old and true,
If you will *France* win,
Then with *Scotland* first begin.
For once the Eagle *England* being in pray,
To his vnfurnisht nest the weazell *Scot*
Would sucke her egs, playing the mouse in absence of the
To spoyle and hauock more then she can eat.　　(cat,

Exe. It followes then, the cat must stay at home,
Yet that is but a curst necessitie.
Since we haue trappes to catch the pretty theeues.
Whilst that the armed hand doth fight abroad,
The aduised head controlles at home:
For gouernment though high, or lowe, being put into parts,
Congrueth with a mutuall confent like musicke.

Bi. True: therefore doth heauen diuide the state of man
　　　　in diuers functions,

Whereto is added as an ayme or butt, obedience:
For so worke the honey Bees creatures that by awe
Ordaine an act of order to a peopled Kingdome:
They haue a King and officers of sorts,
Where some like Magistrates correct at home:
Others like Marchants venture trade abroad:
Others like souldiers armed in their stings,
Make boote vpon the summers velvet buds:
Which pillage they with merry march bring home
To the tent royall of their Emperour,
Who busied in his maiestie, behold
The singing masons building roofes of gold:

The

of Henry the fifth.

The ciuill citizens lading vp the honey;
The sad eyde Iustice with his surly humme,
Deliuering vp to executors pale, the lazy yauning Drone,
This I inferre, that 20. actions once a foote,
May all end in one moment,
As many Arrowes loosed seuerall wayes, flye to one marke,
As many fresh streames runne in one selfe sea:
As many lines close in the dyall center:
So may a thousand actions once a foote,
End in one moment, and be all well borne without defeate.

Therefore, my Liege to *France*.
Diuide your happy England into foure,
Of which take you one quarter into *France*,
And you withall shall make all *Gallia* shake.
If we with thrice that power left at home,
Cannot defend our owne doores from the dogge,
Let vs be beaten, and from henceforth lose
The name of policy and hardinesse.

Ki. Call in the messenger sent from the Dolphin,
And by your ayde, the noble sinewes of our Land,
France being ours, weele bring it to our awe,
Or breake it all in peeces:
Either our Chronicle shall with full mouth speake
Freely of our acts,
Or else like toonglesse mutes
Not worshipt with a paper Epitaph.

Enter the Ambassadors from France.

Now are we well prepared to know the Dolphins pleasure,
For we heare your comming is from him.

Ambass. Please it your Maiestie to giue vs leaue
Freely to render what we haue in charge:
Or shall I sparingly shew a farre off
The Dolphins pleasure, and our Embassage?

King. We are no tyrant, but a Christian King,
Vnto whose grace our passions are as subiect
As our wretches fettred in our prisons:

There

The Chronicle Hiſtorie

Nim. I muſt do as I may, tho patience be a tyred mare,
Yet ſheel plod, and ſome ſay kniues haue edges,
And men may ſleepe and haue their throtes about them
At that time, and there is the humour of it.
Bar. Come yfaith, Ile beſtow a breakfaſt to make *Piſtoll*
And thee friendes. What a plague ſhould we carrie kniues
To cut our owne throates.
Nim. Yfaith Ile liue as long as I may, thats the certaine of it.
And when I cannot liue any longer, Ile do as I may,
And theres my reſt, and the randeuous of it.

Enter Piſtoll and Hoſtes Quickly his wife.

Bar. Godmorrow ancient *Piſtoll.*
Here comes ancient *Piſtoll*, I prithee *Nim* be quiet.
Nim. How do you my Hoſte?
Piſt. Baſe ſlaue, calleſt thou me hoſte?
Now by gads lugges I ſweare, I ſcorne the title,
Nor ſhall my *Nell* keepe lodging.
Hoſt. No by my troath not I,
For we cãnot bed nor boord half a ſcore honeſt gẽtlewomẽ
That liue honeſtly by the prick of their needle,
But it is thought ſtraight we keepe a bawdy-houſe.
O Lord heeres Corporall *Nims*, now ſhall
We haue wilful adultry and murther committed:
Good Corporall *Nim* ſhew the valour of a man,
And put vp your ſword.
Nim. Puſh.
Piſt. What doſt thou puſh, thou prickeard cur of Iſeland?
Nim. Will you ſhog off? I would haue you ſolus.
Piſt. Solus egregious dog, that ſolus in thy throte,
And in thy lungs, and which is worſe, within
Thy meſfull mouth, I do retort that ſolus in thy
Bowels, and in thy Iaw, perdie: for I can talke,
And *Piſtolls* flaſhing firy cock is up.
Nim. I am not *Barbaſom*, you cannot coniure me:
I haue an humour *Piſtoll* to knock you indifferently well,
And you fall foule with me *Piſtoll*, Ile ſcoure you with my
Rapier

of Henry the fift.

Rapier in faire termes. If you will walke off a little,
Ile prick your guts a litle in good termes,
And theres the humour of it.
Piſt. O braggard vile, and damned furious wight,
The Graue doth gape, and groaning
Death is neare, therefore exall.

They drawe.

Bar. Heare me, he that ſtrikes the firſt blow,
Ile kill him, as I am a ſouldier.
Piſt. An oath of mickle might, and fury ſhall abate.
Nim. Ile cut your throat at one time or an other in faire termes,
And theres the humor of it.
Piſt. Couple gorge is the word, I thee defie agen:
A damned hound, thinkſt thou my ſpouſe to get?
No, to the powdering tub of infamy,
Fetch forth the lazar kite of Creſides kinde,
Doll Tear-ſheete, ſhe by name, and her eſpouſe
I haue, and I will hold, the quandom quickly,
For the onely ſhe and Paco, there it is inough.

Enter the Boy.

Boy. Hoſtes you muſt come ſtraight to my maiſter,
And you Hoſt *Piſtoll.* Good *Bardolfe,*
Put thy noſe betweene the ſheetes, and do the office of a warming pan.
Hoſt. By my troath heele yeeld the crow a pudding one of theſe dayes,
Ile go to him, husband youle come?
Bar. Come *Piſtoll* be friends.
Nim prithee be friends, and if thou wilt not be
Enemies with me too.
Ni. I ſhal haue my eight ſhillings I woon of you at beating?
Piſt. Baſe is the ſlaue that payes.
Nim. That now I will haue, and theres the humor of it.
Piſt. As manhood ſhall compound. *They draw.*
Bar. He that ſtrikes the firſt blow,
Ile kill him by this ſword.
Piſt. Sword is an oath, and oathes muſt haue their courſe.

B 2 *Nim.*

Cam. Neuer was Monarch better fear'd and lou'd, then
is your maiestie.

Grey. Euen those that were your Fathers enemies

Haue steeped their galles in honey for your sake.

King. We therefore haue great cause of thankfulnes,

And shall forget the office of our hands:

Sooner then reward and merite,

According to their cause and worthinesse.

Masha. So seruice shall with steeled sinewes

And labour shall refresh it selfe with hope

To do your Grace inceslant seruices.

King. Vncle of Exeter, enlarge the man

Committed yesterday, that rayl'd against our person,

We consider it was the heate of wine that set him on,

And on his more aduice we pardon him.

Masha. That is mercy, but too much securitie:

Let him be punisht Soueraigne, least the example

Breed more of such a kinde.

King. O let vs yet be mercifull.

Cam. So may your highnesse, and yet punish too.

Grey. You shew great mercy if you giue him life,

After the taste of his correction.

King. Alas, your too much loue and care of me,

Are heauy orisons 'gainst the poore wretch:

If little faults proceeding on distemper, should not be

How should we stretch our eye when capitall crimes,

Chew'd, swallowed, and digested, appeare before vs?

Wee'l yet enlarge the man, tho Cambridge and the rest

In their deere care and tender preseruation of our person

Would haue him punisht.

Now to our French causes,

Who are the late Commissioners?

Cam. Me one my Lord, your Highnesse bad me aske for it

to day.

The Chronicle Historie

Nim. I will these my eight shillings I wonne of you at
betting?

Pist. A noble shalt thou haue, and ready pay,

And liquor likewise will I giue to thee,

And friendship shall combind, and brotherhood:

Ile liue by *Nim* as *Nim* shall liue by me:

Is not this iust? for I shall Sutler be

Vnto the Campe, and profit will accrew.

Nim. I shall haue my noble?

Pist. In cash most truly paid.

Nim. Why there's the humor of it.

Enter Hostesse.

Hostes. As euer you came of men, come in,

Sir *Iohn* poore soule is so troubled

With a burning tashan quotidian tertian feuer, it's wonderful:

Pist. Let vs condole the knight, for lambkins we will liue.

Exeunt.

Enter Exeter and Gloster.

Glost. Before God my Lord, his Grace is too bold to trust
these traytors.

Exet. They shall be apprehended by and by.

Glost. But the man that was his bedfellow

Whom he hath cloyd and graced with princely fauours,

That he should for a forraine purse, to sell

His Soueraignes life to death and treachery.

Exet. O the Lord of *Masham.*

Enter the King and three Lords.

King. Now sits the windes faire, and we will aboord,

My Lord of *Cambridge*, and my Lord of *Masham*,

And you my gentle Knight, giue me your thoughts,

Do you not thinke the power that we bring with vs,

Will make vs conquerors in the field of *France*?

Masha. No doubt my Liege, if each man do his best.

Cam. Neuer

The Chronicle History

Mash. So did you my Soueraigne.
Grey. And me my Lord.
   King. Then Richard Earle of Cambridge there is yours.
There is yours my Lord of Masham.
And sir Thomas Grey knight of Northumberland, this same is yours
Read them, and know them know your worthinesse. (you
Vncle Exeter I will abord tonight.
Why how now Gentlemen, why change you colour?
What see you in those papers
That hath so chased your bloud out of apparence
   Cam. I do confesse my fault, and do submit me
To your highnesse mercie.
   Mash. To which we all appeale.
   King. The mercy which was quit in me but late,
By your owne reasons is forestald and done,
You must not dare for shame to talke of mercy,
For your owne conscience turne vpon your bosomes,
As dogs vpon their maisters worrying them.
See you my Princes, and my noble Peeres,
These English monsters:
My Lord of Cambridge here,
You know how apt we were to grace him,
In all things belonging to his honour:
And this vilde man hath for a fewe light crownes,
Lightly conspired and sworne vnto the practises of France,
To kill vs here in Hampton. To the which,
This knight no lesse in bountie bound to vs
Then Cambridge is, hath likewise sworne.
But oh what shall I say to thee false man,
Thou cruell ingratefull and inhumane creature,
Thou that didst beare the key of all my counsell,
That knewst the very secrets of my heart,
That almost mightst a coyned me into gold,
Wouldst thou haue practised on me for thy vse:
Can it be possible that out of thee
Should proceed one sparke that might warme my finger?

Tis

Tis so strange, that tho the truth doth show as grosse
At black from white, mine eye will scarcely see it.
Their faults are open, arrest them to the answer of the law,
And God acquite them of their practise.
   Exe. I arrest thee of high treason,
By the name of Richard, Earle of Cambridge.
I arrest thee of high treason,
By the name of Henry, Lord of Masham.
I arrest thee of high treason,
By the name of Thomas Grey, knight of Northumberland.
   Mash. Our purpose God iustly hath discouered,
And I repent my fault more then my death,
Which I beseech your highnes to forgiue,
Altho my body pay the price of it.
   King. God quite you in his mercy. Heare your sentence.
You haue conspired against our royall person,
Ioyned with an enemy proclaimed and fixed,
And from his coffers receiu'd the golden earnest of our death
Touching our person we seeke no redresse,
But we our kingdomes safetie must tender,
Whose ruine you haue sought,
That to her lawes we do deliuer you.
Get ye therefore hence, poore miserable creatures to your death,
The taste whereof, God in his mercy giue you
Patience to endure, and true repentance of all your deeds
Beare them hence.

Exit three Lords.

Now Lords for France, the enterprise whereof,
Shall be to you as vs, successfull.
Since God so graciously hath brought to light,
This dangerous treason lurking in our way,
Cheerly to sea, the signes of war aduance,
No King of England if not King of France.

Exeunt.

Enter Nim, Pistoll, Bardolfe, Hostesse and a Boy.

Host. I prethy sweete heart, let me bring thee so farre.

Pist. No fur, no fur.

Bar. Well sir *Iohn* is gone. God be with him.

Host. I, he is in *Arthors* bosome, if euer any were:
He went away as if it were a cryscom childe,
Betweene twelue and one,
Iust at turning of the tide:
For when I saw him fumble with the sheetes,
His nose was as sharpe as a pen:
And talk of floures, and smile vpon his fingers ends
I knew there was no way but one.
How now sir *Iohn* quoth I?
And he cryed three times, God, God, God,
Now I to comfort him, bad him not thinke of God,
I hope there was no such need.
Then he bad me put more cloathes at his feete:
And I felt to them, and they were as cold as any stone:
And to his knees, and they were as cold as any stone.

Nim. They say he cried out of Sack.

Host. I that he did.

Bar. And of women.

Host. No that he did not.

Boy. Yes that he did, and he sed they were diuels incarnate.

Host. Indeed carnation was a colour he neuer loued.

Nim. Well he did cry out on women.

Host. Indeed he did in some sort handle women, (*Babylon.*
But then he was rumaticke, and talkt of the whore of

Boy. Histhes do you remember he saw a Flea stand
Vpon *Bardolfes* Nose, and sed it was a blacke soule
Burning in hell fire?

Bar.

Bar. Well, God be with him,
That was all the wealth I got in his seruice.

Nim. Shall we shog off?

Pist. Cleare vp thy christalles,
Looke to my chattels and my moueables:
Trust none the word is pitch and paye,
Mens words are wafer cakes,
And holdfast is the only dog my deare,
Therefore cophetua be thy counseller,
Touch her soft lips and part.

Bar. Farewell hostes.

Nim. I cannot kisse and theres the humor of it.
But adieu.   *Dieu vous.*

Pist. Keepe fast thy buggle boe.

Enter King of France, Bourbon, Dolphin,
and others.

King. Now you Lords of *Orleance,*
Of *Bourbon,* and of *Berry,*
You see the King of England is not slacke,
For he is footed on this land already.

Dolphin. My gracious Lord, tis meet we all goe
(fourth,
And arme vs against the foe:
And view the weak & sickly parts of *France,*
But let vs do it with no show of feare,
No with no more, then if we heard
England were busied with a Morris dance:
For my good Lord she is so idely kingd,
Her scepter so fantastically borne,
So guided by a shallow humorous youth,
That feare attends her not.

Con. O peace Prince *Dolphin,* you deceiue your selfe,

C   Question

381

The Chronicle Historie

Question your grace the late Embassador,
With what great state he heard his Embassage,
How well supplied with aged Counsellours,
And how his resolution answered him,
You then would say that *Harry* was not wilde.
  King. Well thinke we *Harry* strong:
And strongly arme vs to present the foe,
  Com. My Lord here is an Embassador
From the King of England.
  Kin. Bid him come in.
You see this chafe is hotly followed Lords.
  Dol. My gracious father, cut vp this English short,
Selfeloue my Liege is not so vile a thing
As selfe neglecting.

Enter Exeter.

  King. From our brother England?
  Exe. From him, and thus he greets your Maiestie:
He wils you in the name of God Almightie,
That you deuest your selfe and lay apart
That borrowed tytle, which by gift of heauen,
Of lawe of nature, and of nations, longs
To him and to his heires, namely the crowne
And all wide stretched titles that belongs
Vnto the Crowne of *France*, that you may know
Tis no sinister, nor no awkeward claime,
Pickt from the worme-holes of old vanisht dayes,
Nor from the dust of old oblivion rackte,
He sends you these most memorable lynes,
In every branch truly demonstrated.
Willing you ouerlooke this pedigree,
And when you finde him euenly deriued
From his most famed and famous ancestors,
Edward the third, he bids you then resigne
Your crowne and kingdome, indirectly held
From him, the natiue and true challenger.
                        King.

Henry the fift.

  King. If not, what followes?
  Exe. Bloody constraint: for if you hide the crowne
Euen in your hearts, there will he rake for it:
Therefore in fierce tempest is he comming,
In thunder, and in earthquake, like a *Ioue*,
That if requiring faile, he will compell it:
And on your heads turnes he the widowes teares,
The Orphanes cries, the dead mens bones,
The pining maydens grones,
For husbands, fathers, and distressed louers,
Which shall be swallowed in this controuersie.
This is his claime, his threatning, and my message,
Vnles the *Dolphin* be in presence here,
To whom expressly we bring greeting too.
  Dol. For the *Dolphin?* I stand here for him,
What to heare from England?
  Exe. Scorne & defiance, slight regard, contempt,
And any thing that may not misbecome
The mightie sender, doth he prise you at:
Thus faith my King, Vnles your father laughe,
Sweare the bitter mocke you sent his Maiestie,
Heele call you to so loud an answere for it,
That caues and wombely vaultes of *France*,
Shall chide your trespasse, and returne your mocke,
In second accent of his ordenance.
  Dol. Say that my father render faire reply,
It is against my will:
For I desire nothing so much,
As oddes with England.
And for that cause according to his youth
I did present him with those *Paris* balles.
  Exe. Heele make your *Paris Louer* shake for it,
Were it the mistresse Court of mightie *Europe*,
And be assured, you'le finde a difference
As we his subiects haue in wonder found,

                               C 2   Betweene

of Henry the fift.

Flen. Looke you, tell the Duke it is not so good
To come to the mines: the concaueties is otherwise.
You may discusse to the Duke, the enemy is dig'd
Himselfe fine yardes vnder the countermines:
By Iesus I thinke heele blowe vp all
If there be no better direction.

Enter the King and his Lords alarum.

King. How yet resolues the Gouernour of the Towne?
This is the latest parley weele admit:
Therefore to our best mercy giue your selues,
Or like to men proud of destruction, define vs to our worst:
For I am souldier, a name that in my thoughts
Becomes me best, if we begin the battery once againe
I will not leaue the halfe atchieued Harflew,
Till in her ashes she be buried,
The gates of mercy is all shut vp,
What say you, will you yeeld and this auoyde,
Or guiltie in defence be thus destroyd?

Enter Gouernour.

Gouer. Our expectation hath this day an end:
The Dolphin whom of succour we entreated
Returnes vs word, his powers are not yet ready,
To raise so great a siege: therefore dread King,
We yeeld our towne and liues to thy soft mercy:
Enter our gates, dispose of vs and ours,
For we no longer are defensiue now.

Enter Katherine, Alice.

Kate. Alice venies, vous aues cates en,
Vou parte fransoie A signe anglas,
Capam sap allees en crop.

C 3

The Chronicle Historie

Between his yonger dayes and these that he sees now,
Now he weyes time euen to the latest graine,
Which you shall finde in your owne losses
If he stay in France.

King. Well for vs all we shall returne our answere backe
To our brother England.

Exit omnes.

Enter Nim, Bardolfe, Pistoll, Boy.

Nim. Before God here is hote seruice.
Pist. Tis hot indeed, blowe, go and come,
Gods vassals drop and die.
Nim. Tis honour, and theres the humor of it.
Boy. Would I were in London.
I de giue all my honour for a pot of Ale.
Pist. And I, if wishes would preuaile,
I would not stay, but thither would I hie.

Enter Flewellen and beates them in.

Flew. Gods plud vp to the breaches
You rascals, will you not vp to the breaches?

Nim. Abate thy rage.
Boy. Well I would I were once from them
They would haue me as familiar
With mens pockets, as their gloues or
Handkerchers, they will steale any thing.
Bardolfs stole a lute case,
And solde it for three halfpence.
Nim stole a fier shouell.
I knew by that, they meane to carry clothes
Well, if they will not leaue me,
I meane to leaue them.

Exit Nim, Bardolfe, Pistoll and the Boy.

Enter Gower.

Gower, Captain Flewellen, you must come presently
To the Mines, to the Duke of Glocester.

Looke

The Chronicle Historie

Ali. Es main madam de him.

Kate. E da bra.

Alice. De arma madam.

Kate. Le main da han la bras de arma.

Alice. Owy madam.

Kate. E Coman la pella vow la me..on a la coill

Alice. De necke, de cin, madam.

Kate. De necke de cin, de code.

Alice. E de necke de cin, de code.

Alice. De cudie ma foy le oblye mais le remembre,
Le nek, qode elbo madam.

Kate. Ecowte Ie charfera, owte cella que Ie apremdre
De han, de arma, de neck, du cin, de bilke.

Alice. De elbo madam.

Kate. O Iefu, Ie obloye ma foy qoque Ie recommen
De han, de arma, de neck, de cin, de code, e ca bon.

Alice. Ma foy maine, vow pula le bon Anglays.
Afis vous ans estue en Englume.

Kate. Par la grace de dieu an petteteme, Ie pula milue
Coman si pella vowie pude le robe.

Alice. Le foot, che com.

Kate. Le foo, e le con, O Iefu. Ie ne vow pula pro...
Se pius devant le che challino de franse,
Par one million masioy.

Alice. Madam de foo e de con.

Kate. O til au fie, ecowte Allice, de han, de arma,
De neck, de cin, le fonte, e de con.

Alice. Coranbon madam.

Kate. A lone a dinar.

Exit omnes.

Enter King of France Lord Conftable the Dolphin,
and Burbon.

King. Tis certaine he is paft the Riuer Some.

Co. Mordam vie Shall a few fprints of his,

The

Henry the fift.

The emptying of our fathers luxurie,
Oregrow their graffers.

Bur. Normans, baftard Normans, Norman baftardes
And if they paiffe vnfoughtwithall,
Ile fell my Dukedome for a foggy farme
In that fhort nooke Ile of England.

Conf. Why whence haue they this metall?
Is not their clymate raw, foggy and colde,
On whom as in difdaine, the Sunne lookes pale?
Can barley broath, a dr ench for fwolne Iades
Their foddaine water decocts fuch liuely blood?
And fhall our quick blood fpirited with wine
Seeme frofty? O for honour of our names.
Les vs now hang like frozen Iceficles
Vpon our houfes tops while they amore frofty clymate
Sweats drops of youthfull blood.

King. Conftable difpatch, fend Momboy forth,
To know what willing ranfome he will giue?
Sonne Dolphin you fhall ftay in Roan with vne.

Dol. Not fo I do befeech your Maieftie.

King. Well, I fay it fhalbe fo.

Exeunt omnes

Enter Gower,

Go. How now Captain Flewellen, come you fro the bridge?

Flew. By Iefus thers excellEt feruice comitted at y bridge.

Gow. Is the Duke of Exeter fafe?

Flew. The duke of Exeter is a mã whom I loue, & I honour,
And I worfhip with my foule, and my heart, and my life,
And my lands and my liuing,
And my vttermoft powers.
The Duke is looke you,
God be praifed and pleafed for it, no harme in the world
He is maintaine the bridge very gallantly: there is an Enfigne
There,

There, I do not know how you call him, but by Iesu I thinke
He is as valiant a man as *Marke Antonie*, & he doth maintaine
the bridge most gallantly : yet he is a man of no reckoning:
But I did see him do gallant seruice.

Gour. How do you call him?

Flew. His name is ancient *Pistoll.*

Gour. I know him not.

Enter Ancient Pistoll.

Flew. Do you not know him: here comes the man.

Pist. Captaine, I thee beseech to do me fauors,
The Duke of *Exeter* doth loue thee well.

Flew. I, and I praise God I haue merited some loue at
(his hands.

Pist. Bardolfe a souldier, one of buxsome valour,
Hath by furious fate
And giddy Fortunes fickle wheele,
That Goddesse blinde that stands vpon the rowling restlesse
(stone.

Flew. By your patience ancient *Pistoll,*
Fortune, looke you is painted,
Blind with a muffler before her eyes,
To signifie to you, that Fortune is blind :
And she is moreouer painted with a wheele,
Which is the morall that Fortune is turning,
And inconstant, and variation : and mutabilities :
And her fate is fixed at a spherical stone,
Which roules, and roules, and roules :
Surely the Poet is make an excellent description of Fortune,
Fortune looke you is and excellent morall.

Pist. Fortune is *Bardolfes* foe, and frownes on him,
For he hath stolne a packs, and hanged must he bee :
A damned death, let gallowes gape for dogs,
Let man go free, and let not death his windpipe stop.

But

But *Exeter* hath giuen the doome of death,
For packs of petty price :
Therefore go speake, the Duke will heare thy voyce,
And let not *Bardolfes* vitall thread be cut,
With edge of penny-cord, and vile approach.
Speake Captaine for his life, and I will thee requite.

Flew. Captaine *Pistoll,* I partly vnderstand your meaning.

Pist. Why then reioyce therefore.

Flew. Certainly Antient *Pistoll,* tis not a thing to reioyce you,
For if he were my owne brother, I would with the Duke
To do his pleasure, and put him to execution: for looke you,
Disciplines ought to be kept, they ought to be kept.

Pist. Die and be damned, and figa for thy friendshyp.

Flew. That is good.

Pist. The figge of *Spaine* within thy lawe.

Flew. That is very well.

Pist. I say the figge within thy bowels and thy durty maw.
Exit Pistoll.

Flew. Captaine *Gower,* now you know is this the Ancient you told me of?

Gow. Why is this the Ancient you told me of?
I remember him now, he is a bawd, a cutpurse.

Flew. By Iesus he is vtter as prate words vpon the bridge
As you shall desire to see in a Summers day : but tis all one,
What he hath said to me, looke you, is all one.

Go. Why this is a gull, a foole, a rogue that goes to the warrs
Onely to grace himselfe at his returne to London:
And such fellowes as he,
Are perfect in great Commanders names.
They will learne by rote where seruices were done,
At such and such a sconce, at such a breach,
As such a conuoy : who came off brauely, who was shot,
Who disgraced, what termes the enemie stood on.
And this they con perfectly in phrase of warre,
Which they trick vp with new tuned oathes: & what a berd
Of the Generalls cut, and a horride shout of the campe
(will.

D

The Chronicle History

Enter the King disguised, to him Pistoll.

Pist. Ke vela?

King. A friend.

Pist. Discus vnto me, art thou Gentleman?
Or art thou common, base, and popeler?

King. No sir, I am a Gentleman of a Company.

Pist. Trailes thou the puissant pike?

King. Euen so sir, What are you?

Pist. As good a gentleman as the Emperour.

King. O then thou art better then the King?

Pist. The king a bego, and a hart of gold,

Pist. A lad of life, an impe of fame:
Of parents good, of fist most valiant:
I kis his durtie shoe: and from my harte stringes
I loue the louely bully, What is thy name?

King. Harry le Roy.

Pist. Le Roya Cornish name.
Art thou of Cornish crew?

Kin. No sir, I am a Welchman.

Pist. A Welchman: knowst thou *Flewellen*?

Kin. I sir, he's my kinsman.

Pist. Are thou his friend?

Kin. I sir.

Pist. Figa for thee then: my name is *Pistoll*.

Kin. It forts well with your fiercenesse.

Pist. Pistoll is my name.

                 Exit Pistoll.

      Enter Gower and Flewellen.

Gow. Captaine *Flewellen*.

Flu. In the name of Ieshu speake lewer.
It is the greatest folly in the world, when the aunciēt
Prerogatiues of the warres be not kept.
I warrant you, if you looke into the warres of the Romanes,
You shall finde, no tittle tattle, nor pibble bable there:

                         But

of Henry the fift.

But you shall finde the caves, and the feares
And the ceremonies, to be otherwise.

Gow. Why the enemy is loud, you heard him all night.

Flu. Gods sollud, if the enemy be an Asse & a Foole,
And a prating cocks-combe, is it meet that we be also a foole,
And a prating cocks-combe, in your conscience now?

Gow. Ile speake lower.

Flu. I beseech you do, good Captaine *Gower*,

           Exit Gower, and Flewellen.

Kin. Tho it appeare a litle out of fashion,
Yet theres much care in this.

      Enter three Souldiers.

1.Soul. Is not that the morning yonder?

2.Soul. I see the beginning.
God knowes whether we shall see the end or no.

3.Soul. Well I thinke the king could wish himselfe
Vp to the necks in the middle of the Thames,
And so I would he were, at all aduentures, and I with him.

3.S. Ifaith small cheer some of vs is like to haue,
Ere this day ende.

Kin. Why feare nothing man, the king is frolike.

2.S. I he may be, for he hath no such cause as we.

Kin. Nay say not so, he is a man as we are.
The Violet smels to him as to vs:
Therefore if the see reasons, he feares as we do,

2.Sol. But the king hath a heauy reckoning to make,
If his cause be not good, when all those soules
Whose bodies shall be slaughtered here,
Shall ioyne together at the latter day,
And say I dyed at such a place, Some swearing.
Some their wiues rawly left:
Some leauing their children poore behind them

                         Now

The Chronicle Historie

Now if this cause be bad, it will be a grieuous matter
(to him)
King. Why so you may say, if a man send his seruant
As Factor into another Countrey,
And be by any meanes miscarry,
You may say the businesse of the master,
Was the author of his seruants misfortune,
Or if a sonne be imployd by his father,
And the fall into any lewd action, you may say the father
Was the author of his sonnes damnation:
But the master is not to answere for his seruants,
The father for his sonne, nor the king for his subiects:
For they purpose not their deaths, when they craue their ser-
Some there are that haue the gift of premeditated (uices
Murder on them:
Others the broken seale of Forgery, in beguiling maydons.
Now if these outstrip the law,
Yet they escape not Gods punishments.
War is Gods Beadel, War is Gods vengeance
Euery mans seruice is the kings
But euery mans soule is his owne.
Therefore I would haue euery souldier examine himselfe,
And wash euery moath out of his conscience:
That in so dooing, he may but the readier for death
Or not dying, why the time was well spent,
Wherein such preperation was made.
3.Lord. Yfaith he saies true:
Euery mans fault on his owne head,
I would not haue the king answere for me
Yet I intend to fight lustily for him.
King. Well, I heard the King, he would not be ransomde
2.L. I he said so, to make vs fight,
But when our throates be cut, he may be ransomde,
And we neuer the wiser.
King. If I liue to see that, Ile neuer trust his word againe.
2.Lord.

of Henry the fifth

2.Sol. May you be pay him, that is thou tels a greate displeasure
That an elder gun, can do to a guift is common:
Or a sibilies against a mustarde
Youle nere take his word again, you re as well go goe
King. Your reproofe is somewhat too bitter
Were it not at this time I could be angry.
2.Sol. Why let it be a quarrell if thou wilt.
King. How shall I know thee?
2.Sol. Here is my gloue, which if euer I see thy hand,
Ile challenge thee, and strike thee.
Kin. Here is likewise another of mine,
And sure thee Ile weare it.
2.Sol. Thou dar'st as well the hangd.
3.Sol. Be friends you fooles,
We haue French quarrels now inow
We haue no need of English broyles
Kin. Tis no treason to cut French crownes,
For to morrow the king himselfe will be a clipper.
Exit soldiers.

Enter King, Gloster, Epingham, and Attendants.

K. O God of Battels steele my souldiers harts,
Take from them now the sence of reckning,
That the appossed multitudes which stand before them,
May not appall their courage.
O not to day, not to day O God,
Thinke on the fault my father made,
In compassing the crowne.
I Richards bodie haue interred new,
And on it hath bestowed more contrite teares,
Then from it issued forced drops of blood:
A hundred men haue I in yearely pay,
Which

of Henry the fift

We would not die in that mans company,
That feares his fellowship to die with vs.
This day is called the day of Cryspin,
He that out-liues this day, and sees old age,
Shall yeerely on the vigill feast his friends,
And say, to morrow is S. Cryspines day.
Then shall we in their flowing bowles
Be newly remembred. *Henry the King,*
Bedford and Exeter, Clarence and Gloster,
Warwick and Yorke.
Familiar in their mouthes as houshold words,
This story shall the good man tell his sonne:
And from this day, vnto the generall doome:
But we in it shall be remembred:
We fewe, we happie fewe, we band of brothers,
For he to day that sheds his blood by mine,
Shalbe my brother: be he nere so base,
This day shall gentle his condition.
Then shall he strip his sleeues, and shew his skars,
And say, these wounds I had on Crispines day:
And Gentlemen in England now a bed,
Shall thinke themselues accurst,
And hold their manhood cheape,
While any speake, that fought with vs
Vpon Saint Crispines day.
 Glost. My gracious Lord,
The French is in the field.
 Kin. Why all things are readie, if our minds be so.
 War. Perish the man whose mind is backward now.
 King. Thou dost not wish more help fro England consent?
 War. Gods will my Liege, would you and I alone,
Without more helpe, might fight this battaile out.
 King. Why

E. 3

The Chronicle Historie

With thy very day their withered hands hold vp,
To heauen to pardon blood,
And I haue built two chanceries, more will I doe:
Tho all that I can do, is all too little.

 Enter Gloster.

 Glost. My Lord,
 King. My brother *Glosters* voyce,
 Glost. My Lord the Army stayes vpon your presence,
 King. Stay *Gloster* stay, and I will go with thee,
The day my friends, and all things stayes for me.

 Enter Clarence, Gloster, Exeter and Salisburie.

 War. My Lords the French are very strong,
 Exe. There is fiue to one, besides they all are fresh.
 War. Of fighting men they haue full fortie thousand.
 Sal. The ods is all too great. Farewell kind Lords
Braue *Clarence*, and my Lord of *Gloster*,
My Lord of *Warwicke*, and to all farewell.
 Clar. Farewell kind Lord, fight valiantly to day,
And yet in truth, I do thee wrong,
For thou art made on the true sparkes of honour.

 Enter King.

 War. O would we had but ten thousand men in England,
Now this instant, that doth not worke in England.
 King. Whose that, that wishes so my Cousin *Warwick?*
Gods will I would not loose so base honours,
One man would share from me:
Not for my Kingdome.
No faith my Cousin, wish not one man more,
Rather proclaime it presently through out my campe,
That he that hath no stomacke to this feast,
Let him depart, his pasport shall be drawne,
And crownes for conuoy put into his purse,

We

The Chronicle Historie

Why well faid. Thou doth please me better
Then to wish me one. You know your charge,
God be with you all.

Enter the Herald from the French.

Herald. Once more I come to know of thee king Harry,
What thou wilt giue for ranfome?
Kin. Who haft fent thee now?
Her. The Conftable of France.
Kin. I prethy beare my former anfwer backe,
Bid them atchieue me and then fell my bones.
Good God, why fhould they mock good fellowes thus?
The man that once did fell the Lions skin,
While the beaft liu'd, was kild with hunting him.
A many of our bodies fhall no doubt
Finde graues within your realme of France,
Tho buried in your dunghills, fhalbe fam'd,
For there the Sun fhall greet them,
And draw vp their honors reeking vp to heauen,
Leauing their earthly parts to choke your clime,
The fmel whereof, fhall breede a plague in France,
Marke then abundant valour in our English,
That being dead, like to the bullets crafing,
Breakes forth into a fecond courfe of mifchiefe,
Killing in relaps of mortalitie.
Let me fpeake proudly,
Thers not a peece of feather in our campe,
Good argument I hope we wil in fluster,
And time hath worne vs into flouenrie,
But by the mas, our hearts are in the trim,
And my poore fouldiers tell me, yet ere night
Thayle be in frefher robes, or they will plucke
The gay new cloaths ore your French fouldiers eares
And turne them out of feruice. If they do this,
As if it pleafe God they fhall,
Then fhall our ranfome foone be leuied.

A Chronicle Historie

Saue thou thy labour Herauld,
Come thou no more for ranfome gentle Herauld,
They fhall haue nought I fweare but thefe my bones
Which if they haue as I will leaue em them,
Her. I fhall deliuer fo...

Yorke. My gracious Lord, vpon my knee I craue
The leading of the vaward.
Kin. Take it braue Yorke. Come fouldiers lets away,
And as thou pleafeft God difpofe the day.

Enter the foure French Lords.

Ge. O diabello.
Conft. Mor du ma vie.
Or. O what a day is this?
Bur. O iour de hont, all is gone, all is loft.
Con. We are inough yet liuing in the field,
To fmoother vp thefe English...
If any order might be...
Bur. A plague...
And...
Let him go home...
Likewife...
Why halt by...
His faireft daughter is contaminated...
Con. Diforder that hath fpoyl'd vs, friend vs now,
Come we in heapes, weele offer vp our liues
Vnto thefe English, or else die with fame.
Come, come alongs,
Lets dye with honour, our fhame doth laft too long.

E 3

Enter Pistoll, the French man, and the Boy.

Pist. Yeeld cur.

French. O Mounsir ie vous en pri et me petie de moy?

Pist. Moy shall not serue, I will haue fortie moyes.

Boy take him his ...

Boy. Monsieur Fer.

Pist. He sayes his name is Master Fer.

Pist. Ile Fer him, and ferit him, and ferke him.

Boy discus the same in French.

Boy. Sir I do not know what's French

Powder, ferit and ferke.

Pist. Bid him prepare, for I will cut his throate.

Boy. Feare you ...

French. Oye ma toy couple la gorge.

Violette tow giue to me ...

French. Qui dit il monsieur?

Boy ...

French. La grand ...

French. O Ie vous en pri ...

... capitaine ...

A moy ...

Pist. What ...

Boy. Marry sir ...

Crownes ...

House of France ...

He will giue you 200 Crownes

Pist. My ...

And I the Crowne ...

And as I such blood, I will ...

Follow me cur.

Enter the King and his Nobles, Pistoll.

King. What will the French retire?

Yet

Yet all is not done, yet keepe the French the field.

Exe. The Duke of Yorke commends him to your Grace.

King. Lives he good Vnckle, thrice within this houre
I saw him downe, thrice vp againe:
From helmet to the spurre, all bleeding ore.

Exe. In which aray, braue souldier, doth he lye,
Larding the plaines: and by his bloody side,
Yoake-fellow to his honour dying wounds,
The noble Earle of Suffolke also lyes.
Suffolke first dyde, and Yorke all hagled ore,
Comes to him where in blood he lay steepe,
And takes him by the beard, kisses the gashes
That bloodily did yawne vpon his face:
And cryde aloud, tary deare cousin Suffolke:
My soule shall thine keepe company in heauen:
Tary deare soule a while, then flie to rest:
And in this glorious and well-foughten field
We kept together in our chiualry.
Vpon these words I came and cheerd them vp,
He tooke me by the hand, said deare my Lord,
Commend my seruice to my soueraigne,
So did he turne, and ouer Suffolkes necke
He threw his wounded arme, and kist his lips,
With blood he sealed A testament of noble ending loue:
Of neuer ending loue. The pretty and sweet manner of it forc'd
Forst those waters from me, which I would haue stop'd,
But I not so much of man in me,
But all my mother came into mine eyes,
And gaue me vp to teares.

King. I blame you not, for hearing this I must
I must compound to teares.

Alarum soundes.

What new alarum is this?

Bid euery souldier kill his prisoner.

Pist. Couple gorge. *Exeunt.*

The Chronicle Historie

Enter Fluellen, and Captaine Gower.

Flu. Godes plud kill the boyes and the luggage,
Tis the arrants peece of knauery as can be desired,
In the world now, in your conscience now.
Gower. Tis certaine, theres not a boy left aliue,
And the cowardly rascals that ran from the battell,
Themselues haue done this slaughter,
Beside, they haue burned and carried away
All that was in the kings Tent,
Whereupon the king caused euery prisoner
Throat to be cut. O he is a worthy king.
Flu. I he was borne at Monmouth,
Captaine Gower, what call you the place where
Alexander the big was borne?
Gower. Alexander the great.
Flu. Why I pray, is not big great?
As if I say, big or great, or magnanimous,
I hope it is all one reckoning,
Saue the frase is a litle variations.
Gower. I thinke Alexander the great
Was borne at Macedon,
His father was called Phillip of Macedon,
As I take it.
Flu. I thinke it was Macedon indeede where Alexander
Was borne: looke you Captaine Gower,
And if you looke into the mappes of the world well,
You shall finde litle difference
Betweene Macedon and Monmouth: looke you there is
A Riuer in Macedon, and there is also a Riuer
In Monmouth, the Riuers name at Monmouth is
Called Wye.
But tis out of my braine, what is the name of the other
But tis all one, tis so like as my fingers is to my fingers,
And there is Samon in both.
Looke you, if you marke it, Gower, and your

You

You shall finde our King is come after Alexander.
God knowes, and you know, the Alexander in his
Bowles, and his ales, and his wrath, and his displeasures,
And indignacions, was kill his friend Clitus.
Gower. But our King is not like him in that,
For he neuer kill any of his friends.
Flew. Looke you, it is not well done to take the tale out
Of a mans mouth, ere it is made an end and finished.
I speake in the comparison as Alexander is kill
His friend Clitus : so our King being in his ripe
Wits and iudgements, is turne away, the fat knite
With the great belly doublet: I am forget his name.
Gower.   Sir Iohn Falstaffe.
Flew. I, I thinke it is Sir Iohn Falstaffe indeede,
I can tell you, theres good men borne at Monmouth.
        Enter King and the Lords.
King. I was not angry since I came into France,
V ntill this howre.
Take a trumpet Herauld,
And ride vnto the horssemen on yon hill:
If they will fight with vs bid them come downe,
Or leaue the field, they do offend our sight:
Will they do neither, we will come to them,
And make them skyr away as fast
As stones enforst from the old Assirian slings:
Besides, weele cut the throats of those we haue,
And not one aliue shall tast our mercy.
        Enter the Herauld.
Gods will what meanes this? know'st thou not
That we haue fined these bones of ours for ransome?
Herald. I come great king for charitable fauour,
To sort our Nobles from our common men,
We may haue leaue to bury all our dead,
Which in the field lye spoyled and trod on.
Kin. I tell the truly Herald, I do not know whither

F   The

The Chronicle Historie

The day be ours.

For yet a many of your watch do keep the field.

Her. This day is yours.

Kin. Praised be God therefore.

What Castle call you that?

Her. We call it *Agincourt*.

Kin. Then call we this the field of *Agincourt*,

Fought on the day of *Crispin Crispin*.

Flew. Your grandfather of famous memorie,

If your grace be remembred,

Is do good service in *France*.

Kin. I is true *Fluellen*.

Flew. Your Maiestie sayes verie true.

And it please your Maiestie,

The Welchmen there was do good seruice

In a garden where Leekes did grow,

And I thinke your Maiestie wil take no scorne,

To weare a Leeke in your cap vpon S. *Dauies* day.

Kin. No *Fluellen*, for I am welch as well as you.

Flew. All the water in *Wye* will not wash your welch

Blood out of you. God keep it and preserue it.

To his graces will and pleasure.

Kin. Thankes good countrymen.

Flew. By Iesu I am your Maiesties countrieman,

I care not who know it: so long as your maiestie is an honest (man.

K. God keep me do. Our Herald go with him,

And bring vs the number of the slaine of both French (men.

Call yonder souldier hither.

Flew. You fellow, come to the king.

Kin. Fellow why dost thou weare that gloue in thy hat?

Soul. And please your maiestie, tis a raskals that (wronged

With me the other day: and he hath one of mine, (I wear

Which if euer I see, I haue sworne to strike him.

of Henry the fifth.

So hath he sworne the like to weare the like for the oath (vaunt

K. How think you *Fluellen*, is it lawfull he keep his oath?

Fl. And it please your maiesty, tis lawfull he keep his vow.

If he be periur'd once, he is as arrant a beggerly knaue

As treads vpon too blacke shoos.

Flew. His enemy may be a gentleman of worth.

And if he be but of good's gentleman as Lucifer

And *Belzebub*, and the diuell himselfe,

Tis meete he keepe his vowe.

Kin. Well sirrah, keep your word.

Vnder what Captaine seruest thou?

Soul. Vnder Captaine *Gower.*

Flew. Captaine *Gower* is a good Captaine

And hath good litterature in the warres.

Kin. Go call him hither.

Soul. I will my Lord.   *Exit souldier.*

Kin. Captain *Fluellen,* when *Alanson* and my selfe were

Downe together, I tooke this gloue off from his helmet,

Heere *Fluellen,* weare it. If any do challenge it,

He is a friend of *Alansons,*

And do serue me not.

Fle. Your Maiestie doth me as great a fauour

As can be desired in the hearts of his subiects,

I would see that man now that should challenge this gloue,

And it please God of his grace, I would but see him,

That's all.

Kin. Fluellen knowest thou this Captaine *Gower?*

Fle. Captaine *Gower* is my friend,

And if it like your maiestie, I know him very well.

Kin. Go call him hither.

Flew. I will and if that please your maiestie.

Kin. Follow *Fluellen* closely at the heeles,

The gloue he weares, it was this souldiers,

F 2

The Chronicle History

It may be there will be harme betweene them,
For I do know Fluellen valiant,
And being touch't as hot as gunpowder:
And quickly will returne an iniury.
Goe see there be no harme betweene them.

Enter Gower, Fluellen, and the Souldier.

Flew. Captain Gower, in the name of Iesu,
Come to his Maiestie, there is more good toward you,
Then you can dreame off.
Soul. Do you heare you sir? do you know this gloue?
Flew. I know the the gloue is a gloue.
Soul. Sir I know this, and thus I challenge it.

He strike him.

Flew. Gods plut, and his, Captain Gower stand away:
Ile giue treason his due presently.

Enter the King, Warwicke, Clarence, and Exeter.

Kin. How now, what is the matter?
Flew. And it shall please your Maiestie,
Here is the notablest peece of treason come to light,
As you shall desire to see in a sommers day.
Here is a rascall begger, scald beggerly lowsie knaue it is,
Which your Maiestie tooke out of the bridge of *Agincourt*,
And your Maiestie will beare me witnesse and testimonie in A-
And auouchments, this is the gloue of *Alanson*,
Soul. And it please your Maiestie, this is my gloue.
He that I gaue it too in the night,
Promised me to weare it in his hat,
I promised to strike him if he did.
Inter that Gentleman with my gloue in his hat,
And I thinke I haue bene as good as my word.
Flew. Your Maiestie heare now, saving your Maiestie
Manhood, what a beggerly lowsie knaue it is.
Kin. Let me see thy gloue. Looke you,
This is the fellow of it.
It was I indeed you promised to strike.

And.

of Henry the fift.

And thou dost hast giuen me most bitter termes,
How canst thou make vs amends?
Flew. Let his necke answere it.
If there be any marshals lawe in the worell.
Soul. My Liege, all offences come from the heart:
Neuer came any from mine to offend your Maiestie.
You appeard to mee as a common man:
Witnesse the night, your garments, your lowlinesse,
And what soeuer you receiued vnder that habit,
I beseech your Maiestie impute it to your owne fault
And not mine. For your selfe came not like your selfe:
Had you bene as you seemed, I had made no offence.
Therefore I beseech your grace to pardon me.
Kin. Vnckle, fill the gloue with crownes,
And giue it to the souldier. Weare it souldier,
As an honour in thy cap, till I do challenge it.
Giue him the crownes. Come Captaine *Fluellen*,
I must needs haue you friends.
Flew. By Iesu, the fellow hath mettall enough
In his belly. Harke you souldier, there is a shilling for you,
And keepe your selfe out of braules, & brables, & dissentions,
And looke you, it shall be the better for you.
Soul. Ile none of your money sir, nor I
Flew. Why tis a good shilling man,
Why should you be queamish? Your shoes are not so good,
It will serue you to mend your shoes.
Kin. What men of sort are taken vncle?
Exe. (Charge Duke of *Orleance*, Nephew to the King,
Iohn Duke of *Burbon*, and Lord *Bowchwald*,
Of other Lords and Barrons, Knights and Squiers,
Full fifteene hundred, besides common men.
This note doth tell me often thousand
French, that in the field lyes slaine.
Of Nobles bearing banners in the field,

F 3   *Our.*

The Chronicle Historie

Charles de le Brute, the Constable of France,
Iaques of Chatillion, Admirall of France,
The Maister of the crosbowes, Iohn Duke Alson.
Lord Rambures, like Maister of France.
The braue sir Guychard, Dolphin Of Nobelle Charolles,
Gran Prix and Rossi, Fawconbridge and Foy,
Gerard and Verton. Vidancour and Lestreat.
Here was a royall fellowship of death,
Where is the number of our English dead?

Edward the Duke of Yorke, the Earle of Suffolke,
Sir Richard Ketly, Dauy Gam Esquiere:
And of all other, but fiue and twentie.
O God thy arme was here,
And vnto thee alone, ascribe we praise.
When without stratagem,
And in euen shock of battle, was euer heard
So great, and little losse, on one part and an other.
Take it God, for it is onely thine.

Exe. Tis wonderfull.

King. Come let vs go on procession through the camp:
Let it be death proclaimed to any man,
To boast hereof, or take the praise from God,
Which is his due.

Flu. Ait lawfull, and it please your Maiestie,
To tell how many is kild?

King. Yes Flewellan, but with this acknowledgement,
That God fought for vs.

Flu. Yes in my conscience, he did vs great good.

King. Let there be sung Nonnobis, and te Deum,
The dead with charitie enterred in clay,
Weele then to Callice, and to England then,
Where nere from France arriue more happier men.

Exit omnes.

Enter Gower, and Flewellin.

Gower. But why do you weare your Leeke to day?
Saint

of Henry the fifth.

Saint Dauies day is past.

Flew. There is occasion Captaine Gower,
Looke you why, and wherefore.
The other day I looke you Pistoll
Which you know is a man of no merites
In the world, is come where I was the other day,
And brings bread and saule, and bids me
Eate my Leeke: twas in a place looke you.
Where I could mooue no discentious:
But if I can see him, I shall tell him,
A little of my desires.

Gow. Here a comes swelling like a Turkecocke.

Enter Pistoll.

Flew. Tis no matter for his swelling, and his turkecocke,
God plesse you Antient Pistoll, you scall,
Beggerly, lowsie knaue, God plesse you.

Pist. Ha, art thou bedlam?
Dost thou thurst base Troyan,
To haue me foulde vp Parcas fatall web?
Hence, I am qualmish at the smell of Leeke.

Flew. Antient Pistoll, I would desire you because
It doth not agree with your stomacke, and your appetite,
And your digestions, to eate this Leeke.

Pist. Not for Cadwallader and all his goates.

Flew. There is one goate for you Antient Pistoll.

He strikes him.

Pist. Base Troyan, thou shall dye.

Flew. I, I know I shall dye, meane time, I would
Desire you to liue and eate this Leeke.

Gower. Inough Captaine, you haue astonisht him.

Flew. Astonish him, by Iesu, Ile beate his head
Foure dayes and foure nights, but Ile
Make him eate some part of my Leeke.

Pist. Well must I byte?

Flew. I

The Chronicle Historie

Flew. I out of question or doubt yor ambiguities:
You must byte.
Pist. Good good.
Flew. I Leekes are goob Ancient *Pistoll*:
There is a shilling for you to heale your bloudy coxckome,
Pist. Me a shilling.
Flew. If you will not take it,
I haue an other Leeke for you.
Pist. I take thy shilling in earnest of reconing.
Flew. If I owe you any thing, ile pay you in cudgels,
You shalbe a woodmonger,
And buy cudgels. God buy you,
Ancient *Pistoll*, God blesse you,
And heale your broken pate.
Ancient *Pistoll* if you see Leekes an other time,
Mocke at them, ther is all: God bwy you.
                                   Exit Flewellen.
Pist. All hell shall stir for this.
Doth Fortune play the huswyfe with me now?
Is honour cudgeld from my wearie lims?
Well *France* farwell, newes haue I certainly
That Doll is sicke. One mallydie of *France*,
The warres affordeth nought, home will I trug:
Bawd will I turne, and vse the sleyte of hand:
To England will I steale.
And there ile steale.
And patches will I get vnto these skarres,
And sweare I get them in the Gallia warres.   *Exit Pistoll.*

*Enter at one doore the King of England and his Lords. And at
the other doore the King of France, Queene Katherine, the
Duke of Burbon, and others.*

Harry. Peace to this meeting, wherefore we are met:
                                                   And

of Henry the fift.

And to our brother *France*, Faire time of day.
Faire health vnto our louely cousen *Katherine*.
And as a branch, and member of this stock:
We do salue you Duke of *Burgondie*.
Fran. Brother of *England*, right ioyous are we to behold
Your face, so are we Princes English euery one.
Duk. With pardon vnto both your mightines.
Let it not displease you, if I demaund
What rub or bar hath thus far hindred you,
To keepe you from the gentle speech of peace?
Har. If Duke of *Burgondy* you wold haue peace,
You must buy that peace,
According as we haue drawne our articles.
Fran. We haue but with a cursenary eye,
Oreviewd them pleaseth your Grace:
To let some of vs our Councell sit withvs,
We shall returne our peremptory answere.
Har. Go Lords, and sit with them,
And bring vs answere backe.
Yet leaue our cousen *Katherine* here behind.
France. With all our hearts.

*Exis King and the Lords, Henry, Kathe-
rine, and the Gentlewoman.*

Har. Now *Kate*, you haue a blunt wooer here
Left with you.
If I could win thee at leapfrog,
Or with vawting with my armour on my backe,
Into my saddle,
Without brag be it spoken,
Ide make compare with any.
But leauing that *Kate*,
If thou takest me now,
Thou shalt haue me at the worst:
                                              G   And

The Chronicle Historie

And in wearing-shout shalt haue one better and better,
Thou shalt haue a face that is not worth sunne-burning:
But doest thou thinke that thou and I,
Betweene Saint Denis,
And Saint George, shall get a boy,
That shall goe to Constantinople,
And take the great Turke by the beard ha Kate.
Kate. I st possible dat me shall
    Loue de enemie de France.
Harry. No Kate, tis vnpossible
You should loue the enemie of France,
For Kate I loue France so well,
That Ile not leaue a Village,
Ile haue it all mine: then Kate,
When France is mine,
And I am yours,
Then France is yours,
And you are mine.
Kate. I cannot tell what is dat.
Harry. No Kate,
Why Ile tell it you in French,
Which will hang vpon my tongue, like a bride
On her new married Husband,
Let me see Saint Denis be my speed,
Quan France et mon.
Kate. Dat is, when France is yours,
Harry. Et vous estes a moy.
Kate. And I am to you.
Harry. Donck France estes a vous
Kate. Den France sall be mine.
Harry. Et Ie suynes a vous.
Kate. And you will be to me,
Har. Wilt belieue me Kate? tis easier for me
To conquer the kingdome, this to speake so much
More French.

of Henry the fifth.

Kate. A your Maiesty has fallse France inough
To deceiue de best Lady in France,
    Harry. No faith Kate not I. But Kate,
In plaine termes, do you loue me?
Kate. I cannot tell.
    Harry. No, can any of your neighbours tell,
Ile aske them.
Come Kate I know you loue me,
And soone when you are in your closse,
Youle question this Lady of me,
But I pray thee sweete Kate, vse me mercifully,
Because I loue thee cruelly.
That I shall dye Kate Is it fast?
But for thy loue, by the Lord no:no,
What Wench,
A straight blacke will growe crooked,
A round eye will growe hollowe,
A great leg will waxe small,
A curld pate prooue bald:
But a good heart Kate, is the sunne and the moone,
And rather the Sunne and not the Moone:
And therefore Kate take me,
Take a souldier: take a souldier
Take a King.
Therefore tell me Kate, wilt thou haue me?
Kate. Dat is as please the King my father.
    Harry. Nay it will please him Kate.
Ney it sall please him Kate.
And vpon that condition Kate Ile kisse you.
Ka.O mon dela se vo voudoy faire quelke chose
Pour toute le monde,
Come poynt voster seigneur en fonor.
    Harry. What saies she Lady?
    Lady. Dat it is not de fashion en France,
For de maides, before de be married to

G 3

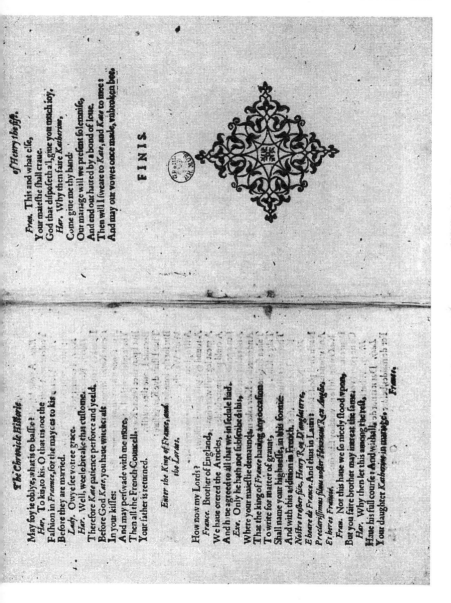

The Chronicle Historie

May fewe oblige, what is to baise?
Kate. To kisse to kis. O that is not the
Fashion in *Fraunce*, for the may es to kis.
Before they are married.
Lady. Owye see votree grace.
Kate. Well, wee lobrake that custome.
Therefore God *Kate* patience perforce and yeeld.
Before God *Kate*, you haue witchcraft
In your kisses:
And may perswade with me more,
Then all the French Councell.
Your father is returned.

Enter the King of France, *and*
the Lords.

How now my Lords?
France. Brother of England,
We haue ored the Articles,
And haue agreede to all that we in sedule had.
Exe. Only he hath not subscribed this.
Where your maiestie demaunds
That the king of *France* having any occasion
To write for matter of graunt,
Shall name your highnesse, in this forme
And with this addition in French,
Nostre treser fise, Henry Roy D'angleterre,
E heere de France. And thus in Latin:
Preclarissimus filius noster Henricus Rex Anglie,
Et heres Franciæ.
Fran. Nor this haue we so nicely stood vpon,
But you faire brother may intreat the same.
Har. Why then let this among the rest.
Haue his full course: And withall,
Your daughter *Katherine* in mariage.
France.

of Henry the fift.

Fran. This and what else,
Your maiestie shall craue.
God that disposeth all, giue you much ioy,
Har. Why then faire *Katherine*,
Come giue me thy hand:
Our mariage will we present solemnise,
And end our hatred by a bond of loue,
Then will I sweare to *Kate*, and *Kate* to mee:
And may our vowes once made, vnbroken bees

FINIS.

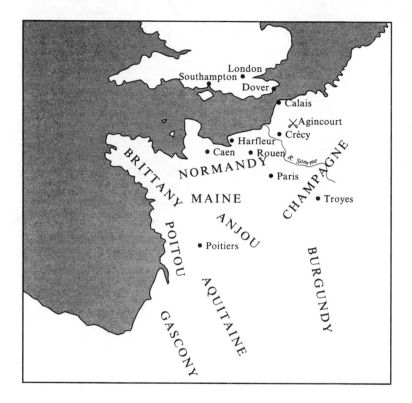

Map of France and the south of England

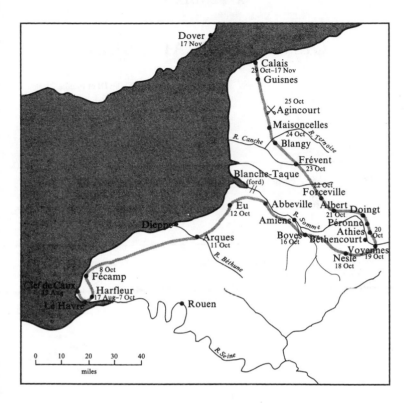

Map of the route of Henry V's army,
from 13 August to 17 November 1415

APPENDIX 4

GENEALOGICAL TABLE

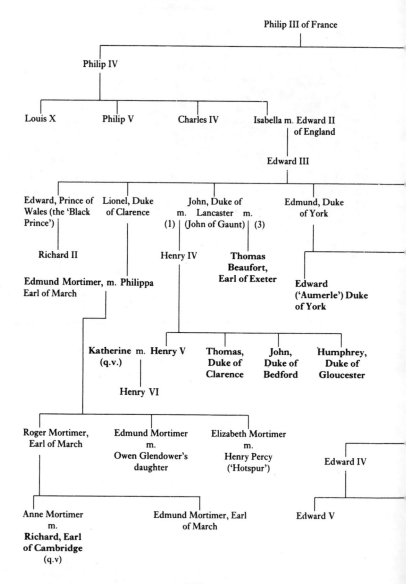

402

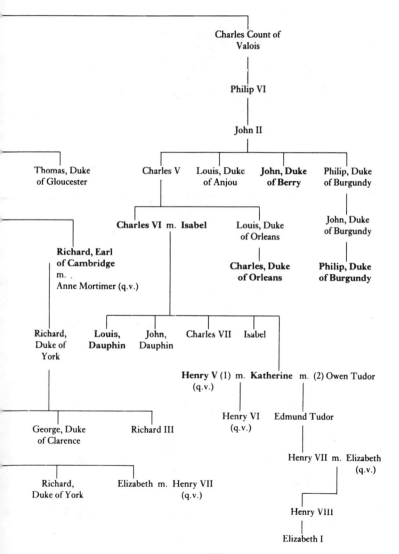

DOUBLING CHART

Actor	Pro	1.1	1.2	2.0	2.1	2.2	2.3	2.4	3.0	3.1	3.2	3.3	3.4	3.5	3.6
1	Cho			Cho		(-*sol-)			Cho						
2			King			-King				King		King			-Mon- -King (-*sol)
3			Exe			Exe		-Exe		*Exe		*Exe			
4			*Cla			(-*Cla)		Dau		(*sol)		(*sol)		Dau	
5			*Glo			(-*Glo)		(-*att)		*Glo		(*Glo)			-Glo (-*sol)
6			*Bed			Bed		(-*att)		*Bed		(*Bed)			
7			(*att)			(-*sol-)		(-*att)			-Flu	(*Flu)			Flu
8			West			West		-Mess-			-Gow	(*Gow)			Gow (-*sol)
9		Cant	-Cant		Nym	(-*sol-)	Nym			(*sol)	Nym-				
10		Ely	-Ely					Fr. K			-Jamy	(*Jamy)		Fr. K	
11					-Pist		Pist				Pi-/-Mc	(*Mac)			-Pist- (-*sol)
12			-1 Am-		Bard	-Cam-	Bard			(*sol)	Bard-			(*lord)	
13			-2 Am-			-Scr-		Cons		(*sol)		(*cit)		Cons	
14			*War			-Grey-		*Ber		(*sol)		(*cit)		(*Ber)	
15								*Brit				Gov		Brit	
†16			(*att)		-Boy-		Boy				Boy-		Kat		
†17			(*att)		-Host-		Host						Ali		
†18															

Actor	3.7	4.0	4.1	4.2	4.3	4.4	4.5	4.6	4.7	4.8	5.0	5.1	5.2	Epi	No. of Lines
1		Cho			-Mon-			(-*sol)	-Mon-		Cho			Cho	275
2			King		-King			King	-King	-King			King		1036
3					Exe			-Exe	-Exe	-Exe			Exe		130
4	Dau			Dau	-York		Dau			(-*Cla)			*Cla		118
5			Glo		Glo			(*Glo)	-Glo	-Glo			*Glo		5
6			*Bed-		Bed		Bou		*Bou				*Bed		16
7			-Flu-		(*Flu)				Flu-	Flu		Flu-	*Hunt		288
8	-Mess-		-Gow-	-Mess-	West				-Gow-	Gow		Gow-	West		96
9			-Erp-	-Gra	*Erp			(*sol-)	(-*sol)	(-*sol)			(*F.lo)		279
10	(*sol-)							(*sol-)	(-*sol)	(-*sol)			Fr.K		160
11	(*sol-)		-Pist-		(*Pist)	Pist-		(*sol-)	(-*sol)	(-*sol)		-Pist			182
12					Sali			(*pris-)	-*Her-	-Her			Burg		111
13	Cons		-Wil-	-Cons		Fr.S-	Cons		-Wil-	Wil			(*F.lo)		227
14	Orl		-Bat-	Orl			Orl		(-*sol)	(-*sol)			(*F.lo)		95
15	Ram		-Cou-	Ram			Ram		-*War	-War			*War		42
†16					(*sol)	Boy			(-*sol)	(-*sol)			Kat		63
†17					(*Boy)			(*pris-)	(*pris)				Ali		104
†18					(*sol)			(*pris-)	(*pris)				Isa		68

† boy actor
* mute
– enters after beginning or exits before end of scene
( ) available either as named character or as unnamed extra

ABBREVIATIONS AND REFERENCES

Quotations and references relating to *Henry V* are keyed to the present edition. Those relating to Shakespeare's other works are keyed to Oxf in the following list; where Oxf's act/scene/line numbering departs from traditional numbering the latter is supplied, in square brackets, from Alexander. Biblical quotations are taken from the 'Bishops' Bible' edition (London, 1568 etc.) except where otherwise stated. Abbreviations of the parts of speech (*a.*, *adv.*, *sb.*, *ppl.*, *a.* etc.) are those used in *OED*. Titles of collected editions of Shakespeare other than the Folios are simplified as *Works* if they include the poems and as *Plays* if they do not; titles of editions of the play alone, including the Quartos, are given as *Henry V*; and variations in the spelling of the name Shakespeare are not recorded.

In all references, place of publication is London unless otherwise stated.

ABBREVIATIONS

ABBREVIATIONS USED IN NOTES

*	Precedes commentary notes involving readings altered from the early edition on which this edition is based
SD	stage direction
SP	speech prefix
subst.	substantively
t.n.	the textual notes at the foot of each page
this edn	a reading adopted for the first time in this edition

SHAKESPEARE'S WORKS

AC	*Antony and Cleopatra*
AW	*All's Well That Ends Well*
AYL	*As You Like It*
CE	*The Comedy of Errors*
Cor	*Coriolanus*
Cym	*Cymbeline*
Ham	*Hamlet*

1H4	*Henry IV, Part 1*
2H4	*Henry IV, Part 2*
H5	*Henry V*
1H6	*Henry VI, Part 1*
2H6	*Henry VI, Part 2*
3H6	*Henry VI, Part 3*
H8	*Henry VIII*
JC	*Julius Caesar*
KJ	*King John*
KL	*King Lear*
LLL	*Love's Labour's Lost*
Luc	*The Rape of Lucrece*
MA	*Much Ado About Nothing*
Mac	*Macbeth*
MM	*Measure for Measure*
MND	*A Midsummer Night's Dream*
MV	*The Merchant of Venice*
MW	*The Merry Wives of Windsor*
Oth	*Othello*
Per	*Pericles*
PP	*The Passionate Pilgrim*
R2	*Richard II*
R3	*Richard III*
RJ	*Romeo and Juliet*
Son	*Sonnets*
TC	*Troilus and Cressida*
Tem	*The Tempest*
TGV	*The Two Gentlemen of Verona*
Tim	*Timon of Athens*
Tit	*Titus Andronicus*
TN	*Twelfth Night*
TNK	*The Two Noble Kinsmen*
TS	*The Taming of the Shrew*
VA	*Venus and Adonis*
WT	*The Winter's Tale*

REFERENCES

EDITIONS OF SHAKESPEARE COLLATED

Alexander	*Works*, ed. Peter Alexander (London and Glasgow, 1951)
Ard[1]	*Henry V*, ed. H. A. Evans, Arden Shakespeare (1903)

Ard[2]	*Henry V*, ed. J. H. Walter, Arden Shakespeare (1954)
Bantam	*Henry V*, ed. David Bevington, Bantam Shakespeare (Toronto etc., 1988)
BBC	*Henry V*, The BBC TV Shakespeare (1979)
Boswell	*Works*, ed. James Boswell, 21 vols (1821)
Branagh	*Henry V*, a screen adaptation by Kenneth Branagh (1989)
Cam	*Works*, ed. William George Clark and William Aldis Wright, 9 vols (Cambridge and London, 1863–6)
Cam[1]	*Henry V*, ed. John Dover Wilson (Cambridge, 1947; repr. with additions, 1955)
Cam[2]	*Henry V*, ed. Andrew Gurr (Cambridge, 1992)
Capell	*Plays*, ed. Edward Capell, 10 vols (1767–8)
Collier	*Works*, ed. John Payne Collier, 8 vols (1842–4)
Collier[2]	*Works*, ed. John Payne Collier, 6 vols (1858)
Craig & Bevington	*Works*, ed. Hardin Craig, rev. David Bevington (Glenview, Ill., 1973)
Deighton	*Henry V*, ed. K. Deighton (1880)
Delius	*Works* (*Werke*), ed. Nicolaus Delius, 7 vols (Elberfeld, 1854–61)
Dyce	*Works*, ed. Alexander Dyce, 6 vols (1857)
Dyce[2]	*Works*, ed. Alexander Dyce, 9 vols (1864–7)
Evans	*see* Ard[1]
F, F1	*Comedies, Histories and Tragedies*, The First Folio (1623)
F2	*Comedies, Histories and Tragedies*, The Second Folio (1632)
F3	*Comedies, Histories and Tragedies*, The Third Folio (1664)
F4	*Comedies, Histories and Tragedies*, The Fourth Folio (1685)
Gurr	*see* Cam[2]
Hanmer	*Works*, ed. Thomas Hanmer, 6 vols (Oxford, 1743–4)
Herford	*Works*, ed. C. H. Herford, 10 vols (1899)
Hudson	*Works*, ed. Henry N. Hudson, 20 vols (Boston and Cambridge, Mass., 1886)
Humphreys	*Henry V*, ed. A. R. Humphreys, New Penguin Shakespeare (Harmondsworth, 1968)
Irving & Marshall	*Works*, ed. Sir Henry Irving and Frank A. Marshall, The Henry Irving Shakespeare, 2nd edn, 14 vols (1906)
Johnson	*Plays*, ed. Samuel Johnson, 8 vols (1765)
Keightley	*Plays*, ed. Thomas Keightley, 6 vols (1864)
Kittredge	*Henry V*, ed. George Lyman Kittredge (Boston, Mass., 1943)
Knight	*Works*, ed. Charles Knight, 8 vols (1838–43)
Malone	*Works*, ed. Edmond Malone, 10 vols (1790)

Moore Smith	*Henry V*, ed. G. C. Moore Smith, Warwick Shakespeare (1893)
Munro	*Works*, ed. John Munro, London Shakespeare, 6 vols (1958)
Oxf	*Works*, ed. Stanley Wells, Gary Taylor, John Jowett and William Montgomery (Oxford, 1986)
Oxf[1]	*Henry V*, ed. Gary Taylor, Oxford Shakespeare (Oxford, 1982)
Pope	*Works*, ed. Alexander Pope, 6 vols (1723–5)
Pope[2]	*Works*, ed. Alexander Pope, 8 vols (1728)
Q, Q1	*Henry V*, The First Quarto (1600)
Q2	*Henry V*, The Second Quarto (1602)
Q3	*Henry V*, The Third Quarto (1619; '1608')
Rann	*Plays*, ed. Joseph Rann, 6 vols (Oxford, 1786–94)
Ridley	*Henry V*, ed. M. R. Ridley, New Temple Shakespeare (1935)
Riv	*Works*, textual editor G. Blakemore Evans, Riverside Shakespeare (Boston, Mass., 1974)
Rowe	*Works*, ed. Nicholas Rowe, 6 vols (1709)
Rowe[3]	*Works*, ed. Nicholas Rowe, 8 vols (1714)
Sisson	*Works*, ed. Charles Jasper Sisson (1954)
Staunton	*Plays*, ed. Howard Staunton, 3 vols (1858–60)
Steevens	*Plays*, ed. Samuel Johnson and George Steevens, 10 vols (1773)
Steevens[2]	*Plays*, ed. Samuel Johnson and George Steevens, 10 vols (1778)
Stone	*Henry V*, ed. Walter George Stone (1880)
Taylor	*see* Oxf[1]
Theobald	*Works*, ed. Lewis Theobald, 7 vols (1733)
Verity .	*Henry V*, ed. A. W. Verity (Cambridge, 1900; rev. 1929)
Walter	*see* Ard[2]
Wilson	*see* Cam[1]
Wordsworth	*Shakespeare's Historical Plays, Roman and English*, ed. Charles Wordsworth, 3 vols (1883)
Wright	*Henry V*, ed. William Aldis Wright (Oxford, 1881)

OTHER WORKS

| Abbott | E. A. Abbott, *A Shakespearian Grammar*, 2nd edn (1870) (References are to numbered sections, not to pages) |
| Babula | William Babula, 'Whatever happened to Prince Hal? An essay on *Henry V*', *SS*, 30 (1977), 47–59 |

Baldwin	T. W. Baldwin, *William Shakspere's 'Small Latine & Less Greeke'* (Urbana, Ill., 1944)
Barton	Anne Barton, 'The king disguised: Shakespeare's *Henry V* and the comical history', in Joseph G. Price (ed.), *The Triple Bond: Plays, mainly Shakespearean, in Performance* (University Park, Penn., 1975)
Beauman	Sally Beauman, *The RSC's Production of 'Henry V' for the Centenary Season of the Royal Shakespeare Theatre* (Oxford, 1976)
Beaumont	Francis Beaumont, *The Knight of the Burning Pestle*, in *Elizabethan Plays*, ed. Hazelton Spencer (Boston, Mass., 1933)
Beaumont & Fletcher	Francis Beaumont and John Fletcher, *The Maid's Tragedy*, ed. T. W. Craik, The Revels Plays (Manchester, 1988)
Berman	Ronald Berman (ed.), *Twentieth Century Interpretations of 'Henry V': A Collection of Critical Essays* (Englewood Cliffs, NJ, 1968)
Berry	Edward Berry, 'Twentieth-century Shakespeare criticism: the histories', in Stanley Wells (ed.), *The Cambridge Companion to Shakespeare Studies* (Cambridge, 1986)
Bevington	David Bevington, *Tudor Drama and Politics: A Critical Approach to Topical Meaning* (Cambridge, Mass., 1968)
Bloom	Harold Bloom, Introduction to *William Shakespeare's 'Henry V'*, Modern Critical Interpretations Series (1987)
Bradley	A. C. Bradley, *Oxford Lectures on Poetry* (1909)
Brissenden	Alan Brissenden, *Shakespeare and the Dance* (1981)
Brooke	C. F. Tucker Brooke (ed.), *The Shakespeare Apocrypha: Being a Collection of Fourteen Plays which have been ascribed to Shakespeare* (Oxford, 1908)
Bullough	Geoffrey Bullough (ed.), *Narrative and Dramatic Sources of Shakespeare*, 7 vols (London and New York, 1966–75)
Cairncross	Andrew S. Cairncross, 'Quarto copy for Folio *Henry V*', *SB*, 8 (1956), 67–94
Candido & Forker	Joseph Candido and Charles R. Forker, *Henry V: An Annotated Bibliography*, Garland Shakespeare Bibliographies 4 (New York, 1983)
Capell, *Notes*	Edward Capell, *Notes and Various Readings to Shakespeare* (1783)
Chambers	E. K. Chambers, *The Elizabethan Stage*, 4 vols (Oxford, 1923)
Chapman's Homer	Chapman's Homer, ed. Allardyce Nicoll, 2 vols (1957)

References

CHEL	*The Cambridge History of English Literature*, ed. A. W. Ward and A. R. Waller, 14 vols (Cambridge, 1907–16)
Craik	T. W. Craik (ed.), *Minor Elizabethan Tragedies* (1974)
Daniel	P. A. Daniel, *Notes and Conjectural Emendations of Certain Doubtful Passages in Shakespeare's Plays* (1870)
David	Richard David, *Shakespeare in the Theatre* (Cambridge, 1978)
Dekker	Thomas Dekker, *The Shoemaker's Holiday*, ed. R. L. Smallwood and Stanley Wells, The Revels Plays (Manchester, 1979)
Dent	R. W. Dent, *Shakespeare's Proverbial Language: An Index* (1981)
Dent, *PLED*	R. W. Dent, *Proverbial Language in English Drama, exclusive of Shakespeare, 1495–1616* (1984)
DNB	*The Compact Edition of the Dictionary of National Biography*, 2 vols (Oxford, 1975)
Donaldson	Peter S. Donaldson, 'Taking on Shakespeare: Kenneth Branagh's *Henry V*', *SQ*, 42 (1991), 60–71
Dutton	Richard Dutton, 'The second tetralogy', in Stanley Wells (ed.), *Shakespeare*, Oxford Bibliographical Guides (Oxford, 1990)
E3	anon., *Edward III*, in C. F. Tucker Brooke (ed.), *The Shakespeare Apocrypha* (Oxford, 1908)
Evans	G. Blakemore Evans, 'Shakespeare's text: approaches and problems', in Kenneth Muir and S. Schoenbaum (eds), *A New Companion to Shakespeare Studies* (Cambridge, 1971)
Famous Victories	anon., *The Famous Victories of Henry the Fifth* (1598) (in Bullough)
Gascoigne	George Gascoigne, *The Complete Works of George Gascoigne*, ed. John W. Cunliffe, 2 vols (Cambridge, 1907–10)
Geneva Bible	*Holy Bible* (1560 and later; edition cited, 1599)
Goddard	Harold C. Goddard, *The Meaning of Shakespeare*, 2 vols (Chicago, 1951)
Golding's Ovid	*Shakespeare's Ovid: Being Arthur Golding's Translation of the Metamorphoses* (1565), ed. W. H. D. Rouse (1961)
Gould	Gerald Gould, 'A new reading of *Henry V*', *The English Review*, 29 (1919), 42–55. (Reprinted, abridged, in Michael Quinn (ed.), *Shakespeare: Henry V: A Selection of Critical Essays*, Casebook Series, 1969)
Granville-Barker	Harley Granville-Barker, 'From *Henry V* to *Hamlet*', in L. Abercrombie, E. K. Chambers, H. Granville-Barker, W. W. Greg, E. Legouis, A. W. Pollard, C. F.

411

	E. Spurgeon, A. Thorndike and J. D. Wilson, *Aspects of Shakespeare: Being British Academy Lectures* (Oxford, 1933)
Greenblatt	Stephen Greenblatt, *Shakespearean Negotiations* (Berkeley and Oxford, 1988)
Greg, 'Principles'	W. W. Greg, 'Principles of emendation in Shakespeare', in L. Abercrombie, E. K. Chambers, H. Granville-Barker, W. W. Greg, E. Legouis, A. W. Pollard, C. F. E. Spurgeon, A. Thorndike and J. D. Wilson, *Aspects of Shakespeare: Being British Academy Lectures* (Oxford, 1933)
Greg, *Problem*	W. W. Greg, *The Editorial Problem in Shakespeare* (Oxford, 1942)
Hall	Edward Hall, *The Union of the Two Noble and Illustre Families of Lancaster and York*, ed. H. Ellis (1809)
Hawkes	Terence Hawkes, 'Shakespeare and new critical approaches', in Stanley Wells (ed.), *The Cambridge Companion to Shakespeare Studies* (Cambridge, 1986)
Hazlitt	William Hazlitt, *Characters of Shakespeare's Plays* (1817), World's Classics (Oxford, 1917)
Heath	anon. (Benjamin Heath), *A Revisal of Shakespear's Text* (1765)
Henslowe	Philip Henslowe, *Henslowe's Diary*, ed. R. A. Foakes and R. T. Rickert (Cambridge, 1968)
Hibbert	Christopher Hibbert, *Agincourt*, British Battles Series (1964, 1968)
Holderness & Loughrey, *Hamlet*	Graham Holderness and Bryan Loughrey (eds), *The Tragical Historie of Hamlet Prince of Denmarke*, Shakespearean Originals: First Editions (Hemel Hempstead, 1992)
Holderness & Loughrey, *Chronicle*	Graham Holderness and Bryan Loughrey (eds), *The Chronicle Historie of Henry the Fift*, Shakespearean Originals: First Editions (Hemel Hempstead, 1993)
Holinshed	Raphael Holinshed, *The Chronicles of England, Scotland and Ireland*, 2nd edn, 3 vols (1587)
Hotson	Leslie Hotson, *I, William Shakespeare...* (etc.) (1937)
Irace	Kathleen Irace, 'Reconstruction and adaptation in Q *Henry V*', *SB*, 44 (1991), 228–49
Jonson	Ben Jonson, *Every Man in his Humour*, in *Elizabethan Plays*, ed. Hazelton Spencer (Boston, Mass., 1933)
Jorgensen	Paul A. Jorgensen, *Shakespeare's Military World* (Berkeley, Calif., 1956)
Keegan	John Keegan, *The Face of Battle* (1976)
Knowles	Richard Knowles (ed.), *As You Like It*, New Variorum Edition of Shakespeare (New York, 1977)

Kyd	Thomas Kyd, *The Spanish Tragedy*, ed. Philip Edwards, The Revels Plays (1959)
Leggatt	Alexander Leggatt, *Shakespeare's Political Drama. The History Plays and the Roman Plays* (1988)
Lever	J. W. Lever, 'Shakespeare's French Fruits', *SS*, 6 (1953), 79–90
Linthicum	M. Channing Linthicum, *Costume in the Drama of Shakespeare and his Contemporaries* (Oxford, 1936)
Liston	William T. Liston, 'Shakespeare in Ohio and Indiana, 1983', *SQ*, 35 (1984), 102–5
Locrine	anon., *Locrine*, in C. F. Tucker Brooke (ed.), *The Shakespeare Apocrypha* (Oxford, 1908)
Lyly, *Endymion*	John Lyly, *Endymion*, in *Elizabethan Plays*, ed. Hazelton Spencer (Boston, Mass., 1933)
Lyly, *Works*	John Lyly, *The Complete Works of John Lyly*, ed. R. Warwick Bond, 3 vols (Oxford, 1902)
Marlowe	Christopher Marlowe, *Complete Plays and Poems*, ed. E. D. Pendry and J. C. Maxwell (1976)
Mason	John Monck Mason, *Comments on the Last Edition of Shakespeare's Plays* (1785)
Middleton & Rowley	Thomas Middleton and William Rowley, *The Changeling*, ed. N. W. Bawcutt, The Revels Plays (1958, 1961)
MLR	*Modern Language Review*
Mucedorus	anon., *Mucedorus*, in C. F. Tucker Brooke (ed.), *The Shakespeare Apocrypha* (Oxford, 1908)
N&Q	*Notes and Queries*
Nashe	R. B. McKerrow (ed.), *The Works of Thomas Nashe*, 5 vols, 1904–10, revised F. P. Wilson (Oxford, 1958)
Noble	Richmond Noble, *Shakespeare's Biblical Knowledge and Use of the Book of Common Prayer* (1935)
ODEP	*The Oxford Dictionary of English Proverbs*, 2nd edn (Oxford, 1948)
OED	*The Compact Edition of the Oxford English Dictionary*, 2 vols (1979)
Onions	C. T. Onions, *A Shakespeare Glossary* (1911), enlarged and revised throughout by Robert D. Eagleson (Oxford, 1986)
Patterson	Annabel Patterson, 'Back by popular demand: the two versions of *Henry V*', *Renaissance Drama*, new series, 19 (1988), 29–62
Potter	Lois Potter, 'Bad and good authority figures: *Richard III* and *Henry V* since 1945', *SJW* (1992), 39–44
Preston	Thomas Preston, *Cambyses*, in *Minor Elizabethan Tragedies*, ed. T. W. Craik (1974)

Price	Hereward T. Price, *The Text of 'Henry V'* (Newcastle-under-Lyme, 1920)
Quinn	Michael Quinn (ed.), *Shakespeare: Henry V: A Selection of Critical Essays*, Casebook Series (1969)
Rabkin	Norman Rabkin, 'Rabbits, ducks and *Henry V*', *SQ*, 28 (1977), 279–96
SB	*Studies in Bibliography*
Scot	Reginald Scot, *The Discovery of Witchcraft* (1584)
Shakespeare's England	*Shakespeare's England: An Account of the Life & Manners of his Age*, gen. ed. C. T. Onions, 2 vols (Oxford, 1916)
Sidney	Sir Philip Sidney, *The Complete Works of Sir Philip Sidney*, ed. Albert Feuillerat, 4 vols (Cambridge, 1912–26)
Simpson	Richard Simpson, 'The politics of Shakspere's historical plays', *Transactions of the New Shakspere Society*, 1st series, 2 (1874), 396–441
Sinfield	Alan Sinfield, *Faultlines: Cultural Materialism and the Politics of Dissident Reading* (Oxford, 1992)
SJO	*Sir John Oldcastle* (A. Munday, M. Drayton, R. Wilson, R. Hathaway), in C. F. Tucker Brooke (ed.), *The Shakespeare Apocrypha* (Oxford, 1908)
SJW	*Shakespeare Jahrbuch West*
Spevack	Marvin Spevack (ed.), *A Complete and Systematic Concordance to the Works of Shakespeare*, 9 vols (Hildesheim, 1968–80)
Sprague	A. C. Sprague, *Shakespeare's Histories: Plays for the Stage*, Society for Theatre Research (1964)
Sprague & Trewin	A. C. Sprague and J. C. Trewin, *Shakespeare's Plays Today: Customs and Conventions of the Stage* (1970)
SQ	*Shakespeare Quarterly*
SS	*Shakespeare Survey*
STM	anon., *Sir Thomas More*, in C. F. Tucker Brooke, *The Shakespeare Apocrypha* (Oxford, 1908)
Taylor, *Moment*	Gary Taylor, *Moment by Moment by Shakespeare* (1985)
TxC	Stanley Wells and Gary Taylor, with John Jowett and William Montgomery, *William Shakespeare: A Textual Companion* (Oxford, 1987)
Theobald, *Shakespeare*	Lewis Theobald, *Shakespeare Restored* (1726)
Thomson	J. A. K. Thomson, *Shakespeare and the Classics* (1952)
Tilley	Morris P. Tilley, *A Dictionary of the Proverbs in England in the Sixteenth and Seventeenth Centuries* (Ann Arbor, Mich., 1950)
Tillyard	E. M. W. Tillyard, *Shakespeare's History Plays* (1944)

References

TLS	*Times Literary Supplement*
Tyrwhitt	Thomas Tyrwhitt, *Observations and Conjectures upon some Passages of Shakespeare* (1766)
Urkowitz	Steven Urkowitz, 'Good news about "bad" quartos', in Maurice Charney (ed.), *Bad Shakespeare: Revaluations of the Shakespeare Canon* (London and Toronto, 1988)
Van Lennep	W. B. Van Lennep, E. L. Avery, A. H. Scouten, G. W. Stone Jr and C. B. Hogan (eds), *The London Stage, 1660–1800: A Calendar of Plays* (etc.), 5 vols (Carbondale, Ill., 1960–8)
Vickers	Brian Vickers (ed.), *Shakespeare: The Critical Heritage, vol. 2 1693–1733* (1974)
Walker	William Sidney Walker, *A Critical Examination of the Text of Shakespeare*, 3 vols (1860)
Walker, 'Principles'	Alice Walker, 'Some editorial principles (with special reference to *Henry V*)', *SB*, 8 (1956), 95–114
Warner & Marten	George Townsend Warner and C. H. K. Marten, *The Groundwork of British History* (1923)
Webster	John Webster, *The White Devil*, ed. John Russell Brown, The Revels Plays (1960)
Werstine	Paul Werstine, 'Narratives about printed Shakespearean texts: "foul papers" and "bad" quartos', *SQ*, 41 (1990), 65–86
Williams	Benjamin Williams (ed.), *Henrici Quinti Angliae regis gesta* (*Gesta Henrici Quinti*), English Historical Society (1850)
Williamson	Marilyn Williamson, 'The courtship of Katherine and the second tetralogy', *Criticism: A Quarterly for Literature and Arts*, 17 (1975), 326–34
Wilson & Dutton	Richard Wilson and Richard Dutton (eds), *New Historicism and Renaissance Drama* (1992)

INDEX
TO INTRODUCTION AND COMMENTARY

417